Quantitative Methods for Business

Quantitative Methods for Business
The A–Z of QM

John Buglear

ELSEVIER
BUTTERWORTH
HEINEMANN

AMSTERDAM • BOSTON • HEIDELBERG • LONDON • NEW YORK • OXFORD
PARIS • SAN DIEGO • SAN FRANCISCO • SINGAPORE • SYDNEY • TOKYO

Elsevier Butterworth-Heinemann
Linacre House, Jordan Hill, Oxford OX2 8DP
30 Corporate Drive, Burlington, MA 01803

First published 2005

British Library Cataloguing in Publication Data
A catalogue record for this book is available from the British Library

Library of Congress Cataloguing in Publication Data
A catalogue record for this book is available from the Library of Congress

ISBN 0 7506 5898 3

For information on all Elsevier Butterworth-Heinemann publications visit our
website at http://books.elsevier.com

Transferred to Digital Print 2007

Printed and bound by CPI Antony Rowe, Eastbourne

Contents

Preface

Quantitative Methods for Business provides an understanding of quantitative business techniques. As the sub-title, *The A–Z of QM* suggests, the book is an accessible guide to the use of a wide variety of quantitative methods that have important and varied business applications. A range of techniques are discussed and demonstrated using worked examples, all set in business contexts. There are 'road test' sections where real uses of the techniques are described.

Quantitative Methods for Business is intended to help readers to use computer software to carry out quantitative work. It provides guidance on the use of the EXCEL, MINITAB and SPSS software packages.

Answers to all review questions, including many fully-worked solutions, are Included. These will help readers monitor their own progress and make the book an effective basis for independent learning.

Acknowledgements

I would like to thank Maggie Smith and Deena Burgess at Elsevier for their support and Elaine Leek for her diligence.

I am grateful to those who reviewed sections of the manuscript for their helpful observations. Particular thanks are due to Heather Owen (Napier University), to Dr Michael Cox (Newcastle University) and to Philip Entwistle and Kazem Shamshiri (University College, Northampton).

Thanks also to my colleagues at Nottingham Trent University. Many of the ideas in this book have evolved through the experience of working with these colleagues and our development of new approaches to teaching and learning quantitative methods.

Finally, thanks to Allison, Max and Tom for their forbearance.

CHAPTER 1

Setting off

This chapter will help you to:

- assess the importance businesses attach to quantitative methods
- make full use of this book
- apply arithmetical procedures
- use the technology: calculators and computer software

Beginning a new programme of study is always something of a challenge. To help ease you into the study of quantitative methods this chapter begins with an outline of the importance of numbers in business life. Following that is an overview of this book and ways in which it can assist in your studies. The next section provides guidance on arithmetical procedures that feature in the techniques you will meet in later chapters. The chapter closes with advice on the use of calculators and software that can take the hard graft out of the analysis to allow you to concentrate on interpreting the results.

1.1 Quantitative methods, numbers and business >

If you are studying business or interested in any aspect of business you need to know about quantitative methods. Why? Because business is all about quantities: quantities of goods produced and services provided, quantities of inputs and costs, quantities of revenues and profit, and so on.

How many times have you seen a news programme that does not mention numbers? How many times have you read a newspaper in which no numbers are quoted? Numbers are integral to our way of life, our understanding of the world around us. This is especially so of the business world that, now and in the future, we relate to as customers, employees, suppliers.

Consider how numbers played a part in the publisher's decision to produce this book. They were interested in the size of the potential market, which meant looking at the number of students on business courses. They needed to set a price, which led them to consider the prices of rival texts on the one hand and their own production costs on the other. The production costs would depend in turn on the number of pages in the book and the number of copies to be produced.

You may feel rather uncomfortable at the prospect of studying numerical subjects. Perhaps memories of Maths at school have left a legacy that leads you to associate analysing numbers with mental numbness. If this is what happened to you, it is best to try to put it behind you. For one thing the focus you will find here is on applications and interpretation rather than proof and derivation. It may help to bear in mind that employers consistently identify numerical and problem-solving skills as highly desirable qualities in potential employees, so try to think of your quantitative studies as building a valuable career asset. For example, in graduate recruitment literature the Exxon Mobil Corporation state that 'Numerical and analytical skills are essential for all vacancies' (Hobsons, 2002, p. 320).

If you do approach the study of quantitative methods with trepidation you may be tempted to think that this is a subject that really doesn't matter because it is of no use to businesses. It might be comforting to think that the subject is irrelevant because this would excuse not bothering with it. In fact the subjects that you will meet in this book have in many cases been forged in and grown up with the business world. The origins of many of the techniques described in this book are embedded in the history of business sectors as diverse as brewing and insurance.

This is not an opinion held only by people who teach it; a number of researchers have tried to establish the use that companies make of quantitative methods. Usually these studies are aimed at finding how widespread is the use of a particular type of technique, but occasionally researchers canvass the application of the spectrum of techniques that comprise quantitative methods. One comprehensive study was a survey of American companies undertaken in the 1980s (Kathawala, 1988).

Kathawala surveyed US companies that were in the 'Fortune 500'. *Fortune* is an American business magazine that periodically compiles lists of the most prominent companies in the USA. He sent questionnaires to firms in the manufacturing and service sectors, as well as a random sample of small companies. Respondents were asked about the extent to which they used a variety of quantitative techniques.

Thirteen of these techniques feature in this book. Approximately half or more of the respondents' organizations put the majority of these to moderate, extensive or frequent use. Some were very widely used; in the case of forecasting only 6% of respondents reported little or no use.

Kathawala found that in general large companies were more likely to use quantitative methods than small companies. He also found that some techniques were widely used in certain sectors; for example, all respondents from the retailing sector reported that they used stock control methods, whereas all the life insurance companies said they used computer simulation.

One interesting aspect of Kathawala's study was the reasons companies gave for not using quantitative techniques. Foremost among these were that managers lacked knowledge of them. In other words, many respondents who reported that particular techniques were not used said that it was because they had no training in them, not that the techniques were considered to be of no value.

The comprehensive nature of the study makes Kathawala's work interesting, but it is now some years old. However, in the years since it was published the quality and availability of computer software that performs quantitative analysis has vastly improved, suggesting that the use to which businesses put quantitative methods has increased rather than decreased.

1.2 Using this book

This first chapter constitutes a prologue or launch pad for your studies. It is designed to help you start with an idea of the relevance of the subject, an outline of the structure and approach used in this book, and what might be termed a refresher course in the basic 'tools of the trade'.

Chapters 2 and 3 cover simple *deterministic* models that can help to represent and understand business operations. The term deterministic is used because the numbers used in such models are fixed or *predetermined*. Chapters 4 to 9 introduce *descriptive* techniques, methods that will enable you to arrange or analyse sets of figures in ways that help to *describe* the situation being studied. These are important because typically figures do vary and the way in which they vary is of interest.

Chapters 10 to 14 deal with techniques and models that allow the risk inherent in business situations to be reflected in the analysis of them. Chapters 15 to 17 are about *inferential* techniques, methods that enable you to make *inferences* or draw conclusions about an issue in general based on the study of a comparatively modest amount of data.

The final chapter is designed to help you tackle numerical aspects of the sort of project or dissertation that you will probably be asked to write towards the end of your course.

The book will introduce you to a variety of analytical techniques drawn from the fields of Business Mathematics, Operational Research and Statistics that together constitute a 'tool-kit' of methods that can be used to investigate situations and help solve problems. Like any other tool-kit, the key to using it properly is to know not only what each tool does, but also how and when to use it. The book will help you develop this ability by illustrating the application of the methods described using business contexts.

To help you appreciate the wider relevance of the methods you will meet, there are sections identified as *Road tests*. These are outlines of applications of the techniques in the business world, drawn from the publications of those who undertook the work. The original sources are listed in the References at the back of the book.

These sections are intended to reassure you that these techniques are important and so your study of them is not in vain. Some of the sources used were published some time ago and describe pioneering work with the techniques concerned; in such cases the use of the techniques has become so commonplace that it does not merit publication. In other cases commercial confidentiality means that illustrative rather than actual data has had to be used. These published accounts of the application of quantitative methods are really only the tip of a sizeable iceberg; the everyday use of the techniques you will be studying is vast, but unseen.

Techniques will be explained and demonstrated using worked examples. Calculations will be outlined in words before symbols are used to represent the process. Techniques will be explained and demonstrated using worked examples. Solutions to these worked examples will be precise or accurate to three decimal places, unless otherwise stated.

Being able to apply a technique, to produce the correct result from a calculation, is important, especially if you find 'learning by doing' useful, but it is by no means all that is involved. It is even more important to be able to interpret the results that the technique has enabled you to produce and to communicate the meaning of those results. In your future career you may be asked to apply techniques of analysis but you are much more likely to need to be able to explain results, perhaps to judge whether appropriate techniques have been used to produce them. The book therefore provides you with not only a description of each technique and an illustration of its use, but also a discussion of the types of results you could get, and what each of them would mean.

At the end of each chapter there are review questions that you can use to confirm your understanding of the methods and ideas featured in the chapter. Questions that relate to particularly important aspects of the chapter content are flagged as *Key* questions. You can find fully worked solutions to these key questions and answers to the other review questions at the back of the book alongside which you will find references to examples in the chapter. In each case the example is very similar to the question, so that if you do not obtain the correct answer you can refer to the example for guidance. All numerical answers are precise or accurate to at least three decimal places unless stated otherwise.

1.3 Key arithmetical procedures

Certain numerical operations feature in many of the techniques that you will meet later on, so this section is designed to help remind you of them and introduce you to some you may not have met.

1.3.1 Addition and subtraction

Addition, represented by the plus sign ' + ', is the process of putting two or more numbers together to make a sum or total. As long as the numbers being added together are positive, i.e. more than zero, the resulting total grows as more numbers are added.

Example 1.1

A sales manager has to drive to a regional office from the company headquarters. The route involves driving 7 miles to a motorway junction, 15 miles along the motorway, 4 miles along a major road, and finally 3 miles across a city. What is the total length of the journey?

You can get the answer by adding together the distances for the four parts of the journey.

$$\text{Total distance} = 7 + 15 + 4 + 3 = 29 \text{ miles}$$

Although you are probably already familiar with addition, you may not have encountered the symbol called 'sigma', which is used to represent it. Sigma is the letter capital S from the Greek alphabet, written as 'Σ'. It is the letter s because s is the first letter of the word 'sum'. It is a Greek letter because at the time that many quantitative techniques were developed, the 'classical' languages of the ancient world were taught in schools and universities. The Greek language, with its specific alphabet, provided the pioneers of these techniques with a source of distinctive symbols.

Although it may seem that the use of letters and symbols by mathematicians is a conspiracy to intimidate the rest of the world, actually they distil the essence of an operation from what would otherwise be a mass of words. The symbol Σ (sigma) simply stands for 'the sum of'. It is a form of shorthand that is used for convenience. Similarly letters are often used in numerical subjects to represent quantities, sometimes to abbreviate a procedure involving specific numbers and sometimes to represent a procedure in general. For instance,

$$\sum x \quad \text{means 'the sum of a series of numbers, each of}$$
which are represented by the letter x'.

Sometimes it is important to identify precisely which of a set of numbers are to be added together. To show this, the letter 'i' is used to count the numbers, for example,

$$\sum_{i=1}^{3} x_i \quad \text{means 'the sum of the first to the third numbers'.}$$

The expression '$i = 1$' below the sigma tells us to start the addition with the first number and the '3' above the sigma sign tells us to finish the addition with the third.

Example 1.2

In the situation described in Example 1.1, we could show that the total distance travelled (which we could represent by 'D') is the sum of the distance for the four parts of the journey (represented by d_1, d_2 etc.) using the expression:

$$D = \sum_{i=1}^{4} d_i = d_1 + d_2 + d_3 + d_4 = 7 + 15 + 4 + 3 = 29$$

If we want to indicate that all of a set of numbers should be added together and we don't know exactly how many there are, we can use the letter 'n' to represent the last number in the set, so

$$\sum_{i=1}^{n} x_i \quad \text{means 'the sum of the first to the last of the numbers'.}$$

At first these types of symbol may appear strange to you, but it is worth learning to recognize and use them as they can become very useful shorthand forms which will save you space and time in future work.

Subtraction, represented by the minus sign '$-$', is the process of subtracting or 'taking away' one or more numbers from another. As long as the numbers being subtracted are positive, i.e. more than zero, the result reduces as more numbers are subtracted.

Example 1.3

An on-line music business has a stock of 49 copies of a CD at the beginning of February. In the first week of the month it received orders for 11 copies, in the second week orders for 6 copies, in the third week orders for 9 copies and in the final week orders for 13 copies. How many copies will be left in stock at the end of the month?

You can get the answer by subtracting the orders from the initial stock:

$$\text{Stock at the end of the month} = 49 - 11 - 6 - 9 - 13 = 10$$

An alternative approach to this operation is to add the orders first and then subtract the total orders from the initial stock. This would be written as:

$$\text{Stock at the end of the month} = 49 - (11 + 6 + 9 + 13)$$
$$= 49 - 39 = 10$$

The round brackets dictate that the operations shown within them have to be carried out first. They are used to indicate priority.

You may well find addition and subtraction fairly easy, but there are cases where they are not so straightforward; first, when negative numbers are involved, and second when the operation involves numbers measured in awkward units, e.g. minutes and hours.

Addition and subtraction may give you some difficulty if negative numbers are involved. If a negative number is added to a total, it reduces the total.

Example 1.4

A customer purchases four items in a supermarket: a pizza costing £2.50, milk costing £1.50, and two deodorants costing £3 each. The deodorants are on a 'two-for-one' special offer. What is the total bill the customer should expect?

Because the till adjusts for the special offer after the second deodorant has been scanned, the answer might be written as:

$$\text{Total bill} = £2.50 + £1.50 + £3 + £3 + (-£3) = £7$$

Here round brackets have been used, both to highlight the fact that there is a negative number in the sequence and to indicate that it must be dealt with first. This means deciding how to tackle the apparently contradictory '+ −' sequence of symbols. In fact the minus sign overrides the plus sign, so adding a negative number is the same as subtracting a number. The arithmetical expression used to find the total amount in Example 1.4 has exactly the same result as the following expression, which combines addition and subtraction:

$$\text{Total bill} = £2.50 + £1.50 + £3 + £3 - £3 = £7$$

But what do you do if you have to subtract a negative number? In fact subtracting a negative number produces the same result as adding a positive number.

Example 1.5

The till operator notices that the deodorants the customer has selected are not those on special offer, the offer applies to a similar product. How will this change the total bill?

The special offer reduction of £3 has to be taken from the previous total, so now:

$$\text{Total bill} = £7 - (-£3) = £10$$

You get exactly the same result if you simply add the amount concerned, £3.

You may find it helpful to think of the two minus signs 'cancelling each other out' to leave you with an addition. This is rather like the interpretation of double negatives in the English language where, for instance the sentence 'I won't do it for nothing' means 'I want something'. Alternatively it may help to think that taking away a negative is always positive.

Addition and subtraction involving time is something many people find difficult because time is measured in hours made up of sixty minutes, and minutes made up of sixty seconds, rather than nice neat numerical parcels of ten. The use of the 24-hour clock on top of all this is simply too much for many people.

Example 1.6

A parcel delivery driver has to deliver packages to four customers. From the depot it takes 15 minutes to reach the first, a further 40 minutes to reach the second, a further 12 minutes to reach the third, and a further 27 minutes to reach the fourth. It takes 1 hour 10 minutes to reach the depot from the last customer. What is the total driving time?

To get the answer we can express all the times mentioned, including the duration of the last stage, in minutes.

$$\text{Total journey time} = 15 + 40 + 12 + 27 + 70 = 164$$

It may be more useful to express the answer in hours and minutes. To do this we need to find how many lots of sixty minutes there are in 164 minutes. The answer is two, so the total journey time is two hours (120 of the total number of minutes) and 44 minutes (the number of minutes left over if 120 is subtracted from 164).

Example 1.7

If the driver in Example 1.6 starts at 11am, at what time will she arrive back at the depot (assuming the time for delivering packages from the van is negligible), and what time is this on the 24-hour clock?

To get the answer, work in hours first, then minutes:

$$\text{Arrival time} = 11 + 2 \text{ hours} = 1\text{pm}$$
$$+44 \text{ minutes} = 1.44 \text{ pm}$$

To express this using the 24-hour clock, add 12 to the number of hours, because the arrival time is after midday:

$$\text{Arrival time} = 1.44 + 12 = 13.44$$

But if the driver started the route at 11.45am what time would she get back to the depot? This is a little more complicated because the departure time and total journey time are measured in both hours and minutes. To find the answer we can start by adding the hours:

$$11 + 2 = 13$$

Then add the minutes together:

$$45 + 44 = 89$$

Since this amount of minutes is more than 60, i.e. longer than an hour, we have to express it in hours and minutes, and add the result to the sum of the hours:

$$89 \text{ minutes} = 1 \text{ hour and } 29 \text{ minutes}$$

$$13 + 1 = 14 \text{ hours}$$
$$+ 29 \text{ minutes} = 14.29, \text{ or } 2.29\text{pm}.$$

1.3.2 Multiplication and division

Multiplication, or 'times-ing', represented either by the asterisk '*' or the 'times' sign '×', is the process of multiplying two or more numbers together. The result is called the *product*. If a number is multiplied by another number that is greater than one, the product will be greater than the original number.

Example 1.8

A domestic heating supplier is replacing gas boilers in a housing complex. A new boiler can supply up to 15 litres of hot water per minute. According to the original specifications an old boiler could supply up to 14 quarts of hot water per minute. There are 1.137 litres in a quart. Will a new boiler supply hot water at a greater rate than an old one?

We need to convert the quarts given for an old boiler into litres by multiplying the number of quarts by the conversion rate:

$$\text{Litres per minute} = 14 * 1.137 = 15.918$$

We can conclude that a new boiler will not supply hot water at a greater rate than an old one.

In this case the number of litres is greater than the number of quarts, the product represents a numerical increase. But if you multiply a number by another number that is less than one, you will get a product that is lower than your first number.

Example 1.9

An exporter needs to send a package weighing 20 lb abroad. The airfreight company they use require the weight to be given in kilograms. If one pound is 0.4536 kilograms, what is the weight of the package in kilograms?

Find the answer by multiplying the number of pounds by the conversion rate:

$$\text{Weight in kilograms} = 20 * 0.4536 = 9.072$$

But what if the multiplication involves negative numbers? If you have to multiply a positive number by a negative number, the product will be negative. However if you multiply two negative numbers together, the product will be positive:

$$4 * (-2) = -8 \quad \text{but} \quad (-4) * (-2) = 8$$

The two negatives 'cancel each other out' when they are multiplied together. If more than two negative figures are multiplied together, whenever the number of figures is odd the result will be negative, whereas when the number of figures is even the result will be positive:

$$(-3) * (-2) * (-2) = -12 \quad \text{but} \quad (-3) * (-2) * (-2) * (-2) = 24$$

Division, or finding how many times one amount 'goes into' another, is the process of dividing one number by another. It is represented either by the forward slash '/' or the sign '÷'.

If you divide a number by another number that is greater than one, the result will be smaller than the original number.

Example 1.10

A small design partnership makes a profit of £94,200. If the profit is shared equally between the six partners in the business, how much should each partner receive?

Find the answer by dividing the profit by the number of partners.

$$\text{Profit share} = £94,200/6 = £15,700$$

If you divide a number by another number that is less than one, the result will be larger than the original number.

Example 1.11

A businessman from abroad travels 341 miles in the UK. On his return he must enter the number of kilometres he has travelled on his expense claim.

A kilometre is 0.62 of a mile (to 2 decimal places), so how many kilometres should he record?

To get this you have to divide 341 by 0.62:

$$\text{Kilometres travelled} = 341/0.62 = 550$$

1.3.3 Squares, powers and roots

Taking the square of a number is the process of multiplying a number by itself. The process is represented by the number with a superscript showing the number two, for example the square of three, or three squared would be written 3^2, which tells us to multiply three by three.

If the number you want to square is more than one, the result will be larger than the number itself, for instance the square of three is nine. However, if the number you want to square is less than one, the result will be smaller than the number itself, for example the square of a half is a quarter.

Example 1.12

A company changes its logo and must order a new square brass plate measuring 65 cm long by 65 cm wide for the main office. The cost of the plate will be based on the area of the plate. There are two possible suppliers: Boldazbrass, who need the area in square centimetres, and Striking Plates, who need the area in square metres. What figures should be given to the suppliers?

To find an area multiply the length by the width. Here because the plate is square, that is, the length and width are the same, we can simply square 65 to get the figure for the first supplier:

$$\text{Plate area for Boldazbrass} = 65^2 = 4225 \text{ square centimetres}$$

To get a figure in square metres for the second supplier we have to divide 65 by 100 so that the dimensions are expressed in metres before we square them:

$$\text{Plate area for Striking Plates} = 0.65^2 = 0.4225 \text{ square metres}$$

Squaring a positive number will always give you a positive result. But because multiplying one negative number by another always gives you a positive product, squaring a negative number will always give you a positive result as well.

So, $3^2 = 9$ and $(-3)^2 = 9$

The fact that we always get a positive result when we square a negative number is worth remembering because it plays a vital role in several techniques you will meet.

The number 2 in 3^2 is known as the *power* to which 3 is *raised*, which means the number of threes that have to be multiplied together. Three to the power three indicates that three should be *cubed*, that is three threes should be multiplied together:

$$3^3 = 3 * 3 * 3 = 27$$

Multiplying with numbers expressed in powers involves adding the powers, so:

$$3^2 * 3^3 = 3^5$$

Three to the power five ($3 * 3 * 3 * 3 * 3$) is 243 so this is simply another way of saying nine times twenty-seven. At first sight it might seem odd to be adding something when the sign '*' says multiply but in adding the powers (two plus two to give four) we are simply counting the number of threes that would have to be multiplied together to get the answer.

Before electronic calculators became widely available powers were used to carry out multiplication because adding powers was easier. This is what logarithms were about; converting numbers into the powers of ten meant that any multiplication, no matter how complex, could be undertaken using only addition.

Whilst our access to calculators today means that we have no such need for logarithms for arithmetical convenience, you will probably find powers of ten used when very large numbers are shown in calculator displays and computer software.

Example 1.13

An economist wants to find how much it would cost to give every resident of the UK half a million pounds, assuming the UK population is 56 million.

If you multiply fifty-six million by half a million on your calculator (56,000,000 * 500,000) it will probably show something like:

$$2.8^{13} \quad \text{or} \quad 2.8^{*10}13 \quad \text{or} \quad 2.8E+13$$

The calculator produces the answer 28000000000000 but has insufficient space to fit in all the zeroes, so it uses powers of ten to represent them and expresses the answer as 2.8 times ten to the power thirteen. The power, thirteen, is the number of times you would have to multiply 2.8 by ten to get 28,000,000,000,000. The letter E in the third version of the expression stands for *exponent*, another word for power.

Large numbers like the result in Example 1.13 are quite common in the business world, for example the Gross Domestic Product (GDP) of a country or the earnings of a large corporation. Such numbers are sometimes expressed in billions, but be careful because in US terms a billion is one thousand million whereas the convention in the UK is that a billion is one million squared, i.e. one million million. The answer in Example 1.13 would therefore be 28,000 'US billion' or 28 'UK billion'. When you use published figures that are quoted in billions it is worth checking which definition has been used. You will probably find that in business and economic figures the US usage prevails.

You will also come across negative powers or exponents in calculator and computer work. To understand negative powers it helps if you are aware that dividing with numbers involving powers means subtracting the powers, for instance:

$$3^3 \div 3^2 = 3^1$$

This is another way of saying three cubed (27) divided by three squared (9) is three; the result is three to the power one since a number raised to the power one is simply the number itself.

If we use the same approach to divide three cubed by three cubed, we get three to the power zero:

$$3^3 \div 3^3 = 3^0$$

Three cubed is twenty-seven, so this is the same as dividing twenty-seven by twenty-seven, which gives us one. So three to the power zero is one; in fact any number to the power zero is one.

If we divide three squared by three cubed we get a negative power:

$$3^2 \div 3^3 = 3^{-1}$$

Here we are dividing nine by twenty-seven, which gives us one-third. A number raised to the power minus one is one over that number, which is known as the *reciprocal* of the number. A number raised to the power minus two is one over the square of the number:

$$3^2 \div 3^4 = 3^{-2}$$

This is the same as saying nine divided by eighty-one is one-ninth, or one over the square of three.

In the same way as positive powers of ten are used in calculator displays and computer software to represent very large numbers, negative powers of ten are used to represent very small numbers.

Example 1.14

Half a kilogram of a hazardous chemical is deposited by accident in a tank holding 800 million litres of water. If the chemical disperses throughout the contents of the tank, how much will there be per litre of water?

If you divide one-half by 800 million on your calculator (0.5 ÷ 800000000) you will probably see:

$$6.25^{-10} \quad \text{or} \quad 6.25^{*10} - 10 \quad \text{or} \quad 6.25\text{E}-10$$

The answer is 0.000000000625 kilograms per litre but there is not enough room for all the zeroes, so the calculator uses negative powers of ten and the answer is shown as 6.25 divided by ten to the power ten, in other words 6.25 divided by ten ten times.

Taking the square root of a number, represented by the radical or 'tick' sign, $\sqrt{}$, means finding what has to be squared to produce the number. The square root of nine, shown as $\sqrt{9}$, is three because the number three multiplied by itself gives you nine. You should bear in mind that the result of $\sqrt{9}$ could be -3, since the square of -3 is also nine. Having said that, in most business contexts it is the positive root that is of interest.

Example 1.15

A mobile phone retailer has been sent a pack of merchandising material that has to be assembled in the shop window for the launch of a new 'Square Deal' product. At the heart of the display is a fluorescent mosaic in the shape of a square that must be made up of centimetre square stickers. If the pack contains 234 stickers, what are the maximum dimensions of the mosaic square, assuming that the stickers cannot be cut?

You can determine the answer by taking the square root of 234:

$$\text{Length/width} = \sqrt{234} = 15.297$$

The maximum dimensions would be 15 centimetres long by 15 centimetres wide. Although $\sqrt{234}$ is also -15.297 the concept of negative dimensions makes no sense here.

An alternative form of representing the square root of a number is to show the number to the power of a half, so:

$$\sqrt{3} = 3^{1/2}$$

If you square the square root of a number you get the number itself, so:

$$\sqrt{3} * \sqrt{3} = 3$$

We get the same result adding powers:

$$3^{1/2} * 3^{1/2} = 3^1 = 3$$

1.3.4 Fractions, proportions and percentages

Fractions, proportions and percentages sound different, but they are only different ways of doing the same thing: expressing a part of something in relation to its whole. If, for example, a company employs 100 people of whom 25 are women, this could be expressed as:

women make up one-quarter of the labour force
or   women make up 0.25 of the labour force
or   women make up 25% of the labour force.

One-quarter is a fraction, 0.25 is a proportion and 25% is a percentage. They are different ways of saying the same thing because there are four quarters in one, four lots of 0.25 in one and four lots of 25% in 100%. You should bear in mind that each of them is a number less than one, including the percentage, which doesn't look as if it is less than one.

It is easier to use percentages if you understand that the literal meaning of 'percent' is per hundred. (*Cent*um meant one hundred in Latin, *cent* is French for a hundred, *cent*o is Italian for a hundred, and a *cent*ury is a hundred years.) This will help especially when you have to perform arithmetical operations using percentages.

Example 1.16

A bookshop gets £20 for every copy of a particular book sold, 70% of which is paid to the publisher. The publisher pays 10% of the 70% they get to the writer of the book. If the bookshop sells 270 copies, how much will the writer get?

The bookshop gets   270 * £20 = £5400

To work out how much of this the publisher will get you may be tempted to multiply £5400 by 70 and get £378,000. Although the publisher would be delighted by your result it far exceeds the amount the bookshop received for the books! The result is distorted because we have multiplied by 70 not 70%.

To do it properly we need to multiply by 0.7, the proportion form of 70%, or by 70/100, the fraction form of 70%.

$$5400 * 0.7 = £3780 = 5400 * 70/100$$

To find the amount the writer will get we need to take 10% or one-tenth of this, £378. We could represent the whole procedure as:

$$270 * 20 * 0.7 * 0.1 = £378$$

Proportions are the easiest form of numbers less than one to deal with because they are 'calculator friendly', but you may occasionally come across arithmetical operations involving fractions.

Addition and subtraction with fractions is straightforward if the figures below the line, the *denominators*, are the same:

$$\frac{1}{5} + \frac{2}{5} = \frac{3}{5}$$

But if the denominators are different we need to make them compatible. The easiest way of doing this is to multiply them together to find a compatible or *common* denominator, a unit that can be used for both numbers.

Example 1.17

A third of visitors to an Internet site use the Alpha service provider and a quarter use Omega. What fraction of visitors uses Alpha or Omega?

To find this we need to add a quarter to a third,

$$\frac{1}{3} + \frac{1}{4}$$

But these are incompatible; thirds are not the same as quarters. If we multiply three by four we get twelve. Since both a third and a quarter can be expressed in twelfths (4/12 and 3/12 respectively), we can conduct the addition using twelfths:

$$\frac{4}{12} + \frac{3}{12} = \frac{7}{12}$$

Subtracting fractions also involves identifying a common denominator, so:

$$\frac{1}{3} - \frac{1}{4} = \frac{4}{12} - \frac{3}{12} = \frac{1}{12}$$

To multiply two fractions, multiply the figures above the line, the numerators, and divide the result by the product you get from multiplying the denominators together, so:

$$\frac{2}{5} * \frac{3}{4} = \frac{2*3}{5*4} = \frac{6}{20}$$

It is better to express fractions in the smallest denominator possible. Here we could divide both the numerator and denominator by two (doing the same thing top and bottom does not alter the value of the expression), giving the answer as 3/10.

Dividing is the reverse of multiplying. If you multiply a number by two then divide the result by two you get the number you started with. Bear this in mind when you divide fractions, as it involves 'reversing' or inverting the second fraction and then multiplying:

$$\frac{1}{4} \div \frac{2}{5} = \frac{1}{4} * \frac{5}{2} = \frac{1*5}{4*2} = \frac{5}{8}$$

1.3.5 Approximation and rounding

You may find it easy to work out numbers in your head, or you may find such a skill incomprehensible and envy those who have it. The truth is that anyone can learn how to carry out mental arithmetic, the tricks are to round the numbers first so they are easier to deal with, and then use them to get a rough figure that can be refined with a little more work.

People who find it easy to work out numerical problems in their head often use rounding and approximation intuitively, that is without thinking about it. In fact you probably round certain numbers automatically. If someone asked your age, you would say '18' or '24' as appropriate, you would not say '18 years, 3 months and 22 days' or '24.12 years'. You round down to the nearest completed year of your age. In the same way when you check how much money you have you probably look at the notes and large denomination coins in your purse or wallet and make an estimate. Only when you are particularly concerned about how much you have, or you have time to spare would you count every coin.

Approximation and rounding are therefore probably familiar to you. If you get used to applying them in your numerical work you will gain a better 'feel' for numbers, become better able to spot mistakes and think numerically 'on your feet'.

Example 1.18

You enter a burger bar where a member of staff asks for your order. You know what you want to order but you don't know how much it will all cost. As you give your order you look at the prices of the things you want: one burger £2.59, another burger £1.99, a portion of fries £0.89, a cold drink £0.99, a hot drink £0.79. You want some idea of the total cost so you know whether to count up your change or get out a note.

To get a quick answer, round up each item to the nearest pound:

$$\text{Rough cost} = £3 + £2 + £1 + £1 + £1 = £8$$

Every figure has been rounded up so this is an over-estimate. We know that the total cost will be no more than this, but it is a rather rough approximation. You could get a more accurate idea if you rounded each figure to the nearest ten pence:

$$\text{Approximate total cost} = £2.60 + £2.00 + £0.90 + £1.00 + £0.80 = £7.30$$

Each of the figures here is rounded up by one penny, so you can get the precise total by taking five pence away from £7.30, which gives you £7.25.

1.3.6 Significant figures and decimal places

We tend to use rounding to produce informative figures when complete precision is not necessary. You should round down figures under 5 and round up figures of 5 and over. The degree of rounding is expressed as the number of *significant figures*.

Example 1.19

A total of 291,538 people visit a trade exhibition. Round this figure so that it is expressed to:
    (a) five significant figures
    (b) four significant figures
    (c) three significant figures

    (a) 291,540   round the 8 up, so 38 becomes 40
    (b) 291,500   round the 4 down, so 540 becomes 500
    (c) 292,000   round the 5 up, so 1500 becomes 2000

If rounding is applied to numbers with figures after the decimal point, the degree of rounding is expressed as the number of *decimal places*.

Example 1.20

A bureau de change offers an exchange rate of 3.2856 for one currency against another. Express this figure to:
- (a) three decimal places
- (b) two decimal places
- (c) one decimal place

(a) 3.286
(b) 3.29
(c) 3.3

Note that in Example 1.20 zeroes have not been written to the right of the last specific or *significant* figure, whereas zeroes were included in the answers to Example 1.19. This is because in Example 1.19 the zeroes are vital in expressing the size of the numbers.

When you are working with numbers involving decimals you will need to work to a certain number of decimal places, in other words a certain degree of precision, but exactly how many decimal places? To ensure that your work is not too approximate, avoid rounding until you have reached the answer, and express the answer to one more place of decimals than the original figures were in. For example, if the numbers you began with were given to two places of decimals, give your answer to three places of decimals.

1.3.7 Precedence of arithmetical operations

Often you will find that the forms of arithmetical operations we have looked at in this chapter are used in combination. An expression may for instance involve addition, multiplication and squaring. If this is the case it is important that you carry out the operations in the right sequence, with some operations preceding others. This order of precedence can be summarized as:

- First carry out any operations in brackets.
- Then do any squaring and square rooting.

■ Then multiplication and division.
■ Finally, addition and subtraction.

The priority given to brackets is particularly important because they can be used to change the sequence of other operations completely, for example:

$$4 + 7 + 2 * 3 = 17 \quad \text{but} \quad (4 + 7 + 2) * 3 = 39$$

In the first case the multiplication is carried out before the additions. The effect of the brackets is to prioritize the addition over the multiplication. Addition would normally be undertaken after multiplication, but enclosing the additions in brackets makes them 'jump the queue' ahead of the multiplication.

You may find *nested* brackets used to specify a sequence of operation, for instance:

$$((3 + 2) * 4)^2 = (5 * 4)^2 = 20^2 = 400$$

You need to carry out this sort of sequence by starting inside the innermost brackets and working outwards. Note that without the brackets we would get a completely different answer:

$$3 + 2 * 4^2 = 3 + 2 * 16 = 3 + 32 = 35$$

If you come across an expression involving operations with equal priority, carry them out from left to right, for example:

$$16/2 * 4 = 8 * 4 = 32 \quad \text{not} \quad 16/2 * 4 = 16/8 = 2$$

If we wanted to specify that the multiplication should be undertaken first, we should use brackets:

$$16/(2 * 4) - 16/8 = 2$$

Example 1.21

A contractor has to prepare an estimate for resealing the damaged floor of a square swimming pool that has an area measuring 17 metres by 17 metres. The cost of sealing materials is £15 per square metre. He estimates the job will take 3 days. The cost of labour will be £80 per day and equipment hire will cost £50 per day. He adds a mark-up of 35% to the total cost to cover overheads and profit. Work out his estimate.

$$\text{Total cost} = 17^2 * 15 + 3 * 80 + 3 * 50$$

The mark-up of 35% means that to get the estimate we must take the total cost and increase it by 35%. We can do this by taking 135% of the total cost, in other words multiplying by 135/100 or 1.35. Since we should only do this after the total cost has been worked out, we will use brackets to clarify the sequence:

$$1.35 * (17^2 * 15 + 3 * 80 + 3 * 50)$$

Start inside the brackets, squaring first:

$$\text{Estimate} = 1.35 * (289 * 15 + 3 * 80 + 3 * 50)$$

Then multiplying:

$$\text{Estimate} = 1.35 * (4335 + 240 + 150)$$

Then adding:

$$\text{Estimate} = 1.35 * (4725)$$

Finally the multiplication outside the brackets:

$$\text{Estimate} = £6378.75$$

The rules about precedence apply where capital sigma (Σ) is used to represent addition. You may find the process of taking a set of numbers and multiplying them in turn by a set of related numbers before adding up the resulting set of products is expressed as:

$$\sum_{i=1}^{n} x_i y_i$$

Here the x values, x_1 to x_n are the numbers in the first set and the y values, y_1 to y_n are the numbers in the second set. When you see an expression like this remember that the multiplication must be carried out before the addition. You should note that when we use letters to represent numbers as we have done here, the multiplication is implicit or assumed because the y_i is written right after the x_i. This convention avoids the confusion that might arise from using one 'x' to represent a number and another 'x' to represent multiply.

Example 1.22

A cinema manager checks the revenue, R, from the screening of a film by working out:

$$R = \sum_{i=1}^{3} p_i q_i$$

The p values are the ticket prices; p_1 is the adult price of £6, p_2 the children's price of £3, p_3 is the concessionary price of £4 for pensioners. The q values are the quantities of tickets sold; q_1 the number of adult tickets, q_2 the number of children's tickets and q_3 the number of concessionary tickets. What is the revenue from a screening attended by 25 adults, 32 children and 15 pensioners?

$$R = \sum_{i=1}^{3} p_i q_i = p_1 * q_1 + p_2 * q_2 + p_3 * q_3$$
$$= 6 * 25 + 3 * 32 + 4 * 15$$
$$= 150 + 96 + 60 = £306$$

The review questions at the end of this chapter cover the techniques dealt with in this section. You may like to use them to consolidate your understanding.

Whilst this section has covered the arithmetical material you will need in order to follow and apply the techniques you will encounter later in the book it is not intended to be a comprehensive guide to basic maths. If you would like to look at these topics in greater detail you might find Lawlor (1999) or Curwin and Slater (2000) useful.

1.4 Using the technology: calculators, EXCEL, MINITAB and SPSS

Although quantitative methods is about numbers, the amount of time you spend actually performing calculations during your study of the subject can be reduced by using readily available technology, specifically a suitable calculator and appropriate computer software.

If you do not already have a calculator you need to get one. It is an essential tool for the numerical aspects of your course. To be of use to you in later work you need one with a square root function and a memory, and it really is worth spending a little more money to get one with statistical functions. Sometimes this facility is described as a 'statistical mode' or an 'SD' (Standard Deviation) mode. This will assist you immensely in later work.

When you have bought your calculator the first thing you should do is make sure you hang on to the instructions. Your calculator is a sophisticated tool that can do much more for you than you might imagine, but you can only find out how if you have the instructions. Keep a photocopy of them in a safe place in case you mislay the originals.

You will most likely have access to a computer, perhaps at home but almost certainly at your place of study. Because today computers are used so widely to send messages and to access Internet facilities, it is easy to forget that computers were originally developed as machines to process data.

The computers of today still possess that capability. With the right software the machine you use should become an invaluable aid to you in carrying out quantitative work. It will do most of the laborious calculations for you, leaving you free to concentrate on learning how to understand and interpret the results.

This reflects how you are likely to be involved in using quantitative methods in your professional life; it is your perception and interpretation of results that will be important, rather than whether you can compete with a computer to do the calculations. Of course it is important to be able to understand how the computer has arrived at the results, but let the technology do the hard work for you.

So, what is the right software? There are two types of software that can help you with quantitative methods: specialist software such as statistical packages, and spreadsheet packages.

Statistical packages such as MINITAB and SPSS offer a full range of statistical functions and can do just about all of the statistical work you are likely to carry out during your studies.

Spreadsheet packages such as EXCEL are intended primarily for accounting work and offer a more limited range of statistical functions, but none the less can perform many of the methods you will probably need to use.

Although these two types of package offer different ranges of functions and different styles of output, they have become increasingly similar in some respects. The data storage layouts in statistical packages have become more like spreadsheets; numbers are usually stored in the rows and columns of a 'spreadsheet' in EXCEL, in the rows and columns of a 'worksheet' in MINITAB and in the rows and columns of a 'data file' in SPSS. Similarly the statistical output generated by spreadsheet packages has become more like the output from statistical packages.

Example 1.23

Use the relevant commands in EXCEL and/or MINITAB and/or SPSS to store the prices of the items listed in Example 1.18, and to produce the total cost of the order.

Using EXCEL:

- Enter the first price, 2.59, in cell A1 then press **Enter**. Enter the next price in cell A2, press **Enter**, and repeat until all five prices are stored in Cells A1 to A5 and the cursor is resting in cell A6.

- Click the **Autosum** button (labelled Σ) that is located amongst the toolbars at the top of the screen. The message '=SUM(A1:A5)' will appear in cell A6.
- Press the **Enter** key. The figure that now appears in cell A6 should be 7.25, the total cost of the items.

Using MINITAB:

- Enter the first price, 2.59, in row 1 of column 1 (C1) of the worksheet that occupies the lower half of the screen, and then press **Enter**. Enter the next price in row 2 of C1, press **Enter**, and repeat until all the prices are stored in rows 1 to 5 of C1.
- Click on **Calc** (Calculations) in the menu at the top of the screen.
- Click on **Column Statistics** in the **Calc** pull-down menu.
- In the command window that appears select **Sum**, click on the box beside **Input variable**, type C1 in the box and click the **OK** button. A message telling you that the sum of C1 is 7.25 appears in the Session window that occupies the upper half of the screen.

Using SPSS:

- In the initial command window click the button to the left of **Type in data** then click **OK**. An empty data file appears on the screen with the cursor located in the cell in the top left hand corner.
- Type the first price, 2.59, into this first cell then press **Enter**. As you do this, the package inserts the name **var00001** at the top of the column. (This is short for 'variable 1', the default name the package gives to the first column of figures. The word variable is used in Statistics to describe a quantity, in this case price, which varies from one item to another. You can change the variable name to 'price' by clicking the **Variable View** tab to the bottom left of the screen and typing price in the cell below **Name**. To return to the previous display click the **Data View** tab to the bottom left of the screen.) The cursor moves down to the next cell where you should type the second value then press **Enter**. Continue until all five numbers are in the top five cells of the first column.
- Click on **Analyze** in the menu along the top of the screen then select **Reports** from the pull-down menu. Click **Case Summaries** and a command window headed **Summarize Cases** appears. In this you will see **var00001** listed on the left hand side. Click the ▶ button and **var00001** appears in the **Variables** box on the right. Click on the **Statistics** button to the bottom of the window and a window headed **Summary Report: Statistics** appears. Click on **Sum** in the list under **Statistics** on the left then click ▶ and then the **Continue** button below. This returns you to the **Summarize Cases** window where you need to click **OK**. The package then presents you with its 'output viewer' that contains the sum, 7.25, in the lower table. To return to the data editor, minimize the output viewer.

If you have a choice, learn how to use specialist software like MINITAB or SPSS. If you have time and access, learn to use both the specialist software and the statistical functions of the spreadsheet package. In the course of your professional life the software you use will change and you will need to adapt to it, so it is a good idea to learn how to use a variety of software while you are studying.

If you have to choose between a spreadsheet and a statistical package, it may help to consider some of the pros and cons of each.

Spreadsheets are fairly straightforward to use, basic calculations and diagrams can be produced quickly and easily, and they are useful for more than statistical work, e.g. for accounting or human resources planning. But they can perform only a limited range of statistical tasks, and you have limited control over the composition of some output, particularly diagrams.

Statistical packages can carry out a comprehensive range of statistical operations, and the output they produce is statistically meticulous. But they can be more difficult to learn to use and transferring output into other software may not be straightforward.

Because computer software is continually being upgraded and improved the disadvantages are being reduced and the advantages extended, so check the latest available versions before making your decision.

Whatever package you use for your quantitative work, don't expect to know how to use all its functions straight away. It is worth investing some time in learning how to get the best out of the software you use.

Any package should have a help facility; use it to search for advice. It is really an on-line user manual available at your fingertips! You will find that what you regard as awesome when you begin will very soon become familiar. For further guidance on using these packages try Middleton (2003) or Walkenbach (1999) for EXCEL, Ryan and Joiner (2000) for MINITAB, and Pallant (2001) for SPSS.

Review questions

Answers to these questions, including fully worked solutions to the Key questions marked with an asterisk (*), are on pages 626–628.

1.1*   Match the expressions listed below on the left to the answers listed to the right. Try it without a calculator first then use your calculator to check your solutions.

(i) $4 + 3 + 8 * 2 - 5$ (a)   14
(ii) $15/3 * 2 - 4 + 6$ (b)   8 or -8
(iii) $3 * 8/6 + 1 - 5$ (c)   1.5 or -1.5
(iv) $(4 + 3 + 8) * 2 - 10$ (d)   48
(v) $(2 * 8) + (3 - 5)$ (e)   20
(vi) $(((5 - 2) + 7) * 4)$ (f)   0
(vii) $(6 - 2)^2 * 3$ (g)   18
(viii) $\sqrt{64}$ (h)   12
(ix) $\sqrt{36}/4$ (i)   3 or -3
(x) $\sqrt{(36/4)}$ (j)   40

1.2   Pair up the expressions listed below on the left to the alternative forms of them listed on the right.

(i) 0.00000045   (a) $4.5 * 10^{10}$
(ii) 45   (b) $4.5 * 10^{-7}$
(iii) 450,000   (c) $4.5 * 10^1$
(iv) $\sqrt{45}$ (d) $4.5 * 10^{-1}$
(v) 0.0045   (e) $4.5 * 10^0$
(vi) 45,000,000,000   (f) $4.5 * 10^{1/2}$
(vii) 4.5   (g) $4.5 * 10^{-3}$
(viii) 0.45   (h) $4.5 * 10^5$

1.3* Match the operations on the left below to the answers on the right.

(i) 40% of 200   (a)   120
(ii) $2/3 * 3/5$ (b)   2/15
(iii) 120% of 100   (c)   5/3
(iv) $5/4 \div 3/4$ (d)   8%
(v) $1/5 + 1/4$ (e)   80
(vi) $1/3 - 1/5$ (f)   9/20
(vii) 20% of 40%   (g)   2/5

1.4   Annual world wine output recently was 6,875,396 thousand gallons, of which Italy produced 1,439,911 thousand gallons, the USA produced 543,408, and Australia produced 197,035.
      (a) Express the total production and the production of Italy, the USA, and Australia to (i) four significant figures (ii) two significant figures.
      (b) What is the proportion of world output produced by each of these countries, to three decimal places?

1.5* You are to fly from London to Tokyo. The plane is due to depart at 17.30 and you have to check in two hours before take off. You reckon that it will take an hour and a quarter to drive to the airport and a further 30 minutes to get from the car park to the check-in desk.

(a) What time should you start your journey to the airport?

(b) The flight is scheduled to take eleven and a half hours. Going through passport control and baggage collection should take an hour. If local time is nine hours ahead of UK time, when should the person meeting you aim to be at the airport in Tokyo?

1.6*   According to college regulations, to pass a module a student must get at least 40% of the credit for the module, and at least 35% in each assessed element. In one module the assessment consists of an essay worth 40% of the total credit for the module and an exam worth the remaining 60% of the credit for the module. The following students have completed the module and the marks awarded are listed below. Determine who will pass and who will fail the module, identifying the reason for each failure.

Student	Essay mark (%)	Exam mark (%)
Alexander	57	47
Bukhtar	68	38
Ciani	43	36
Dalkiro	65	33
Elchin	51	39
Franklin	40	37

1.7*   A summary of payroll data for a retail store contains the following list:

Department	Number of operatives	Weekly wage per operative
(1) Goods Received	5	£230
(2) Sales – Electricals	8	£310
(3) Sales – Furniture	3	£300
(4) Sales – Textiles	6	£280
(5) Cleaning	4	£200

If x represents the number of operatives in a department and y represents the weekly wage of an operative, find

(a) $\sum_{i=1}^{n} x_i$, the total number of operatives

(b) $\displaystyle\sum_{i=2}^{4} x_i$, and explain what your answer means

(c) $\displaystyle\sum_{i=1}^{n} x_i y_i$, the total weekly wage bill for the operatives.

1.8   A feature of a new office complex is a square piazza made of specially imported marble slabs that are one metre square.

(a) According to the architect's plan the piazza should be 35 metres wide and 35 metres long. How many slabs will be needed?

(b) Supply difficulties mean that only 1100 slabs will be available. What are the dimensions of the largest square piazza that can be built assuming the slabs cannot be cut?

1.9   An insurance company claims department reports that 45% of the claims they dealt with over the last month related to motor policies, and 30% of those involved drivers under 25 years of age. The claims department dealt with 2400 claims last month, so how many were motor policy claims involving drivers under 25?

1.10*   The price of a new Sabaka car purchased from a car supermarket is £12,500. Against this a customer is offered a trade-in of £1700 for her current vehicle. Later the customer visits a brand dealership where the same car is on sale at the full list price of £14,995. The salesperson is prepared to offer a discount of 8% off this price. What is the least that the customer should accept as a trade-in price for her current vehicle to make it worth her while to buy the car from the dealership?

1.11   The loyalty card scheme operated by a retail grocery chain offers customers one point for every £10 of purchases. Occasionally double or triple points are offered on some products. If a customer spent £3700 over a year, of which £290 worth earned double points and £130 worth earned triple points, how many points would he have accumulated?

1.12   A public sector organization has a pension scheme under which the amount of pension is determined by taking 1/80 of the final salary for each year of service. Find the pension that would be paid to:

(a) an employee on a final salary of £28,600 who had 34 years' service

(b) a senior manager on a final salary of £65,000 who had 22 years' service

1.13   An energy company charges households a quarterly fee of £9.20 for providing an electricity supply and 7.11 pence for every unit of electricity consumed. The billed amount is then subject to a 5% tax. If one domestic consumer uses 631 units in a quarter, how big will their total bill be, including tax?

1.14   A Malaysian businessman visiting the UK wants to buy some gifts in a department store. He chooses a man's suit costing £179.99, a lady's coat costing £99.99, and a piece of jewellery costing £69.99. The store allows visitors from abroad to purchase goods 'VAT-free'. If the rate of VAT is 17.5%, what will be the total cost of his purchases?

1.15   After promotion a single graduate has an annual salary of £21,000. He wants to check his monthly take-home pay. He finds out that:

- A single person is entitled to a tax allowance of £4615, which is deducted from total annual pay to give the taxable pay for the year.
- The tax rate applied to the first £1920 of taxable pay is 10%.
- Remaining taxable pay is taxed at 22%.
- The National Insurance is 10% of total pay, deducted from pay after tax.

How much will he take home each month?

1.16   Members of the sales team at a car dealership receive commission of 7% of the profits made on the cars they sell. If the profit margin on the cars sold is 30%, how much commission will be paid to a sales person who sells cars to the value of £94,000?

1.17   A visitor to a Central Asian republic is offered a new vehicle for 600,000 zoom, the national currency. She can buy zoom from a bank at the official exchange rate of 150 zoom per US dollar, but in the bazaar she could get 200 zoom to the dollar. If one dollar is worth 63 pence, what is the cost of the vehicle in pounds:
  (a) if she buys zoom at the official rate?
  (b) if she uses the bazaar?

1.18   The monthly interest rate on a credit card is 1.45% charged on any amount unpaid after the payment deadline. One customer has no outstanding balance at the beginning of July. During the month he spends £410 on his card and pays off £250 within the payment deadline. During August he spends £397 on his card.
  (a) How much will he owe at the end of August?
  (b) What is the minimum he has to pay at the end of August if at least 5% of the balance must be cleared?

1.19   Ray von Mann wants to throw a party. He would like to mix 5 litres of punch using a recipe that requires 2 parts gin to 3 parts red wine to 1 part lemon cordial to 1 part tomato juice to 3 parts lemonade. In his cupboard there is a half-full 75 cl bottle of gin, a full litre bottle of red wine, a three-quarters full litre bottle of lemon cordial, a full litre carton of tomato juice, and a half-full litre bottle of lemonade. What else, if anything, does he need to get?

1.20   A consumer magazine launches an investigation into the efficiency of vehicle breakdown recovery services. They have collected the following data and intend to publish it, identifying those services who take more than an hour to reach more than 5% of their call-outs as 'poor' and those who take more than an hour to reach more than 15% of their call-outs as 'very poor'.

Service	Total call-outs	Number reached in more than an hour
Crews Control	7144	528
Highway Help	3497	541
RAP	9277	462
Road Relief	14125	1816
Wheel Rights	5713	758

Work out the percentage of call-outs each service takes more than an hour to reach and indicate which will be labelled 'poor' and which will be labelled 'very poor'.

1.21   A UK courier delivery service uses vans that will soon need to be replaced and the fleet manager has obtained details of a new van that is currently only available in continental Europe. The fuel economy is given as 8.2 litres of fuel per 100 kilometres travelled. What is the fuel economy of the van in miles per gallon? (There are 4.546 litres in a gallon and 1.609 kilometres in a mile, both to 3 decimal places.)

CHAPTER 2

Getting linear models straight

This chapter will help you to:

- plot and solve linear equations
- apply basic break-even analysis
- interpret inequalities
- undertake simple linear programming using graphs
- use the technology: Solver in EXCEL
- become acquainted with business uses of linear programming

This chapter is intended to introduce you to the use of algebra in solving business problems. For some people the very word algebra conjures up impressions of abstract and impenetrable jumbles of letters and numbers that are the preserve of mathematical boffins. Certainly parts of the subject of algebra are complex, but our concern here is with algebraic techniques that help to represent or *model* business situations.

In doing this we are following in the footsteps of the 'father of algebra', Mohammed ibn-Musa al-Khwarizmi. In the ninth century al-Khwarizmi wrote *Al-jabr wa'l-muqabala*, which might be translated as 'Calculation Using Balancing and Completion'. The first part of the Arabic title gives us the word algebra. Although al-Khwarizmi was a scholar working at the House of Wisdom in Baghdad, he saw his task in very practical terms, namely to focus on

... what is easiest and most useful in arithmetic, such as men constantly require in cases of inheritance, legacies, partitions, law-suits, and trade, and in all their dealings with one another... (cited in Boyer, 1968, p. 252)

In the course of this chapter we will confine our attention to simple algebra and how you can use it to solve certain types of business problem. We will focus on linear equations, which are those that are straight lines when they are plotted graphically. They form the basis of linear models that assist business problem-solving.

2.1 Linear equations

Central to algebra is the use of letters, most frequently x and y, to represent numbers. Doing this allows us to deal systematically with quantities that are unknown yet of importance in an analysis. These unknown quantities are often referred to as *variables*, literally things that vary over a range of numbers or *values*. Sometimes the point is to express a quantitative procedure in a succinct way, and the use of letters merely constitutes convenient shorthand.

Example 2.1

A sales agent is paid a basic wage of £200 per week plus 10% commission on sales. The procedure for working out his/her total wage could be written as:

$$\text{Total wage} = 200 + 10\% \text{ of sales}$$

It is often more useful to abbreviate this by using letters. If y is used to represent the total wage and x to represent sales we can express the procedure as:

$$y = 200 + 0.1x$$

Using this we can find the total wage for a week when sales were £1200:

$$y = 200 + 0.1 * 1200 = 200 + 120 = £320$$

These types of expression are called equations because of the equals sign, '=', which symbolizes equality between the quantity to its left and the quantity to its right. An equation is literally a state of equating or being equal.

An equation that involves just two unknown quantities can be drawn as a line or a curve on a graph. Each point along it represents a combination of x and y values that satisfies, or fits the equation.

To plot an equation start by setting out a scale of possible values of one unknown along one *axis*, or dimension, and a scale of the possible values of the other unknown along the other axis. Ensure the scales cover the range of plausible values, and start them at zero unless interest in the line is limited to part of it well away from zero. Plot the *x* values along the horizontal axis, known as the *x axis*, and the *y* values along the vertical axis, known as the *y axis*. This conveys that *y* depends on *x*.

Once each axis has been prepared, portraying an equation in its graphical form involves finding two points that lay along the line that will represent the equation. This means you have to identify two pairs of *x* and *y* values both of which satisfy the equation. The way to do this is to specify an *x* value and use the equation to work out what value *y* would have to take in order to satisfy the equation, then repeat the process for another *x* value. To ensure that your line is accurate it is important to take one *x* value from the far left hand side of the horizontal axis and the other from the far right hand side.

Example 2.2

Plot the equation that represents the procedure for working out the weekly wage for the sales agent in Example 2.1.

The equation is:

$$y = 200 + 0.1x$$

where *y* represents the wage and *x* the sales.

To help us design the *x* axis let us suppose that the maximum sales the agent could achieve in a week is £5000. Using the equation we can use this to find the maximum wage:

$$y = 200 + 0.1(5000) = 700$$

This means the highest value we need to include in the scale on the *y* axis is £700.

We are now in a position to construct the framework for our graph, which might look like Figure 2.1.

To plot the line that represents the equation we need to find two points that lie on the line. One of these should be on the left hand side. The lowest number on the left of the horizontal axis is zero, so we could use the equation to work out the wage when sales are zero:

$$y = 200 + 0.1(0) = 200$$

When sales are £0 the wage is £200, this pair of values gives us the position, or *coordinates* of one point on the line. The sales value, 0, positions the point along the horizontal axis and the wage value, 200, positions the point along the vertical axis.

To get a second set of coordinates we should take a sales figure from the right hand side of the horizontal axis, say the maximum figure of 5000, and work out the wage when sales are £5000, again using the equation:

$$y = 200 + 0.1(5000) = 700$$

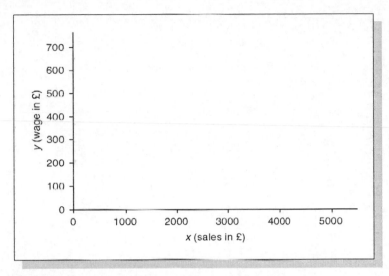

Figure 2.1
Framework for plotting the equation in Example 2.1

When sales are £5000 the wage is £700. The point we plot to represent this pair of values will be positioned at 5000 along the horizontal axis and at 700 along the vertical axis. We can now plot both points as in Figure 2.2:

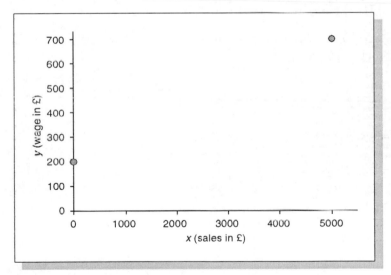

Figure 2.2
Points on the line of the equation in Example 2.1

If plotting an equation is new to you, or just something you haven't done for a while, it is a good idea to plot a third point between the first two. A third point should lie in line with the first two so it is a good way of checking that you have plotted the other points correctly. A suitable position for our third point in this case might be when sales are £2000 and the wage will be:

$$y = 200 + 0.1(2000) = 400$$

The point that represents these coordinates, sales of £2000 and a wage of £400, has been plotted in Figure 2.3.

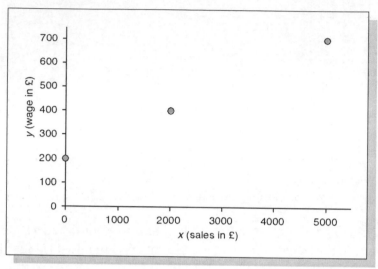

Figure 2.3
Three points on the line of the equation in Example 2.1

The final stage in plotting the equation is to draw a straight line linking the plotted points. This is shown in Figure 2.4:

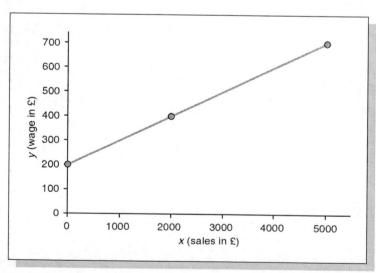

Figure 2.4
The line of the equation in Example 2.1

Lines that represent simple linear equations, such as the one plotted in Figure 2.4, have two defining characteristics: a starting point, or *intercept*, and a direction, or *slope*. We can think of the intercept as specifying the point the line begins, and the slope as specifying the way in which the line travels. In Figure 2.4 the line begins at 200, when sales are zero, and travels upwards at a rate of 0.1 for every one-unit increase in sales, reflecting the fact that the sales agent receives an extra £0.10 for every additional £1 of sales.

Different lines will have different intercepts and slopes. It will help you interpret results of this type of analysis if you can associate basic types of intercept and slope in linear equations with their plotted forms. To illustrate this we can extend the sales agent example to include contrasting approaches to wage determination.

Example 2.3

Suppose the basic wage of the sales agent in Example 2.1 is increased to £300 and the commission on sales remains 10%. Express the procedure for determining the wage as an equation and plot it.

The total wage (y) in terms of sales (x) is now:

$$y = 300 + 0.1x$$

The line representing this has an intercept of 300 and a slope of 0.1. It is the upper line in Figure 2.5.

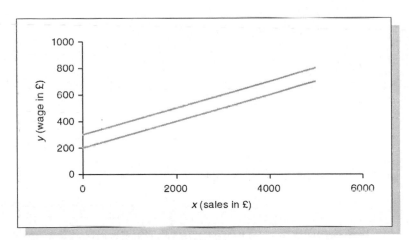

Figure 2.5
The lines of the equations in Examples 2.1 and 2.3

You can see two lines plotted in Figure 2.5. The lower is the line plotted in Figure 2.4, the original formulation for finding the wage. The upper represents the equation from Example 2.3, where the basic wage is increased to £300. It is higher because the intercept is 300 compared to the 200 in the original equation but note that the two lines are parallel since they have exactly the same slope. Lines that have the same slope will be parallel whatever their intercept.

Example 2.4

Identify the equation that would express the calculation of the wages of the sales agent in Example 2.1 if there were no basic wage and the commission rate remained 10%.

The total wage would be:

$$y = 0 + 0.1x$$

This is plotted in Figure 2.6 together with the equations from Examples 2.1 and 2.3.

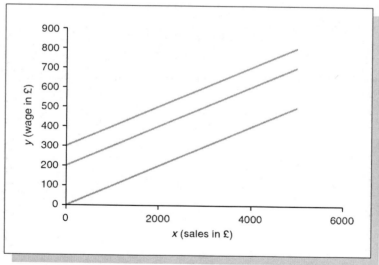

Figure 2.6
The lines of the equations in Examples 2.1, 2.3 and 2.4

The bottom line in Figure 2.6 represents the equation from Example 2.4. It starts from the point where both wage and sales are zero, known as the *origin*, since the intercept of the line is zero. It is parallel to the lines above it because it has the same slope as them.

Example 2.5

The basic wage of the sales agent in Example 2.1 is to remain at £200, but the rate of commission increases to 20%. Express the procedure for determining the wage as an equation and plot it.

The total wage (y) in terms of sales (x) is now:

$$y = 200 + 0.2x$$

The line representing this has an intercept of 200 and a slope of 0.2. It is plotted in Figure 2.7 together with the equation from Example 2.1.

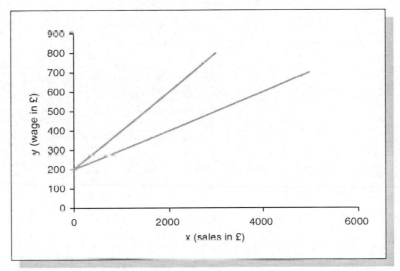

Figure 2.7
The lines of the equations in Examples 2.1 and 2.5

The equations plotted in Figure 2.7 have the same intercept, 200, but different slopes. This means they start at the same point on the left hand side of the graph but their paths diverge. The upper, steeper line represents the equation from Example 2.5. It has a slope of 0.2, twice the slope of the line representing the equation in Example 2.1, 0.1, reflecting the greater rate at which commission is earned, 20% rather than 10%. The slope is twice as steep since the same sales will result in the sales agent earning double the commission.

Example 2.6

Identify the equation that would express the calculation of the wages of the sales agent in Example 2.1 if the basic wage is £200 and there is no commission.

The total wage would be:

$$y = 200 + 0x$$

This is plotted in Figure 2.8 together with the equation from Example 2.1.

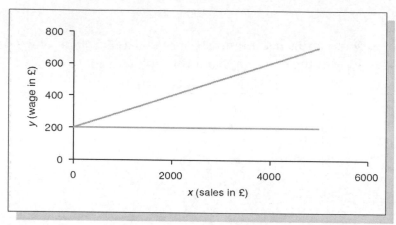

Figure 2.8
The lines of the equation in Examples 2.1 and 2.6

The equation in Example 2.6 is plotted as the bottom, horizontal line in Figure 2.8. It has a zero slope; literally it goes neither up nor down. Whatever the level of sales the wage will be unaffected.

The slopes in the equations we have looked at so far have been upward, or *positive*, and in the case of Example 2.6, zero. You will also come across equations that have *negative*, or downward slopes.

Example 2.7

The company that employs the sales agent in Example 2.1 believes that its sales vary according to the price charged for its product. They summarize the relationship in the form of the following equation:

$$y = 800 - 10x$$

where y represents the number of units sold and x the price at which they are sold in £. The equation is plotted in Figure 2.9.

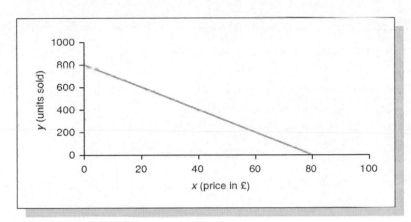

Figure 2.9
The line of the equation in Example 2.7

In Figure 2.9 the line slopes downwards because the slope, -10, is negative. It means that for every increase of £1 in the price of the product the number of units sold will decrease by ten.

At this point you may find it useful to try **Review Questions 2.1 and 2.2** at the end of the chapter.

2.2 Simultaneous equations

In the previous section we looked at how linear equations can be used to show the connection between two variables. Such equations represent the relationship in general terms; they are in effect recipes or formulae that specify how the value of one quantity can be established with reference to another quantity. This is how a wage that consists of a basic component plus sales commission can be calculated or how a phone bill made up of a fixed charge plus a cost per unit can be worked out. In each case a single linear equation provides a clear numerical definition of the process involved and can be used to work out the appropriate y value for any given x value.

Sometimes it is necessary to consider two linear equations jointly, or simultaneously, hence the fact that such combinations of equations are known as *simultaneous equations*. Typically the aim is to find a pair of specific values of x and y that satisfy both equations. You can achieve this by plotting both equations on the same pair of axes and identifying the point where the lines cross.

Example 2.8

The sales agent in Example 2.1, currently receiving a wage of £200 plus 10% commission on sales, is offered the alternative of receiving 20% commission on sales with no basic wage. What is the minimum level of sales the agent would have to reach to make the alternative commission-only wage attractive?

The existing arrangement can be represented as:

$$y = 200 + 0.1x$$

where y represents the wage and x the sales.

The alternative can be expressed as:

$$y = 0 + 0.2x$$

Both equations are plotted in Figure 2.10.

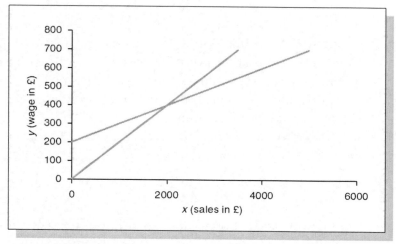

Figure 2.10
The lines of the equations in Example 2.8

In Figure 2.10 the lines cross at the point representing sales of £2000 and a wage of £400. The line representing the current method of determining the wage is the higher line when sales are below £2000, indicating that it would be the better arrangement for the agent when sales are less than £2000. The line representing the alternative arrangement is the higher line when sales are greater than £2000, indicating that it would be the better arrangement when sales exceed £2000. The minimum level of sales the agent would have to reach to make the alternative commission-only wage attractive is therefore £2000.

Finding values that fit both of two equations is known as solving simultaneous equations. In Example 2.8 the point where the lines cross meets the requirements of both equations because it is a point on both lines. The fact that it is the only point where the lines cross tells us that it represents the only combination of wage level and sales that fits both equations.

You can solve simultaneous equations without plotting their lines on a graph using a method known as *elimination*. As the name implies this involves removing or eliminating one of the unknown quantities with the intention of leaving a numerical value for the other.

In order to end up with a clear result conventionally simultaneous equations are arranged so that the unknown quantities and the factors applied to them, their *coefficients*, are located on the left hand side of the equals sign and the intercept, or *constant* appears to its right. This may involve rearranging the equations. In doing this we need to ensure that any manipulation preserves the equality inherent in the equation by balancing every operation performed on one side with the exact same operation on the other side.

Following this we proceed to the removal of one of the unknown quantities, either x or y. This is straightforward if the number of x's or y's in both equations is the same, in which case if you subtract one equation from the other you will be left with an expression which has just one unknown on the left of the equals sign and a number on its right. Using suitable multiplication or division you can then establish the value of this remaining unknown, one of the pair of x and y values that fits both equations.

Having found one of the pair of values mutually compatible with both equations you can substitute it into one of the original equations and find the value of the other unknown that, in combination with the value of the first unknown, satisfies the original equations jointly, or *simultaneously*.

Example 2.9

In Example 2.8 the sales agent is presented with two possible wage arrangements represented as:

$$y = 200 + 0.1x \quad \text{(the original arrangement)}$$

and

$$y = 0 + 0.2x \quad \text{(the commission-only alternative)}$$

where y represents the wage and x the sales.

We will start by rearranging both equations so the components, or *terms*, involving x and y are on the left of the equals sign and the 'stand-alone' numbers are on the right. In the case of the first equation, representing the original arrangement, this entails moving the $0.1x$ from the right of the equals sign over to the left. In doing this we have to reverse the sign in front of it, as strictly speaking we are subtracting $0.1x$ from both sides of the equation, and hence preserving the balance:

$$y = 200 + 0.1x$$

Subtract $0.1x$ from both sides:

$$y - 0.1x = 200 + 0.1x - 0.1x$$

to get:

$$y - 0.1x = 200$$

For the second equation:

$$y = 0 + 0.2x$$

Subtract $0.2x$ from both sides:

$$y - 0.2x = 0 + 0.2x - 0.2x$$

to get:

$$y - 0.2x = 0$$

We can now set these rearranged equations alongside each another and subtract one from the other to eliminate y:

$$
\begin{aligned}
y - 0.1x &= 200 \\
y - 0.2x &= 0 \\
\hline
+0.1x &= 200
\end{aligned}
$$

We can break this operation down into three parts:

$$y - y = 0y \quad \text{no } y$$
$$-0.1x - (-0.2x) = +0.1x$$
$$200 - 0 = 200$$

giving us:

$$0.1x = 200$$

This tells us that one-tenth of x is 200. If we multiply both sides of this by ten we find that a 'whole' x is worth 2000:

$$0.1x * 10 = 200 * 10 \quad \text{so} \quad 1x = 2000$$

In other words both wage determination models produce the same wage when sales are £2000. But what will the wage be? To find this put the sales figure of 2000 into the equation representing the original arrangement:

$$y = 200 + 0.1 * 2000 = 200 + 200 = 400$$

The original approach to establishing the sales agent's wage will produce a wage of £400 when sales are £2000. The alternative, commission-only formulation will of course yield the same wage when sales are £2000:

$$y = 0 + 0.2 * 2000 = 400$$

The values of 2000 and 400 for sales and wages respectively therefore satisfy both wage determination equations simultaneously.

Applying elimination in Example 2.9 was made easier because in both equations there was only one 'y', that is the coefficient on y in each equation was one. If the coefficients on an unknown are different you have to apply multiplication or division to one or both equations to make the coefficients on the unknown you wish to eliminate equal before you can use subtraction to remove it.

Example 2.10

Find the level of wages at which the two procedures for determining the sales agent's wage in Example 2.8 result in the same wage by eliminating x, the level of sales.

The equations representing the procedure, as rearranged in Example 2.9, are:

$$y - 0.1x = 200$$
$$y - 0.2x = 0$$

If we multiply the first equation by two we get:

$$2y - 0.2x = 400$$

Subtracting the second equation from this:

$$
\begin{aligned}
2y - 0.2x &= 400 \\
y - 0.2x &= 0 \\
\hline
y &= 400
\end{aligned}
$$

Again we find that the wage level at which the two wage determination models produce the same result is £400. If we substitute this value of y into the equation representing the original arrangement we can find the level of sales that will yield a wage of £400:

$$400 - 0.1x = 200$$

Subtract 400 from both sides:

$$400 - 400 - 0.1x = 200 - 400$$
$$-0.1x = -200$$

Multiply both sides by minus one:

$$(-1) * (-0.1x) = (-1) * (-200)$$
$$0.1x = 200$$

Multiply both sides by ten:

$$x = 2000$$

The level of sales at which both approaches to wage determination will produce a wage of £400 is therefore £2000.

Not all pairs of equations can be solved simultaneously. These are either cases where one equation is a multiple of another, such as:

$$3x + 2y = 10 \quad \text{and} \quad 6x + 4y = 20$$

or cases where one equation is inconsistent with the other, such as:

$$2x + y = 14 \quad \text{and} \quad 2x + y = 20$$

In the first case the equations are the same; if you try to plot them you will find they produce the same line. In the second case plotting them produces lines that are parallel and therefore do not cross.

At this point you may find it useful to try **Review Question 2.3** at the end of the chapter.

2.3 Break-even analysis

The type of linear model that we have looked at in the previous section can be used to analyse the relationship between the costs and revenue of a company. The aim in doing this is to identify the point at which the revenue matches the costs, known as the break-even point, the output level at which the company makes neither profit nor loss but breaks even.

In setting up a break-even analysis we need to make several definitions and assumptions. First we assume that there are two types of cost, fixed and variable. Fixed costs, as the name implies, are those costs that are constant whatever the level of production. These might be the costs of setting up the operation such as the purchase of machinery as well as expenses, such as business rates, that do not vary with the level of output. Variable costs on the other hand are costs that change in relation to the amount produced, such as the costs of raw materials and labour.

We can define the total costs (TC) as the sum of the total fixed costs (TFC) and the total variable costs (TVC):

$$TC = TFC + TVC$$

The total variable costs depend on the quantity of output. We will assume that the variable cost of producing an extra unit is the same however many units we produce; in other words, it is linear or varies in a straight line with the amount produced. We can therefore express the total variable cost as the variable cost per unit produced, known as the average variable cost (AVC) multiplied by the quantity produced (Q), so the total cost is:

$$TC = TFC + AVC * Q$$

The total revenue (TR) is the price per unit (P) at which the output is sold multiplied by the quantity of output (Q):

$$TR = P * Q$$

Once we have defined the total cost and total revenue equations we can plot them on a graph and look at exactly how total revenue compares to total cost. This is a key comparison as the total revenue minus the total cost is the amount of profit made:

$$Profit = TR - TC$$

The point at which the lines representing the two equations cross is the point at which total cost is precisely equal to total revenue, the break-even point.

Example 2.11

The Ackrana Security Company intends to manufacture video security cameras. The costs of acquiring the necessary plant and machinery and meeting other fixed costs are put at £4.5 million. The average variable cost of producing one of their cameras is estimated to be £60 and the company plans to sell them at £150 each. How many will they need to produce and sell in order to break even?

Total cost, TC = 4500000 + 60Q
Total revenue, TR = 150Q

These equations are plotted in Figure 2.11. Conventionally the money amounts, cost and revenue are plotted on the vertical or y axis and the output is plotted on the horizontal or x axis. This arrangement reflects the assumption that the money amounts depend on the output and makes it easier to interpret the diagram.

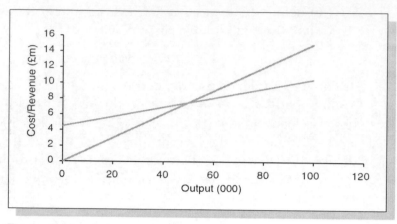

Figure 2.11
Total cost and total revenue lines in Example 2.11

In Figure 2.11 the steeper line that starts from the origin represents the total revenue equation and the other line represents the total cost equation. You can see that the lines cross when output is about 50,000 units. At this level of production both the total cost and total revenue are equal, at about £7.5 million. This is the break-even point, at which costs precisely match revenues.

We can verify the break-even point by solving the total cost and total revenue equations simultaneously:

$$TC = 4500000 + 60Q \quad \text{so} \quad TC - 60Q = 4500000$$
$$TR = 150Q \qquad\qquad\quad \text{so} \quad TR - 150Q = 0$$

When total cost and total revenue are equal, subtracting one from the other will leave us with an expression in which the only unknown is the level of output, Q:

$$TC - \ \ 60Q = 4500000$$
$$\underline{TR - 150Q = \qquad\quad 0}$$
$$+90Q = 4500000$$

Dividing both sides by 90 means that the level of output at which total cost and total revenue are equal is 50,000:

$$4500000/90 = 50000$$

The total cost and total revenue when 50000 units are produced will be:

$$TC = 4500000 + 60 * 50000 = 4500000 + 3000000 = £7,500,000$$
$$TR = 150 * 50000 = £7,500,000$$

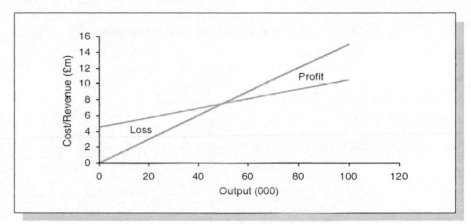

Figure 2.12
Break-even graph
for Example 2.11
with areas
representing profit
and loss

Break-even analysis can be extended to illustrate the levels of output that will yield a loss and those that will yield a profit. A level of output less than the break-even level, and hence to the left of the position of the break-even point along the horizontal axis of the graph, will result in a loss. A level of output higher than the break-even level, to the right of the break-even point on the horizontal axis, will yield a profit.

At any point to the left of the break-even point the total cost line is the higher line indicating that total cost is higher than total revenue; the greater the difference between the two lines, the larger the loss. At any point to the right of the break-even point the total revenue is the higher line, which means that the total revenue is higher than the total cost; the bigger the difference between the two lines, the larger the profit. The areas representing loss and profit are shown in Figure 2.12.

Using Figure 2.12 you can establish how much profit or loss will be achieved at a particular level of production. If for instance production were 30,000 units the graph suggests that the total cost would be £6.3 million and the total revenue would be £4.5 million resulting in a loss of £1.8 million.

We expect that a company would seek to operate at a level of production at which they would make a profit. The difference between the output they intend to produce, their *budgeted output*, and the break-even level of output is their safety margin. This can be expressed as a percentage of the budgeted output to give a measure of the extent to which they can fall short of their budgeted output before making a loss.

Example 2.12

If the Ackrana Security Company in Example 2.11 aims to produce 80,000 cameras what profit should they expect and what is their safety margin?

$$
\begin{aligned}
\text{TR} &= 4500000 + 60 * 80000 = 9,300,000 \\
\text{TC} &= 150 * 80000 \qquad\qquad = 12,000,000 \\
\text{Profit} &= 12000000 - 9300000 \;\; = 2,700,000 \quad \text{that is £2.7 million}
\end{aligned}
$$

In Example 2.11 we found that their break-even point was 50,000 cameras so their safety margin is:

$$
\frac{\text{budgeted output} - \text{break-even output}}{\text{budgeted output}} * 100 = \frac{80000 - 50000}{80000} * 100 = 37.5\%
$$

The break-even analysis we have considered is the simplest case, where both costs and revenue are assumed to be linear, that is to form straight lines when plotted graphically. In practice companies might find that with greater levels of production come economies of scale that mean their variable cost per unit is not constant for every unit produced but falls as output increases. Furthermore, they may have to reduce their price if they want to sell more products so that their total revenue would not have a linear relationship to their output level.

Despite these shortcomings the basic model can be a useful guide to the consequences of relatively modest changes in output as well as a framework for considering different levels of initial investment, pricing strategies and alternative sources of raw materials.

At this point you may find it useful to try **Review Questions 2.4 to 2.9** at the end of the chapter.

2.4 Inequalities

So far we have concentrated on the use of equations to model business situations. Under some circumstances it is appropriate to use *inequalities*, also known as *inequations*, expressions of relationships in which one or more unknowns are not necessarily equal to a specific numerical value.

The basic forms of inequalities are *not equal* ($\neq$), *less than* ($<$), and *greater than* ($>$):

$$
\begin{aligned}
x \neq 10 \quad &\text{means } x \text{ must take a value other than } 10 \\
x < 10 \quad &\text{means } x \text{ must be less than } 10 \\
x > 10 \quad &\text{means } x \text{ must be greater than } 10
\end{aligned}
$$

It may help you to distinguish between $<$ and $>$ if you think of the sharp end of each symbol as pointing to the lesser quantity, and the open end to the greater. In $x < 10$ the sharp end points the x so it is the smaller quantity and 10 is the larger quantity whereas in $x > 10$ the sharp end points to 10 so that is the smaller quantity and x is the larger.

There are two types of composite inequality that you will meet later in this chapter. These are *less than or equal to* ($\leq$) and *greater than or equal to* ($\geq$). In both cases the lines beneath the $<$ and $>$ signs signifies the possibility that the two sides in the relationship are equal is included.

These composite inequalities are useful for representing ways in which business operations might be limited or constrained by factors such as the amount of raw material or time available for the production of different products or services. In such cases all or some of the limited resource might be used, but it is not possible to use more than the amount on hand. The available quantity of resource is a ceiling or *constraint* on the business activity. An inequality can be used to represent the relationship between the amounts of the resource required for the products and the quantity in stock so that we can tell which combinations of products or services can be produced with the given materials, in other words what output levels are *feasible*.

Example 2.13

The Sirdaria Citrus Company produces juices using exotic fruits including two made from hoormah, 'Anelle' and 'Emir'. Fruit concentrate for these products is imported and the supply is erratic. Sirdaria has 4000 litres of hoormah concentrate in stock. The Anelle brand consists of 8% concentrate. Emir, the luxury product, consists of 10% concentrate.

Represent the fruit concentrate constraint as an inequality.

Since we don't know exactly how much of each product can be produced, indeed we want an inequality to identify what the possibilities are, we must start by defining the key variables: the amounts of each product produced. We will use x to represent the amount of Anelle produced and y to represent the amount of Emir produced.

Anelle requires 0.08 litres of concentrate per litre, so if we produce x litres of Anelle we will need $0.08x$ litres of concentrate. Emir requires 0.1 litres of concentrate per litre so producing y litres of Emir will use up $0.1y$ litres of concentrate. Whatever the volume of Anelle and Emir produced the amount of concentrate needed will be the amount required for Anelle production added to the amount required for Emir production:

$$\text{Concentrate required} = 0.08x + 0.1y$$

The concentrate required must be balanced against the available supply of 4000 litres. To be feasible the output of products must not give rise to a demand for concentrate that exceeds the available supply, in other words the demand must be less than or equal to the available supply:

$$0.08x + 0.1y \leqslant 4000$$

Inequalities, like equations, represent the connection or relationship between amounts either side of the appropriate sign. Like equations they can also be represented graphically, but whereas the graphical form of an equation is a line the graphical form of an inequality is an area bounded or limited by a line. To portray an inequality graphically you have to start by plotting the line that bounds the area. If the inequality is a composite type the line to plot is the line for the equation that represents the limits of feasibility, output combinations that use up all of the available resource.

Example 2.14

Show the inequality in Example 2.13 in graphical form.

If all the hoormah concentrate that the Sirdaria Citrus Company have in stock is used then the amounts of concentrate required for Anelle and Emir production will equal 4000 litres:

$$0.08x + 0.1y = 4000$$

The best way to plot this equation is to work out how many litres of each product could be produced using this amount of concentrate if none of the other product were made. You can work out how many litres of Anelle could be produced from 4000 litres of concentrate by dividing 4000 by the amount of concentrate needed for each litre of Anelle, 0.08 litres:

$$4000/0.08 = 50,000$$

So if only Anelle were made, 50,000 litres could be produced using the 4000 litres of concentrate, but there would be no concentrate remaining for Emir production. The point on the graph representing 50,000 litres of Anelle and zero litres of Emir is the intercept of the line of the equation on the x axis.

If all the concentrate were committed to the manufacture of Emir the number of litres produced would be:

$$4000/0.1 = 40,000$$

At this level of output there would be no concentrate available for Anelle production. The point on the graph representing 40,000 litres of Emir and zero litres of Anelle is the intercept of the line on the *y* axis.

The line can be plotted using these two points.

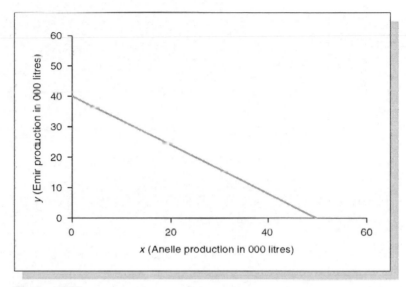

Figure 2.13
The line of the equation in Example 2.14

Each point on the line plotted in Figure 2.13 represents a combination of Anelle and Emir output that would use up the entire stock of concentrate. It is of course feasible to produce output combinations that require a lesser amount of concentrate than 4000 litres, for instance producing 20,000 litres of each product would require only 3600 litres of concentrate. We can confirm this by putting these output levels in the expression representing the concentrate requirement in Example 2.13:

$$\text{Concentrate required} = 0.08x + 0.1y$$

For 20,000 litres of both products:

$$\text{Concentrate required} = 0.08 * 20000 + 01 * 20000 = 1600 + 2000 = 3600$$

Look at Figure 2.14 and you can see that the point representing this combination lies below the line.

The line represents all production combinations that use precisely 4000 litres of concentrate. All the points below it represent combinations that require less than 4000 litres of concentrate. All the points above it represent combinations that require more than 4000 litres of concentrate and are therefore not feasible. An example of this is the manufacture of 30,000 litres of each product, which would require:

$$0.08 * 30000 + 0.1 * 30000 = 2400 + 3000 = 5400$$

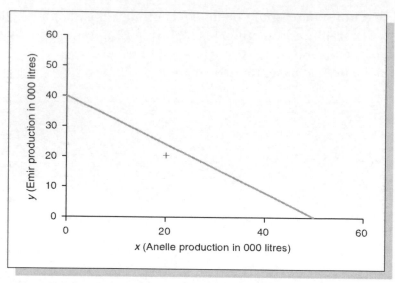

Figure 2.14
A feasible production mix in Example 2.14

Clearly 5400 litres of concentrate is considerably higher than the available stock of 4000 so it is simply not possible to produce these quantities.

The graphical representation of the inequality that expresses the constraint is therefore the line that defines the limits to the production possibilities and the area underneath it. In Figure 2.15 the shaded area represents the output combinations that are feasible given the amount of concentrate available.

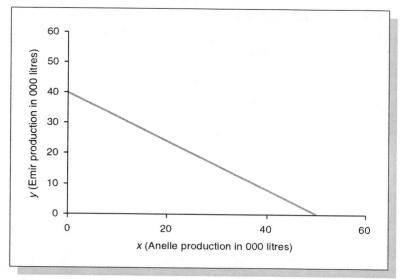

Figure 2.15
The concentrate constraint in Example 2.14

The constraint analysed in Examples 2.13 and 2.14 is an example of a *less than or equal to* form of inequality. Other constraints might take a *greater than or equal to* form of inequality.

Example 2.15

The Sirdaria Citrus Company has a contractual obligation to produce 10,000 litres of Anelle for an important customer.

This is a constraint on production because it obliges Sirdaria to produce at least 10,000 litres of Anelle. If x represents the litres of Anelle produced then the inequality for this constraint is that x must be greater than or equal to 10,000 litres:

$$x \geq 10000$$

Given this limitation any output mix is feasible if it involves producing 10,000 or more litres of Anelle. Were they to produce only 8000 litres, for instance, they would have insufficient to fulfil their commitment to the customer.

To represent this constraint on a graph we need to plot the limit to the constraint ($x = 10000$) and identify which side of it represents production combinations that are feasible.

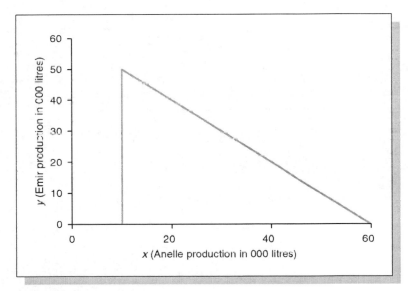

Figure 2.16
The contractual constraint in Example 2.15

In Figure 2.16 the vertical line represents the lower limit on Anelle production resulting from the contractual commitment. Any point to its left would result in too little

Anelle being produced to meet the commitment. Any point to its right enables them to fulfil their obligation and is therefore feasible.

Typically companies face not one single constraint on their operations but several. It can be helpful to display the constraints in a single diagram rather than separately.

Example 2.16

Show the two constraints faced by the Sirdaria Citrus Company, the 4000 litres of concentrate available and their contractual commitment to produce 10,000 litres of Anelle, in graphical form. Identify the production combinations that would be possible taking both constraints into account.

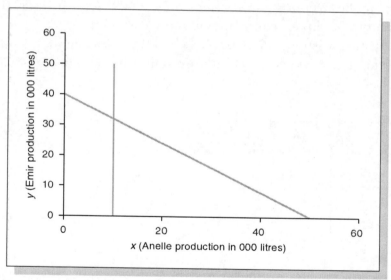

Figure 2.17
Feasible output combinations in Example 2.16

The shaded area in Figure 2.17 represents the production mixes that meet both constraints. There are some output combinations for which they have sufficient concentrate that do not allow them to satisfy their contractual commitments, such as producing 40,000 litres of Emir and no Anelle. Other combinations allow them to produce enough to fulfil their contract but require more concentrate than they have available, such as producing 30,000 litres of each product.

2.5 Linear programming

The inequalities we considered in the last section are important ways of representing the factors that can constrain or limit business operations, but they only demonstrate the possibilities open to a company. They do not indicate which possible, or feasible arrangement would be best for the company.

To provide guidance on making the best choice between the available alternatives we need to bring the intentions or objectives the company wants to achieve into the analysis. This can be done using a technique called *linear programming* that is designed to solve problems of *constrained optimality*, problems in which best, or *optimal* choice has to be made from the alternatives that the constraints collectively permit, the *feasible solutions*.

As the name implies, linear programming assumes that the problem to be solved involves linear or straight-line relationships. Constraints in linear programming are portrayed as inequalities in exactly the same way as we used in the examples in the previous section. Figure 2.17 is the sort of diagram that forms the basis for solving linear programming problems by graphical means.

The constraints we have considered so far reflect tangible limitations to operations. There are also *non-negativity* constraints that reflect the logical limitation that the output quantities cannot be negative. They simply state that each variable representing output of a product must be more than or equal to zero, for instance if x represents the quantity of a product made, then $x \geqslant 0$.

Once the constraints have been plotted and the area representing all the operational possibilities that the constraints collectively allow, the *feasible region*, has been identified, the company objective can be brought into consideration. To do this we need to specify it in algebraic form, as what is called an *objective function*. We assume that the company objective might involve maximizing something, like profit or revenue, but it could be to minimize something, such as cost.

If the company whose operations are being modelled want to maximize their profit they will want to select the feasible solution that yields the most profit. To help them find this we need to know the amount of profit generated from units of the different products they can produce with their limited resources. These figures are key components of the objective function.

The objective function is the profit per unit from the first product multiplied by the quantity of that product made, added to the profit per unit of the second product multiplied by the quantity of the second product made. Since we do not know the level of output for each product when we represent or *formulate* the problem, indeed the point of the analysis is to establish exactly what are the best levels of output, we have to use symbols for the amounts produced. An objective function will look like:

Maximize: $ax + by$

where a is the profit per unit of the first product
         x is the quantity of the first product made
         b is the profit per unit of the second product
         y is the quantity of the second product made

Whatever the level of output, we can use the objective function to find the resulting profit.

Example 2.17

The Sirdaria Citrus Company wants to maximize profits from its production of Anelle and Emir juices. It makes a profit of £0.20 per litre on Anelle and £0.30 per litre on Emir.

Set out the objective function for the company and use it to find the total profit it would make by producing 10,000 litres of Anelle and 20,000 litres of Emir.

The objective function is:

Maximize: $0.20x + 0.30y$

where x is the number of litres of Anelle produced
         y is the number of litres of Emir produced

When the value of x is 10,000 and the value of y is 20,000 total profit will be:

$$0.20 * 10000 + 0.30 * 20000 = 2000 + 6000 = 8000$$

Producing 10,000 litres of Anelle and 20,000 litres of Emir will yield a total profit of £8000.

Formulating the objective function is one thing, but how can we use it to find the best feasible solution, the optimal solution? There are two ways of doing this: either using the objective function to work out the total profit for each feasible solution, or plotting the objective function graphically. We will look at both methods.

The first approach seems daunting because there are simply so many feasible solutions that working out the total profit for each one would be laborious. In fact the vast majority of feasible solutions can be ruled out because logically they cannot be the optimal solution. These are the feasible solutions that are inside, as against on the edges of, the feasible region. Any solution within the feasible region is surrounded by other feasible solutions, including solutions with higher output levels of one or both products. As long as the products yield a profit, a higher level of output of them will yield a higher profit, so a feasible solution inside the feasible region can always be bettered.

Example 2.18

If you look at Figure 2.18 you can see point P inside the feasible region for the Sirdaria Citrus Company problem. If the company were producing the output combination represented by P, it would have fruit concentrate spare to increase Anelle production and move to somewhere like point Q, or to increase Emir production and move to somewhere like point R, or to increase output of both products and move to somewhere like point S. Combinations Q, R and S will all yield a higher profit than combination P, so P cannot possibly be the optimal, maximum profit solution.

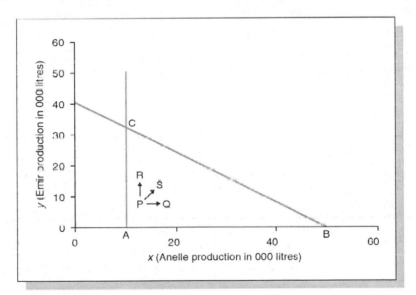

Figure 2.18
The feasible region in Example 2.18

Excluding the solutions inside the feasible region still leaves us with all the solutions along its edges, which still amount to so many that working out the profit for each one of them would be tedious. Fortunately we can ignore the vast majority of these because the optimal solution will be located at one of the corners of the feasible region, except in special circumstances that we will consider later. Because the corners are fundamental to solving the problem they are referred to as *basic feasible solutions.*

Since one corner will be the optimal solution we need only work out the total profit for the output mixes represented by the corner points. The optimal solution is the one that results in the highest profit.

Example 2.19

In Figure 2.18 the corners of the feasible region are labelled A, B and C. Identify the production mixes they represent, work out how much profit each of them will yield, and find the optimal solution.

| | Output (litres) | | Profit (£) | | Total |
Corner	Anelle	Emir	Anelle	Emir	profit (£)
A	10,000	0	2000	0	2000
B	50,000	0	10,000	0	10,000
C	10,000	32,000	2000	9600	11,600

The optimal solution is point C, which represents the production of 10,000 litres of Anelle and 32,000 litres of Emir, and yields a profit of £11,600.

To understand why the solution is one of the corner points rather than somewhere along an edge of the feasible region we can consider the points between points B and C in Figure 2.18. If the company were producing the output represented by corner B, 50,000 litres of Anelle and no Emir, but wanted to produce some Emir they would have to reduce the amount of Anelle produced. They would have no concentrate available for producing Emir as producing 50,000 litres of Anelle would use up all 4000 litres of concentrate at their disposal. Reducing Anelle production to allow some Emir to be produced would amount to moving from corner B in Figure 2.18 along the edge of the feasible region in the direction of corner C.

Would it be worth doing this? In this case yes, because the profit will increase. Suppose the company decreased Anelle production by 100 litres. Since each litre of Anelle requires 0.08 litres of concentrate this reduction will release 8 litres of concentrate. This is enough to make 80 litres of Emir, as each litre of Emir requires 0.1 litres of concentrate. The company would lose £0.20 profit for each litre less of Anelle they produce, a total of £20 profit lost for the 100 litres decrease, but they will gain £0.30 profit for each litre of Emir produced, a total of £24 on the 80 litres they produce. The substitution of Anelle production for Emir production would be worth making and should be continued as far as possible, which is all the way to corner C. Corner B cannot be the optimal solution because from point B swapping Anelle production for Emir production increases profit. Any point between B and C represents a better solution than B, but none will be as good as corner C.

The only case where the optimal solution will not be a corner of the feasible region will be when the ratio of the profits per unit for the products are the same as the ratio of the scarce resource usage. If, for instance, the profit per litre from Emir were £0.25 the amount of profit gained from producing 80 litres would be only £20, exactly the same as the profit from the 100 litres of Anelle that they would have sacrificed to make the Emir. With these profits per litre all the solutions along the edge running from B to C in Figure 2.18 would produce the same total profit, so there would be no unique optimal solution.

Instead of working out the total profit for each corner of the feasible region it is possible to identify the optimal solution by plotting the objective function. This approach is more elegant and can be quicker, especially when the feasible region has more corners. But before you can do this you have to assign a value to the objective function.

Example 2.20

The objective function in Example 2.17, $0.20x + 0.30y$, cannot be plotted on a graph in its current form because it is not an equation, but a general definition of total profit. It has no equals sign or right hand side. Without these we can't identify points on a graph to use to plot a line.

To get us out of this difficulty we need only specify a figure for the total profit. In Example 2.17 we can't plot:

$$0.20x + 0.30y$$

but we can plot:

$$0.20x + 0.30y = 12,000$$

The figure of 12,000 is an arbitrary one that happens to be a convenient round number that is easy to divide by both 0.2 and 0.3. We could choose 15,000 or 18,000 or indeed any other figure to make our *general* objective function into a *specific* equation. These specific values of the objective function are plotted in Figure 2.19. As you can see they are parallel to each other and the higher the profit, the higher the line representing it.

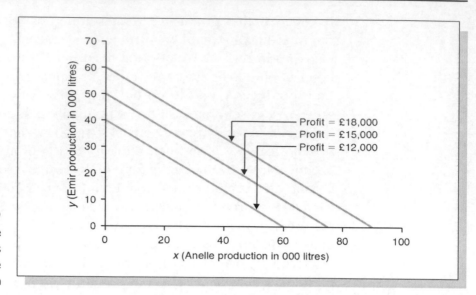

Figure 2.19
Values of the
Sirdaria Citrus
Company objective
function

When an objective function is given a value and plotted the resulting line is called an *iso-profit line*. The points on such a line all have one thing in common: they represent output combinations that yield exactly the same profit. The prefix iso- means equal so an iso-profit line shows production mixes that give equal profit, in the same way as iso-bars on weather maps link places with the same level of atmospheric pressure. In Figure 2.19 the points along the lower line are all different ways in which the company could make a profit of £12,000.

By plotting an iso-profit line that runs through the feasible region we can identify those feasible combinations giving that level of profit. You can use such a line to see how far above it you can go without leaving the feasible region; the furthest you can go is the optimal solution.

However, you may find it easier to plot a value of the objective function that is above the feasible region and look for the point on the feasible region that is nearest to the plotted iso-profit line. This point is the optimal solution. Once we have identified it we can find the levels of production it represents by reading from the graph or solving simultaneously the equations of the lines that cross at the optimal solution.

Example 2.21

Plot the iso-profit line showing product combinations yielding a profit of £12,000 for the Sirdaria Citrus Company and use it to identify the optimal solution. Confirm the levels of output at which profit will be maximized by solving the relevant equations.

In Figure 2.20 the iso-profit line is an unattainable level of profit because nowhere across its length does it even touch the feasible region, so it is not possible for the

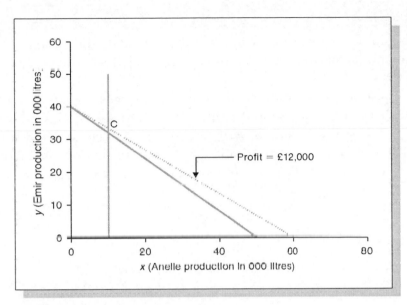

Figure 2.20
The feasible region and iso-profit line in Example 2.21

company to make a profit of £12,000. The nearest we can get to it is to produce combination C, where the lines representing the limits of the contractual obligation to produce 10,000 litres of Anelle and the concentrate constraint meet. At point C:

$$x = 10000 \quad \text{(contract)}$$
and
$$0.08x + 0.1y - 4000 \quad \text{(concentrate)}$$

The first expression defines the Anelle output at point C. To find the Emir output, substitute 10,000 for x in the concentrate equation:

$$0.08 * 10000 + 0.1y = 4000$$
$$800 + 0.1y = 4000$$

subtract 800 from both sides

$$0.1y = 4000 - 800$$
$$= 3200$$

multiply both sides by 10

$$y = 32000$$

This confirms that point C, the optimal solution, depicts the production of 32,000 litres of Emir as well as 10,000 litres of Anelle.

Plotting an iso-profit line to identify the optimal solution is particularly useful if the problem is a little more complex.

Example 2.22

The Sirdaria Citrus Company has encountered another factor that limits its operations; they only have 480 kg of sweetener. A litre of Anelle requires 8 grams and a litre of Emir requires 15 grams.

Show this constraint graphically, and identify the feasible region that results when it is combined with the concentrate and contract constraints. Use the iso-profit line for £12,000 to find the optimal solution, verify it by solving the relevant equations, and work out how much profit the company would make by producing the optimal output mix.

Using x to represent the litres of Anelle produced and y to represent the litres of Emir, the sweetener constraint is:

$$0.008x + 0.015y \leqslant 480$$

The equation representing the limits of this constraint is:

$$0.008x + 0.015y = 480$$

This is represented by the bold line in Figure 2.21

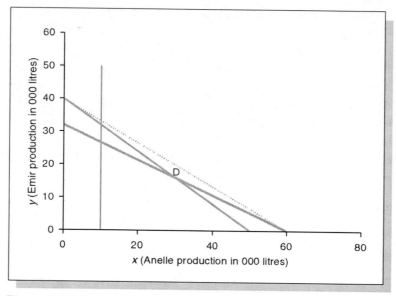

Figure 2.21
The feasible region in Example 2.22

The feasible region is now rather smaller than it was in Figure 2.20. There are production combinations that previously were feasible but are now not possible because they require too much sweetener. Among these is the previous optimal solution. You can check this by working out how much sweetener would be needed to produce 10,000 litres of Anelle and 32,000 litres of Emir:

$$0.008 * 10000 + 0.015 * 32000 = 80 + 480 = 560 \, \text{kg}$$

Since the company only have 480 kg they need to look for a new optimal solution. The point on the feasible region that is closest to the iso-profit line for £12,000 represents the combination of 30,000 litres of Anelle and 16,000 litres of Emir, marked as point D in Figure 2.21. We can check the exact production levels by solving simultaneously the equations of the lines that cross at that point:

$$0.08x + 0.1y = 4000 \text{ (concentrate)}$$
$$0.008x + 0.15y = 480 \quad \text{(sweetener)}$$

Multiply the sweetener equation by 10 and subtract from it the concentrate equation:

$$0.08x + 0.15y = 4800$$
less $$0.08x + 0.1y = 4000$$
gives $$0.05y = 800$$
multiply by 20 $$y = 16000$$

Substitute this in the concentrate equation:

$$0.08x + 0.1 * 16000 = 4000$$
$$0.08x + 16000 \qquad = 4000$$

Subtract 1600 from both sides:

$$0.08x = 2400$$

Divide both sides by 0.08:

$$x = 2400/0.08 = 30000$$

This confirms that the optimal solution is to produce 30,000 litres of Anelle and 16,000 litres of Emir. The profit they would make is:

$$0.20 * 30,000 + 0.3 * 16,000 = 6000 + 4800 = £10,800$$

Note that the amount of Anelle produced is above that specified in the contract constraint, 10,000. This type of constraint, one that does not actually constrain the solution, is known as a *slack* constraint. In contrast concentrate and sweetener are *tight* constraints.

At this point you may find it useful to try **Review Questions 2.10 to 2.19** at the end of the chapter.

2.5.1 Minimization problems

The examples in the previous section featured a maximization problem, one in which the company was seeking to maximize its profits. There also are linear programming problems in which the objective is to minimize something, typically total costs.

The approach to solving a minimization problem is essentially the same as that we use for a maximization problem. We start by formulating the problem, i.e. defining the variables, then setting out the constraints and the objective function. We can then proceed to represent the problem graphically, indicate the feasible region, and use the objective function to find the optimal solution.

Apart from the contrasting form of the objective the main difference between maximization and minimization problems is the type of constraint involved. In maximization problems the constraints are typically 'less than' constraints that impose upper limits on output that generates profit. In minimization problems the constraints are usually 'more than' constraints that impose lower limits on inputs that incur costs.

Example 2.23

The Pamoch Aid Agency has to evacuate the residents of a volcanic island and their belongings by boat. The island's small harbour can only handle small boats. There are two types of boat the agency can hire locally: the Lotka and the Soodna. A Lotka can take 25 passengers and 10 tons of cargo, and costs £800 per day to charter. A Soodna can take 40 passengers and 4 tons of cargo, and costs £1000 per day to charter. The agency needs capacity for at least 2000 passengers and 440 tons of cargo. How many of each type of boat should be chartered to minimize the agency's costs per day, and what is the minimum daily cost?

If we define x as the number of Lotkas they charter and y as the number of Soodnas they charter then their objective is to minimize:

$$800x + 1000y$$

Subject to the following constraints:

$$25x + 40y \geq 2000 \quad \text{(passengers)}$$
$$10x + 4y \geq 440 \quad \text{(cargo)}$$
$$x \geq 0 \text{ and } y \geq 0$$

Figure 2.22 shows the constraints and the feasible region. You can see that the feasible region is above the plotted constraints, which is typical for a minimization problem. Note that it has no upper boundary.

The objective is to minimize cost, so a specific value of the objective function line that we plot is called an *iso-cost* line. The value we choose should be easy to divide by the coefficients in the objective function, in this case 800 and 1000, and should be large

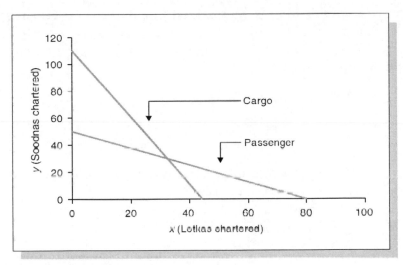

Figure 2.22
The feasible region in Example 2.23

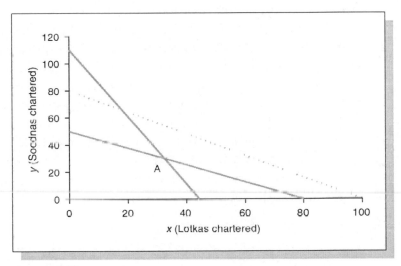

Figure 2.23
The feasible region and iso-cost line for £80,000 in Example 2.23

enough to position the line near the edges of the feasible region. The iso-cost line for £80,000 will meet both requirements; it is the dotted line in Figure 2.23.

Much of the iso-cost line passes through the feasible region, which means that the agency can charter sufficient capacity for £80,000, but much of the feasible region lies below the iso-cost line, which suggests they can do better than that. Finding the optimal solution means locating the point in the feasible region that is as far *below* the iso-cost line as possible as we are trying to find the lowest possible cost.

The lowest cost combination is represented by point A and entails chartering 32 Lotka and 30 Soodna boats. (You could verify these figures by solving simultaneously the equations that cross at point A.) Putting these figures into the objective function will give us the minimum total cost:

$$800 * 32 + 1000 * 30 = 25600 + 30000 = £55,600$$

At this point you may find it useful to try **Review Questions 2.20** and **2.21** at the end of the chapter.

If you want to read more about linear programming you may find Wisniewski (2001) helpful.

2.6 Using the technology: Solver in Excel

The linear programming problems we have considered so far are relatively simple in that they involve deciding the optimal values of two variables, so-called *decision variables* that represent different products. In such cases we can solve the problems graphically, one decision variable on each axis. But there could well be three or more products to consider, in which case a two-dimensional graph would be wholly inadequate.

To deal with more complicated linear programming problems we need computer facilities to help. In this section we will look at one such facility, the *Solver* tool in the EXCEL package, and illustrate how it can be used to solve the Sirdaria Citrus Company problem from the last section.

To try this you need to first ensure that Solver is available to you.

- Enter EXCEL and click the **Tools** pull-down menu.
- If you cannot see **Solver** on the menu click **Add-Ins**.
- On the alphabetical list of tools that appears under **Add-Ins available** click **Solver Add-in** then **OK**.
- Check the **Tools** menu again; **Solver** should now be installed.

Example 2.24

Solve the Sirdaria Citrus Company problem, using Solver.

Step 1: The formulated problem
Define x as the number of litres of Anelle produced and y as the number of litres of Emir produced.

The objective is to maximize: $0.2x + 0.3y$

Subject to the constraints:

$$0.08x + 0.1y \leqslant 4000 \quad \text{(concentrate)}$$
$$x \geqslant 10,000 \quad \text{(contract)}$$
$$0.008x + 0.015y \leqslant 480 \quad \text{(sweetener)}$$

Step 2: Setting up the worksheet

- Set out three headings, Anelle, Emir and Profit, in three adjacent cells near the top of the worksheet, say in columns A, B and C of row 2.
- Make the cell immediately below the Profit heading, C3, the active cell by clicking it then click the Formula bar, the long window immediately above the row of column labels (A, B, C etc.) and to the right of the f_x button. Type **=0.2 * A3 + 0.3 * B3** into the formula bar and click the √ button, two buttons to the left of the Formula bar. This tells the package how to calculate the figure to put in cell C3, the total profit.
- A couple of rows below type in three headings, Concentrate, Contract and Sweetener in the adjacent cells A5, B5 and C5.
- Make the cell beneath the Concentrate heading, A6, the active cell, then click on the Formula bar and type **=0.08 * A3 + 0.1 * B3** and click the √ button. This tells the package how to calculate the amount of concentrate used, which will be put in cell A6.
- Similarly make cell B6 active and type **=A3** and click the √ button, which tells the package that the output level of Anelle should be put in cell B6.
- Finally make cell C6 active and type **=0.008 * A3 + 0.015 * B3** and click the √ button, which tells the package how to calculate the amount of sweetener used and to store it in cell C6.

Step 3: Instructing Solver

- Click the **Tools** menu and click **Solver**.
- The **Solver Parameters** window will appear with the cursor located in the window to the right of **Set Target Cell**.
- Click on cell C3 to make this the target cell, the target being profit. In the next row check that to the right of **Equal To:**, the button indicating **Max** is selected.
- Under **By Changing Cells** type **A3:B3**.
- Click the **Add** button to the right of **Subject to the Constraints**, which brings up the **Add Constraint** window. With the cursor in the **Cell Reference** window click the A6 cell, select **<=** in the window to the left, type **4000** in the window beneath **Constraint** then click the **Add** button.
- The **Add Constraint** window is blank again. Make B6 the active cell, select **>=**, type **10000** under **Constraint** and click **Add**.
- Make C6 the active cell, select **<=**, type **480** under **Constraint** and click **OK**.
- You return to the **Solver Parameters** window and now there are entries under **Subject to the Constraints**.

■ Click the **Options** button to the right of the window, and click **Assume Linear Model** and **Assume Non-Negative**, then **OK**.

■ Back in the **Solver Parameters window** click the **Solve** button on the top right of the window. The solution will appear in the worksheet.

■ The **Solver Results** window appears. Click **OK** to retain the solution.

Step 4: Interpreting the solution

You should see the following details:

Anelle	Emir	Profit	Concentrate	Contract	Sweetener
30000	16000	10800	4000	30000	480

The figures under the Anelle and Emir headings are the number of litres of each that should be produced, the figure under the Profit heading is the amount of profit that would be made. Under the Concentrate heading is the amount of it used – all 4000 litres, which makes this a tight constraint. Under the Contract heading is the Anelle output, which is well in excess of the minimum required, 10,000, making this a slack constraint. Under the Sweetener heading is the amount of it used, all 480 kg, making this a tight constraint. If you look back at Example 2.22 you will see that these are the same as the results we obtained using the graphical approach.

The optimal solution to a linear programming problem like the result we obtained in Example 2.24 is fixed or *static*. As long as the constraints and objective function stay the same so will the optimal solution.

In practice businesses operate in environments that change, that are *dynamic*. The profit levels in an objective function may need to change because new competition is squeezing margins. Constraints may relax if new sources of supply can be located. To cope with such eventualities and answer questions beginning 'what if', we can use *sensitivity analysis* to explore around the optimal solution of a linear programming problem.

When *Solver* produces the solution to a linear programming problem it displays the **Solver Results** window. To the right of it, in the list of **Reports** is **Sensitivity**. Click on this then **OK** and a report will be stored for you in another worksheet, look at the bottom of the screen for **Sensitivity Report** tab and click on it. The contents of such a report enable you to predict the consequences of a greater or lesser amount of the constrained resources and changes in the profitability of the products.

Example 2.25

Use the Solver Sensitivity Report on the problem in Example 2.24 to advise Sirdaria:
- (a) Whether it is worth acquiring more concentrate and if so how much extra profit they would gain?
- (b) Whether it would be worth producing Emir if the profit per litre on it fell below £0.25?

There are two sections to the Sensitivity Report. The lower of the two, titled Constraints, will help us deal with (a). The section looks like:

Name	Final Value	Shadow Price	Constraint R.H. Side	Allowable Increase	Allowable Decrease
Concentrate	4000	1.5	4000	800	533.333333
Contract	30000	0	10000	20000	1E+30
Sweetener	480	10	480	80	80

The figures of central interest here are the *shadow prices*. There is one listed for each of the three constraints. A shadow price is the amount of extra profit that can be obtained by acquiring an extra unit of the resource, or the profit lost if the amount of resource available is reduced by one unit.

In the case of the concentrate the shadow price is £1.50 (it is in pounds, the same units as the profit figures in the formulation of the problem), which means that the answer to (a) is yes, if an extra litre of concentrate were obtained it would be possible to expand production to a new optimal level that would deliver an extra £1.50 profit. In practice, the shadow price is used to show the rate at which profit will increase if the extra resource were available, but only up to a point. Clearly we could increase the amount of concentrate to the stage where we would have insufficient sweetener to go with it. The Allowable Increase and Allowable Decrease figures in the table give the range of resource availability within which the shadow price applies.

The other section of the Sensitivity Report can help us answer (b). It looks like this:

Name	Final Value	Reduced Cost	Objective Coefficient	Allowable Increase	Allowable Decrease
Anelle	30000	0	0.2	0.04	0.04
Emir	16000	0	0.3	0.075	0.05

In this table the Objective Coefficient column reminds us of the original profit figures, in the case of Emir, £0.30. The Allowable Decrease figure of £0.05 is the amount by which the profit per litre can fall, yet still be worth making. In this case Emir would not be worth making if the profit per litre were less than £0.25.

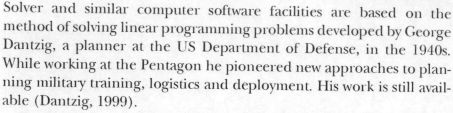

2.7 Road test: Do they really use linear programming?

Solver and similar computer software facilities are based on the method of solving linear programming problems developed by George Dantzig, a planner at the US Department of Defense, in the 1940s. While working at the Pentagon he pioneered new approaches to planning military training, logistics and deployment. His work is still available (Dantzig, 1999).

The Esso Standard Oil Company (the forerunner of Exxon) took up Dantzig's ideas with some enthusiasm in the early 1950s, so much so that they published a book about them (Symonds, 1955) for their managers. The introduction begins:

> Linear programming is a new mathematical method for solving problems concerned with decision-making. It is, therefore, of great interest to management people and their staff advisors. (Symonds, 1955, p. 1)

The book contains applications of linear programming in the refining of oil. One specific case concerns the use of pitch, one of the products from distilling crude oil. Pitch might be combined with a flux product to make fuel oil or used to make tar. The constraints include technical restrictions on viscosity and quantity of the flux. Pitch, fuel oil and tar yield different amounts of profit. The aim was to decide how much pitch should be used to make fuel oil and how much used to make tar in order to maximize profits (Symonds, 1955, pp. 4–11).

The UK Forestry Commission applied linear programming in their management of the New Forest in Hampshire, a case described by Wardle (1965). The problem, in simplified form, was to decide the optimal felling pattern for the mature hardwood stock in the forest; how much should be felled and replaced with pine, how much felled and regenerated, and how much should be retained. Their objective was to maximize the net return. The constraints included restrictions on the total area planted with conifers, and their total felling capacity.

Linear programming has been used in property development, an example being the Highlands project in New York State (Heroux and Wallace, 1975). The developer could build different types of houses and service buildings (commercial and social), each type generating different amounts of profit. The objective was to maximize the developer's profits. The constraints included the total area available for development, maximum school population and maximum local employment opportunities.

The Turkish Ministry of Tourism commissioned a linear programming model for allocating public funds to tourism development projects that involved, for instance, restoration of ruins, improving transport access and building accommodation (Swart *et al.*, 1975). The model was designed to decide which among a set of rival projects should be selected for support from public funds. The principal constraint was the amount of funds available. The objective was to maximize 'tourist attractiveness', the quantification of which the authors discuss at some length.

These are a few examples drawn from the very many applications of linear programming in different business sectors. You can find references to many other pioneering uses of the technique in Gass (1970, pp. 158–168), and a good general discussion of the types of use to which it can be put is in Taha (1997, pp. 39–53). Chvatal (1983) presents a thorough technical guide.

Although linear programming is an important technique you should be aware of its limitations. Some of these have to do with the assumption that profits and resource use are linear. In the case of profits, a company may offer discounts for purchases or enjoy discounts from suppliers for bulk orders or incur disproportionately higher selling costs in achieving high sales. All of these will alter profit margins. In the case of resource use a company may benefit from economies of scale at high volumes of output or have to meet new set-up costs if production is expanded beyond a certain point.

The products a company produces may compete with one another, implying that increasing production of one will reduce profit margins on others. Perhaps it would be costly or difficult to stop and start production in the short-term. The technique takes no account of sequencing production. It may be desirable to have a sustained presence in a market even if it means making a loss, indicating that a company may well have several objectives rather than one. There may indeed be uncertainty about the market for the product.

Despite these shortcomings linear programming is an important technique. It is not only immensely useful in its own right, but it is the basis of other techniques of *mathematical programming* such as *integer programming*, which allows for options to be limited to whole numbers of products, and *transportation*, which is used to find optimal routes for goods to be moved between numbers of sources and numbers of destinations. You will find a good coverage of these in Taha (1997), and Bronson and Naadimuthu (1997).

Review questions

Answers to these questions, including fully worked solutions to the Key questions marked with an asterisk (*), are on pages 629–633.

2.1*   The current system for allocating budgets for the local depots of a national office-cleaning company gives each depot a fixed sum of £35,000 plus an extra £500 for each corporate client in the area the depot covers.

(a) Express the budget allocation model as an equation and portray it graphically.

(b) Use your equation from (a) to work out the budget allocations for the following depots:

(i) Ashford, which has 43 corporate clients

(ii) Byfleet, which has 29 corporate clients

(iii) Croydon, which has 66 corporate clients

(c) A new accountant at the company head office wants to alter the budget allocation model by reducing the fixed sum to £20,000 and increasing to £800 the extra for each corporate client. What changes will these alterations mean for the depots in (b)?

2.2*   A domestic consumer is offered two alternative methods of paying for her annual water bill. The first option is to make 8 payments of £32 at certain points over the forthcoming year. The second is to have her water metered and pay £0.08 for each cubic metre of water used plus an annual standing charge of £20. What is the maximum amount of water she would have to use over the year to make it economical for her to choose the second payment method?

2.3   Solve each of the following pairs of simultaneous equations by elimination:

(a) $3x + 2y = 7$ (b) $5x + 3y = 19$ (c) $2x + 7y = 3$
     $x + y = 3$ $2x - y = 1$ $4x + 3y = 17$

(d) $6x + 6y = 27$ (e) $3x - 2y = 8$ (f) $12x + 4y = 2$
     $4x + 5y = 22$ $x + 4y = 26$ $2x - y = 0$

2.4   Following a crash, the owner of the Skorrost Courier Service has to purchase a new van. The make and model have already been decided, but there is a choice between petrol and diesel versions. The petrol version costs £10,000 to buy and will incur fuel costs of £0.12 per mile. The diesel version costs £11,000 and will incur fuel costs of £0.08 per mile. What is the minimum number of miles that the vehicle must travel to make purchasing the diesel version the more economical choice?

2.5*   The Pasuda Porcelain Company is about to launch a new luxury tableware range. The selling price for a set will be £90. To make the range the company has invested £319,000 in new equipment. Variable production costs will be £35 per set.
  (a)   What number of sets must they sell to break even?
  (b)   What profit will they make if they sell 6000 sets, and what is their margin of safety?

2.6   Samocat Automotive want to move the production of their motor scooters to a purpose-built new plant that will cost £24 m to construct. The scooters sell for £1850 and variable costs of production amount to £1100 per scooter.
  (a)   What is the break-even point for scooter production at the new plant?
  (b)   How will the break-even point change if the costs of the new plant rise to £30 m?

2.7   A plant hire company purchases a mobile crane for £120,000. It plans to charge £190 a day for hiring out the crane. For each day on which it is hired out the company expects to incur variable costs of £40.
  (a)   Work out how many days the company needs to hire out the crane in order to break even.
  (b)   If the variable costs are actually £55 and the hire charge has to be reduced to £180 per day, what is the new break-even point?

2.8   Holly buys a hot dog stall for £360. In addition she has to pay a fixed charge of £200 to the local council to secure her pitch. She plans to sell her hot dogs at £1 each and the cost of preparing each one is £0.60.
  (a)   How many hot dogs will she need to sell to break even?
  (b)   She finds a supplier that can provide cheaper hot dog sausages, enabling her to save 10 p per hot dog on the preparation cost. What effect does this have on the break-even point?

2.9   Volna Appliances want to take over a competitor that makes microwave ovens. They have bid £48 m for the company and expect their offer to be accepted. The microwave ovens are sold for £85 and variable costs amount to £25 per unit.

(a) Work out the break-even point for microwave production.

(b) Volna plan to introduce a rationalization plan that will reduce variable costs by £6 and a price reduction of £16 to increase market share. What is the new break-even point?

2.10* Pianni Beverages produce two ready-mixed cocktail drinks; the Zombie and the Skyjack. Each is a mixture of vodka, vermouth and ginger. It takes 3 litres of vodka, 6 litres of vermouth and 1 litre of ginger to make 10 litres of Zombie, and 5 litres of vodka, 3 litres of vermouth and 2 litres of ginger to make 10 litres of Skyjack. The company makes £15 profit per 10 litres of Zombie and £20 profit per 10 litres of Skyjack. The maximum available supplies per day are: 1500 litres of vodka, 1500 litres of vermouth and 400 litres of ginger. How much of each cocktail should be made to maximize profit per day, and what is the maximum profit per day it can make?

2.11   A company specializing in lubrication products for vintage motors produce two blended oils, Smazka and Neftianikov. They make a profit of £5 per litre of Smazka and £4 per litre of Neftianikov. A litre of Smazka requires 0.4 litres of heavy oil and 0.6 litres of light oil. A litre of Neftianikov requires 0.8 litres of heavy oil and 0.2 litres of light oil. The company has 100 litres of heavy oil and 80 litres of light oil. How many litres of each product should they make to maximize profits and what level of profit will they obtain?

2.12   Gutbucket Gastronomics is a contract caterer that produces cook–chill meals. They make a standard meal selling at £1.60 per portion and an executive meal selling at £2.40 per portion. The products are made up and transported in trays. Each tray can accommodate either 10 executive portions or 20 standard portions. The company has capacity to transport up to 800 trays of product per day. The company employs three chefs to make the meals, each working an 8-hour day. Between them the chefs could produce 24,000 portions of the standard product per day. It takes a chef ten times as long to produce an executive portion as it does to produce a standard portion. If the com-pany wants to maximize its revenue what combination of products should it produce per day and what revenue will be generated?

2.13   Domar Properties plc have a site covering 20,000 m² on which they intend to build a mixed estate of 2- and 4-bedroom houses. The 2-bedroom houses will each occupy a plot of 60 m² and will be sold at a profit of £15,000. On average each will house 2 people owning 1.2 cars. The 4-bedroom houses will each occupy a plot of $300\,\text{m}^2$ and will be sold at a profit of £50,000. On average each will house 5 people owning between them 1.5 cars.

They anticipate that roads, verges, play areas and other communal facilities will occupy 40% of the total site. Water and sewage considerations mean that the total number of residents on the estate should not exceed 250. The local authority has told Domar that the road entrance is unsuitable for more than 120 cars to be based on the estate.

How many houses of each type should Domar build in order to maximize their profit, and how much profit should they expect if they did so?

2.14 The Ooze Haircraft Corporation make two brands of hair treatment: Volossy, which is produced under licence, and its own products Sedina. The company is in dispute with its supplier of colourant and solidifier as a result of which the supplier is no longer taking their orders. An alternative source of supply cannot be arranged for a month and Ooze must plan production for the month with their stock of 480 litres of colourant and 900 litres of solidifier.

A bottle of Volossy requires 3 millilitres of colourant and 9 millilitres of solidifier. A bottle of Sedina requires 4 millilitres of colourant and 6 millilitres of solidifier. The licensing agreement restricts production of Volossy to no more than 60,000 bottles a month and commitments to existing customers mean that at least 20,000 bottles of Sedina must be produced.

The company makes £0.40 profit per bottle of Volossy and £0.20 profit per bottle of Sedina.

(a) How many bottles of each product should they produce and how much profit will they make?

(b) Identify which constraints are tight and which are slack.

2.15 Roo Satellite Systems manufacture two types of broadcast receiving system, the 'Soap Dish' and the 'Houston'. The production process for each includes wiring, assembly and inspection, the times in hours required in each section are:

	Soap Dish	*Houston*
Wiring	3	3
Assembly	1.2	3
Inspection	0.4	0.5

Each month the company has 4500 hours of wiring labour, 3000 hours of assembly labour and 600 hours of inspection labour available. They make a profit of £16 from each Soap Dish and £12 from each Houston. How many of each system should they make per month in order to maximize their profit, and what is the maximum profit?

2.16 The Reklama Advertising Agency has a client who wants to buy TV advertisement slots. The client wants to reach the largest possible target audience within their budget of £3 m. Reklama have been offered peak and off-peak slots by one network. These slots reach 14 million and 4 million people respectively. A peak slot costs £150,000 and an off-peak slot £50,000. The network only has twelve peak slots available within the timescale the client wants and they insist that at least ten of the slots they sell to Reklama are off-peak.

   (a) How many of each type of slot should Reklama book to maximize the audience for the client, and what is the maximum total audience?

   (b) Independent analysis suggests that the audiences are actually 12 million for the peak and 5 million for the off-peak slots. Should Reklama change the booking in the light of this new information, and if so, to what?

2.17 Tapachki & Sons produce handmade clogs in Lancashire. They produce two types of clog, the Nelson and the Oldham. The profits per pair are £10 and £12 respectively. The company employs 2 leather-cutters, 4 sole-makers and 3 stitchers. Each works a 40-hour week. The amount of labour time in hours required for a pair of each type of clog is:

	Nelson	Oldham
Leather-cutting	0.40	0.25
Sole-making	1.00	0.80
Stitching	0.80	0.50

Work out the optimal weekly production mix for the company to make the highest level of profit possible and state the maximum weekly profit they can expect.

2.18* The Chic Sheet Company have to plan production for the next week. The firm produces two types of sheet, standard and luxury, in packs that are sold to retailers for £80 and £145 respectively. The costs of materials are £25 per pack of standard sheets and £45 per pack of luxury sheets. These materials are available in unlimited amounts.

   There are three production departments, cutting, machining and packing. The workforce includes 10 cutters, 150 machinists and 40 packers. The labour required per pack for each product and the labour charges for each department are:

	Standard	*Luxury*	*Charge per hour* (£)
Cutting	0.25	0.375	40
Machining	2.50	6.250	8
Packing	1.25	1.250	12

The factory works a 37.5-hour week.

(a) Work out the profit per pack for each product.

(b) Find the production mix that will enable the company to maximize its profit for the week, and determine the level of profit that would result.

(c) Identify which constraints are tight and which are slack.

2.19   Wooffer & Tweeter make speakers for the specialist audio market. Following the death of the founder of their rival, they have acquired the assets of his company, the Croaker Can & Cab Co. These assets consist of raw materials used to make the two types of speaker produced by Croaker, the Cosmic and the Celestial. The assets and their value are:

Item	*Quantity*	*Total value* (£)
Speaker unit	3000	27,000
Birch ply	$1200\,m^2$	12,000
Grille sheet	$320\,m^2$	1600

Wooffer & Tweeter plan to use these materials to make a final consignment of Croaker speakers. The production requirements for the products are:

Item	*Cosmic (per pair)*	*Celestial (per pair)*
Speaker units	6	4
Birch ply	$2.4\,m^2$	$1.0\,m^2$
Grille sheet	$0.4\,m^2$	$0.8\,m^2$
Labour[†]	1 hour	1.6 hours

[†]An unlimited supply of labour is available at a cost of £10 per hour

Croaker had an outstanding order for 200 pairs of Cosmic speakers for the Asteroid retail group, and have agreed to fulfil this order as they are anxious to do further business with Asteroid.

(a) If Cosmic speakers sell for £100 a pair and Celestial speakers sell for £91 a pair, what production combination will maximize revenue, and what will the maximum revenue be?

(b) Work out the variable cost for each product and subtract it from the selling price to find the profit from each product.

(c) Find the number of pairs of each type of speaker that should be made to maximize profit, and work out what the profit would be.

(d) How much, if any, extra profit would be made by not fulfilling the Asteroid order?

2.20* Kolbasnik the pig farmer needs to add 36 kg of protein and 10 kg of vitamin to the pig feed. There are two possible additives. The cost and protein and vitamin content of each are:

Additive	Cost per kg (£)	Protein content	Vitamin content
Seelni-swine	20	60%	40%
Vita-sosiska	15	90%	10%

How much of each additive should be used in order to minimize costs, and what is the lowest cost of ensuring that the protein and vitamin requirements are met?

2.21 Stroika Concrete makes bags of easy-use concrete for the DIY market. The company mixes their concrete using two ingredients, 'Great Grit' and 'A1 Aggregate'. Great Grit costs £1 per kilogram and consists of 20% fine sand, 40% coarse sand and 40% gravel. A1 Aggregate costs £0.75 per kilogram and consists of 10% fine sand, 50% coarse sand and 40% gravel. Each bag of Stroika concrete must contain at least 2 kg of fine sand, 2 kg of coarse sand and 6 kg of gravel. What is the least cost combination of ingredients that will satisfy the minimum requirements, and what will be the cost of these ingredients per bag of concrete produced?

CHAPTER 3

Dealing with curves without going round the bend

This chapter will help you to:

- deal with types of non linear equations
- interpret and analyse non-linear business models
- apply differential calculus to non-linear business models
- use the Economic Order Quantity (EOQ) model for stock control
- become acquainted with business uses of EOQ model

In the last chapter we looked at how linear equations, equations that represent straight lines, can be used to model business situations and solve business problems. Although important, their limitation is that the relationships they are used to model need to be linear for them to be appropriate. There are circumstances when this is not the case, for instance the sort of model economists use to represent the connection between volume of production and cost per unit. In such a model economies of scale mean that the average cost of production per unit gets lower as output increases. The equation representing the situation would be non-linear and we might be interested in analysing it to find the least cost level of output.

In this chapter we will look at the features of basic non-linear equations and use them to analyse business operations. Following this we will consider how to find optimal points in non-linear business models using simple calculus. Later in the chapter you will meet the Economic Order Quantity model, a non-linear business model that organizations can use in determining their best stock ordering policy.

3.1 Simple forms of non-linear equations

One thing you might have noticed about the linear equations that featured in Chapter 2 was the absence of powers. We met terms like 60Q and $0.08x$ but not $3Q^2$ or $3/x$. The presence of powers (or for that matter other non-linear forms like sines and cosines, although we will not be concerned with them here) distinguishes a non-linear equation. In order to appreciate why, consider two possible relationships between x and y:

$$y = x$$
$$y = x^2$$

In the first case we have a linear equation: y will increase at the same pace with x however big x is. If x is 4, y will be 4. If x goes up to 5, so will y. If x is 10 and goes up to 11, so will y. Even if we had something that looks more elaborate, the effect on y that is caused by a change in x is the same, whether x is small or large.

Example 3.1

A train operating company sets ticket prices using the equation:

$$y = 0.8 + 0.2x$$

where y is the ticket price in £ and x is the number of miles travelled.

To use this equation to work out the cost of a ticket for a 4-mile journey we simply substitute the 4 for x:

$$y = 0.8 + 0.2 * 4 = 0.8 + 0.8 = £1.60$$

The cost of a 5-mile journey will be:

$$y = 0.8 + 0.2 * 5 = 0.8 + 1.0 = £1.80$$

The cost of a 10-mile journey will be:

$$y = 0.8 + 0.2 * 10 = 0.8 + 2.0 = £2.80$$

The cost of an 11-mile journey will be:

$$y = 0.8 + 0.2 * 11 = 0.8 + 2.2 = £3.00$$

Notice that the difference an extra mile makes to the cost, £0.20, is the same whether the difference is between 4 and 5 miles or between 10 and 11 miles. This is because the equation is linear; the slope is constant so the rate at which the value of y changes when x is changed is the same however big or small the value of x. The equation is plotted in Figure 3.1.

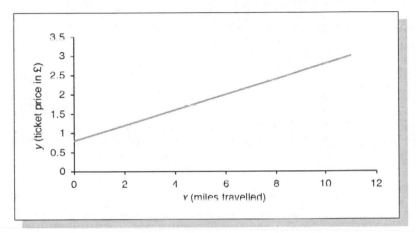

Figure 3.1
The ticket price equation in Example 3.1

If an equation is not linear the size of the change in y that comes about when x changes does depend on how big x is. With a non-linear equation a one-unit increase in x when x is small may result in a modest change in y whereas a one-unit change in x when x is large may cause a much larger change in y.

Example 3.2

The inventor of the new Slugar household labour-saving gadget prepares a business plan to attract investors for the venture. She anticipates that over time sales of the product will grow according to the equation:

$$y = 2 + x^2$$

where y is the sales in thousands of units and x is the number of years elapsed since the product launch.

Show the expected sales growth over 9 years graphically.

To plot a linear equation you only need two points since the line is straight. To plot a non-linear equation we need a series of points that track the path of the curve that represents it. This entails calculating y values using the range of x values in which we are interested, in this case from 0 (product launch) to 9.

x (years since product launch)	y (sales in 000s)
0	2
1	3
2	6
3	11
4	18
5	27
6	38
7	51
8	66
9	83

These points are plotted in Figure 3.2.

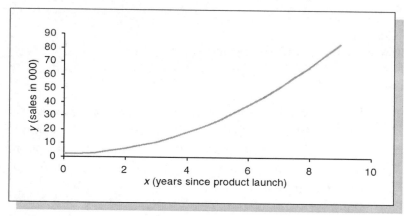

Figure 3.2
The sales growth equation in Example 3.2

An equation that includes x to the power two is called a *quadratic* equation, derived from the Latin word *quadrare*, which means to square. Similarly an equation that includes x to the power three is known as *cubic*. You may also meet reciprocal or *hyperbolic* equations. These include x to a negative power, for instance:

$$y = x^{-1} = 1/x$$

Example 3.3

An economist studying the market for a certain type of digital camera concludes that the relationship between demand for the camera and its price can be represented by the equation:

$$y = 800/x$$

where y is the demand in thousands of units and x is the price in £.

To plot this equation we need a series of points such as the following:

x (price in £)	y (demand in 000s)
100	8.000
200	4.000
300	2.667
400	2.000
500	1.600
600	1.333
700	1.143
800	1.000

The equation is plotted in Figure 3.3.

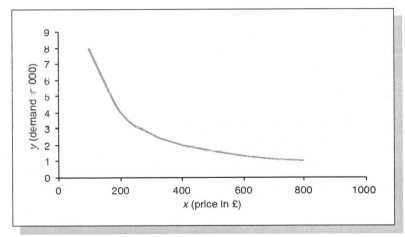

Figure 3.3
The demand equation in Example 3.3

Some curves feature peaks and troughs, known as maximum and minimum points respectively. These sorts of points are often of particular interest as they may represent a maximum revenue or a minimum cost, indeed later in the chapter we will be looking at how such points can be identified exactly using *calculus*.

Example 3.4

The project manager of the new Machinar car plant suggests to the board of directors that the production costs per car will depend on the number of cars produced according to the equation:

$$y = x^2 - 6x + 11$$

where y is the cost per car in thousands of pounds and x is the number of cars produced in millions.

The equation is plotted in Figure 3.4.

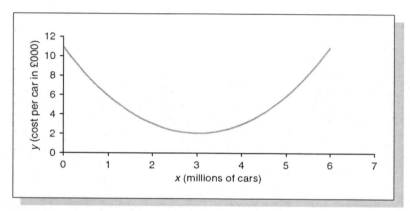

Figure 3.4
The curve representing the equation in Example 3.4

Figure 3.4 show the sort of curve that economists might use to represent economies of scale. The minimum point represents the minimum cost per unit and the point below it on the horizontal axis the level of output that should be produced if the firm wants to produce at that cost. Other models economists use include maximum points.

Example 3.5

Pustinia plc sell adventure holidays. The company accountant believes that the relationship between the prices at which they could sell their holidays and the total revenue that the firm could earn is defined by the equation:

$$y = -x^2 + 4x$$

where y is the total revenue in millions of pounds and x is the price per holiday in thousands of pounds.

The equation is plotted in Figure 3.5.

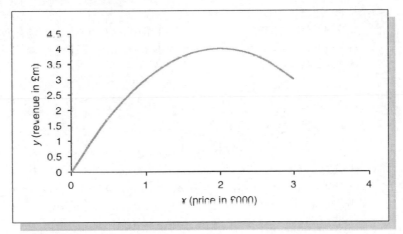

Figure 3.5
The curve representing the equation in Example 3.5

The maximum point in Figure 3.5 represents the maximum revenue the firm could earn and the point below it on the horizontal axis the price the firm should set in order to maximize its revenue.

3.2 Basic differential calculus

We can find the approximate location of the maximum and minimum points in Examples 3.4 and 3.5 by studying the graphs carefully, marking the maximum or minimum point then identifying the values of x and y at which the point is located using the scales along the axes. At best this would give us an idea of where the point lies in relation to x and y, but it is almost impossible to pinpoint it accurately by inspecting the graph.

To find the precise location of maximum and minimum points we can use techniques from the branch of mathematics known as calculus. The word calculus conveys an impression of mystery to some people. In fact it, like the word calculate, is derived from the Latin word *calculare* which means to reckon with little stones, a reflection of the method of counting in ancient times. *Calculare* is related to the Latin word *calx* which means a stone, the source of the word calcium.

Calculus has two branches, *differential* calculus and *integral* calculus. The former, which involves the process of *differentiation*, is about finding how curves change, whereas the latter is about finding areas underneath curves. Our concern in this section is with differentiation. If you would like to find out about integration you may find Croft and Davison (2003) helpful.

Differentiation is concerned with slopes, and slopes in equations reflect the way that the x variable changes the y variable. In a simple equation such as:

$$y = 5 + 3x$$

the slope, $+3$, tells us that an increase of one in the value of x will result in the value of y increasing by three. The slope is the *rate of change* in y that is brought about by a unit change in x. The other number in the equation, 5, is a constant or fixed component; whatever the value of x, the amount added to three lots of x to get y is always 5.

The slopes of more elaborate equations are not so straightforward. If you look carefully at Figure 3.5 you will see that the slope changes as the line moves from left to right across the graph. It begins by climbing upward then reaches a maximum before altering course to descend. To start with it has a positive slope then at the maximum it has a zero slope, it 'stands still', and finally it has a negative slope. The nature of the slope therefore depends on where we are along the horizontal scale, in other words, the value of x. For the lower values of x the slope is positive, for the higher ones it is negative.

Figure 3.4 shows a similar pattern. To begin with the slope is downwards, or negative, then it 'bottoms out' at a minimum and finally becomes upwards, or positive. In this case the minimum is the point where the slope is momentarily zero, it is a point of transition between the negative-sloping and positive-sloping parts of the curve. The maximum point in Figure 3.5 is a similar point of transition, or *turning point* in the line.

So how does differential calculus help us find slopes? It consists of a fairly mechanical procedure that is applied to all the components in an equation that contains x in one form or another; either simply with a coefficient, like $3x$, or perhaps raised to a power, like x^2. The procedure involves taking the power to which x is raised and making it the new coefficient on x then reducing the original power by one. When this is applied to x^2 the result is $2x$. The power, 2, is placed in front of the x, forming the coefficient, and the power reduced from 2 to 1:

$$x^2 \quad \text{becomes} \quad 2x^{2-1} \quad \text{or simply} \quad 2x$$

This means that for the equation:

$$y = x^2$$

the slope, or the rate at which y changes in response to a unit change in x, is $2x$. This is the difference to y that a change in x makes, the differential of the equation, which is represented as dy/dx:

$$y = x^2 \qquad \frac{\mathrm{d}y}{\mathrm{d}x} = 2x$$

You may find it helpful to associate the process of differentiation as finding such a difference. A more exact definition is that it is the marginal change in y resulting from an infinitely small marginal change in x. Because the differential is derived from the original equation it is also known as the *derivative*.

If the expression already includes a coefficient for x, like $2x^2$, we multiply the power by the existing coefficient to give us the new coefficient:

$$y = 2x^2 \qquad \frac{\mathrm{d}y}{\mathrm{d}x} = 2 * 2x = 4x$$

In this case the differential includes x, so the slope of the equation depends on the size of x; whatever x is, the rate of change in y arising from a change in x is four times the value of x. If we apply the same procedure to $3x$, the result is a constant, 3. In carrying out the differentiation of $3x$ remember that $3x$ is 3 times x to the power one so the power reduces to zero, and that any quantity raised to the power zero is one:

$$y = 3x^1 \qquad \frac{\mathrm{d}y}{\mathrm{d}x} = 1 * 3x^{1-1} = 3x^0 = 3$$

In this case the slope is simply 3, and does not depend on the value of x: whether x is small or large the slope will always be 3.

The other type of differentiation result that you should know concerns cases where x is raised to a negative power, such as the reciprocal of x, $1/x$, which can be written as x^{-1}. The process is the same, take the original power and multiply it by the existing coefficient then reduce the power by one:

$$y = \frac{2}{x^2} = 2x^{-2} \qquad \frac{\mathrm{d}y}{\mathrm{d}x} = (-2) * 2x^{-2-1} = -4x^{-3} = \frac{-4}{x^3}$$

When you differentiate expressions like this the key is to remember that a constant divided by x raised to a positive power is simply the constant times x raised to the negative power. When x is taken above the line the power becomes negative.

Some of the equations you may have to differentiate will consist of several different parts, not necessarily all involving x. For the types of equation we shall look at you need only deal with the parts one at a time to reach the differential.

Example 3.6

The production cost equation for the car plant in Example 3.4 was:

$$y = x^2 - 6x + 11$$

where y is the cost per car in thousands of pounds and x is the number of cars produced in millions.

Differentiate this equation.

$$\frac{dy}{dx} = 2x^{2-1} - 6x^{1-1} = 2x - 6$$

Note that in Example 3.6 the constant of 11 is not represented in the derivative. The derivative tells us how y changes with respect to x. When x changes so will x^2 and $6x$ but the constant remains 11.

At this point you may find it useful to try **Review Question 3.1** at the end of the chapter.

When an equation has a turning point, a maximum or a minimum, we can use the differential to find the exact position of the turning point. At the turning point the slope is zero, in other words the differential, the rate of change in y with respect to x, is zero. Once we know the differential we can find the value of x at which the slope is zero simply by equating it to zero and solving the resulting equation.

Example 3.7

Find the location of the turning point of the production cost equation for the car plant in Example 3.4.

From Example 3.6 we know that the derivative is:

$$\frac{dy}{dx} = 2x - 6$$

The value of x at which this is equal to zero is the position of the turning point along the horizontal axis:

$$2x - 6 = 0 \quad \text{so} \quad 2x = 6 \quad \text{and} \quad x = 3$$

The turning point is located above 3 on the horizontal axis. If you look back to Figure 3.4 you can see that the plotted curve reaches its minimum at that point. We can conclude that the minimum production cost per car will be achieved when 3 million cars are produced.

The cost per car at that level of production is something we can establish by inserting the value of x at the turning point into the original production cost equation:

$$y = x^2 - 6x + 11$$

$$\text{Minimum cost} = 3^2 - 6*3 + 11 = 9 - 18 + 11 = 2$$

If 3 million cars are produced the cost per car will be £2000.

In Example 3.7 we were able to refer back to Figure 3.4 and see from the graph that the turning point was a minimum. But what if the cost equation had not been plotted, how could we tell that it was a minimum and not a maximum? We take the derivative and differentiate again to produce a *second derivative*. If the second derivative is positive the turning point is a minimum, if it is negative the turning point is a maximum. It may help to think that after a minimum the only way to go is up, so the second derivative is positive whereas after a maximum the only way to go is down, so the second derivative is negative.

Example 3.8

Find the second derivative of the production cost equation from Example 3.4.
   The first derivative of the cost equation was:

$$\frac{dy}{dx} = 2x - 6$$

If we differentiate this again we get 2, which is of course positive, confirming that the turning point is a minimum.

To distinguish the second from the original or first derivative the notation representing it is:

$$\frac{d^2 y}{dx^2} = 2$$

The inclusion of the 2s on the left hand side signifies that the process of differentiation has been applied twice in reaching the result.

Example 3.9

The total revenue for the firm in Example 3.5 was:

$$y = -x^2 + 4x$$

where y is the total revenue in millions of pounds and x is the price per holiday in thousands of pounds.

Find the first order derivative and use it to locate the turning point. Confirm that the turning point is a maximum by finding the second derivative, and work out the maximum revenue.

The first derivative is:

$$\frac{dy}{dx} = -2x + 4$$

Turning point location:

$$-2x + 4 = 0$$
$$-2x = -4$$
$$x = 2$$

Revenue will be maximized when the price is £2000.
The second derivative is:

$$\frac{d^2y}{dx^2} = -2$$

Since the second derivative is negative, the turning point is a maximum.
The revenue when the price is £2000:

$$y = -(2)^2 + 4 * 2 = -4 + 8 = 4$$

The maximum revenue is £4 million.

At this point you may find it useful to try **Review Questions 3.2 to 3.11** at the end of the chapter.

3.3 The Economic Order Quantity model

An important application of the calculus we looked at in the previous section occurs in a technique companies use to manage inventories, the Economic Order Quantity (EOQ) model. This model was developed to help companies manage stocks of materials and components, specifically by enabling managers to work out the quantity to order each time if they want to minimize costs.

Before we look at the model in detail it is worth reflecting on the reasons companies keep stocks or inventories. Most companies keep some stock of the materials they need for their operations; a bus company will probably have a stock of diesel fuel, a furniture maker will probably have a stock of wood. Such stocks are important because being without the material would disadvantage the company. On the other hand, if a company keeps a large amount of stock the costs of holding it are likely to be very high. The stock would have to be stored somewhere, perhaps under certain temperature or security constraints, and these facilities will have a cost.

For sound business reasons then a company will not want to run out of stock, yet will not want to hold too much. To resolve this, a company might consider placing small, regular orders with their supplier. Whilst this would mean that stock would never be very high, and hence stock-holding costs would be modest, it will probably cost money every time an order is made; a requisition may have to be processed, a delivery charge met, a payment authorized. They would find that the more orders they make, the higher the cost of making them.

The dilemma they face is to decide how much material should be ordered each time they place an order, the order quantity, so that the combined costs of making the orders and holding the stock, the *total stock cost*, is at a minimum. To see how this can be resolved we need to start by examining how the total stock-holding costs and the total order costs vary in relation to the quantity ordered.

We shall concentrate on the simplest Economic Order Quantity model, in which we assume that the rate at which the material is used is constant. The amount used in one week is the same as the amount used in any other week. We also assume that once an order is placed the material will be delivered right away, there is no time lag for delivery. This latter assumption means that the company can wait until their stock runs out before placing an order for its replenishment.

Taking these assumptions together we can conclude that the highest amount that could be in stock would be the order quantity, which we will refer to as Q, the amount that is ordered every time an order is placed. The lowest level of stock will be zero, since they don't need to order more until they run out. The rate of use is constant, so the fluctuations in the stock level will follow the pattern shown in Figure 3.6.

The repeating saw-tooth pattern that you can see in Figure 3.6 consists of a series of vertical lines each of which represents a delivery of the order quantity, Q. The stock level peaks at Q at the point of each delivery and then declines at a constant rate as the material is taken out of the store and used until the stock level is zero and another delivery comes in.

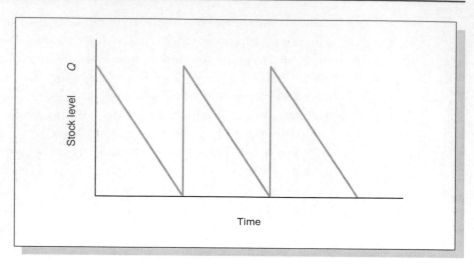

Figure 3.6
Stock levels
over time

The level of stock fluctuates between Q and 0. The even rate of depletion means that the average stock level will be midway between these extremes, half of Q.

If we use S to represent the cost of storing one unit of the material for a year then the cost of storing an average of $Q/2$ units in stock for a year, the total annual stock-holding cost, is:

$$\frac{SQ}{2}$$

The implication of this expression is that the bigger the order quantity, the larger the average stock and hence the greater the total annual stock cost.

The other part of the total stock cost is the total order cost, which again we shall express for a whole year. If we use Y to represent the number of units of the material that are used over a year, then the number of orders made during a year will be Y divided by the amount that is ordered on each occasion, the order quantity:

$$\frac{Y}{Q}$$

If we use C to represent the cost of making an order, the total order cost for a year will be the number of orders multiplied by the order cost:

$$\frac{CY}{Q}$$

The implication of this expression is that the larger the order quantity the fewer the number of orders and hence the lower the total annual order cost. Note that the total order cost for the year is the total cost of making the orders and not the total purchase cost of the items bought.

We will assume for the time being that the purchase cost of the items will be the same whether they are bought ten at a time or a hundred at a time.

The total stock cost for a year is the sum of the total annual stock-holding cost and the total annual order cost:

$$\text{Total stock cost} = \frac{SQ}{2} + \frac{CY}{Q}$$

This total cost will vary according to the size of Q, the order quantity. We assume that in any given context the other factors, the storage cost, annual demand and so on, are fixed, so we can focus on how big the order quantity should be if the total stock cost is to be minimized.

Example 3.10

The Cheesty Cleaning Company uses 200 gallons of floor cleaner over a year. The company would like to find out how many gallons of floor cleaner they should order at a time to minimize their total stock costs.

The cost of storing one gallon of floor cleaner for a year is £50. We will begin by showing graphically how the total annual stock-holding costs are related to the quantity ordered.

$$\text{The total annual stock cost} = \frac{SQ}{2} = \frac{50Q}{2} = 25Q$$

Using this expression we can work out the total annual stock-holding cost for a given order quantity, for instance if the order quantity is 5 the total annual stock-holding cost will be £125. The expression is plotted in Figure 3.7.

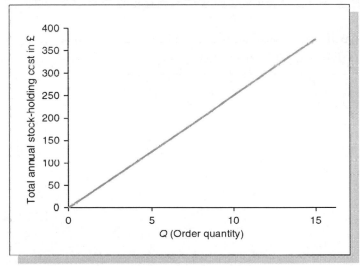

Figure 3.7
Total annual stock-holding cost and order quantity in Example 3.10

The cost of processing an order for a consignment of floor cleaner is £12.50. We can show graphically how the total annual order costs are related to the quantity ordered.

$$\text{Total annual order cost} = \frac{CY}{Q} = \frac{12.50 * 200}{Q} = \frac{2500}{Q}$$

From this we can find the total annual order cost for a given order quantity. If, say, the order quantity is 5 gallons the total annual order cost will be 2500/5, £500. The expression is plotted in Figure 3.8.

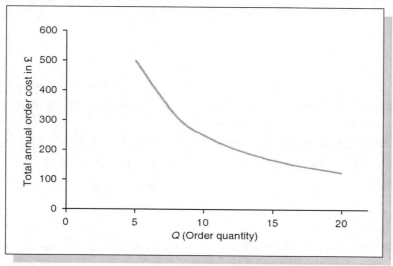

Figure 3.8
Total annual order cost and order quantity in Example 3.10

The company will have both stock-holding and order costs so we need to see how these costs combined, the total annual stock cost, are related to the order quantity.

$$\text{Total annual stock cost} = \frac{CY}{Q} + \frac{SQ}{2} = \frac{12.5 * 240}{Q} + \frac{50Q}{2} = \frac{3000}{Q} + 25Q$$

We can use this to determine the total annual stock costs for a specific order quantity, for instance 5 gallons:

$$\text{Total annual stock cost} = \frac{3000}{5} + 25 * 5 = 600 + 125 = £725$$

Figure 3.9 shows the relationship between total annual stock cost and order quantity. The uppermost line in Figure 3.9 represents the total annual stock cost. The lower straight line represents the total annual stock holding cost, the lower curve represents

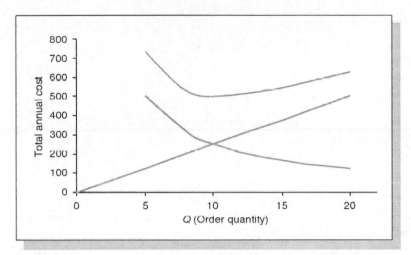

Figure 3.9
Total annual stock cost and order quantity in Example 3.10

the total annual order cost. These lines reflect the fact that as the order quantity is increased the holding costs will rise and the order costs will fall.

If you look carefully at Figure 3.9 you will see that the curve representing the total annual stock cost does reach a minimum when the order quantity is about 10 gallons.

To ascertain the exact position of the minimum point of the total stock cost equation we can differentiate it:

$$\text{Total annual stock cost} = \frac{CY}{Q} + \frac{SQ}{2} = CYQ^{-1} + \frac{SQ}{2}$$

$$\frac{\text{dCost}}{\text{d}Q} = -CYQ^{-2} + \frac{S}{2} = \frac{CY}{Q^2} + \frac{S}{2}$$

At the minimum point of the curve this derivative will be equal to zero:

$$-\frac{CY}{Q^2} + \frac{S}{2} = 0$$

We can rearrange this to obtain a definition of the least-cost order quantity:

$$\frac{S}{2} = \frac{CY}{Q^2}$$

$$\frac{S}{2CY} = \frac{1}{Q^2}$$

$$\frac{2CY}{S} = Q^2$$

$$\sqrt{\frac{2CY}{S}} = Q$$

So Q, the least cost or *economic order quantity* is:

$$Q = \sqrt{\frac{2CY}{S}}$$

This is the Economic Order Quantity (EOQ) model.

Of course, the square root of the expression on the left of the EOQ model can in theory be either positive or negative, but since only a positive order quantity makes practical sense the positive root is the only relevant one.

We can confirm that at this value of Q the total stock cost is at a minimum by finding the second derivative of the total stock cost equation:

$$\frac{d^2\text{Cost}}{dQ^2} = (-2) - CYQ^{-3} = \frac{CY}{Q^3}$$

If this is positive it means that the turning point is indeed a minimum. This will be the case because C, the order cost, and Y, the annual demand for the item, and all plausible values of Q will be positive so the second derivative will always have a positive value.

Example 3.11

Use the Economic Order Quantity model to find the order quantity Cheesty Cleaners should use in purchasing their supplies of floor cleaner, and find out the total annual stock costs they will incur by implementing that stock control policy.

The order cost, C, in this case is £12.50, the annual demand, Y, is 200 gallons and the stock holding cost, S, is £50. Their economic order quantity is:

$$Q = \sqrt{\frac{2CY}{S}} = \sqrt{\frac{2 * 12.50 * 200}{50}} = \sqrt{\frac{5000}{50}} = \sqrt{10} = 10$$

To minimize its total stock costs the company should order 10 gallons of floor cleaner at a time.

The total annual stock costs when Q is 10 will be:

$$\text{Total annual stock cost} = \frac{CY}{Q} + \frac{SQ}{2} = \frac{12.50 * 200}{10} + \frac{50 * 10}{2} = 250 + 250 = £500$$

Note that in Example 3.11 both elements of the total annual stock cost, the total annual order cost and the total annual stock-holding cost, are equal when the amount ordered is the economic order quantity. This is no accident; in the EOQ model the minimum point of the total annual stock cost curve is always directly above the point where the lines representing the total annual order cost and the total annual stock-holding cost cross. You can see this if you look back at Figure 3.9.

At this point you may find it useful to try **Review Questions 3.12 to 3.20** at the end of the chapter.

3.4 Road test: Do they really use the Economic Order Quantity model?

The Economic Order Quantity model is a well-established technique that dates back about a century. Its invention is usually credited to Ford Whitman Harris, a production engineer at Westinghouse, the US electrical goods manufacturer. In 1913 the journal *Factory, The Magazine of Management* published an article by Harris in which he described a systematic approach to calculating the optimal size of production runs, a technique that is sometimes called the Economic Batch Quantity model. Harris used examples drawn from his experience at Westinghouse, specifically dealing with small copper components, to show how mathematics could be used to identify the least-cost production run that balanced the cost of storing the output against the cost of setting up the production run (Harris, 1990).

Some years later R.H. Wilson independently reported essentially the same approach to finding the optimal quantity to purchase, rather than the optimal quantity to make (Wilson, 1934). Both models involve storage costs, in the first case of output, in the second case of bought-in items, but whereas the batch quantity model includes set-up costs incurred prior to manufacture, the purchase quantity model includes the cost of making an order.

Wilson reported that the Western Electric Company had developed a model similar to the one he described, some years previously (Wilson, 1934, p. 122 *fn4*). Western Electric was for many years the largest electrical equipment manufacturer in the USA. Originally the supplier of telegraph equipment to Western Union it became the manufacturing arm of the group of corporations known as the Bell System, which built and operated the telephone networks of the USA. It had a reputation for innovations, both technical and managerial. As well as stock control it was the seedbed for breakthroughs in product quality control and industrial psychology. The Hawthorne experiments that were the foundation of the human relations theory of management were conducted at the Western Electric plant at Hawthorne on the outskirts of Chicago.

Other major US manufacturers adopted the EOQ model as a key element in the management of their stocks and purchasing decision-making. It was attractive because it was a technique that reduced the chances of being out of stock and at the same time avoided holding too large an amount of stock. Berk and Berk (1993), who are highly critical of the model, concede that:

> For most of America's manufacturing history, industry has followed the economic ordering quantity (or EOQ for short) philosophy of inventory management. (Berk and Berk, 1993, p. 186)

Despite its widespread use both in the USA and elsewhere the EOQ model has serious limitations. These might be subdivided between the practical and the philosophical. The practical limitations arise because some of the assumptions that are made in deriving the basic EOQ model are simply unrealistic.

One assumption is that demand for the item is constant. Whilst there are some situations where this may be true, such as items used on a consistent basis by maintenance departments, typically demand for items is variable rather than fixed. Although this is a common criticism of the model it was a limitation that Wilson recognized:

> This system is not intended to apply to stock control of style, seasonal, or perishable goods, but has found its chief application in the field of routine orders and of goods not subject to the vagaries of fashion. (Wilson, 1934, p. 116)

In practice, forecasting the demand for the item concerned became an important adjunct of the EOQ model.

A further assumption is that delivery of the item by the supplier is immediate. In practice there was typically some time lag between the placing of an order and its being delivered, and to complicate matters further the delivery time could vary. To allow for this uncertainty the idea of a reorder level, a volume of stock at which the placing of a new order was triggered, was built into the model.

More complications arise in applying the EOQ model when the costs of running out of stock are very high, perhaps the loss of important customers. Such a possibility is simply not catered for in the EOQ model. The model also did not allow for the common practice of securing a discount for buying in bulk, since it excludes the purchase price of the item. Such a saving might be so significant that it outweighs the costs that are the focus of the EOQ model.

Most organizations of any size are likely to store many different items at many different locations, perhaps involving different costs of capital. This makes it very difficult to identify even an approximate storage cost for a given item.

The limitations in the EOQ model meant that it came to be regarded as a rough guide to stock control policy rather than the source of a definitive solution. This is in part because the optimal order policy shown in a diagram like Figure 3.9 is at the bottom of a shallow curve, particularly along the section to the right of the minimum point on the curve. This suggests that even if the actual order quantity is a little higher than the EOQ, the resulting increase in total stock costs is modest.

To find out more about the practical limitations of the EOQ model, and how it was adapted to deal with some of them, you may find Lewis (2001) helpful.

The philosophical limitations of the EOQ model relate to the assumptions, but to the influence they had on stock control management rather than their practical feasibility. One of the things that the EOQ model assumes is that delivery times are outside the control of the purchasing organization, whereas it may be possible to negotiate the reduction or even eradication of delivery lags with a supplier, particularly if the purchasing organization is a particularly important customer for the supplier.

Despite the criticisms levelled at it the EOQ model remains an important topic. Historically it can be seen as a springboard for the development of the more comprehensive Materials Requirements Planning and Just-in-time inventory management techniques. The EOQ model provided a key benchmark for one of the US pioneers of Just-in-time production management, Dennis Butt, the manager of the Kawasaki Heavy Industries plant in the USA. The plant was set up to manufacture motorcycles, jet skis and snowmobiles for the American market and had a troubled early history. The way Butt used EOQ as a reference point is described in Schonberger (1982). Hall (1987) provides a fuller account of the improvements introduced at the Kawasaki factory.

Answers to these questions, including fully worked solutions to the Key questions marked with an asterisk(*), are on pages 633–636.

3.1*   Differentiate each of the equations listed below on the left and match your answers to the derivatives listed on the right.

(i) $y = 3x$

(a) $\dfrac{dy}{dx} = \dfrac{-1}{x^2}$

(ii) $y = 4x^2$

(b) $\dfrac{dy}{dx} = 2x^3$

(iii) $y = 2x^3$

(c) $\dfrac{dy}{dx} = 8x$

(iv) $y = \dfrac{1}{x}$

(d) $\dfrac{dy}{dx} = 2x + 4$

(v) $y = \dfrac{x^4}{2}$

(e) $\dfrac{dy}{dx} = \dfrac{-10}{x^3} - 1$

(vi) $y = 3x^3 + 2$

(f) $\dfrac{dy}{dx} = 3$

(vii) $y = x^2 + 4x$

(g) $\dfrac{dy}{dx} = 6x^2$

(viii) $y = \dfrac{5}{x^2} - x$

(h) $\dfrac{dy}{dx} = \dfrac{-2}{3x^2} + 10x$

(ix) $y = \dfrac{2}{3x} + 5x^2$

(i) $\dfrac{dy}{dx} = 16x^3 + 9x^2$

(x) $y = 4x^4 + 3x^3$

(j) $\dfrac{dy}{dx} = 9x^2$

3.2*   Ackno Fenestrations manufacture garden conservatories to order. Their production costs per unit vary with the number of conservatories they produce per month according to the equation:

$$y = 2x^2 - 280x + 16000$$

where y is the cost per conservatory in £, and x is the monthly output.

(a) Find the least cost level of output.

(b) Obtain the second derivative and use it to demonstrate that at the level of output you identify in (a) the cost per conservatory will be minimized.

(c) Work out the minimum cost per conservatory.

3.3 Glazzy Opticon performs laser eye surgery in a purpose-built facility. The cost per operation in £, y, depends on the number of operations conducted per week, x, as follows:

$$y = \frac{x^2}{2} - 36x + 1300$$

(a) How many operations should be undertaken per week to minimize the cost per operation?

(b) Confirm by means of the second derivative that the cost equation will reach a minimum when this many operations are performed.

(c) What is the minimum cost per operation?

3.4 Cartina Technologies make digital cameras. The cost of manufacture per unit at their factory in £, y, is related to output per hour, x, in line with the equation:

$$y = 0.8x^2 - 16x + 150$$

(a) How many cameras should be made per hour if they are to minimize the cost per camera?

(b) Determine the second derivative and use it to confirm that the cost equation will be at a minimum when this many cameras are produced.

(c) Calculate the minimum cost per camera.

3.5* The 2Flee Footwear Company intends to launch a new brand of designer shoes. They anticipate that revenue from the sale of these shoes will vary with the selling price in the following way:

$$y = -4x^2 + 960x$$

where y is revenue and x is the selling price (both in £).

(a) At what price will revenue be maximized?

(b) Demonstrate with reference to the second derivative that the revenue equation will be at a maximum at this price.

(c) What is the maximum revenue?

3.6 Varota United Football Club want to set a price for a season ticket that will maximize their revenue from season tickets.

Past experience suggests that total season ticket revenue in £, y, is related to the price in £, x, in keeping with the equation:

$$y = -3x^2 + 3000x$$

(a) What season ticket price will maximize revenue?
(b) Show that the revenue equation will be maximized at this price using the second derivative.
(c) Calculate the maximum revenue.

3.7   The Mashinar Garage provides an exhaust system replacement service for the Bistri car. The revenue from this operation in thousands of pounds, y, depends on the price of the service in £, x, in line with the equation:

$$y = -\frac{x^2}{5} + 10x - 90$$

(a) How much should they charge for this service to maximize their revenue from it?
(b) Find the second derivative and use it to show that the revenue equation will be at a maximum at the price established in (a).
(c) What is the maximum revenue they can expect?

3.8*   Peridatt Audio manufactures specialist sound amplifiers. The company have identified the following expressions to represent the demand for their products and the total cost of their operations:

$$\text{Price (£)} = 500 - 3x$$

$$\text{Cost (£)} = 150 + 20x + x^2$$

where x is the number of amplifiers produced and sold. (Production is to order only.)

(a) Determine the profit equation for the company.
(b) Use the profit equation to find the profit maximizing level of output and price, and the optimum profit.
(c) Find the second derivative of the profit equation and use it to confirm that the output level in (b) does occur at a maximum.

3.9   Gladeet Domestic offers busy professionals a clothes-ironing service. The equations that represent the connections between their volume of business in thousands of clients (x), and firstly the price they charge, and secondly the total cost they incur are:

$$\text{Price (£)} = 60 - x$$

$$\text{Cost (£000)} = 80 + 6x + 2x^2$$

(a) Derive the profit equation for their business.
(b) What are the profit maximizing levels of output and price, and the maximum profit they can obtain?
(c) Obtain the second derivative of the profit equation and use it to prove that the output level in (b) occurs at a maximum.

3.10　Avaria Autosports sell rally-driving adventure weekends to companies looking for incentive gifts for staff. Careful study of their past sales suggests that the price per weekend is based on the number of weekends sold, x, in line with:

$$\text{Price (£)} = 635 - 3x$$

Their costs depend on the weekends sold according to the expression:

$$\text{Cost(£)} = 450 + 5x + \frac{x^2}{2}$$

(a) Obtain the profit equation for the company.
(b) Use this equation to find the number of sales and the price at which they would maximize their profit, as well as the maximum profit.
(c) By means of the second derivative of the profit equation demonstrate that the sales level in (b) is at a maximum point on the profit equation.

3.11　Soumotchka Accessories make customized handbags to order. The price they can charge depends on how many they sell, x, consistent with the expression:

$$\text{Price (£)} = 242 - 0.4x$$

The total cost of producing the handbags is:

$$\text{Cost (£)} = 300 + 2x + 0.1x^2$$

(a) What is the profit equation for the company?
(b) What are the number of bags sold and the selling price at which they would maximize their profit?
(c) What is the maximum profit?
(d) Find the second derivative of the profit equation and use it to ascertain that the number of bags sold in (b) does occur at a maximum point of the profit equation.

3.12*　Doroga City Council Highways Department uses 2000 litres of yellow road paint a year at a constant rate. It costs the council £50 per litre to store the paint for a year. Each time a purchase order for paint is processed the cost to the council is £20. What is the optimal order quantity of paint that will allow the council to minimize its total stock cost?

3.13   The annual demand for dog biscuits at Dogwatch Security amounts to 1690 kg. The cost of the manager going to collect a supply of dog biscuits in her company car is reckoned to be £40 per trip. The cost of storing the biscuits is estimated to be £8 per kilogram per year. The dog biscuits come in sealed packs and last indefinitely. How many kilograms of dog biscuits should the manager collect at a time to minimize their total stock costs?

3.14   Twenty packs of paper towels are used in the washrooms in an office block every week. The cost of making an order for them is £6, and the cost of storing one pack for a year is £0.30. If the building is in use 50 weeks of the year, what quantity of towels should be ordered each time new supplies are required?

3.15   A film-processing laboratory uses 37.5 litres of developer per week and is open for business 50 weeks in a year. Administrative and other costs of ordering a consignment of developer are £15 and it costs £10 to keep one litre of developer in stock for a year. Use the Economic Order Quantity formula to work out how much developer should be ordered each time they need to replenish their stock.

3.16   Mechanics at a large vehicle repair and servicing centre use 56 kg of grease-remover a year. Storage costs for the grease-remover are £2 per kilogram per year, and the cost of putting in an order to the supplier is £14.

      (a) If the centre is open for 50 weeks of the year how much grease-remover should be ordered on each occasion that an order is made?

      (b) If they use the order quantity from (a), how many orders would need to be made in a year?

3.17   The Pratchka Laundry uses 2205 kg of industrial detergent per year. The cost of processing an order for the detergent is £50 per order, and the cost of storage works out at £5 per kilogram per year.

      (a) Assuming that the laundry operates for 52 weeks a year, what, according to the Economic Order Quantity model, is the amount that should be ordered each time?

      (b) If they followed this practice what would their total annual stock cost be?

3.18   The manager of a garden centre expects that sales of barbecue fuel will reach 16,000 bags for the year. The cost of keeping a bag of barbecue fuel in stock for a year is put at £5 and the administrative and other costs associated with implementing an order amount to £25.

(a) Use the EOQ model to advise the proprietor how many bags should be ordered each time an order is made.

(b) What will be the average stock level if the proprietor does as you advise in (a)?

(c) In the light of the assumptions on which the EOQ model is based, how valid is its application to this case?

3.19 The kitchen at a children's hospital used 12,800 kg of ice cream last year and expects to use approximately the same amount this year. The storage costs incurred by keeping 1 kg of ice cream in the freezer for a year are estimated to be £7. To process an order to the supplier costs £28.

(a) Use the EOQ formula to ascertain how much ice cream (to the nearest kg) should be ordered each time to minimize costs.

(b) Scrapping obsolete equipment means that maximum storage capacity has recently been reduced to 350 kg. Will this be sufficient for the stocks that will accumulate if your recommendation in (a) is implemented?

(c) The storage cost has been recalculated to be £10 per kilogram per year. What is the new EOQ?

3.20 Aptieka Chemicals uses 80 litres of a solvent per week in a continuous process. Storing the solvent in accordance with fire and safety requirements costs £5 per litre per annum. The cost of administering an order is £26.

(a) Assuming the process operates for all 52 weeks of the year, how much of the solvent should the company order each time if total stock costs are to be minimized?

(b) How will a 25% increase in the price of the solvent affect the Economic Order Quantity?

CHAPTER 4

Filling up — fuelling quantitative analysis

This chapter will help you to:

- understand key statistical terms
- distinguish between primary and secondary data
- recognize different types of data
- arrange data using basic tabulation and frequency distributions
- use the technology: arrange data in EXCEL, MINITAB and SPSS.

In previous chapters we have concentrated on techniques or models involving single values that are known with certainty. Examples of these are break-even analysis and linear programming, which we looked at in Chapter 2, and the Economic Order Quantity model featured in Chapter 3. In break-even analysis the revenue per unit, the fixed cost and the variable cost per unit are in each case a specified single value. In linear programming we assume that both profit per unit and resource usage are constant amounts. In the Economic Order Quantity model the order cost and the stock-holding cost per unit are each known single values. Because these types of models involve values that are fixed or *predetermined* they are called *deterministic* models.

Deterministic models can be useful means of understanding and resolving business problems. Their reliance on known single value inputs makes them relatively easy to use but is their key shortcoming. Companies simply cannot rely on a figure such as the amount of raw material used per unit of production being a single constant value. In practice, such an amount may not be known with certainty, because it is subject to chance variation. Because of this company managers may well need to study the variation and incorporate it within the models they use to guide them.

Models that use input values that are uncertain rather than certain, values that are subject to chance variation rather than known, are called *probabilistic* models, after the field of *probability*, which involves the measurement and analysis of chance. We shall be dealing with probability in later chapters.

Before you can use probability to reflect the chance variation in business situations you need to know how to get some idea of the variation. To do this we have to start by ascertaining where relevant information might be found. Having identified these sources you need to know how to arrange and present what you find from them in forms that will help you understand and communicate the variation. In order to do this in appropriate ways it is important that you are aware of the different types of data that you may meet.

The purpose of this chapter is therefore to acquaint you with some essential preliminaries for studying variation. We will start with definitions of some key terms, before looking into sources of data and considering the different types of data. Subsequently we shall look at basic methods of arranging data.

4.1 Some key words you need to know

There are several important terms that you will find mentioned frequently in this and subsequent chapters. They are:

Data   The word data is a plural noun (the singular form is *datum*), which means a set of known or given things, facts. Data can be numerical (e.g. wages of employees) or non-numerical (e.g. job titles of employees).

Variable   A variable is a quantity that varies, the opposite of a constant. For example, the number of telephone calls made to a call centre per hour is a variable, whereas the number of minutes in an hour is a constant. Often a capital letter, usually X or Y, is used to represent a variable.

Value   A value is a specific amount that a variable could be. For example the number of telephone calls made to a call centre per hour could be 47 or 71. These are both possible values of the variable 'number of calls made'.

Observation or *Observed value*   This is a value of a variable that has actually occurred, i.e. been counted or measured. For example, if 58 telephone calls are made to a call centre in a particular hour that is an observation or observed value of the variable 'number of calls made'.

An observation is represented by the lower case of the letter used to represent the variable; for instance 'x' represents a single observed value of the variable 'X'. A small numerical suffix is added to distinguish particular observations in a set; x_1 would represent the first observed value, x_2 the second and so on.

Data set   A data set consists of all the observations of all the variables collected in the course of a study or investigation, together with the variable names.

Random   This describes something that occurs in an unplanned way, by chance.

Random variable   A random variable has observed values that arise by chance. The number of new cars a car dealer sells during a month is a random variable; whereas the number of days in a month is a variable that is not random because its observed values are pre-determined.

Distribution   The pattern exhibited by the observed values of a variable when they are arranged in order of magnitude. A *theoretical* distribution is one that has been deduced, rather than compiled from observed values.

Population   Generally this means the total number of persons residing in a defined area at a given time. In quantitative methods a *population* is the complete set of things or *elements* we want to investigate. These may be human, such as all the people who have purchased a particular product, or inanimate, such as all the cars repaired at a garage.

Sample   A sample is a subset of a population, that is, a smaller number of items picked from the population. A *random sample* is a sample that has components chosen in a random way, on the basis that any single item in the population has no more or less chance than any other to be included in the sample.

A typical quantitative investigation of a business problem might involve defining the *population* and specifying the *variables* to be studied. Following this a *sample* of *elements* from the *population* is selected and *observations* of the *variables* for each element in the sample recorded. Once the data set has been assembled work can begin on arranging and presenting the data so that the patterns of variation in the *distributions* of values can be examined.

At this point you may find it useful to try **Review Question 4.1** at the end of the chapter.

4.2 Sources of data

The data that form the basis of an investigation might be collected at first hand in response to a specific problem. This type of data, collected by direct observation or measurement, is known as *primary data*. The procedures used to gather primary data are surveys, experiments and observational methods. A survey might involve asking consumers their opinion of a product. A series of experiments might be conducted on products to assess their quality. Observation might be used to ascertain the hazards at building sites.

The advantages of using primary data are that they should match the requirements of those conducting the investigation and they are up-to-date. The disadvantages are that gathering such data is both costly and time-consuming.

An alternative might be to find data that have already been collected by someone else. This is known as *secondary data*. A company looking for data for a specific study will have access to internal sources of secondary data, but as well as those there are a large number of external sources; government statistical publications, company reports, academic and industry publications, and specialist information services such as the Economist Intelligence Unit. The advantages of using secondary data are that they are usually easier and cheaper to obtain. The disadvantages are that they could be out of date and may not be entirely suitable for the purposes of the investigation.

4.3 Types of data

Collecting data is usually not an end in itself. When collected the data will be in 'raw' form, a state that might lead someone to refer to it as 'meaningless data'. Once it is collected the next stage is to begin transforming it into *information*, literally to enable it to *inform* us about the issue being investigated.

There is a wide range of techniques that you can use to organize, display and represent data. Selecting which ones to use depends on the type of data you have. The nature of the raw material you are working with determines your choice of tools. Scissors are fine for cutting paper but no good for cutting wood. A saw will cut wood but is useless for cutting paper. It is therefore essential that you understand the nature of the data you want to analyse before embarking on the analysis, so in this section we will look at several ways of distinguishing between different types of data.

There are different types of data because there are different ways in which facts are gathered. Some data may exist because specific things have characteristics that have been categorized whereas other data may exist as a result of things being counted, or measured, on some sort of scale.

Example 4.1

Holders of a certain type of investment account are described as 'wealthy'.

To investigate this we could use socio-economic definitions of class to *categorize* each account holder, or we could *count* the number of homes owned by each account holder, or we could *measure* the income of each account holder.

Perhaps the most important way of contrasting data types is on the basis of the scales of measurement used in obtaining them. The acronym *NOIR* stands for *N*ominal, *O*rdinal, *I*nterval, *R*atio; the four basic data types. Nominal is the 'lowest' form of data, which contains the least amount of information. Ratio is the 'highest' form of data, which contains the most amount of information.

The word nominal comes from the same Latin root as the word name. Nominal data are data that consist solely of names or labels. These labels might be numeric such as a bank account number, or they might be non-numeric such as gender. Nominal data can be categorized using the labels themselves to establish, for instance the number of males and females. It is possible to represent and analyse nominal data using proportions and modes (the modal category is the one that contains the most observations), but carrying out more sophisticated analysis such as calculating an average is inappropriate; for example, adding a set of telephone numbers together and dividing by the number there are to get an average would be meaningless.

Like nominal data, ordinal or 'order' data consist of labels that can be used to categorize the data, but order data can also be ranked. Examples of ordinal data are academic grades and finishing positions in a horse race. An academic grade is a label (an 'A' grade student) that also belongs to a ranking system ('A' is better than 'B'). Because ordinal data contain more information than nominal data we can use a wider variety of techniques to represent and analyse them. As well as proportions and modes we can also use *order statistics*, such as identifying the middle or *median* observation. However, any method involving arithmetic is not suitable for ordinal data because although the data can be ranked the intervals between the ranks are not consistent. For instance, the difference between the horse finishing first in a race and the one finishing second is one place. The difference between the horse finishing third and the one finishing fourth is also one place, but this does not mean that there is the same distance between the third- and fourth-placed horses as there is between the first- and second-placed horses.

Interval data consist of labels and can be ranked, but in addition the intervals are measured in fixed units so the differences between values have meaning. It follows from this that unlike nominal and ordinal, both of which can be either numeric or non-numeric, interval data are always numeric. Because interval data are based on a consistent numerical scale, techniques using arithmetical procedures can be applied to them. Temperatures measured in degrees Fahrenheit are interval data. The difference between 30° and 40° is the same as the difference between 80° and 90°.

What distinguishes interval data from the highest data form, ratio data, is that interval data are measured on a scale that does not have a meaningful zero point to 'anchor' it. The zero point is arbitrary, for instance 0° Fahrenheit does not mean a complete lack of heat, nor is it the same as 0° Celsius. The lack of a meaningful zero also means that ratios between the data are not consistent, for example 40° is not half as hot as 80°. (The Celsius equivalents of these temperatures are 4.4° and 26.7°, the same heat levels yet they have a completely different ratio between them.)

Ratio-type data has all the characteristics of interval data – it consists of labels that can be ranked as well as being measured in fixed amounts on a numerical scale. The difference is that the scale has a meaningful zero and ratios between observations are consistent. Distances are ratio data whether we measure them in miles or kilometres. Zero kilometres and zero miles mean the same – no distance. Ten miles is twice as far as five, and their kilometre equivalents, 16 and 8, have the same ratio between them.

Example 4.2

Identify the data types of the variables in Example 4.1.

The socio-economic classes of account holders are ordinal data because they are labels for the account holders and they can be ranked.

The numbers of homes owned by account holders and the incomes of account holders are both ratio data. Four homes are twice as many as two, and £60,000 is twice as much income as £30,000.

At this point you may find it useful to try **Review Question 4.2** at the end of the chapter.

Another important distinction you need to make is between *qualitative* data and *quantitative* data. Qualitative data consist of categories or types of a characteristic or attribute and are always either nominal or ordinal. The categories form the basis of the analysis of qualitative data. Quantitative data are based on counting 'how many' or measuring 'how much' and are always of interval or ratio type. The numerical scale used to produce the figures forms the basis of the analysis of quantitative data.

There are two different types of quantitative data: *discrete* and *continuous*. Discrete data are quantitative data that can take only a limited number of values because they are produced by counting in distinct or 'discrete' steps, or measuring against a scale made up of distinct steps.

There are three types of discrete data that you may come across. First, data that can only take certain values because other values simply cannot occur, for example the number of hats sold by a clothing retailer in a day. There could be 12 sold one day and 7 on another, but selling 9.3 hats in a day is not possible because there is no such thing as 0.3 of a hat. Such data are discrete by definition.

Secondly, data that take only certain values because those are the ones that have been established by long-standing custom and practice, for example bars in the UK sell draught beer in whole and half pints. You could try asking for three-quarters of a pint, but the bar staff would no doubt insist that you purchase the smaller or larger quantity. They simply would not have the equipment or pricing information to hand to do otherwise.

There are also data that only take certain values because the people who have provided the data or the analysis have decided, for convenience, to round values that do not have to be discrete. This is what you are doing when you give your age to the last full year. Similarly, the temperatures given in weather reports are rounded to the nearest degree, and the distances on road signs are usually rounded to the nearest mile. These data are discrete by convention rather than by definition. They are really *continuous* data.

Discrete data often but not always consist of whole number values. The number of visitors to a website will always be a whole number, but shoe sizes include half sizes. In other cases, like the UK standard sizes of women's clothing, only some whole numbers occur.

The important thing to remember about discrete data is that there are gaps between the values that can occur, that is why this type of data is sometimes referred to as *discontinuous* data. In contrast, continuous data consist of numerical values that are not restricted to specific numbers. Such data are called continuous because there are no gaps between feasible values. This is because measuring on a continuous scale such as distance or temperature yields continuous data.

The precision of continuous data is limited only by how precisely the quantities are measured. For instance, we measure both the length of bus journeys and athletic performances using the scale of time. In the first case a clock or a wristwatch is sufficiently accurate, but in the second case we would use a stopwatch or an even more sophisticated timing device.

The terms *discrete variable* and *continuous variable* are used in describing data sets. A discrete variable has discrete values whereas a continuous variable has continuous values.

Example 4.3

A motoring magazine describes cars using the following variables:

> Type of vehicle – Hatchback/Estate/MPV/Off-Road/Performance
> Number of passengers that can be carried
> Fuel type – petrol/diesel
> Fuel efficiency in miles per gallon

Which variables are qualitative and which quantitative?
The type of car and fuel type are qualitative; the number of passengers and the fuel efficiency are quantitative.

Which quantitative variables are discrete and which continuous?
The number of passengers is discrete; the fuel efficiency is continuous.

At this point you may find it useful to try **Review Questions 4.3 and 4.4** at the end of the chapter.

In most of your early work on analysing variation you will probably be using data that consist of observed values of a single variable. However you may need to analyse data that consist of observed values of two variables in order to find out if there is a connection between them. For instance, we might want to ascertain how cab fares are related to journey times.

In dealing with a single variable we apply *univariate* analysis, whereas in dealing with two variables we apply *bivariate* analysis. The prefixes uni- and bi- in these words convey the same meanings as they do in other words like unilateral and bilateral. You may also find reference to *multivariate* analysis, which involves exploring relationships between more than two variables.

You may come across data referred to as either *hard* or *soft*. Hard data are facts, measurements or characteristics arising from situations that actually exist or were in existence. Temperatures recorded at a weather station and the nationalities of tourists are examples of hard data. Soft data are about beliefs, attitudes and behaviours. Asking consumers what they know about a product or how they feel about an advertisement will yield soft data. The implication of this distinction is that hard data can be subjected to a wider range of quantitative analysis. Soft data is at best ordinal and therefore offers less scope for quantitative analysis.

A further distinction you need to know is between *cross-section* and *time series* data. Cross-section data are data collected at the same point in time or based on the same period of time. Time series data consist of observations collected at regular intervals over time. The volumes of wine produced in European countries in 2002 are cross-section data whereas the volumes of wine produced in Italy in the years 1992 to 2002 are time series data.

At this point you may find it useful to try **Review Question 4.5** at the end of the chapter.

4.4 Arrangement of data

Arranging or *classifying* data in some sort of systematic manner is the vital first stage you should take in transforming the data into information, and hence getting it to 'talk to you'. The way you approach this depends on the type of data you wish to analyse.

4.4.1 Arranging qualitative data

Dealing with qualitative data is quite straightforward as long as the number of categories of the characteristic being studied is relatively small. Even if there are a large number of categories, the task can be made easier by merging categories.

The most basic way you can present a set of qualitative data is to *tabulate* it, to arrange it in the form of a summary table. A summary table consists of two parts, a list of categories of the characteristic, and the number of things that fall into each category, known as the *frequency* of the category. Compiling such a table is simply a matter of counting how many elements in the study fall into each category.

Example 4.4

Suppose we want to find how many different types of retail outlet in an area sell trainers.

We could tour the area or consult the telephone directory in order to compile a list of outlets, but the list itself may be too crude a form in which to present our results.

By listing the types of outlet and the number of each type of outlet we find we can construct a summary table:

Table 4.1
The number of outlets selling trainers by type of outlet

Type of outlet	Frequency	Relative frequency (%)
Shoe shops	12	30.8
Sports shops	11	28.2
Department stores	6	15.4
Other	10	25.6
Total number of outlets	39	100.0

In Table 4.1 the outlet types are qualitative data. The 'Other' category, which might contain several different types of outlet, such as hypermarkets and market stalls, has been created in order to keep the summary table to manageable proportions.

Notice that for each category, the number of outlets as a percentage of the total, the *relative frequency* of the category, is listed on the right hand side. This is to make it easier to communicate the contents; saying 30.8% of the outlets are shoe shops is more effective than saying 12/39ths of them were shoe shops, although they are different ways of saying the same thing.

You may want to use a summary table to present more than one attribute. Such a two-way tabulation is also known as a *contingency table* because it enables us to look for connections between the attributes, in other words to find out whether one attribute is *contingent* upon another.

Example 4.5

Four large retailers each operate their own loyalty scheme. Customers can apply for loyalty cards and receive points when they present them whilst making purchases. These points are accumulated and can subsequently be used to obtain gifts or discounts.

A survey of usage levels of loyalty cards provided the information in the following table:

Table 4.2
Number of transactions by loyalty card use

Retailer	Transactions		
	With card	**Without card**	**Total**
Aptyeka	236	705	941
Botinky	294	439	733
Crassivy	145	759	904
Total	675	1903	2578

At this point you may find it useful to try **Review Questions 4.6 to 4.8** at the end of the chapter.

4.4.2 Arranging quantitative data

The nature of quantitative data is different to qualitative data and therefore the methods used to arrange quantitative data are rather different. However, the most appropriate way of arranging some quantitative data is the same as the approach we have used to arrange qualitative data.

This applies to the analysis of a discrete quantitative variable that has a very few feasible values. You simply treat the values as you would the categories of a characteristic and tabulate the data to show how often each value occurs. When quantitative data are tabulated, the resulting table is called a *frequency distribution* because it demonstrates how frequently each value in the distribution occurs.

Example 4.6

The UREA department store offers free refills when customers purchase hot beverages in its cafe. The numbers of refills taken by 20 customers were:

0   1   3   1   2   0   2   2   0   1   0   3   1   0   1   2   1   1   0   2

These figures can be tabulated as follows:

Table 4.3
Number of hot beverage refills taken

Number of refills	Number of customers
0	6
1	7
2	5
3	2
Total number of customers	20

At this point you may find it useful to try **Review Questions 4.9 to 4.11** at the end of the chapter.

We can present the data in Example 4.6 in the form of a simple table because there are only a very limited number of values. Unfortunately this is not always the case, even with discrete quantitative data.

For instance, if Example 4.6 included customers who spent all day in the café and drank 20 or so cups of coffee each then the number of refills might go from none to 30. This would result in a table with far too many rows to be of use.

To get around this problem we can *group* the data into fewer categories or *classes* by compiling a *grouped* frequency distribution. This shows the frequency of observations in each class.

Example 4.7

The numbers of email messages received by 22 office workers in one day were:

50 14 25   8 10 33 52 12 45 15   7
 5 98 13 31 52   6 75 17 20 12 64

Produce a grouped frequency distribution to present these data.

Number of messages received	Frequency
0–19	11
20–39	4
40–59	4
60–79	2
80–99	1
Total frequency	22

In order to compile a grouped frequency distribution you will need to exercise a little judgement because there are many sets of classes that could be used for a specific set of data. To help you, there are three rules:

1 Don't use classes that overlap.
2 Don't leave gaps between classes.
3 The first class must begin low enough to include the lowest observation and the last class must finish high enough to include the highest observation.

In Example 4.7 it would be wrong to use the classes 0–20, 20–40, 40–60 and so on because a value on the very edge of the classes like 20 could be put into either one, or even both, of two classes. Although there are numerical gaps between the classes that have been used in Example 4.7, they are not real gaps because no feasible value could fall into them. The first class finishes on 19 and the second begins on 20, but since the number of messages received is a discrete variable a value like 19.6, which would fall into the gap, simply will not occur. Since there are no observed values lower than zero or higher than 99, the third rule is satisfied.

We could sum up these rules by saying that anyone looking at a grouped frequency distribution should be in no doubt where each feasible value belongs. Every piece of data must have one and only one place for it to be. To avoid any ambiguity whatsoever, you may like to use the phrase 'and under' between the beginning and end of each class. The classes in Example 4.7 could be rewritten as:

---

0 and under 20
20 and under 40 … and so on.

It is especially important to apply these rules when you are dealing with continuous quantitative data. Unless you decide to use 'and under' or a similar style of words, it is vital that the beginning and end of each class is specified to at least the same degree of precision as the data.

Example 4.8

The results of measuring the contents (in millilitres) of a sample of 30 bottles of 'Nogat' nail polish labelled as containing 10 ml were:

10.30	10.05	10.06	9.82	10.09	9.85	9.98	9.97	10.28	10.01	9.92
10.03	10.17	9.95	10.23	9.92	10.05	10.11	10.02	10.06	10.21	10.04
10.12	9.99	10.19	9.89	10.05	10.11	10.00	9.92			

Arrange these figures in a grouped frequency distribution.

Nail polish (ml)	Frequency
9.80–9.89	3
9.90–9.99	7
10.00–10.09	11
10.10–10.19	5
10.20–10.29	3
10.30–10.39	1
Total frequency	30

When you construct a grouped frequency distribution you will also need to decide how many classes to use and how wide they are. These are related issues: the fewer the number of classes the wider each one needs to be. It is a question of balance. You should avoid having a very few very wide classes because they will only convey a crude impression of the distribution. On the other hand, if you have very many narrow classes you will be conveying too much detail. So, what is too few and what is too many? As a guide, take the square root of the number of observations in the set of data. In Example 4.8 there are 30 observations. The square root of 30 is 5.48, so we should round down to 5 or up to 6 because we can only have whole numbers of classes. We have actually used six classes for these data, which according to this guide is about right.

Once you have some idea of the number of classes, the width of the classes has to be decided. It is useful if all the classes have the same width, especially if the frequency distribution is going to be the basis for further work on the data.

The set of classes you use must cover all the observations from lowest to highest, so to help you decide the width of classes, subtract the lowest observation from the highest observation to give you the difference between the two, known as the *range* of the values. Divide this by the number of classes you want to have and the result will be the minimum class width you must use. If you look back at Example 4.7 the range of observations is 93 (98 minus 5) which, when divided by 5 gives 18.6. So if we want a set of five classes of equal width to cover the range from 5 to 98, each class must be at least 18.6 wide.

This number, 18.6, is not particularly 'neat', so to make our grouped frequency distribution easier to interpret we can round it up. The most obvious number to take is 20, so 5 classes 20 units wide will be sufficient to cover the range. In fact because these classes will combine to cover a range of 100, whereas the range of our data is 93 we have some flexibility when it comes to deciding where the first class should start.

The first class must begin at or below the lowest observation in the set, in Example 4.7 this means it must start at 5 or below. Because 5 is a fairly 'neat' round number it would make a perfectly acceptable start for our first class, which would then be '5–24', the second class would be 25–44' and so on. But what if the first observed value was 3 or 7? Starting a set of classes with such a value would result in a grouped frequency distribution that would look rather ungainly. If we start the classes at a round number lower than the lowest value in the distribution, for instance zero in Example 4.7, we can guarantee that the resulting set of classes will have 'neat' beginnings.

Grouped frequency distributions are very useful for comparing two or more sets of data because the classes provide a common framework. The best way of using grouped frequency distributions in this way is to calculate the relative frequencies of the number of observations in every class for each set of data.

Example 4.9

A rival brand of nail polish, Pallyets, also comes in 10 ml bottles. The contents in millilitres of a sample of 26 bottles of this product were:

10.19	9.92	10.22	10.39	9.95	10.15	10.12	10.25	9.94
9.88	9.92	10.23	9.86	10.34	10.37	10.38	10.34	10.08
10.23	10.05	9.86	9.92	10.35	10.07	9.93	10.14	

Classify these data using the classes from Example 4.8 and work out the relative frequencies for both distributions.

Nail polish (ml)	Frequency (Nogat)	Relative frequency (%) (Nogat)	Frequency (Pallyets)	Relative frequency (%)
9.80–9.89	3	10.0	3	11.5
9.90–9.99	7	23.3	6	23.1
10.00–10.09	11	36.7	3	11.5
10.10–10.19	5	16.7	4	15.4
10.20–10.29	3	10.0	4	15.4
10.30–10.39	1	3.3	6	23.1
Total	30	100.0	26	100.0

The use of relative frequencies in Example 4.9, given in percentages to one place of decimals, makes direct comparison of the two sets of data much easier. Saying for instance that 3.3% of the sample of Nogat and 34.6% of the sample of Pallyets contained 10.3 ml or more is more straightforward than comparing 1/30 with 6/26.

At this point you may find it useful to try **Review Questions 4.12 to 4.20** at the end of the chapter.

4.5 Using the technology: arranging data in EXCEL, MINITAB and SPSS

4.5.1 EXCEL

The PivotTable facility in EXCEL enables you to compile simple tabulations. Click on **Data** at the top of the screen and you will find it listed as **PivotTable and PivotChart Report** on the pull-down menu. Prior to using it the data you want to tabulate should be entered into a column under a suitable variable name. In Example 4.10 we will use the facility to produce a table for the data in Example 4.6.

Example 4.10

In Example 4.6 the number of hot beverage refills taken by 20 customers were:

0   1   3   1   2   0   2   2   0   1   0   3   1   0   1   2   1   1   0   2

- Enter the variable name (Refills) in the first cell of a column and the figures into the cells beneath.
- Click **Data** and select **PivotTable and PivotChart Report** from the pull-down menu.
- In the **PivotTable and PivotChart Wizard Step 1 of 3** window that appears the default settings should be **Microsoft Excel list or database** under the question **Where is the data that you want to analyze?**, and **PivotTable** under the question **What kind of report do you want to create?**. If these are not the default settings select them by clicking on the buttons to their left. Click the **Next>** button.
- In the **PivotTable and PivotChart Wizard Step 2 of 3** window that appears the cursor should be positioned in the window to the right of **Range:**. Specify the range of cells containing the data by clicking at the top of the column where the data are located and dragging the mouse down to cover all the entries in the column. When you release the mouse button the cell range appears in the window. Make sure you have included the variable name in the specified range. Click the **Next>** button.
- In the **PivotTable and PivotChart Wizard Step 3 of 3** window that appears select **Existing worksheet** to locate the table the package will produce in the worksheet

you can see. The cell location in the window beneath **Existing worksheet** is the position the package will use to locate the table in your worksheet. If it obscures any of the existing entries in your worksheet simply click on a cell a suitable distance away and the table location will be altered automatically.

- Click the **Layout** button to the bottom left of the **PivotTable and PivotChart Wizard Step 3 of 3** window. The **PivotTable and PivotChart – Layout** window that appears shows the framework that will be used to construct the table. It should also have a button to the left with the name of the variable, Refills, on it. Click on this button and drag it to the area of the table framework labelled **ROW**. This will ensure that the values from the Refills column will be used as the rows in the table. The Refills button now appears at the top of the **ROW** area and in its original position. Click on the button in its original position and drag it to the **DATA** area of the table framework, which tells the package to use the data in the Refills column to compile the table. When you do this you should see a button labelled **Sum of Refills** in the **DATA** area. This means that the package will add up the values in the Refills column rather than count them. Double left click on **Sum of Refills** and the **PivotTable Field** window appears. Select **Count** from the list of options under **Summarize by** then click **OK**. The button in the **DATA** area should now be labelled **Count of Refills**. Click **OK** in the **PivotTable and PivotChart – Layout** window.

- Click on the **Finish** button in the **PivotTable and PivotChart Step 3 of 3** window. The following table should appear in the worksheet:

Count of Refills	
Refills	**Total**
0	6
1	7
2	5
3	2
Grand total	20

The small **PivotTable** window that appears in the worksheet at the same time as the table is of no immediate use and can be deleted.

The same EXCEL facility can be used to create a two-way or contingency table. Such a table might be helpful to the researchers who had gathered the data used in Example 4.10 if they were interested in whether female and male customers appeared to take similar numbers of refills and they had noted the gender of each customer in their sample.

Example 4.11

The refills data from Example 4.6 and the genders of the customers are:

```
0   1   3   1   2   0   2   2   0   1   0   3   1   0   1   2   1   1   0   2
F   F   M   F   F   M   M   M   F   F   M   F   F   F   M   F   M   M   M   M
```

▦ Enter the variable name Gender at the top of a column next to the column in which you have located the refills figures. Enter the gender of each customer, F or M as appropriate, alongside the number of refills taken by the customer.

▦ Follow the procedure outlined in Example 4.10. When you reach the **PivotTable and PivotChart Wizard Step 2 of 3** window click and drag across the columns containing the variable names and data for *both* Refills *and* Gender so that the cells specified in the window to the right of **Range:** cover two columns.

▦ When you reach the **PivotTable and PivotChart Wizard Step 3 of 3** window click the **Layout** button and in the **PivotTable and PivotChart – Layout** window you should see two buttons on the right, one labelled Refills and the other labelled Gender. Click and drag the Refills button into both the **ROW** and **DATA** areas of the table framework, then click and drag the Gender button to the **COLUMN** area of the table framework. Double left click on **Sum of Refills** and select **Count** from the list of options under **Summarize by** in the **PivotTable Field** window then click **OK**. The button in the **DATA** area should now be labelled **Count of Refills**. Click **OK** in the **PivotTable and PivotChart – Layout** window.

▦ Click on the **Finish** button in the **PivotTable and PivotChart Step 3 of 3** window. The following table should appear in the worksheet:

Count of Refills	Gender		
Refills	F	M	Grand total
0	3	3	6
1	4	3	7
2	2	3	5
3	1	1	2
Grand total	10	10	20

4.5.2 MINITAB

The MINITAB package has a Tables facility that you can use to compile summary tables. You will find it listed as **Tables** on the **Stat** pull-down menu. The Tables sub-menu includes **Tally** for simple tables and **Cross**

Tabulation for two-way tables. In Example 4.12 we will outline the procedures for using these tools using the data from Example 4.6.

Example 4.12

The refills data from Example 4.6 and the genders of the customers are:

```
0   1  3   1   2  0   2   2   0   1   0   3   1   0   1   2   1   1   0   2
F   F  M   F   F  M   M   M   F   F   M   F   F   F   M   F   M   M   M   M
```

- Enter the variable name (Refills) in the unnumbered grey cell at the top of a column of the worksheet and enter the figures into the column cells beneath.
- Click on **Stat** at the top of the screen and select **Tables** from the pull-down menu that appears. Click on **Tally** in the sub-menu.
- In the **Tally** window that appears you will see the name Refills on the left-hand side with the number of the column where the values of the variable are stored. Double left click on Refills and it will appear in the window below **Variables:**, which tells the package that you want a table compiled from the values in that column.
- Ensure that the **Counts** option under **Display** is ticked then click **OK** and the following table should appear in the session window in the upper part of the screen:

Refills	Count
0	6
1	7
2	5
3	2
	$N = 20$

The letter N in this output represents the total number of observations counted. To obtain a two-way table showing gender and numbers of refills:

- Enter the variable name Gender in the unnumbered grey cell at the top of a column next to the column in which you have entered the refills figures. Enter the gender of each customer, F or M as appropriate, alongside the number of refills taken by the customer.
- Select **Tables** from the **Stat** pull-down menu, and select **Cross Tabulation** from the **Tables** sub-menu.
- In the **Cross Tabulation** window both Refills and Gender variable names are listed in the space on the right-hand side. Click on the upper variable name and drag down to cover both variable names then click the **Select** button below. They will appear in the window under **Classification variables:**.

■ Click the space to the left of **Counts** under **Display** then click **OK** and the following table should appear in the session window in the upper part of the screen:

Refills	Gender		
	F	M	All
0	3	3	6
1	4	3	7
2	2	3	5
3	1	1	2
All	10	10	20

4.5.3 SPSS

The SPSS package has a **Tables of Frequencies** facility that can produce simple and two-way tables. You can find it in the **Custom Tables** option listed on the **Analyze** pull-down menu. Example 4.13 below outlines how it can be used to produce tables for the data from Example 4.6.

Example 4.13

The refills data from Example 4.6 and the genders of the customers are:

```
0   1   3   1   2   0   2   2   0   1   0   3   1   0   1   2   1   1   0   2
F   F   M   F   F   M   M   M   F   F   M   F   F   F   M   F   M   M   M   M
```

■ On entering SPSS you will be presented with a window with the question **What would you like to do?** at the top. Click the button to the left of **Type in data** then click the **OK** button.

■ Enter the refills observations into the cells of a column of the worksheet.

■ Click the **Variable View** tab at the bottom left of the screen. On the left of the screen that appears you will see a column headed **Name**. Type **Refills** over the default name that appears there. Click on the **Data View** tab at the bottom left of the screen and you will return to the data worksheet.

■ Click on **Analyze** at the top of the screen and from the pull-down menu select **Custom Tables**. Click on **Tables of Frequencies**.

■ In the **Tables of Frequencies** window that appears you will see the variable name refills highlighted in the space on the left. Click the ▶ button to the left of **Frequencies for:** and the refills name should be switched to the space below

Frequencies for:. Click **OK** and you should see the following table in the output viewer screen:

	Count
0.00	6
1.00	7
2.00	5
3.00	2

To obtain a two-way table showing gender and numbers of refills:

▢ Put the gender data into a column adjacent to the one you used to store the refills data. Enter the gender of each customer, F or M as appropriate, alongside the number of refills taken by the customer.

▢ Click the **Variable View** tab at the bottom left of the screen. In the column headed **Name** type **Gender** over the default name given to the new row. Click on the **Data View** tab at the bottom left of the screen to return to the data worksheet.

▢ Click **Analyze** at the top of the screen and select **Custom Tables** and click on **Tables of Frequencies**.

▢ In the **Tables of Frequencies** window the refills variable name is highlighted in the space on the left. Click the ▶ button to the left of **Frequencies for:** to select refills name.

▢ Click on the gender variable name in the space on the left then click the ▶ button to the left of **In Each Table** and gender should now appear in the space below **In Each Table:**. Click **OK** and you should see the following table in the output viewer screen:

	Count	
	F	M
0.00	3	3
1.00	4	3
2.00	2	3
3.00	1	1

Review questions

Answers to the following questions, including fully worked solutions to the Key questions marked with an asterisk (*), are on pages 636–637.

4.1   Match the definitions listed below on the right-hand side to the words listed on the left-hand side.

(a)	distribution	(i)	something that occurs by chance
(b)	element	(ii)	a subset of a population
(c)	random	(iii)	a complete set of things to study
(d)	sample	(iv)	a value of a variable that has occurred
(e)	population	(v)	a systematic arrangement of data
(f)	observation	(vi)	a single member of a population

4.2 Identify the type of scale of measurement (nominal, ordinal, interval or ratio) appropriate for each of the following types of data.

(a) Star ratings of hotels

(b) Sales revenues of companies

(c) Grades of officers in armed forces

(d) House numbers in a street

(e) Prices of cars

(f) Classes of accommodation on passenger flights

(g) Passport numbers

(h) Numbers in a rating scale on a questionnaire

(i) Index numbers such as the FTSE100 ('Footsie')

4.3 Indicate which of the variables below will have discrete values and which will have continuous values.

(a) Time taken to answer telephone calls

(b) Clothing sizes for female apparel

(c) Age of consumers

(d) Calories in foodstuffs

(e) Shoe sizes

(f) Visitors to a theme park

(g) Interest rates

(h) Transactions in a supermarket

4.4 Indicate which of the variables below are qualitative, discrete quantitative or continuous quantitative.

(a) Duration of telephone calls

(b) Modes of travel to work

(c) The alcohol contents of beers

(d) Sizes of theatre audiences

(e) Places of birth of passport applicants

(f) Numbers of websites found in a search

4.5 Select which of the statements listed below on the right-hand side best describes each of the terms on the left-hand side.

(a)	time series data	(i)	concern attitudes and beliefs
(b)	nominal data	(ii)	are limited to distinct numerical values
(c)	hard data	(iii)	consist of values of two variables

(d)	discrete data	(iv)	are collected at regular intervals
(e)	cross-sectional data	(v)	are factual
(f)	bivariate data	(vi)	are based on a scale with an arbitrary zero
(g)	soft data	(vii)	are only labels
(h)	interval data	(viii)	relate to a specific point or period of time

4.6* A bus company operates services to and from the East, North, South and West of a city. A recent report from the Chief Executive contains the following summary of their operations. (All figures have been rounded to the nearest thousand.)

The total number of passenger journeys made on our services was 430,000. Of these, 124,000 were to and from the North, 63,000 to and from the South, and 78,000 to and from the East. Passengers used bus passes to pay for 158,000 of the total number of journeys: 43,000 on northern services, 51,000 on western services, and 35,000 on eastern services. Passengers who did not use a bus pass paid for their journeys in cash.

   Construct a two-way tabulation with rows for the city areas and columns for the method of payment. Work out the figures that are not quoted in the summary by using the information provided.

4.7 A hotel had 1360 bookings for accommodation in a month. Of these 940 were for one night. Business bookings amounted to 813 of the total number, all but 141 being for one night. Leisure bookings amounted to a further 362, the remaining bookings being associated with functions (weddings etc.). Only 23 of these latter bookings were for more than one night.

   Draw up a two-way table for these figures with rows for the types of booking and columns for the length of stay. Deduce the figures that are not given by using the information provided.

4.8 A total of 127 people applied for several jobs at a new clothing retail outlet. Seventy-four applicants were female, and of these 32 had previous experience of clothing retail and 19 had no previous retail experience. A total of 45 applicants had previous retail experience but not in the clothing sector. Of the males only 9 had no previous retail experience.

Use the information given to construct a contingency table showing the breakdown of applicants by gender and experience.

4.9*   The numbers of people in 95 passenger cars travelling along a road during the morning rush hour were:

1 1 2 1 2   1 3 5 1 1   2 1 1 4 1 2 1 1 1   4 1 2 1 1   4 1 1 2 3   2 3 1 4 1

Compile a frequency distribution for this set of data.

4.10   The 'To Let' column in the accommodation pages of a local newspaper contains details of 20 houses available to rent. The numbers of bedrooms in these properties are:

2	3	5	2	4	2	4	4	4	3
2	5	3	2	3	4	4	3	2	4

Arrange these data into a frequency distribution.

4.11   The ages of 28 applicants for a graduate management trainee post are:

21 23 21 21 23   21 24 22 21 24   21 26 23 22 21   22 23 21 22 21   22 25 21 22 21   22 21 24

Produce a frequency distribution for these figures.

4.12   The number of business trips abroad taken in the last year by each of a sample of 41 executives were:

3	11	1	10	14	14	12	6	1	10	7
11	9	2	7	11	17	12	13	2	0	14
6	4	3	12	14	8	7	11	9	6	9
15	0	4	9	7	10	4	5			

(a) Arrange these data into a frequency distribution.
(b) Classify these data into a grouped frequency distribution using the classes 0–2, 3–5, 6–8, 9–11, 12–14 and 15–17.

4.13* The speeds (in miles per hour) of 24 cars travelling along a road that has a 30 mph speed limit were:

31	35	35	27	26	30	36	23	36	33	27	31
32	38	26	40	21	39	33	24	28	23	28	35

Construct a grouped frequency distribution for these data.

4.14   The numbers of laptops sold during a week in each of the 37 outlets of a chain of computer dealers were:

6	14	22	17	15	12	18	11	23	10	13	17	8

25	13	0	13	20	18	13	16	15	0	15	14
15	9	7	14	17	13	3	15	7	23	10	15

Present these data in the form of a grouped frequency distribution.

4.15　The rates of growth in revenue (%) of 25 companies over a year were:

4.22　3.85　10.23　5.11　7.91　4.60　8.16　5.28　3.98　2.51　9.95
6.98　6.06　9.24　3.29　9.75　0.11　11.38　1.41　4.05　1.93　5.16
1.99　12.41　7.73

Compile a grouped frequency distribution for these figures.

4.16　The prices (in £s) of 27 second-hand 'Krushenia' cars on sale at a car hypermarket are:

4860　1720　2350　2770　3340　4240　4850　4390　3870
2790　3740　2230　1690　2750　1390　4990　3660　1900
5200　4390　3690　1760　4800　1730　2040　4070　2670

Create a frequency distribution to present these data.

4.17　The hourly wages (in £s) of 32 jobs offered by an employment agency are:

6.28　4.90　4.52　5.11　5.94　5.82　7.14　7.28　8.15　7.04
4.41　4.67　6.90　5.85　5.65　5.50　4.12　5.27　5.25　6.43
5.73　4.65　5.37　4.24　6.45　4.70　5.09　4.82　6.23　5.40
6.48　5.26

Construct a grouped frequency distribution for these figures.

4.18*　The monthly membership fees in £s for 22 health clubs are:

32　43　44　22　73　69　48　67　33　56　67
28　78　60　63　32　67　41　65　48　48　77

(a) Arrange these data into a grouped frequency distribution. Use classes £10 wide starting at £20.

(b) The monthly membership fees in £s for 17 fitness centres in local authority leisure centres are:

27　50　44　32　31　55　21　36　24
56　51　55　32　39　42　28　55

Arrange these data into a grouped frequency distribution using the same classes as in (a).

(c) Work out the relative frequencies for every class in the distributions and use them to compare the percentage of clubs charging £50 or more with the percentage of health centres charging £50 or more.

4.19   A company has plants in Manchester and Southampton. Thirty staff from Manchester and 24 staff from Southampton attended a training course at the end of which they were each given a proficiency test.

The marks for the test (out of 100) for the staff from Manchester were:

49	53	70	35	55	38	44	79	67	85
67	72	49	62	87	64	67	70	57	63
35	50	58	47	54	39	44	40	64	34

The marks for the staff from Southampton were:

51	65	74	24	45	66	75	39	52	59
85	78	75	46	28	51	22	70	89	38
29	49	08	81						

(a) Classify both sets of data into grouped frequency distributions using classes 10 marks wide.

(b) Find the relative frequency for each class of the distributions.

(c) The company considers marks of less than 40 in this test to be unsatisfactory. Using your relative frequency figures compare the proportions of staff obtaining unsatisfactory results from the two locations.

4.20   A leisure company operates three amusement arcades in the UK: at Redcar, Skegness and Torquay. As part of a performance review the duration in minutes of the period spent in the arcades by each of a sample of customers visiting was recorded. The durations of visits made by 21 customers visiting the Redcar arcade were:

23	8	39	72	73	13	44	74	37	21
21	27	27	34	31	32	43	74	44	36
23									

The figures for 18 customers visiting the Skegness arcade were:

31	51	69	12	53	28	36	28	36	30
35	45	48	25	9	32	60	66		

The figures for 20 customers visiting the Torquay arcade were:

3	19	1	15	21	9	7	20	10	2
6	2	11	37	10	6	10	14	3	5

(a) Classify both sets of data into grouped frequency distributions.

(b) Calculate the relative frequency for each class of all three distributions.

(c) The company expects customers to spend at least 20 minutes on visits to their arcades. Use your relative frequency figures to compare the performances of the arcades in this respect.

CHAPTER 5

Good visibility — pictorial presentation of data

This chapter will help you to:

- illustrate qualitative data using pictographs, bar charts and pie charts
- portray quantitative data using histograms, cumulative frequency charts and stem and leaf displays
- present bivariate quantitative data using scatter diagrams
- display time series data using time series charts
- use the technology: data presentation in EXCEL, MINITAB and SPSS
- become acquainted with business uses of pictorial data presentation

In the last chapter we looked at arranging and tabulating data, taking the first steps in transforming raw data into information, bringing meaning to the apparently meaningless. In this chapter we will continue this theme by considering various ways of portraying data in visual form. Used appropriately the diagrams and charts you will find here are very effective means of communicating the patterns and meaning contained in data, specifically the patterns and sequences in distributions.

There are techniques that are very common in business documents so being able to understand what they mean is an important skill.

There are many different diagrams and charts that can be used to do this, so it is important to know when to use them. The techniques we use depend on the type of data we want to present, in the same way as the suitability of the methods of arranging data featured in the last chapter depended on the type of data. Essentially, the simpler the data, the simpler the presentational tools that can be used to represent them: simple nominal data restricted to a few categories can be shown effectively in the form of a simple bar chart whereas ratio data require the more rigorous scaling of something like a histogram.

5.1 Displaying qualitative data

Section 4.4.1 of Chapter 4 covered the arrangement of qualitative data in the form of summary tables. As well as being a useful way of displaying qualitative data, a summary table is an essential preliminary task to preparing a diagram to portray the data.

A diagram is usually a much more effective way of communicating data because it is easier for the eye to digest than a table. This will be important when you have to include data in a report or presentation because you want your audience to focus their attention on what you are saying. They can do that more easily if they don't have to work too hard to understand the form in which you have presented your data.

Displaying qualitative data is fairly simple if there are few categories of the attribute or characteristic being investigated. With more categories, the task can be simplified by merging categories.

There are three types of diagram that you can use to show qualitative data: *pictographs*, *pie charts* and *bar charts*. We will deal with them in this section in order of increasing sophistication.

5.1.1 Pictographs

A pictograph is little more than a simple extension of a summary table. The categories of the attribute are listed as they are in a summary table, and we use symbols to represent the number of things in each category. The symbols you use in a pictograph should have a simple and direct visual association with the data.

A pictograph like Figure 5.1 can be an effective way of presenting a simple set of qualitative data. The symbols are a simple way of representing

Example 5.1

The table below lists four racehorse trainers and the number of horses they trained that won races at a horse race meeting.

Trainer	Number of winners
Nadia Amazonka	5
Freddie Conn	3
Lavinia Loshart	1
Victor Sedlow	2

Show this set of data in the form of a pictograph.

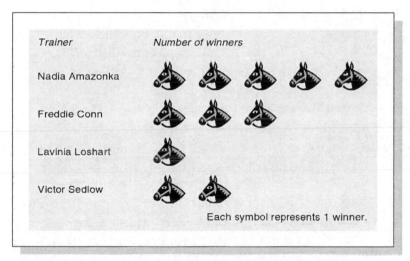

Figure 5.1
Pictograph of the number of winners by each trainer

the number in each category and have the extra advantage of emphasizing the context of the data.

Pictographs do have some drawbacks that may put you off using them. Unless you are artistically gifted and can create appropriate images by hand, you will probably have to rely on computer software to produce them for you. Creating a pictograph using a PC can be a laborious process. Spreadsheet and statistical packages cannot produce a pictograph for you directly from data, so symbols have to be grafted alongside text in a word processing package.

If you do use pictographs you need to choose the symbols carefully. They should be easy to associate with the context of the data and not so elaborate that the symbols themselves become the focus of attention rather than the data they are supposed to represent.

You may occasionally see a pictograph in academic and business documents; you are more likely to see them on television and in newspapers. The computer graphics software reporters and editors use is much more sophisticated than any that you are likely to have access to during your studies.

5.1.2 Pie charts

The second method of displaying qualitative data that we will look at is the pie chart. Pie charts are used much more than pictographs in part because they can be produced using widely available computer software.

A pie chart, like a pictograph, is designed to show how many things belong to each category of an attribute. It does this by representing the entire set of data as a circle or 'pie' and dividing the circle into segments or 'slices'. Each segment represents a category, and the size of the segment reflects the number of things in the category.

Just about every spreadsheet or statistical package can produce a pie chart like Figure 5.2 either from the original data or from a summary table. You will find guidance on doing this using EXCEL, MINITAB and SPSS in the final section of this chapter. These packages provide various ways of enhancing pie charts: colour and shading patterns, 3D effects, and detached or 'exploded' slices to emphasize a particular segment.

With practice you will be able to use these options in creating pie charts, but don't overdo it. Remember that the pattern of the data is what you want to convey not your ability to use every possible gimmick in the package.

Pie charts are so widely used and understood that it is very tempting to regard them as an almost universal means of displaying qualitative

Example 5.2

The Steeralny Appliance Repair Service has depots in Crewe, Doncaster, Exeter and Frome. The numbers of call-outs from each depot on one day are given in the following table:

Depot	Call-outs
Crewe	36 (26.1%)
Doncaster	57 (41.3%)
Exeter	28 (20.3%)
Frome	17 (12.3%)
Total	138 (100.0%)

These data are presented in the form of a pie chart in Figure 5.2.

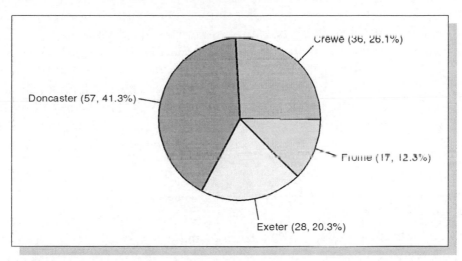

Figure 5.2
Number of call-outs by depot

data. In many cases they are appropriate and effective, but in some situations they are not.

Because the role of a pie chart is to show how different components make up a whole, you should not use one when you cannot or do not want to show the whole. This may be because there are some values missing from the data or perhaps there is an untidy 'Other' category for data that do not fit in the main categories. In leaving out any data, either for administrative or aesthetic reasons, you would not be presenting the whole, which is exactly what pie charts are designed to do.

One reason that people find pie charts accessible is that the analogy of cutting up a pie is quite an obvious one. As long as the pie chart looks like a pie it works. However if you produce a pie chart that has too many categories it can look more like a bicycle wheel than a pie, and confuses rather than clarifies the data. If you have a lot of categories to present, say more than ten, either merge some of the categories in order to reduce the number of segments in the pie chart or consider an alternative way of presenting your data.

5.1.3 Bar charts

Another method of portraying qualitative data is the bar chart. Like pie charts, bar charts are widely used, fairly simple to interpret, and can be produced using spreadsheet and statistical packages. However because there are several different varieties of bar charts, they are more flexible tools. We can use bar charts to portray not only simple categorizations but also two-way classifications.

The basic function of a bar chart is the same as that of a pie chart, and for that matter a pictograph; to show the number or frequency of things in each of a succession of categories of an attribute. It represents the frequencies as a series of bars. The height of each bar is in direct proportion to the frequency of the category; the taller the bar that represents a category, the more things there are in that category.

Example 5.3

Produce a bar chart to display the data from Example 5.2.

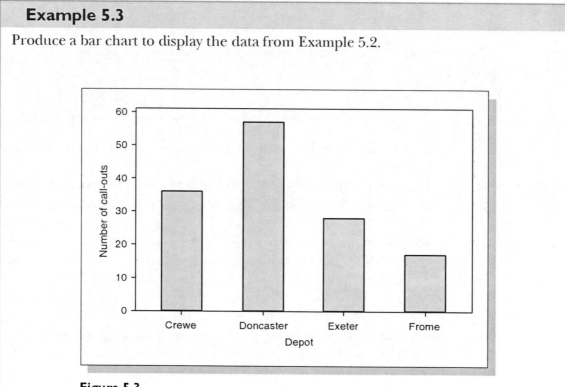

Figure 5.3
A bar chart of call-outs by depot

The type of bar chart shown in Figure 5.3 is called a *simple* bar chart because it represents only one attribute. If we had two attributes to display we might use a more sophisticated type of bar chart, either a *component* bar chart or a *stack* bar chart.

The type of bar chart shown in Figure 5.4 is called a component bar chart because each bar is divided into parts or components. The

Example 5.4

The call-outs data in Example 5.2 have been scrutinized to establish how many call-outs from each depot concerned washing machines and how many concerned other appliances. The numbers of the two call-out types from each depot are:

Depot	Washing machine call-outs	Other appliance call-outs
Crewe	21	15
Doncaster	44	13
Exeter	13	15
Frome	10	7

Display these data as a component bar chart.

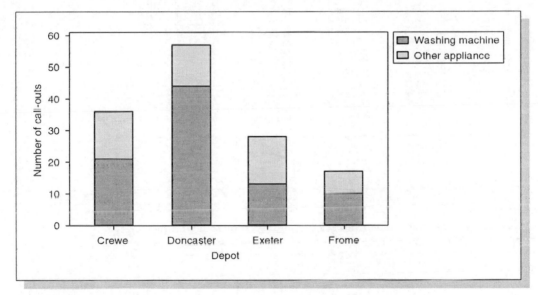

Figure 5.4
A component bar chart of call-outs by depot and appliance type

alternative name for it, a stacked bar chart, reflects the way in which the components of each bar are stacked on top of one another.

A component bar chart is particularly useful if you want to emphasize the relative proportions of each category, in other words to show the balance *within* the categories of one attribute (in the case of Example 5.4 the depot) *between* the categories of another attribute (in Example 5.4 the type of call-out).

If you want to focus on this balance exclusively and are not too concerned about the absolute frequencies in each category you could use a component bar chart in which each bar is subdivided in percentage terms.

Example 5.5

Produce a component bar chart for the data in Example 5.4 in which the sections of the bars represent the percentages of call-outs by appliance type.

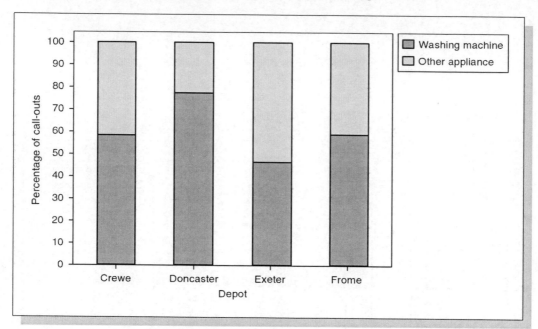

Figure 5.5
A component bar chart of percentages of call-outs by depot and appliance type

If you want to emphasize the absolute differences *between* the categories of one attribute (in Example 5.4 the depots) *within* the categories of another (in Example 5.4 the types of call-out) you may find a *cluster* bar chart more useful.

The type of bar chart shown in Example 5.6 is called a cluster bar chart because it uses a group or cluster of bars to show the composition of each category of one characteristic by categories of a second characteristic. For instance in Figure 5.6 the bars for Crewe show how the call-outs from the Crewe depot are composed of call-outs for washing machines and call-outs for other appliances.

At this point you may find it useful to try **Review Questions 5.1 to 5.3** at the end of the chapter.

Example 5.6

Produce a cluster bar chart to portray the data from Example 5.4.

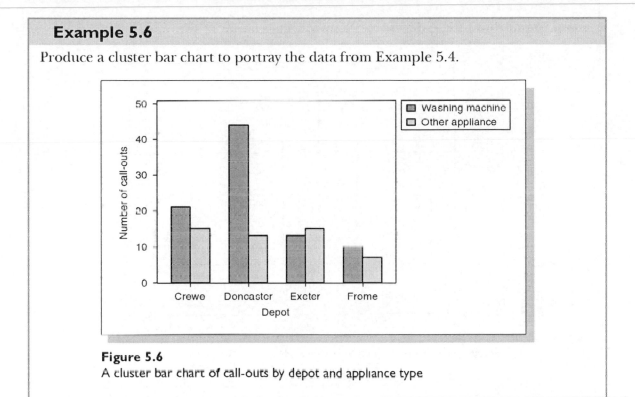

Figure 5.6
A cluster bar chart of call-outs by depot and appliance type

5.2 Displaying quantitative data

Quantitative data are more sophisticated data than qualitative data and therefore the methods used to present quantitative data are generally more elaborate. The exception to this is where you want to represent the simplest type of quantitative data, discrete quantitative variables that have very few feasible values. You can treat the values in these data

Example 5.7

In Example 4.6 the numbers of free refills taken by 20 customers visiting the UREA department store cafe were tabulated as follows:

Number of refills	Number of customers
0	6
1	7
2	5
3	2

Figure 5.7 shows these data in the form of a bar chart.

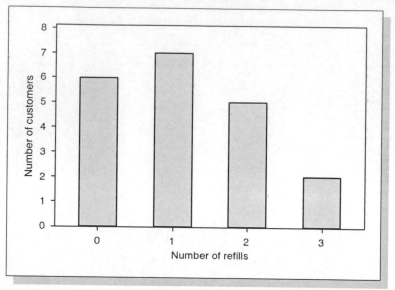

Figure 5.7
Number of customers by number of refills

as you would categories in qualitative data, using them to construct a bar chart or pie chart.

5.2.1 Histograms

In general quantitative data consist of a rather larger variety of values than the data portrayed in Figure 5.7. In section 4.4.2 of Chapter 4 we saw how grouped frequency distributions could be used to arrange quantitative data. Here we will look at what is probably the most widely used way of displaying data arranged in a grouped frequency distribution, the *histogram*. This is a special type of bar chart where each bar or *block* represents the frequency of a class of values rather than the frequency of a single value. Because they are composed in this way histograms are sometimes called *block diagrams*.

You can see that in Figure 5.8 there are no gaps between the blocks in the histogram. The classes on which it is based start with '0–19' then '20–39' and so on. When plotting such classes you may be tempted to leave gaps to reflect the fact that there is a numerical gap between the end of the first class and the beginning of the next but this would be

Example 5.8

In Example 4.7 the numbers of email messages received by 22 office workers were arranged in the following grouped frequency distribution.

Number of messages received	Frequency
0–19	11
20–39	4
40–59	4
60–79	2
80–99	1
Total frequency	22

Show this grouped frequency distribution as a histogram

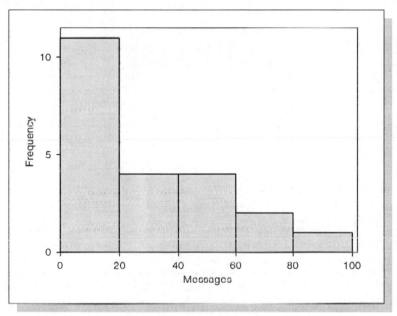

Figure 5.8
Histogram of email messages sent by 22 office workers

wrong because the gap would be meaningless as it is simply not possible to receive say 19.2 messages.

A histogram is a visual tool that displays the pattern or distribution of observed values of a variable. The larger the size of the block that represents a class, the greater the number of values that has occurred in that class. Because the connection between the size of the blocks and the frequencies of the classes is the key feature of the diagram the scale along the vertical or 'Y' axis must start at zero, as in Figure 5.8.

As long as the classes in a grouped frequency distribution are of the same width it is simply the heights of the blocks of the histogram that reflect the frequencies of observed values in the classes. If the classes have different widths it is important that the areas of the blocks are proportional to the frequencies of the classes. The best way of ensuring this is to represent the *frequency density* rather than the frequency of the classes. The frequency density is the frequency of values in a class divided by the width of the class. It expresses how densely the values are packed in the class to which they belong.

Example 5.9

The table below shows the distribution of ages of customers opening accounts at a bank:

Age range	Frequency
Under 15	0
15–24	5
25–44	20
45–64	18
Over 64	7

Calculate frequency density figures for the classes in the distribution and use them to produce a histogram to portray the distribution.

In this distribution the classes have different widths, but an additional complication is that the first class has no numerical beginning and the last class has no numerical end, they are both 'open-ended' classes.

Before we can proceed we need to 'close' these classes. In the case of the first class this is straightforward; we can simply express it as '0 to 14'. The last class poses more of a problem. If we knew the age of the oldest person we could use that as the end of the class, but as we don't we have to select an arbitrary yet plausible end of the class. In keeping with the style of some of the other classes we could use '65 to 84'.

The amended classes with their frequency densities are:

Age range	Frequency	Frequency density
0–14	0	0/15 = 0.00
15–24	5	5/10 = 0.50
25–44	20	20/20 = 1.00
45–64	18	18/20 = 0.90
65–84	7	7/20 = 0.35

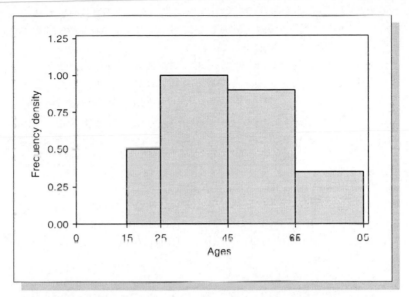

Figure 5.9
Histogram of ages of customers opening bank accounts

Using frequency densities in Figure 5.9 means that the height of the block representing the '15 to 24' class is increased to reflect the fact that it is narrower than the other classes. Despite having only *one quarter* of the frequency of the '25–44' class the height of the block representing the '15–24' class is *half* the height of the block representing the '25–44' class. The class is *half* the width of the classes to the right of it, so to keep the area in proportion to the frequency the height of the block has to be *doubled*.

In Figure 5.9 there are no gaps between the classes, although it might be tempting to insert them as each class finishes on the number before the next class begins. This would be wrong because, for instance, people are considered to be 14 years old right up until the day before their fifteenth birthday.

The pattern of the distribution shown in Figure 5.9 is broadly balanced or *symmetrical*. There are two large blocks in the middle and smaller blocks to the left and right of the 'bulge'. From this we would conclude that the majority of observed values occur towards the middle of the age range, with only a few relatively young and old customers.

In contrast, if you look back at Figure 5.8, the histogram showing the numbers of email messages received, you will see an asymmetrical or *skewed* pattern. The block on the left-hand side is the largest and the size of the blocks gets smaller to the right of it. It could be more accurately described as *right* or *positively* skewed. From Figure 5.8 we can conclude that the majority of office workers receive a relatively modest number of email messages and only a few office workers receive large numbers of email messages.

You may come across distributions that are *left* or *negatively* skewed. In these the classes on the left-hand side have smaller frequencies and those on the right-hand side have larger frequencies.

In Figure 5.10 there are no gaps between the classes because there are no numerical gaps between the classes; they are seamless.

Example 5.10

Raketa Airlines say they allow their passengers to take up to 5 kg of baggage with them into the cabin. The weights of cabin baggage taken onto one flight were recorded and the following grouped frequency distribution compiled from the data:

Weight of cabin baggage (kg)	Number of passengers
0 and under 1	2
1 and under 2	3
2 and under 3	8
3 and under 4	11
4 and under 5	20
5 and under 6	18

Portray this distribution in the form of a histogram.

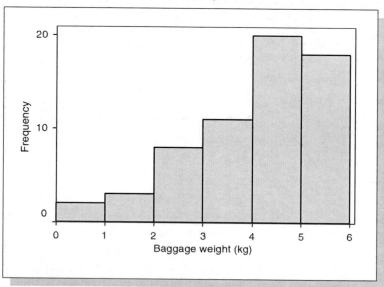

Figure 5.10
Histogram of weights of cabin baggage

5.2.2 Cumulative frequency graphs

An alternative method of presenting data arranged in a grouped frequency distribution is the *cumulative frequency graph*. This diagram shows the way in which the data *accumulates* through the distribution from the first to the last class in the grouped frequency distribution. It uses the same horizontal axis as you would use to construct a histogram to present the same data, but you have to make sure that the vertical axis, which must begin at zero, extends far enough to cover the total frequency of the distribution.

To plot a cumulative frequency graph you must begin by working out the cumulative frequency of each class in the grouped frequency distribution. The cumulative frequency of a class is the frequency of the class itself added to the cumulative, or combined frequency of *all* the preceding classes.

The cumulative frequency of the first class is simply the frequency of the first class because it has no preceding classes. The cumulative frequency of the second class is the frequency of the second class added to the frequency of the first class. The cumulative frequency of the third class is the frequency of the third class added to the cumulative frequency of the second class, and so on.

Example 5.11

Find the cumulative frequencies of each class in the grouped frequency distribution in Example 5.8.

Number of messages sent	Frequency	Cumulative frequency
0–19	11	11
20–39	4	15
40 59	4	19
60–79	2	21
80–99	1	22

Note that the cumulative frequency of the last class in the distribution in Example 5.11 is 22, the total frequency of values in the distribution. This should always be the case. Once we have included the values in the final class in the cumulative total we should have included every value in the distribution.

The cumulative frequency figures represent the number of values that have been accumulated by the end of a class. A cumulative frequency graph is a series of single points each of which represents the cumulative frequency of its class plotted above the very end of its class. There should be one plotted point for every class in the distribution. The final step is to connect the points with straight lines.

Example 5.12

Plot a cumulative frequency graph for the data in Example 5.8.

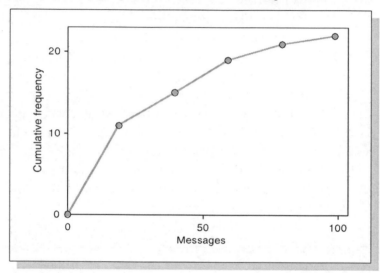

Figure 5.11
Cumulative frequency graph of email messages sent by 22 office workers

If you look carefully at Figure 5.11 you will see that the line begins at zero on the horizontal axis, which is the beginning of the first class, and zero on the vertical axis. This is a logical starting point. It signifies that no values have been accumulated before the beginning of the first class. The line then climbs steeply before flattening off. The steep climb represents the concentration of values in the first class, which contains half of the values in the distribution. The flatter sections to the right represent the very few values in the later classes.

The line in Figure 5.12 starts with a gentle slope then rises more steeply before finishing with a gentle slope. This signifies that the first classes contain few values, the middle classes contain many values, and the final classes contain few values. This is a symmetrical distribution, whereas the distribution shown in Figure 5.11 is a skewed distribution.

Example 5.13

Plot a cumulative frequency graph for the distribution of contents of bottles of 'Nogat' nail polish in Example 4.8.

Nail polish (ml)	Frequency	Cumulative frequency
9.80–9.89	3	3
9.90–9.99	7	10
10.00–10.09	11	21
10.10–10.19	5	26
10.20–10.29	3	29
10.30–10.39	1	30

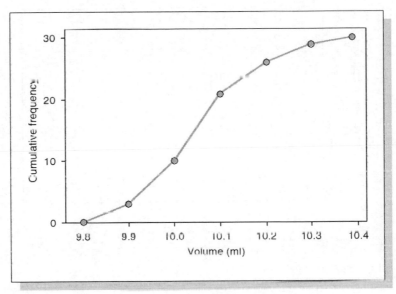

Figure 5.12
Cumulative frequency graph of contents of nail varnish bottles

It may be more convenient to plot a cumulative *relative* frequency graph, in which the points represent the proportions of the total number of values that occur in and prior to each class. This is particularly useful if the total number of values in the distribution is an awkward number. You will find further discussion of cumulative frequency graphs in the next chapter because they offer an easy way of finding the approximate values of medians, quartiles and other order statistics.

At this point you may find it useful to try **Review Questions 5.4 to 5.9** at the end of the chapter.

Example 5.14

The size of cash payments made by 119 customers at a petrol station is summarized in the following grouped frequency distribution. Plot a cumulative relative frequency graph.

Payment (£)	Frequency	Relative frequency	Cumulative relative frequency
5.00–9.99	15	15/119 = 0.126	0.126
10.00–14.99	37	37/119 = 0.311	0.437
15.00–19.99	41	41/119 = 0.344	0.781
20.00–24.99	22	22/119 = 0.185	0.966
25.00–29.99	4	4/119 = 0.034	1.000

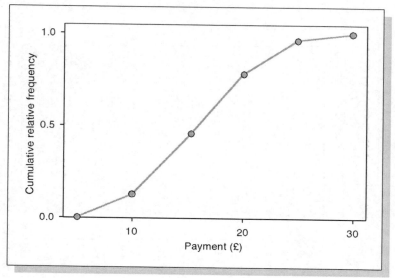

Figure 5.13
Cumulative relative frequency graph of cash payments at a petrol station

5.2.3 Stem and leaf displays

Histograms and cumulative frequency graphs are effective and widely used means of presenting quantitative data. Until fairly recently they could be described as unrivalled. However, there is an alternative way of presenting quantitative data in visual form, the *stem and leaf display*. This is one of a number of newer techniques known collectively as *Exploratory Data Analysis (EDA)*. If you want to know more about EDA, the books by Tukey (1977), and Velleman and Hoaglin (1981) provide a thorough introduction.

The role of a stem and leaf display is the same as the role of a histogram, namely to show the pattern of a distribution. But unlike a histogram, a stem and leaf display is constructed using the actual data as building blocks, so as well as showing the pattern of a distribution it is also a list of the observations that make up that distribution. It is a very useful tool for making an initial investigation of a set of data as it portrays the shape of the distribution, identifies unusual observations and provides the basis for judging the suitability of different types of averages.

The basis of a stem and leaf display is the structure of numbers, the fact that a number is made up of units, tens, hundreds and so on. For instance the number 45 is composed of two digits, the 4 tens and the 5 units. Using the analogy of a plant, the stem of the number 45 is the number on the left-hand side, 4 (the number of tens) and the leaf is the number on the right hand side, 5 (the number of units). A stem on a plant can have different leaves; in the same way the numerical stem 4 can have different numerical leaves. The number 48 has the same stem as the number 45, but a different leaf, 8.

To produce a stem and leaf display for a set of data we have to list the set of stem digits that appear in the data and then record each observation by putting its leaf digit alongside its stem digit. When we have done this for every observed value in the set of data the result is a series of 'stem lines' each of which consists of a stem digit and the leaf digits of all the observations sharing that particular stem. The final stage in the process is to arrange the leaf digits on each stem line in order of magnitude.

The message 'leaf unit = 1' on the final version of the stem and leaf display in Example 5.15 has the same role as the scale on the horizontal or 'X' axis of a histogram, in that it specifies the order of magnitude

Example 5.15

Musor Burgers operate fast food restaurants. The seating capacities of the 27 restaurants they operate in East Anglia are:

53	38	59	62	51	51	28	45	61	39
59	50	48	74	52	41	73	68	47	48
52	56	52	55	47	52	41			

Produce a stem and leaf display for these data.

Every value consists of two digits: tens and units. The tens are the stem digits and the units are the leaf digits. The lowest value is 28 and the highest is 74 so the first stem line will be for the stem digit 2, and the last one for the stem digit 7. The first stem line will have a leaf digit for the lowest value, the 8 from 28. The second stem line, for the stem digit 3, will have two leaf digits, the 8 from 38 and the 9 from 39, and so on.

Stem	Leaves
2	8
3	8 9
4	8 7 1 1 5 7 8
5	3 9 2 0 6 9 2 5 1 2 1 2
6	2 8 1
7	4 3

This is a stem and leaf display, but it is not yet finished. We need to rearrange the leaf digits so they are listed from the smallest to the largest.

Stem	Leaves
2	8
3	8 9
4	1 1 5 7 7 8 8
5	0 1 1 2 2 2 2 3 5 6 9 9
6	1 2 8
7	3 4

Leaf unit = 1

of the data. Without this message someone might look at the display, see that the highest value in the distribution has the stem digit 7 and the leaf digit 4, but be unclear whether the value is 0.74, 7.4, 74, 740, 7400, or any other number with a 7 followed by a 4. It is only when you know that the leaf digits are units in this display that you can be sure the stem digit 7 and the leaf digit 4 represents the number 74.

Although a stem and leaf display may appear a little strange it is a tool that is well worth learning to use because it has two advantages over a histogram: particular values can be highlighted and two distributions can be shown in one display. A histogram simply cannot do the former because it consists of blocks rather than data. It is possible to

Example 5.16

Five of the Musor restaurants whose seating capacities are given in Example 5.15 are in city centre locations. The seating capacities for these five restaurants are shown in bold type below:

53	38	**59**	**62**	51	51	28	45	61	39
59	**50**	48	74	52	41	**73**	68	47	48
52	56	52	55	47	52	41			

We can embolden these values in the stem and leaf display.

Stem	Leaves
2	8
3	8 9
4	1 1 5 7 7 8 8
5	0 1 1 2 2 2 2 3 5 6 9 9
6	1 2 8
7	3 4

Leaf unit = 1

You can see from the display in Example 5.15 that the city centre restaurants are among those with larger seating capacities.

plot a histogram showing two distributions but the result is cumbersome and you would do better to plot two separate histograms.

To show two distributions in one stem and leaf display you simply list the leaf digits for one distribution to the left of the list of stem digits and the leaf digits for the other distribution to the right of the stem digits.

Example 5.17

The seating capacities for the 22 Musor restaurants in the Bristol area are:

61	54	73	78	59	49	51	58	75	67
60	87	61	70	52	56	86	91	55	76
69	82								

Produce a stem and leaf display to show these data alongside the seating capacity data from the Musor restaurants in East Anglia given in Example 5.15.

East Anglia	Stem	Bristol
8	2	
9 8	3	
8 7 7 5 1 1	4	9
9 9 6 5 3 2 2 2 2 1 1 0	5	1 2 4 5 6 8 9
8 2 1	6	0 1 1 7 9
4 3	7	0 3 5 6 8
	8	2 6 7
	9	1

Leaf unit = 1

By looking at the display in Example 5.17 you can see that in general the restaurants in the Bristol area have larger seating capacities than those in East Anglia.

On the left-hand side of the stem and leaf display in Example 5.17 stem line 5 is heavily loaded with leaf digits. You can modify stem and leaf displays to reduce long rows of leaf digits by stretching the stems.

Example 5.18

Produce a stem and leaf display to show the seating capacities of the Musor restaurants in East Anglia. Use two stems for each stem digit.

Stem	Leaves
2	8
3	
3	8 9
4	1 1
4	7 7 8
5	0 1 1 2 2 2 2 3
5	5 6 9 9
6	1 2
6	8
7	3 4

Leaf unit = 1

In Example 5.18 the stem and leaf display contains two stem lines for each stem digit, except 2 and 7. The first stem line for a stem digit contains leaf units 0 to 4 inclusive. The second stem line contains leaf units 5 to 9 inclusive. There is only one stem line for stem digit 2 because the stem digit 2 has no leaf digits less than 5. There is only one stem line for stem digit 7 because the stem digit 7 has no leaf digits more than 4.

The data we have used so far to construct stem and leaf displays has consisted of two-digit numbers which makes it fairly easy: the left-hand digit is the stem and the right-hand digit is the leaf. But what if you have to deal with more complex figures? In the same way as we can experiment with different classes to produce a suitable histogram, we can try rounding, dividing stem lines, having longer stems or longer leaves to produce a suitable stem and leaf display. Just as we can have too many or too few classes in a histogram, we can have too many or too few stem lines in a stem and leaf display. The important thing is to construct the display so that it is an effective way of presenting the data we have.

You can see by looking at the stem and leaf display in Example 5.19 that there are many cheaper but few expensive quotations. This is an example of a positively skewed distribution.

Example 5.19

The prices in £s of 16 different motor insurance quotations received by a motorist were:

| 448 | 423 | 284 | 377 | 502 | 459 | 278 | 268 |
| 374 | 344 | 256 | 228 | 380 | 286 | 219 | 352 |

Produce a stem and leaf display to show these data.

There are two ways to approach this task. You could try longer, two-digit stems and one-digit leaves, so for instance the value 448 will have a stem of 44 and a leaf of 8. This means that your list of stem lines will start with 21 (the stem of 219, the lowest value) and finish with 50 (the stem of 502, the highest value). You would have a very long list of stem lines (30) with only 16 leaf digits shared between them.

Alternatively you might try one-digit stems and longer, two-digit leaves, so 448 will have a stem of 4 and a leaf of 48. This is much more promising in this case.

Stem	Leaves
2	19 28 56 68 78 84 86
3	44 52 74 77 80
4	23 48 59
5	02

Leaf unit – 1.0

Although a stem and leaf display is essentially an alternative to a histogram, it can be used instead of a grouped frequency distribution as a way of sorting the data before plotting a histogram.

At this point you may find it useful to try **Review Questions 5.10 to 5.13** at the end of the chapter.

5.3 Presenting bivariate quantitative data

The techniques for presenting quantitative data that you have met so far in this chapter have one thing in common: they are all designed to portray the observed values of one variable. They are sometimes called tools of *univariate* analysis.

But what if you want to present values of two variables in one diagram in order to illustrate a connection (or maybe a lack of connection) between them? In that case you need another type of graph, the *scatter diagram*, which is a tool of *bivariate*, that is, two-variable, analysis. The word scatter is used because the intention of the diagram is to show how the observed values of one variable are distributed or *scattered* in relation to the observed values of another variable.

Example 5.20

Produce a histogram to portray the data in Example 5.19.

To do this we can use each stem line in the stem and leaf display as a class, which will be represented as a block in the histogram. The first stem line will be the class '200 and under 300' and so on.

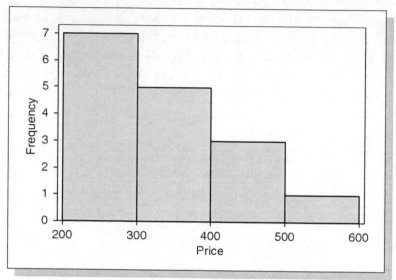

Figure 5.14
Histogram of prices of motor insurance quotations

A set of bivariate data consists of two sets of observed values, a pair of values for each item or thing or person that has been studied. A scatter diagram is constructed by plotting a point for each pair of observed values in the set of data. One value in the pair is plotted against the horizontal axis, the other against the vertical axis. The result is a *scatter* of points that will form some pattern if there is a connection between the variables.

Typically when we plot a scatter diagram we do so because we have a specific notion about the possible connection between the two variables. If we believe that one variable depends in some way on the other variable we refer to one of the variables as the *dependent* variable whose values we think depend on the values of the other, which is called the *independent* variable. The dependent variable is known as the Y variable and its observed values are plotted against the Y, or vertical, axis. The independent variable is known as the X variable and its values are plotted against the X, or horizontal, axis.

Example 5.21

The maximum daytime temperatures (in degree Celsius) and the quantities of barbecue fuel (in kg) sold at a service station on 13 days were:

Temperature (°C)	15	17	18	18	19	20	21	22	24	25	27	27	28
Fuel sold (kg)	10	15	25	20	45	50	40	85	130	135	170	195	180

Decide which is the dependent (Y) variable and which is the independent (X) variable then produce a scatter diagram to portray this set of data.

Fuel sold is the dependent (Y) variable because logically it depends on the temperature, which is the independent (X) variable.

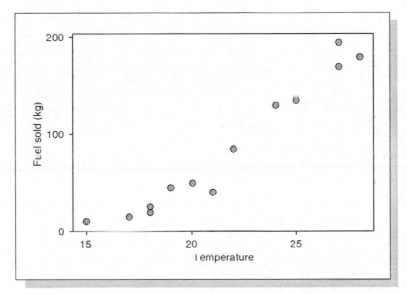

Figure 5.15
A scatter diagram of temperature and barbecue fuel sold

In Figure 5.15 you can see 13 points in the diagram, one for each of the 13 days in the set of data. Each point represents both the temperature and the amount of barbecue fuel sold for a particular day. The position of the point along the vertical or Y axis tells you the quantity sold on the day and the position of the point along the horizontal or X axis tells you the temperature on the day, for instance the point on the bottom left of the diagram represents the day when the temperature was 15 degrees Celsius and the quantity sold was 10 kg.

The diagram shows us that there appears to be a clear connection between the temperature and the quantity of barbecue fuel sold. The quantity sold appears to be higher when the temperature is higher. This is an example of a *direct* relationship, where the values of one variable increases as the values of the other variable increase. A relationship in which the values of one variable decrease as the values of the other increase is an *inverse* relationship.

At this point you may find it useful to try **Review Questions 5.14 to 5.16** at the end of the chapter.

5.4 Presenting time series data

A time series is a set of data that consists of observations collected over a period, usually at regular intervals. It is bivariate data in which one of the variables is time. Businesses of all kinds collect this sort of data as a matter of course – for instance weekly sales, monthly output, annual profit – so presenting time series data is important.

The type of graph used to portray time series data is a *time series plot*. It is similar to a scatter diagram in that it consists of a set of plotted points each of which represents a pair of values of two variables plotted against a pair of axes.

However there are key differences. In a time series plot the time variable is always plotted on the horizontal, or X, axis which represents the passage of time from left (the first observation) to right (the last observation). The points that represent the data are joined up to emphasize the flow of time, whereas in a scatter diagram they are never joined up. The scale of the vertical, or Y, axis should begin at zero so that the fluctuations over time are not over-emphasized, whereas the scales on the axes of a scatter diagram do not need to start at zero.

You can see from Figure 5.16 that the company has undergone a dramatic growth in its number of employees over this period. In other words there has been a strong upward *trend*, or basic movement. Plots of

Example 5.22

The numbers of employees of a biomedical company over nine years were:

Year	1995	1996	1997	1998	1999	2000	2001	2002	2003
Employees	7	15	38	112	149	371	371	508	422

Produce a time series chart to show these data.

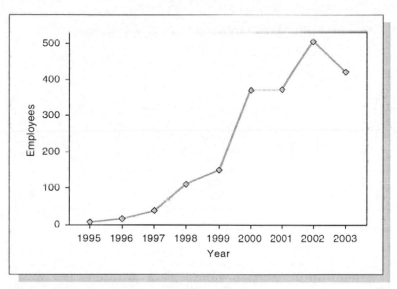

Figure 5.16
Employees of a biomedical company

other time series might show a more fluctuating pattern, perhaps with *seasonal* variations, that is a recurrent pattern within each year, or *cyclical* variations, that is recurrent variations over periods of years.

You can tell by looking at Figure 5.17 that the energy costs for this building are far higher in the autumn and winter months (quarters 1 and 4) than in the spring and summer months (quarters 2 and 3), and that this pattern occurs in both years.

At this point you may find it useful to try **Review Questions 5.17 to 5.19** at the end of the chapter.

Example 5.23

The quarterly costs of energy supplied to the Komnata office building over two years were:

	Quarter			
Year	**1**	**2**	**3**	**4**
1	£6375	£2791	£7964	£8283
2	£6941	£2309	£3128	£8537

Produce a time series plot to show these data.

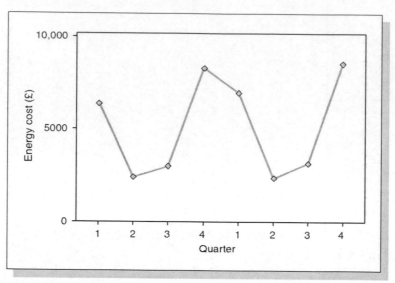

Figure 5.17
Quarterly energy costs

5.5 Using the technology: presenting data in EXCEL, MINITAB and SPSS

In this section you will find out about using EXCEL, MINITAB and SPSS to produce the diagrams introduced in this chapter. For each of these packages, producing the diagrams is discussed in the same sequence as the diagrams were introduced in the chapter, starting with pie charts and concluding with time series plots.

5.5.1 EXCEL

To produce a pie chart like Figure 5.2 start by storing the categories in one column of the spreadsheet and the frequencies in another, then

■ select **Chart** from the **Insert** menu. A sequence of windows called **Chart Wizard** will appear. Choose **Pie** as the type of chart in the **Step 1** window then click the **Next >** button at the bottom of the window.

■ The **Step 2** window that appears gives you a preview of the chart. If it is what you expect click **Next >** to move on to **Step 3** where you can embellish the chart with a title and other features.

■ Click **Next >** to get to **Step 4** where you can specify whether the chart will appear in the existing worksheet (the default setting) or in a new one.

■ Click **Finish** and the chart will appear.

Producing a bar chart like Figure 5.3 involves carrying out the same procedure as you would use to produce a pie chart. Store the summary table in a spreadsheet then select **Chart** from the **Insert** menu. In **Step 1** of the **Chart Wizard** sequence, choose **Column** as the type of chart (or **Bar** if you prefer a chart with horizontal bars) then proceed through **Step 1** to **Step 4**.

To get a component or stacked bar chart like Figure 5.4, put the categories in one column of a spreadsheet and the first and second sets of frequencies in adjacent columns, for instance the data from Example 5.4 would be entered as:

	A	B	C
1	Crewe	21	15
2	Doncaster	44	13
3	Exeter	13	15
4	Frome	10	7

■ Select **Chart** from the **Insert** menu then **Column** in **Step 1** of the **Chart Wizard** sequence. Pick the **Stacked Column** chart sub-type from the selection in the window and click the **Next >** button.

■ If the preview in the **Step 2** is not what you expect check that the **Data range** is correctly specified by clicking and dragging your mouse over the cell locations of the data in the spreadsheet.

■ Continue through the remaining **Chart Wizard** windows and the chart should appear on screen once you click **Finish** in **Step 4**.

To obtain a component or stacked bar chart with the bars subdivided by percentages like Figure 5.5, proceed exactly as you would to produce a component but in the **Step 1** window of the **Chart Wizard** sequence select **Column** then pick the **100% Stacked Column** chart sub-type.

For a cluster bar chart like Figure 5.6 carry out the same sequence of operations as you would to obtain a component or stacked bar chart but you need only choose **Column** as the chart type in the **Step 1** window of the **Chart Wizard** sequence as the default chart sub-type is the **Clustered Column**.

To plot a histogram like Figure 5.8 put your data into a column of the spreadsheet then

- Select **Data Analysis** from the **Tools** menu. (If you cannot find **Data Analysis** click **Add-Ins** in the **Tools** menu and look for **Analysis ToolPak**.) **Click** on **Histogram** in the list of techniques that appears in the **Data Analysis** window.
- In the **Histogram** window that appears specify the location of the data in **Input Range** and click the space to the left of **Chart Output** to request a histogram.
- In the **Output options** section of the **Histogram** window the **New Worksheet Ply** option is the default setting. This will locate your histogram and the grouped frequency distribution the package compiles to create it in a new worksheet when you click **OK**.
- If you are not satisfied with the classes the package has used you can alter them by choosing your own classes and putting their starting points in a column of the spreadsheet then putting the column location in the **Bin Ranges** box in the command window. The word 'bin' is used as a synonym for class in EXCEL because putting observations into classes is the same sort of thing as sorting objects into different bins.

For a scatter diagram like Figure 5.15 enter the values of the two variables into two columns of the spreadsheet then

- Select **Chart** from the **Insert** menu. Choose **XY(Scatter)** from the **Step 1** window of the **Chart Wizard** sequence and click **Next >** to continue through the sequence.
- In the **Step 3** window you can remove the default gridlines by clicking the **Gridlines** tab and clicking to remove the tick in the space to the left of **Major gridlines** for the **Y axis**.

To obtain a simple time series plot like Figure 5.16 put your data in a single column of the worksheet in chronological order then select **Chart** from the **Insert** menu then the **Line** chart type and continue through the **Chart Wizard** sequence.

5.5.2 MINITAB

For a pie chart like Figure 5.2 put the categories in one column of the worksheet and their frequencies in another.

- Click the **Graph** pull-down menu and select **Pie Chart**.
- In the **Pie Chart** command window click the button to the right of **Chart table** and then click in the window to the right

of **Categories in** and type in the column location of the categories, e.g. c1. Click in the window to the right of **Frequencies in** and type in the column location of the frequencies.

▪ Click the **OK** button and the graphic will appear.

To produce a bar chart like Figure 5.3 store the categories and frequencies in two columns in the worksheet then select **Chart** from the **Graph** menu. You will need to put the column location of the frequencies in the **Y (Measurement)** box and the column location of the categories in the **X (Categories)** box then click the **OK** button.

You can produce a component or stack bar chart like Figure 5.4 by following the same procedure to produce a simple bar chart, but you need to put the data in three columns: one for the main categories, a second for the frequencies and a third for the sub-divisions within the categories. To illustrate, the data from Example 5.4 would be entered like this:

C1-T Depot	C2 Call-outs	C3-T Appliance
Crewe	21	Washing machine
Doncaster	44	Washing machine
Exeter	13	Washing machine
Frome	10	Washing machine
Crewe	15	Other
Doncaster	13	Other
Exeter	15	Other
Frome	7	Other

Because a depot has *two* numbers associated with it, every depot appears *twice*. Because each appliance type has *four* numbers associated with it, appliance type categories appear *four times*. Note that the two columns containing the non-numeric data have '-T' added to their column names to indicate that the columns contain text. This happens whenever you put non-numeric data onto a MINITAB column to tell you that you will not be allowed to carry out techniques based on arithmetical operations on the data in these columns.

To obtain the component or stack bar chart,

▪ Choose **Chart** from the **Graph** menu.
▪ Type the column location of the frequencies in the **Y (measurement)** box and the column location of the categories in the **X (category)** box.
▪ Click the ▼ button by **For each** and choose **Group**.
▪ Click the space below **Group variables** and type in the column location of the category sub-divisions then click the **Options** button.

- Select **Stack** in the **Options** window and specify the column where the category sub-divisions are stored in the box to the right of **Stack**.
- Click the **OK** buttons on first the **Options** window then the **Chart** window.

For a component or stacked bar chart with the bars subdivided by percentages, like Figure 5.5, proceed exactly as you would to produce a component bar chart but when you reach the **Options** window click the button to the left of **Total Y to 100% within each X category**.

To get a cluster bar chart like Figure 5.6 follow the procedure for obtaining a component or stack bar chart, but select **Cluster** instead of **Stack** in the **Options** window. Put the column location of the category sub-divisions in the box alongside **Cluster** and click the **OK** buttons on first the **Options** window then the **Chart** window.

To produce a histogram like Figure 5.8 put the data into one of the columns of the worksheet and

- Select **Histogram** from the **Graph** menu.
- Specify the column location of the data in the command window that appears and click **OK**.
- Clicking on the **Options** button in the command window will allow you to choose how to arrange your classes by modifying the **Definition of Intervals** if you are not satisfied with the diagram the package produces for you.

To obtain a stem and leaf display like the one in Example 5.15 put your data into a column of the worksheet then select **Stem-and-Leaf** from the **Graph** menu and specify in the command window the column location of your data then click **OK**. You can modify the stem lines by inserting an appropriate figure in the **Increment:** window.

You can produce a scatter diagram like Figure 5.15 by entering the values of one variable in one column of the worksheet and the values of the other variable in another. Select **Plot** from the **Graph** menu and then specify the column locations of the observed values of the Y and X variables in the appropriate boxes of the **Plot** window and click **OK**.

For a time series chart like Figure 5.16 enter the data in a column of the worksheet in chronological order then

- Select **Time Series Plot** from the **Graph** menu.
- Specify the column location of the time series in the command window. The time scale along the axis will be plotted for you, but you need to specify the intervals of time under **Time Scale** and then click **Options** and enter the first time period.

For the data in Example 5.22 these are 'year' and '1995' respectively.

▪ Click **OK** and the graph will appear.

5.5.3 SPSS

For a pie chart like Figure 5.2 put the categories in one column of the worksheet and their frequencies in another.

▪ Click the **Graph** pull-down menu and select **Pie...**.

▪ In the **Pie Charts** window that appears the **Summaries for groups of cases** should be selected.

▪ Click the **Define** button and in the **Define Pie** window that appears the columns listed on the left hand side should be those containing your data.

▪ Click on the one containing your categories and then click ▶ to the left of **Define Slices by:**.

▪ In the section headed **Slices Represent** click the button to the left of **Other summary function** then click on the column location of your frequencies on the left-hand side of the window and click ▶ to the left of **Variable:**.

▪ Click the **OK** button and the graphic will appear in the output viewer.

To produce a bar chart like Figure 5.3 store the categories and frequencies in two columns in the worksheet then

▪ Select **Bar...** from the **Graph** menu.

▪ In the **Bar Charts** window **Simple** chart type and **Summaries for groups of cases** should be the default settings, if not, select them.

▪ Click the **Define** button and in the **Define Simple Bar** window that comes up the columns listed on the left should be those containing your data.

▪ Click on the one containing your categories and then click ▶ to the left of **Category Axis:**.

▪ In the section headed **Bars Represent** click the button to the left of **Other summary function** then click on the column location of your frequencies on the left-hand side of the window and click ▶ to the left of **Variable:**.

▪ Click the **OK** button and the graphic will appear in the output viewer.

To produce a component or stacked bar chart like Figure 5.4 you need to put the data in three columns: one for the main categories, a second for the frequencies and a third for the sub-divisions within the categories. To illustrate, the data from Example 5.4 would be entered like this:

Depot	Call-outs	Appliance
Crewe	21	Washing machine
Doncaster	44	Washing machine
Exeter	13	Washing machine
Frome	10	Washing machine
Crewe	15	Other
Doncaster	13	Other
Exeter	15	Other
Frome	7	Other

- Select **Bar...** from the **Graphs** menu and in the **Bar Charts** window click the **Stacked** style of chart.
- Check that **Summaries for groups of cases** is selected then click **Define**.
- In the **Define Stacked Bar** window click on the column name of the categories then click ▶ to the left of **Category Axis:**.
- Click on the column name of the sub-divisions then click ▶ to the left of **Define Stacks by:**.
- In the section headed **Bars Represent** click the button to the left of **Other summary function** then click on the column name of your frequencies and click ▶ to the left of **Variable:**.
- Click the **OK** button and the graphic will appear.

For a cluster bar chart like Figure 5.6 follow the procedure for obtaining a component or stacked bar chart, but in the **Bar Charts** window click the **Clustered** style of chart. The **Define Clustered Bar** window that appears is almost the same as the **Define Stacked Bar** window and should be completed in the same way. The only difference is that you have to enter the column name of the sub-divisions in the **Define Cluster by:** window.

To get a histogram like Figure 5.8 put the data into one of the columns of the worksheet and select **Histogram ...** from the **Graphs** menu. In the **Histograms** window click on the column name of the column where your data are located then click ▶ to the left of **Variable:** and click **OK**.

For a stem and leaf display like the one in Example 5.15 put your data into a worksheet column then

- Select **Descriptive Statistics** from the **Analyze** menu.
- Choose **Explore ...** from the sub-menu.

■ In the **Explore** window click on the column name of the column where your data are located then click ▶ to the left of **Dependent List:**.

■ Click the **Plots** button in the lower part of the window and check that **Stem-and-leaf** is ticked.

■ Click the **Continue** button then **OK**. The stem and leaf display for your data will appear in the output viewer below a summary of your data.

You can produce a scatter diagram like Figure 5.15 by entering the values of one variable in one column of the worksheet and the values of the other variable in another.

■ Choose **Scatter ...** from the **Graphs** menu, take the default (**Simple**) chart type in the **Scatterplot** window then click the **Define** button.

■ In the **Simple Scatterplot** window click on the name of the column location of your y values then click ▶ to the left of **Y Axis:**.

■ Click on the name of the column location of your x values and click ▶ to the left of **X Axis:** then click **OK**.

For a time series chart like Figure 5.16 enter the data in one column of the worksheet in chronological order and the corresponding time periods in another.

■ Select **Line ...** from the **Graphs** menu.

■ In the **Line Charts** window check that the default setting is the **Simple** chart type then click on **Define**.

■ In the **Define Simple Line** window click **Other summary function** then click on the column name of the location of your time series data and click ▶ to the left of **Variable:**.

■ Click on the column name of the column location of your time periods then click ▶ to the left of **Category Axis:** then click **OK**.

5.6 Road test: Do they really use pictorial presentation?

The techniques we have considered in this chapter are very widely used in a range of documents produced by and for businesses. Pick up a company report and you will probably see the profile of the company depicted in the form of pie charts, bar charts and histograms and the progress of the company depicted in the form of time series charts. Pick up a copy of the *Financial Times* and you will find time series plots of movements in stock markets, pie and bar charts in company profiles. These are publicly available materials, but the organizations you work for will produce departmental reports, share issue prospectuses and development studies in which data are portrayed in visual form.

This extensive usage of visual tools to display data stretches back as far as the origins of modern business organizations. An early pioneer was the Scottish draughtsman William Playfair (1759–1823), who worked for the Birmingham engineering firm Boulton & Watt. He developed charting methods that he used to depict, among other things, the trading fortunes of the East India Company. You can read more about him and see some of his work in Holmes (1991) and Tufte (1983). Both books give a good historical perspective of pictorial presentation of data. The Tufte text is a particularly helpful guide to good practice in the construction of statistical diagrams.

Review questions

Answers to these questions, including fully worked solutions to the Key questions marked with an asterisk (*), are on pages 638–641.

5.1*   Vorovka Direct Marketing has offices in Liverpool, Motherwell and Newbury. The number of employees in each location and their genders are tabulated below:

	Number of employees		
Office	*Females*	*Males*	*Total*
Liverpool	12	8	20
Motherwell	9	15	24
Newbury	23	6	29

(a) Plot a simple bar chart to show the total number of employees in each office.

(b) Plot a component bar chart to show the number of employees in each office by gender.

(c) Plot a cluster bar chart to show the number of employees at each office by gender.

5.2   Tourists seeking holiday accommodation in a self-catering complex in the resort of Zidania can make either a one- or two-week booking. The manager of the complex has produced the following table to show the bookings she received last season:

	Type of booking	
Tourist's home country	*One-week*	*Two-week*
France	13	44
Germany	29	36
Holland	17	21
Ireland	8	5

(a) Produce a simple bar chart to show the total number of bookings by home country.

(b) Produce a component bar chart to show the number of bookings by home country and type of booking.

(c) Produce a cluster bar chart to show the number of bookings by home country and type of booking.

5.3   A machine vending company operates three hot drinks machines, one at a bus station, a second at a train station and a third at a leisure centre. The numbers of coffee, tea and chocolate drinks dispensed from each in a single day are given in the following table.

	Number of drinks		
Location of machine	*Coffee*	*Tea*	*Chocolate*
Bus station	68	91	23
Train station	105	74	47
Leisure centre	49	67	89

(a) Plot a simple bar chart to portray the total number of drinks dispensed at each location.

(b) Plot a cluster bar chart to portray the number of drinks dispensed at each location by the type of drink.

(c) Plot a component bar chart to portray the number of drinks dispensed at each location by the type of drink.

5.4   The manager of the customer service department at Prastudar Promotions submits the following frequency distribution for the number of days in the previous week staff in the department were off sick:

Days off	Number of staff
0	17
1	4
2	2
3	1
4	0
5	2

Construct a bar chart to display this distribution.

5.5* A roadside breakdown assistance service answers 37 calls in Derbyshire on one day. The response times taken to deal with these calls were noted and have been arranged in the grouped frequency distribution below.

Response time (minutes)	Number of calls
20 and under 30	4
30 and under 40	8
40 and under 50	17
50 and under 60	6
60 and under 70	2

(a) Produce a histogram to portray this distribution and describe the shape of the distribution.
(b) Find the cumulative frequency for each class.
(c) Produce a cumulative frequency graph of the distribution.

5.6 Rents per person (to the nearest £) for 83 flats and houses advertised on the notice boards at a university were collected and the following grouped frequency distribution compiled:

Rent per person (£)	Frequency
35–39	13
40–44	29
45–49	22
50–54	10
55–59	7
60–64	2

(a) Plot a histogram to portray this distribution and comment on the shape of the distribution.
(b) Find the cumulative frequency for each class.
(c) Plot a cumulative frequency graph of the distribution.

5.7   The company marketing the revolutionary 'Girth Control' diet have distributed a press release that includes a grouped frequency distribution showing the weight losses achieved by the 56 participants in the trial of the diet.

Weight lost (kg)	*Number of participants*
0 and under 2	3
2 and under 4	3
4 and under 6	4
6 and under 8	8
8 and under 10	27
10 and under 12	11

(a) Draw a histogram to portray this distribution and comment on the shape of the distribution.
(b) Calculate the cumulative frequency for each class.
(c) Draw a cumulative frequency graph of the distribution.

5.8   A video rental shop has 312 different feature films that are available for hire overnight. The number of times these videos were rented out during a month is presented in the following grouped frequency distribution:

Number of rentals	*Number of videos*
0–4	169
5–9	71
10–14	39
15–19	18
20–24	11
25–29	4

(a) Construct a histogram for this distribution.
(b) Calculate the cumulative relative frequency for each class.
(c) Plot a cumulative relative frequency graph of the distribution.

5.9   One branch of a bank has 849 customers who have credit balances in a certain type of current account. The sizes of the balances in these accounts, to the nearest £, have been arranged in the following grouped frequency distribution:

Size of balance (£)	*Number of accounts*
0–249	88
250–499	153
500–749	202
750–999	174
1000–1499	160
1500–1999	72

(a) Plot a histogram to represent this distribution.

(b) Find the cumulative relative frequency for each class.

(c) Plot a cumulative relative frequency distribution of the distribution.

5.10*   Monthly membership fees in £s for 22 health clubs are:

34	**43**	44	**22**	73	69	48	67	33	56	67
27	78	60	63	**32**	67	41	65	**48**	48	77

(a) Compile a stem and leaf display of these data.

(b) The clubs whose fees appear in bold do not have a swimming pool. Highlight them in your display.

5.11   The monthly membership fees in £s for 17 fitness centres in local authority leisure centres are:

28	50	44	32	31	55	21	36	24
55	51	55	32	39	42	28	55	

(a) Compile a stem and leaf display to show these figures and the set of data in the previous question. List the leaf digits for this distribution to the left of the stem digits and the leaf digits for the data in question 5.10 to the right.

(b) Compare the two distributions.

5.12   The hourly wages (in £s) of 32 jobs advertised by a 'temp' agency are:

6.26	4.90	4.52	5.11	5.94	5.82	7.14	7.28	5.15	7.04
4.47	4.67	6.90	5.85	5.65	5.50	4.12	5.27	5.25	6.43
5.65	4.65	5.37	4.24	6.45	4.70	5.09	4.82	6.23	5.40
6.22	5.26								

(a) Compile a stem and leaf display to present these figures using the figures in pounds (4, 5, 6, 7) as stem digits and a single line for each stem digit.

(b) Modify your stem and leaf display so that there are two stem lines for each stem digit.

5.13   The prices (in £s) of 27 second-hand small hatchback cars on sale at a garage are:

4960	1720	2350	2770	3340	4240	4850	4390	3870
2990	3740	2230	1690	2750	1590	4990	3660	1900
4250	4390	3690	1760	4800	1730	2040	4070	2670

(a) Compile a stem and leaf display for these figures using thousands as stem digits.

(b) Modify your display by using two stem lines for each stem digit.

(c) Construct a histogram using classes based on the stem lines used in (b).

5.14* Levels of expenditure on domestic fuel (in $'000m) and the populations (in millions) of nine countries are:

Expenditure
($'000m)   5.2 4.1   1.9 1.4 27.2 0.5 11.1 10.2 20.4
Population
(m)   10.6 5.4 10.3 4.2 55.9 0.4 15.3 40.1 56.3

(a) Identify the dependent (Y) variable,
(b) Plot a scatter diagram to portray these figures.
(c) Describe the type of relationship between the two variables.

5.15 A catalogue shop sells 9 brands of television sets with 14" screens. The prices of these (to the nearest £), and the number of each sold are:

Price (£)	75	80	85	100	100	120	140	200	220
Number sold	48	31	39	28	24	17	11	6	2

(a) Which is the independent (X) variable?
(b) Draw a scatter diagram to represent these sets of data.
(c) Is the relationship between the two variables direct or inverse?

5.16 The top speeds and engine sizes of 12 performance cars are:

Top speed (mph)	137	165	185	118	168	155	125
Engine size (litres)	2.0	5.9	3.6	1.7	3.2	4.2	1.8

Top speed (mph)	177	129	163	157	134
Engine size (litres)	4.2	1.8	5.5	2.7	2.2

(a) Which variable is the independent (X) variable?
(b) Draw a scatter diagram to represent these sets of data.
(c) Is there a direct or inverse relationship between the two variables?

5.17* The sales of organic vegetables (in £'000) by a fruit and vegetable wholesaler over 10 years were:

Year	1994	1995	1996	1997	1998	1999	2000	2001
Sales	0.0	0.0	1.2	1.7	3.2	5.1	10.4	12.2

Year	2002	2003
Sales	26.9	47.1

Construct a time series plot to present this set of data.

5.18   The quarterly sales (in £'000) of greeting cards in a supermarket were:

	Quarter			
Year	*1*	*2*	*3*	*4*
1	12.0	14.8	9.6	19.2
2	13.1	16.3	9.2	20.8

Produce a time series plot to show these figures.

5.19   Sales of cold and flu treatments (in £'000) in a Manchester pharmacy during the last three years were:

	Quarter			
Year	*1*	*2*	*3*	*4*
1	11.3	5.1	3.9	9.5
2	12.6	7.9	3.7	8.8
3	10.9	6.2	4.7	9.3

Draw a time series plot for these data.

5.20   Select which of the statements listed below on the right-hand side describes the words listed on the left-hand side.

(i) histogram	(a) can only take a limited number of values
(ii) time series	(b) segments or slices represent categories
(iii) pictogram	(c) each plotted point represents a pair of values
(iv) discrete data	(d) separates parts of each observation
(v) stem and leaf display	(e) each block represents a class
(vi) scatter diagram	(f) data collected at regular intervals over time
(vii) pie chart	(g) comprises a set of small pictures

CHAPTER 6

General directions — summarizing data

This chapter will help you to:

- understand and use summary measures of location; the mode, median and arithmetic mean
- understand and use summary measures of spread; the range, quartiles, semi inter-quartile range, standard deviation, variance
- present order statistics using boxplots
- find summary measures from grouped data
- use the technology: summarize data in EXCEL, MINITAB and SPSS
- become acquainted with business uses of summary measures in control charts

This chapter is about using figures known as *summary measures* to represent or *summarize* quantitative data. Because they are used to *describe* sets of data they are also called *descriptive measures*. The summary measures that you will come across are very effective and widely used methods of communicating the essence or gist of a set of observations in just one or two figures, particularly when it is important to compare two or more distributions. Knowing when to use them and how to interpret them will enable you to communicate quantitative information effectively.

There are two basic ways of summarizing data. The first is to use a figure to give some idea of what the values within a set of data are like.

This is the idea of an average, something you are probably familiar with; you may have achieved an average mark, you may be of average build etc.

The word average suggests a 'middle' or 'typical' level. An average is a representative figure that summarizes a whole set of numbers in a single figure. There are two other names for averages that you will meet. The first is *measures of location*, used because averages tell us where the data are positioned or *located* on the numerical scale. The second is *measures of central tendency*, used because averages provide us with some idea of the *centre* or middle of a set of data.

The second basic way of summarizing a set of data is to measure how widely the figures are spread out or dispersed. Summary measures that do this are known as *measures of spread* or *measures of dispersion*. They are single figures that tell us how broadly a set of observations is scattered.

These two types of summary measures, measures of location and measures of spread, are not alternatives; they are complementary to each other. That is, we don't use either a measure of location or a measure of spread to summarize a set of data. Typically we use both a measure of location and a measure of spread to convey an overall impression of a set of data.

6.1 Measures of location

There are various averages, or measures of location, that you can use to summarize or describe a set of data. The simplest both to apply and to interpret is the mode.

6.1.1 The mode

The *mode*, or *modal value*, is the most frequently occurring value in a set of observations. You can find the mode of a set of data by simply inspecting the observations.

Example 6.1

The ages of 15 sales staff at a cell phone shop are:

17   18   21   18   16   19   17   28   16   20   18   17   17   19   17

What is the mode?

The value 17 occurs more often (5 times) than any other value, so 17 is the mode.

If you want an average to represent a set of data that consists of a fairly small number of discrete values in which one value is clearly the most frequent, then the mode is a perfectly good way of describing the data. Looking at the data in Example 6.1, you can see that using the mode, and describing these workers as having an average age of 17, would give a useful impression of the data.

The mode is much less suitable if the data we want to summarize consist of a larger number of different values, especially if there is more than one value that occurs the same number of times.

Example 6.2

The ages of 18 sales staff at a car showroom are:

39	17	44	22	39	45	40	37	31
33	39	28	32	32	31	31	37	42

What is the mode?

The values 31 and 39 each occur three times.

The data set in Example 6.2 is *bimodal*, that is to say, it has two modes. If another person aged 32 joined the workforce there would be three modes. The more modes there are, the less useful the mode is to use. Ideally we want a single figure as a measure of location to represent a set of data.

If you want to summarize a set of continuous data, using the mode is going to be even more inappropriate; usually continuous data consist of different values so every value would be a mode because it occurs as often as every other value. If two or more observations take precisely the same value it is something of a fluke.

6.1.2 The median

Whereas you can only use the mode for some types of data, the second type of average or measure of location, the *median*, can be used for any set of data.

The median is the middle observation in a set of data. It is called an *order statistic* because it is chosen on the basis of its *order* or position within the data. Finding the median of a set of data involves first establishing *where* it is then *what* it is. To enable us to do this we must arrange the data in order of magnitude, which means listing the data in order from the lowest to the highest values in what is called an *array*. The exact position of the median in an array is found by taking the number of observations, represented by the letter *n*, adding one and then dividing by two.

$$\text{Median position} = (n + 1)/2$$

Example 6.3

Find the median of the data in Example 6.1.

Array:

   16   16   17   17   17   17   17   **18**   18   18   19   19   20   21   28

Here there are 15 observations, that is $n = 15$, so:

$$\text{Median position} = (15 + 1)/2 = 16/2 = 8$$

The median is in the eighth position in the array, in other words the eighth highest value, which is the first 18, shown in bold type. There are seven observations to the left of it in the array, and seven observations to the right of it, making it the middle value.

The median age of these workers is 18.

In Example 6.3 there are an odd number of observations, 15, so there is one middle value. If you have an even number of observations there is no single middle value, so to get the median you have to identify the middle pair and split the difference between them.

Example 6.4

Find the median of the data in Example 6.2.

Array:

   17   22   28   31   31   31   32   32   **33**   **37**   37   39
   39   39   40   42   44   45

In this case there are 18 observations, $n = 18$, so:

$$\text{Median position} = (18 + 1)/2 = 9.5$$

Although we can find a ninth observation and a tenth observation there is clearly no 9.5th observation. The position of the median is 9.5th so the median is located half way between the ninth and tenth observations, 33 and 37, which appear in bold type in the array. To find the half way mark between these observations, add them together and divide by two.

$$\text{Median} = (33 + 37)/2 = 35$$

The median age of this group of workers is 35.

6.1.3 The arithmetic mean

Although you have probably come across averages before, and you may already be familiar with the mode and the median, they may not be the first things to come to mind if you were asked to find the average of a set of data. Faced with such a request you might well think of adding the observations together and then dividing by the number of observations there are.

This is what many people think of as 'the average', although actually it is one of several averages. We have already dealt with two of them, the mode and the median. This third average, or measure of location, is called the *mean* or more specifically the *arithmetic mean* in order to distinguish it from other types of mean. Like the median the arithmetic mean can be used with any set of quantitative data.

The procedure for finding the arithmetic mean involves calculation so you may find it more laborious than finding the mode, which involves merely inspecting data, and finding the median, which involves putting data in order. To get the arithmetic mean you first get the sum of the observations and then divide by n, the number of observations in the set of data.

$$\text{Arithmetic mean} = \Sigma x/n$$

The symbol x is used here to represent an observed value of the variable X, so Σx represents the sum of the observed values of the variable X. The arithmetic mean of a sample is represented by the symbol $\bar{x}$, 'x-bar'. The arithmetic mean of a population is represented by the Greek letter μ, 'mu', which is the Greek 'm' (m for mean). Later on we will look at how sample means can be used to estimate population means, so it is important to recognize this difference.

The mean is one of several statistical measures you will meet which have two different symbols, one of which is Greek, to represent them. The Greek symbol is always used to denote the measure for the population. Rarely do we have the time and resources to calculate a measure for a whole population so almost invariably the ones we do calculate are for a sample.

Example 6.5

In one month the total costs (to the nearest £) of the calls made by 23 male mobile phone owners were:

| 17 | 17 | 14 | 16 | 15 | 24 | 12 | 20 | 17 | 17 | 13 | 21 |
| 15 | 14 | 14 | 20 | 21 | 9 | 15 | 22 | 19 | 27 | 19 | |

Find the mean monthly cost:

The sum of these costs: $\sum x = 21 + 19 + 22 + \cdots + 5 + 17 = 398$

The arithmetic mean: $\sum x/n = 398/23 = £17.30$ (to the nearest penny)

6.1.4 Choosing which measure of location to use

The whole point of using a measure of location is that it should convey an impression of a distribution in a single figure. If you want to communicate this it won't help if you quote the mode, median and mean and then leave it to your reader or audience to please themselves which one to pick. It is important to use the right average.

Picking which average to use might depend on a number of factors:

- The type of data we are dealing with.
- Whether the average needs to be easy to find.
- The shape of the distribution.
- Whether the average will be the basis for further work on the data.

As far as the type of data is concerned, unless you are dealing with fairly simple discrete data the mode is redundant. If you do have to analyse such data the mode may be worth considering, particularly if it is important that your measure of location is a feasible value for the variable to take.

Example 6.6

The numbers of days that 16 office workers were absent through illness were:

    1   1   9   0   2   1   1   4   0   2   4   1   4   3   2   1

Find the mode, median and mean for this set of data.

The modal value is 1, which occurs six times.

Array:

0   0   1   1   1   1   1   1   2   2   2   3   4   4   4   9

The median position is: $(16 + 1)/2 = 8.5$th position
The median is: (8th value + 9th value)$/2 = (1 + 2)/2 = 1.5$
The arithmetic mean $= (0 + 0 + 1 + 1 + \cdots + 4 + 9)/16 = 36/16 = 2.25$

In Example 6.6 it is only the mode that has a value that is both feasible and actually occurs, 1. Although the value of the median, 1.5 may be feasible if the employer recorded half-day absences, it is not one of the observed values. The value of the mean, 2.25 is not feasible and therefore cannot be one of the observed values.

The only other reason you might prefer to use the mode rather than the other measures of location, assuming that you are dealing with discrete data made up of a relatively few different values, is that it is the easiest of the measures of location to find. All you need to do is to look at the data and count how many times the values occur. Often with the sort of simple data that the mode suits it is fairly obvious which value occurs most frequently and there is no need to count the frequency of each value.

There are more reasons for not using the mode than there are for using the mode. First, it is simply not appropriate for some types of data, especially continuous data. Secondly, there is no guarantee that there is only one mode; there may be two or more in a single distribution. Thirdly, only the observations that have the modal value 'count', the rest of the observations in the distribution are not taken into account at all. In contrast, when we calculate a mean we add all the values in the distribution together; none of them is excluded.

In many cases you will find that the choice of average boils down to either the median or the mean. The shape of the distribution is a factor that could well influence your choice. If you have a distribution that is skewed rather than symmetrical, the median is likely to be the more realistic and reliable measure of location to use.

Example 6.7

Produce a histogram to display the data from Example 6.6 and comment on the shape of the distribution.

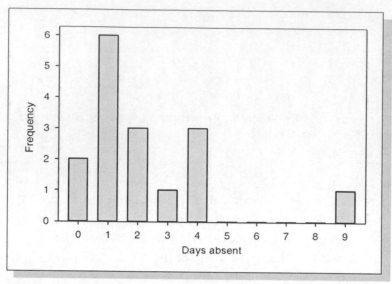

Figure 6.1
Bar chart of the number of days absent

The distribution of days absent is positively skewed, with the majority of the observations occurring to the left of the distribution.

The median and mean for the data in Example 6.6 were 1.5 and 2.25 respectively. There is quite a difference between them, especially when you consider that the difference between the lowest and highest values in the distribution is only 9. The difference between the median and the mean arises because the distribution is skewed.

When you find a median you concentrate on the middle of the distribution, you are not concerned with the observations to either side of the middle, so the pattern of the distribution at either end of the distribution does not have any effect on the median. In Example 6.6 it would not matter if the highest value in the distribution were 99 rather than 9, the median would still be 1.5. The value of the median is determined by *how many* observations lie to the left and right of it, not the *values* of those observations.

The mean on the other hand depends entirely on all of the values in the distribution, from the lowest to the highest; they all have to be added together in order to calculate the mean. If the highest value in the distribution were 99 rather than 9 it would make a considerable difference to the value of the mean (in fact it would increase to 7.875).

Because calculating the mean involves adding all the observations together the value of the mean is sensitive to unusual values or *outliers*. Every observation is equal in the sense that it contributes 1 to the value of n, the number of observations. However if an observation is much lower than the rest, when it is added into the sum of the values it will contribute relatively little to the sum and make the value of the mean considerably lower. If an observation is much higher than the rest, it will contribute disproportionately more to the sum and make the value of the mean considerably higher.

Example 6.8

One of the observed values in the data in Example 6.6 has been recorded wrongly. The figure '9' should have been '2'. How does this affect the values of the mode, median and mean?

The mode is unaffected, the value '1' still occurs more frequently than the other values.

The median is unaffected because the eighth and ninth values will still be '1' and '2' respectively.

The mean will be affected because the sum of the observations will reduce by 7 to 29, so the mean is $29/16 = 1.8125$.

In Example 6.8 only one value was changed yet the mean drops from 2.25 to 1.8125.

In a skewed distribution there are typically unusual values so if you use a mean to represent a skewed distribution you should bear in mind that it will be disproportionately influenced or 'distorted' by the relatively extreme values or outliers in the distribution. This is why the median for the data in Example 6.6 was 1.5 and the mean was 2.25. The higher values in the distribution, the '9' and the '4's, have in effect 'pulled' the mean away from the median.

In general the mean will be higher than the median in positively skewed distributions such as the one shown in Figure 6.1. In negatively skewed distributions, where the greater accumulation of values is to the right of the distribution, the mean will be lower than the median.

So, should you use the median or the mean to represent a skewed distribution? The answer is that the median is the more representative of the two. Consider the values of the median and mean in relation to Figure 6.1. The median, 1.5, is by definition in the middle of the distribution, with eight observations below it and 8 observations above it. The mean, 2.25, in contrast has eleven observations below it and only five above it.

If you are dealing with a symmetrical distribution you will find that the mean is not susceptible to distortion because by definition there is roughly as much numerical 'weight' to one side of the distribution as there is to the other. The mean and median of a symmetrical distribution will therefore be close together.

Example 6.9

Produce a histogram to portray the data in Example 6.5. Find the median and compare it to the mean.

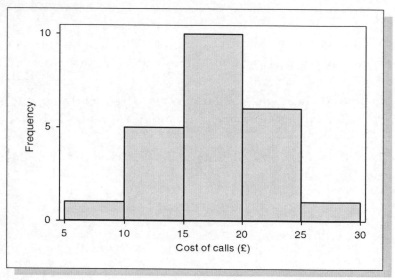

Figure 6.2
Histogram of the monthly costs of calls

There are 23 observations so the median is the $(23 + 1)/2 = $ 12th observation.

Array

9	12	13	14	14	14	15	15	15	16	17	**17**	17
17	19	19	20	20	21	21	22	24	27			

The median is 17, which also happens to be the mode as the value 17 occurs four times, and is close to the mean:

$$(9 + 12 + \cdots + 24 + 27)/23 = 398/23 = £17.30 \text{ (to the nearest penny).}$$

Figure 6.2 shows a much more symmetrical distribution than the one in Figure 6.1. This symmetry causes the mean and the median to be close together.

There is one further factor to consider when you need to choose a measure of location, and that is whether you will be using the result as the basis for further statistical analysis. If this were the case you would be well advised to use the mean because it has a more extensive role within statistics as a representative measure than the median.

You will find that choosing the right measure of location is not always straightforward. The conclusions from the discussion in this section are

- Use a mode if your data set is discrete and has only one mode.
- It is better to use a median if your data set is skewed.
- In other cases use a mean.

At this point you may find it useful to try **Review Questions 6.1 to 6.4** at the end of the chapter.

6.1.5 Finding measures of location from classified data

You may find yourself in a situation where you would like to use a measure of location to represent a distribution but you only have the data in some classified form, perhaps a frequency distribution or a diagram. Maybe the original data has been mislaid or discarded, or you want to develop work initiated by someone else and the original data is simply not available to you.

If the data is classified in the form of a stem and leaf display finding a measure of location from it is no problem since the display is also a list of the observed values in the distribution. Each observation is listed, but in a detached form so all you have to do is to put the stems and their leaves back together again to get the original data from which they were derived.

You can find the mode of a distribution from its stem and leaf display by looking for the most frequently occurring leaf digits grouped together on a stem line. Finding the median involves counting down (or up) to the middle value. To get the mean you have to reassemble each observation in order to add them up.

Example 6.10

Construct a stem and leaf display to show the data in Example 6.5. Use the display to find the mode, median and mean of the distribution.

Stem and leaf of cost of calls $n = 23$

```
0   9
1   2 3 4 4 4
1   5 5 5 6 7 7 7 7 8 9 9
2   0 0 1 1 2 4
2   7
```

Leaf unit $= 1.0$

The modal value is 17, the leaf digit '7' appears four times on the lower of the two stem lines for the stem digit '1'.

We know from the calculation $(23 + 1)/2 = 12$ that the median is the twelfth observation, which is also 17. To find it we can count from the top. The leaf digit on the first stem line, which represents the observed value '9' is the first observed value in the distribution in order of magnitude. The five leaf digits on the next stem line, the first of the two stem lines for the stem digit '1', are the second to the sixth observed values in order of magnitude. The first leaf digit on the third stem line, the second of the two for the stem digit '1', is the seventh observed value, so if we count a further five values along that stem line we come to the twelfth observation, the median value. The leaf digit that represents the median value in the display is shown in bold type.

To get the mean we have to put the observed values back together again and add 9, 12, 13, 14, 14 etc. to get the sum of the values, 398, which when divided by 23, the number of values, is £17.30 (to the nearest penny), the same result as we obtained in Example 6.5.

In Example 6.10 you can see that we can get the same values for the mode, median and mean as we obtained from the original data because the stem and leaf display is constructed from the parts of the original data. Even if the stem and leaf display were made up of rounded versions of the original data we would get a very close approximation of the real values of the measures of location.

But what if you didn't have a stem and leaf display to work with? If you had a frequency distribution that gave the frequency of every value in the distribution, or a bar chart that depicted the frequency distribution, you could still find the measures of location.

Example 6.11

Use Figure 6.1 to find the mode, median and mean of the distribution of days absence through illness.

Figure 6.1 shows the frequency with which each number of days absence occurs, in the form of a bar. By checking the height of the bar against the vertical axis we can tell exactly how many times that number of days absence has occurred. We can put that information in the form of a frequency distribution:

Number of days absent	Frequency
0	2
1	6
2	3
3	1
4	3
5	0
6	0
7	0
8	0
9	1

We can see that the value '1' has occurred six times, more than any other level of absence, so the mode is 1.

The median position is $(16 + 1)/2 = 8.5$th. To find the median we have to find the eighth and ninth values and split the difference. We can find these observations by counting down the observations in each category, in the same way as we can with a stem and leaf display. The first row in the table contains two '0's, the first and second observations in the distribution in order of magnitude. The second row contains the third to the eighth observations, so the eighth observation is a '1'. The third row contains the ninth to the eleventh observations, so the ninth observation is a '2'. The median is therefore half way between the eighth value, 1, and the ninth value, 2, which is 1.5.

To find the mean from the frequency distribution we could add each number of days absence into the sum the same number of times as its frequency. We add two '0's, six '1's and so on. There is a much more direct way of doing this involving multiplication, which is after all collective addition. We simply take each number of days absent and multiply it by its frequency, then add the products of this process together. If we use 'x' to represent days absent, and 'f' to represent frequency we can describe this procedure as $\sum fx$. Another way of representing n, the number of observations, is $\sum f$, the sum of the frequencies, so the procedure for calculating the mean can be represented as $\sum fx/\sum f$.

Number of days absent (x)	Frequency (f)	fx
0	2	0
1	6	6
2	3	6
3	1	3
4	3	12
5	0	0
6	0	0
7	0	0
		(Continued)

Number of days absent (x)	Frequency (f)	fx
8	0	0
9	1	9
	$\Sigma f = 16$	$\Sigma fx = 36$

$$\text{The mean} = \frac{\Sigma fx}{\Sigma f} = \frac{36}{16} = 2.25.$$

You can see that the results obtained in Example 6.11 are exactly the same as the results found in Example 6.6 from the original data. This is possible because every value in the distribution is itself a category in the frequency distribution so we can tell exactly how many times it occurs.

But suppose you need to find measures of location for a distribution that is only available to you in the form of a grouped frequency distribution? The categories are not individual values but classes of values. We can't tell from it exactly how many times each value occurs, only the number of times each class of values occurs. From such limited information we can find measures of location but they will be approximations of the true values that we would get from the original data.

Because the data used to construct grouped frequency distributions usually include many different values, hence the need to divide them into classes, finding an approximate value for the mode is a rather arbitrary exercise. It is almost always sufficient to identify the **modal class**, which is the class that contains most observations.

Example 6.12

Use Figure 6.2 to find the modal class of the monthly costs of calls.

The grouped frequency distribution used to construct Figure 6.2 was:

Cost (£)	Frequency
5 and under 10	1
10 and under 15	5
15 and under 20	10
20 and under 25	6
25 and under 30	1

The modal class is '15 and under 20' because it contains more values, ten, than any other class.

Since a grouped frequency distribution does not show individual values we cannot use it to find the exact value of the median, only an approximation. To do this we need to identify the median class, the class in which the median is located, but first we must find the median location. Once we have this we can use the fact that, although the values are not listed in order of magnitude the classes that make up the grouped frequency distribution are. So it is a matter of looking for the class that contains the middle value.

When we know which class the median is in we need to establish its likely position within that class. To do this we assume that all the values belonging to the median class are spread out evenly over the width of the class. How far we go through the class to get an approximate value for the median depends on how many values in the distribution are located in the classes before the median class. Subtracting this from the median position gives us the number of values we need to 'go into' the median class to get our approximate median. The distance we need to go into the median class is the median position less the number of values in the earlier classes divided by the number of values in the median class, which we then multiply by the width of the median class. We can express the procedure as follows:

$$\text{Approximate median} = \text{start of MC}$$
$$+ \frac{\left(\begin{array}{cc}\text{median} & \text{number of} \\ \text{position} & \text{values up to MC}\end{array}\right)}{\text{frequency of MC}}$$
$$* \text{width of MC}$$

where MC stands for Median Class.

Example 6.13

Find the approximate value of the median from the grouped frequency distribution in Example 6.12.

There are 23 observations in the distribution so the median is the $(23 + 1)/2 = 12$th value in order of magnitude.

The median value does not belong to the first class, '5 and under 10' because it contains only the first observation, the lowest one in the distribution. Neither does it belong to the second class, which contains the second to the sixth values. The median is in the third class, which contains the seventh to the sixteenth values.

The first value in the median class is the seventh value in the distribution. We want to find the twelfth, which will be the sixth observation in the median class. We know it must be at least 15 because that is where the median class starts so all ten observations in it are no lower than 15.

We assume that all ten observations in the median class are distributed evenly through it. If that were the case the median would be 6/10ths the way along the median class. To get the approximate value for the median:

begin at the start of the median class   15
add 6/10ths of the width of the median class   6/10 * 5   3
                                                                                          18

Alternatively we can apply the procedure:

$$\text{start of MC} + \frac{(\text{median position} - \text{number of values up to MC})}{\text{frequency of MC}} * \text{width of MC}$$

In this case the start of the median class is 15, the median position is 12, there are 6 values in the classes up to the median class, 10 values in the median class and the median class width is 5, so the approximate median is:

$$= 15 + \frac{(12-6)}{10} * 5 = 15 + \frac{6}{10} * 5 = 18$$

This is quite close to the real value we obtained from the original data, 17.

There is an alternative method that you can use to find the approximate value of the median from data presented in the form of a grouped frequency distribution. It is possible to estimate the value of the median from a cumulative frequency graph or a cumulative relative frequency graph of the distribution. These graphs are described in section 5.2.2 of Chapter 5.

To obtain an approximate value for the median, plot the graph and find the point along the vertical axis that represents half the total frequency. Draw a horizontal line from that point to the line that represents the cumulative frequency and then draw a vertical line from that point to the horizontal axis. The point at which your vertical line meets the horizontal axis is the approximate value of the median.

This approach is easier to apply to a cumulative *relative* frequency graph as half the total frequency of the distribution is represented by the point '0.5' on the cumulative relative frequency scale along the vertical axis.

Example 6.14

Draw a cumulative relative frequency graph to represent the grouped frequency distribution in Example 6.12 and use it to find the approximate value of the median monthly cost of calls.

Cost (£)	Frequency	Cumulative frequency	Cumulative relative frequency
5 and under 10	1	1	0.04
10 and under 15	5	6	0.26
15 and under 20	10	16	0.70
20 and under 25	6	22	0.96
25 and under 30	1	23	1.00

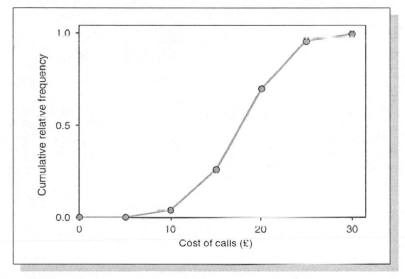

Figure 6.3
Cumulative relative frequency graph of the monthly costs of calls

The starting point on the left of the horizontal dotted line on the graph in Figure 6.3 is '0.5' on the vertical axis, midway on the cumulative relative frequency scale. At the point where the horizontal dotted line meets the cumulative relative frequency line, the vertical dotted line drops down to the x axis. The point where this vertical dotted line reaches the horizontal axis is about 17.5, which is the estimate of the median. The graph suggests that half of the values in the distribution are accumulated below 17.5 and half are accumulated above 17.5.

If you look back to Example 6.9 you will find that the actual median is 17.

To obtain an approximate value for the mean from a grouped frequency distribution we apply the same frequency-based approach as we used in Example 6.11, where we multiplied each value, *x*, by the number of times it occurred in the distribution, *f*, added up these products and divided by the total frequency of values in the distribution:

$$\bar{x} = \frac{\sum fx}{\sum f}$$

If we have data arranged in a grouped frequency distribution we have to overcome the problem of not knowing the exact values of the observations in the distribution as all the values are in classes. To get around this we assume that all the observations in a class take, on average, the value in the middle of the class, known as the class midpoint. The set of class midpoints is then used as the values of the variables, x, that are contained in the distribution.

Example 6.15

Find the approximate value of the mean from the grouped frequency distribution in Example 6.12.

Cost of calls (£)	Midpoint (x)	Frequency (f)	fx
5 and under 10	7.5	1	7.5
10 and under 15	12.5	5	62.5
15 and under 20	17.5	10	175.0
20 and under 25	22.5	6	135.0
25 and under 30	27.5	1	27.5
		$\Sigma f = 23$	$\Sigma fx = 407.5$

The approximate value of the mean $= \Sigma fx / \Sigma f = 407.5/23 = £17.72$ (to the nearest penny), which is close to the actual value we obtained in Example 6.5, £17.30 (to the nearest penny).

At this point you may find it useful to try **Review Questions 6.5 and 6.6** at the end of the chapter.

6.2 Measures of spread

Just as there are several measures of location you can use to convey the central tendency of a distribution, there are several measures of spread to convey the dispersion of a distribution. They are used alongside measures of location in order to give an overall impression of a distribution; where its middle is and how widely scattered the observations are around the middle. Indeed, the two most important ones are closely linked to the median and the mean.

6.2.1 The range

The simplest measure of spread is the *range*. The range of a distribution is the difference between the lowest and the highest observations in the distribution, that is:

Range = highest observed value − lowest observed value

The range is very easy to use and understand, and is sometimes a perfectly adequate method of measuring dispersion. However, it is not a wholly reliable or thorough way of assessing spread because it is based on only two observations. If, for instance, you were asked to compare the spread in two different sets of data you may find that the ranges are very similar but the observations are spread out very differently.

Example 6.16

Two employment agencies, Rabota Recruitment and Slugar Selection, each employ nine people. The length of service that each of the employees of these companies has with their agencies (in years) is:

Rabota	0	4	4	5	7	0	10	11	15
Slugar	0	0	4	4	7	10	10	14	15

Find the range and plot a histogram for each set of data and use them to compare the lengths of service of the employees of the agencies.

Range (Rabota) = 15 − 0   Range (Slugar) = 15 − 0

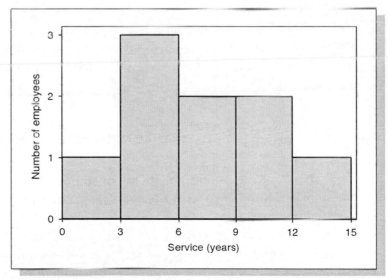

Figure 6.4
Lengths of service of Rabota staff

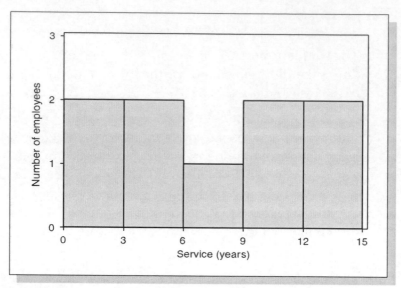

Figure 6.5
Lengths of service of Slugar staff

The ranges are exactly the same, but this does not mean that the observations in the two distributions are spread out in exactly the same way.

If you compare Figure 6.4 and Figure 6.5 you can see that the distribution of lengths of service of the staff at Rabota has a much more pronounced centre whereas the distribution of lengths of service of staff at Slugar has much more pronounced ends.

Although the ranges for the distributions in Example 6.15 are identical, the histograms show different levels of dispersion. The figures for Slugar are more widely spread or dispersed than the figures for Rabota. The range is therefore not a wholly reliable way of measuring the spread of data, because it is based on the extreme observations only.

6.2.2 Quartiles and the semi-interquartile range

The second measure of dispersion at our disposal is the *semi-interquartile range*, or SIQR for short. It is based on *quartiles*, which are order statistics like the median.

One way of looking at the median, or middle observation, of a distribution is to regard it as the point that separates the distribution into two equal halves, one consisting of the lower half of the observations and the other consisting of the upper half of the observations. The median, in effect, cuts the distribution in two.

If the median is a single cut that divides a distribution in two, the quartiles are a set of three separate points in a distribution that divide it into four equal quarters. The first, or lower quartile, known as $Q1$, is the point that separates the lowest quarter of the observations in a distribution from the rest. The second quartile is the median itself; it separates the lower two quarters (i.e. the lower half) of the observations in the distribution from the upper two quarters (i.e. the upper half). The third, or upper quartile, known as $Q3$, separates the highest quarter of observations in the distribution from the rest.

The median and the quartiles are known as *order statistics* because their values are based on the order or sequence of observations in a distribution. You may come across other order statistics such as *deciles*, which divide a distribution into tenths, and *percentiles*, which divide a distribution into hundredths.

You can find the quartiles of a distribution from an array or a stem and leaf display of the observations in the distribution. The quartile position is half way between the end of the distribution and the median, so it is defined in relation to the median position, which is $(n + 1)/2$, where n is the number of observations. To find the approximate position of the quartiles take the median position, *round it down to the nearest whole number if it is not already a whole number*, add one and divide by two, that is:

$$\text{Quartile position} = (\text{median position} + 1)/2$$

Once you know the quartile position you can find the lower quartile by counting up to the quartile position from the lowest observation and the upper quartile by counting down to the quartile position from the highest observation.

Example 6.17

In one month the total costs (to the nearest £) of the calls made by 23 female mobile phone owners were:

14	5	15	6	17	10	22	10	12	17	13	29
7	27	33	16	30	9	15	7	33	28	21	

Find the median and upper and lower quartiles for this distribution.

Array

5	6	7	7	9	10	10	12	13	14	15	15
16	17	17	21	22	27	28	29	30	33	33	

The median position $= (23 + 1)/2 = 12$th position, so the median value is the value '15'. This suggests that the monthly cost of calls for half the female owners is below £15, and the monthly costs for the other half is above £15.

The quartile position $= (12 + 1)/2 = 6.5$th position, that is midway between the sixth and seventh observations.

The lower quartile is half way between the observations sixth and seventh from the lowest, which are both 10, so the lower quartile is 10. This suggests that the monthly cost of calls for 25% of the female owners is below £10.

The upper quartile is half way between the observations sixth and seventh from the highest, which are 27 and 22 respectively. The upper quartile is midway between these values, i.e. 24.5, so the monthly cost of calls for 25% of the female owners is above £24.50.

If the upper quartile separates off the top quarter of the distribution and the lower quartile separates off the bottom quarter, the difference between the lower and upper quartiles is the range or span of the middle half of the observations in the distribution. This is called the *interquartile range*, which is the range between the quartiles. The semi-interquartile range (SIQR) is, as its name suggests, half the interquartile range, that is:

$$\text{SIQR} = (Q3 - Q1)/2$$

Example 6.18

Find the semi-interquartile range for the data in Example 6.17.

The lower quartile monthly cost of calls is £10 and the upper quartile monthly cost of calls is £24.5.

$$\text{SIQR} = (£24.5 - £10)/2 = £14.5/2 = £7.25$$

The semi-interquartile range is a measure of spread. The larger the value of the SIQR, the more dispersed the observations in the distribution are.

Example 6.19

Find the SIQR of the data in Example 6.5 and compare this to the SIQR of the data in Example 6.17.

Array

9	12	13	14	14	14	15	15	15	16	17	17
17	17	19	19	20	20	21	21	22	24	27	

There are 23 observations, so the median position is the $(23 + 1)/2 = 12$th position.

The quartile position is the $(12 + 1)/2 = 6.5$th position.

$$Q1 = (£14 + £15)/2 = £14.5 \quad Q3 = (£20 + £20)/2 = £20$$
$$\text{SIQR} = (£20 - £14.5)/2 = £2.75$$

The SIQR for the data for the males (£2.75) is far lower than the SIQR for the data for the females (£7.25) indicating that there is more variation in the cost of calls for females.

There is a diagram called a *boxplot*, which is a very useful way of displaying order statistics. In a boxplot the middle half of the values in a distribution are represented by a box, which has the lower quartile at one end and the upper quartile at the other. A line inside the box represents the median. The top and bottom quarters are represented by straight lines called 'whiskers' protruding from each end of the box. A boxplot is a particularly useful way of comparing distributions.

Example 6.20

Produce boxplots for the monthly costs of calls for females and males.

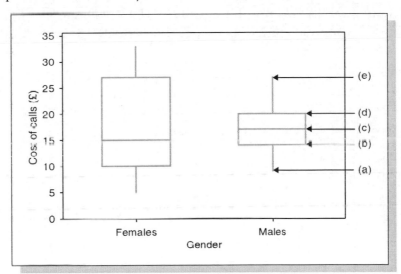

Figure 6.6
Monthly costs of calls for female and male mobile phone owners

Look carefully at the boxplot to the right in Figure 6.6, which represents the monthly costs of calls for males. The letter (a) indicates the position of the lowest observation, (b) indicates the position of the lower quartile, (c) is the median, (d) is the upper quartile and (e) is the highest value.

In Figure 6.6 the diagram representing the costs of calls for females is larger than the diagram representing the costs of calls for males, emphasizing the greater variation in costs for females. The fact that the median line in the costs of calls for females box is positioned low down within the box suggests that the middle half of the distribution is skewed. The quarter of observations between the median and the upper quartile are more widely spread than the quarter of observations between the median and the lower quartile. In contrast, the median line in the box that represents the costs of calls for males is midway between the top and the bottom of the box and indicates that the spread of values in the middle half of the costs for males is symmetrical.

A boxplot is particularly useful for identifying outliers, observed values that seem detached from the rest of the distribution. If you have outliers in a distribution it is important to check firstly that they have not been written down wrongly and secondly, assuming that they are accurately recorded, what reasons might explain such an unusual observation.

Example 6.21

If the lowest value in the set of monthly costs of calls for male mobile phone owners in Example 6.5 was wrongly recorded as £9 but was actually £4, how does the boxplot change?

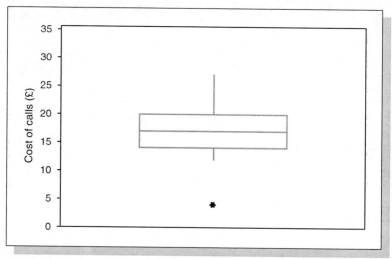

Figure 6.7
Monthly costs of calls for male mobile phone owners

If you look at Figure 6.7 you will see that now the lowest observation, 4, is represented as an asterisk to emphasize its relative isolation from the rest of the observations.

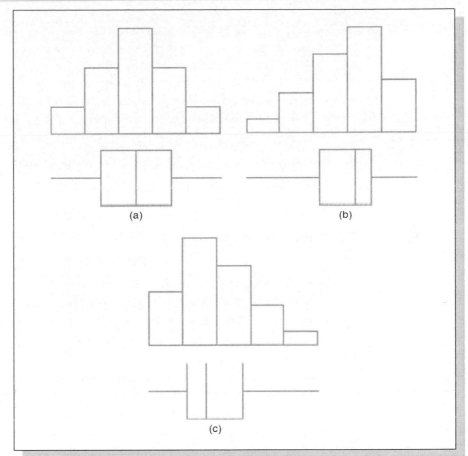

Figure 6.8
Boxplots and
histograms for
symmetrical (a),
negatively skewed
(b) and positively
skewed (c)
distributions

The shape of a boxplot is a good guide to the shape of the distribution it represents. Figure 6.8 shows example boxplots for symmetrical, negative skewed and positive skewed distributions in each case compared to a histogram portraying the same distribution.

The semi-interquartile range (SIQR), based like boxplots on quartiles, is a useful way of measuring spread and, together with the median, is often the best way of summarizing skewed distributions. However, just like the range, the SIQR is based on selected observations in a distribution so it cannot always detect dispersion in data.

Example 6.22

Find the SIQR for the lengths of service of staff in each of the employment agencies in Example 6.16.

There are nine observations in each distribution, so the median position is $(9 + 1)/2 = 5$th and the quartile position is $(5 + 1)/2 = 3$rd position for both distributions.

| Rabota | 0 | 4 | 4 | 5 | 7 | 8 | 10 | 11 | 15 |
| Slugar | 0 | 0 | 4 | 4 | 7 | 10 | 10 | 14 | 15 |

In both distributions the lower quartile is 4 and the upper quartile is 10, giving an SIQR of 3 years service for each agency. Despite these identical SIQR results, Figures 6.4 and 6.5 clearly showed that the distributions are not spread out in the same way.

At this point you may find it useful to try **Review Questions 6.7 and 6.8** at the end of the chapter.

6.2.3 The standard deviation

In order to avoid the shortcomings of the range and the SIQR we have to turn to a measure of spread that is based on including every observation rather than selecting just a few. That measure, the most important measure of spread in Statistics, is known as the *standard deviation*.

As the name suggests, the standard deviation is based on the idea of measuring the typical, or standard, amount of deviation, or difference, in a set of observations. But deviation from what? Deviation from the arithmetic mean.

We can find the standard deviation by first calculating the mean and then finding how far each observation deviates or varies from it.

Example 6.23

Six newsagents sell the following number of boxes of plain potato crisps in a particular week:

$$2 \quad 5 \quad 6 \quad 4 \quad 3 \quad 4$$

The mean, $\bar{x} = 24/6 = 4$

Observation (x)	Mean ($\bar{x}$)	Deviation ($x - \bar{x}$)
2	4	−2
5	4	1
6	4	2
4	4	0
3	4	−1
4	4	0

To get a single measure of spread from deviation figures like those in Example 6.23 it would be very convenient to add up the deviations and divide the sum of the deviations by the number of them to get a sort of 'average' deviation. Unfortunately, as you will find out if you try it with the deviations in Example 6.23, it doesn't work because the deviations add up to zero.

This will always happen because the mean is, in effect, the centre of gravity of a distribution. In the same way that the centre of gravity of an object has as much weight to one side as it does to the other, the mean has as much numerical 'weight' below it as it has above it. The result is that the deviations between the mean and the observations that are lower than the mean, which are always negative, cancel out the deviations between the mean and the observations that are higher than the mean, which are always positive. You can see in Example 6.23 that the negative deviations (-1 and -2) would be cancelled out by the positive deviations (1 and 2) if we added all the deviations together.

To get around this problem we square the deviations before adding them up, since any number squared is positive. The sum of the squared deviations, $\sum(x - \bar{x})^2$, is the basis of the standard deviation.

Example 6.24

Find the sum of the squared deviations, $\sum(x - \bar{x})^2$, from the mean for the data in Example 6.23.

Observation (x)	Mean (x)	Deviation (x − x)	Squared deviation $(x - \bar{x})^2$
2	4	−2	4
5	4	1	1
6	4	2	4
4	4	0	0
3	4	−1	1
4	4	0	0

$$\sum(x - \bar{x})^2 = 4 + 1 + 4 + 0 + 1 + 0 = 10$$

Now we have a way of measuring total deviation it would be convenient to simply divide by the number of deviations that have been added together, which is the same as n, the number of observations. However, we actually divide the sum of the squared deviations by *one less than n* instead of *n* itself.

The reason for this is that any set of data starts off with the same number of *degrees of freedom* as it has observations, n. The implication is that if you wanted to specify all the figures in the set of data yourself you can do so freely. However, once you have found the mean you could only specify one less than the number of figures freely. The last one would have to be the only figure that combines with the ones you have specified to keep the mean the same, so you have 'lost' a degree of freedom. For instance if we know that the mean of a set of three figures is 5, and we suggest that 2 and 7 are the first two figures in the set, the third value has to be 6 in order that the mean is still 5. Choose any other value for third figure and the mean will be different.

When we calculate a standard deviation we are using the mean and we lose one degree of freedom, so the procedure that we use to calculate the standard deviation, s, of a sample involves dividing the sum of squared deviations by $(n - 1)$. The only exception is the rare occasion when we need to calculate the population standard deviation, σ (the lower case of the Greek letter s), in which case the sum of squared deviations is divided by n.

In later work you will find that a sample standard deviation can be used as an estimate of a population standard deviation. This can save time and money, but it can only be done if the sample standard deviation is calculated properly.

The final part of the procedure you follow to obtain a sample standard deviation is to take the square root of the sum of squared deviations divided by $(n - 1)$. You have to do this to get a figure that is in the same units as your original data. For instance, the squared deviation figures in Example 6.24 are in 'boxes of crisps squared'. It is much more useful to have a figure measured in boxes of crisps.

We can sum up the procedure that is used to obtain a sample standard deviation in the following expression

$$s = \sqrt{\frac{\sum(x - \bar{x})^2}{(n - 1)}}$$

Example 6.25

Calculate the standard deviation for the data in Example 6.23.

The sum of squared deviations is 10 and the number of observations is 6, so the standard deviation of this sample is:

$$s = \sqrt{\frac{10}{5}} = \sqrt{2} = 1.414$$

Calculating standard deviations as we have done so far is rather cumbersome, especially for large sets of data, because it involves subtracting the mean from every observation. An alternative way of obtaining a sample standard deviation is to square the observations and add them up to get the sum of the squared observations and then take the sum of the observations and square that. This latter amount is the square of the sum of the observations. We divide it by the number of observations we have and subtract the result from the sum of the squared observations. Finally, multiply by one divided by the number of degrees of freedom and take the square root. We can express the procedure as:

$$s = \sqrt{\frac{1}{n-1}\left(\sum x^2 - \frac{(\sum x)^2}{n}\right)}$$

Example 6.26

Calculate the standard deviation for the data in Example 6.23 without subtracting each observation from the mean.

Observation (x)	x^2
2	4
5	25
6	36
4	16
3	9
4	16
$\sum x - 24$	$\sum x^2 - 106$

$$s = \sqrt{\frac{1}{6-1}\left(106 - \frac{(24)^2}{6}\right)} = \sqrt{\frac{1}{5}\left(106 - \frac{576}{6}\right)} = \sqrt{\frac{1}{5}(106 - 96)}$$

$$= \sqrt{\frac{1}{5}(10)} = \sqrt{2} = 1.414$$

This is exactly the same as the result we obtained in Example 6.25 using the original approach.

If your data come from an entire population you do not have to worry about degrees of freedom and the procedure you need to apply to find the population standard deviation, sigma (σ), is:

$$\sigma = \sqrt{\frac{\sum(x - \mu)^2}{n}}$$

Note that to get the *population* standard deviation you have to subtract the *population* mean, μ, from every value. The alternative approach, which does not involve subtracting every value from the mean, is:

$$\sigma = \sqrt{\left(\sum x^2 - \frac{(\sum x)^2}{n} \right)}$$

If you use any of these expressions to calculate the standard deviation of a set of data with many observations you will find the experience laborious. It really is a task that should be carried out with the aid of calculator or computer software.

If your calculator has statistical functions look for a key with *s* or $x\sigma_{n-1}$ or σ_{xn-1} or **S-VAR** above or below it.

- Access the statistical functions of your calculator using the **MODE** key. Pressing it should display a menu of options that are probably numbered. The key to the options will be in the display or immediately above or beneath it.
- One of the mode options should be **SD** (for standard deviation) or **STAT**. Press the appropriate number key to access this mode. Your calculator will now operate differently. Look for the memory key (**M** or **M+**). Above or below it you may see **DATA** or **DT**. This key now operates like the **Enter** key on a PC.
- Type in the values in your data set one at a time and press the memory key after you enter each one.
- When you have entered the last value and press the memory key your data is stored in the memory and can be processed using the statistical functions.
- Look for a **SHIFT** key and press it then press the key with s or $x\sigma_{n-1}$ or σ_{xn-1} above or below it to get the standard deviation. If your calculator has a key with **S-VAR** press **SHIFT** then this key and you should see several numbered options in the display. Select the one for $x\sigma_{n-1}$ or σ_{xn-1}.

Note that calculator procedures vary depending on the model and manufacturer so you will need to check the instructions for your model.

In later quantitative work you may encounter something called a *variance*. The variance is the square of the standard deviation. The expression for the variance looks like the expression for the standard deviation and in fact the only difference is that finding the variance does not involve taking a square root.

The sample variance, $s^2 = \dfrac{\sum(x - \bar{x})^2}{n - 1}$

$$\text{The population variance,} \quad \sigma^2 = \frac{\Sigma(x - \mu)^2}{n}$$

The standard deviation is widely used with the mean to provide an overall summary of a distribution. Indeed, for many distributions the mean and the standard deviation are the key defining characteristics or *parameters* of the distribution.

One of the reasons the standard deviation has become such an important measure of spread is that it is a reliable way of detecting dispersion.

Example 6.27

Find the mean and the standard deviation of the data from Example 6.16 and compare the results for the two agencies.

Rabota: Mean = $(0 + 4 + 4 + 5 + 7 + 8 + 10 + 11 + 15)/9 = 7.111$

Length of service (x)	x^2
0	0
4	16
4	16
5	25
7	49
8	64
10	100
11	121
15	225
64	616

$$s = \sqrt{\frac{1}{8}\left(616 - \frac{(64)^2}{9}\right)} = \sqrt{\frac{1}{8}(616 - 455.111)} = \sqrt{\frac{1}{8}(160.889)}$$
$$= \sqrt{20.111} = 4.485$$

Slugar: Mean = $(0 + 0 + 4 + 4 + 7 + 10 + 10 + 14 + 15)/9 = 7.111$

Length of service (x)	x^2
0	0
0	0
4	16
4	16
7	49
10	100
10	100
14	196
15	225
64	702

$$s = \sqrt{\frac{1}{8}\left(702 - \frac{(64)^2}{9}\right)} = \sqrt{\frac{1}{8}(702 - 455.111)} = \sqrt{\frac{1}{8}(246.889)}$$
$$= \sqrt{30.861} = 5.555$$

The means are the same, 7.111, but the standard deviation for Slugar is higher than the standard deviation for Rabota, 5.555 compared to 4.485. The difference between the standard deviations reflects the contrasting spread we saw in Figures 6.4 and 6.5.

The mean and standard deviation can be used to approximate the overall spread of observations in a distribution. Typically, nearly all the observations will lie between the point three standard deviations below the mean and the point three standard deviations above the mean. Another way of saying this is to say that almost the entire distribution is located within three standard deviations of the mean. Another rule of thumb is that 90% or so of a distribution will be within two standard deviations of the mean.

In further work you will find that the mean and the standard deviation can be used to define the positions of values in a distribution. For instance, if the mean of a set of examination marks is 55 and the standard deviation is 10 a result of 75 marks could be described as being two standard deviations above the mean. A result of 40 could be described as being one and a half standard deviations below the mean.

You may meet the *coefficient of variation*, which is sometimes used to compare distributions, especially where the units of measurement differ. This is simply the standard deviation as a percentage of the mean:

$$\text{Coefficient of variation (CV)} = \frac{s}{x} * 100$$

Example 6.28

A transport consultant is asked to compare car use in the UK with that in the Netherlands. The mean annual mileage of a sample of motorists living in London was 12,466 with a standard deviation of 3281. The mean number of kilometres travelled by a sample of Amsterdam motorists was 15,170 with a standard deviation of 3594.

Calculate the coefficient of variation for each sample of motorists and use them to compare the annual distances travelled.

$$\text{London} \quad \text{CV} = \frac{3281}{12466} * 100 = 26.320\%$$

$$\text{Amsterdam} \quad CV = \frac{3549}{15170} * 100 = 23.395\%$$

The distances travelled by the Amsterdam motorists vary slightly less in relation to the mean.

At this point you may find it useful to try **Review Questions 6.9 to 6.11** at the end of the chapter.

6.2.3 Finding measures of spread from classified data

You may need to determine measures of spread for data that are already classified. The ease of doing this and the accuracy of the results depend on the type of data and the form in which they are presented.

If you have a frequency distribution that shows the number of times each one of a small number of discrete values occurs then you will be able to identify all the values in the distribution and carry out the appropriate procedures and calculations on them. Similarly, if you have data in the form of a stem and leaf display you should be able to identify at least the approximate values of the data. In either case the results you obtain should be identical to, or at least very close to the real values.

If, however, the data you have are in the form of a grouped frequency distribution then it is possible to find measures of spread, but these will be approximations. Here we will consider how to find an approximate value of a standard deviation from a grouped frequency distribution and how to find approximate values for quartiles, and hence the semi-interquartile range, from a cumulative relative frequency graph.

A grouped frequency distribution shows how many observed values in the distribution fall into a series of classes. It does not show the actual values of the data. Since calculating a standard deviation does usually require the actual values, we have to find some way of representing the actual values based on the classes to which they belong. In fact the midpoint of each class is used as the approximate value of every value in the class. This is the same approach as we used to find the mean from a grouped frequency distribution in section 6.1.5 of this chapter.

The approximate value of the standard deviation is:

$$s = \sqrt{\frac{1}{\Sigma f - 1}\left[\Sigma fx^2 - \frac{(\Sigma fx)^2}{\Sigma f}\right]}$$

where f represents the frequency of a class and x its midpoint.

Example 6.29

Find the approximate value of the standard deviation of the data represented in the grouped frequency distribution in Example 6.12.

Cost of calls	Midpoint (x)	Frequency (f)	fx	x²	fx²
5 and under 10	7.5	1	7.5	56.25	56.25
10 and under 15	12.5	5	62.5	156.25	781.25
15 and under 20	17.5	10	175.0	306.25	3062.50
20 and under 25	22.5	6	135.0	506.25	3037.50
25 and under 30	27.5	1	27.5	756.25	756.25
		$\Sigma f = 23$	$\Sigma fx = 407.5$		$\Sigma fx^2 = 7693.75$

$$s = \sqrt{\frac{1}{23-1}\left[7693.75 - \frac{(407.5)^2}{23}\right]} = \sqrt{\frac{1}{22}\left[7693.75 - \frac{166056.25}{23}\right]}$$

$$= \sqrt{\frac{1}{22}[7693.75 - 7219.837]} = \sqrt{21.5415} = 4.641$$

You may like to work out the actual standard deviation using the original data, which are given in Example 6.5. You should find it is 4.128.

You can find the approximate values of the quartiles of a distribution from a cumulative frequency graph or a cumulative relative frequency graph by employing the same approach as we used to find the approximate value of the median in section 6.1.5 of this chapter. The difference is that to approximate the quartiles we start from points one-quarter and three-quarters the way up the vertical scale.

Example 6.30

Use the cumulative relative frequency graph shown in Example 6.14 (Figure 6.3) to estimate the values of the lower and upper quartiles for the distribution of costs of calls made by female mobile phone owners and produce an approximate value of the semi-interquartile range.

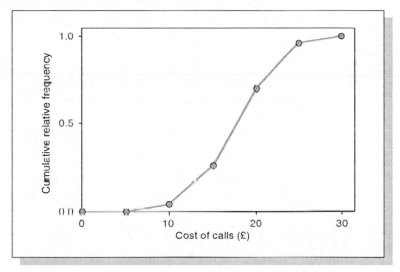

Figure 6.9
Monthly costs of calls made by male mobile phone owners

In Figure 6.9 the approximate value of the lower quartile is the point where the vertical dotted line to the left meets the horizontal axis, at about £14. The approximate value of the upper quartile is the point where the vertical dotted line to the right meets the horizontal axis, at about £21. The semi-interquartile range is half the difference between these two, £3.5.

If you look back at Examples 6.17 and 6.18, you will see that the true values of the lower and upper quartiles are £14.5 and £20 respectively, and that the semi-interquartile range is £2.75.

At this point you may find it useful to try **Review Questions 6.12 to 6.19** at the end of the chapter.

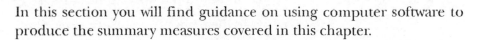

6.3 Using the technology: summarizing data in EXCEL, MINITAB and SPSS

In this section you will find guidance on using computer software to produce the summary measures covered in this chapter.

6.3.1 EXCEL

You can use the **Descriptive Statistics** facility in EXCEL to obtain the mode, median and mean, as well as the range, standard deviation and variance of a set of data. Enter the data into a column of the spreadsheet then

- Select **Data Analysis** from the **Tools** menu and choose **Descriptive Statistics** from the menu in the **Data Analysis** command window.
- In the **Descriptive Statistics** command window specify the cell locations of your data in the box alongside **Input Range** and tick **Summary statistics** in the lower part of the window. The default output setting, **New Worksheet Ply** will place your output in a new worksheet.

To obtain quartiles click on an empty cell of the worksheet then click in the formula bar to the right of *fx* (or = in some versions) in the upper part of the screen. To get the first quartile of a set of data stored in cells A1 to A12 of the spreadsheet type = **QUARTILE(A1:A12,1)** in the formula bar and press Enter. The first quartile should appear in the empty cell you clicked before clicking the formula bar. To get the third quartile type = **QUARTILE(A1:A12,3)** in the formula bar and press Enter.

6.3.2 MINITAB

MINITAB will provide you with a selection of summary measures including mode, median, mean, quartiles and standard deviation by means of a single command sequence. Store your data in a column of the worksheet then

- Click the **Stat** pull-down menu and select **Basic Statistics**.
- In the sub-menu that appears click **Display Descriptive Statistics**.
- In the **Display Descriptive Statistics** window the number of the column containing your data should be listed in the space on the left. Double left click on it and it will appear in the space below **Variables:**.
- Click **OK** and the summary measures will appear in the output window in the upper part of the screen.

If you only want the median, mean, range or standard deviation, choose **Column Statistics** from the **Calc** menu. In the command window select the summary measure you require and specify the column location of your data in the box alongside **Input variable**.

You can produce a boxplot using MINITAB by selecting **Boxplot** from the **Graph** menu and entering the column location of your data under **Y** in the **Graph variables:** section in the upper section of the command window then clicking **OK**.

6.3.3 SPSS

The **Descriptive Statistics** facility in SPSS will give you the median, mean, range, interquartile range, standard deviation and variance as well as a boxplot. Enter your data into a column of the worksheet then

- Select **Descriptive Statistics** from the **Analyze** menu and choose **Explore ...** from the sub-menu.
- In the Explore window click on the column location of your data then click ▶ to the left of **Dependent list:**.
- In the lower part of the window under **Display** click on the button to the left of **Both** then click **OK**.

6.4 Road test: Do they really use summary measures?

The concept of summary measures stretches back centuries. The use of the arithmetic mean goes back to the ancient world. It was used in astronomy and surveying as a way of balancing out discrepancies in observations of the positions of stars and landmarks. In the sixteenth, seventeenth and eighteenth centuries these were matters of considerable importance for navigation and disputed territory.

The subject of errors in measurement was an important one for astronomers in those days and they were interested in the spread in their measurements, attempting to minimize what they called the *probable error*. In the wake of Charles Darwin's work on heredity there was great interest in the measurement of and variation in human characteristics with a view to establishing whether they were inherited. Pioneers in this field, notably Francis Galton, developed the notion of the standard deviation of a set of observations. He also developed the median and quartiles in the measurement of human characteristics that he ranked in order rather than measured. You can find out more about these developments in Mackenzie (1981).

In the 1920s summary measures were used to apply *statistical quality control* in manufacturing industry. A prominent pioneer in this field was Yasushi Ishida who worked for the Tokyo Shibaura Electric Company (which later became the Toshiba Corporation). Ishida used statistical methods to improve the quality of the light-bulbs the company produced. At the time these were among the company's most important products and the company wanted him to ensure that they lasted longer (for more about Ishida see Nonaka, 1995). At about the same time Walter Shewhart, an engineer who worked for the Bell System telephone combine in the USA, developed *control charts* that enabled managers to improve quality by using summary measures as benchmarks against which to judge the goods produced (Juran, 1995).

In many fields of business the quality of the product is paramount. Improving quality often means increasing the consistency of the product, or to put it another way, reducing the variation of the product. Measures of spread like the standard deviation and the variance are important factors in product quality because they measure variation. Increasing consistency may mean implementing changes that reduce standard deviations and variances. Monitoring quality may involve comparing current performance with previous performance, which can be described using a mean and standard deviation.

The *control chart* is based on the distribution of the variable being measured to assess quality. Such a chart consists of a horizontal line representing the mean of the variable, which is the performance target, and lines three standard deviations above and below the mean, which are the control limits. As products are produced or services delivered they are measured and the observations plotted on the chart. If a plotted point lies beyond either of the control limits, the process is considered to be out of control and either corrective action must be taken or the process must be shut down.

Example 6.31

A film processing shop promises to deliver photographs in half an hour. The mean and standard deviation of the processing times are 22 minutes and 3 minutes respectively. The layout of the machines in the shop has been altered. The processing times of the first ten films to be developed after the reorganization are:

> 32.6   28.2   30.8   28.1   27.0   25.1   23.2   32.5   24.9   32.8

Plot a control chart based on these data and use it to ascertain whether the reorganization has affected the processing times.

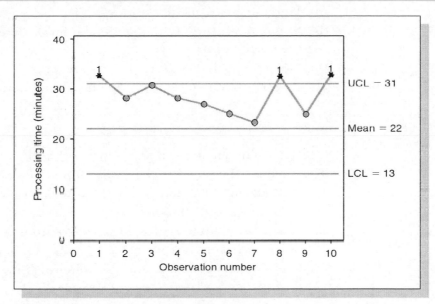

Figure 6.10
Control chart for film processing times

Figure 6.10 shows that the first processing time is too high, then the times improve so that they are within the control limits until the erratic pattern in the last three observations, which suggests the process is going out of control.

In practice control charts are rather more complicated than in Example 6.31 because the monitoring process involves taking samples rather than individual values, but the role of the standard deviation is essentially the same. For a good introduction to statistical quality control, see Montgomery (2000).

At this point you may find it useful to try **Review Question 6.21** at the end of the chapter.

Review questions

Answers to these questions, including fully worked solutions to the Key questions marked with an asterisk (*), are on pages 641–644.

6.1*   A supermarket sells kilogram bags of pears. The numbers of pears in 21 bags were:

7	9	8	8	10	9	8	10	10	8	9
10	7	9	9	9	7	8	7	8	9	

    (a) Find the mode, median and mean for these data.

    (b) Compare your results and comment on the likely shape of the distribution.

    (c) Plot a simple bar chart to portray the data.

6.2   The numbers of credit cards carried by 25 shoppers are:

```
2   5   2   0   4   3   0   1   1   7   1   4   1
3   9   4   1   4   1   5   5   2   3   1   1
```

    (a) Determine the mode and median of this distribution.

    (b) Calculate the mean of the distribution and compare it to the mode and median. What can you conclude about the shape of the distribution?

    (c) Draw a bar chart to represent the distribution and confirm your conclusions in (b).

6.3   Twenty-six dental patients require the following numbers of fillings during their current course of treatment:

```
2   3   2   2   3   1   2   2   1   3   2   2   2
2   4   3   2   2   2   2   2   1   1   0   1   1
```

    (a) Identify the mode, find the median, and calculate the mean of these figures.

    (b) Compare the results you obtained for (a). What do they tell you about the shape of the distribution?

    (c) Compile a bar chart to display the distribution.

6.4   A supermarket has one checkout for customers who wish to purchase 10 items or less. The numbers of items presented at this checkout by 19 customers were:

```
10   8    7    7    6    11   10   8    9    9
 9   6   10    9    8    9    10   10   10
```

    (a) Find the mode, median and mean for these data.

    (b) What do your results for (a) tell you about the shape of the distribution?

    (c) Plot a simple bar chart to portray the distribution.

6.5*   The numbers of driving tests taken to pass by 28 clients of a driving school are given in the following table:

Tests taken	Number of clients
1	10
2	8
3	4
4	3
5	3

(a) Obtain the mode, median and mean from this frequency distribution and compare their values.

(b) Plot a simple bar chart of the distribution.

6.6   Spina Software Solutions operate an on-line help and advice service for PC owners. The numbers of calls made to them by subscribers in a month are tabulated below:

	Number of subscribers	
Calls made	*Female*	*Male*
1	31	47
2	44	42
3	19	24
4	6	15
5	1	4

Find the mode, median and mean for both distributions and use them to compare the two distributions.

6.7*   Toofley the Chemists own 29 pharmacies. The numbers of packets of a new skin medication sold in each of their shops in a week were:

7	22	17	13	11	20	15	18	5	22
6	18	10	13	33	13	9	8	9	19
19	8	12	12	21	20	12	13	22	

(a) Find the mode and range of these data.

(b) Identify the median of the data.

(c) Find the lower and upper quartiles.

(d) Determine the semi-interquartile range.

6.8   The crowd sizes for the 22 home league games played by Athletico Almaz were:

1976	2162	1502	1782	1523	2033	1564	1320
1951	1714	1841	1648	1345	1837	1718	2047
1954	2000	1479	2571	1739	1781		

The crowd sizes for the 22 home fixtures played by a rival club, Red Star Rubine, were:

1508	2055	2085	2098	1745	1939	2116	1956
2075	1702	1995	2391	1964	1879	1813	2144
1958	2203	2149	2064	1777	1989		

(a) Find the median, quartiles and semi-interquartile range for each team.

(b) Compare and contrast the two distributions using your results from (a).

6.9* Voditel International own a large fleet of company cars. The mileages, in thousands of miles, of a sample of 17 of their cars over the last financial year were:

11	31	27	26	27	35	23	19	28	25
15	36	29	27	26	22	20

Calculate the mean and standard deviation of these mileage figures.

6.10 Two friends work in the same office. One travels to work by bus, the other cycles. The times taken (in minutes) by each to get to work on a sample of 8 days were:

Bus passenger	33	28	40	32	41	32	38	42
Cyclist	26	33	27	31	31	30	28	24

Calculate the mean and standard deviation for each set of times and use them to compare the travel times for the two commuters.

6.11* Three credit card companies each produced an analysis of its customers' bills over the last month. The following results have been published:

Company	Mean bill size	Standard deviation of bill sizes
Akula	£559	£172
Bremia	£612	£147
Dolg	£507	£161

Are the following statements true or false?
(a) Dolg bills are on average the smallest and vary more than those from the other companies.
(b) Bremia bills are on average the largest and vary more than those from the other companies.
(c) Akula bills are on average larger than those from Dolg and vary more than those from Bremia.
(d) Akula bills are on average smaller than those from Bremia and vary less than those from Dolg.
(e) Bremia bills are on average larger than those from Akula and vary more than those from Dolg.
(f) Dolg bills vary less than those from Akula and are on average smaller than those from Bremia.

6.12* The kilocalories per portion in a sample of 32 different breakfast cereals were recorded and collated into the following grouped frequency distribution:

Kcal per portion	Frequency
80 and under 120	3
120 and under 160	11
160 and under 200	9
200 and under 240	7
240 and under 280	2

(a) Obtain an approximate value for the median of the distribution.

(b) Calculate approximate values for the mean and standard deviation of the distribution.

6.13 The playing times of a sample of 57 contemporary pop albums and a sample of 48 reissued 'classic' pop albums are summarized in the following grouped frequency distributions:

Playing time (minutes)	Frequency (Contemporary)	Frequency (Reissue)
30 and under 35	0	4
35 and under 40	7	9
40 and under 45	13	17
45 and under 50	22	15
50 and under 55	10	3
55 and under 60	4	0
60 and under 65	1	0

(a) Find approximate values of the median and mean for each distribution.

(b) Calculate approximate values of the standard deviation of each distribution.

(c) Use your results to compare the distributions.

6.14 The time in seconds that a sample of 79 callers trying to contact an insurance company had to wait was recorded. After introducing new procedures the waiting time for a sample of 61 callers was recorded. The results are presented in the following grouped frequency distribution:

Waiting time (seconds)	Frequency (before change)	Frequency (after change)
0 and under 10	2	7
10 and under 20	15	19
20 and under 30	23	31
30 and under 40	24	3
40 and under 50	11	1
50 and under 60	4	0

(a) Determine values for the mean and median of the distributions.

(b) Find an approximate value for the standard deviation of each distribution.

(c) Use the figures you obtain for (a) and (b) to compare the two distributions.

6.15   The total spend of a sample of 110 customers of the Peeshar supermarket and the total spend of a sample of 128 customers of the Peevar supermarket were analysed and the following grouped frequency distribution produced:

Total spend (£)	Frequency (Peeshar)	Frequency (Peevar)
0.00 to 19.99	13	35
20.00 to 39.99	27	61
40.00 to 59.99	41	17
60.00 to 79.99	17	14
80.00 to 99.99	10	1
100.00 to 119.99	2	0

(a) Find values for the mean and standard deviation of each distribution and use them to compare the distributions.

(b) One of these supermarkets attracts customers doing their weekly shopping whereas the other attracts customers seeking alcoholic beverages and luxury food purchases. From your answers to (a), which supermarket is which?

6.16*   The stem and leaf display below shows the Friday night admission prices for 31 clubs.

Stem	Leaves
0	44
0	5555677789
1	000224444
1	5555588
2	002

Leaf unit = £1.0

Find the values of the median and semi-interquartile range.

6.17   The costs of work done at a garage on 33 vehicles to enable them to pass the MOT test of roadworthiness were:

482 471 277 230   357 491 213 386 357 141 282
184 324 426 408   213 155 287 415 499 470 461
233 314 240 107   113 314 242 112 289 283 389

Identify the median and quartiles of this set of data and use them to compile a boxplot to represent the data.

6.18   The credit balances in the current accounts of customers of a bank are summarized in the following grouped relative frequency distribution:

Balance (£)	Relative frequency
0 and under 500	0.12
500 and under 1000	0.29
1000 and under 1500	0.26
1500 and under 2000	0.19
2000 and under 2500	0.09
2500 and under 3000	0.05

Plot a cumulative relative frequency graph to portray this distribution and use it to find approximate values of the median, quartiles and semi-interquartile range.

6.19   A report on usage of glass recycling bins contains the following grouped relative frequency distribution:

Weight of glass deposited per week (kg)	Proportion of bins
0 and under 400	0.23
400 and under 800	0.34
800 and under 1200	0.28
1200 and under 1600	0.11
1600 and under 2000	0.04

Compile a cumulative relative frequency graph for this distribution and use it to determine approximate values of the median, quartile and semi-interquartile range.

6.20   The ages of holidaymakers staying at two Adriatic resorts on a particular day were taken and the boxplots on the following page were produced. Study the diagram and say whether each of the following is true or false.

(a) The youngest holidaymaker is in Journost.

(b) The SIQR for Vozrast is larger.

(c) There is one outlier, the youngest holidaymaker in Journost.

(d) The middle half of the ages of holidaymakers in Vozrast is more symmetrically distributed.

(e) The upper quartile of ages in Vozrast is about 25.

(f) The median age in Journost is about 19.

(g) The median age in Vozrast is higher than the upper quartile age in Journost.

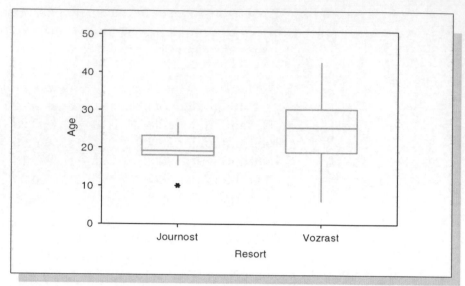

Figure 6.11

6.21   A 'while-you-wait' shoe repair service offers to replace certain types of heels on ladies' shoes in three minutes. Long experience has shown that the mean replacement time for these heels is 2.8 minutes and the standard deviation is 0.15 minutes. A trainee achieves the following times on her first day:

2.5	3.2	2.9	3.0	2.7	3.1	2.4	3.2
2.7	3.2	2.6	3.0	3.1	3.2	3.5	

Construct a control chart using these figures and use it to assess the performance of the new trainee.

6.22   Select which of the statements on the right-hand side best defines the words on the left-hand side.

(i) median   (a) the square of the standard deviation

(ii) range   (b) a diagram based on order statistics

(iii) variance   (c) the most frequently occurring value

(iv) boxplot   (d) the difference between the extreme observations

(v) SIQR   (e) the middle value

(vi) mode   (f) half the difference between the first and third quartiles

Two-way traffic — summarizing and representing relationships between two variables

This chapter will help you to:

- explore links between quantitative variables using bivariate analysis
- measure association between quantitative variables using Pearson's product moment correlation coefficient and the coefficient of determination
- quantify association in ordinal data using Spearman's rank correlation coefficient
- represent the connection between two quantitative variables using simple linear regression analysis
- use the technology: correlation and regression in EXCEL, MINITAB and SPSS
- become acquainted with business uses of correlation and regression

This chapter is about techniques that you can use to study relation-ships between two variables. The types of data set that these techniques are intended to analyse are called *bivariate* because they consist of observed values of two variables. The techniques themselves are part of what is known as bivariate analysis.

Bivariate analysis is of great importance to business. The results of this sort of analysis have affected many aspects of business consider-ably. The establishment of the relationship between smoking and health problems transformed the tobacco industry. The analysis of sur-vival rates of micro-organisms and temperature is crucial to the setting of appropriate refrigeration levels by food retailers. Marketing strate-gies of many organizations are often based on the analysis of consumer expenditure in relation to age or income.

The chapter will introduce you to some of the techniques that com-panies and other organizations use to analyse bivariate data. The tech-niques you will meet here are *correlation* analysis and *regression* analysis.

Suppose you have a set of bivariate data that consist of observations of one variable, *X*, and the associated observations of another variable, *Y*, and you want to see if *X* and *Y* are related. For instance, the *Y* vari-able could be sales of ice cream per day and the *X* variable the daily temperature, and you want to investigate the connection between tem-perature and ice cream sales. In such a case correlation analysis enables us to assess whether there is a connection between the two vari-ables and, if so, how strong that connection is.

If correlation analysis tells us there is a connection we can use regres-sion analysis to identify the exact form of the relationship. It is essential to know this if you want to use the relationship to make predictions, for instance if we want to predict the demand for ice cream when the daily temperature is at a particular level.

The assumption that underpins bivariate analysis is that one variable depends on the other. The letter *Y* is used to represent the *dependent* variable, the one whose values are believed to depend on the other variable. This other variable, represented by the letter *X*, is called the *independent* variable. The *Y* or dependent variable is sometimes known as the *response* because it is believed to *respond* to changes in the value of the *X* variable. The *X* variable is also known as the *predictor* because it might help us to predict the values of *Y*.

7.1 Correlation analysis

Correlation analysis is a way of investigating whether two variables are cor-related, or connected with each other. We can study this to some extent by using a scatter diagram to portray the data, but such a diagram can only give us a visual 'feel' for the association between two variables, it doesn't actually measure the strength of the connection. So, although a scatter diagram is the thing you should begin with to carry out bivariate analysis, you need to calculate a *correlation coefficient* if you want a precise way of assessing how closely the variables are related.

In this section we shall consider two correlation coefficients. The first and more important is *Pearson's* product moment correlation coefficient, related to which is the coefficient of determination. The second is *Spearman's* rank correlation coefficient. Pearson's coefficient is suitable for assessing the strength of the connection between quantitative variables, variables whose values are interval or ratio data (you may find it helpful to refer back to section 4.3 of Chapter 4 for more on types of data). Spearman's coefficient is designed for variables whose values are ranked, and is used to assess the connection between two variables, one or both of which have ordinal values.

7.1.1 Pearson's product moment correlation coefficient

Pearson's correlation coefficient is similar to the standard deviation in that it is based on the idea of dispersion or spread. The comparison is not complete because bivariate data are spread out in two dimensions; if you look at a scatter diagram you will see that the points representing the data are scattered both vertically and horizontally.

The letter r is used to represent the Pearson correlation coefficient for sample data. Its Greek counterpart, the letter ρ ('rho') is used to represent the Pearson correlation coefficient for population data. As is the case with other summary measures, it is very unlikely that you will have to find the value of a population correlation coefficient because of the cost and practical difficulty of studying entire populations.

Pearson's correlation coefficient is a ratio; it compares the co-ordinated scatter to the total scatter. The co-ordinated scatter is the extent to which the observed values of one variable, X, vary in co-ordination with, or 'in step with' the observed values of a second variable, Y. We use the *covariance* of the values of X and Y, Cov_{XY} to measure the degree of co-ordinated scatter.

To calculate the covariance you have to multiply the amount that each x deviates from the mean of the X values, $\bar{x}$, by the amount that its corresponding y deviates from the mean of the Y values, $\bar{y}$. That is, for every pair of x and y observations you calculate:

$$(x - \bar{x})(y - \bar{y})$$

The result will be positive whenever the x and y values are both bigger than their means, because we will be multiplying two positive deviations together. It will also be positive if both the x and y values are smaller than their means, because both deviations will be negative and the result of multiplying them together will be positive. The result will only be negative if one of the deviations is positive and the other negative.

The covariance is the total of the products from this process divided by n, the number of pairs of observations, minus one. We have to divide by $n - 1$ because the use of the means in arriving at the deviations results in the loss of a degree of freedom.

$$\text{Cov}_{XY} = \sum \frac{(x - \bar{x})(y - \bar{y})}{(n - 1)}$$

The covariance is positive if values of X below $\bar{x}$ tend to be associated with values of Y below $\bar{y}$, and values of X above $\bar{x}$ tend to be associated with values of Y above $\bar{y}$. In other words if high x values occur with high y values and low x values occur with low y values we will have a positive covariance. This suggests that there is a positive or *direct* relationship between X and Y, that is, if X goes up we would expect Y to go up as well, and vice versa. If you compared the income of a sample of consumers with their expenditure on clothing you would expect to find a positive relationship.

The covariance is negative if values of X below $\bar{x}$ are associated with values of Y above $\bar{y}$, and vice versa. The low values of X occur with the high values of Y, and the high values of X occur with the low values of Y. This is a negative or *inverse* relationship. If you compared the prices of articles of clothing with demand for them, economic theory suggests you might expect to find an inverse relationship.

Example 7.1

Courtka Clothing sells six brands of shower-proof jacket. The prices and the numbers sold in a week are:

Price	18	20	25	27	28	32
Number sold	8	6	5	2	2	1

Plot a scatter diagram and calculate the covariance.

In Figure 7.1 number sold has been plotted on the Y, or vertical, axis and price has been plotted on the X, or horizontal, axis. We are assuming that number sold depends on price rather than the other way round.

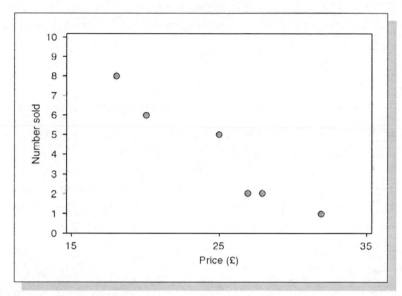

Figure 7.1
Prices of jackets and numbers sold

To calculate the covariance we need to calculate deviations from the mean for every x and y value.

$$\bar{x} = (18 + 20 + 25 + 27 + 28 + 32)/6 = 150/5 = 25$$

$$\bar{y} = (8 + 6 + 5 + 2 + 2 + 1)/6 = 24/6 = 4$$

Price (x)	$\bar{x}$	$(x - \bar{x})$	Numbers sold (y)	$\bar{y}$	$(y - \bar{y})$	$(x - \bar{x})(y - \bar{y})$
18	25	−7	8	4	4	−28
20	25	−5	6	4	2	−10
25	25	0	5	4	1	0
27	25	2	2	4	−2	−4
28	25	3	2	4	−2	−6
32	25	7	1	4	−3	−21
					$\Sigma(x - \bar{x})(y - y) =$	−69

$$\text{Covariance} = \Sigma(x - \bar{x})(y - \bar{y})/(n - 1) = -69/5 = -13.8$$

The other input we need to obtain a Pearson correlation coefficient is some measure of total scatter, some way of assessing the horizontal and vertical dispersion. We do this by taking the standard deviation of the x values, which measures the horizontal spread, and multiplying by the standard deviation of the y values, which measures the vertical spread.

The Pearson correlation coefficient, r, is the covariance of the x and y values divided by the product of the two standard deviations.

$$r = \frac{\text{Cov}_{XY}}{(s_x * s_y)}$$

There are two important things you should note about r:

- It can be either positive or negative because the covariance can be negative or positive.
- It cannot be larger than 1 or -1 because the co-ordinated scatter, measured by the covariance, cannot be larger than the total scatter, measured by the product of the standard deviations.

Example 7.2

Calculate the correlation coefficient for the data in Example 7.1.
We need to calculate the sample standard deviation for X and Y.

Price (x)	$\bar{x}$	$(x - \bar{x})$	$(x - \bar{x})^2$	Number sold (y)	$\bar{y}$	$(y - \bar{y})$	$(y - \bar{y})$
18	25	-7	49	8	4	4	16
20	25	-5	25	6	4	2	4
25	25	0	0	5	4	1	1
27	25	2	4	2	4	-2	4
28	25	3	9	2	4	-2	4
32	25	7	49	1	4	-3	9
			136				38

From Example 7.1:   Covariance $= -13.8$

Sample standard deviation of X: $s_x = \sqrt{\Sigma(x - \bar{x})^2/(n - 1)} = \sqrt{136/5} = 5.215$

Sample standard deviation of Y: $s_y = \sqrt{\Sigma(y - \bar{y})^2/(n - 1)} = \sqrt{38/5} = 2.757$

Correlation coefficient: $r = (-13.8)/(5.215 * 2.757)$
$$= -13.8/14.41 = -0.960$$

A more direct approach to calculating the value of the Pearson correlation coefficient is to use the following formula, which is derived from the approach we used in Examples 7.1 and 7.2:

$$r = \frac{n\,\Sigma xy - (\Sigma x * \Sigma y)}{\sqrt{\left(n\,\Sigma x^2 - (\Sigma x)^2\right) * \left(n\,\Sigma y^2 - (\Sigma y)^2\right)}}$$

The advantage of this approach is that there are no subtractions between the observations and their means as it involves simply adding up the observations and their squares.

Example 7.3

Calculate the Pearson correlation coefficient for the data in Example 7.1 without subtracting observations from means.

Price (x)	x^2	Number sold (y)	y^2	xy
18	324	8	64	144
20	400	6	36	120
25	625	5	25	125
27	729	2	4	54
28	784	2	4	56
32	1024	1	1	32
$\Sigma x = 150$	$\Sigma x^2 = 3886$	$\Sigma y = 24$	$\Sigma y^2 = 134$	$\Sigma xy = 531$ $\quad n = 6$

$$r = \frac{6 * 531 - 150 * 24}{\sqrt{\left(6 * 3886 - 150^2\right) * \left(6 * 134 - 24^2\right)}}$$

$$= \frac{3186 - 3600}{\sqrt{(23316 - 22500) * (804 - 576)}}$$

$$= \frac{-414}{\sqrt{816 * 228}} = \frac{-414}{\sqrt{186048}}$$

$$= \frac{-414}{431.333} = -0.960$$

As you can see, calculating a correlation coefficient, even for a fairly simple set of data, is quite laborious. In practice Pearson correlation coefficients are seldom calculated in this way because many calculators and just about all spreadsheet and statistical packages have functions to produce them. Try looking for two-variable functions on your calculator and refer to section 7.3 later in this chapter for guidance on software facilities.

What should we conclude from the analysis of the data in Example 7.1? Figure 7.1 shows that the scatter of points representing the data nearly forms a straight line, in other words, there is a pronounced linear pattern. The diagram also shows that this linear pattern goes from the top left of the diagram to the bottom right, suggesting that fewer of the more expensive garments are sold. This means there is an inverse relationship between the numbers sold and price.

What does the Pearson correlation coefficient in Example 7.2 tell us? The fact that it is negative, -0.96, confirms that the relationship between the numbers sold and price is indeed an inverse one. The fact that it is very close to the maximum possible negative value that a Pearson correlation coefficient can take, -1, indicates that there is a strong association between the variables.

The Pearson correlation coefficient measures linear correlation, the extent to which there is a straight-line relationship between the variables. Every coefficient will lie somewhere on the scale of possible values, that is between -1 and $+1$ inclusive.

A Pearson correlation coefficient of $+1$ tells us that there is a *perfect positive linear association* or *perfect positive correlation* between the variables. If we plotted a scatter diagram of data that has such a relationship we would expect to find all the points lying in the form of an upward-sloping straight line. You can see this sort of pattern in Figure 7.2. A correlation coefficient of -1 means we have *perfect negative correlation*, which is illustrated in Figure 7.3.

In practice you are unlikely to come across a Pearson correlation coefficient of precisely $+1$ or -1, but you may well meet coefficients that are positive and fairly close to $+1$ or negative and fairly close to -1. Such values reflect good positive and good negative correlation respectively.

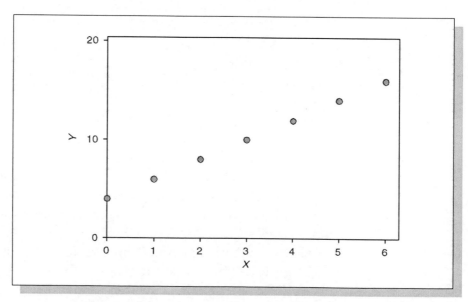

Figure 7.2
Perfect positive
correlation

Figure 7.4 shows a set of data with a correlation coefficient of +0.9. You can see that although the points do not form a perfect straight line they form a pattern that is clearly linear and upward sloping.

Figure 7.5 portrays bivariate data that has a Pearson correlation coefficient of −0.9. The points do not lie in a perfect straight downward line but you can see a clear downward linear pattern.

The closer your Pearson correlation coefficient is to +1 the better the positive correlation. The closer it is to −1 the better the negative correlation. It follows that the nearer the coefficient is to zero the weaker

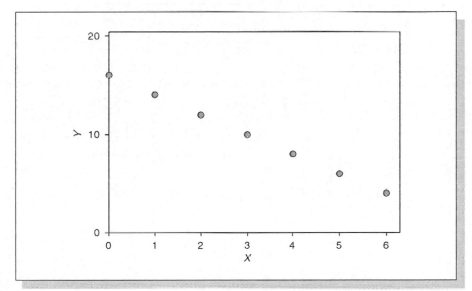

Figure 7.3
Perfect negative
correlation

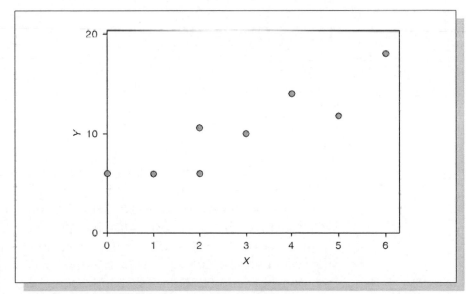

Figure 7.4
Good positive
correlation

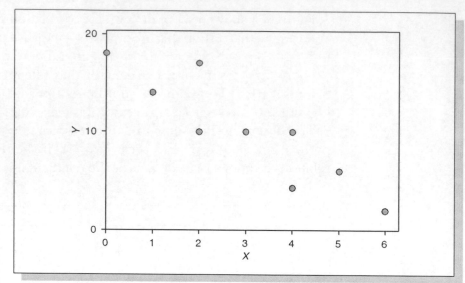

Figure 7.5
Good negative
correlation

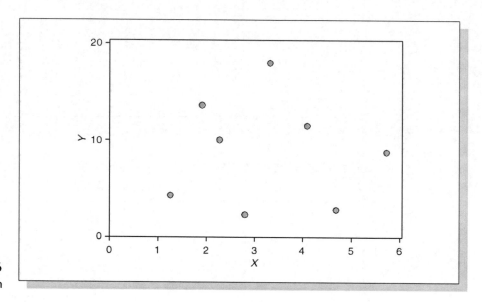

Figure 7.6
Zero correlation

the connection between the two variables. Figure 7.6 shows a sample of observations of two variables with a coefficient close to zero, which provides little evidence of any correlation.

It is important to bear in mind that the Pearson correlation coefficient assesses the strength of linear relationships between two variables. It is quite possible to find a low or even zero correlation coefficient where the scatter diagram shows a strong connection. This happens when the relationship between the two variables is not linear.

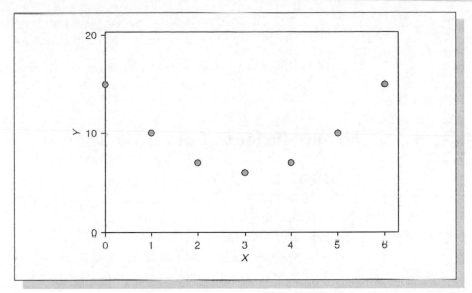

Figure 7.7
A non-linear
relationship

Figure 7.7 shows that a clear non-linear relationship exists between the variables yet the Pearson correlation coefficient for the data it portrays is zero.

If you have to write about correlation analysis results you may find the following descriptions useful:

Values of r	Suitable adjectives
+0.9 to +1.0	Strong, positive
+0.6 to +0.89	Fair/moderate, positive
+0.3 to +0.59	Weak, positive
0.0 to +0.29	Negligible/scant positive
0.0 to −0.29	Negligible/scant negative
−0.3 to −0.59	Weak, negative
−0.6 to −0.89	Fair/moderate, negative
−0.9 to −1.0	Strong, negative

The things to remember about the sample Pearson correlation coefficient, r, are:

- It measures the strength of the connection or association between observed values of two variables.
- It can take any value from −1 to +1 inclusive.
- If it is positive it means there is a direct or upward-sloping relationship.
- If it is negative it means there is an inverse or downward-sloping relationship.

■ The further it is from zero the stronger the association.
■ It only measures the strength of linear relationships.

At this point you may find it useful to try **Review Questions 7.1 to 7.5** at the end of the chapter.

7.1.2 The coefficient of determination

The square of the Pearson correlation coefficient is also used as a way of measuring the connection between variables. Although it is the square of r, the upper case is used in representing it, R^2. It is called the *coefficient of determination* because it can help you to assess how much the values of one variable are decided or *determined* by the values of another.

As we saw, the Pearson correlation coefficient is based on the standard deviation. Similarly the square of the correlation coefficient is based on the square of the standard deviation, the variance.

Like the correlation coefficient, the coefficient of determination is a ratio, the ratio of the amount of the variance that can be explained by the relationship between the variables to the total variance in the data. Because it is a ratio it cannot exceed one and because it is a square it is always a positive value. Conventionally it is expressed as a percentage.

Example 7.4

Calculate the coefficient of determination, R^2, for the data in Example 7.1.

In Example 7.2 we calculated that the Pearson correlation coefficient for these data was -0.960. The square of -0.960 is 0.922 or 92.2%. This is the value of R^2. It means that 92.2% of the variation in the numbers of jackets sold can be explained by the variation in the prices.

You may find R^2 an easier way to communicate the strength of the relationship between two variables. Its only disadvantage compared to the correlation coefficient is that the figure itself does not convey whether the association is positive or negative. However, there are other ways of showing this, including the scatter diagram.

7.1.3 Spearman's rank correlation coefficient

If you want to investigate links involving ordinal or ranked data you should not use the Pearson correlation coefficient as it is based on the arithmetic measures of location and spread, the mean and the standard deviation. Fortunately there is an alternative, the Spearman rank correlation coefficient.

It is possible to use the Spearman coefficient with interval and ratio data provided the data are ranked. You find the value of the coefficient from the ranked data rather than the original observations you would use to get the Pearson coefficient. This may be a preferable alternative as you may find calculating the Spearman coefficient easier. If your original observations contain extreme values the Pearson coefficient may be distorted by them, just as the mean is sensitive to extreme values, in which case the Spearman coefficient may be more reliable.

To calculate the Spearman coefficient, usually represented by the symbol r_s, subtract the ranks of your y values from the ranks of their corresponding x values to give a difference in rank, d, for each pair of observations. Next square the differences and add them up to get Σd^2. Multiply the sum of the squared differences by 6 then divide the result by n, the number of pairs of observations, multiplied by the square of n minus one. Finally subtract the result from one to arrive at the coefficient. The procedure can be expressed as follows:

$$r_s = 1 - \frac{6 \Sigma d^2}{n(n^2 - 1)}$$

Example 7.5

The total annual cost of players' wages for eight football clubs and their final league positions are as follows:

Wages bill (£m)	Final league position
45	1
32	2
41	3
13	4
27	5
15	6
18	7
22	8

Work out the Spearman coefficient for the correlation between the league positions and wages bills of these clubs.

One variable, league position, is already ranked, but before we can calculate the coefficient we have to rank the values of the other variable, the wage bill.

Rank of wages bill	League position	d	d^2
1	1	0	0
3	2	+1	1
2	3	+1	1
8	4	+4	16
4	5	−1	1
7	6	+1	1
6	7	−1	1
5	8	−3	9
		$\Sigma d^2 = 30$	$n = 8$

$$r_s = 1 - \frac{6 * 30}{8(8^2 - 1)} = 1 - \frac{180}{8(64 - 1)} = 1 - \frac{180}{8 * 63}$$

$$= 1 - \frac{180}{504} = 1 - 0.357 = 0.643$$

The interpretation of the Spearman coefficient is the same as we use for the Pearson coefficient. In Example 7.5 the coefficient is positive, indicating positive correlation and rather less than +1 suggesting the degree of correlation is modest.

Using the Spearman coefficient with ranked data that contains ties is not quite as straightforward. The ranks for the tied elements need to be adjusted so that they share the ranks they would have had if they were not equal. For instance if two elements are ranked second equal in effect they share the second and third positions. To reflect this we would give them a rank of 2.5 each.

Example 7.6

Rank the data in Example 7.1 from lowest to highest and find the Spearman rank correlation coefficient for the prices of the jackets and the number of jackets sold.

Price (x)	Rank (x)	Number sold (y)	Rank (y)	d	d^2
18	1	8	6	$1 - 6 = -5$	25
20	2	6	5	$2 - 5 = -3$	9

(Continued)

Price (x)	Rank (x)	Number sold (y)	Rank (y)	d	d²
25	3	5	4	3 – 4 = –1	1
27	4	2	2.5	4 – 2.5 = 1.5	2.25
28	5	2	2.5	5 – 2.5 = 2.5	6.25
32	6	1	1	6 – 1 = 5	25
				$\sum d^2 = 68.5$	$n = 6$

$$r_s = 1 - \frac{6 * 68.5}{6(6^2 - 1)} = 1 - \frac{411}{6(36 - 1)} = 1 - \frac{411}{6 * 35}$$

$$= 1 - \frac{411}{210} = 1 - 1.957 = -0.957$$

In Example 7.6 the Spearman coefficient for the ranked data is very similar to the value of the Pearson coefficient we obtained in Example 7.2 for the original observations – 0.960. Both results show that the correlation between prices and sales is strong and negative.

At this point you may find it useful to try **Review Questions 7.6 to 7.9** at the end of the chapter.

7.2 Simple linear regression analysis

Measuring correlation tells you how strong the linear relationship between two variables might be but it doesn't tell us exactly what that relationship is. If we need to know about the way in which two variables are related we have to use the other part of basic bivariate analysis, *regression analysis*.

The simplest form of this technique, *simple linear regression* (which is often abbreviated to SLR), enables us to find the straight line most appropriate for representing the connection between two sets of observed values. Because the line that we 'fit' to our data can be used to represent the relationship it is rather like an average in two dimensions, it summarizes the link between the variables.

Simple linear regression is called *simple* because it analyses two variables, it is called *linear* because it is about finding a straight line, but why is it called *regression*, which actually means going backwards? The answer is that the technique was first developed by the nineteenth century scientist Sir Francis Galton, who wanted a way of representing how the heights of children were genetically constrained or 'regressed' by the heights of their parents.

In later work you may encounter *multiple* regression, which is used to analyse relationships between more than two variables, and *non-linear* regression, which is used to analyse relationships that do not have a straight-line pattern.

You might ask why it is necessary to have a technique to fit a line to a set of data? It would be quite easy to look at a scatter diagram like Figure 7.1, lay a ruler close to the points and draw a line to represent the relationship between the variables. This is known as fitting a line 'by eye' and is a perfectly acceptable way of getting a quick approximation, particularly in a case like Figure 7.1 where there are few points which form a clear linear pattern.

The trouble with fitting a line by eye is that it is inconsistent and unreliable. It is inconsistent because the position of the line depends on the judgement of the person drawing the line. Different people will produce different lines for the same data.

For any set of bivariate data there is one line that is the most appropriate, the so-called 'best-fit' line. There is no guarantee that fitting a line by eye will produce the best-fit line, so fitting a line by eye is unreliable.

We need a reliable, consistent way of finding the line that best fits a set of plotted points, which is what simple linear regression analysis is. It is a technique that finds the line of best-fit, the line that travels as closely as possible to the plotted points. It identifies the two defining characteristics of that line, its *intercept*, or starting point, and its *slope*, or rate of increase or decrease. These are illustrated in Figure 7.8.

We can use these defining characteristics to compose the equation of the line of best fit, which represents the line using symbols. The equation enables us to plot the line itself.

Simple linear regression is based on the idea of minimizing the differences between a line and the points it is intended to represent. Since

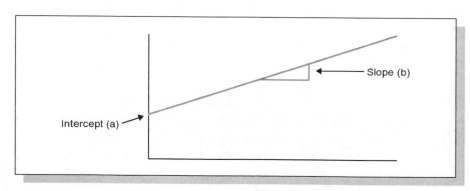

Figure 7.8
The intercept and slope of a line

all the points matter, it is the sum of these differences that needs to be minimized. In other words, the best-fit line is the line that results in a lower sum of differences than any other line would for that set of data.

The task for simple linear regression is a little more complicated because the difference between a point and the line is positive if the point is above the line, and negative if the point is below the line. If we were to add up these differences we would find that the negative and positive differences cancel each other out.

This means the sum of the differences is not a reliable way of judging how well a line fits a set of points. To get around this problem, simple linear regression is based on the squares of the differences because they will always be positive.

The best-fit line that simple linear regression finds for us is the line which takes the path that results in there being the least possible sum

---

Example 7.7

The amount of profit tax (in £m) paid by three companies in the current financial year and their respective gross profits (in £m) were:

| Profit tax paid (Y) | 4.0 | 3.0 | 6.5 |
| Gross profit (X) | 15.0 | 20.0 | 25.0 |

Which of the two lines best fits the data, the one in Figure 7.9 or the one in Figure 7.10?

The deviations between the points and the line in Figure 7.9 ($y = -3.5 + 0.4x$) are, from left to right, $+1.5$, -1.5 and 0. The total deviation is:

$$+1.5 + (-1.5) + 0.0 = 0.0$$

The deviations between the points and the line in Figure 7.10 ($y = 0.2x$) are, from left to right, $+1$, -1 and $+1$. The total deviation is:

$$+1.0 + (-1.0) + 1.5 = 1.5$$

The fact that the total deviation is smaller for Figure 7.9 suggests that its line is the better fit. But if we take the sum of the squared deviations the conclusion is different.

Total squared deviation in Figure 7.9

$$= 1.5^2 + (-1.5)^2 + 0.0^2 = 2.25 + 2.25 + 0.00 = 4.50$$

Total squared deviation in Figure 7.10

$$= 1.0^2 + (-1.0)^2 + 1.5^2 = 1.00 + 1.00 + 2.25 = 4.25$$

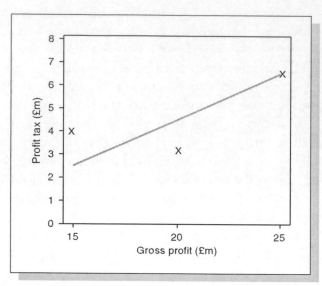

Figure 7.9
Profit tax and profit

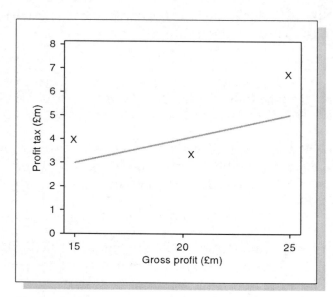

Figure 7.10
Profit tax and gross profit

This apparent contradiction has arisen because the large deviations in Figure 7.9 cancel each other out when we simply add them together.

of squared differences between the points and the line. For this reason the technique is sometimes referred to as *least squares regression.*

For any given set of data, as you can imagine, there are many lines from which the best-fit line could be chosen. To pick the right one we could plot each of them in turn and measure the differences using a ruler. Fortunately, such a laborious procedure is not necessary. Simple linear regression uses calculus, the area of mathematics that is partly about finding minimum or maximum values, to find the intercept and slope of the line of best fit directly from the data.

The procedure involves using two expressions to find, first, the slope and then the intercept. Since simple linear regression is almost always used to find the line of best fit from a set of sample data the letters used to represent the intercept and the slope are *a* and *b* respectively. The equivalent Greek letters, α and β, are used to represent the intercept and slope of the population line of best fit.

According to simple linear regression analysis the slope of the line of best fit:

$$b = \frac{\sum xy - (\sum x * \sum y)/n}{\sum x^2 - (\sum x)^2/n}$$

And the intercept: $a = (\sum y - b\sum x)/n$

These results can then be combined to give the equation of the line of best fit, which is known as the *regression equation*:

$$Y = a + bX$$

The expressions for getting the slope and intercept of the line of best fit look daunting, but this need not worry you. If you have to find a best fit line you can use a statistical or a spreadsheet package, or even a calculator with a good statistical facility to do the hard work for you. They are quoted here, and used in Example 7.8 below, merely to show you how the procedure works.

Example 7.8

Find the equation of the line of best fit for the data in Example 7.1 and plot the line.

We need to find four summations: the sum of the *x* values, the sum of the *y* values, the sum of the *x* squared values and the sum of the products of each pair of *x* and *y* values multiplied together.

Price (x)	x^2	Number sold (y)	xy
18	324	8	144
20	400	6	120
			(Continued)

Price (x)	x^2	Number sold (y)	xy
25	625	5	125
27	729	2	54
28	784	2	56
32	1024	1	32
$\Sigma x = 150$	$\Sigma x^2 = 3886$	$\Sigma y = 24$	$\Sigma xy = 531$

$$b = \frac{\Sigma xy - (\Sigma x * \Sigma y)/n}{\Sigma x^2 - (\Sigma x)^2/n} = \frac{531 - (150 * 24)/6}{3886 - 150^2/6}$$

$$= \frac{531 - 3600/6}{3886 - 22500/6} = \frac{531 - 600}{3886 - 3750} = \frac{-69}{136} = -0.507$$

$$a = (\Sigma y - b\Sigma x)/n = (24 - (-0.507)150)/6 = (24 + 76.103)/6$$

$$= 100.103/6 = 16.684$$

The equation of the line of best fit is: $Y = 16.684 - 0.507X$

Or, in other words, Number sold $= 16.684 - 0.507$ Price

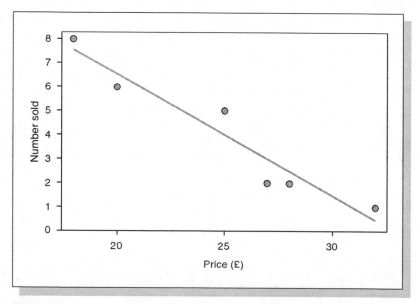

Figure 7.11
The line of best fit for the numbers of jackets sold and their prices

Once we have the equation of a regression line we can use its components, its intercept and slope, to describe the relationship between the variables. For instance, the slope of the equation in Example 7.8 suggests that for every £1 increase in the price of a jacket the number sold will drop by 0.507 jackets, and for every £1 decrease in the price of a jacket the number sold will increase by 0.507 jackets. Since the slope is the *rate of change* in jacket sales with respect to price, the fact that it is not a whole number is not important.

The intercept of the equation of a regression line is the value that the *Y* variable is predicted to take if the *X* variable has the value zero. In Example 7.8 the intercept of 16.684 suggests that roughly seventeen jackets would be 'sold' if the price was zero.

You can use a diagram like Figure 7.11 to compare the individual points of data to the line of best fit. A point below the line indicates that the *y* value is relatively low compared to what we would expect given the *x* value, for instance in Figure 7.11 the sales of the jacket priced at £27 are a little lower than we might expect. A point above the line suggests a *y* value rather greater than we would expect, such as the jacket priced at £25 in Figure 7.11. Any point far above or below the line would represent a *possible outlier*. If, for example, sales of seven jackets priced at £30 were plotted the point would be far above the line in Figure 7.11 and would be a possible outlier.

The process of finding a best fit line with regression analysis is a laborious procedure, even with a relatively simple set of data. It is best performed using appropriate computer software or two-variable calculator functions.

The equation of the line of best fit we derived in Example 7.8 is an example of a regression 'model'. It represents how the two variables are connected based on the sample evidence in Example 7.1. It is the best linear model that can be found for that set of data.

We can use such an equation to predict values of *Y* that should occur with values of *X*. These are known as *expected* values of *Y* because they are what the line leads us to *expect* to be associated with the *X* values. The symbol $\hat{y}$, '*y*-hat', is used to represent a value of *Y* that is predicted using the regression equation, so that we can distinguish it from an actual *y* value. That is to say, the regression equation

$$Y = a + bX$$

can be used to predict an individual *y* value that is expected to occur with an observed *x* value:

$$\hat{y} = a + bx$$

Example 7.9

Use the regression equation from Example 7.8 to find how many jackets priced at £23 Courtka can expect to sell.

The regression equation tells us that: Number sold = 16.684 − 0.507 Price

If we insert the value '23' where 'Price' appears in the equation we can work out what, according to the equation, the number sold should be.

$$\text{Number sold (if price is 23)} = 16.684 - 0.507(23)$$

$$= 16.684 - 11.661 = 5.023$$

This suggests the expected number sold will be 5, as jackets sales must be in whole numbers.

7.3 Using the technology: correlation and regression in EXCEL, MINITAB and SPSS

7.3.1 Excel

For a Pearson correlation coefficient store the observations of your two variables in adjacent columns of the spreadsheet then

- Select **Data Analysis** from the **Tools** menu.
- Choose **Correlation** from the menu in the **Data Analysis** command window, click **OK** and the **Correlation** window will appear. The cursor should be in the **Input range:** box.
- Click and drag your mouse across the cells in the spreadsheet that contain your data then click **OK**.

To produce a regression equation using EXCEL

- Choose **Data Analysis** from the **Tools** pull-down menu and select **Regression** from the **Data Analysis** menu. Click **OK**.
- In the **Regression** window that appears the cursor should be in the **Input Y Range:** box.
- Click and drag your mouse down the column where your *y* values are stored then click the **Input X Range:** box and click and drag your mouse down the column containing your *x* values. Click **OK** and the output that appear includes the intercept and slope of the line of best-fit in the **Coefficient** column towards the bottom left of the screen. The intercept is in the first row and the slope is in the second row.

If you would like the line of best fit shown graphically with the scatter of points representing your data follow the **Regression** sequence as above but in the **Regression** command window look for the **Residuals** section towards the bottom and in it click the box to the left of **Line Fit Plots** then **OK**. The graph should appear to the right of the main regression output. In it the line of best fit is represented as a series of points. To get a line through these double click on any one of them and the **Format Data Series** command window should appear with the **Pattern** tab displayed. Look for the section headed **Line** to the left of the window and in it click the button to the left of **Automatic** then click **OK**.

7.3.2 MINITAB

You can use MINITAB to produce a correlation coefficient by storing your *x* and *y* values in two columns of the worksheet and selecting **Basic Statistics** from the **Stat** menu. Choose **Correlation** from the sub-menu then give the column location of both sets of observations in the command window and click **OK**.

For the equation of a line of best fit

- Select **Regression** from the **Stat** menu and choose **Regression** from the **Regression** sub-menu.
- Specify the column locations of the **Response**, i.e. the values of *Y*, and the **Predictor**, i.e. the values of *X*.
- Click **OK** and the output that appears has the regression equation, the equation of the line of best fit, at the top.

If you want a scatter diagram with the line of best fit superimposed on the scatter, follow the **Stat – Regression** sequence but choose **Fitted Line Plot** from the **Regression** sub-menu. Specify the column locations of the **Response (Y):** and **Predictor (X):** observations in the boxes to the right of these labels and click **OK**. The diagram that appears includes the regression equation and the value of R^2 for the data.

7.3.3 SPSS

To get a correlation coefficient store the values of your two variables in the worksheet then

- Choose **Correlate** from the **Analyze** pull-down menu and select **Bivariate** from the sub-menu.

▓ In the **Bivariate Correlations** window that appears the locations of your data are listed on the left.

▓ Click the ▶ symbol to bring them into the **Variables**: box on the right.

▓ Check that the default setting under **Correlation coefficients** is **Pearson** and click **OK**.

Note that you can obtain a Spearman coefficient by clicking the button to the left of **Spearman** in this part of the window. The results appear in the output viewer.

For a regression line

▓ Choose **Regression** from the **Analyze** pull-down menu and select **Linear**.

▓ In the **Linear Regression** window click on the column location of your dependent (Y) variable on the left-hand side then click the ▶ symbol to the left of the **Dependent** box. Click on the column location of your independent (X) variable then click the ▶ symbol to the left of the **Independent** box then click **OK**.

▓ Look for the table headed **Coefficients** and the two columns in it labelled **Unstandardized coefficients**. In the left-hand column, headed **B**, you will find two figures. The upper one, in the row labelled (**Constant**), is the intercept of the model and the lower one is the slope.

If you would like your regression line fitted to the scatter,

▓ Obtain a scatter diagram by choosing **Scatter** from the **Graphs** pull-down menu then click the **Simple** plot type and click **Define**.

▓ In the **Scatterplot** window select your *Y* **axis**: and *X* **axis**: variables and click **OK**. The scatter diagram should be in the output viewer.

▓ Double left click on it and the **Chart 1 – SPSS Chart Editor** window should appear.

▓ Click on its **Chart** pull-down menu and select **Options**.

▓ In the **Scatterplot Options** window that you should see, click the button to the left of **Total** under **Fit Line** then click the **Fit Options** button and click the **Linear Regression** fit type.

▓ Click **Continue** to get back to the **Scatterplot Options** window where you need to click **OK**.

▓ Minimize or delete the **Chart 1 – SPSS Chart Editor** window and your scatter plot should now have a line of best fit.

7.4 Road test: Do they really use correlation and regression?

In the Kathawala study (1988), 65% of the respondents reported either moderate, frequent or extensive use of correlation and regression by their companies, making it one of the most widely used techniques considered in that survey. They are techniques that you may well encounter in many business contexts.

In Human Resources Management correlation analysis has been used to assess the relationship between the performances applicants achieve in recruitment and selection procedures and how well they perform as employees following appointment. Simpson (2002) gives correlation coefficients for a variety of selection methods from interview performance to handwriting. The results suggest that more systematic approaches like structured interviews are more effective predictors of job performance than references.

There are laws that prohibit employers from discriminating against people on the basis of, *inter alia*, their gender or their ethnicity. Since these laws were introduced there have been many legal cases based on alleged discrimination in appointment and promotion procedures. Conway and Roberts (1986) illustrate how regression analysis has been used in some of these cases to demonstrate how an individual has not reached the salary level or grade they might expect given the time they had worked for their employer. In such models the salary or grade is the dependent (Y) variable and the length of service is the independent (X) variable.

Health and safety is another area of business in which correlation and regression is used extensively. In industries where employees are exposed to hazards the effects on health may well depend on the extent of exposure to those hazards. This type of analysis is extensively used in mining. Kuempel *et al.* (2003) report the results of a recent study of the relationship between exposure to coal mine dust and lung disorders in coal miners.

The performance of different sales territories or areas is an important issue for sales managers in many organizations. It can have a bearing on, among other things, the allocation of sales staff and commission levels. Cravens *et al.* (1972) used regression analysis to examine how a variety of factors, including the market potential of the sales areas, the experience of the sales staff working in the areas and the advertising expenditure in the areas, might influence sales performance in the areas. They developed a multiple regression model that was able to predict 72% of the variation in sales territory performance.

In product testing it is often important to investigate the relationships between the lifetime of the product and its operating characteristics. In the offshore oil industry the durability of ropes for long-term mooring of floating structures such as mobile drilling units is an important issue, specifically the performance of synthetic ropes and the more traditional steel ropes. Ming-Yao *et al.* (2000) use regression analysis to relate the minimum break strength to the duration of use.

Review questions

Answers to these questions, including fully worked solutions to the Key questions marked with an asterisk (*), are on pages 644–649.

7.1   Consider which of the relationships below are likely to have a positive and which are likely to have a negative correlation coefficient.
(a) The distance a vehicle travels and the fuel consumed
(b) The demand for laptop computers and their price
(c) The average temperature of countries and the sales of warm clothing
(d) The amount consumers spend on motor insurance and their age
(e) The population of countries and the amount of electricity used
(f) The income of people and the amount of income tax they pay
(g) The fuel efficiency of cars and their engine size

7.2*   Outstanding balances on the monthly bills of nine credit card accounts and the household income of the account holders are:

Balance (£)	250	1630	970	2190	410	830	0	550	0
Income (£000)	15	23	26	28	31	35	37	38	42

(a) Plot these figures on a scatter diagram with outstanding balance as the dependent variable (Y).
(b) Calculate the Pearson correlation coefficient and comment on its value.

7.3   Car parking spaces in a city centre are at a premium. The costs of parking a car for a whole day in ten public car parks within the city, and the distances between those car parks and the city centre are:

Cost (£)	5	5	7	8	10	12	15	15	18	20
Distance (km)	1.5	1.2	1.0	1.1	0.8	0.5	0.4	0.2	0.1	0.1

(a) Assuming that the cost of parking is dependent on the distance the car park is from the city centre, plot the data on a scatter diagram.

(b) Find the value of the Pearson correlation coefficient and indicate what conclusions should be drawn from it.

7.4   The weekly turnover and the total display area, in square metres, of eight 'late night' grocery shops are:

Turnover (£000)	23	37	33	41	47	86	72	95
Display area (m^2)	15	21	30	45	61	77	79	92

(a) Identify which variable is the dependent variable (Y).

(b) Plot a scatter diagram to portray these figures.

(c) Calculate the Pearson correlation coefficient and discuss its value.

7.5   The cost of placing a full-page colour advertisement and the circulation figures of nine magazines are:

Cost (£000)	9	43	16	17	19	13	20	44	35
Circulation (000)	135	2100	680	470	450	105	275	2250	695

(a) Which of these variables should be the dependent variable (Y), and why?

(b) Plot a scatter diagram to portray the data.

(c) Determine the Pearson correlation coefficient and assess its value.

7.6*   A panel of film critics ranked what they consider the six best new films. Their rankings and the box office takings of the films to date are:

Critics' rank	Takings ($m)
1	2.2
2	0.8
3	7.3
4	1.6
5	1.0
6	0.5

Calculate the Spearman correlation coefficient for these data and comment on its value.

7.7   There are eight electoral wards in a town. The crime levels in these wards have been ranked by the local police, with the lowest crime area ranked 1, and the level of house prices ranked by a local estate agent, with the lowest price level ranked 1. The results are:

Crime level:	1	2	3	4	5	6	7	8
House price level:	7	6	8	3	5	1	4	2

Find the value of the Spearman correlation coefficient for these figures and assess its meaning.

7.8   The ten best-selling cars were studied by a team of designers who ranked them for design and style. The same cars were studied by a team of road accident investigators who ranked them for safety. The results are set out below:

Design ranking:	1	2	3	4	5	6	7	8	9	10
Safety ranking:	4	6	1	5	2	3	10	7	9	8

Work out the value of Spearman's rank correlation coefficient and explain how it should be interpreted.

7.9   Eight companies dominate a particular industry. The annual revenue and annual gross profit for these companies are as follows:

Company	Revenue (£m)	Gross profit (£m)
Mirovoy	2815	322
Materique	1139	198
Strannar	626	73
Malenky	557	41
Ribar	291	47
Krevetka	172	25
Meesh	144	33
Blochar	85	9

(a) Rank the revenues and profits of these companies and use your results to calculate the Spearman's rank correlation coefficient.

(b) What does the value of the coefficient suggest about the association between revenue and profit?

7.10*   A consumer group has tested nine makes of personal stereo. The prices and the scores (out of 100) awarded to them by a panel of experts the group commissioned to test them, are:

Price (£)	95	69	18	32	27	70	49	35	50
Score	74	63	28	33	37	58	38	43	50

(a) Plot a scatter diagram to portray the data taking score as the dependent variable (Y).
(b) Find the equation of the line of best fit using simple linear regression.
(c) Plot the line of best fit on the scatter diagram produced for (a).
(d) Use the regression equation from (c) to predict the score that the panel of experts would award to a personal stereo priced £45.

7.11   Eight prominent football teams play in the same division. The total number of goals scored by each team last season and the league position each was in at the end of the season are:

Goals scored	75	60	56	44	43	40	37	52
League position	2	5	9	10	14	16	17	22

(a) Produce a scatter diagram to display the data taking league position as the dependent variable (Y).
(b) Using simple linear regression, determine the line of best fit and plot it on your scatter diagram.
(c) Predict the final position of a team that scored 50 goals using your regression equation.

7.12   In a survey of commuting patterns ten respondents say that they cycle to work. The distances they travel and the mean journey times they report are:

Distance (miles)	2	2	3	4	5	6	7	8	8	10
Mean journey time (minutes)	10	15	15	20	25	25	30	40	45	50

(a) Which of these is the dependent variable (Y)?
(b) Portray the data on a scatter diagram.
(c) Calculate the slope and intercept of the line of best fit using simple linear regression analysis.
(d) Plot the line of best fit and use it to estimate the time that a journey of 9 miles would take.

7.13   The classified advertisement columns of a local paper contain details of 12 used cars of a particular make and model. The prices of these cars and the numbers of miles they have travelled are:

Price (£000)	6.8	6.2	5.7	4.7	6.0	5.9	7.0	4.5	5.0	3.0	3.8	3.5
Mileage (000)	9	13	11	33	14	11	3	19	22	35	40	44

(a) Identify the independent variable (X).
(b) Present these data in the form of a scatter diagram.
(c) Find the least squares line of best fit and plot it on your scatter diagram.
(d) Predict the price of a car of this type that has travelled 25,000 miles.

7.14* An estate agency employs ten qualified sales consultants. The annual salaries and years of experience in the business of these ten are as follows:

Salary (£000): 13 18 19 22 25 27 31 36 38 42
Experience
(years):   1   4   3   2   7   8   5   13 20 22

(a) Which variable is the independent (X) variable?
(b) Portray the data in the form of a scatter diagram.
(c) Work out the best fit equation and plot it on the diagram.
(d) Calculate the coefficient of determination for these data and comment on its value.

7.15   The percentages of workers in trade unions and the mean hourly wage in nine US states are:

Union membership (%):   7.5   17.2   9.1   16.1   25.4
Mean hourly wage ($):   13.80 16.81 13.40 18.00 20.00

Union membership (%):   16.9   23.7   19.5   9.2
Mean hourly wage ($):   15.60 16.63 16.07 11.51

(a) Which one of these should be the dependent variable (Y)?
(b) Plot the data on a scatter diagram.
(c) Determine the equation of the line of best fit and plot it on your diagram.
(d) Find the coefficient of determination and assess its value.

7.16   The annual turnovers (in £000m) and numbers of employees (in 000s) of 12 major retail companies are:

Turnover: 20.1 14.0 10.7 10.6 8.6 8.1 5.5 4.9 4.6 4.5 4.3 4.1
Employees: 126 141 107 101 92 70 52 34 57 32 47 26

(a) Which variable should be the independent (X) variable?
(b) Portray these data in the form of a scatter diagram.
(c) Find the equation of the line of best fit and plot the line on your scatter diagram.
(d) Work out the coefficient of determination and outline what it tells you about the relationship between the two variables.

7.17   A leak of a hazardous substance at a chemical plant means that all employees working in the area of the plant affected have been tested for contamination. The following figures are the hours worked in the affected area since the leak and the contamination levels (in parts per million) of the first ten workers to be tested:

Hours worked:	1	2	3	3	4	4	6	6	8	8
Contamination level:	15	18	27	29	36	38	61	58	75	82

(a) Which variable should be the dependent variable (Y), and why?

(b) Show these data on a scatter diagram.

(c) Work out the equation of the line of best fit and plot it on your scatter diagram.

(d) Calculate the coefficient of determination and interpret its meaning.

7.18   An international road transport consultant wants to see if the extent of a country's motorway network (in kilometres) depends on its land area (in thousands of square kilometres). She has collected figures for a selection of European countries:

Land area:	84	31	43	337	544	357	132	41	69	301
Motorway network:	1596	1666	930	394	9140	11200	420	2300	70	8860

(a) Plot the data on a scatter diagram.

(b) Ascertain the line of best fit and plot it on your scatter diagram.

(c) Find the coefficient of determination and use it to advise the consultant.

(d) Identify any possible outliers.

7.19   An economist studying the market for designer watches has produced a regression model to describe the relationship between sales of the different brands of watch (in thousands of units) and the advertising expenditure used to promote them (in £m).

$$\text{Sales} = 4.32 + 6.69 \text{ Advertising expenditure}$$

$$R^2 = 64.8\%$$

(a) If there was no advertising expenditure to promote a brand of watch, what sales could be expected?

(b) By how many units would sales be expected to increase for every extra £1m spent on advertising?

(c) What is the value of the Pearson correlation coefficient?

7.20   Select the appropriate definition for each term on the left-hand side from the list on the right-hand side.

(i)	regression equation	(a)	another name for Y
(ii)	Pearson correlation coefficient	(b)	measures association in ranked data
(iii)	coefficient of determination	(c)	X increases as Y increases
(iv)	inverse relationship	(d)	the square of r
(v)	predictor	(e)	defines the line of best fit
(vi)	response	(f)	measures association in quantitative data
(vii)	Spearman correlation coefficient	(g)	Y increases as X decreases
(viii)	direct relationship	(h)	another name for X

Counting the cost — summarizing money variables over time

This chapter will help you to:

- employ simple and aggregate index numbers to measure price changes over time
- work out weighted aggregate price indices: Laspeyre and Paasche indices
- adjust figures for the effects of inflation using price indices
- apply methods of investment appraisal: accounting rate of return, payback period, net present value, and internal rate of return
- use the technology: investment appraisal methods in EXCEL
- become acquainted with business uses of investment appraisal

In the last two chapters we have looked at ways of summarizing data. In Chapter 6 we concentrated on measuring the location and spread in univariate (single variable) data, in Chapter 7 we focused on measuring the strength and direction in bivariate data. In both chapters the data concerned were cross-sectional data, data relating to the same point or period of time. In this chapter and the next we will consider ways of summarizing data relating to different periods of time.

Time-based data consist of numerical observations that can be measured and summarized using the techniques you met in the previous two chapters. We could, for instance, collect the price of gold at various points in time and calculate the mean price of gold over the period, or use correlation analysis to measure the association between the price of gold and the price of silver at various points in time. However, often the most important aspect of time-based data is the time factor and the techniques in the previous two chapters would not allow us to bring that out of the data.

In this chapter we will look at techniques to summarize money variables that relate to different time periods. We will start by exploring index numbers and how they can be used to summarize the general movements in prices over time. Then we will look at how such price indices can be used to adjust money amounts for the effects of inflation. Later in the chapter we will consider summarizing amounts of interest accumulated over time and how this approach is used to assess the worth of investment projects.

8.1 Index numbers

Data collected over time are very important for the successful performance of organizations. For instance, such data can reveal trends in consumer expenditure and taste that companies need to follow.

Businesses use information based on data collected by other agencies over time to help them understand and evaluate the environment in which they operate. Perhaps the most important and widespread example of this is the use of *index numbers* to monitor general trends in prices and costs. For instance, the Retail Price Index is used as a benchmark figure in the context of wage bargaining, and Share Price Indices are reference points in financial decisions companies face.

Most businesses attach a great deal of importance to changes in the costs of things they buy and the prices of things they sell. During periods of high inflation these changes are more dramatic; in periods of low inflation they are modest. Over recent decades, when the level of inflation has fluctuated, companies have had to track general price and cost movements carefully. To help them do this they use index numbers.

Index numbers can be used to represent movements over time in a series of single figures. A simple index number is the value of something at one point in time, maybe the current value, in relation to its value at another point in time, the base period, multiplied by 100 to give a percentage (although the percent sign, %, is not usually written alongside it).

$$\text{Simple price index} = \frac{\text{current price}}{\text{base period price}} * 100 = \frac{p_c}{p_0} * 100$$

where p_c represents the price in the current year and p_0 represent the price in the base year (i.e. period zero).

Example 8.1

Full exhaust systems cost the Remont Repairs garage £156 each in 2003. They cost £125 in 2000. Calculate a simple price index to represent the change in price over the period.

$$\text{Simple price index} = \frac{\text{current price}}{\text{base period price}} * 100 = \frac{p_c}{p_0} * 100$$

$$= \frac{156}{125} * 100 = 124.8 \text{ to 1 decimal place}$$

This tells us that the price of an exhaust system has increased by 24.8% over this period.

At this point you may find it useful to try **Review Question 8.1** at the end of the chapter.

Since businesses usually buy and sell more than a single item, a simple price index is of limited use. Of much greater importance are *aggregate* indices that summarize price movements of many items in a single figure.

We can calculate a simple aggregate price index for a combination of goods by taking the sum of the prices for the goods in the current period and dividing it by the sum of the prices of the same goods in the base period. That is

$$\text{Simple aggregate price index} = \frac{\Sigma p_c}{\Sigma p_0} * 100.$$

Example 8.2

Remont Repairs regularly buys exhaust systems, car batteries and tyres. The prices of these goods in 2003 and 2000 are given in the following table.

Calculate a simple aggregate price index to compare the prices in 2003 to the prices in 2000.

	2000	2003
Exhaust system	£125	£156
Battery	£25	£35
Tyre	£28	£32

Simple aggregate price index:

$$\frac{\Sigma p_c}{\Sigma p_0} * 100 = \frac{156 + 35 + 32}{125 + 25 + 28} * 100 = \frac{223}{178} * 100 = 125.3 \text{ to 1 decimal place}$$

This result indicates that prices paid by the garage increased by 25.3% from 2000 to 2003.

At this point you may find it useful to try **Review Questions 8.2 and 8.3** at the end of the chapter.

The result we obtained in Example 8.2 may well be more useful because it is an overall figure that includes all the commodities. However, it does not differentiate between prices of items that may be purchased in greater quantity than other items, which implies that their prices are of much greater significance than prices of less important items.

In a simple aggregate price index each price is given equal prominence, you can see that it appears once in the expression. Its numerical 'clout' depends simply on whether it is a large or small price. In Example 8.2, the result, 125.3, is close to the value of the simple price index of the exhaust system calculated in Example 8.1, 124.8. This is because the exhaust system happens to have the largest price in the set.

In practice, the importance of the price of an item is a reflection of the quantity that is bought as well as the price itself. To measure changes in movements of prices in a more realistic way we need to *weight* each price in proportion to the quantity purchased and calculate a weighted aggregate price index.

There are two ways we can do this. The first is to use the quantity figure from the base year, represented by the symbol q_0, to weight the price of each item. This type of index is known as the Laspeyre price index. To calculate it we need to work out the total cost of the base period quantities at current prices, divide that by the total cost of the base period quantities at base period prices, and multiply the result by 100:

$$\text{Laspeyre price index} = \frac{\Sigma q_0 p_c}{\Sigma q_0 p_0} * 100$$

Example 8.3

The garage records show that in 2000 50 exhaust systems, 400 batteries and 1000 tyres were purchased. Use these figures and the price figures from Example 8.2 to produce a Laspeyre price index to compare the prices of 2003 to those of 2000.

$$\frac{\Sigma q_0 p_c}{\Sigma q_0 p_0} * 100 = \frac{(50 * 156) + (400 * 35) + (1000 * 32)}{(50 * 125) + (400 * 25) + (1000 * 28)} * 100$$

$$= \frac{53800}{44250} * 100$$

$$= 121.6 \text{ to 1 decimal place}$$

This suggests that the prices have increased by 21.6% between 2000 and 2003.

The result is lower than the figure obtained in Example 8.2, 125.3, because the exhaust system price has the lowest weighting and tyres, which have the lowest price change, have the highest weighting.

The Laspeyre technique uses quantities that are historical. The advantage of this is that such figures are usually readily available. The disadvantage is that they may not accurately reflect the quantities used in the current period.

The alternative approach, which is more useful when quantities used have changed considerably, is to use quantity figures from the current period, q_c. This type of index is known as the Paasche price index. To calculate it you work out the total cost of the current period quantities at current prices, divide that by the total cost of the current period quantities at base period prices, and multiply the result by 100:

$$\text{Paasche price index} = \frac{\Sigma q_c p_c}{\Sigma q_c p_0} * 100$$

Example 8.4

In 2003 the garage purchased 50 exhaust systems, 600 batteries and 750 tyres. Use these figures and the price figures from Example 8.2 to produce a Paasche price index to compare the prices of 2003 to those of 2000.

$$\frac{\Sigma q_c p_c}{\Sigma q_c p_0} * 100 = \frac{(50 * 156) + (600 * 35) + (750 * 32)}{(50 * 125) + (600 * 25) + (750 * 28)} * 100$$

$$= \frac{52800}{42250} * 100 = 125.0 \text{ to 1 decimal place}$$

This result suggests that the prices have increased by 25.0% between 2000 and 2003.

The figure is higher than the result in Example 8.3 because there is a greater weighting on the battery price, which has changed most, and a lower weighting on the tyre price, which has changed least.

The advantage of using a Paasche price index is that the quantity figures used are more up-to-date and therefore realistic. But it is not always possible to get current period quantity figures, particularly when there is a wide range of items and a large number of organizations or consumers that buy them.

The other disadvantage of using the Paasche price index is that new quantity figures must be available for each period we want to compare with the base period. If the garage proprietor wants a Paashce price index for prices in 2004 compared to 2000 you could not provide one until you know both the quantities and the prices used in 2004. By contrast, to calculate a Laspeyre price index for 2004 you only need to know the prices in 2004 because you would use quantities from 2000.

If you look carefully at Example 8.3 and 8.4 you will see that whichever index is used the same quantity figures weight the prices from the different years. This is an important point; they are *price* indices and they are used to compare prices across the time period, not quantities.

At this point you may find it useful to try **Review Questions 8.4 to 8.7** at the end of the chapter.

Organizations tend to use index numbers that have already been compiled rather than construct their own. Probably the most common use of index numbers that you will meet is in the adjustment of financial amounts to take into account changes in price levels.

A sum of money in one period is not necessarily the same as the same amount in another period because its purchasing power changes. This means that if we want to compare an amount from one period with an amount from another period we have to make some adjustment for price changes. The most common way of doing this is to use the Retail Price Index (RPI), an index the Government Statistical Service calculates to monitor price changes, changes in the cost of living.

Example 8.5

The annual salary of the manager of the Zdorovy sports goods shop has changed in the following way between 2000 and 2003. Use the RPI figures for those years to see whether the increases in her salary have kept up with the cost of living.

	2000	2001	2002	2003
Salary (£000)	27	29	30	33
RPI (1987 – 100)	170.3	173.3	176.2	181.3

(*Source:* 'Retail Price Index', Office for National Statistics, © Crown Copyright 2003)

We can 'deflate' the figures for 2001, 2002 and 2003 so that they are expressed in '2000 pounds' by multiplying each of them by the ratio between the RPI for 2000 and the RPI for the year concerned.

$$\text{Adjusted 2001 salary} = 29 * \frac{170.3}{173.3} = 28.498 \text{ i.e. } £28,498$$

$$\text{Adjusted 2002 salary} = 30 * \frac{170.3}{176.2} = 28.995 \text{ i.e. } £28,995$$

$$\text{Adjusted 2003 salary} = 33 * \frac{170.3}{181.3} = 30.998 \text{ i.e. } £30,998$$

These results suggest that her salary has increased more than the cost of living throughout the period.

At this point you may find it useful to try **Review Questions 8.8 to 8.11** at the end of the chapter.

8.2 Investment appraisal

Almost every organization at one time or another has to take decisions about making investments. These decisions may involve something as big as the construction of a new plant or something more mundane like the purchase of a new piece of machinery. One of the main difficulties that managers face when taking these sorts of decisions is that the cost of making the investment is incurred when the plant is built or the machine is purchased, yet the income which it is intended to help generate arises in the future, perhaps over many years.

In this section we will look at techniques that enable managers to appraise, or weigh up, investment in long-lasting assets by relating the initial outlay to the future revenue. These techniques are used by businesses both to assess specific investments and to decide between alternative investments. Companies take these decisions very seriously because they involve large amounts of resources and once made they cannot be reversed.

We will begin with the accounting rate of return method then we will consider the payback period approach, and finally the more sophisticated discounting techniques. Despite the differences between them they all involve the determination of single figures that summarize the financial appeal of an investment project.

8.2.1 The accounting rate of return

Generally, a rate of return expresses the *return* or profit resulting from the use of assets such as machinery or equipment in terms of the expenditure involved in purchasing them, usually in percentage terms. You will find that accountants make extensive use of these types of summary measure; look at a business newspaper or a company report and you will probably find reference to measures like the ROCE (Return on Capital Employed). These measures are used by companies to indicate how effectively they have managed the assets under their control.

The accounting rate of return, often abbreviated to ARR, is the use of this approach to weigh up the attraction of an investment proposal. To apply it we need to establish the average (mean) profit per year and divide that by the average level of investment per year.

To calculate the average profit per year we add up the annual profits and divide by the number of years over which the investment will help generate these revenues. Having said that, the profit figures we use must be profits after allowing for *depreciation*. Depreciation is the spreading of the cost of an asset over its useful life. The simplest way of doing this is to subtract the *residual value* of the asset, which is the amount that the company expects to get from the sale of the asset when it is no longer of use, from the purchase cost of the asset and divide by the number of years of useful life the asset is expected to have. This approach is known as *straight-line depreciation* and it assumes that the usefulness of the asset, in terms of helping to generate profits, is reasonably consistent over its useful life.

To work out the average level of investment, we need to know the cost of the asset and the residual value of the asset. The average investment value is the difference between the initial cost and the residual value divided by two, in other words we split the difference between the highest and lowest values of the asset while it is in use. After dividing the average return by the average investment we multiply by 100 so that we have a percentage result. The procedure can be represented as:

$$\text{accounting rate of return} = \frac{\text{average annual return}}{\text{average annual investment}} * 100$$

where

$$\text{average annual investment} = \frac{(\text{purchase cost} - \text{residual value})}{2}$$

Example 8.6

The Budisha Bus Company is thinking of purchasing a new luxury coach to sustain its prestige client business. The purchase cost of the vehicle, including licence plates and delivery, is £120,000. The company anticipates that it will use the vehicle for five years and be able to sell it at the end of that period for £40,000. The revenue the company expects to generate using the coach is as follows:

By the end of year	Net profit before depreciation (£)
1	30,000
2	30,000
3	30,000
4	25,000
5	20,000

What is the accounting rate of return for this investment?
The average annual profit before depreciation is:

$$\frac{(30000 + 30000 + 30000 + 25000 + 20000)}{5} = \frac{135000}{5} = £27000$$

From this amount we must subtract the annual cost of depreciation, which is:

$$\frac{120000 - 40000}{5} = \frac{80000}{5} = £16000$$

The annual average profit after depreciation is: $27000 - 16000 = £11000$
The average annual investment is:

$$\frac{(120000 - 40000)}{2} = \frac{80000}{2} = £40000$$

The accounting rate of return is:

$$\frac{11000}{40000} * 100 = 27.5\%$$

Should the company in Example 8.6 regard the accounting rate of return for this project as high enough to make the investment worth its while? In practice they would compare this figure to accounting rates of return for alternative investments that it could make with the same money, or perhaps they have a company minimum rate that any project has to exceed to be approved.

The accounting rate of return is widely used to evaluate investment projects. It produces a percentage figure which managers can easily compare to interest rates and it is essentially the same approach to future investment as accountants take when working out the ROCE (Return on Capital Employed) to evaluate a company's past performance.

The critical weakness in using the accounting rate of return to appraise investments is that it is completely blind to the timing of the initial expenditure and future income. It ignores what is called the *time value of money*. The value that an individual or business puts on a sum of money is related to when the money is received; for example if you were offered the choice of a gift of £1000 now or £1000 in two year's time you would most likely prefer the cash now. This may be because you need cash now rather than then, but even if you have sufficient funds now you would still be better off having the money now because you could invest the money in a savings account and receive interest on it.

The other investment appraisal techniques we shall examine have the advantage of bringing the time element into consideration. The other difference between them and the accounting rate of return approach is that they are based on net cash flows into the company, which are essentially net profits before depreciation.

8.2.2 Payback period

The payback period approach to investment appraisal does take the timing of cash flows into account and is based on a straightforward concept – the time it will take for the net profits earned using the asset to cover the purchase of the asset. We need only accumulate the negative (expenditure) and positive (net profits before depreciation) cash flows relating to the investment over time and ascertain when the cumulative cash flow reaches zero. At this point the initial outlay on the asset will have been paid back.

Example 8.7

Work out the payback period for the investment proposal being considered by the Budisha Bus Company in Example 8.6.

The net cash flows associated with the acquisition of the luxury coach can be summarized as follows:

End of year	Cost/receipt	Net cash flow (£)	Cumulative cash flow (£)
0	Cost of coach	−120,000	−120,000
1	Net profit before depreciation	30,000	−90,000
2	Net profit before depreciation	30,000	−60,000
3	Net profit before depreciation	30,000	−30,000
4	Net profit before depreciation	25,000	−5000
5	Net profit before depreciation	20,000	+15,000
5	Sale of coach	40,000	+55,000

Payback is achieved in year 5. We can be more precise by adding the extra cash flow required after the end of year four to reach zero cumulative cash flow (£5000) divided by the net cash flow received by the end of the fifth year (£20,000):

$$\text{Payback period} = 4 + \frac{5000}{20000} = 4.25 \text{ years}$$

Note that in the net cash flow column of the table in Example 8.7 the initial outlay for the coach has a negative sign to indicate that it is a flow of cash out of the business. You will find that accountants use round brackets to indicate an outflow of cash, so where we have written −120000 for the outgoing cash to buy the coach an accountant would represent it as (120000).

The payback period we found in Example 8.7 might be compared with a minimum payback period the company required for any investment or with alternative investments that could be made with the same resources.

At this point you may find it useful to try **Review Questions 8.12** at the end of the chapter.

The payback period is a simple concept for managers to apply and it is particularly appropriate when firms are very sensitive to risk because it indicates the time during which they are exposed to the risk of not recouping their initial outlay. A cautious manager would probably be comfortable with the idea of preferring investment opportunities that have shorter payback periods.

The weakness of the payback approach is that it ignores cash flows that arise in periods beyond the payback period. Where there are two alternative projects it may not suggest the one that performs better overall.

Example 8.8

Gravura Print specialize in precision graphics for the art poster market. To expand their business they want to purchase a flying-arm stamper. There are two manufacturers that produce such machines: Smeshnoy and Pazorna. The cash flows arising from the two ventures are expected to be as follows:

Smeshnoy machine

End of year	Cost/receipt	Net cash flow (£)	Cumulative cash flow (£)
0	Cost of machine	−30,000	−30,000
1	Net profit before depreciation	7000	−23,000
2	Net profit befzore depreciation	8000	−15,000
3	Net profit before depreciation	8000	−7000
4	Net profit before depreciation	7000	0
5	Net profit before depreciation	7000	+7000
5	Sale of machine	5000	+12000

Pazorna machine

End of year	Cost/receipt	Net cash flow (£)	Cumulative cash flow (£)
0	Cost of machine	−30,000	−30,000
1	Net profit before depreciation	12,000	−18,000
2	Net profit before depreciation	12,000	−6000
3	Net profit before depreciation	6000	0
4	Net profit before depreciation	2000	+2000
5	Net profit before depreciation	1000	+3000
5	Sale of machine	2000	+5000

In Example 8.8 the payback period for the Smeshnoy machine is four years and for the Pazorna machine three years. Applying the payback period criterion we should choose the Pazorna machine, but in doing so we would be passing up the opportunity of achieving the rather higher returns from investing in the Smeshnoy machine.

A better approach would be to base our assessment of investments on all of the cash flows involved rather than just the earlier ones, and to bring into our calculations the time value of money. Techniques that allow us to do this adjust or *discount* cash flows to compensate for the time that passes before they arrive. The first of these techniques that we shall consider is the net present value.

8.2.3 Net present value

The net present value (NPV) of an investment is a single figure that summarizes all the cash flows arising from an investment, both expenditure and receipts, each of which have been adjusted so that whenever they arise in the future it is their current or *present* value that is used in the calculation. Adjusting, or *discounting* them to get their present value means working out how much money would have to be invested now in order to generate that specific amount at that time in the future.

To do this we use the same approach as we would to calculate the amount of money accumulating in a savings account. We need to know the rate of interest and the amount of money initially deposited. The amount in the account at the end of one year is the original amount deposited plus the rate of interest, r, applied to the original amount:

$$\text{Amount at the end of the year} = \text{Deposit} + (\text{Deposit} * r)$$

We can express this as:

$$\text{Amount at the end of the year} = \text{Deposit} * (1 + r)$$

If the money stays in the account for a second year:

$$\text{Amount at the end of the second year} = \text{Deposit} * (1 + r) * (1 + r)$$

$$= \text{Deposit} * (1 + r)^2$$

Example 8.9

If you invested £1000 in a savings account paying 5% interest per annum, how much money would you have in the account after two years?

$$\text{Amount at the end of the first year} = 1000 * (1 + 0.05) = £1050$$

If we invested £1050 for a year at 5%, at the end of one year it would be worth:

$$1050 * (1 + 0.05) = £1102.5$$

We can combine these calculations:

$$\text{Amount at the end of the second year} = 1000 * (1 + 0.05)^2$$
$$= 1000 * 1.05^2 = 1000 * 1.1025 = £1102.5$$

In general if we deposit an amount in an account paying an annual interest rate r for n years, the amount accumulated in the account at the end of the period will be:

$$\text{Deposit} * (1 + r)^n$$

The deposit is, of course, the sum of money we start with, it is the *present value* (PV) of our investment, so we can express this procedure as:

$$\text{Amount at the end of year } n = \text{PV} * (1 + r)^n$$

This expression enables us to work out the future value of a known present value, like the amount we deposit in an account. When we assess investment projects we want to know how much a known (or at least expected) amount to be received in the future is worth now. Instead of knowing the present value and wanting to work out the future, we need to reverse the process and determine the present value of a known future amount. To obtain this we can rearrange the expression we used to work out the amount accumulated at the end of a period:

$$\text{Present value (PV)} = \frac{\text{Amount at the end of year } n}{(1 + r)^n}$$

Example 8.10

You are offered £1000 to be paid to you in two years' time. What is the present value of this sum if you can invest cash in a savings account paying 5% interest per annum?

$$\text{Present value} = \frac{1000}{(1 + 0.05)^2} = \frac{1000}{1.05^2} = \frac{1000}{1.1025} = 907.029$$

The present value of £1000 received in two years' time is £907.03, to the nearest penny. In other words, if you invested £907.03 at 5% now in two years' time the amount would be worth

$$\text{Amount at the end of year two} = 907.03 * (1 + 0.05)^2 = 907.03 * 1.1025$$

$$= \text{£}1000.00 \text{ to the nearest penny}$$

When companies use net present value (NPV) to assess investments they discount future cash flows in the same way as we did in Example 8.10, but before they can do so they need to identify the appropriate rate of interest to use. In Example 8.10 we used 5% as it was a viable alternative that in effect reflected the *opportunity cost* of not receiving the money for two years, that is, the amount you have had to forego by having to wait.

The interest, or *discount*, rate a company uses is likely to reflect the opportunity cost, which may be the interest it could earn by investing the money in a bank. It may also reflect the prevailing rate of inflation and the risk of the investment project not working out as planned.

Example 8.11

What is the net present value of the proposed investment in a luxury coach by the Budisha Bus Company in Example 8.6? Use a 10% interest rate.

The cash flows involved in the project were:

End of year	Cash flow (£)	Calculation for PV	PV (to the nearest £)
0	−120,000	$-120{,}000/(1 + 0.1)^0$	−120,000
1	30,000	$30{,}000/(1 + 0.1)^1$	27,273
2	30,000	$30{,}000/(1 + 0.1)^2$	24,794
3	30,000	$30{,}000/(1 + 0.1)^3$	22,539
4	25,000	$25{,}000/(1 + 0.1)^4$	17,075
5	20,000	$20{,}000/(1 + 0.1)^5$	12,418
5	40,000	$40{,}000/(1 + 0.1)^5$	24,837
		Net present value =	8936

The net present value of the project in Example 8.11 is £8936. The initial outlay of £120,000 in effect purchases future returns that are worth £128,936. Because the discount rate used is in effect a threshold of acceptable returns from a project, any opportunity that results in a positive NPV such as in Example 8.11 should be approved and any opportunity producing a negative NPV should be declined.

The calculation of present values of a series of cash flows is an arduous process, so it is easier to use *discount tables*, tables that give values of the discount factor, $1/(1 + r)^n$ for different values of r and n. You can find discount tables in Table 1 on page 617.

Example 8.12

Use Table 1 in Appendix 1 to find the net present values for the company in Example 8.8. Apply a discount rate of 8%.

Gravura Print can purchase two makes of flying-arm stamper. The cash flows involved and their present values are:

Purchase the Smeshnoy machine

End of year	Cash flow (£)	Discount factor	PV (Cash flow * discount factor)
0	−30,000	1.000+	−30,000
1	7000	0.926	6482
2	8000	0.857	6856
3	8000	0.794	6352
4	7000	0.735	5145
5	6000	0.681	4086
5	5000	0.681	3405
		Net present value =	2326

Purchase the Pazorna machine

End of year	Cash flow (£)	Discount factor	PV (Cash flow * discount factor)
0	−30,000	1.000+	−30000
1	12,000	0.926	11112
2	12,000	0.857	10284
3	6000	0.794	4764
4	2000	0.735	1470
5	1000	0.681	681
5	2000	0.681	1362
		Net present value = −327	

+ no adjustment necessary, initial outlays

The company in Example 8.12 should choose the Smeshnoy machine as it will deliver not only a better NPV than the other machine, but an NPV that is positive.

8.2.4 The internal rate of return

A fourth investment appraisal method widely used by businesses is the internal rate of return (IRR). It is closely related to the net present value approach; indeed the internal rate of return is the discount rate at which the total present value of the cash flows into a business arising from an investment precisely equals the initial outlay. To put it another way, the internal rate of return is the discount rate that would result in a net present value (NPV) of zero for the investment. Because the concept of discounting is at the heart of both NPV and IRR they are known as *discounted cash flow* (DCF) methods.

Finding the internal rate of return for a project is a rather hit and miss affair. We try out one discount rate and if the result is a positive NPV we try a higher discount rate; if the result is negative, we try a lower discount rate.

Example 8.13

Find the internal rate of return for the proposed luxury coach purchase by the Budisha Bus Company project in Example 8.6.

We know from Example 8.11 that if we apply a discount rate of 10% the net present value of the project is £8936. Since this is positive the internal rate of return will be higher, so we might try 15%:

End of year	Cash flow (£)	Discount factor	PV (Cash flow * discount factor)
0	−120,000	1.000	−120,000
1	30,000	0.870	26,100
2	30,000	0.756	22,680
3	30,000	0.658	19,740
4	25,000	0.572	14,300
5	20,000	0.497	9940
5	40,000	0.497	19,880
			Net present value = −7360

This negative NPV suggest that the internal rate of return is not as high as 15%. We could try a lower discount rate such as 12% or 13%, but it is easier to use the NPV figures we have for the discount rates of 10% and 15% to approximate the internal rate of return.

Using the discount rate of 10% the NPV for the project was £8936 and using the discount rate of 15% the NPV is −£7360. The difference between these two figures is:

$$8936 - (-7360) = 8936 + 7360 = £16,296$$

This difference arises when we change the discount rate by 5%. The change in NPV per 1% change in discount rate is £16,296 divided by five, roughly £3260. We can conclude from this that for every 1% increase in the discount rate there will be a drop of £3000 or so in the NPV of the project. The NPV at the discount rate of 10% was just under £9000 so the discount rate that will yield an NPV of zero is about 13%.

Often it is sufficient to find an approximate value of the IRR, as we have done in Example 8.13. If you need a precise value you can try several discount rates and plot them against the resulting NPV figures for the project.

Example 8.14

The net present values for the coach purchase by the Budisha Bus Company were calculated using different discount rates. The results are:

Discount rate	Net present value (£)
10%	8936
12%	1980
13%	−1265
15%	−7360

Plot these and use the graph to estimate the internal rate of return for the project.

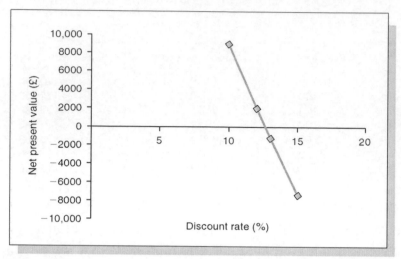

Figure 8.1
Net present values and discount rates in Example 8.14

Look carefully at Figure 8.1 and you will see that the plotted line crosses the horizontal axis about midway between 10 and 15. This suggests that the internal rate of return for the project, the discount rate that produces a zero net present value, is about 12.5%.

The result we obtained in Example 8.14 could be used to assess the coach purchase in comparison with other investment opportunities open to the company, or perhaps the cost of borrowing the money to make the investment, if they needed to do so. In general, the higher the internal rate of return, the more attractive the project.

The internal rate of return and the net present value methods of investment appraisal are similar in that they summarize all the cash flows associated with a venture and are therefore superior to the payback method. They also take the time value of money into account and are therefore superior to the accounting rate of return approach.

The drawback of the internal rate of return technique compared to the net present value method is that the IRR is an interest rate, a relative amount, which unlike the NPV gives no idea of the scale of the cash flows involved. Both IRR and NPV are rather laborious to calculate. Companies may well use the fairly basic approach of the payback period as the threshold that any proposed investment must meet, and then use either NPV or IRR to select from those that do.

At this point you may find it useful to try **Review Questions 8.13 to 8.20** at the end of the chapter.

If you want to find out more about investment appraisal, you will probably find Drury (2000) helpful.

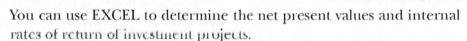

8.3 Using the technology: investment appraisal in EXCEL

You can use EXCEL to determine the net present values and internal rates of return of investment projects.

To obtain the net present value of a project enter the discount rate you wish to use followed by the initial outlay, as a negative amount, then the annual cash flows from the venture into a single column of the spreadsheet. We would enter the data from Example 8.11 in the following way:

	A	B	C
1	0.1		
2	120000		
3	30000		
4	30000		
5	30000		
6	25000		
7	60000		

Note that cell A7 contains the total cash flow in at the end of the fifth year, the sum of the £20,000 net profit from operating the coach and the £40,000 the company expects to sell the coach for at the end of the fifth year.

Once you have entered the data click on the empty cell A8 then click in the formula bar and type in:

$$= NPV(A1, A3:A7) + A2$$

Press **Enter** or click the green √ button to the left of the formula bar to the right of f_x in the upper part of the screen and the net present value figure, £8936.18, should appear in cell A8. The answer we reached in Example 8.11 was £8936. The small difference is the result of rounding.

For an internal rate of return the procedure is very similar, except that we do not enter a discount rate as we do for a net present value. The data for the Budisha Bus Company might be entered as overleaf.

Click in cell A7 then click in the formula bar. Type = IRR(A1:A6) in the formula bar then click the green tick to the left of the formula bar

	A	B	C
1	−120000		
2	30000		
3	30000		
4	30000		
5	25000		
6	60000		

and 13%, the internal rate of return to the nearest per cent, should appear in cell A7.

8.4 Road test: Do they really use investment appraisal?

The origins of the discounting methods of investment appraisal, net present value and internal rate of return go back some time. Parker (1968) identifies the concept of present value in the appendix to a set of interest tables published by the Dutch mathematician Simon Stevin in 1582. Tables like those produced by Stevin were used extensively by the banking and insurance companies of the time.

Discounting in the assessment of industrial as against financial investment begin considerably later, and specifically in the UK railway industry. Many pioneers, such as Brunel, assumed that once built, railways would last so long that there was no need to worry about investing in the replacement and upgrading of track. Within twenty or so years of the first passenger railway journeys it was clear to Captain Mark Huish, General Manager of the London and North Western Railway, that as locomotives and wagons became heavier, trains longer and journeys more frequent the original track was wearing out faster than anticipated. In 1853 Huish and two colleagues produced a report on the investment needs the company ought to address. In making their calculations they determined

> the annual reserve which, at either 4 or 4½ per cent compound interest, would be necessary in order to reproduce, at the end of the period, the total amount required to restore the [rail]road. (Huish *et al.*, 1853, p. 273)

Rail companies had to make large-scale investments that paid off over long periods. Weighing up the returns against the original investment was no simple matter. Similar concerns arose in the South African gold mining industry in the early twentieth century. Frankel reported that:

> The present value criterion was applied in the first attempt to measure the return to capital invested in the Witwatersrand gold mining industry [...] on behalf of the Mining Industry Commission of 1907/8. (Frankel, 1967, p. 10)

Later in the twentieth century engineers working in capital-intensive industries, primarily oil and chemicals, developed and applied discounting approaches to investment decisions. Johnson and Kaplan (1991) refer to three major US oil companies (ARCO, Mobil and Standard Oil of Indiana) where this occurred, and Weaver and Reilly (1956) of the Atlas Powder Company of Delaware were advocates in the chemical industry.

Recent surveys of company practice suggest that both net present value and internal rate of return are widely used. In his 1992 survey of UK companies Pike (1996) discovered that 81% used internal rate of return and 74% used net present value. The equivalent figures in his survey of usage in 1980 were 57% and 39% respectively.

In a study of large US industrial companies Klammer *et al.* (1991) found that the great majority (80% or so) used discounting in appraising investment in the expansion of existing operations and in the setting up of new operations and operations abroad.

Review questions

Answers to these questions, including fully worked solutions to the Key questions marked with an asterisk (*), are on pages 649–651.

8.1   An oil refining company buys crude oil to process in its refineries. The price they have paid per barrel has been:

Year	1997	1999	2001	2003
Cost ($)	22	13	28	25

(a) Calculate a simple price index for
     (i) the price in 2003 relative to 1997

(ii) the price in 2001 relative to 1997

(iii) the price in 2003 relative to 1999

(iv) the price in 2001 relative to 1999

(b) Compare your answers to (a) (i) and (ii) with your answers to (a) (iii) and (iv).

8.2*   An office manager purchases regular supplies of paper and toner for the photocopier. The prices of these supplies (in £) over the years 2001 to 2003 were:

	2001	2002	2003
Paper (per 500 sheets)	9.99	11.99	12.99
Toner (per pack)	44.99	48.99	49.99

Calculate a simple aggregate price index for the prices in 2002 and 2003 using 2001 as the base period.

8.3   A pizza manufacturer purchases cheese, pepperoni and tomato paste. The prices of these ingredients in 1999, 2001 and 2003 were:

	1999	2001	2003
Cheese (per kg)	£1.75	£2.65	£3.10
Pepperoni (per kg)	£2.25	£2.87	£3.55
Tomato paste (per litre)	£0.60	£1.10	£1.35

(a) Calculate a simple aggregate price index for the prices in 2001 and 2003 using 1999 as the base period.

(b) What additional information would you need in order to calculate a weighted aggregate price index to measure these price changes?

8.4*   Zackon Associates, international corporate lawyers, use both email and fax to transmit documents. The company accountant has worked out that the price of sending a document by fax has increased from £0.25 in 1998 to £0.45 in 2003. The price of sending a document by email has increased from £0.50 in 1998 to £0.60 in 2003.

In 1998 the company sent 23,000 documents by fax and 1500 documents by email. In 2003 they sent 12,000 documents by fax and 15,000 by email.

(a) Calculate the weighted aggregate price index for the prices in 2003 based on the prices in 1998 using the Laspeyre method.

(b) Calculate the weighted aggregate price index for 2003 with 1998 as the base year using the Paasche method.

(c) Compare the answers you get for (a) and (b). Which method would be more appropriate in this case, and why?

8.5   A cab driver pays for fuel, vehicle servicing and maintenance every 3 months, and an annual operating licence. The prices of these in 2003 and in 1999, together with the quantity of each that was purchased during 1999, are:

	Price in 2003 (£)	Price in 1999 (£)	Quantity bought in 1999
Fuel (litre)	0.76	0.48	4100
Servicing (visit)	115.00	83.00	4
Licence	750.00	500.00	1

(a) Calculate the weighted aggregate price index for the prices in 2003 based on the prices in 1999 using the Laspeyre method.

(b) In 2003 the driver purchased 4000 litres of fuel, had the vehicle serviced 4 times and bought the annual licence. Use these figures to calculate the weighted aggregate price index for 2003 with 1999 as the base year using the Paasche method.

(c) Compare the results to (a) and (b) and advise the driver, who is not good at keeping records, which method of assessing overall changes in costs would be more suitable.

8.6   A textile manufacturer makes casual jackets. The company buys lining fabric, interfacing fabric and outer fabric. These fabrics are cut and machined to make the garments. The prices per metre of these materials in 2001, 2002 and 2003 were:

	2001	2002	2003
Lining	£2.20	£2.30	£2.35
Interfacing	£0.92	£0.95	£1.00
Outer	£6.50	£7.25	£7.95

In 2001 the company purchased 2500 metres of lining fabric, 400 metres of interfacing fabric and 2750 metres of outer fabric. In 2002 these quantities were 2800, 500 and 3200 respectively. In 2003 they were 3000, 500 and 5000 respectively.

(a) Calculate Laspeyre price indices for 2002 and 2003 using 2001 as the base period.

(b) Calculate Paasche price indices for 2002 and 2003 using 2001 as the base period.

(c) Compare your answers to (a) and (b) and account for any differences between the values of the price indices.

8.7   A confectioner buys cocoa, cocoa butter, sugar and milk solids. The prices per kilogram of these ingredients in 1997, 2000 and 2003 were:

	1997	2000	2003
Cocoa	£1.50	£1.45	£1.70
Cocoa butter	£1.30	£1.95	£2.05
Sugar	£0.45	£0.50	£0.55
Milk solids	£0.35	£0.62	£0.68

The quantities that were purchased in 1997 were 7500 kg of cocoa, 4200 kg, of cocoa butter, 12,000 kg of sugar and 5700 kg of milk solids. The purchased amounts of these items in 2000 were 8000 kg, 4000 kg, 13,000 kg and 6000 kg respectively. In 2003 they were 8800 kg, 3100 kg, 15,000 kg and 4500 kg respectively.

(a) Compile Laspeyre price indices for 2000 and 2003 using 1997 as the base year.

(b) Compile Paasche price indices for 2000 and 2003 using 1997 as the base year.

(c) Compare your results for (a) and (b) suggesting reasons for any differences between them.

8.8*   The turnover figures provided in the annual accounts of a large retail grocer over the six years from 1998 to 2003 were:

Year	1998	1999	2000	2001	2002	2003
Turnover (£m)	7022	7101	7350	7844	8249	8598

The values of the Retail Price Index (RPI) for this period were:

Year	1998	1999	2000	2001	2002	2003
RPI	162.9	165.4	170.3	173.3	176.2	181.3

Use the RPI values to deflate the turnover figures so that they are all expressed in 1998 pounds.

8.9   An enthusiast paid £5000 for a classic car in 1993. Since that time the car has been kept carefully and been valued every two years. The valuations were:

Year	1995	1997	1999	2001	2003
Valuation (£)	£5800	£5200	£5500	£6200	£6000

The values of the Retail Price Index (RPI) for these years were:

Year	1995	1997	1999	2001	2003
RPI	149.1	157.5	165.4	173.3	181.3

Use the values of the RPI to adjust the valuations of the car so that they are all expressed in 1993 pounds. The value of the RPI in 1993 was 140.7.

8.10   A media and entertainments company operates two theme parks in two different countries: Dorrogoy and Stoymost. The annual profits of each theme park over the first five years of operations, in millions of units of local currency (the Lukar in Dorrogoy and the Diyengi in Stoymost) were:

	1998	*2003*
Dorrogoy (m Lukars)	46.1	182.2
Stoymost (m Diyengi)	15.2	51.4

The governments of the two countries each monitor the general level of prices using a weighted aggregate price index. Values of these indices for the years 1998 and 2003 are:

	1998	*2003*
Dorrogoy	112.7	281.4
Stoymost	103.4	192.3

(a) Deflate the profits for Dorrogoy so that the profit figures are expressed in 1998 Lukars.

(b) Deflate the profits for Stoymost so that the profit figures are expressed in 1998 Diyengi.

(c) Compare the results you obtain for (a) and (b), and comment on the relative success of the two theme parks over the period 1998 to 2003.

8.11   Select the appropriate definition for each term on the left-hand side from the list on the right-hand side.

(i) a simple price index	(a) uses current period weights
(ii) a Laspeyre price index	(b) an un-weighted index of prices of several items
(iii) the base period	(c) using an index to adjust for inflation
(iv) the Retail Price Index	(d) measures the changes in the price of one item

(v) a Paasche price index

(e) measures changes in the UK cost of living

(vi) deflating

(f) uses base period weights

(vii) a simple aggregate price index

(g) the point of comparison for subsequent prices

8.12   A young aspiring DJ has saved up £4000 to buy the equipment she needs. She anticipates that the equipment will last for five years, after which it will be obsolete and have no disposal value. During these five years she believes she can use it to earn the following amounts, after allowing for her own wages and costs of travelling to clubs and events:

End of year	Net cash flow (£)
1	1200
2	1800
3	2000
4	2000
5	2000

(a) Work out the accounting rate of return for the investment, allowing for depreciation of one-fifth of the cost of the equipment per year.

(b) Find the payback period for the investment.

8.13*   An advertisement offers a time share investment in a luxury apartment in the Algarve region of Portugal. Investors can purchase the use of the apartment for an eight-week period each year to rent out to tourists. The cost of the time share is £15,000 for five years and it is claimed that the net rental income will be £4000 per year.

(a) What is the payback period for the investment?

(b) What is the net present value of the investment to an investor who would otherwise be able to earn 5% on their money?

(c) In the small print of the advertisement it says 'a service charge of £1000 per annum is charged for the cleaning and general maintenance of the property'. Work out how this will alter the net present value of the investment.

8.14   After a bad accident Anton receives a large sum in compensation. He is thinking about using it to invest in a stretch limousine to hire out for special occasions. The cost of the limousine is £100,000. Anton is due to retire in six years, at which stage he thinks he will be able to sell the limousine for £40,000. The net cash inflows for the venture, after allowing for the driver's wages and other direct expenses are:

End of year	Net cash flow (£)
1	10,000
2	15,000
3	20,000
4	20,000
5	20,000
6	15,000

(a) Find the payback period for this venture.

(b) Calculate the net present value using a discount rate of 8%.

8.15   Ricky Sadovnik, a geologist, discovered a deposit of decorative stone during a holiday in Scotland. He wants to establish a quarry to extract the stone and sell it to gardeners. The owner of the land is prepared to allow him to open and operate a quarry on the site for five years for a fee of £150,000. In addition he must landscape the site at the end of the period, at a cost of £50,000. Ricky intends to hire the digging equipment for the quarry. The net cash flows from the sale of the stone are predicted to be:

End of year	Net cash flow (£)
1	30,000
2	50,000
3	60,000
4	60,000
5	60,000

(a) Determine the net present value for this project based on a discount rate of 15%.

(b) Find the net present value using a discount rate of 10% and by comparing this figure to your answer to (a) estimate the internal rate of return for the project.

8.16   A Russian businessman offers a major Japanese car manufacturer an eight-year lease on a disused tank factory in Southern Russia. The company could refit the factory and use it to manufacture low-cost recreational off-road vehicles for the holiday car-hire market in Southern Europe. The total cost of the investment, including the lease and the installation of equipment is $55 m. Once the plant is operational the following net cash flows are expected:

End of year	Net cash flow ($m)
1	8
2	12
3	15
4	20
5	20
6	10
7	10
8	5

At the end of the eighth year the lease would expire. The disposal value of the equipment is likely to be $5 m.

(a) Using a discount rate of 20%, work out the net present value for this proposal.

(b) Work out the net present value applying a discount rate of 15% and estimate the internal rate of return by comparing this to your answer to (a).

8.17   A pub management company acquired a derelict public house when they took over a rival business. They want to renovate it as either a cafe bar offering a wide range of drinks or a family pub concentrating on food. The cost of fitting it out as a cafe bar is £200,000, the cost of making it into a family pub is £300,000. The income anticipated from each of these options (in £000s) is:

End of year	Net cash flow (cafe bar)	Net cash flow (family pub)
1	50	100
2	60	100
3	75	100
4	75	60
5	60	60
6	60	50

The company believes in theme pubs and refits all its sites after six years. They do not expect any of the fixtures and fittings to have a disposal value.

(a) Identify the payback period for each option.

(b) Calculate the net present value of each options using a discount rate of 12%.

8.18   Otto Carr owns a chain of car parks in small towns. He wants to expand his business by leasing a suitable site in a city centre. There are two sites that would be appropriate. There is a six-year lease available on the Markets site for £200,000 and a seven-year lease available on the Riverside site for £300,000. The cost of clearing, marking out and equipping Markets is £120,000. The equivalent figure for Riverside is £100,000. The cash flows (in £000s) arising from these projects are:

End of year	Net cash flow (Markets)	Net cash flow (Riverside)
1	60	120
2	80	120
3	80	80
4	90	80
5	90	40
6	80	40
6	10[†]	
7		40
7		10[†]

[†]disposal value of equipment

(a)　Determine the payback period for each site.

(b)　Using a discount rate of 8% calculate the net present value for each site.

(c)　Which site should Otto acquire and why?

8.19　Screbro Screen Films is an independent company specializing in the speedy production of low-budget films. Currently they have three film proposals and need to select which, if any, to make. The first is an occult thriller, the second a romantic comedy and the third a science fiction feature. The outlay and returns from each of these projects are:

	Net cash flows ($m)		
Year (expense/income)	Occult thriller	Romantic comedy	Science fiction
0 (production)	−5	−4	−6.5
1 (box office)	2	1.5	2
2 (DVD and video)	3	0.5	2
3 (sales to satellite TV stations)	1	2	3
4 (sales to terrestrial TV stations)	1	1	2

Work out the net present value for each film using a discount rate of 14%. Use your results to suggest which films the company should make.

8.20　Lovekey Home Service is new firm set up to provide on-line emergency domestic assistance from plumbers, locksmiths, electricians etc. They need to invest in a website to operate their business. They have been offered three website designs, with different layouts and interactive features, and need to choose which one to purchase. Whichever one they select it would operate for five years then be replaced. The disposal value of the software at the end of this period is zero. The costs and returns for each of the systems (in £000s) are:

End of year	e-mergency	e-ssential	e-xpeditious
0 (outlay)	−60	−80	−100
1	10	15	40
2	30	40	40
3	30	30	30
4	20	20	20
5	20	20	20

Find the net present value of each design using a discount rate of 18% and suggest, with reference to your results, which design the company should choose.

Long distance — analysing time series data

This chapter will help you to:

- identify the components of time series
- employ classical decomposition to analyse time series data
- produce forecasts of future values of time series variables
- apply exponential smoothing to analyse time series data
- use the technology: time series analysis in MINITAB and SPSS
- become acquainted with business uses of forecasting

Organizations collect time series data, which is data made up of observations taken at regular intervals, as a matter of course. Look at the operations of a company and you will find figures such as daily receipts, weekly staff absences and monthly payroll. If you look at the annual report it produces to present its performance you will find more time series data such as quarterly turnover and annual profit.

The value of time series data to managers is that unlike a single figure relating to one period a time series shows changes over time; maybe improvement in the sales of some products and perhaps deterioration in the sales of others. The single figure is like a photograph that captures a single moment, a time series is like a video recording that shows events unfolding. This sort of record can help managers review the company performance over the period covered by the time series and it offers a basis for predicting future values of the time series.

By portraying time series data in the form of a time series chart it is possible to use the series to both review performance and anticipate future direction. If you look back at the time series charts in Figures 5.16 and 5.17 in Chapter 5 you will see graphs that show the progression of observations over time. You can use them to look for an overall movement in the series, a *trend*, and perhaps recurrent fluctuations around the trend.

When you inspect a plotted time series the points representing the observations may form a straight line pattern. If this is the case you can use the regression analysis that we looked at in section 7.2 of Chapter 7, taking time as the independent variable, to model the series and predict future values. Typically time series data that businesses need to analyse are seldom this straightforward so we need to consider different methods.

9.1 Components of time series

Whilst plotting a time series graphically is a good way to get a 'feel' for the way it is behaving, to analyse a time series properly we need to use a more systematic approach. One way of doing this is the *decomposition* method, which involves breaking down or *decomposing* the series into different *components*. This approach is suitable for time series data that has a repeated pattern, which includes many time series that occur in business.

The components of a time series are:

- a *trend* (T), an underlying longer-term movement in the series that may be upward, downward or constant
- a *seasonal* element (S), a short-term recurrent component, which may be daily, weekly, monthly as well as seasonal
- a *cyclical* element (C), a long-term recurrent component that repeats over several years
- an *error* or *random* or *residual* element (E), the amount that isn't part of either the trend or the recurrent components.

The type of 'seasonal' component we find in a time series depends on how regularly the data are collected. We would expect to find daily components in data collected each day, weekly components in data collected each week and so on. Seasonal components are usually a feature of data collected quarterly, whereas cyclical components, patterns that recur over many years, will only feature in data collected annually.

It is possible that a time series includes more than one 'seasonal' component, for instance weekly figures may exhibit a regular monthly fluctuation as well as a weekly one. However, usually the analysis of a time series involves looking for the trend and just one recurrent component.

Example 9.1

A 'DIY' superstore is open seven days every week. The following numbers of customers (to the nearest thousand) visited the store each day over a three-week period:

Week	Day	Number of customers (000s)
1	Monday	4
	Tuesday	6
	Wednesday	6
	Thursday	9
	Friday	15
	Saturday	28
	Sunday	30
2	Monday	3
	Tuesday	5
	Wednesday	7
	Thursday	11
	Friday	14
	Saturday	26
	Sunday	34
3	Monday	5
	Tuesday	8
	Wednesday	7
	Thursday	8
	Friday	17
	Saturday	32
	Sunday	35

Construct a time series chart for these data and examine it for evidence of a trend and seasonal components for days of the week.

If you look carefully at Figure 9.1 you can see that there is a gradual upward drift in the points that represent the time series. This suggests that the trend is that the numbers of customers is increasing.

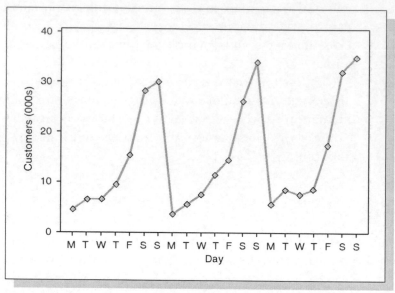

Figure 9.1
Customers visiting the DIY store in Example 9.1

You can also see that within the figures for each week there is considerable variation. The points for the weekdays are consistently lower than those for the weekend days.

Note that in Example 9.1 it is not possible to look for cyclical components as the data cover only three weeks. Neither is it possible to identify error components as these 'leftover' components can only be discerned when the trend and seasonal components have been 'sifted out'. We can do this using classical decomposition analysis.

9.2 Classical decomposition of time series data

Classical decomposition involves taking apart a time series so that we can identify the components that make it up. The first stage we take in decomposing a time series is to separate out the trend. We can do this by calculating a set of *moving averages* for the series. Moving averages are sequential; they are means calculated from sequences of values in a time series.

A moving average (MA) is the mean of a set of values consisting of one from each time period in the time series. For the data in Example 9.1

each moving average will be the mean of one figure from each day of the week. Because the moving average will be calculated from seven observations it is called a *seven-point* moving average.

The first moving average in the set will be the mean of the figures for Monday to Sunday of the first week. The second moving average will be the mean of the figures from Tuesday to Sunday of the first week and Monday of the second week. The result will still be the mean of seven figures, one from each day. We continue doing this, dropping the first value of the sequence out and replacing it with a new figure until we reach the end of the series.

Example 9.2

Calculate moving averages for the data in Example 9.1 and plot them graphically.

Day   M   T   W   T   F   S   S   M   T

The first MA $= (4 + 6 + 6 + 9 + 15 + 28 + 30)/7$ $= 98/7 = 14.000$
The second MA $=$ $(6 + 6 + 9 + 15 + 28 + 30 + 3)/7$ $= 97/7 = 13.856$
The third MA $=$ $(6 + 9 + 15 + 28 + 30 + 3 + 5)/7 = 96/7 = 13.714$ etc.

Week	Day	Number of customers (000s)	7-point MA
1	Monday	4	
	Tuesday	6	
	Wednesday	6	
	Thursday	9	14.000
	Friday	15	13.857
	Saturday	28	13.714
	Sunday	30	13.857
2	Monday	3	14.143
	Tuesday	5	14.000
	Wednesday	7	13.714
	Thursday	11	14.286
	Friday	14	14.571
	Saturday	26	15.000
	Sunday	34	15.000
3	Monday	5	14.571
	Tuesday	8	15.000
	Wednesday	7	15.857
	Thursday	8	16.000
	Friday	17	
	Saturday	32	
	Sunday	35	

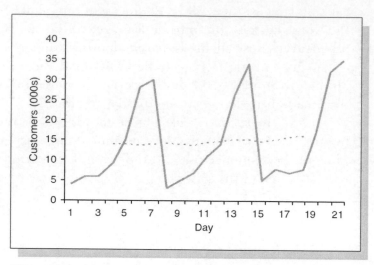

Figure 9.2
The moving averages and series values in Example 9.2

In Figure 9.2 the original time series observations appear as the solid line, the moving average estimates of the trend are plotted as the dashed line.

There are three points you should note about the moving averages in Example 9.2. The first is that whilst the series values vary from 3 to 35 the moving averages vary only from 13.714 to 16.000. The moving averages are estimates of the trend at different stages of the series. The trend is in effect the backbone of the series that underpins the fluctuations around it. When we find the trend using moving averages we are 'averaging out' these fluctuations to leave a relatively smooth trend.

The second point to note is that, like any other average, we can think of a moving average as being in the middle of the set of data from which it has been calculated. In the case of a moving average we associate it with the middle of the period covered by the observations that we used to calculate it. The first moving average is therefore associated with Thursday of Week 1 because that is the middle day of the first seven days, the days whose observed values were used to calculate it, the second is associated with Friday of Week 1 and so on. The process of positioning moving averages in line with the middle of the observations they summarize is called *centring*.

The third point to note is that there are fewer moving averages (15) than series values (21). This is because each moving average summarizes seven observations that come from different days. In Example 9.2 we need a set of seven series values, one from each day of the week, to find a moving average. Three belong to days before the middle day of the seven; three belong to days after the middle. There is no moving average to associate with the Monday of Week 1 because we do not have observations for three days before. There is no moving average to associate with the Sunday of Week 3 because there are no observations after it. Compared with the list of customer numbers the list of moving averages is 'topped and tailed'.

In Example 9.1 there were seven daily values for each week; the series has a *periodicity* of seven. The process of centring is a little more complicated if you have a time series with an even number of smaller time periods in each larger time period. In quarterly time series data the periodicity is four because there are observations for each of four quarters in every year. For quarterly data you have to use four-point moving averages and to centre them you split the difference between two moving averages because the ones you calculate are 'out of phase' with the time series observations.

Example 9.3

Sales of beachwear (in £000s) at a department store over three years were:

Year	Winter	Spring	Summer	Autumn
1	14.2	31.8	33.0	6.8
2	15.4	34.8	36.2	7.4
3	14.8	38.2	41.4	7.6

Plot the data then calculate and centre four-point moving averages for them.

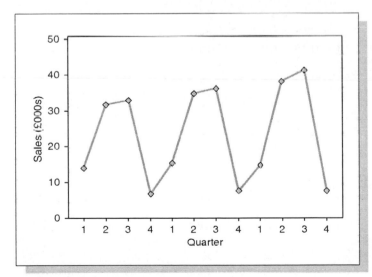

Figure 9.3
Sales of beachwear

First MA $= (14.2 + 31.8 + 33.0 + 6.8)/4$ $= 85.8/4 = 21.450$
Second MA $=$ $(31.8 + 33.0 + 6.8 + 15.4)/4 = 87.0/4 = 21.750$ etc.

Year	Quarter	Sales	4-point MA
1	Winter	14.2	
1	Spring	31.8	
			21.450
1	Summer	33.0	
			21.750
1	Autumn	6.8	
			22.500
2	Winter	15.4	
			23.300
2	Spring	34.8	
			23.450
2	Summer	36.2	
			23.300
2	Autumn	7.4	
			24.150
3	Winter	14.8	
			25.450
3	Spring	38.2	
			25.500
3	Summer	41.4	
3	Autumn	7.6	

The moving averages straddle two quarters because the middle of four periods is between two of them. To centre them to bring them in line with the series itself we have to split the difference between pairs of them.

The centred four-point MA for the Summer of Year 1 $= (21.450 + 21.750)/2 = 21.600$
The centred four-point MA for the Autumn of Year 1 $= (21.750 + 22.500)/2 = 22.125$
and so on.

Year	Quarter	Sales	4-point MA	Centred 4-point MA
1	Winter	14.2		
1	Spring	31.8		
			21.450	
1	Summer	33.0		21.600
			21.750	
1	Autumn	6.8		22.125
			22.500	
2	Winter	15.4		22.900
			23.300	

(*Continued*)

Year	Quarter	Sales	4-point MA	Centred 4-point MA
2	Spring	34.8		23.375
			23.450	
2	Summer	36.2		23.375
			23.300	
2	Autumn	7.4		23.725
			24.150	
3	Winter	14.8		24.800
			25.450	
3	Spring	38.2		25.475
			25.500	
3	Summer	41.4		
3	Autumn	7.6		

At this point you may find it useful to try **Review Questions 9.1 to 9.6** at the end of the chapter.

Centring moving averages is important because the moving averages are the figures that we need to use as estimates of the trend at specific points in time. We want to be able to compare them directly with observations in order to sift out other components of the time series.

The procedure we use to separate the components of a time series depends on how we assume they are combined in the observations. The simplest case is to assume that the components are added together with each observation, y, being the sum of a set of components:

$$Y = \text{Trend component } (T) + \text{Seasonal component } (S) + \text{Cyclical component } (C) + \text{Error component } (E)$$

Unless the time series data stretch over many years the cyclical component is impossible to distinguish from the trend element as both are long-term movements in a series. We can therefore simplify the model to:

$$Y = \text{Trend component } (T) + \text{Seasonal component } (S) + \text{Error component } (E)$$

This is called the *additive* model of a time series. Later we will deal with the *multiplicative* model. If you want to analyse a time series which you assume is additive, you have to *subtract* the components from each other to decompose the time series. If you assume it is multiplicative, you have to *divide* to decompose it.

We begin the process of decomposing a time series assumed to be additive by subtracting the centred moving averages, which are the estimated trend values (T), from the observations they sit alongside (Y). What we are left with are deviations from the trend, a set of figures that contain only the seasonal and error components, that is

$$Y - T = S + E$$

Example 9.4

Subtract the centred moving averages in Example 9.3 from their associated observations.

Year	Quarter	Sales (Y)	Centred 4-point MA (T)	$Y - T$
1	Winter	14.2		
1	Spring	31.8		
1	Summer	33.0	21.600	11.400
1	Autumn	6.8	22.125	−15.325
2	Winter	15.4	22.900	−7.500
2	Spring	34.8	23.375	11.425
2	Summer	36.2	23.375	12.875
2	Autumn	7.4	23.725	−16.325
3	Winter	14.8	24.800	−10.000
3	Spring	38.2	25.475	12.725
3	Summer	41.4		
3	Autumn	7.6		

The next stage is to arrange the $Y - T$ results by the quarters of the year and calculate the mean of the deviations from the trend for each quarter. These will be our estimates for the seasonal components for the quarters, the differences we expect between the trend and the observed value in each quarter.

Example 9.5

Find estimates for the seasonal components from the figures in Example 9.4. What do they tell us about the pattern of beachwear sales?

	Winter	Spring	Summer	Autumn
Year 1			11.400	−15.325
Year 2	−7.500	11.425	12.875	−16.325
Year 3	−10.000	12.725		
Total seasonal deviation	−17.500	24.150	24.275	−31.650
Mean seasonal deviation	−8.750	12.075	12.1375	−15.825

These four figures mean seasonal deviations add up to −0.3625. Because they are variations around the trend they really should add up to 0, otherwise when they are used together they suggest a deviation from the trend. To overcome this problem, we simply divide their total by 4, as there are four seasonal components, and add this amount (0.090625) to each component. After this modification the components should add up to zero:

Adjusted winter component = −8.750 + 0.090625 = −8.659375
Adjusted spring component = 12.075 + 0.090625 = 12.165625
Adjusted summer component = 12.1375 + 0.090625 = 12.228125
Adjusted autumn component = −15.825 + 0.090625 = −15.734375

$$\text{———————}$$
$$0.000000$$

These are the seasonal components (S) for each quarter. They suggest that beach-wear sales are £8659 below the trend in winter quarters, £12,166 above the trend in spring quarters, £12,228 above the trend in summer quarters and £15,734 below the trend in autumn quarters.

We can take the analysis a stage further by subtracting the seasonal components, S from the $Y - T$ figures to isolate the error components, E. That is:

$$E = Y - T - S$$

The T components are what the model suggests the trend should be at a particular time and the S components are the deviations from the trend that the model suggests occur in the different quarters, the T and S values combined are the predicted values for the series. The error components are the differences between the actual values (Y) and the predicted values ($T + S$):

$$E = \text{Actual sales} - \text{Predicted sales} = Y - (T + S)$$

Example 9.6

Find the error components for the data in Example 9.3 using the table produced in Example 9.4 and the seasonal components from Example 9.5.

Year	Quarter	Actual sales (Y)	T	S	Predicted sales ($T + S$)	Error = Actual − Predicted
1	Winter	14.2				
1	Spring	31.8				
1	Summer	33.0	21.600	12.228	33.828	−0.828
1	Autumn	6.8	22.125	−15.734	6.391	0.409
2	Winter	15.4	22.900	−8.659	14.241	1.159
2	Spring	34.8	23.375	12.166	35.541	−0.741
2	Summer	36.2	23.375	12.228	35.603	0.597
2	Autumn	7.4	23.725	−15.734	7.991	−0.591
3	Winter	14.8	24.800	−8.659	16.141	−1.341
3	Spring	38.2	25.475	12.166	37.641	0.559
3	Summer	41.4				
3	Autumn	7.6				

The error components enable us to review the performance over the period. A negative error component such as in the summer quarter of year 1 suggests the store under-performed in that period and might lead them to investigate why that was. A positive error component such as in the spring quarter of year 3 suggests the store performed better than expected and they might look for reasons to explain the success. This type of evaluation should enable the store to improve sales performance because they can counter the factors resulting in poor performances and build on the factors that contribute to good performances.

Occasionally the analysis of a time series results in a very large error component that reflects the influence of some unusual and unexpected external influence such as a fuel shortage or a sudden rise in exchange rates. You can usually spot the impact of such factors by looking for prominent peaks or troughs, sometimes called spikes, when the series is plotted.

The error components terms have another role in time series analysis; they are used to judge how well a time series model fits the data. If the model is appropriate the errors will be small and show no pattern of variation. You can investigate this by plotting them graphically.

Example 9.7

Plot the errors in Example 9.6 and comment on the result.

The errors in Figure 9.4 show no systematic pattern and are broadly scattered.

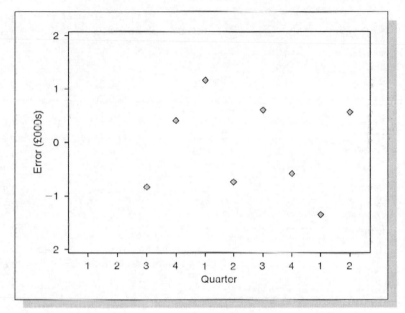

Figure 9.4
The error components for the beachwear sales

There are statistical measures that you can use to summarize the errors; they are called *measures of accuracy* because they help you to assess how accurately a time series model fits a set of time series data. The most useful one is the mean squared deviation (MSD). It is similar in concept to the standard deviation that we met in section 6.2.3 of Chapter 6, but instead of measuring deviation from the mean of a distribution it measures deviation between actual and predicted values of a time series.

The standard deviation is based on the squared differences between observations and their mean because deviations from the mean can be positive or negative, and can thus cancel each other out. In the same way deviations between actual and predicted time series values can be negative and positive, so in calculating the MSD we square the deviations. The MSD is the sum of the squared deviations divided by the number of deviations (n):

$$\text{MSD} = \frac{\sum(\text{Error})^2}{n}$$

Example 9.8

Calculate the MSD of the decomposition model of the beachwear data.
   From Example 9.6:

Year	Quarter	Actual sales (Y)	Predicted	Error = Actual − Predicted	Squared error
1	Winter	14.2			
1	Spring	31.8			
1	Summer	33.0	33.828	−0.828	0.686
1	Autumn	6.8	6.391	0.409	0.167
2	Winter	15.4	14.241	1.159	1.343
2	Spring	34.8	35.541	−0.741	0.549
2	Summer	36.2	35.603	0.597	0.356
2	Autumn	7.4	7.991	−0.591	0.349
3	Winter	14.8	16.141	−1.341	1.798
3	Spring	38.2	37.641	0.559	0.312
3	Summer	41.4			
3	Autumn	7.6			
				Total squared deviation	5.560
				Mean squared deviation (MSD)	0.695

At this point you may find it useful to try **Review Questions 9.7 to 9.9** at the end of the chapter.

There are other measures of accuracy that you may meet. The mean absolute deviation (MAD) is the mean of the absolute values of the errors, which means ignoring any negative signs when you add them up. There is also the mean absolute percentage error (MAPE) which is the mean of the errors as percentages of the actual values they are part of. As with the MSD, the lower the values of these measures, the better the model fits the data.

The MSD result in Example 9.8 is a figure that we can compare to the MSD figures we get when other models are applied to the time series. The best model is the one that produces the smallest MSD.

The model we have applied so far is the additive decomposition model that assumes the components of a time series are added together. This model is appropriate for series that have regular and constant fluctuations around a trend. The alternative form of the decomposition model is the multiplicative model in which we assume that the components of the series are multiplied together. This is appropriate for series that have regular but increasing or decreasing fluctuations around a trend.

To apply the multiplicative model we need exactly the same centred moving averages as we need for the additive model, but instead of subtracting them from the actual series values to help us get to the seasonal components we divide each actual value by its corresponding centred moving average to get a *seasonal factor*. We then have to find the average seasonal factor for each quarter, adjusting as necessary. Once we have the set of seasonal factors we multiply them by the trend estimates to get the predicted series values, which we can subtract from the actual values to get the errors.

Example 9.9

Apply the multiplicative model to the beachwear sales data. Obtain the errors, plot them and use them to calculate the mean squared deviation (MSD) for the model.

The first stage is to calculate the seasonal factors:

Year	Quarter	Actual sales (Y)	Centred 4-point MA (T)	Y/T
	Winter	14.2		
1	Spring	31.8		
1	Summer	33.0	21.600	1.528
1	Autumn	6.8	22.125	0.307
2	Winter	15.4	22.900	0.672
2	Spring	34.8	23.375	1.489
2	Summer	36.2	23.375	1.549
2	Autumn	7.4	23.725	0.312
3	Winter	14.8	24.800	0.597
3	Spring	38.2	25.475	1.500
3	Summer	41.4		
3	Autumn	7.6		

The next stage is to find the mean seasonal factor for each quarter and adjust them so that they add up to 4, since the average should be one, the only factor that makes no difference to the trend when applied to it.

	Winter	Spring	Summer	Autumn
Year 1			1.528	0.307
Year 2	0.672	1.489	1.549	0.312
Year 3	0.597	1.500		
Total	1.269	2.989	3.077	0.619
Mean	0.6345	1.4945	1.5385	0.3095

Sum of the means = 0.6345 + 1.4945 + 1.5385 + 0.3095 = 3.977

To ensure they add up to four, add one-fourth of the difference between 3.977 and 4, 0.00575 to each mean:

Adjusted winter factor $= 0.6345 + 0.00575 = 0.64025$
Adjusted spring factor $= 1.4945 + 0.00575 = 1.50025$
Adjusted summer component $= 1.5385 + 0.00575 = 1.54425$
Adjusted autumn component $= 0.3095 + 0.00575 = \underline{0.31525}$

$$4.00000$$

We can now use these adjusted factors to work out the predicted values and hence find the error terms:

Year	Quarter	Actual sales (Y)	T	S	Predicted sales (T * S)	Error = Actual − Predicted
1	Winter	14.2				
1	Spring	31.8				
1	Summer	33.0	21.600	1.544	33.350	−0.350
1	Autumn	6.8	22.125	0.315	6.969	−0.169
2	Winter	15.4	22.900	0.640	14.656	0.744
2	Spring	34.8	23.375	1.500	35.063	−0.263
2	Summer	36.2	23.375	1.544	36.091	0.109
2	Autumn	7.4	23.725	0.315	7.473	−0.073
3	Winter	14.8	24.800	0.640	15.872	−1.072
3	Spring	38.2	25.475	1.500	38.213	−0.013
3	Summer	41.4				
3	Autumn	7.6				

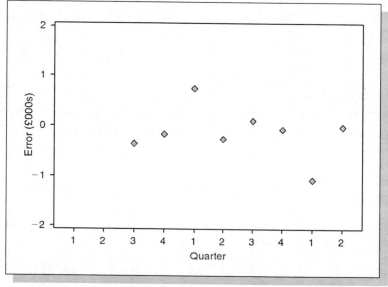

Figure 9.5
The error terms for the multiplicative model

The error terms are plotted in Figure 9.5. The absence of a systematic pattern and the lesser scatter than in Figure 9.4 indicates that the multiplicative model is more appropriate for this set of data than the additive model.

Year	Quarter	Actual sales (Y)	Predicted	Error = Actual − Predicted	Squared error
1	Winter	14.2			
1	Spring	31.8			
1	Summer	33.0	33.350	−0.350	0.123
1	Autumn	6.8	6.969	−0.169	0.029
2	Winter	15.4	14.656	0.744	0.554
2	Spring	34.8	35.063	−0.263	0.069
2	Summer	36.2	36.091	0.109	0.012
2	Autumn	7.4	7.473	−0.073	0.005
3	Winter	14.8	15.872	−1.072	1.149
3	Spring	38.2	38.213	−0.013	0.002
3	Summer	41.4			
3	Autumn	7.6			
			Total squared deviation		1.943
			Mean squared deviation (MSD)		0.243

This MSD is smaller than the MSD for the additive model from Example 9.8, 0.695, confirming that the multiplicative is the more appropriate model.

At this point you may find it useful to try **Review Questions 9.10 to 9.12** at the end of the chapter.

We can use decomposition models to construct forecasts for future periods. There are two stages in doing this. The first is to project the trend into the periods we want to predict, and the second is to add the appropriate seasonal component to each trend projection, if we are using the additive model:

$$\hat{y} = T + S$$

If we are using the multiplicative model we multiply the trend projection by the appropriate seasonal factor:

$$\hat{y} = T * S$$

Here $\hat{y}$ is the estimated future value, and T and S are the trend and seasonal components or factors. You can see there is no error component. The error components are, by definition, unpredictable.

You could produce trend projections by plotting the centred moving averages and fitting a line to them by eye, then simply continuing the line into the future periods you want to predict. An alternative approach that does not involve graphical work is to take the difference between the first and last trend estimates for your series and divide by the number of periods between them; if you have n trend estimates you divide the difference between the first and last of them by $n - 1$. The result is the mean change in the trend per period. To forecast a value three periods ahead you add three times this amount to the last trend estimate, four periods ahead, add four times this to the last trend estimate and so on.

Example 9.10

Use the additive and multiplicative decomposition models to forecast the sales of beachwear at the department store in Example 9.3 for the four quarters of year 4.

The first trend estimate was for the summer quarter of year 1, 21.600. The last trend estimate was for the spring quarter of year 3, 25.475. The difference between these figures, 3.875, is the increase in the trend over the seven quarters between the summer of year 1 and the spring of year 3. The mean change per quarter in the trend is one-seventh of this amount, 0.554.

To forecast the winter quarter sales in year 4 using the additive model we must add three times the trend change per quarter, since the winter of year 4 is three quarters later than the spring quarter of year 3, the last quarter for which we have a trend estimate. Having done this we add the seasonal component for the winter quarter:

$$\text{Forecast for winter, year 4} = 25.475 + (3 * 0.554) + (-8.659) = 18.478$$

Forecasting the three other quarters of year four involves adding more trend change and the appropriate seasonal component:

$$\text{Forecast for spring, year 4} = 25.475 + (4 * 0.554) + 12.166 = 39.857$$
$$\text{Forecast for summer, year 4} = 25.475 + (5 * 0.554) + 12.228 = 40.473$$
$$\text{Forecast for autumn, year 4} = 25.475 + (6 * 0.554) + (-15.734) = 13.065$$

To obtain forecasts using the multiplicative model we project the trend as we have done for the additive model, but multiply by the seasonal factors:

$$\text{Forecast for winter, year 4} = [25.475 + (3 * 0.554)] * 0.640 = 17.386$$
$$\text{Forecast for spring, year 4} = [25.475 + (4 * 0.554)] * 1.500 = 41.537$$
$$\text{Forecast for summer, year 4} = [25.475 + (5 * 0.554)] * 1.544 = 43.610$$
$$\text{Forecast for autumn, year 4} = [25.475 + (6 * 0.554)] * 0.315 = 9.072$$

At this point you may find it useful to try **Review Questions 9.13 to 9.15** at the end of the chapter.

Another method of projecting the trend is to use regression analysis to get the equation of the line that best fits the moving averages and use the equation to project the trend. The regression equation in this context is called the *trend line equation*.

Forecasts like the ones we have obtained in Example 9.10 can be used as the basis for setting budgets, for assessing future order levels and so forth. In practice, computer software would be used to derive them.

9.3 Exponential smoothing of time series data

The decomposition models we considered in the last section are called static models because in using them we assume that the components of the model are fixed over time. They are appropriate for series that have a clear structure. They are not appropriate for series that are more erratic. To produce forecasts for these types of series we can turn to dynamic models such as *exponential smoothing* which use recent observations in the series to predict the next one.

In exponential smoothing we create a forecast for the next period by taking the forecast we generated for the previous period and adding a proportion of the error in the previous forecast, which is the difference between the actual and forecast values for the previous period. We can represent this as:

$$\text{New forecast} = \text{Previous forecast} + \alpha * (\text{Previous actual} - \text{Previous forecast})$$

The symbol α represents the *smoothing constant*, the proportion of the error we add to the previous forecast to adjust for the error in the previous forecast. Being a proportion, α must be between 0 and 1 inclusive. If it is zero then no proportion of the previous error is added to the previous forecast to get the new forecast, so the forecast for the new period is always the same as the forecast for the previous period. If α is one, the entire previous error is added to the previous forecast so the new forecast is always the same as the previous actual value.

When we forecast using exponential smoothing every new forecast depends on the previous one, which in turn depends on the one before that and so on. The influence of past forecasts diminishes with time; mathematically the further back the forecast the greater the power or exponent of an expression involving α that is applied to it, hence the term exponential in the name of the technique.

The lower the value of α we use the less the weight we attach to the previous forecast and the greater the weight we give to forecasts before it.

The higher the value of α, the greater the weight we attach to the previous forecast relative to forecasts before it. This contrast means that lower values of α produce smoother sequences of forecasts compared to those we get with higher values of α. On the other hand, higher values of α result in forecasts that are more responsive to sudden changes in the time series.

Selecting the appropriate α value for a particular time series is a matter of trial and error. The best α value is the one that results in the lowest values of measures of accuracy like the mean squared deviation (MSD).

Before we can use exponential smoothing we need a forecast for the previous period. The easiest way of doing this is to take the actual value for the first period as the forecast for the second period.

Example 9.11

The numbers of customers paying home contents insurance premiums to the Domashny Insurance Company by telephone over the past ten weeks are:

Week	1	2	3	4	5	6	7	8	9	10
Customers	360	410	440	390	450	380	350	400	360	420

Use a smoothing constant of 0.2, produce forecasts for the series to week 11, calculate the mean squared deviation for this model, and plot the forecasts against the actual values.

If we take the actual value for week 1, 360, as the forecast for week 2, the error for week 2 is:

Error (week 2) = Actual (week 2) − Forecast (week 2) = 410 − 360 = 50

The forecast for week 3 will be:

Forecast (week 3) = Forecast (week 2) + 0.2 * Error (week 2)
= 360 + 0.2 * 50 = 370

Continuing this process we can obtain forecasts to week 11:

Week	Acutal	Forecast	Error (Actual − Forecast)	0.2 * Error	Error²
1	360	–	–	–	–
2	410	360.000	50.000	10.000	2500.000
3	440	370.000	70.000	14.000	4900.000
4	390	384.000	6.000	1.200	36.000
5	450	385.200	64.800	12.960	4199.040

(Continued)

Week	Acutal	Forecast	Error (Actual − Forecast)	0.2 * Error	Error²
6	380	398.160	−18.160	−3.632	329.786
7	350	394.528	−44.528	−8.906	1982.743
8	400	385.622	14.378	2.876	206.727
9	360	388.498	−28.498	−5.700	812.136
10	420	382.798	37.202	7.440	1383.989
11		390.238			
					16350.408

The mean squared deviation (MSD) = 16350.408/9 = 1816.712
Figure 9.6 shows the forecasts against the actual values:

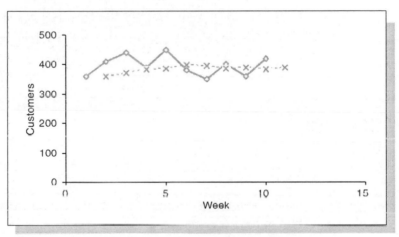

Figure 9.6
Actual values and forecasts of customer calls in Example 9.11

We could try other smoothing constants for the series in Example 9.11 to see if we could improve on the accuracy of the forecasts. If you try a constant of 0.3 you should obtain an MSD of around 1613, which is about the best; a higher constant for this series results in a higher MSD, for instance a constant of 0.5 gives an MSD of around 1674.

At this point you may find it useful to try **Review Questions 9.16 to 9.19** at the end of the chapter.

In this chapter we have concentrated on relatively simple methods of analysing time series data. The field of time series analysis is substantial and contains a variety of techniques. If you would like to read more about it, try Chatfield (1996) and Cryer (1986).

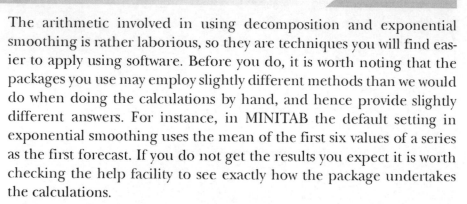

9.4 Using the technology: time series analysis in MINITAB and SPSS

The arithmetic involved in using decomposition and exponential smoothing is rather laborious, so they are techniques you will find easier to apply using software. Before you do, it is worth noting that the packages you use may employ slightly different methods than we would do when doing the calculations by hand, and hence provide slightly different answers. For instance, in MINITAB the default setting in exponential smoothing uses the mean of the first six values of a series as the first forecast. If you do not get the results you expect it is worth checking the help facility to see exactly how the package undertakes the calculations.

9.4.1 MINITAB

If you want decomposition analysis

- Click **Decomposition** on the **Time Series** sub-menu of the **Stat** menu.
- In the command window that appears you need to insert the column location of your data in the window to the right of **Variable:** and specify the **Seasonal length:**, which will be 4 if you have quarterly data.
- Under **Model Type** the default setting is **Multiplicative**, click the button to the left of **Additive** to choose the alternative model. You don't need to adjust the default setting under **Model Components**. Neither do you need to change the default for **First obs. is in seasonal period** unless your first observation is not in quarter 1.
- Click the box to the left of **Generate forecasts** and type in the space to the right of **Number of forecasts** how many you want to obtain. The package will assume that you want forecasts for the periods beginning with the first period after the last actual value you have in your series. If you want the forecasts to start

at any other point you should specify it in the space to the right of **Starting from origin**.

▦ You will see **Results** and **Storage** buttons in the lower part of the **Decomposition** command window. Click the former and you can choose not to have a plot of your results and whether to have a results table as well as a summary.

▦ Clicking the **Storage** button allows you to store results in the worksheet.

▦ When you have made the necessary settings click the **OK** button.

▦ You should see three graph windows appear on the screen. The uppermost two contain plots of the model components. Delete or minimize these and study the third plot, which should show the series, predicted values of the actual observations, forecasts of future values and measures of accuracy. In the output window in the upper part of the screen you should see details of the model.

For exponential smoothing

▦ Click on **Single Exp Smoothing** on the **Time Series** sub-menu in the **Stat** menu.

▦ In the command window that appears type the column location of your data in the space to the right of **Variables:**.

▦ Under **Weight to Use in Smoothing** the default setting is **Optimize**. To specify a value click the button to the left of **Use:** and type the smoothing constant you want to try in the space to the right.

▦ Click **Generate forecasts** and specify the **Number of forecasts** you want.

▦ If you want these forecasts to start at some point other than at the end of your series data type the appropriate period in the space to the right of **Starting from origin**.

▦ If you click the **Options** button you will be able to **Set initial smoothed value**.

▦ If you type 1 in the space in **Use average of first observations** the first forecast will be the first actual value. The default setting is that the average of the first six values in the series is the first forecast. Note that if you choose the **Optimize** option under **Weight to Use in Smoothing** you cannot alter this default setting.

▦ Click the **OK** button when you have made your selections then *OK* in the command window.

▦ You should see a plot showing the series, predicted values of the actual observations, forecasts of future values and measures of accuracy. In the output window in the upper part of the screen you should find details of the model.

9.4.2 SPSS

Before you can obtain decomposition analysis you need to set up the worksheet.

- Enter the package and click **Type in data** under **What would you like to do?** in the initial dialogue box and type your data into a column of the worksheet.
- For decomposition you will need to add a time variable to the worksheet by clicking **Define Dates** on the **Data** pull-down menu. If you have quarterly data click **Years, quarters** on the list under **Cases Are:** in the command window that appears. Note that you should have data for four years.
- Specify the year and the quarter of your first observation in the spaces to the right of **Year:** and **Quarter:** under **First Case Is:** and check that the **Periodicity at higher level** is 4 then click **OK**.
- The addition of new variables will be reported in the output viewer.
- You will see the new variables if you minimize the output viewer.

For decomposition output

- Click **Time Series** on the **Analyze** pull-down menu and choose **Seasonal Decomposition**.
- In the list of variables on the left-hand side of the command window that appears click on the column name of the data you entered originally and click the ▶ to the right. The variable name should now be listed in the space under **Variable(s):**.
- The default model should be **Multiplicative**, click the button to the left of **Additive** for the alternative model.
- You do not need to change the default setting under **Moving Average Weight**.
- Click **OK** and you will see a list of seasonal components appear in the output viewer as well as a key to the names of columns, including one containing the errors that are added to the worksheet.
- Minimize the output viewer and you will see these in the worksheet.

For exponential smoothing

- Enter your data into a column of the worksheet then choose **Time Series** from the **Analyze** pull-down menu and select **Exponential Smoothing**.
- In the command window that comes up click on the column name of the data you entered and click on ▶ to the right. The variable name should now be listed in the space under **Variable(s):**.
- The default model should be **Simple**, if not select it.
- Click the **Parameters** button and in the **Exponential Smoothing: Parameters** window under **General (Alpha)** type your choice of smoothing constant in the space to the right of **Value:**.
- If you would like the package to try a variety of α values click the button to the left of **Grid Search** at this stage.
- Click on the **Continue** button then on **OK** in the **Exponential Smoothing** window. The output viewer will appear with the SSE (sum of squared errors) for the model and the key to two new columns added to the worksheet. One of these contains the errors, the other contains the forecasts.
- If you have used the **Grid Search** facility the output viewer provides you with the SSE figures for the models the package tried and the error and prediction values for the model with the lowest SSE are inserted in the worksheet.

9.5 Road test: Do they really use forecasting?

For most businesses time series data, and forecasting future values from them, are immensely important. If sales for the next period can be forecast then managers can order the necessary stock. If future profits can be forecast, investment plans can be made. It is therefore not surprising that in Kathawala's study of the use of quantitative techniques by American companies 92% of respondents reported that they made moderate, frequent or extensive use of forecasting (Kathawala, 1988).

In a more specific study, Sparkes and McHugh (1984) conducted a survey of members of the Institute of Cost and Management Accountants (ICMA) who occupied key posts in the UK manufacturing sector. They found that 98% of respondents had an awareness or working knowledge of moving averages, and 58% of these used the technique. Also, 92% of their respondents had an awareness or working knowledge of trend analysis, 63% of whom used it. The respondents reported that they used these time series analysis techniques to forecast market share, production and stock control, and financial projections.

Forecasting is particularly important in industries where large-scale investment decisions depend on demand many years into the future. A good example is electricity supply, where constructing new generating capacity may take ten years or so, and minimizing costs depends on forecasting peak demand in the future. In a survey of US electricity supply companies Huss (1987) found that nearly 98% of managers regarded forecasting as either very important or critical for electricity generation planning and 93% regarded it as very important or critical for financial planning.

According to a manager at the Thames Water Authority in the UK, the water industry had similar concerns. Million (1980) explained that justification of investment in new reservoirs depended on forecast water demand 20 years or so into the future.

The Corporate Planning Director of the French paper company Aussedat-Rey described decomposition as

---

the oldest and most commonly used approach to forecasting. (Majani, 1987, p. 219)

He shows how decomposition was used to analyse the changes in the consumption of newsprint in France (Majani, 1987, pp. 224–228).

The role of forecasting is not restricted to strategic planning. Zhongjie (1993) outlines the problems of overloading on the Chinese rail network and demonstrates how time series analysis was used to forecast freight traffic at a railway station in southern China in order to promote better utilization rates of freight cars. Sutlieff (1982) illustrates how forecasting emergency jobs at North Thames Gas in the UK enabled the company to plan the workload of its fitters more effectively.

A consistent feature of time series data is seasonal variation. Consumer purchasing patterns are highly seasonal, as are levels of activity in the construction business. You will find a rich variety of examples of seasonal fluctuation in both business and other spheres in Thorneycroft (1987).

Review questions

Answers to these questions, including fully worked solutions to the Key questions marked with an asterisk (*), are on pages 652–655.

9.1* The revenue (in £) from newspaper sales at a new service station for the morning, afternoon and evening periods of the first three days of operation are:

	Morning	Afternoon	Evening
Day 1	320	92	218
Day 2	341	101	224
Day 3	359	116	272

(a) Construct a time series chart and examine it for evidence of a trend and recurring components for parts of the day.
(b) Calculate three-point moving averages for the series and plot them on the chart.

9.2 Sales of alcoholic beverages (in £) at an off-licence during the course of three days were:

	Morning	Afternoon	Evening
Day 1	204	450	939
Day 2	261	459	1056
Day 3	315	522	1114

(a) Plot a graph to display the time series.
(b) Calculate three-point moving averages for the series and plot them on the graph.

9.3 A body-piercing and tattoo studio is open each day of the week except Sundays and Mondays. The number of customers visiting the studio per day over a period of three weeks is:

	Tuesday	Wednesday	Thursday	Friday	Saturday
Week 1	5	8	9	18	34
Week 2	4	8	11	22	39
Week 3	7	9	14	21	42

(a) Plot this time series.
(b) Calculate five-point moving averages for the series and plot them on your graph.

9.4 The amounts of gas (in thousands of gigawatt hours) sold to domestic consumers by a regional energy company over three years were:

	Quarter			
	Winter	Spring	Summer	Autumn
Year 1	28	12	7	23
Year 2	27	14	7	24
Year 3	28	13	6	24

(a) Produce a graph to represent these data.

(b) Determine centred four-point moving averages for the time series and plot them on your graph.

9.5   A High Street chemist sells travel first aid packs. The numbers of these sold over three years were:

	Quarter			
	Winter	Spring	Summer	Autumn
Year 1	11	37	61	18
Year 2	13	49	58	16
Year 3	16	53	66	18

(a) Plot a graph to portray the data.

(b) Calculate centred four-point moving averages for the time series and plot them on your graph.

9.6   The quarterly sales (in £000) of greeting cards in a supermarket were:

	Quarter			
	1	2	3	4
Year 1	12.0	14.8	9.6	19.2
Year 2	13.1	16.3	8.2	22.8
Year 3	14.8	18.9	6.9	25.1

(a) Produce a time series plot to show these figures.

(b) Work out centred four-point moving averages for this series and plot them on your graph

9.7*   Using the results from Review Question 9.1 and applying the additive decomposition model:

(a) Determine the recurring components for each part of the day.

(b) Calculate the mean squared deviation (MSD) for the model.

9.8   Draw on your answers to Review Question 9.4 and apply the additive decomposition model to:

(a) Identify the seasonal components for each quarter.

(b) Work out the mean squared deviation (MSD) for the model.

9.9   Use the additive decomposition model and your answers to Review Question 9.5 to:

(a) Ascertain the seasonal components for each quarter.

(b) Compute the mean squared deviation (MSD) for the model.

9.10*   Using the multiplicative model and your answers to Review Question 9.1:
   (a) Evaluate the recurring factors for the parts of the day.
   (b) Calculate the mean squared deviation (MSD) for the model.
   (c) Compare the MSD for this model with your answer to Review Question 9.7 part (b) and say which model is more appropriate for the newspaper sales data.

9.11   Building on your answers to Review Question 9.4, use the multiplicative decomposition model to:
   (a) Find the seasonal factors for each quarter.
   (b) Calculate the mean squared deviation (MSD) for the model.
   (c) By contrasting your answer to part (b) with the MSD for the additive model you obtained for Review Question 9.8 part (b) state which is the better model for the gas consumption series.

9.12   Building on your answers to Review Question 9.5, use the multiplicative decomposition model to:
   (a) Establish the seasonal factors for each quarter.
   (b) Work out the mean squared deviation (MSD) for the model.
   (c) Refer to your answers to part (b) and the MSD for the additive model you obtained for Review Question 9.9 part (b). Which is the better model for these sales data?

9.13*   Basing your work on the answers you obtained to Review Questions 9.1, 9.7 and 9.10, use the more appropriate decomposition model to produce forecasts for the newspaper sales in the morning, afternoon and evening of day 4.

9.14   Referring to your answers to Review Questions 9.4, 9.8 and 9.11, generate forecasts for the gas consumption in the quarters of year 4 using the more appropriate decomposition model.

9.15   Making use of your answers to Review Questions 9.5, 9.9 and 9.12, develop forecasts for the sales of travel packs in the four quarters of the fourth year using the more appropriate decomposition model.

9.16*   A new security system was installed at the Platia Clothing Store eight weeks ago. The numbers of items stolen from the store in the period since are:

Week	1	2	3	4	5	6	7	8
Items stolen	63	56	49	45	51	36	42	37

(a) Use the exponential smoothing model with a smoothing constant of 0.8 to predict values of the series to week 9.

(b) Plot the series and the forecasts on the same graph.

(c) Calculate the mean squared deviation (MSD) for the model.

9.17   In the nine months since new parking regulations were introduced the numbers of vehicles impounded by a city highways department were:

Month	1	2	3	4	5	6	7	8	9
Vehicles	207	246	195	233	218	289	248	292	276

(a) Apply the exponential smoothing model with an alpha value of 0.5 to predict values of the series to the tenth month.

(b) Portray the actual values and the forecasts on the same graph.

(c) Work out the mean squared deviation (MSD) for the model.

9.18   The bookings taken by an airline on the first eight days after a well-publicized aviation accident were:

Day	1	2	3	4	5	6	7	8
Bookings	78	33	41	86	102	133	150	210

(a) Produce predictions up to and including day 9 using the exponential smoothing model with a smoothing constant of 0.3 and calculate the mean squared deviation (MSD) of the errors.

(b) Construct predictions to day 9 using a smoothing constant of 0.6 and compute the MSD of the errors. Is this a better model?

9.19   To minimize the risk of accidents from their activities pigeons nesting in the tunnels of an underground railway system are culled every night. The numbers of birds shot over recent weeks has been:

Week	1	2	3	4	5	6	7	8	9
Birds shot	260	340	190	410	370	280	330	400	450

(a) Generate predictions for weeks 2 to 10 by means of an exponential smoothing model with a smoothing constant of 0.5 and compute the mean squared deviation (MSD) of the errors.

(b) Use a smoothing constant of 0.2, calculate the MSD for this model and comment on whether it is more suitable than the model in (a).

9.20   Select the appropriate definition for each term on the left-hand side from the list on the right-hand side.

(i) a trend component	(a) an actual value minus a predicted value
(ii) an additive model	(b) an underlying movement in a time series
(iii) a moving average	(c) a long-term repeating effect in a time series
(iv) a smoothing constant	(d) decomposition with sums of components
(v) a seasonal factor	(e) a mean of a sequence of time series values
(vi) an error component	(f) decomposition with products of factors
(vii) a multiplicative model	(g) a proportion of an error added into a forecast
(viii) a cyclical component	(h) a short-term repeating effect in a time series

CHAPTER 10

Is it worth the risk? — introducing probability

This chapter will help you to:

- measure risk and chance using probability
- recognize the types of probability
- use Venn diagrams to represent alternatives and combinations
- apply the addition rule of probability: chances of alternatives
- apply the multiplication rule of probability: chances of combinations
- calculate and interpret conditional probabilities and apply Bayes' rule
- construct and make use of probability trees
- become acquainted with business uses of probability

This chapter is intended to introduce you to the subject of probability, the branch of mathematics that is about finding out how *likely* real events or theoretical results are to happen. The subject originated in gambling, in particular the efforts of two seventeenth-century French mathematical pioneers, Fermat and Pascal, to calculate the odds of certain results in dice games.

Probability may well have remained a historical curiosity within mathematics, little known outside casinos and race-tracks, if it were not for the fact that probability has proved to be invaluable in fields as varied as psychology, economics, physical science, market research and medicine. In these and other fields, probability offers us a way of analysing chance and allowing for risk so that it can be taken into account whether we are investigating a problem or trying to make a decision.

Probability makes the difference between facing *uncertainty* and coping with *risk*. Uncertainty is a situation where we know that it is possible that things could turn out in different ways but we simply don't know how probable each result is. Risk, on the other hand, is when we know there are different outcomes but we also have some idea of how likely each one is to occur.

Business organizations operate in conditions that are far from certain. Economic circumstances change, customer tastes shift, employees move to other jobs. New product development and investment projects are usually rather a gamble.

As well as these examples of what we might call normal commercial risk, there is the added peril of unforeseen risk. Potential customers in developing markets may be ravaged by disease, an earthquake may destroy a factory, strike action may disrupt transport etc.

The topics you will meet in this chapter will help you to understand how organizations can measure and assess the risks they have to deal with. But there is a second reason why probability is a very important part of your studies: because of the role it plays in future statistical work.

Almost every statistical investigation that you are likely to come across during your studies and in your future career, whether it is to research consumer behaviour, employee attitudes, product quality, or any other facet of business, will have one important thing in common; it will involve the collection and analysis of a sample of data.

In almost every case both the people who commission the research and those who carry it out want to know about an entire population. They may want to know the opinions of all customers, the attitudes of all employees, the characteristics of all products, but it would be far too expensive or time-consuming or simply impractical to study every item in a population. The only alternative is to study a sample and use the results to gain some insight into the population.

This can work very well, but only if we have a sample that is random and we take account of the risks associated with sampling.

A sample is called a random sample if every item in the population has the same chance of being included in the sample as every other item in the population. If a sample is not random it is of very little use in helping us to understand a population.

Taking samples involves risk because we can take different random samples from a single population. These samples will be composed of different items from the population and produce different results.

Some samples will produce results very similar to those that we would get from the population itself if we had the opportunity to study all of it. Other samples will produce results that are not typical of the population as a whole.

To use sample results effectively we need to know how likely they are to be close to the population results even though we don't actually know what the population results are. Assessing this involves the use of probability.

10.1 Measuring probability

A *probability*, represented by capital *P*, is a measure of the likelihood of a particular result or outcome. It is a number on a scale that runs from zero to one inclusive, and can be expressed as a percentage.

If there is a probability of zero that an outcome will occur it means there is literally no chance that it will happen. At the other end of the scale, if there is a probability of one that something will happen, it means that it is absolutely certain to occur. At the half-way mark, a probability of one half means that a result is equally likely to occur as not to occur. This probability literally means there is a fifty-fifty chance of getting the result.

So how do we establish the probability that something happens? The answer is that there are three distinct approaches that can be used to attach a probability to a particular outcome. We can describe these as the *judgemental, experimental* and *theoretical* approaches to identifying probabilities.

The judgemental approach means evaluating the chance of something happening on the basis of opinion alone. Usually the something is relatively uncommon, which rules out the use of the experimental approach, and doesn't occur within a context of definable possibilities, which rules out the use of the theoretical approach. The source of the opinion on which the probability is based is usually an expert.

You will often find judgemental probabilities in assessments of political stability and economic conditions, perhaps concerning investment prospects or currency fluctuations. You could, of course, use a judgemental approach to assessing the probability of any outcome even when there are more sophisticated means available. For instance, some people assess the chance that a horse wins a race solely on their opinion of the name of the horse instead of studying the horse's record or 'form'.

If you use the horse's form to work out the chance that it wins a race you would be using an experimental approach, looking into the results of the previous occasions when the 'experiment', in this case the horse entering a race, was conducted. You could work out the number of races the horse has won as a proportion of the total number of races it has entered. This is the *relative frequency* of wins and can be used to estimate the probability that the horse wins its next race.

A relative frequency based on a limited number of experiments is only an estimate of the probability because it approximates the 'true' probability, which is the relative frequency based on an infinite number of experiments.

Example 10.1

The horse 'Starikaziole' has won 6 of the 16 races it entered. What is the probability that it will win its next race?

The relative frequency of wins is the number of wins, six, divided by the total number of races, sixteen:

$$\text{Relative frequency} = \frac{6}{16} = 0.375 \text{ or } 37.5\%$$

We can conclude therefore that on the basis of its record, the probability that this horse wins its next race:

$$P(\text{Starikaziole wins its next race}) = 0.375$$

In other words, better than a one-third or a one in three chance.

Of course Example 10.1 is a simplified version of what horse racing pundits actually do. They would probably consider ground conditions, other horses in the race and so on, but essentially they base their assessment of a horse's chances on the experimental approach to setting probabilities.

There are other situations when we want to establish the probability of a certain result of some process and we could use the experimental approach. If we wanted to advise a car manufacturer whether they should offer a three-year warranty on their cars we might visit their dealers and find out the relative frequency of the cars that needed major repairs before they were three years old. This relative frequency would be an estimate of the probability of a car needing major repair before it is three years old, which the manufacturer would have to pay for under a three-year warranty.

We don't need to go to the trouble of using the experimental approach if we can deduce the probability using the theoretical approach. You can deduce the probability of a particular outcome if the process that produces it has a constant, limited and identifiable number of possible outcomes, one of which must occur whenever the process is repeated.

There are many examples of this sort of process in gambling, including those where the number of possible outcomes is very large indeed, such as in bingo and lotteries. Even then, the number of outcomes is finite, the possible outcomes remain the same whenever the process takes places, and they could all be identified if we had the time and patience to do so.

Probabilities of specific results in bingo and lotteries can be deduced because the same number of balls and type of machine are used each time. In contrast, probabilities of horses winning races can't be deduced because horses enter only some races, the length of races varies and so on.

Example 10.2

A 'Wheel of Fortune' machine in an amusement arcade has forty segments. Five of the segments would give the player a cash prize. What is the probability that you win a cash prize if you play the game?

To answer this we could build a wheel of the same type, spin it thousands of times and work out what proportion of the results would have given us a cash prize. Alternatively, we could question people who have played the game previously and find out what proportion of them won a cash prize. These are two ways of finding the probability experimentally.

It is far simpler to deduce the probability. Five outcomes out of a possible forty would give us a cash prize so:

$$P(\text{cash prize}) = \frac{5}{40} = 0.125 \text{ or } 12.5\%$$

This assumes that the wheel is fair, in other words, that each outcome is as likely to occur as any other outcome.

Gambling is a rich source of illustrations of the use of probabilities because it is about games of chance. However, it is by no means the only field where you will find probabilities. Whenever you buy insurance you are buying a product whose price has been decided on the basis of the rigorous and extensive use of the experimental approach to finding probabilities.

At this point you may find it useful to try **Review Questions 10.1 to 10.3** at the end of the chapter.

10.2 The types of probability

So far the probabilities that you have met in this chapter have been what are known as *simple* probabilities. Simple probabilities are probabilities of single outcomes. In Example 10.1 we wanted to know the chance of the horse winning its next race. The probability that the horse wins its next two races is a *compound* probability.

A compound probability is the probability of a compound or combined outcome. In Example 10.2 winning a cash prize is a simple outcome, but winning cash or a non-cash prize, like a cuddly toy, is a compound outcome.

To illustrate the different types of compound probability we can apply the experimental approach to bivariate data. We can estimate compound probabilities by finding appropriate relative frequencies from data that have been tabulated by categories of attributes, or classes of values of variables.

Example 10.3

The Shirokoy Balota shopping mall has a food hall with three fast food outlets; Bolshoyburger, Gatovielle and Kuriatina. A survey of transactions in these establishments produced the following results.

Customer profile	Bolshoyburger	Gatovielle	Kuriatina	Total
Lone	87	189	15	291
Couple	11	5	62	78
Family	4	12	115	131
Total	102	206	192	500

What is the probability that the customer profile is Family?

What is the probability that a transaction is in Kuriatina?

These are both simple probabilities because they each relate to only one variable – customer profile in the first case, establishment used in the second.

According to the totals column on the right of the table, in 131 of the 500 transactions the customer profile was Family, so

$$P(\text{Family}) = \frac{131}{500} = 0.262 \text{ or } 26.2\%$$

which is the relative frequency of Family customer profiles.

Similarly, from the totals row along the bottom of the table, we find that 192 of the transactions were in Kuriatina, so

$$P(\text{Kuriatina}) = \frac{192}{500} = 0.384 \text{ or } 38.4\%$$

which is the relative frequency of transactions in Kuriatina.

If we want to use a table such as in Example 10.3 to find compound probabilities we must use figures from the cells within the table, rather than the column and row totals, to produce relative frequencies.

Example 10.4

What is the probability that the profile of a customer in Example 10.3 is Lone and their purchase is from Bolshoyburger?

The number of Lone customers in the survey who made a purchase from Bolshoyburger was 87 so:

$$P(\text{Lone customer profile and Bolshoyburger purchase}) = \frac{87}{500} = 0.174 \text{ or } 17.4\%$$

It is laborious to write full descriptions of the outcomes so we can abbreviate them. We will use 'L' to represent Lone customers, 'C' to represent Couple customers and 'F' for Family customers. Similarly, we will use 'B' for Bolshoyburger, 'G' for Gatovielle and 'K' for Kuriatina. So we can express the probability in Example 10.4 in a more convenient way.

$$P(\text{Lone customer profile and Bolshoyburger purchase}) = P(L \text{ and } B)$$
$$= 0.174$$

The type of compound probability in Example 10.4, which includes the word 'and', measures the chance of the *intersection* of two outcomes. The relative frequency we have used as the probability is based on the number of people who are in two specific categories of the 'customer profile' and 'establishment' characteristics. It is the number of people who are at the 'cross-roads' or intersection between the 'Lone' and the 'Bolshoyburger' categories.

Finding the probability of an intersection of two outcomes is quite straightforward if we apply the experimental approach to bivariate data. In other situations, for instance where we only have simple probabilities to go on, we need to use the *multiplication rule* of probability, which we will discuss later in the chapter.

There is a second type of compound probability, which measures the probability that one out of two or more alternative outcomes occurs. This type of compound probability includes the word 'or' in the description of the outcomes involved.

Example 10.5

Use the data in Example 10.3 to find the probability that a transaction involves a Couple or is in Kuriatina.

The probability that one (and by implication, both) of these outcomes occurs is based on the relative frequency of the transactions in one or other category. This implies that we should add the total number of transactions at Kuriatina to the total number of transactions involving customers profiled as Couple, and divide the result by the total number of transactions in the survey.

$$\text{Number of transactions at Kuriatina} = 15 + 62 + 115 = 192$$

$$\text{Number of transactions involving Couples} = 11 + 5 + 62 = 78$$

Look carefully and you will see that the number 62 appears in both of these expressions. This means that if we add the number of transactions at Kuriatina to the number of transactions involving Couples to get our relative frequency figure we will double-count the 62 transactions involving both Kuriatina and Couples. The probability we get will be too large.

The problem arises because we have added the 62 transactions by Couples at Kuriatina in twice. To correct this we have to subtract the same number *once*.

$$P(K \text{ or } C) = \frac{(15 + 62 + 115) + (11 + 5 + 62) - 62}{500} = \frac{192 + 78 - 62}{500}$$

$$= \frac{208}{500} = 0.416 \text{ or } 41.6\%$$

The type of compound probability in Example 10.5 measures the chance of a *union* of two outcomes. The relative frequency we have used as the probability is based on the combined number of transactions in two specific categories of the 'customer profile' and 'establishment' characteristics. It is the number of transactions in the union or 'merger' between the 'Couple' and the 'Kuriatina' categories.

To get a probability of a union of outcomes from other probabilities, rather than by applying the experimental approach to bivariate data, we use the *addition rule* of probability. You will find this discussed later in the chapter.

The third type of compound probability is the *conditional* probability. Such a probability measures the chance that one outcome occurs given that, or on *condition* that, another outcome has already occurred.

Example 10.6

Use the data in Example 10.3 to find the probability that a transaction in Gatovielle involves a Lone customer.

Another way of describing this is that given (or on condition) that the transaction is in Gatovielle, what is the probability that a Lone customer has made the purchase. We represent this as:

$$P(L|G)$$

Where '|' stands for 'given that'.

We find this probability by taking the number of transactions involving Lone customers as a proportion of the total number of transactions at Gatovielle.

$$P(L|G) = \frac{189}{206} = 0.9175 \text{ or } 91.75\%$$

This is a proportion of a subset of the 500 transactions in the survey. The majority of them, the 294 people who did not use Gatovielle, are excluded because they didn't meet the condition on which the probability is based, i.e. purchasing at Gatovielle.

At this point you may find it useful to try **Review Questions 10.4 to 10.9** at the end of the chapter.

It is always possible to identify compound probabilities directly from the sort of bivariate data in Example 10.3 by the experimental approach. But what if we don't have this sort of data? Perhaps we have some probabilities that have been obtained judgementally or theoretically and we want to use them to find compound probabilities. Perhaps there are some probabilities that have been obtained experimentally but the original data are not at our disposal. In such circumstances we need to turn to the rules of probability.

10.3 The rules of probability

In situations where we do not have experimental data to use we need to have some method of finding compound probabilities. There are two rules of probability: the addition rule and the multiplication rule.

10.3.1 The addition rule

The addition rule of probability specifies the procedure for finding the probability of a union of outcomes, a compound probability that is defined using the word 'or'.

According to the addition rule, the compound probability of one or both of two outcomes, which we will call A and B for convenience, is the simple probability that A occurs added to the simple probability that B occurs. From this total we subtract the compound probability of the intersection of A and B, the probability that both A and B occur. That is:

$$P(A \text{ or } B) = P(A) + P(B) - P(A \text{ and } B)$$

Example 10.7

Use the addition rule to calculate the probability that a transaction in the food hall in Example 10.3 is at Kuriatina or involves a Couple.

Applying the addition rule:

$$P(K \text{ or } C) = P(K) + P(C) - P(K \text{ and } C)$$

The simple probability that a transaction is at Kuriatina: $P(K) = \dfrac{192}{500}$

The simple probability that a transaction involves a Couple: $P(C) = \dfrac{78}{500}$

The probability that a transaction is at Kuriatina and involves a Couple:

$$P(K \text{ and } C) = \frac{62}{500}$$

So:

$$P(K \text{ or } C) = \frac{192}{500} + \frac{78}{500} - \frac{62}{500}$$

$$= \frac{192 + 78 - 62}{500} = \frac{208}{500} = 0.416 \text{ or } 41.6\%$$

If you compare this answer to the answer we obtained in Example 10.5 you will see they are exactly the same. In this case the addition rule is an alternative means of getting to the same result. In some ways it is more convenient because it is based more on row and column totals of the table in Example 10.3 rather than numbers from different cells within the table.

The addition rule can look more complicated than it actually is because it is called the addition rule yet it includes a subtraction. It may help to represent the situation in the form of a *Venn* diagram, the sort of diagram used in part of mathematics called *set theory*.

In a Venn diagram the complete set of outcomes that could occur, known as the *sample space*, is represented by a rectangle. Within the rectangle, circles are used to represent sets of outcomes.

In Figure 10.1 the circle on the left represents the Kuriatina transactions, and the circle on the right represents the Couple transactions. The area covered by both circles represents the probability that a transaction is at Kuriatina or involves a Couple. The area of overlap represents the probability that a transaction is both at Kuriatina and involves a Couple. The area of the rectangle outside the circles contains transactions that are not at Kuriatina and do not involve Couples.

By definition the area of overlap is part of both circles. If you simply add the areas of the two circles together to try to get the area covered by both circles, you will include the area of overlap twice. If you subtract it once from the sum of the areas of the two circles you will only have counted it once.

The addition rule would be simpler if there were no overlap; in other words, there is no chance that the two outcomes can occur together. This is when we are dealing with outcomes that are known as *mutually exclusive*. The probability that two mutually exclusive outcomes both occur is zero.

In this case we can alter the addition rule:

$$P(A \text{ or } B) = P(A) + P(B) - P(A \text{ and } B)$$

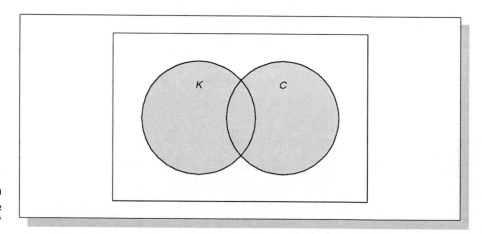

Figure 10.1
A Venn diagram
to illustrate
Example 10.7

to $P(A \text{ or } B) = P(A) + P(B)$

because $P(A \text{ and } B) = 0.$

Example 10.8

One weekend a total of 178 prospective car-buyers visit a car showroom. They are offered the chance to test drive one of three vehicles: the off-road 'Almiak', the 'Balanda' saloon, or the 'Caverza' sports car. When invited to select the car they would like to drive, 43 chose the 'Almiak', 61 the 'Balanda' and 29 the 'Caverza'.

What is the probability that a prospective car-buyer from this group has chosen the 'Balanda' or the 'Caverza'?

We can assume that the choices are mutually exclusive because each prospective buyer can only test drive one car. We can therefore use the simpler form of the addition rule.

For convenience we can use the letter A for 'Almiak', B for 'Balanda' and C for 'Caverza'.

$$P(B \text{ or } C) = P(B) + P(C) = \frac{61}{178} + \frac{29}{178} = \frac{90}{178} = 0.5056 \text{ or } 50.56\%$$

If you read Example 10.8 carefully you can see that although the three choices of car are mutually exclusive, they do not constitute all of the alternative outcomes. That is to say, they are not *collectively exhaustive*. As well as choosing one of the three cars each prospective car-buyer has a fourth choice, to decline the offer of a test drive. If you subtract the number of prospective car-buyers choosing a car to drive from the total number of prospective car-buyers you will find that 45 of the prospective car-buyers have not chosen a car to drive.

A footnote to the addition rule is that if we have a set of mutually exclusive and collectively exhaustive outcomes their probabilities must add up to one. A probability of one means certainty, which reflects the fact that in a situation where there are a set of mutually exclusive and collectively exhaustive outcomes, one and only one of them is certain to occur.

Example 10.9

What is the probability that one of the prospective car-buyers in Example 10.8 chooses the 'Almiak' or the 'Balanda' or the 'Caverza' or chooses not to take a test drive? For convenience we will use the letter N to denote the latter.

The simple probability that a prospective car-buyer picks the 'Almiak' = $P(A) = \dfrac{43}{178}$

The simple probability that a prospective car-buyer picks the 'Balanda' $= P(B) = \dfrac{61}{178}$

The simple probability that a prospective car-buyer picks the 'Caverza' $= P(C) = \dfrac{29}{178}$

The simple probability that a prospective car-buyer declines a test drive $= P(N) = \dfrac{45}{178}$

$$P(A \text{ or } B \text{ or } C \text{ or } N) = \frac{43 + 61 + 29 + 45}{178} = \frac{178}{178} = 1$$

This footnote to the addition rule can be used to derive probabilities of one of a set of mutually exclusive and collectively exhaustive outcomes if we know the probabilities of the other outcomes.

Example 10.10

Deduce the probability that a prospective car-buyer in Example 10.8 declines to take a test drive using the simple probabilities of the other outcomes.

$$
\begin{aligned}
P(\text{Prospective car - buyer declines a test drive}) &= 1 - P(A) - P(B) - P(C) \\
&= 1 - \frac{43}{178} - \frac{61}{178} - \frac{29}{178} \\
&= 1 - 0.2416 - 0.3427 - 0.1629 \\
&= 1 - 0.7472 = 0.2528 \text{ or } 25.28\%
\end{aligned}
$$

The result we obtained in Example 10.10, 0.2528, is the decimal equivalent of the figure of 45/178 that we used for $P(N)$ in Example 10.9.

10.3.2 The multiplication rule

The multiplication rule of probability is the procedure for finding the probability of an intersection of outcomes, a compound probability that is defined using the word 'and'.

According to the multiplication rule the compound probability that two outcomes both occur is the simple probability that the first one occurs multiplied by the *conditional* probability that the second outcome occurs, given that the first outcome has already happened:

$$P(A \text{ and } B) = P(A) * P(B|A)$$

The multiplication rule is what bookmakers use to work out odds for 'accumulator' bets, bets that a sequence of outcomes, like several specific horses winning races, occurs. To win the bet the first horse must win the first race; the second horse must win the second race and so on. The odds of this sort of thing happening are often something like five hundred to one. The numbers, like five hundred, are large because they are obtained by multiplication.

Example 10.11

Use the multiplication rule to calculate the probability that a transaction at the food hall in Example 10.3 involved a Lone customer and was at Bolshoyburger.

$$P(L \text{ and } B) = P(L) * P(B|L)$$

From the table in Example 10.3:

$$P(L) = \frac{291}{500}$$

which is the relative frequency of transactions involving a Lone customer

and

$$P(B|L) = \frac{87}{291}$$

which is the relative frequency of transactions involving Lone customers that were at Bolshoyburger.

So

$$P(L \text{ and } B) = \frac{291}{500} * \frac{87}{291} = 0.582 * 0.299 = 0.174 \text{ or } 17.4\%$$

If you compare this figure to the answer we obtained in Example 10.4 you will see that they are exactly the same.

The multiplication rule can look more complex than it actually is because it includes a conditional probability. We use a conditional probability for the second outcome because the chances of it occurring could be influenced by the first outcome. This is called *dependency*; in other words, one outcome is dependent on the other.

You can find out whether two outcomes are dependent by comparing the conditional probability of one outcome given that the other has happened, with the simple probability that it happens. If the two figures are different, the outcomes are dependent.

Example 10.12

At a promotional stall in a supermarket shoppers are invited to taste ostrich meat. A total of 200 people try it and 122 of them say they liked it. Of these, 45 say they would buy the product. Overall 59 of the 200 shoppers say they would buy the product.

Are liking the product and expressing the intention to buy it dependent?

The simple probability that a shopper expresses an intention to buy is 59/200 or 29.5%.

The conditional probability that a shopper expresses an intention to buy given that they liked the product is 45/122 or 36.9%.

There is a difference between these two figures, which suggests that expressing an intention to buy is dependent on liking the product.

The multiplication rule can be rearranged to provide us with a way of finding a conditional probability:

if
$$P(A \text{ and } B) = P(A) * P(B|A)$$

then if we divide both sides by $P(A)$ we get

$$\frac{P(A \text{ and } B)}{P(A)} = P(B|A)$$

so
$$P(B|A) = \frac{P(A \text{ and } B)}{P(A)}$$

Example 10.13

What is the probability that a transaction at Gatovielle in the food hall in Example 10.3 involves a Lone customer?

$$P(L|G) = \frac{P(L \text{ and } G)}{P(G)}$$

From the table in Example 10.3

$$P(L \text{ and } G) = \frac{189}{500} = 0.378$$

and
$$P(G) = \frac{206}{500} = 0.412$$

so
$$P(L|G) = \frac{0.378}{0.412} = 0.9175 \text{ or } 91.75\%$$

You might like to compare this to the answer we obtained in Example 10.6, which is exactly the same.

If there had been no difference between the two probabilities in Example 10.12 there would be no dependency; that is, the outcomes would be *independent*. In situations where outcomes are *independent*, the conditional probabilities of the outcomes are the same as their simple probabilities. This means we can simplify the multiplication rule when we are dealing with independent outcomes. We can replace the conditional probability of the second outcome given that the first outcome has occurred with the simple probability that the second outcome occurs. That is:

instead of	$P(A \text{ and } B) = P(A) * P(B|A)$
we can use	$P(A \text{ and } B) = P(A) * P(B)$
because	$P(B) = P(B|A).$

Example 10.14

What is the probability that a player who plays the Wheel of Fortune in Example 10.2 twice, wins cash prizes both times?

Five of the forty segments give a cash prize, so the probability of a cash prize in any one game is 5/40.

The conditional probability that a player gets a cash prize in their second game given that they have won a cash prize in their first game is also 5/40. The outcomes are independent; in other words, the result of the second game is not influenced, or conditioned by the result of the first. (If this is not clear because you feel there is a connection, you might ask yourself how the Wheel of Fortune remembers what it did the first time!)

We will use the letter C to represent a cash prize. The first cash prize the player wins can then be represented as C_1, and the second as C_2.

$$P(C_1 \text{ and } C_2) = P(C) * P(C) = \frac{5}{40} * \frac{5}{40} = 0.016 \text{ or } 1.6\%$$

Conditional probabilities are particularly important if you want to work out the chance of a sequence of outcomes involving a limited number of elements. In these cases the selection of one of the elements alters the probabilities of further selections.

Example 10.15

Bella is taking her friend out for the evening but has forgotten to take some cash out of her bank account. She reaches the cash machine, but can't remember the exact sequence of her PIN number. She knows that the digits in her PIN number are 2, 7, 8 and 9. What is the probability that Bella enters the correct PIN number?

There are four digits in Bella's PIN number so the chance that she keys in the correct first digit is one chance in four. The conditional probability that, assuming she has keyed in the correct first digit she then keys in the correct second digit is one in three as there are three possible digits remaining and only one of them is the correct one. The conditional probability that given she gets the first two right she then keys in the correct third digit is one in two as she is left with two digits, one of which is the correct one. The conditional probability that she gets the last one right, assuming that she has keyed in the first correctly is one since there is only one digit left and it must be the correct fourth digit.

$$P(\text{PIN number correct}) = \frac{1}{4} * \frac{1}{3} * \frac{1}{2} * 1 = 0.042$$

At this point you may find it useful to try **Review Questions 10.10 to 10.15** at the end of the chapter.

10.3.3 Bayes' rule

In the last section we looked at how the multiplication rule, which enables us to find the compound probability that both of two outcomes occur, could be rearranged to provide a definition of the conditional probability that the second outcome occurs given that the first outcome had already occurred. That is, if

$$P(A \text{ and } B) = P(A) * P(B|A)$$

then $$P(B|A) = \frac{P(A \text{ and } B)}{P(A)}$$

In this context we normally assume that outcome A occurs before outcome B, for instance the probability that a person buys a car (B) given that they have test driven it (A).

Thanks to the work of the eighteenth-century clergyman and mathematician Thomas Bayes, we can develop this further to say that:

$$P(B \text{ and } A) = P(B) * P(A|B)$$

so $$P(A|B) = \frac{P(B \text{ and } A)}{P(B)}$$

This means that we can find the probability that outcome A happened given that we know outcome B has subsequently happened. This is known as a *posterior*, or 'after-the event' probability. In contrast, the simple probability that outcome *A* happens is a *prior*, or 'before-the event' probability.

The compound probability that both *A* and *B* occur is the same whether it is described as the probability of *A* and *B* or the probability of *B* and *A*. That is:

$$P(A \text{ and } B) = P(B \text{ and } A)$$

The multiplication rule tells us that:

$$P(A \text{ and } B) = P(A) * P(B|A)$$

We can therefore express the conditional probability that A has occurred given that we know B has subsequently occurred as:

$$P(A|B) = \frac{P(A) * P(B|A)}{P(B)}$$

This definition of the posterior probability of an outcome is known as Bayes' rule or Bayes' theorem.

Example 10.16

A financial services ombudsman is investigating the mis-selling of pension schemes some years previously. Some buyers of these pension schemes were sold the schemes on the basis of misleading information, and would have been better off had they made alternative arrangements.

The pension schemes being investigated were provided by one company but actually sold by two brokers, Copilka, who sold 80% of the schemes, and Denarius, who sold 20% of the schemes. Some of the pension schemes sold by these brokers were appropriate for the customers who bought them, but the ombudsman has established that 30% of the schemes sold by Copilka and 40% of the schemes sold by Denarius have turned out to be inappropriate for the customers who bought them.

The ombudsman wishes to apportion liability for compensation for mis-sold pension schemes between the two brokers and wants to do so on the basis of the following:

(a) If a pension scheme was mis-sold what is the probability that it was sold by Copilka?
(b) If a pension scheme was mis-sold what is the probability that it was sold by Denarius?

We will use *M* to represent a pension scheme that was mis-sold, *C* to denote that a pension scheme was sold by Copilka, and *D* to denote that a pension scheme was sold by Denarius.

The first probability that the ombudsman needs to know is $P(C|M)$.

Using Bayes' rule:

$$P(C|M) = \frac{P(C) * P(M|C)}{P(M)}$$

We know that the probability that a pension scheme was sold by Copilka, $P(C)$, is 0.8. We also know that the probability that a pension scheme was mis-sold given that it was sold by Copilka, $P(M|C)$ is 0.3. The only other probability that we need in order to apply Bayes' rule in this case is $P(M)$, the probability that a pension scheme was mis-sold.

A pension scheme that was mis-sold must have been sold by either Copilka or Denarius. The probability that a pension scheme was mis-sold must therefore be the sum of the probability that a pension scheme was mis-sold and it was sold by Copilka and the probability that a pension scheme was mis-sold and it was sold by Denarius. That is:

$$P(M) = P(C \text{ and } M) + P(D \text{ and } M)$$

Although we do not know these compound probabilities we can derive them by applying the multiplication rule:

$$P(C \text{ and } M) = P(C) * P(M|C) = 0.8 * 0.3 = 0.24$$

The probability that a pension scheme was sold by Denarius, $P(D)$ is 0.2, and the probability that a pension scheme was mis-sold given that it was sold by Denarius, $P(M|D)$ is 0.4, so:

$$P(D \text{ and } M) = P(D) * P(M|D) = 0.2 * 0.4 = 0.08$$

so $$P(M) = 0.24 + 0.08 = 0.32$$

We can now work out the first of the two probabilities that the ombudsman needs; the probability that if a pension scheme was mis-sold it was sold by Copilka, $P(C|M)$:

$$P(C|M) = \frac{P(C) * P(M|C)}{P(M)} = \frac{0.8 * 0.3}{0.32} = \frac{0.24}{0.32} = 0.75$$

A mis-sold pension scheme must have been sold by Denarius if it was not sold by Copilka, they are mutually exclusive and collectively exhaustive outcomes. This means that we can deduce that the probability that if a pension scheme was mis-sold it was sold by Denarius, $P(D|M)$ is one less $P(C|M)$:

$$P(D|M) = 1 - 0.75 = 0.25$$

On the basis of these results the ombudsman should apportion 75% of the liability for compensation to Copilka and 25% of the liability for compensation to Denarius.

At this point you may find it useful to try **Review Questions 10.16 and 10.17** at the end of the chapter.

10.3.4 Applying the rules of probability

Although we have dealt separately with different types of probability, rules of probability and so on, when it comes to applying them to solve problems involving sequences of outcomes you may well have to use them together. You may like to look at Example 10.17, which brings together many of the topics that you have met in this chapter to solve an apparently straightforward problem.

Example 10.17

Twenty-five graduates join a company at the same time. During their training programme friendships are established and they decide that when one of them has a birthday they will all dine at a restaurant chosen by the person whose birthday is being celebrated. One of the graduates asks what will happen if two or more of them share a birthday. In response another says that it won't happen because there are only 25 of them and 365 days in the year.

What is the probability that there will be at least one clash of birthdays in a year?

This is quite a complex question because of the sheer variety of ways in which there could conceivably be a clash of birthdays. We could have a clash on the 1st of January, the 2nd of January and so on. Maybe three graduates could share the same birthday? It would be extremely difficult and tedious to work out all these probabilities separately.

In fact we don't need to. One of the phrases you may remember from the discussion of the addition rule was 'mutually exclusive and collectively exhaustive'. Such outcomes rule each other out and have probabilities that add up to one. We can use this here.

We have two basic outcomes: either some birthdays clash or none do. They are mutually exclusive because it is impossible to have both clashes and no clashes. They are collectively exhaustive because we must have either clashes or no clashes.

This makes things easier. We want the probability of clashes, but to get that we would have to analyse many different combinations of outcomes and put their probabilities together. Instead we can work out the probability than there are no clashes and take it away from one. This is easier because there is only one probability to work out.

What is the probability that there are no clashes?

Imagine if there was just one graduate and we introduced the others one at a time. The first graduate can have a birthday on any day; there are no other graduates whose birthdays could clash.

The probability that the second graduate has a birthday on a different day is 364/365 because one day is already 'occupied' by the birthday of the first graduate, leaving 364 'free' days.

The probability that the third graduate has a birthday on a different day to the other two graduates assuming that the first two graduates' birthdays don't clash is 363/365. This is the conditional probability that the third graduate's birthday misses those of both the first and second graduates, given that the birthdays of the first and second graduates don't clash. The number 363 appears because that is the number of 'free' days remaining if the birthdays of the first two graduates don't clash.

Continuing the process, the probability that the fourth graduate's birthday doesn't clash with those of the first three, assuming the first three are on different days, is 362/365. The probability that the fifth graduate's birthday doesn't clash with those of the first four is 361/365, and so on.

Eventually we reach the probability that the twenty-fifth graduate's birthday doesn't clash with those of the other twenty-four, assuming none of the previous twenty-four birthdays clash, which is 341/365.

The probabilities that we now have are probabilities that the birthdays of specific graduates don't clash with those of other specific graduates. What we want is the probability that there are no clashes at all. To get this we have to put these probabilities together. But how? Should we multiply or add?

The answer is that we multiply them together. We want the probability that the second graduate's birthday misses that of the first graduate *and* the third graduate's birthday misses those of the first two and so on.

So
$$P(\text{no clashes}) = \frac{364}{365} * \frac{363}{365} * \frac{362}{365} * \ldots * \frac{342}{365} * \frac{341}{365}$$
$$= 0.4252 \text{ or } 42.52\%$$

This is the probability that there are no clashes, but we wanted to find the probability that there is at least one clash. For this we use the addition rule. It is certain that there is either at least one clash *or* no clash:

$$P(\text{at least one clash}) + P(\text{no clash}) = 1$$

So
$$P(\text{at least one clash}) = 1 - P(\text{no clash})$$
$$= 1 - 0.4252 = 0.5748 \text{ or } 57.48\%$$

10.4 Tree diagrams

If you have to investigate the probabilities of sequences of several outcomes it can be difficult to work out the different combinations of outcomes in your head. It helps if you write down all the different varia-tions, and you may find a Venn diagram a useful way of arranging them in order to work out probabilities of certain types of combinations. But perhaps the best way of sorting out this kind of problem is to use a *tree diagram*.

A tree diagram, which is sometimes called a *probability tree*, repre-sents the different sequences of outcomes in the style of a tree that 'grows' from left to right. Each branch of the tree leads to a particular result.

On the right hand side of the diagram, at the end of each branch, we can insert the combination of outcomes that the sequence of branches represents and, using the multiplication rule, the probability that the sequence of outcomes happens.

Example 10.18

Three friends start Higher Education courses at the same time in the same institution. Armand is studying Architecture, Brendan is studying Banking and Chloe is studying Chemistry. Seventy per cent of students who begin the Architecture course complete it successfully, 80% of students who begin the Banking course complete it successfully and 60% of students who begin the Chemistry course complete it successfully. Construct a tree diagram and use it to work out:

▦   The probability that all three friends successfully complete their courses.
▦   The probability that two of the friends successfully complete their courses.
▦   The probability that only one of the friends successfully completes their course.

We will use *A* to represent Armand, *B* for Brendan and *C* for Chloe. To indicate some-one failing their course we will use the appropriate letter followed by a 'mark, so *A*' rep-resents the outcome that Armand fails his course, whereas *A* alone represents the outcome that Armand completes his course successfully.

The completion rate suggests the probability that Armand passes the Architecture course is 0.7, and given that the 'pass' and 'fail' outcomes are mutually exclusive and col-lectively exhaustive, the probability he fails is 0.3. The probability that Brendan passes the Banking course is 0.8, and the probability that he fails is 0.2. The probability that Chloe passes the Chemistry course is 0.6 and the probability that she fails is 0.4.

In Figure 10.2 the probability that all three pass, $P(ABC)$, is the probability at the top on the right-hand side, 0.336 or 33.6%.

The probability that two of the friends pass is the probability that one of three sequences, either ABC' or $AB'C$ or $A'BC$ occurs. Since these combinations are mutually

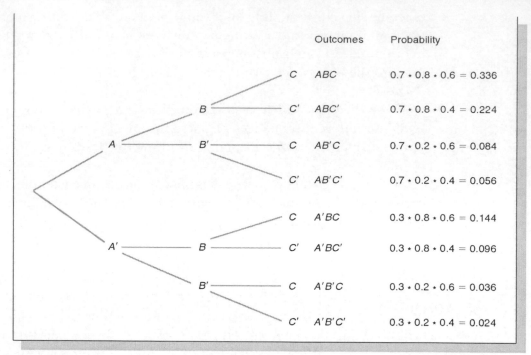

Figure 10.2
Tree diagram for Example 10.18

exclusive we can apply the simpler form of the addition rule:

$$P(ABC' \text{ or } AB'C \text{ or } A'BC) = 0.224 + 0.084 + 0.144 = 0.452 \text{ or } 45.2 \text{ per cent}$$

The probability that only one of the friends passes is the probability that either $AB'C'$ or $A'BC'$ or $A'B'C$ occurs. These combinations are also mutually exclusive, so again we can apply the simpler form of the addition rule:

$$P(AB'C' \text{ or } A'BC' \text{ or } A'B'C) = 0.056 + 0.096 + 0.036 = 0.188 \text{ or } 18.8 \text{ per cent}$$

A tree diagram should include all possible sequences. One way you can check that it does is to add up the probabilities on the right-hand side. Because these outcomes are mutually exclusive and collectively exhaustive their probabilities should add up to one. We can check that this is the case in Example 10.18.

$$0.336 + 0.224 + 0.084 + 0.056 + 0.144 + 0.096 + 0.036 + 0.024 = 1$$

At this point you may find it useful to try **Review Questions 10.18 and 10.19** at the end of the chapter.

10.5 Road test: Do they really use probability?

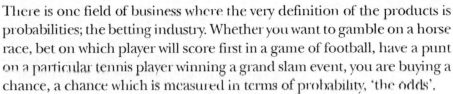

There is one field of business where the very definition of the products is probabilities; the betting industry. Whether you want to gamble on a horse race, bet on which player will score first in a game of football, have a punt on a particular tennis player winning a grand slam event, you are buying a chance, a chance which is measured in terms of probability, 'the odds'.

Another industry delivering products based on probability is the insurance industry. When you buy insurance you are paying the insurer to meet the financial consequences of any calamity that may be visited upon you. When you buy motor insurance, for example, you are paying for the insurance company to cover the costs you might incur if you have an accident. Clearly the company would be rash to offer you this cover without weighing up the chances of your having an accident, which is why when you apply for insurance you have to provide so much information about yourself and your vehicle. If you don't have an accident the company makes a profit from you, if you do it will lose money. Insurance companies have extensive records of motor accidents. They reference the information you give them, your age and gender, the type of car you use, etc. against their databases to assess the probability of your having an accident and base the cost of your insurance on this probability.

The legal context within which businesses operate places obligations on them to ensure their operations do not endanger the health and safety of their workers, and their products are not harmful to their customers or the wider environment. For this reason companies undertake risk assessments. These assessments typically involve using probability to define the risks that their activities may pose. Boghani (1990) describes how probability has been employed in assessing the risks associated with transporting hazardous materials on special trains. North (1990) explains how the process of judgemental evaluation was used to ascertain probabilities of potential damage to forestry production and fish stocks in the lakes of Wisconsin from sulphur dioxide emissions. In the same paper North shows how experimental data were used to assess the health risks arising from the use of a particular solvent in dry-cleaning.

Review questions

Answers to these questions, including fully worked solutions to the Key questions (marked *), are on pages 656–657.

10.1   An electrical goods retailer sold DVD systems to 8200 customers last year and extended warranties to 3500 of these customers. When the retailer sells a DVD system, what is the probability that:

(a) the customer will buy an extended warranty?

(b) the customer will not buy an extended warranty?

10.2   Since it was set up 73,825 people have visited the website of a music and fashion magazine and 6301 of them purchased goods on-line. When someone visits the site what is the probability that:

(a) they do not purchase goods on-line?

(b) they do purchase goods on-line?

10.3   A direct marketing company produces leaflets offering membership of a book club. These leaflets are then inserted into the magazine sections of two Sunday newspapers, the *Citizen* and the *Despatch*, 360,000 leaflets being put in copies of the *Citizen* and 2,130,000 put in copies of the *Despatch*. The company receives 19,447 completed leaflets from *Citizen* readers and 58,193 completed leaflets from *Despatch* readers. What is the probability that:

(a) a *Citizen* reader returns a leaflet?

(b) a *Despatch* reader returns a leaflet?

10.4*   A garage offers a breakdown recovery service for motorists that is available every day of the year. According to their records the number of call-outs they received per day last year were:

Number of call-outs	0	1	2	3	4
Number of days	68	103	145	37	12

What is the probability that:

(a) they receive two call-outs in a day?

(b) they receive two or fewer call-outs in a day?

(c) they receive one or more call-outs in a day?

(d) they receive less than four call-outs in a day?

(e) they receive more than two call-outs in a day?

10.5   Last year 12,966 people opened new accounts at a building society. Of these 5314 were branch-based accounts, 4056 were postal accounts and 3596 were Internet accounts. What is the probability that when a customer opens a new account:

(a) it is a postal account?

(b) it is an Internet account?

(c) it is either branch-based or postal?

10.6* The 120 employees at a factory were asked which would best improve their working life: better promotion prospects, higher pay or more respect from other staff. The results are tabulated below.

	Job type		
Response	*Manual*	*Clerical*	*Managerial*
Better promotion prospects	12	12	3
Higher pay	53	19	2
More respect	7	6	6

(a) What is the probability that an employee selected more respect?

(b) What is the probability that an employee is a clerical worker or selected better promotion prospects?

(c) What is the probability that a manual employee selected higher pay?

(d) What is the probability that an employee selected more respect and is a manager.

(e) What is the probability that a managerial employee selected higher pay?

10.7 A soft drinks company has commissioned an investigation of the level of recognition of one of its brands in various countries that are considered important markets. Random samples of respondents in each country were asked to identify the product from the brand image. The results are:

	Brand recognition	
Country	*Yes*	*No*
Czech Republic	115	29
Estonia	66	35
Hungary	87	61
Poland	131	20

(a) What is the probability that a respondent recognizes the brand?

(b) What is the probability that a respondent is from Hungary?

(c) What is the probability that a respondent recognizes the brand and is from Estonia?

(d) If a respondent is from Poland, what is the probability that s/he recognizes the brand?

(e) Compare your answers to (a) and (d), and comment on whether the country of residence of a respondent and brand recognition are independent.

10.8 A safety agency analysed road traffic accidents involving injury to pedestrians by private cars and produced the following table:

	Type of car		
Degree of injury	*4 * 4*	*Sports*	*Other*
Fatal	8	5	14
Serious	21	9	38
Non-serious	13	7	95

What is the probability that:
(a) an injury to a pedestrian proves fatal?
(b) an accident involved a sports car?
(c) an accident involved a 4 * 4 car or resulted in a non-serious injury?
(d) an accident resulted in serious injury and involved an 'other' type of car?
(e) an accident that involved a 4 * 4 car resulted in a fatal injury? Compare this figure and your answer to (a), and comment on whether the type of car and degree of injury are independent.

10.9 The following survey results show the social class and type of main holiday destination of 250 adult holidaymakers.

	Social class		
Destination	*AB*	*C1C2*	*DE*
UK	13	25	26
The rest of Europe	29	60	23
Other	55	14	5

Use these figures to estimate:
(a) the probability that a holidaymaker belongs to social class *DE*
(b) the probability that a holidaymaker takes a main holiday in the UK
(c) the probability that a holidaymaker is in social class *AB* or takes a main holiday outside Europe
(d) the probability that a holidaymaker takes a main holiday in the rest of Europe or is in social class *DE*

(c) the probability that a holidaymaker is in social class *C1C2* and takes a main holiday in the UK

(f) the probability that a holidaymaker takes a main holiday in the rest of Europe and is in social class *AB*

(g) the probability that a holidaymaker in social class DE takes a main holiday outside Europe

(h) the probability that a holidaymaker in social class DE takes a main holiday in the UK

(i) Compare your answers to (b) and (h). Are social class and main holiday destination independent?

10.10 A final year undergraduate applies for a well-paid job with a large and reputable organization in a highly desirable location. Competition for the job is expected to be fierce. The probability that a candidate is selected for first interview is 0.10. The probability that a candidate is then selected for second interview is 0.4. The probability that a candidate then passes the psychometric test is 0.8. The probability that a candidate then passes the selection procedure at the assessment centre and is offered the job is 0.25. What is the probability that the undergraduate will get the job?

10.11 A commuter's journey to work consists of driving her car to her local train station, taking a train to the city, and catching a bus to her place of work. If her car trip is delayed she misses the train and is late for work. If the train is delayed, she misses the bus and is late for work. If the bus is delayed she is late for work. The probability that her car journey is delayed is 0.05, the probability that the train is delayed is 0.1, and the probability that the bus is delayed is 0.07.

(a) What is the probability that she arrives at work on time?

(b) What is the probability that she is late for work?

(c) What is the probability that she is late for work because the bus is delayed?

10.12* Declan, Emily and Farid each intend to start their own business after leaving college. Declan wants to start a computer software company, Emily intends to open a recruitment agency, and Farid would like to launch a graphic design business. According to available evidence 60% of computer software companies, 75% of recruitment agencies, and 80% of graphic design businesses fail within their first trading year. What is the probability that:

(a) the businesses that Declan, Emily and Farid start all stay in operation for at least a year?

(b) the businesses that two of them start are still trading after a year?

(c) all three businesses fail within a year?

10.13 Two friends have a favourite compilation *CD* that contains some of their all-time favourite tracks. There are 20 tracks on the album. Sam likes five tracks and Chris likes six other tracks. If they program their *CD* player to play three tracks selected at random from the album, and assuming that the *CD* player can only select a track once, what is:

(a) the probability that none of their favourites is selected?

(b) the probability that at least one of Sam's favourites is selected?

(c) the probability that at least one of Chris' favourites is selected?

10.14 Every morning Jack makes tea for the other five people in his section. Two of them take sugar. Jack always forgets which teas he has sugared. One of the two senior members of the section, Alicia, takes sugar in her tea; the other, Bashir, does not. If Jack takes tea first to Alicia and then to Bashir, what is the probability that:

(a) he gives them both the right tea?

(b) he gets one wrong?

(c) he gets both wrong?

10.15 As a result of flood damage a supermarket has a very large stock of tins without labels. Forty per cent of the tins contain soup, 30% contain carrots, 25% contain raspberries and 5% contain asparagus. The tins are to be offered for sale at three for 50 pence. If a customer buys three tins estimate the probability that:

(a) none of the tins contains asparagus?

(b) all three tins contain soup?

(c) one tin contains raspberries?

(d) two tins contain carrots?

(e) the contents of the three tins are different?

10.16 Florrie's Fashion Store and Mary's market stall both sell a particular style of sweatshirt. They are the only outlets for the garment in the area, with Florrie's accounting for 70% of the total number sold and Mary's accounting for the remainder. Unfortunately colour dye that faded prematurely was used to manufacture the first batches of the product. The supplier estimates that 15% of the stock supplied to Florrie and 25% of the stock supplied to Mary have this problem. Use Bayes' rule to find the probability that if a sweatshirt is defective it was sold by Mary.

10.17 The Strachovania Insurance Company offers quotations for motor insurance by telephone. The company employs permanent staff to do this work but as a result of a dramatic rise in the number of telephone enquiries 35% of quotations are provided by temporary staff. Unfortunately 22% of the quotations provided by temporary staff prove to be wrong, compared to the 8% of the quotations provided by full-time staff that turn out to be wrong. Under the contract with the agency supplying the temporary staff, the agency will pay a proportion of the total costs of mistakes based on the proportion of them that are made by the temporary staff. Use Bayes' rule to determine the probability that if a mistake has been it has been made by one of the temporary staff and use it to suggest what proportion of the total costs of mistakes the agency should pay.

10.18 Thursday, Friday and Saturday are the busiest nights at the Jopper bar. Police records show that on 12 of the last 50 Thursdays, 15 of the last 50 Fridays, and 16 of the last 50 Saturdays they were summoned to deal with a disturbance at the bar. Construct a tree diagram and use it to find the probability that over the next Thursday, Friday and Saturday nights there will be:

(a) no trouble

(b) trouble on Thursday only

(c) trouble on one night only

(d) trouble on Friday and Saturday only

(e) trouble on two nights only

Assume that events on any one night are independent of events on any other night.

10.19 You win a prize in a raffle. The prize, donated by an airline, consists of three return tickets to a destination in Africa; Cairo, Dar-es-salaam and Entebbe. The seats you are allocated on the journeys will be either Business or Economy, the only seat types the airline offers, and will be picked at random by the airline. The flight to Cairo has 200 seats, 50 of which are Business. The flight to Dar-es-salaam has 300 seats, 90 of which are Business. The flight to Entebbe has 150 seats, of which 60 are Business. Assuming that if you are allocated a Business seat it is for both the outward and return parts of the journey:

(a) What is the probability that you are allocated a Business seat on none of the journeys?

(b) What is the probability that you are allocated a Business seat on one of the journeys?

(c) What is the probability that you are allocated a Business seat on two or more of the journeys?

10.20 Select the appropriate definition for each term on the left-hand side from the list on the right-hand side.

    (i) compound probability   (a) basing a probability on opinion

   (ii) multiplication rule   (b) outcomes that cannot occur together

 (iii) collectively exhaustive   (c) $P(A \text{ and } B) = P(A) * P(B|A)$

 (iv) dependency   (d) a probability of a single outcome

   (v) judgemental   (e) basing a probability on deduction

 (vi) simple probability   (f) all possible outcomes

(vii) mutually exclusive   (g) $P(A \text{ or } B) = P(A) + P(B) - P(A \text{ and } B)$

(viii) experimental   (h) when $P(B|A)$ is not equal to $P(B)$

 (ix) addition rule   (i) a probability of more than one outcome

  (x) theoretical   (j) basing a probability on evidence

CHAPTER 11

Finding the right way — analysing decisions

This chapter will help you to:

- work out expected values using probabilities
- appreciate attitudes to risk and apply decision rules
- construct decision trees and use them to decide between alternative strategies
- ask 'what if' question about conclusions from decision trees by employing sensitivity analysis
- make use of Bayes' rule to find posterior probabilities for decision trees
- become acquainted with business uses of decision analysis

In the previous chapter we looked at how probability can be used to assess risk. In this chapter we will consider how probability is used in the analysis of decisions. We will begin with *expectation*, the process of multiplying probabilities by the tangible results of the outcomes whose chances they measure to obtain *expected values* of the process or situation under investigation. We will move on to examine various quantitative approaches to taking decisions, including decision trees.

11.1 Expectation

A probability assesses the chance of a certain outcome in general. Expectation is using a probability to produce a predicted or expected value of the outcome.

To produce an expected value we have to apply the probability to something specific. If the probability refers to a process that is repeated, we can predict how many times a certain outcome will occur if the process happens a specific number of times by multiplying the probability by the number of times the process happens.

Example 11.1

The probability that a customer visiting the Kenigar Bookshop makes a purchase is 0.35. If 500 customers visit the shop one day, how many should be expected to make a purchase?

Expected number of customers making a purchase = 0.35 * 500 = 175

The result we obtained in Example 11.1 is a prediction, and like any prediction it will not always be true. We should not therefore interpret the result as meaning that out of every 500 customers that visit the store exactly 175 will make a purchase. What the result in Example 11.1 does mean is that in the long run we would expect that the average number of customers making a purchase in every 500 that visit the store will be 175.

In many business situations outcomes are associated with specific financial results. In these cases the probabilities can be applied to the monetary consequences of the outcomes to produce a prediction of the average amount of money income or expenditure. These types of prediction are called *expected monetary values (EMVs)*.

Example 11.2

A rail operating company incurs extra costs if its long-distance trains are late. Passengers are given a voucher to put towards the cost of a future journey if the delay is between thirty minutes and two hours. If the train is more than two hours late the company refunds the cost of the ticket for every passenger. The cost of issuing vouchers costs the company £500. The cost of refunding all the fares costs the company £6000.

The probability that a train is between thirty minutes and two hours late is 10% and the probability a train is more than two hours late is 2%. What is the expected monetary value of the operating company's extra costs per journey?

To answer this we need to take the probability of each of the three possible outcomes (less than thirty minutes late, thirty minutes to two hours late, more than two hours late) and multiply them by their respective costs (£0, £500 and £6000). The expected monetary value is the sum of these results.

EMV = (0.88 * 0) + (0.1 * 500) + (0.02 * 6000) = 0 + 50 + 120 = 170

The company can therefore expect that extra costs will amount to £170 per journey.

At this point you may find it useful to try **Review Questions 11.1 to 11.4** at the end of the chapter.

11.2 Decision rules

From time to time companies are faced with decisions that are pivotal to their future. These involve developing new products, building new facilities, introducing new working practices and so on. In most cases the managers who take these decisions will not know whether they have made the right choices for many months or years to come. They have to take these decisions against a background of either uncertainty, where they cannot attach a probability to each of the outcomes, or risk, where they can put a probability to each of the outcomes.

In this section we will look at decision rules, techniques available to managers taking decisions under conditions of both uncertainty and risk. All of these techniques assist managers by helping them analyse the decisions and the possible outcomes in a systematic way. The starting point is the *pay-off table* in which the results or pay-offs of the different possibilities or *strategies* that could be chosen are arranged according to the conditions or *states of nature* affecting the pay-off that might prevail.

Example 11.3

Following the success of their CeeZee Seafood fast food restaurant in London, the proprietors, Soll and Perretts, are thinking of expanding the business. They could do this by investing in new sites or by franchising the operation to aspiring fast food entrepreneurs who would pay a fee to Soll and Perretts. The estimated profits for each strategy depend on the future demand for healthy fast food, which could increase, remain stable, or decline. Another possibility for Soll and Perretts is to accept the offer of £20m that a major international fast food company has made for their business. The expected profits are shown in Table 11.1.

Table 11.1
Expected profits (in £m) for Soll and Perretts

Strategy	State of future demand		
	Increasing	Steady	Decreasing
Invest	100	40	−30
Franchise	60	50	0
Sell	20	20	20

The pay-off table in Example 11.3 does not in itself indicate what strategy would be best. This is where decision rules can help. When you apply them remember that the decision you are analysing involves choosing between the available strategies not between the states of nature, which are by definition beyond the control of the decision-maker.

11.2.1 The maximax rule

According to the maximax rule the best strategy is the one that offers the highest pay-off irrespective of other possibilities. We apply the max-imax rule by identifying the best pay-off for each strategy and choosing the strategy that has the best among the best, or *maxi*mum among the *maxi*mum, pay-offs.

Example 11.4

Which strategy should be selected in Example 11.3 according to the maximax decision rule?

The best pay-off available from investing is £100m, from franchising, £50m and from selling, £20m, so according to the maximax rule they should invest.

The attitude of the decision-maker has a bearing on the suitability of deci-sion rules. The maximax rule is appropriate for decision-makers who are risk-seekers; those who are prepared to accept the chance of losing money in gambling on the biggest possible pay-off. However, we should add that the attitude of the decision-maker may well be influenced by the financial state of the business. If it is cash-rich, the maximax approach would make more sense than if it were strapped for cash. In the former case it would have the resources to cushion the losses that may result in choosing the strategy with the highest pay-off.

11.2.2 The maximin rule

If maximax is the rule for the optimists and the gamblers, maximin is for the pessimists and the risk-avoiders. The maximin rule is to pick the strategy that offers the best of the worst returns for each strategy, the *maxi*mum of the *mini*mum pay-offs.

Example 11.5

Which strategy should be selected in Example 11.3 according to the maximin decision rule?

The worst pay-off available from investing is −£30m, from franchising, £0m and from selling, £20m, so according to the maximin rule they should sell.

This approach would be appropriate for a business that does not have large cash resources and would therefore be especially vulnerable to taking a loss. It would therefore make sense to pass up the opportunity to gain a large pay-off if it carries with it a risk of a loss and settle for more modest prospects without the chance of losses.

11.2.3 The minimax regret rule

This rule is a compromise between the optimistic maximax and the pessimistic maximin. It involves working out the opportunity loss or *regret* you would incur if you selected any but the best strategy for the conditions that come about. To apply it you have to identify the best strategy for each state of nature. You then allocate a regret of zero to each of these strategies, as you would have no regret if you had picked them and it turned out to be the best thing for that state of nature, and work out how much worse off you would be under that state of nature had you chosen another strategy. Finally look for the largest regret figure for each strategy and choose the strategy with the lowest of these figures, in doing so you are selecting the strategy with the *mini*mum of the *maxi*mum *regret*s.

Example 11.6

Which strategy should be selected in Example 11.3 according to the minimax regret decision rule?

If they knew that demand would increase in the future they should choose to invest, but if instead they had chosen to franchise they would be £40m worse off (£100m − £60m), and if they had chosen to sell they would be £80m (£100m − £20m) worse off.

These figures are the opportunity losses for the strategies under the increasing demand state of nature.

The complete set of opportunity loss figures are given in Table 11.2.

Table 11.2
Opportunity loss figures (in £m) for Example 11.3

Strategy	State of future demand		
	Increasing	Steady	Decreasing
Invest	0	10	50
Franchise	40	0	20
Sell	80	30	0

From Table 11.2 the maximum opportunity loss from investing is £80m, from franchising, £30m and from selling, £50m. The minimum of these is the £30m from franchising, so according to the minimax regret decision rule this is the strategy they should adopt.

11.2.4 The equal likelihood decision rule

In decision-making under uncertainty there is insufficient information available to assign probabilities to the different states of nature. The equal likelihood approach involves assigning probabilities to the states of nature on the basis that, in the absence of any evidence to the contrary, each state of nature is as likely to prevail as any other state of nature; for instance if there are two possible states of nature we give each of them a probability of 0.5. We then use these probabilities to work out the expected monetary value (EMV) of each strategy and select the strategy with the highest EMV.

Example 11.7

Which strategy should be selected in Example 11.3 according to the equal likelihood decision rule?

In this case there are three possible states of nature – increasing, steady and decreasing future demand – so we assign each one a probability of one-third. The investing strategy represents a one-third chance of a £100m pay-off, a one-third chance of a £60m pay-off and a one-third chance of a −£30m pay-off. To get the EMV of the strategy we multiply the pay-offs by the probabilities assigned to them:

EMV(Invest) = 1/3 * 100 + 1/3 * 60 + 1/3 * (−30) = 33.333 + 20 + (−10) = 43.333

Similarly, the EMVs for the other strategies are:

EMV(Franchise) = 1/3 * 40 + 1/3 * 50 + 1/3 * 0 = 13.333 + 16.667 + 0 = 30

EMV(Sell) = 1/3 * 20 + 1/3 * 20 + 1/3 * 20 = 20

According to the equal likehood approach they should choose to invest, since it has the highest EMV.

At this point you may find it useful to try **Review Questions 11.5 to 11.9** at the end of the chapter.

11.3 Decision trees

The decision rules we examined in the previous section help to deal with situations where there is uncertainty about the states of nature and no probabilities are available to represent the chances of their happening. If we do have probabilities for the different states of nature we can use these probabilities to determine expected monetary values (EMVs) for each strategy. This approach is at the heart of decision trees.

As their name implies, decision trees depict the different sequences of outcomes and decisions in the style of a tree, extending from left to right. Each branch of the tree represents an outcome or a decision. The junctions, or points at which branches separate, are called *nodes*. If the branches that stem from a node represent outcomes, the node is called a *chance node* and depicted using a small circle. If the branches represent different decisions that could be made at that point, the node is a *decision node* and depicted using a small square.

All the paths in a decision tree should lead to a specific monetary result that may be positive (an income or a profit) or negative (a cost or a loss). The probability that each outcome occurs is written alongside the branch that represents the outcome. We use the probabilities and the monetary results to work out the expected monetary value (EMV) of each possible decision. The final task is to select the decision, or series of decisions if there is more than one stage of decision-making, that yields the highest EMV.

Example 11.8

The proprietors of the business in Example 11.3 estimate that the probability that demand increases in the future is 0.4, the probability that it remains stable is 0.5 and the probability that it decreases is 0.1. Using this information construct a decision tree to represent the situation and use it to advise Soll and Perrets.

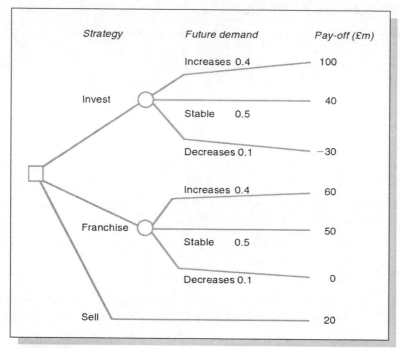

Figure 11.1
Decision tree for Example 11.8

EMV for the Invest strategy $= 0.4 * 100 + 0.5 * 40 + 0.1 * (-30) = £57$m

EMV for the Franchise strategy $= 0.4 * 60 + 0.5 * 50 + 0.1 * 0 = £49$m

EMV for the Sell strategy $= £20$m

The proprietors should choose to invest.

The probabilities of the states of nature in Example 11.8 were provided by the decision-makers themselves, but what if they could commission an infallible forecast of future demand? How much would this be worth to them? This is the value of perfect information, and we can put a figure on it by working out the difference between the EMV of the best strategy and the expected value with perfect information.

This latter amount is the sum of the best pay-off under each state of nature multiplied by the probability of that state of nature.

Example 11.9

Work out the expected value of perfect information for the proprietors of the fast food business in Example 11.3.

We will assume that the proprietors' probability assessments of future demand are accurate; the chance of increasing demand is 0.4 and so on. If they knew for certain that future demand would increase they would choose to invest, if they knew demand was definitely going to remain stable they would franchise, and if they knew demand would decrease they would sell. The expected value with perfect information is:

$$0.4 * 100 + 0.5 * 50 + 0.1 * 20 = £67m$$

From Example 11.8 the best EMV was £57m, for investing. The difference between this and the expected value with perfect information, £10m, is the value to the proprietors of perfect information.

The decision tree we used in Example 11.8 is a fairly basic one, representing just one point at which a decision has to be made and the ensuing three possible states of nature. Decision trees really come into their own when there are a number of stages of outcomes and decisions; when there is a multi-stage decision process.

Example 11.10

Sam 'the Chemise' has a market stall in a small town where she sells budget clothing. Unexpectedly the local football team have reached the semi-finals of a major tournament. A few hours before the semi-final is to be played a supplier offers her a consignment of the team's shirts at a good price but says she can have either 500 or 1000 and has to agree to the deal right away.

If the team reach the final, the chance of which a TV commentator puts at 0.6, and Sam has ordered 1000 shirts she will be able to sell all of them at a profit of £10 each. If the team do not reach the final and she has ordered 1000 she will not sell any this season but could store them and sell them at a profit of £5 each next season, unless the team change their strip in which case she will only make a profit of £2 per shirt. The probability of the team changing their strip for next season is 0.75. Rather than store the shirts she could sell them to a discount chain at a profit of £2.50 per shirt.

If Sam orders 500 shirts and the teams reach the final she will be able to sell all the shirts at a profit of £10 each. If they do not make the final and she has ordered 500 she will not have the option of selling to the discount chain as the quantity would be too small for them. She could only sell them next season at a profit of £5 each if the team strip is not changed and at a profit of £2 each if it is. Sam could of course decline the offer of the shirts.

Draw a decision tree to represent the situation Sam faces.

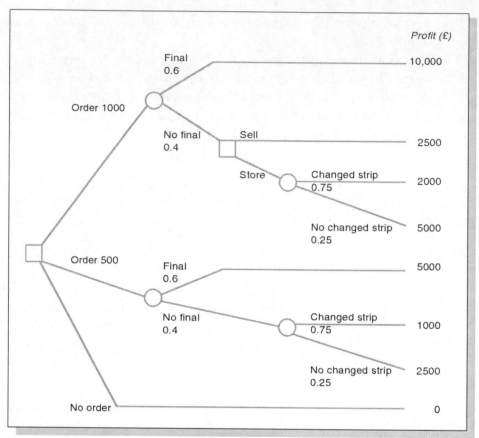

Figure 11.2
Decision tree for Example 11.10

A decision tree like the one in Figure 11.2 only represents the situation; the real point is to come to some recommendation. This is a little more complex when, as in Figure 11.2, there is more than one point at which a decision has to be made. Since the consequences for the first decision, on the left-hand side of the diagram, are influenced by the later decision we have to work back through the diagram using what is called *backward induction* or the *roll back* method to make a recommendation about the later decision before we can analyse the earlier one. We assess each strategy by determining its EMV and select the one with the highest EMV, just as we did in Example 11.8.

Example 11.11

Find the EMV for each decision that Sam, the market trader in Example 11.10, could take if she had ordered 1000 shirts and the team did not make it to the final.

$$\text{EMV(Store)} = 0.75 * 2000 + 0.25 * 5000 = £2750$$

Since this figure is higher than the value of selling the shirts to the discount chain, £2500, Sam should store rather than sell the shirts at this stage.

Once we have come to a recommendation for the later course of action we assume that the decision-maker would follow our advice at that stage and hence we need only incorporate the preferred strategy in the subsequent analysis. We work out the EMV of each decision open to the decision-maker at the earlier stage and recommend the one with the highest EMV.

Example 11.12

Find the EMV for each decision that Sam, the market trader in Example 11.10, could take concerning the offer made to her by the supplier.

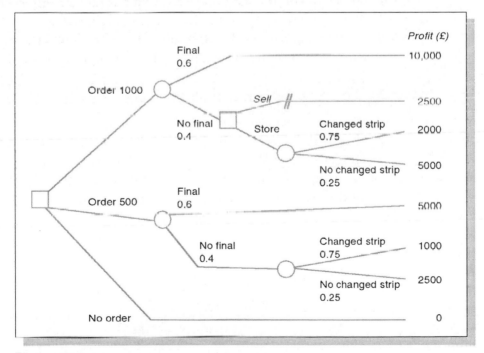

Figure 11.3
Amended decision tree for Example 11.10

We can indicate as shown in Figure 11.3 that the option of selling the stock if she were to order 1000 and the team does not reach the final, should be excluded. This makes the EMV of the decision to order 1000 shirts much easier to ascertain. In working it out we use the EMV of the preferred strategy at the later stage, storing the shirts, as the pay-off if the team were not to make the final.

$$EMV(\text{Order } 1000) = 0.6 * 10000 + 0.4 * 2750 = £7100$$

In identifying the EMV of the decision to order 500 shirts we have to take account of the chance of the team strip being changed as well as the chance of the team reaching the final. This involves applying the multiplication rule of probability; the probability that Sam makes a profit of £2500 is the chance that the team fail to reach the final *and* don't change their strip next season.

$$EMV(\text{Order } 500) = 0.6 * 5000 + 0.4 * 0.75 * 1000 + 0.4 * 0.25 * 2500 = £3550$$

We would recommend that Sam orders 1000 as the EMV for that strategy is higher, £7100, than the EMV for ordering 500, £3550, and the EMV of not making an order, £0.

The probabilities used in decision trees are often little more than educated guesses, yet they are an integral part of the analysis. It is therefore useful to see how the recommendation might change if the probabilities of the relevant outcomes are altered, in other words to see how sensitive the recommendation is to changes in these probabilities. *Sensitivity analysis* involves finding out by how much the probabilities would have to change for a different decision to be recommended.

Example 11.13

In Example 11.11 we recommended that Sam, the market trader in Example 11.10, should store rather than sell the shirts if she had ordered 1000 shirts and the team did not make it to the final. We worked out the EMV that led to this conclusion using the probability that the team would change its strip, 0.75. But what if it changed? At what point would we alter our advice and say she should sell the shirts to the discount chain instead?

If we use p to represent the probability the team strip changes and $1 - p$ to represent the probability it doesn't, then the point at which the sell and store strategies have equal value is when:

$$p * 2000 + (1 - p) * 5000 = 2500$$
$$2000p + 5000 - 5000p = 2500$$
$$-3000p = -2500$$
$$p = \frac{2500}{3000} = 0.833$$

This result suggests that if the probability of the team changing its strip is more than 0.833, then Sam should sell the shirts to the discount chain rather than store them. We can check this by taking a higher figure:

$$\text{EMV(Store)} = 0.9 * 2000 + 0.1 * 5000 = \pounds2300$$

This is lower than the value of selling the shirts to the discount chain, £2500, so if the probability of the team changing its strip were 0.9, Sam should sell the shirts.

The probability in Example 11.13 would not have to change by very much, from 0.75 to 0.833, for our advice to change; the decision is *sensitive* to the value of the probability. If it needed a substantial shift in the value of the probability we would consider the decision to be *robust*.

The probabilities that we have used in the decision trees we have studied so far have been prior, or before-the-event, probabilities, and conditional probabilities. There are situations where we need to include prior, or after-the-event probabilities, which we can work out using the Bayes' rule that we looked at in section 10.3.3 of Chapter 10.

Example 11.14

Karovnick Construction has acquired a piece of land where a disused warehouse currently stands. They plan to build apartments in the shell of the warehouse building. It is a speculative venture which depends on the existing building being sound enough to support the new work. Karovnick's own staff put the probability of the building being sound at 0.5. The company can sell the building for £4m without doing any work on the site or they could go ahead and build.

If the building proves to be sound they will make a profit of £15m, but if it is not sound the extra costs of extensive structural work will result in a profit of only £1m. They could decide at the outset to commission a full structural survey. The firm they would hire to carry this out have a good record, but they are not infallible; they were correct 80% of the time when a building they surveyed turned out to be sound and 90% of the time when a building they surveyed turned out to be unsound. The surveyor's report would only be available to Karovnick, so whatever the conclusions it contains the company could still sell the site for £4m.

We can draw a decision tree to represent this situation:

The decision nodes in Figure 11.4 have been labelled A, B, C and D to make it easier to illustrate the subsequent analysis. Note that although we have included all the pay-offs in this decision tree, the majority of outcomes do not have probabilities. This is because we do not know for instance the probability that the building turns out to be sound given that the surveyor's report predicts the building is sound. This probability

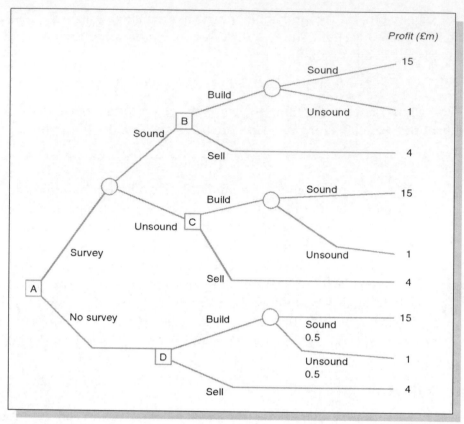

Figure 11.4
Decision tree for Example 11.14

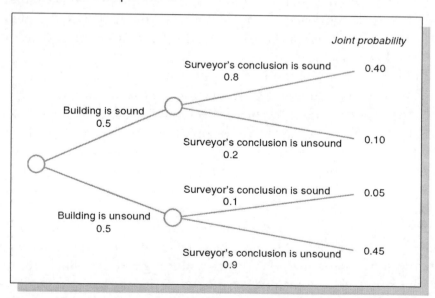

Figure 11.5
Probability tree for Example 11.14

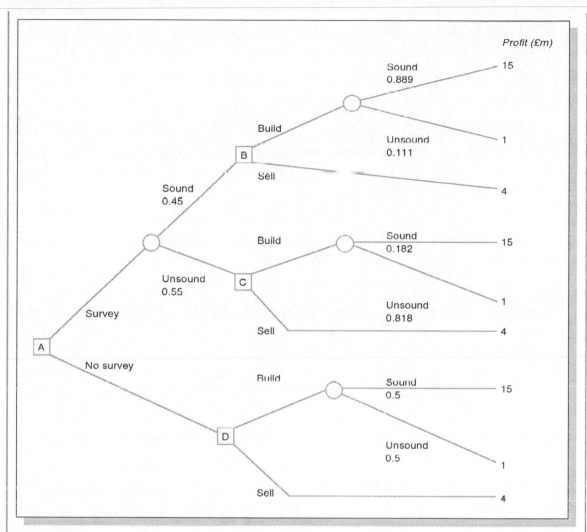

Figure 11.6
Amended decision tree for Example 11.14

depends on the probability that the surveyor predicts the building is sound, which is
either accurate or inaccurate. To help us sort out the probabilities we need we can construct a probability tree:

Using the joint probabilities on the right-hand side of Figure 11.5 we can work out:

$$P(\text{Surveyor's conclusion is sound}) \quad = 0.40 + 0.05 = 0.45$$

$$P(\text{Surveyor's conclusion is unsound}) = 0.10 + 0.45 = 0.55$$

Using Bayes' rule:

$$P(A|B) = \frac{P(B \text{ and } A)}{P(B)}$$

We can work out:

P(Building is sound|Surveyor's conclusion is sound)   = 0.40/0.45 = 0.889

P(Building is unsound|Surveyor's conclusion is sound) = 0.05/0.45 = 0.111

P(Building is sound|Surveyor's conclusion is unsound) = 0.10/0.55 = 0.182

P(Building is sound|Surveyor's conclusion is sound)   = 0.45/0.55 = 0.818

We now have the probabilities we need to complete the decision tree as in Figure 11.6.

We are now in a position to work out the expected monetary values for the decisions represented in the upper part of the diagram by nodes B and C.

At node B EMV(Build) = 0.889 * 15 + 0.111 * 1 = £13.446m

This is much higher than the value of the alternative Sell strategy, £4 m, so if the surveyor finds the building sound, they should Build.

At node C EMV(Build) = 0.182 * 15 + 0.818 * 1 = £3.548m

This is lower than the value of the Sell strategy, £4m, so should the surveyor find the building unsound, they should Sell.

We now need to use the EMVs of the preferred strategies at nodes B and C, Build and Sell respectively, as the pay-offs to work out the EMV for the Survey strategy at node A:

EMV(Survey) = 0.45 * 13.446 + 0.55 * 4 = £8.251m

We need to compare this to the EMV of the alternative strategy at node A, No survey. (At node D the Sell strategy will only yield £4m, so the preferred strategy is to Build.)

EMV(No survey) = 0.5 * 15 + 0.5 * 1 = £8m

Since this is lower than the EMV for the Survey strategy we would advise the company to commission a survey. In the event that the surveyor finds the building sound, they should Build; if the surveyor finds the building unsound, they should Sell.

As a footnote to Example 11.14, you may notice that the EMV figures for the two possible decisions at node A are very close, suggesting that the conclusion is highly sensitive to changes in the probability values. We can interpret the difference between the two figures, £0.251m or £251,000, as the most it is worth the company paying for the surveyor's report.

Although decision trees can be a useful approach to weighing up decisions, they do have some shortcomings as techniques for taking decisions.

Their first weakness is that they are only as good as the information that you put into them. If the probabilities and monetary figures are not reliable then the conclusion is also unreliable. This is an important issue when, as in Example 11.8, the figures are speculative assessments of future events over a considerable period of time.

The second shortcoming is that they take no account of the attitude that the people making the decision have towards risk. For instance, if Soll and Perrets in Example 11.8 had made high profits and were cash-rich they might be more prepared to accept the risk of a loss more readily than if they had made low profits and had a liquidity problem.

The third drawback is that it is difficult to introduce factors that are non-quantifiable or difficult to quantify into the process. For instance, the area where the company in Example 11.14 wants to build may be one in which skilled building workers are in short supply.

Despite these weaknesses decision trees can help to investigate decisions and their consequences, especially when we are interested in the effects of altering some of the figures to see whether the conclusion changes.

At this point you may find it useful to try **Review Questions 11.10 to 11.19** at the end of the chapter.

11.4 Road test: Do they really use decision analysis?

As well as providing an authoritative and detailed coverage of decision analysis Brown, Kahr and Peterson (1974) describe its use in several major US corporations; to determine the scale of pilot production of a new product at Du Pont, to decide which type of packaging was more appropriate for certain grocery products at Pillsbury, to find an optimal pricing and production strategy for a maturing product at General Electric, and identifying a product policy to deal with increasing competition at the Tractor Division of the Ford Motor Company.

The UK confectionery company Cadbury is a good example of a company that launches new products on a regular basis. The decision whether to launch a new product might begin with relatively small-scale consumer testing using samples of the product from a pilot production run. Beattie (1969) explains how decision tree analysis was applied to the next stage in the product launch, deciding whether to proceed directly to a full national launch of the product or to test market the product in a UK region and decide whether or not to go for a full launch on the basis of the performance of the product in the test market. If they went directly to a full launch then, assuming it proved a success, they would earn profits on the product earlier, but they would risk a large financial outlay on full-scale production and promoting the product on a national basis. According to Beattie the main advantage that Cadbury staff gained from using decision tree analysis was that the framework offered a systematic way of examining the problem and investigating it from different perspectives.

The case Phillips (1982) describes stands in marked contrast to the situation the marketing analysts at Cadbury faced. The company produced outboard motors for boats. For a long time the greater part of their revenue was from the sales of a particular engine, which sold in large quantities across the world. When this engine was banned in the USA on the grounds of its failure to meet federal emission constraints, the company had to decide whether to continue producing the engine or to replace it with a new and technologically superior product that had already been designed. The problem was that customers who had valued the reliable old product might be unwilling to accept a new product that was yet to prove to be as robust. A further complication was that a rival company was believed to be about to launch a product with similar specifications but more advanced technology. There were also limited resources available to the company to invest in the manufacturing equipment for making the new product. Phillips recounts the stages involved in the company's use of decision tree analysis, from formulating the problem to using sensitivity analysis to explore the results.

In more recent times the oil and gas industry, especially the exploration and production arm of it, has used decision analysis extensively. The decisions they have to make involve bidding procedures, drilling decisions, when to increase capacity and the length of supply contracts. These decisions have to be taken against a background of fluctuating oil and gas prices and uncertainty about the scale of reserves in new fields. Coopersmith *et al.* (2000) provide an interesting overview of these applications and illustrate the use of decision tree analysis by Aker Maritime Inc., a US manufacturer of offshore platforms, to advise a customer on the selection of the most appropriate deepwater oil production system for a new oilfield off the West African coast. The customer, the operating company, had to decide whether to purchase an adaptable system that could be installed relatively quickly and would enable production to be increased if the reserves were larger than anticipated. If they did this they would produce oil and earn revenue earlier than if they adopted the alternative strategy of drilling more wells to get a better idea of the size of the reservoir of oil in the field and then purchase a production system that would be optimal for the scale of reserves they could tap.

The types of decisions that decision trees are intended to help resolve are typically key decisions that affect the future of the organization facing them. These decisions are often contentious and involve a variety of staff with different expertise and perspectives. The way the decision is taken, and indeed the definition of what information is relevant, reflects the balance of power and influence within the organization. For a useful insight into these issues, try Jennings and Wattam (1998).

Review questions

Answers to these questions, including fully worked solutions to the Key questions marked with an asterisk (*), are on pages 658–660.

11.1*   Heemy Pharmaceuticals marketed a drug that proved to be an effective treatment but unfortunately resulted in side effects for some patients. On the basis of initial clinical research the probability that a patient who is treated with the drug suffers no side effect is 0.85, the probability of a minor side effect is 0.11, and the probability of a major side effect is 0.04. Under an agreement with the appropriate authorities the company has agreed to pay £2500 in compensation to patients who suffer a minor side effect and £20,000 in compensation to patients who suffer a major side effect. What is the expected value of the compensation per patient?

11.2   A graduate wants to pursue a career in a profession. She will need to gain membership of the professional institute by passing three stages of examinations. If she becomes a full member of the institute she anticipates that she will be able to earn £50,000 per year. If she fails the final stage of the examinations, but passes the first two stages she can become an associate member of the institute. An associate member earns about £32,000 per year. If she fails at the second stage but passes the initial stage she can obtain a certificate of competence from the institute and probably earn £24,000. If she fails the initial stage of the examinations she will have to consider other employment and anticipates that she would be able to earn £18,000. The pass rates for the initial, second and final stages of the institute's examinations are 70%, 55% and 80% respectively. What is the expected value of her annual earnings?

11.3   An insurance company calculates that the probability that in a year a motor insurance policyholder makes a claim arising from a major accident is 0.03, the probability that s/he makes a claim as a result of a minor accident is 0.1, and the probability that s/he makes a claim as a result of vehicle theft is 0.05. The typical payment for a major accident claim is £4500, for a minor accident claim is £800, and for theft £4000. The probability that a policyholder makes more than one claim in a year is zero. What is the expected value of claims per policy?

11.4   A film production company is about to release a new movie. They estimate that there is a 5% chance that the film will make a profit of $14m, a 30% chance that it will make a profit of $1m, a 25% chance that it will break even and a 40% chance that it will make a loss of $2 m. What is the expected return from the film?

11.5* Ivana Loyer claims she has been unfairly dismissed by her employers. She consults the law firm of Zackon and Vorovat, who agree to take up her case. They advise her that if she wins her case she can expect compensation of £15,000, but if she loses she will receive nothing. They estimate that their fee will be £1500, which she will have to pay whether she wins or loses. Under the rules of the relevant tribunal she cannot be asked to pay her employer's costs. As an alternative they offer her a 'no win no fee' deal under which she pays no fee but if she wins her case Zackon and Vorovat take one-third of the compensation she receives. She could decide against bringing the case, which would incur no cost and result in no compensation. Advise Ivana what to do:

(a) using the maximax decision rule

(b) using the maximin decision rule

(c) using the minimax regret decision rule

(d) using the equal likelihood decision rule

11.6   Zak 'the Snack' Cusker rents out a pitch for his stall at a music festival. The night before the festival he has to decide whether to load his van with ice-cream products, or burgers or a mix of burgers and ice-cream products. The takings he can expect (in £) depend on the weather, as shown in the following table:

	Weather	
Load	*Sun*	*Showers*
Ice cream	2800	1300
Mix	2100	2200
Burgers	1500	2500

Recommend which load Zak should take using:

(a) the maximax decision rule

(b) the maximin decision rule

(c) the minimax regret decision rule

(d) the equal likelihood decision rule

11.7   V. Nimania plc builds water treatment facilities throughout the world. One contract it has concerns an installation in an area prone to outbreaks of a dangerous disease. The company has to decide whether or not to vaccinate the employees who will be working there. Vaccination will cost £200,000, which will be deducted from the profit it makes from the venture. The company expects a profit of £1.2m from the contract but if there is an outbreak of the disease and the workforce has not been vaccinated, delays will result in the profit being reduced to £0.5m. If the workforce has been vaccinated and there is an outbreak of the disease, the work will progress as planned but disruption to infrastructure will result in their profit being reduced by £0.2m. Advise the company using:

(a) the maximax decision rule

(b) the maximin decision rule

(c) the minimax regret decision rule

(d) the equal likelihood decision rule

11.8   Pashley Package Holidays has to decide whether to discount its holidays to destinations abroad next summer in response to poor consumer confidence in international travel following recent military events. If they do not discount their prices and consumer confidence in air travel remains low the company expects to sell 1300 holidays at a profit of £60 per holiday. However, if they discount their prices and confidence remains low they expect that they could sell 2500 holidays at a profit of £35 per holiday. If they do not discount their prices and consumer confidence in air travel recovers they could expect to sell 4200 holidays at a profit of £50. If they do discount their prices and consumer confidence recovers, they could expect to sell 5000 holidays at a profit of £20. Recommend which course of action the company should take with the aid of:

(a) the maximax decision rule

(b) the maximin decision rule

(c) the minimax regret decision rule

(d) the equal likelihood decision rule

11.9   Cloppock Cotton is a farming collective in a central Asian republic. Their operations have been reliant on a government subsidy paid out to cotton farmers to support the production since cotton is a key export commodity. There are rumours that the government will reduce the subsidy for the next crop. The

Cloppock farmers have to decide whether to increase or decrease the number of hectares it farms, or to keep it the same. The pay-offs (in Soom, the national currency) for these strategies under the same subsidy regime and under reduced subsidies are:

Area	Same subsidy	Reduced subsidy
Increased	80000	−40000
The same	40000	15000
Decreased	20000	17000

Suggest what the farmers should do using:
(a) the maximax decision rule
(b) the maximin decision rule
(c) the minimax regret decision rule
(d) the equal likelihood decision rule

11.10* A sportswear company markets a premium brand of trainers. At present the revenue from sales of these trainers is £17m a year. They have been negotiating with representatives of a top US sports star in order to obtain his endorsement of the product. The cost to the company of the endorsement would be £3m a year, a cost that would be met from the sales revenue from the trainers. If the star endorses the trainers the company expects that the sales revenue will rise to £30m a year. However, just as the deal is about to be signed a regional US news agency runs a story alleging that the star has taken bribes. The sportswear company understand from their US representatives that there is a 60% chance that the star will be able to successfully refute the allegation, in which case sales of the trainers will still be £30m. If the star is unable to refute the allegation the negative publicity is likely to reduce sales revenue from the trainers to £10m a year.
(a) Should the company cancel or complete the endorsement deal?
(b) What should the company do if the chance of the star successfully refuting the allegations is 40%?

11.11 A freight company has to transport a container by road from Amsterdam to Tabriz. There are two routes that are viable. Route A is longer but less dangerous than Route B. If the container reaches its destination successfully the company will receive a fee of €15,000. Fuel and other direct costs incurred amount to €6000 on Route A and €4500 on Route B. The probability that the container is hijacked on Route A is put at 0.2; on Route B it is estimated to be 0.5. If the container is hijacked the company will receive no fee but anticipates it will only have to meet two-thirds of the fuel and other direct costs. The company will not be insuring the container because of the prohibitive cost of cargo insurance for such a journey.

(a) Draw a decision tree to represent the situation the company faces.

(b) Calculate the Expected Monetary Value for each route and use these to advise the company which route they should take.

(c) There are reports of armed incursions across a border at a critical point on Route A. As a result, the probability of the container being hijacked on Route A must be revised to 0.4. Explain what effect, if any, this has on the advice you gave in your answer to (b).

11.12   A member of a successful girl band is considering leaving the band to pursue a solo career. If she stays with the band she estimates that there is a 60% chance that the band will continue to be successful and she would earn £1.7m over the next three years. If the band's success does not continue she would still earn £0.6m over the next three years under her existing contract. If she embarks on a solo career she estimates that the chance of success is 20%. A successful solo career would bring her £4m in the next three years. If her solo career is not successful she can expect to earn only £0.25m in the next three years. What should she do?

11.13   Kholodny plc installs ventilation systems. At present its order book is rather thin and it has no work for the forthcoming period. It has been offered two contracts abroad, of which it can take only one. The first contract is to install a ventilation system in the Presidential Palace of the republic of Sloochai. The contract should earn the company a profit of £8m but the country is unstable and there is a 70% probability that the president will be overthrown before the work is finished. If the president is overthrown his opponents are not expected to pay for the work and the company would face a loss of £0.5m. The second contract is to install a ventilation system in an administration building in the republic of Parooka. The company can expect a profit of £6m from this contract unless the local currency is devalued during the completion of the project in which case the profit will fall to £3m. Financial experts put the probability of devaluation at 0.5.

(a) Construct a decision tree to portray the situation the company faces.

(b) Calculate the Expected Monetary Value for each project and use them to suggest which project the company should take.

(c) The President of Sloochai gives a key opponent a prominent post in his government. As a result the probability of the President being overthrown is revised to 40%. Does this new information alter the advice you gave in your answer to (b)? If so, why?

11.14 An arable farmer is thinking of sowing scientifically modified crops next year. She believes that if she did so her profits would be £75,000, compared to £50,000 if she sowed unmodified crops. A neighbouring farmer has made it clear that if his crops are contaminated he will demand compensation. The arable farmer guesses the probability of contamination to be 40%. In the event that the neighbouring farmer claims compensation there is a 30% chance that the arable farmer would have to pay £25,000 in compensation and a 70% chance she would have to pay £50,000 in compensation.

(a) Construct a decision tree and use it to advise the arable farmer.

(b) An expert puts the probability that there will be contamination of the crops of the neighbouring farmer at 60%. Should the arable farmer change her strategy in the light of this information?

11.15* Miners at the Gopher Gold Mine in Siberia have put in a series of wage and condition demands that would cost $50m to the management and threaten to strike if the demands are not met. The management have to decide right away whether to increase short-term production to build up a stockpile of output to reduce the impact of a strike, a move that would cost $20m in overtime and other extra costs. If they build a stockpile they estimate that the probability that the strike goes ahead is 0.6, whereas if they don't build a stockpile the chance of a strike is put at 0.7. Once the workers decide to strike the management have to decide whether to accept the miners' demands or to take them on. If the management decide to fight, the chance that they win is estimated to be 0.75 if they have built a stockpile and 0.5 if they have not. Whether the management win or lose the cost of the strike to them will be $10m in lost production and geological problems. If management win the miners' demands will not be met, if they lose they will. If the miners do not strike their demands will not be met.

(a) Use a decision tree to advise the management of the company.

(b) How sensitive are your recommendations to changes in the probability of the management winning if they have built a stockpile?

11.16   Kenny Videnia, a film producer, has to decide whether to bid for the film rights of a modestly successful novel. He believes that there is a 0.9 chance that he will be successful. If the bid is unsuccessful he will have to meet legal and administrative costs of $0.5m. If he is successful he has to decide whether to engage a big star for the main role. If he hires a big star the probability that the movie will be successful and make a profit of $50m is 0.3 and the chance that it fails and makes a loss of $20m is 0.7. If he doesn't hire a big star there is a 0.2 chance of the film making a profit of $30m and a 0.8 chance that it makes a loss of $10m.

(a) Suggest what Kenny should do using a decision tree.

(b) How sensitive is your advice to changes in the probability of the film making a profit if Kenny does not hire a big star?

11.17   Scientists at the Medicament Drug Company have synthesized a new drug which they believe will be an effective treatment for stress and anxiety. The company must decide whether to proceed with the commercial development of the new drug or not. If they decide not to develop it, no further costs will be incurred. If they decide to develop it, they have to submit it for clinical testing before they can sell it. The probability that it will pass the tests is estimated to be 0.75. If it fails the tests the costs incurred will be £2m. If it passes the test the company has to decide whether to set up a small-scale or a large-scale production facility. The money it will make from the drug depends on whether it is approved for National Health Service use. If it is approved and they have set up large-scale production they will make a profit of £60m, compared to the £20m they will make if they have only small-scale production. If the drug is not approved they will make a loss of £40m if they have large-scale production and a profit of £5m if they have small-scale production. The probability of getting approval for NHS use is 0.4.

(a) Advise the company using a decision tree.

(b) How sensitive is the choice of large- or small-scale production to a change in the probability of the drug being approved for NHS use?

11.18   Seela Energy wants to build a nuclear power station on a remote coastline in Northern Europe. They need new capacity, as without it they will incur a loss of €100m because they will have to use inefficient old capacity to meet demand. At an early stage during the time it will take to build the station a general election is due. The main opposition party are against the expansion of the nuclear industry and will withdraw the permission the existing government has given for the project. The probability of the opposition winning the election is put at 0.5. If they do win the company will incur losses of €20m in addition to the losses incurred by meeting demand using inefficient capacity. If the same government is re-elected Seela can continue with the project and will need to decide whether to build a 5 MW or a 2 MW reactor. The smaller reactor is a proven design and there is a 0.95 chance it will operate without difficulty and yield a profit of €200m, although there is a 0.05 chance it will be have to be shut down for long periods if there is a backlog of spent fuel rods. If this happens the company will incur a loss of €40m. If they build the larger reactor there is a 0.89 chance of fault-free operation and a profit of €500m. However it is a new design and experience with the prototype suggest there is a 0.1 chance of long shut-downs and hence a loss of €80m, and a 0.01 chance of premature permanent closure and a loss of €400m. Represent the situation using a decision tree and use it to advise the company what to do.

11.19   Lord Du Raq owns a crumbling castle in Scotland. The revenue from visitors is no longer sufficient to cover the upkeep of the property and he must decide what to do. A national heritage organization has offered to buy the property for £8m. Alternatively he could have a theme park constructed in the grounds. If this proves to be a success he will make a profit of £25m, but if it is not he will incur a loss of £5m. He estimates that the chance of success in the venture will be 0.6. He could start building the theme park right away, but a tourist authority contact has suggested that before he decides whether or not to build the park he should hire Baz Umney, an expert on leisure developments, to assess the prospects of the venture. Baz has a distinguished record, accurately predicting the success of similar ventures 70% of the time and accurately predicting the failure 80% of the time. Create a decision tree to model the situation Lord Du Raq faces and, using Bayes' rule, suggest what he should do.

11.20　Select the appropriate description for each term on the left-hand side from the list on the right-hand side.

(i)	maximax	(a)	a decision rule based on lowest pay-offs
(ii)	sensitivity analysis	(b)	the expected monetary value of a decision
(iii)	minimax regret	(c)	working out EMVs in a multi-stage decision tree
(iv)	EMV	(d)	a decision rule based on highest pay-offs
(v)	maximin	(e)	represent decisions and outcomes
(vi)	decision trees	(f)	ascertains the robustness of a decision
(vii)	backward induction	(g)	a decision rule based on opportunity losses

CHAPTER 12

Accidents and incidence — discrete probability distributions and simulation

This chapter will help you to:

- work out the probabilities for a basic discrete probability distribution
- calculate the mean and standard deviation of a discrete probability distribution
- model business processes with the binomial distribution
- model business processes with the Poisson distribution
- simulate simple random business processes with random numbers
- use the technology: discrete probability distributions in EXCEL, MINITAB and SPSS, random number generation in EXCEL
- become acquainted with business uses of discrete probability distributions and simulation

In this chapter we will bring together two key concepts from earlier chapters. The first of these is the idea of a frequency distribution, which shows the frequency or regularity with which the values of a variable occur, in other words how they are distributed across their range. The second key concept is that of probability, which we considered in Chapter 9. Here we will be looking at *probability distributions* which portray not the frequency with which values of a distribution actually occur but the probability with which we predict they will occur.

Probability distributions are very important tools for modelling or representing processes that occur at random, such as customers visiting a website or accidents on a building site. These are examples of *discrete random variables* as they vary in a random fashion and can have only certain values, whole numbers in both cases; we cannot conceive of half a customer visiting a website or 0.3 of an accident happening. We use *discrete probability distributions* to model these sorts of variables.

In studying probability distributions we will look at how they can be derived and how we can *model* or represent the chances of different combinations of outcomes using the same sort of approach as we use to arrange data into frequency distributions. Following that we will examine two standard discrete probability distributions; the binomial and the Poisson. Lastly we will look at how random numbers and discrete probability distributions can be used to simulate the operation of random business processes.

12.1 Simple probability distributions

In section 4.4.2 of Chapter 4 we looked at how we could present data in the form of a frequency distribution. This involved defining categories of values that occurred in the set of data and finding out how many observed values fell into each category, in other words, the frequency of each category of values in the set of data. The results of this process enabled us to see how the observations were distributed over the range of the data, hence the term frequency distribution.

A *probability distribution* is very similar to a frequency distribution. Like a frequency distribution, a probability distribution has a series of categories, but instead of categories of values it has categories of types of outcomes. The other difference is that each category has a probability instead of a frequency.

In the same way as a frequency distribution tells us how frequently each type of value occurs, a probability distribution tells us how probable each type of outcome is.

In section 5.2.1 of Chapter 5 we saw how a histogram could be used to show a frequency distribution. We can use a similar type of diagram to portray a probability distribution.

In Chapter 6 we used summary measures, including the mean and standard deviation, to summarize distributions of data. We can use the mean and standard deviation to summarize distributions of probabilities.

Just as we needed a set of data to construct a frequency distribution, we need to identify a set of compound outcomes in order to create a probability distribution. We also need the probabilities of the simple outcomes that make up the combinations of outcomes.

Example 12.1

Imported Loobov condoms are sold in packets of three. Following customer complaints the importer commissioned product testing which showed that due to a randomly occurring manufacturing fault 10% of the condoms tear in use. What are the chances that a packet of three includes zero, one, two and three defective condoms?

The probability that a condom is defective (D) is 0.1 and the probability it is good (G) is 0.9.

The probability that a packet of three contains no defectives is the probability that a sequence of three good condoms were put in the packet.

$$P(GGG) = 0.9 * 0.9 * 0.9 = 0.729$$

The probability that a packet contains one defective is a little more complicated because we have to take into account the fact that the defective one could be the first or the second or the third condom to be put in the packet.

so $P(1 \text{ Defective}) = P(DGG \text{ or } GDG \text{ or } GGD)$

Because these three sequences are mutually exclusive, according to the addition rule of probability (you may like to refer back to section 10.3.1 of Chapter 10):

$$P(1 \text{ Defective}) = P(DGG) + P(GDG) + P(GGD)$$

The probability that the first of these sequences occurs is:

$$P(DGG) = 0.1 * 0.9 * 0.9 = 0.081$$

The probability of the second:

$$P(GDG) = 0.9 * 0.1 * 0.9 = 0.081$$

It is no accident that the probabilities of these sequences are the same. Although the exact sequence is different the elements that make up both are the same. To work out the compound probabilities that they occur we use the same simple probabilities but in a different order, and the order does not affect the result when we multiply them together. If you work out $P(GGD)$ you should find that it also is 0.081.

The probability of getting one defective is therefore:

$$P(1 \text{ Defective}) = 0.081 + 0.081 + 0.081 = 3 * 0.081 = 0.243$$

We find the same sort of thing when we work out the probability that there are two defectives in a packet.

$$P(2 \text{ Defectives}) = P(DDG \text{ or } DGD \text{ or } GDD)$$
$$P(DDG) = 0.1 * 0.1 * 0.9 = 0.009$$
$$P(DGD) = 0.1 * 0.9 * 0.1 = 0.009$$
$$P(GDD) = 0.9 * 0.1 * 0.1 = 0.009$$

So $\qquad P(2 \text{ Defectives}) = 3 * 0.009 \qquad = 0.027$

Finally $\qquad P(3 \text{ Defectives}) = 0.1 * 0.1 * 0.1 \quad = 0.001$

We can bring these results together and present them in the form of a probability distribution.

Number of defectives (x)	P(x)
0	0.729
1	0.243
2	0.027
3	0.001
	1.000

Note that the sum of these probabilities is 1 because they are mutually exclusive (we cannot have both one defective and two defectives in a single packet of three) and collectively exhaustive (there can be only none, one, two or three defectives in a packet of three).

In Example 12.1 the probability distribution presents the number of defectives as a variable, X, whose values are represented as x. The variable X is a *discrete random variable*. It is discrete because it can only take a limited number of values – zero, one, two or three. It is random because the values occur as the result of a random process.

The symbol '$P(x)$' represents the probability that the variable X takes a particular value, x. For instance, we can represent the probability that the number of females is one, as

$$P(X = 1) = 0.243$$

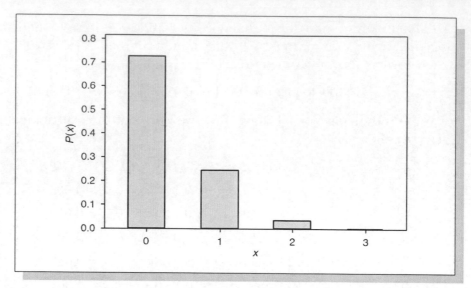

Figure 12.1
The probability distribution of *X*, the number of defectives

Figure 12.1 shows the probability distribution we compiled in Example 12.1 in graphical form.

We can find summary measures to represent this distribution, in the same way as we could use summary measures to represent distributions of data. However, as we don't have a set of data to use to get our summary measures we use the probabilities to 'weight' the values of *X*, just as we would use frequencies to obtain the mean from a frequency distribution. You work out the mean of a probability distribution by multiplying each value of *x* by its probability and then adding up the products:

$$\mu = \sum x\, P(x)$$

Notice that we use the Greek symbol μ to represent the mean of the distribution. The mean of a probability distribution is a population mean because we are dealing with a distribution that represents the probabilities of all possible values of the variable.

Once we have found the mean we can proceed to find the variance and standard deviation. We can obtain the variance, σ^2, by squaring each *x* value, multiplying the square of it by its probability and adding the products. From this sum we subtract the square of the mean.

$$\sigma^2 = \sum x^2\, P(x) - \mu^2$$

The standard deviation, σ, is simply the square root of the variance.

Again you can see that we use a Greek letter in representing the variance and the standard deviation because they are population measures.

Example 12.2

Calculate the mean and the standard deviation for the probability distribution in Example 12.1.

x	P(x)	x P(x)	x^2	$x^2 P(x)$
0	0.729	0.000	0	0.000
1	0.243	0.243	1	0.243
2	0.027	0.054	4	0.108
3	0.001	0.003	9	0.009
		0.300		0.360

The mean, μ, is 0.300, the total of the $x P(x)$ column.

The variance, σ^2, is 0.360, the total of the $x^2 P(x)$ column minus the square of the mean:

$$\sigma^2 = 0.360 - 0.300^2 = 0.360 - 0.090 = 0.270$$

The standard deviation: $\sigma = \sqrt{\sigma^2} = \sqrt{0.270} = 0.520$

The mean of a probability distribution is sometimes referred to as the *expected value* of the distribution. Unlike the mean of a set of data, which is based on what the observed values of a variable actually were, the mean of a probability distribution tells us what the values of the variable are likely, or *expected* to be.

We may need to know the probability that a discrete random variable takes a particular value or a lower value. This is known as a *cumulative* probability because in order to get it we have to add up or *accumulate* other probabilities. You can calculate cumulative probabilities directly from a probability distribution.

Example 12.3

Calculate a set of cumulative probabilities from the probability distribution in Example 12.1.

Suppose we want the probability that X, the number of defectives, is either two or less than two. Another way of saying this is the probability that X is less than or equal to two. We can use the symbol '$\leq$' to represent 'less than or equal to', so we are looking for $P(X \leq 2)$. (It may help you to recognize this symbol if you remember that the small end of the '$<$' part is pointing at the X and the large end at the 2, implying that X is smaller than 2.)

We can find the cumulative probabilities for each value of X by taking the probability that X takes that value and adding the probability that X takes a lesser value. You can see these cumulative probabilities in the right-hand column of the following table:

Number of defectives (x)	P(x)	P(X ⩽ x)
0	0.729	0.729
1	0.243	0.972
2	0.027	0.999
3	0.001	1.000

The cumulative probability that X is zero or less, $P(X \leqslant 0)$, is the probability that X is zero, 0.729, plus the probability that X is less than zero, but since it is impossible for X to be less than zero we do not have to add anything to 0.729.

The second cumulative probability, the probability that X is one or less, $P(X \leqslant 1)$, is the probability that X is one, 0.243, plus the probability that X is less than one, in other words, that it is zero, 0.729. Adding these two probabilities together gives us 0.972.

The third cumulative probability is the probability that X is two or less, $P(X \leqslant 2)$. We obtain this by adding the probability that X is 2, 0.027, to the probability that X is less than 2, in other words that it is one or less. This is the previous cumulative probability, 0.972. If we add this to the 0.027 we get 0.999.

The fourth and final cumulative probability is the probability that X is three or less. Since we know that X cannot be more than three (there are only three condoms in a packet), it is certain to be three or less, so the cumulative probability is one. We would get the same result arithmetically if we add the probability that X is three, 0.001, to the cumulative probability that X is less than three, in other words that it is two or less, 0.999.

The cumulative probabilities like those we worked out in Example 12.3 are perfectly adequate if we want the probability that a variable takes a particular value or a lower one, but what if we need to know the probability that a variable is higher than a particular value?

We can use the same cumulative probabilities if we manipulate them using our knowledge of the addition rule of probability. If, for instance, we want to know the probability that a variable is more than two, we can find it by taking the probability that it is two or less away from one.

$$P(X > 2) = 1 - P(X \leqslant 2)$$

We can do this because the two outcomes (X being greater than two and X being less than or equal to two) are mutually exclusive and collectively exhaustive. One and only one of them must occur. There are no other possibilities so it is certain that one of them happens.

In the expression $P(X > 2)$, which represents the probability that X is greater than two, we use the symbol '>' to represent 'greater than'. (It may help you to recognize this symbol if you remember that the larger end of it is pointing to the X and the smaller end is pointing to the 2, implying than X is bigger than 2.)

Although the situation described in Example 12.1, considering packets of just three condoms, was quite simple, the approach we used to obtain the probability distribution was rather laborious. Imagine that you had to use the same approach to produce a probability distribution if there were five or six condoms in a packet instead of just three. We had to be careful enough in identifying the three different ways in which there could be two defectives in a packet of three. If the packets contained five condoms, identifying the different ways that there could be say two defectives in a packet would be far more tedious.

Fortunately there are methods of analysing such situations that do not involve strenuous mental gymnastics. These involve using a type of probability distribution known as the *binomial* distribution.

At this point you may find it useful to try **Review Questions 12.1 and 12.2** at the end of the chapter.

12.2 The binomial distribution

The binomial distribution is the first of a series of 'model' statistical distributions that you will meet in this chapter and the two that follow it. The distribution was first derived theoretically but is widely used in dealing with practical situations. It is particularly useful because it enables you not only to answer a specific question but also to explore the consequences of altering the situation without actually doing it.

You can use the binomial distribution to solve problems that have what is called a *binomial structure*. These types of problems arise in situations where a series of finite, or limited number of 'experiments', or 'trials' take place repeatedly. Each trial has the same two mutually exclusive and collectively exhaustive outcomes, as the *bi* in the word binomial might suggest. By convention one of these outcomes is referred to as 'success'; the other as 'failure'.

To analyse a problem using the binomial distribution you have to know the probability of each outcome and it must be the same for every trial. In other words, the results of the trials must be independent of each other.

Words like 'experiment' and 'trial' are used to describe binomial situations because of the origins and widespread use of the binomial distribution in science. Although the distribution has become widely used in many other fields, these scientific terms have stuck.

The process in Example 12.1 has a binomial structure. Putting three condoms in a packet is in effect conducting a series of three trials. In each trial, that is, each time a condom is put in a packet, there can be only one of two outcomes: either it is defective or it is good.

In practice, we would use tables such as Table 2 in Appendix 1 on page 618 to apply the binomial distribution. These are produced using an equation, called the binomial equation, which you will see below. You won't need to remember it, and you shouldn't need to use it. We will look at it here to illustrate how it works.

We will use the symbol X to represent the number of 'successes' in a certain number of trials, n. X is what is called a binomial random variable. The probability of success in any one trial is represented by the letter p.

The probability that there are x successes in n trials is:

$$P(X = x) = \frac{n!}{x!(n - x)!} * p^x(1 - p)^{n-x}$$

You will see that an exclamation mark is used several times in the equation. It represents a *factorial*, which is a number multiplied by one less than itself then multiplied by two less itself and so on until we get to one. For instance four factorial, 4!, is four times three times two times one, $4 * 3 * 2 * 1$, which comes to 24.

Example 12.4

Use the binomial equation to find the first two probabilities in the probability distribution for Example 12.1.

We will begin by identifying the number of trials to insert in the binomial equation. Putting three condoms in a packet involves conducting three 'trials', so $n = 3$.

The variable X is the number of defectives in a packet of three. We need to find the probabilities that X is 0, 1, 2 and 3, so these will be the x values.

Suppose we define 'success' as a defective, then p, the probability of success in any one trial, is 0.1.

We can now put these numbers into the equation. We will start by working out the probability that there are no defectives in a packet of three, that is $X = 0$.

$$P(X = 0) = \frac{3!}{0!(3 - 0)!} * 0.1^0(1 - 0.1)^{3-0}$$

This expression can be simplified considerably. Any number raised to the power zero is one, so $0.1^0 = 1$. Conveniently zero factorial, 0!, is one as well. We can also carry out the subtractions.

$$P(X=0) = \frac{3!}{1(3)!} * 1(0.9)^3$$
$$= \frac{3*2*1}{3*2*1} * (0.9*0.9*0.9)$$
$$= 1 * 0.729 = 0.729$$

If you look back at Example 12.1, you will find that this is the same as the first figure in the probability distribution. The figure below it, 0.243, is the probability that there is one defective in a packet of three, that is $X = 1$. Using the binomial equation:

$$P(X=1) = \frac{3!}{1!(3-1)!} * 0.1^1(1-0.1)^{3-1}$$
$$= \frac{3*2*1}{1(2!)} * 0.1(0.9)^2$$
$$= \frac{6}{1(2*1)} * 0.1(0.81) = 3 * 0.081 = 0.243$$

Look carefully at this expression. You can see that the first part of it, which involves the factorials, is there to reflect the number of ways there are of getting a packet with one defective, 3(*DGG*, *GDG* and *GGD*). In the earlier expression, for $P(X = 0)$, the first part of the expression came to one, since there is only one way of getting a packet with no defectives (*GGG*).

You may like to try using this method to work out $P(X = 2)$ and $P(X = 3)$.

Finding binomial probabilities using printed tables means we don't have to undertake laborious calculations to obtain the figures we are looking for. We can use them to help us analyse far more complex problems than Example 12.1, such as the problem in Example 12.5.

Example 12.5

Melloch Aviation operates commuter flights out of Chicago using aircraft that can take ten passengers. During each flight passengers are given a hot drink and a 'Snack Pack' that contains a ham sandwich and a cake. The company is aware that some of their passengers may be vegetarians and therefore every flight is stocked with one vegetarian Snack Pack that contains a cheese sandwich in addition to ten that contain ham.

If 10% of the population are vegetarians, what is the probability that on a fully booked flight there will be at least one vegetarian passenger for whom a meat-free Snack Pack will not be available?

This problem has a binomial structure. We will define the variable X as the number of vegetarians on a fully booked flight. Each passenger is a 'trial' that can be a 'success', a vegetarian, or a 'failure', a non-vegetarian. The probability of 'success', in this case the probability that a passenger is a vegetarian, is 0.1. There are ten passengers on a fully booked flight, so the number of trials, n, is 10.

The appropriate probability distribution for this problem is the binomial distribution with $n = 10$ and $p = 0.1$. Table 2 on page 618 contains the following information about the distribution:

For 10 trials ($n = 10$); $p = 0.1$

	$P(x)$	$P(X \leqslant x)$
$x = 0$	0.349	0.349
$x = 1$	0.387	0.736
$x = 2$	0.194	0.930
$x = 3$	0.057	0.987
$x = 4$	0.011	0.998
$x = 5$	0.001	1.000
$x = 6$	0.000	1.000
$x = 7$	0.000	1.000
$x = 8$	0.000	1.000
$x = 9$	0.000	1.000
$x = 10$	0.000	1.000

The column headed $P(x)$ provides the probabilities that a specific number of 'successes', x, occurs, e.g. the probability of three 'successes' in ten trials, $P(3)$, is 0.057. The column headed $P(X \leqslant x)$ provides the probability that x or fewer 'successes' occur, e.g. the probability that there are 3 or fewer 'successes', $P(X \leqslant 3)$, is 0.987.

If there is only one vegetarian passenger they can be given the single vegetarian Snack Pack available on the plane. It is only when there is more than one vegetarian passenger that at least one of them will object to their Snack Pack. So we need the probability that there is more than one vegetarian passenger, which is the probability that X is greater than one, $P(X > 1)$. We could get it by adding up all the probabilities in the $P(x)$ column except the first and second ones, the probability that X is zero, $P(0)$, and the probability that X is one, $P(1)$. However, it is easier to take the probability of one or fewer, $P(X \leqslant 1)$, away from one:

$$P(X > 1) = 1 - P(X \leqslant 1) = 1 - 0.736 = 0.254 \quad \text{or} \quad 25.4\%$$

We can show the binomial distribution we used in Example 12.5 graphically.

In Figure 12.2 the block above 0 represents the probability that $X = 0$, $P(0)$, 0.349. The other blocks combined represent the probability that X is larger than 0, $P(X > 0)$, 0.651.

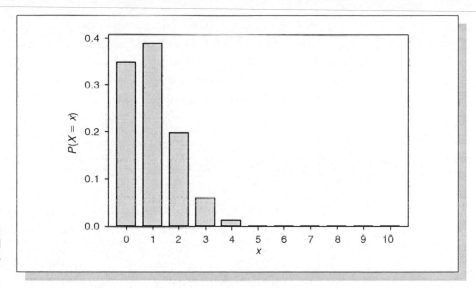

Figure 12.2
The binomial
distribution for
$n = 10$ and $p = 0.1$

It is quite easy to find the mean and variance of a binomial distribution. The mean, μ, is simply the number of trials multiplied by the probability of success:

$$\mu = n * p$$

The variance is the number of trials multiplied by the probability of success times one minus the probability of success:

$$\sigma^2 = n * p(1 - p).$$

Example 12.6

Calculate the mean, variance and standard deviation of the binomial distribution in Example 12.5.

In Example 12.5 the number of trials, n, was 10 and the probability of success, p, was 0.1, so the mean number of vegetarians on fully booked flights is:

$$\mu = n * p = 10 * 0.1 = 1.0$$

The variance is: $\sigma^2 = n * p(1 - p) = 10 * 0.1(1 - 0.1) = 1.0 * 0.9 = 0.9$

The standard deviation is: $\sigma = \sqrt{\sigma^2} = \sqrt{0.9} = 0.949$

The binomial distribution is called a *discrete probability distribution* because it describes the behaviour of certain types of discrete random variables, binomial variables. These variables concern the number of times certain outcomes occur in the course of a finite number of trials.

But what if we need to analyse how many things happen over a period of time? For this sort of situation we use another type of discrete probability distribution known as the *Poisson* distribution.

At this point you may find it useful to try **Review Questions 12.3 to 12.8** at the end of the chapter.

12.3 The Poisson distribution

Some types of business problem involve the analysis of incidents that are unpredictable. Usually they are things that can happen over a period of time, such as the number of telephone calls coming through to an office worker. However, it could be a number of things over an area, such as the number of stains in a carpet.

The Poisson distribution describes the behaviour of variables like the number of calls per hour or the number of stains per square metre. It enables us to find the probability that a specific number of incidents happen over a particular period. The distribution is named after the French mathematician Simeon Poisson, who outlined the idea in 1837, but the credit for demonstrating its usefulness belongs to the Russian statistician Vladislav Bortkiewicz, who applied it to a variety of situations including famously the incidence of deaths by horse kicks amongst soldiers of the Prussian army.

Using the Poisson distribution is quite straightforward. In fact you may find it easier than using the binomial distribution because we need to know fewer things about the situation. To identify which binomial distribution to use we had to specify the number of trials and the probability of success; these were the two defining characteristics, or *parameters* of the binomial distribution. In contrast, the Poisson distribution is a single parameter distribution, the one parameter being the mean.

If we have the mean of the variable we are investigating we can obtain the probabilities of the Poisson distribution using Table 3 on page 619 in Appendix 1.

Example 12.7

The medical tent at the Paroda music festival has the capacity to deal with up to three people requiring treatment in any one hour. The mean number of people requiring treatment is 2 per hour. What is the probability that they will not be able to deal with all the people requiring treatment in an hour?

The variable, X, in this case is the number of people per hour that require treatment. We can use the Poisson distribution to investigate the problem because it involves a discrete number of occurrences, or incidents over a period of time. The mean of X is 2.

The medical facility can deal with three people an hour, so the probability that there are more people requiring treatment than they can handle is the probability that X is more than 3, $P(X > 3)$.

The appropriate distribution is the Poisson distribution with a mean of 2. Table 3 on page 619 contains the following information about the distribution:

$$\mu = 2.0$$

	P(x)	P(X ⩽ x)
x = 0	0.135	0.135
x = 1	0.271	0.406
x = 2	0.271	0.677
x = 3	0.180	0.857
x = 4	0.090	0.947
x = 5	0.036	0.983
x = 6	0.012	0.995
x = 7	0.003	0.999
x = 8	0.001	1.000

The column headed $P(x)$ provides the probabilities that a specific number of incidents, x, occurs e.g. the probability of four incidents, $P(4)$, is 0.090. The column headed $P(X \leq x)$ provides the probability that x or fewer incidents occur, e.g. the probability that there are 4 or fewer incidents, $P(X \leq 4)$, is 0.947.

To obtain the probability that more than three people require treatment at the first aid tent, $P(X > 3)$, we subtract the probability of X being 3 or fewer, $P(X \leq 3)$, which is the probability that the number of people requiring treatment in an hour can be dealt with, from one.

$$P(X > 3) = 1 - P(X \leq 3) = 1 - 0.857 = 0.143 \quad \text{or} \quad 14.3\%$$

If we had to produce the Poisson probabilities in Example 12.7 without the aid of tables we could calculate them using the formula for the distribution. You won't have to remember it, and probably won't need to use it, but it may help your understanding if you know where the figures come from.

The probability that the number of incidents, X, takes a particular value, x, is:

$$P(X = x) = \frac{e^{-\mu} * \mu^x}{x!}$$

The letter e is the mathematical constant known as Euler's number. The value of this, to 4 places of decimals, is 2.7183, so we can put this in the formula:

$$P(X = x) = \frac{2.7183^{-\mu} * \mu^{x}}{x!}$$

The symbol μ represents the mean of the distribution and x is the value of X whose probability we want to know. In Example 12.7 the mean is 2, so the probability that there are no people requiring treatment, in other words the probability that X is zero, is:

$$P(X = 0) = \frac{2.7183^{-\mu} * \mu^{0}}{0!} = \frac{2.7183^{-2} * 2^{0}}{1}$$

To work this out you need to know that if you raise any number (in this case μ) to the power zero the answer is one, so:

$$P(X = 0) = \frac{2.7183^{-2} * 2^{0}}{1} = \frac{2.7183^{-2} * 1}{1}$$

The first part of the expression, 2.7183^{-2}, is $1 / 2.7183^2$ since any number raised to a negative power is a reciprocal, so:

$$P(X = 0) = \frac{1}{2.7183^2} = 0.135 \text{ to 3 decimal places}$$

If you are unsure of the arithmetic we have used here you may find it helpful to refer back to section 1.3.3 of Chapter 1.

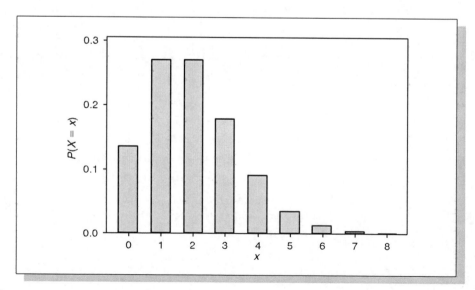

Figure 12.3
The Poisson
distribution for
$\mu = 2.0$

If you look back to the extract from Table 3 in Example 12.7 you can check that this is the correct figure. The figure $P(0)$, 0.135, in the extract from Table 3 is $P(1)$, 0.271, which can be calculated as follows:

$$P(X = 1) = \frac{2.7183^{-\mu} * \mu^1}{1!} = \frac{2.7183^{-2} * 2}{1}$$

$$- \frac{2}{2.7183^2} = 0.271$$

We can portray the Poisson distribution used in Example 12.7 graphically. See Figure 12.3.

At this point you may find it useful to try **Review Questions 12.9 to 12.14** at the end of the chapter.

12.4 Simulating business processes

Most businesses conduct operations that involve random variables; the numbers of customers booking a vehicle service at a garage, the number of products damaged in transit, the number of workers off sick etc. The managers of these businesses can use probability distributions to represent and analyse these variables. They can take this approach a stage further and use the probability distributions that best represent the random processes in their operations to *simulate* the effects of the variation on those operations.

Simulation is particularly useful where a major investment such as a garage building another service bay is under consideration. It is possible to simulate the operations of the vehicle servicing operation with another service bay so that the benefits of building the extra bay in terms of increased customer satisfaction and higher turnover can be explored before the resources are committed to the investment.

There are two stages in simulating a business process; the first is setting up the structure or framework of the process, the second is using random numbers to simulate the operation of the process. The first stage involves identifying the possible outcomes of the process, finding the probabilities for these outcomes and then allocating bands of random numbers to each of the outcomes in keeping with their probabilities. In making such allocations we are saying that whenever a random number used in the simulation falls within the allocation for a certain outcome, for the purposes of the simulation that outcome is deemed to have occurred.

Example 12.8

The Munich company AT-Dalenni Travel specialize in organizing adventure holidays for serious travellers. They run 'Explorer' trips to the Tien Shan mountain range in Central Asia. Each trip has 10 places and they run 12 trips a year. The business is not seasonal, as customers regard the experience as the 'trip of a lifetime' and demand is steady. The number of customers wanting to purchase a place on a trip varies according to the following probability distribution:

Number of customers	Probability
8	0.15
9	0.25
10	0.20
11	0.20
12	0.20

Use this probability distribution to set up random number allocations for simulating the operation.

The probabilities in these distributions are specified to two places of decimals so we need to show how the range of two-digit random numbers from 00 to 99 should be allocated to the different outcomes. It is easier to do this if we list the cumulative probabilities for the distribution:

Number of customers	Probability	Cumulative probability	Random number allocation
8	0.15	0.15	00–14
9	0.25	0.40	15–39
10	0.20	0.60	40–59
11	0.20	0.80	60–79
12	0.20	1.00	80–99

Notice how the random number allocations match the probabilities; we allocate one of the hundred possible two-digit random variables for every one-hundredth (0.01) measure of probability. The probability of 8 customers is 0.15 or fifteen hundredths so the random number allocation is fifteen, 00 to 14 inclusive. The probability of 9 customers is 0.25 or twenty-five hundredths so the allocation is twenty-five random numbers, 15 to 39 inclusive, and so on.

In Example 12.8 we have set up the simulation, but what we actually need to run it are random numbers. We could generate some random numbers using a truly random process such as a lottery machine or a roulette wheel. Since we are unlikely to have such equipment to hand it is easier to use tables of them such as Table 4 on page 620 in

Appendix 1, which have been generated using computer software (see Section 12.5.1).

Example 12.9

Use the following random numbers to simulate the numbers of customers on 12 trips undertaken by AT-Dalenni.

06   18   15   50   06   46   63   92   67   12   91   70

We will take each random number in turn and use it to simulate the number of customers on one trip. Since it is possible for there to be more customers wanting to take a trip than there are places on it we will include a column for the number of disappointed customers. To keep things simple we will assume that customers who do not get on the trip are not prepared to wait for the next one. The results are tabulated below.

Trip number	Random number	Number of customers	Disappointed customers
1	06	8	0
2	18	9	0
3	15	9	0
4	50	10	0
5	06	8	0
6	46	10	0
7	63	11	1
8	92	12	2
9	67	11	1
10	12	8	0
11	91	12	2
12	70	11	1

The results of this simulation suggest that there are few disappointed customers, only seven in twelve trips, or on average 0.583 per trip.

The simulation in Example 12.9 is relatively simple, so instead of simulating the process we could work out the mean of the probability distribution and subtract 10 from it to find the average number of disappointed customers per trip. (If you want to try it you should get an answer of 0.05.) Simulation really comes into its own when there is an interaction of random variables.

Example 12.10

The profit AT-Dalenni makes each trip varies; weather conditions, availability of local drivers and guides, and currency fluctuations all have an effect. The profit per customer varies according to the following probability distribution:

Profit per customer (€)	Probability
400	0.25
500	0.35
600	0.30
700	0.10

Make random number allocations for this distribution and use the following random numbers to extend the simulation in Example 12.9 and work out the simulated profit from the twelve trips.

85   25   63   11   35   12   63   00   38   80   26   67

Profit per customer	Probability	Cumulative probability	Random numbers
400	0.25	0.25	00–24
500	0.35	0.60	25–59
600	0.30	0.90	60–89
700	0.10	1.00	90–99

Trip	Random number (1)	Customers	Random number (2)	Profit (€)
1	06	8	85	600 * 8 = 4800
2	18	9	25	500 * 9 = 4500
3	15	9	63	600 * 9 = 5400
4	50	10	11	400 * 10 = 4000
5	06	8	35	500 * 8 = 4000
6	46	10	12	400 * 10 = 4000
7	63	11	63	600 * 10 = 6000
8	92	12	00	400 * 10 = 4000
9	67	11	38	500 * 10 = 5000
10	12	8	80	600 * 8 = 4800
11	91	12	26	500 * 10 = 5000
12	70	11	67	600 * 10 = 6000
				57500

The simulated total profit is €57,500.

You may notice that in working out the profit for trips 7, 8, 9, 11 and 12 we have multiplied the simulated profit per customer by ten customers rather than the simulated number of customers. This is because they can only take ten customers per trip.

Simulation allows us to investigate the consequences of making changes. The company in Example 12.10 might, for instance, want to consider acquiring vehicles that would allow them to take up to 12 customers per trip.

Example 12.11

How much extra profit would AT-Dalenni have made, according to the simulation in Example 12.10, if they had the capacity to take 12 customers on each trip?

In Example 12.12 there are five trips that had more customers interested than places available. The simulated numbers of customers and profit per customer for these trips were:

Trip	Number of customers	Profit per customer	Extra profit
7	11	600	600
8	12	400	800
9	11	500	500
11	12	500	1000
12	11	600	600
			3500

The extra profit they could have made is €3,500.

In practice, simulations are performed on computers and the runs are much longer than the ones we have conducted in this section, and in practice there would be many runs carried out. Much of the work in using simulation involves testing the appropriateness or *validity* of the model; only when the model is demonstrated to be reasonably close to the real process can it be of any use. For more on simulation try Brooks and Robinson (2001) and Oakshott (1997).

At this point you may find it useful to try **Review Questions 12.15 to 12.19** at the end of the chapter.

12.5 Using the technology: discrete probability distributions and random number generation in EXCEL, discrete probability distributions in MINITAB and SPSS

In analysing the examples in section 12.2 and 12.3 of this chapter we have used Tables 2 and 3 on pages 618–619 of Appendix 1. These tables should be sufficient for your immediate requirements, but it is useful to know how to produce such information using software because space constraints mean that printed tables can only contain a limited number of versions of the distributions.

12.5.1 EXCEL

You can obtain binomial probabilities one at a time in EXCEL.

■ Click on an empty cell in the spreadsheet then type **=BINOMDIST(x,n,p,FALSE)** in the Formula Bar, where the numbers you put in for x, n and p depend on the problem. For instance, to get the probability of there being one defective in a packet of three in Example 12.1 type in **=BINOMDIST(1,3,0.1,FALSE)** then press Enter. **FALSE** denotes that we don't want a cumulative probability, **TRUE** denotes that we do.

■ For the probability that there is more than one vegetarian on a flight in Example 12.5 type **=BINOMDIST(1,10, 0.1,TRUE)** then press Enter. The result you should get, 0.736, is the probability of 0 or 1 successes (in this case the number of vegetarians), which when subtracted from 1 gives you 0.254, the probability of more than one vegetarian.

To get Poisson probabilities in EXCEL

■ Click on an empty cell in the spreadsheet then type **=POISSON(x,Mean,FALSE)** in the Formula Bar, where x is the value of the variable. For the probability of no people calling at the first aid tent in Example 12.7 type **=POISSON(0,2,FALSE)** then press Enter. Again **FALSE** denotes that we don't want a cumulative probability and **TRUE** denotes that we do.

■ For the probability of more than three people calling at the first aid tent in Example 12.7 type **=POISSON(3,2,TRUE)** then press Enter and subtract the answer you get, 0.857, which is the probability of three or fewer, from one to give you the answer, 0.143.

For random numbers,

■ Choose the **Data Analysis** option from the **Tools** pull-down menu.

■ Under **Analysis Tools** select **Random Number Generation** and click **OK**.

In the window that appears type 1 in the space to the right of **Number of Variables:** and specify the **Number of Random Numbers:** you require. Click the ▼ button to the right of **Distribution:** and choose **Uniform**. Type 99 in the space to the right under **Parameters** then pick one of the **Output options**, by either specifying an **Output Range:** in the existing worksheet or accepting the default of a new worksheet, then click **OK**.

12.5.2 MINITAB

You can obtain binomial probabilities by

- Selecting the **Probability Distributions** option from the **Calc** menu and then picking the **Binomial** option from the sub-menu.
- In the command window you can choose to obtain probabilities or cumulative probabilities. You will need to specify the **Number of trials** and the **Probability of success** in the spaces provided. If you only want one probability, click the button to the left of **Input constant:**, type the value of x in the space to the right and click **OK**. For the probability that there is one defective in a packet of three in Example 12.1 the **Number of trials:** is 3, the **Probability of success:** is 0.1, and the **Input constant:** is 1.
- If you want a table of probabilities put the x values in a column of the worksheet, select **Input column:** in the **Binomial Distribution** command window and enter the column location of your x values in the space to the right of **Input column:**.

For Poisson probabilities

- Select **Probability Distributions** from the **Calc** menu, and then pick **Poisson** from the sub menu.
- In the command window you can choose to obtain probabilities or cumulative probabilities. You will need to provide the **Mean** as well as the column location of your x values if you want probabilities for several x values.
- If you only require one probability you can click the button to the left of **Input constant:** and enter the x value in the space to the right of it.

12.5.3 SPSS

For a single binomial probability

- Choose the **Compute** option from the **Transform** pull-down menu.

▨ In the **Compute Variable** window click on **PDF.BINOM(q,n,p)** in the long list under **Functions:** on the right-hand side of the window and click the ▲ button to the right of **Functions:**. The command should now appear in the space under **Numeric Expression:** to the top right of the window with three question marks inside the brackets. Replace these question marks with the value of x whose probability you want (referred to as q in SPSS), the number of trials (n) and the probability of success (p), respectively. For instance, to use this facility to get the probability of three vegetarian passengers in Example 12.5 your command should be **PDF.BINOM(3,10,0.1)**. You will need to enter the name of a column to store the answer in the space under **Target Variable:**, this can be a default name like **var00001**.

▨ Click **OK** and the probability should appear in the column you have targeted.

You can get a cumulative binomial probability if you

▨ Select **CDF.BINOM(q,n,p)** from the list below **Functions:** and proceed as outlined in the previous paragraph.

▨ If you want to get binomial probabilities for a list of x values, put the x values in a column and type the name of this column first in the brackets. Alternatively, look in the space to the lower left of the command window for the name of the column where you have stored your x values, click in front of the first question mark in the brackets and click the ▶ button to the right of the space. The column name should now appear inside the brackets.

▨ Once you have done this carry on as in the previous paragraph.

Obtaining Poisson probabilities in SPSS is very similar to finding binomial probabilities.

▨ Select the **Compute** option from the **Transform** pull-down menu and select **PDF.POISSON(q,mean)** from the **Functions:** list, or **CDF.POISSON(q,mean)** for a cumulative probability. In the brackets you will need to specify the value of x for the probability you require (q) and the mean of the distribution you want to use. To get the probability of four people seeking treatment in one hour at the medical tent in Example 12.7 the command would be **PDF.POISSON(4,2)**. You have to provide a column location for the answer in the space below **Target Variable:** and finally click **OK**.

■ If you want Poisson probabilities for a set of x values, store them in a column and insert the column name for q in the brackets after the command.

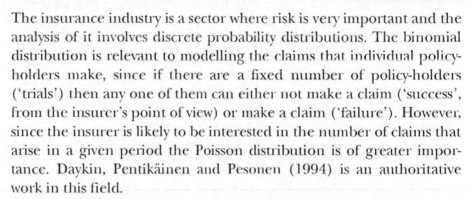

12.6 Road test: Do they really use discrete probability distributions and simulation?

The insurance industry is a sector where risk is very important and the analysis of it involves discrete probability distributions. The binomial distribution is relevant to modelling the claims that individual policy-holders make, since if there are a fixed number of policy-holders ('trials') then any one of them can either not make a claim ('success', from the insurer's point of view) or make a claim ('failure'). However, since the insurer is likely to be interested in the number of claims that arise in a given period the Poisson distribution is of greater importance. Daykin, Pentikäinen and Pesonen (1994) is an authoritative work in this field.

Tippett (1935) applied a number of statistical techniques in his work on variation in the manufacture of cotton. The quality of yarn varied as a result of a number of factors, including changing humidity and differences in the tension of the yarn during the production process. He studied yarn production in Lancashire mills that spun American and Egyptian cotton in order to analyse quality variation. In part of his work he applied the Poisson distribution to the incidence of faults in cloth arising from deficiencies in cotton yarn.

The dramatic increase in demand for lager in the UK during the 1980s presented problems for brewers in terms of building new capacity or switching capacity from the production of ale, a product that was experiencing some decline in demand. MacKenzie (1988) describes how simulation was used to address this dilemma at the Edinburgh brewing complex of Scottish and Newcastle Breweries. The company was looking at a variety of proposals for expanding the tank capacity for the fermentation and maturation of their lager products. The simulation had to take into account factors that included the number of different products made at the plant, variation in the processing time, maintenance breaks and the finite number of pipe routes through the plant. The problem was made more complex by a number of other factors, including the introduction of new filtration facilities, longer processing times to enhance product quality and a new packaging facility that required different supply arrangements. The result of the analysis enabled the company to meet demand even during a period when lager production at another plant suffered a short-term halt.

Gorman (1988) explains how simulation was used to resolve the design of a production unit for the engineering firm Mather and Platt. The unit was to consist of a suite of new technology machines, including a laser cutter and robots, for the production of parts of electric motors. The simulation was used to model the performance of two possible scenarios, one based on the existing arrangements and the other with the new equipment. The aim was to investigate the efficiency of the systems and to identify bottlenecks that might build up. Running simulations of a variety of scenarios enabled the company to ascertain the best way of setting up the unit and the optimal level of staffing support for it.

Review questions

Answers to these questions, including fully worked solutions to the Key questions marked with an asterisk (*), are on pages 660–662.

12.1   There are three very old X-ray security machines in the departure complex of an airport. All three machines are exactly the same. The probability that a machine breaks down in the course of a day is 0.2. If they are all in working order at the beginning of a day, and breakdowns are independent of each other, find the probability that during the day:
(a) there are no breakdowns
(b) one machine breaks down
(c) two machines break down
(d) all three machines break down

12.2*   If 30% of the adult population have made an airline booking through the Internet work out the probability that out of four people:
(a) none has made an Internet booking
(b) one has made an Internet booking
(c) two have made an Internet booking
(d) three have made an Internet booking
(e) all four have made an Internet booking

12.3   A lingerie manufacturer produces ladies' knickers in packs of five pairs. Quality control has been erratic and they estimate that one in every ten pairs of knickers leave the factory without

the trim sewn on. What is the probability that in a pack of five pairs of knickers:
(a) there are no pairs without the trim?
(b) there are two or fewer pairs without the trim?
(c) there is more than one pair without the trim?
(d) the majority of pairs are without the trim?

12.4 A large party of Russian managers is to visit a car plant in the UK. They will be shown round the plant in small groups of five. Twenty per cent of the managers speak English. If the groups are selected at random, what is the probability that:
(a) there is no English speaker in a group?
(b) there is at least one English speaker in a group?
(c) all but one of the group speaks English?

12.5 'Fast' Gary and Mickey 'the Mule' import alcoholic beverages from France into the UK. They are offered a consignment of packs of bottled beers. Each pack contains ten bottles. The price for the consignment is low because due to problems at the bottling plant 20% of the bottles have no labels. What is the probability that in a pack from this consignment:
(a) no bottles are without labels?
(b) three or fewer bottles are without labels?
(c) more than one bottle is without a label?
(d) less than five bottles are without labels?
(e) the majority of bottles are without labels?

12.6 The producers of a TV survival programme advertise for potential participants and then select random samples of ten people to appear in the programme. If 30% of the people who apply to take part in the programme are smokers, what is the probability that:
(a) a team consists entirely of non-smokers?
(b) a team includes only one smoker?
(c) a team includes no more than three smokers?
(d) a team includes more than four smokers?
(e) the majority of a team are non-smokers?

12.7 An egg packing company thinks that a tenth of all the eggs they buy from farms are contaminated with harmful bacteria that could result in food poisoning. What is the probability that in a pack of ten eggs:
(a) none of the eggs contains harmful bacteria?
(b) more than two eggs contain harmful bacteria?
(c) half the eggs contain harmful bacteria?
(d) less than two eggs contain harmful bacteria?

12.8   Two in five people can associate a particular piece of music with the product it is used to promote in an advertising campaign. Identify the probability that in a group of ten people:

(a) none will recognize it

(b) less than half will recognize it

(c) exactly six will recognize it

(d) more than six will recognize it

12.9*   The mean number of accidents per day at a large building site is 1.0. What is the probability that a day passes when there are:

(a) no accidents?

(b) two accidents?

(c) four or fewer accidents?

(d) more than three accidents?

12.10   Wasim's word processing skills are good. On average he only makes 0.5 mistakes on each page he types. What is the probability that in a document ten pages long he makes:

(a) no mistakes?

(b) less than four mistakes?

(c) no more than six mistakes?

(d) at least eight mistakes?

12.11   An office worker receives an average of 22.5 email messages per day. If his working day lasts seven and a half hours, what is the probability that:

(a) he receives no emails in an hour?

(b) he receives one email in an hour?

(c) he receives two or fewer emails in an hour?

(d) he receives more than four emails in an hour?

12.12   The mean number of violent incidents at the Koshmar pub is 14 per week. As a result of being injured at work the pub bouncer will be off for a day.

(a) What is the probability that the day passes without any violent incidents?

(b) What is the probability that the day passes with no more than one violent incident?

(c) If his doctor says the bouncer needs two days off work, what is the probability that these two days pass without any violent incidents?

(d) What is the probability that these two days pass with more than one violent incident?

12.13   Everyone working in a large open plan office takes cups of tea or coffee back to their desk to drink. The mean number of spilled cups of hot drinks in an eight-hour working day is 24. What is the probability that an hour passes in which:

(a) there are no spillages?

(b) there are two spillages?

(c) there are less than four spillages?

(d) there is at least one spillage?

12.14 A company produces mouse mats that are 20 cm long and 20 cm wide. These mats are cut from sheets of material that are one metre long and one metre wide. Precise machine setting means that 25 mouse mats can be cut from each sheet of material. Problems that have arisen in the laminating process mean that the sheets of material contain small holes. The mean number of holes per sheet is 25. What is the probability that:

(a) a mouse mat has no holes?

(b) a mouse mat has two or fewer holes?

(c) a mouse mat has more than one hole?

12.15* Furgon Van Hire rents out trucks and vans. One service they offer is a same-day rental deal under which account customers can call in the morning to hire a van for the day. Five vehicles are available for hire on these terms. The demand for the service varies according to the following distribution:

Demand (vans):	0	1	2	3	4	5	6	7	8
Probability:	0.05	0.05	0.10	0.15	0.20	0.20	0.15	0.05	0.05

Simulate the demand for this service over a period of ten days and using your results work out the average number of disappointed customers per day. Use random numbers from Table 4 on page 620 in Appendix 1, starting at the top of column 10 and working down.

12.16 Orders for the Potchtar Mail Order Company are sent in batches of 50 by the Post Office. The number of orders arriving each working day varies according to the following probability distribution:

Number of orders	Probability
150	0.05
200	0.15
250	0.30
300	0.30
350	0.15
400	0.05

These orders are opened and keyed into the company's system by a data entry assistant who, following the departure of a colleague, will handle this task by himself. The rate per day at which he processes orders varies as follows:

Orders processed	Probability
100	0.1
150	0.2
200	0.4
250	0.2
300	0.1

Any orders that are not processed by the end of one day are held over and dealt with first on the following day.

(a) Simulate the operation of this system for ten working days using two streams of random numbers from Table 4 on page 620 in Appendix 1. Start at the top of column 2 and go down the column for the orders received and start at the top of column 5 and go down the column for the orders processed. From your results work out the average number of orders held over per day.

(b) A new assistant may be appointed to help out. If this happened the distribution of processing times is expected to be:

Orders processed	Probability
200	0.15
250	0.15
300	0.40
350	0.20
400	0.10

Simulate the operation of the new arrangement for ten days using the same sets of random numbers you used in part (a). Work out the average number of orders held over per day and compare your result to those you obtained for part (a).

12.17 A restaurant serves fresh locally grown strawberries as part of its 'Wimbledon working lunch' menu for ten working days in the early summer. The supplier provides 100 kg per day and sells to the hotel at a price that varies according to the probability distribution:

Price per kg (£)	1.00	1.10	1.20	1.30	1.40
Probability	0.1	0.25	0.35	0.20	0.10

The number of portions sold per day at £3 per 250 g per portion varies according to the probability distribution:

Portions ordered	200	240	280	320	400
Probability	0.30	0.20	0.20	0.20	0.10

Any strawberries not sold during the lunch are sold to a jammaker the same day for £0.50 per kilogram.

Using simulation, estimate the profit that the restaurant can expect to make over the ten days. [The answer to this question in Appendix 2 is based on using random numbers from Table 4 on page 620 in Appendix 1, starting with row 3 column 1 and moving right for the price and row 9 column 2 and moving right for the portions ordered.]

12.18   A book trader has taken out a 13-week lease on a small unit in a shopping mall prior to it being fitted out as a new outlet by a major retailer. The trader intends to sell remaindered books, 'coffee table classics' selling for £3 each and children's books selling at £1 each. She has a stock consisting of 2000 of the former and 5000 of the latter. The demand for the books per week is expected to vary as follows:

Demand (£3 books)	Probability	Demand (£1 books)	Probability
100	0.10	300	0.20
120	0.10	325	0.20
140	0.20	350	0.30
160	0.30	375	0.10
180	0.15	400	0.12
200	0.15	425	0.08

Simulate the sales and use them to estimate the total revenue over the 13 weeks the shop will be open. [The answer to this question in Appendix 2 is based on using random numbers from Table 4 on page 620 in Appendix 1, starting with column 1 row 2 and going to the right for the £3 books, and starting with column 1 row 7 and going to the right for the £1 books.]

12.19   A builder completes a large project for a property company who, due to cash flow problems, offer him a small seaside hotel in lieu of payment. The builder, who has no desire to enter the hotel business, has found a buyer for the hotel, but this deal will not be completed until 12 weeks after the hotel is due to open for the summer season. The builder has decided to operate the hotel himself for these 12 weeks. To keep this simple he has decided to accept only one-week bookings. There are 8 double rooms and 3 single rooms in the hotel. The cost of a double room for one week will be £300, and the cost of a single room for one week, £200. The numbers of rooms of each type booked per week varies according to the following distributions:

Double rooms	Probability	Single rooms	Probability
1	0.05	0	0.10
2	0.10	1	0.40
3	0.10	2	0.30
4	0.15	3	0.20
5	0.25		
6	0.20		
7	0.10		
8	0.05		

Simulate the operation of the hotel for these 12 weeks and work out the total revenue. [The answer to this question in Appendix 2 was obtained using random numbers from Table 4 on page 620 in Appendix 1, starting at the top of column 8 and going down for the double rooms and starting at the top of column 11 and going down for the single rooms.]

12.20   Select the appropriate description for each term on the left-hand side from the list on the right-hand side.

(i)	simulation	(a)	consists of probabilities of incidents over time
(ii)	np	(b)	four factorial, twenty-four
(iii)	the binomial distribution	(c)	the variance of the binomial distribution
(iv)	the Poisson distribution	(d)	consists of probabilities of successes in trials
(v)	$np(1 - p)$	(e)	modelling distributions using random numbers
(vi)	4!	(f)	another name for a probability distribution mean
(vii)	expected value	(g)	the mean of the binomial distribution

CHAPTER 13

Smooth running — continuous probability distributions and basic queuing theory

This chapter will help you to:

- make use of the normal distribution and appreciate its importance
- employ the Standard Normal Distribution to investigate normal distribution problems
- apply the exponential distribution and be aware of its usefulness in analysing queues
- analyse a simple queuing system
- use the technology: continuous probability distribution
- become acquainted with business uses of the normal distribution

In the previous chapter we looked at how two different types of theoretical probability distributions, the binomial and Poisson distributions, can be used to model or simulate the behaviour of discrete random variables. These types of variable can only have a limited or finite number of values, typically only whole numbers like the number of defective products in a pack or the number of telephone calls received over a period of time.

Discrete random variables are not the only type of random variable. You will also come across continuous random variables, variables whose possible values are not confined to a limited range. In the same way as we used discrete probability distributions to help us investigate the behaviour of discrete random variables we use continuous probability distributions to help us investigate the behaviour of continuous random variables. Continuous probability distributions can also be used to investigate the behaviour of discrete variables that can have many different values.

The most important continuous probability distribution in Statistics is the normal distribution. As the name suggests, this distribution represents the pattern of many 'typical' or 'normal' variables. You may find the distribution referred to as the Gaussian distribution after the German mathematician Carl Friedrich Gauss (1777–1855) who developed it to model observation errors that arose in surveying and astronomy measurements.

The normal distribution has a very special place in Statistics because as well as helping us to model variables that behave in the way that the normal distribution portrays, it is used to model the way in which results from samples vary. This is of great importance when we want to use sample results to make predictions about entire populations.

13.1 The normal distribution

Just as we saw that there are different versions of the binomial distribution that describe the patterns of values of binomial variables, and different versions of the Poisson distribution that describe the behaviour of Poisson variables, there are many different versions of the normal distributions that display the patterns of values of normal variables.

Each version of the binomial distribution is defined by n, the number of trials, and p, the probability of success in any one trial. Each version of the Poisson distribution is defined by its mean. In the same way, each version of the normal distribution is identified by two defining characteristics or parameters: its mean and its standard deviation.

The normal distribution has three distinguishing features:

  ▪ It is unimodal, in other words there is a single peak.
  ▪ It is symmetrical, one side is the mirror image of the other.

    ■   It is asymptotic, that is, it tails off very gradually on each side but the line representing the distribution never quite meets the horizontal axis.

Because the normal distribution is a symmetrical distribution with a single peak, the mean, median and mode all coincide at the middle of the distribution. For this reason we only need to use the mean as the measure of location for the normal distribution. Since the average we use is the mean, the measure of spread that we use for the normal distribution is the standard deviation.

The normal distribution is sometimes described as bell-shaped. Figure 13.1 illustrates the shape of the normal distribution. It takes the form of a smooth curve. This is because it represents the probabilities that a continuous variable takes values right across the range of the distribution.

If you look back at the diagrams we used to represent discrete probability distributions in Figures 12.1 and 12.2 in Chapter 12 you will see that they are bar charts that consist of separate blocks. Each distinct block represents the probability that the discrete random variable in question takes one of its distinct values. Because the variable can only take discrete, or distinct, values we can represent its behaviour with a diagram consisting of discrete, or distinct, sections.

If we want to use a diagram like Figure 12.1 or 12.2 to find the probability that the discrete variable it describes takes a specific value, we can simply measure the height of the block against the vertical axis. In contrast, using the smooth or continuous curve in Figure 13.1 to find the probability that the continuous variable it describes takes a particular value is not so easy.

To start with we need to specify a range rather than a single value because we are dealing with continuous values. For instance, referring to the probability of a variable, X being 4 is inadequate as in a continuous

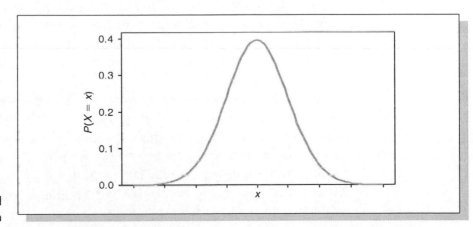

Figure 13.1
The normal
distribution

distribution it implies the probability that X is precisely 4.000. Instead we would have to specify the probability that X is between 3.500 and 4.499. This probability would be represented in a diagram by the area below the curve between the points 3.500 and 4.499 on the horizontal axis as a proportion of the total area below the curve. The probability that a continuous variable takes a precise value is, in effect zero. This means that in practice there is no difference between, say, the probability that X is less than 4, $P(X < 4.000)$ and the probability that X is less than or equal to 4, $P(X \leqslant 4.000)$. Similarly the probability that X is more than 4, $P(X > 4.000)$ is essentially indistinguishable from the probability that X is more than or equal to 4, $P(X \geqslant 4.000)$. For convenience the equalities are left out of the probability statements in what follows.

When we looked at the binomial and Poisson distributions in Chapter 12 we saw how it was possible to calculate probabilities in these distributions using the appropriate formulae. In fact, in the days before the sort of software we now have became available, if you needed to use a binomial or a Poisson distribution you had to start by consulting published tables. However, because of the sheer number of distributions, the one that you wanted may not have appeared in the tables. In such a situation you had to calculate the probabilities yourself.

Calculating the probabilities that make up discrete distributions is tedious but not impossible, especially if the number of outcomes involved is quite small. The nature of the variables concerned, the fact that they can only take a limited number of values, restricts the number of calculations involved.

In contrast, calculating the probabilities in continuous distributions can be daunting. The variables, being continuous, can have an infinite number of different values and the distribution consists of a smooth curve rather than a collection of detached blocks. This makes the mathematics involved very much more difficult and puts the task beyond many people.

Because it was so difficult to calculate normal distribution probabilities, tables were the only viable means of using the normal distribution. However, the number of versions of the normal distribution is literally infinite, so it was impossible to publish tables of all the versions of the normal distribution.

The solution to this problem was the production of tables describing a benchmark normal distribution known as the *Standard Normal Distribution*. The advantage of this was that you could analyse any version of the normal distribution by comparing points in it with equivalent points in the Standard Normal Distribution. Once you had these equivalent points you could use published Standard Normal Distribution tables to assist you with your analysis.

Although modern software means that the Standard Normal Distribution is not as indispensable as it once was, it is important that you know something about it. Not only is it useful in case you do not have access to appropriate software, but more importantly, there are many aspects of further statistical work you will meet that are easier to understand if you are aware of the Standard Normal Distribution.

13.2 The Standard Normal Distribution

The Standard Normal Distribution describes the behaviour of the variable Z, which is normally distributed with a mean of zero and a standard deviation of one. Z is sometimes known as the *Standard Normal Variable* and the Standard Normal Distribution is known as the *Z Distribution*. The distribution is shown in Figure 13.2.

If you look carefully at Figure 13.2 you will see that the bulk of the distribution is quite close to the mean, 0. The tails on either side get closer to the horizontal axis as we get further away from the mean, but they never meet the horizontal axis. They are what are called asymptotic.

As you can see from Figure 13.2, half of the Standard Normal Distribution is to the left of zero, and half to the right. This means that half of the z values that make up the distribution are negative and half are positive.

Table 5 on pages 621–622, Appendix 1 provides a detailed breakdown of the Standard Normal Distribution. You can use it to find the probability that Z, the Standard Normal Variable, is more than a certain value, z,

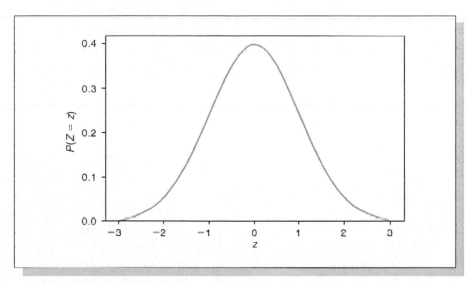

Figure 13.2
The Standard
Normal Distribution

or less than z. In order to show you how this can be done, a section of Table 5 is printed below:

z	0.00	0.01	0.02	0.03	0.04	0.05	0.06	0.07	0.08	0.09
0.0	0.5000	0.4960	0.4920	0.4880	0.4840	0.4801	0.4761	0.4721	0.4681	0.4641
0.1	0.4602	0.4562	0.4522	0.4483	0.4443	0.4404	0.4364	0.4325	0.4286	0.4247
0.2	0.4207	0.4168	0.4129	0.4090	0.4052	0.4013	0.3974	0.3936	0.3897	0.3859
0.3	0.3821	0.3783	0.3745	0.3707	0.3669	0.3632	0.3594	0.3557	0.3520	0.3483
0.4	0.3446	0.3409	0.3372	0.3336	0.3300	0.3264	0.3228	0.3192	0.3156	0.3121
0.5	0.3085	0.3050	0.3015	0.2981	0.2946	0.2912	0.2877	0.2843	0.2810	0.2776
0.6	0.2743	0.2709	0.2676	0.2643	0.2611	0.2578	0.2546	0.2514	0.2483	0.2451
0.7	0.2420	0.2389	0.2358	0.2327	0.2297	0.2266	0.2236	0.2206	0.2177	0.2148
0.8	0.2119	0.2090	0.2061	0.2033	0.2005	0.1977	0.1949	0.1922	0.1894	0.1867
0.9	0.1841	0.1814	0.1788	0.1762	0.1736	0.1711	0.1685	0.1660	0.1635	0.1611
1.0	0.1587	0.1562	0.1539	0.1515	0.1492	0.1469	0.1446	0.1423	0.1401	0.1379

Suppose you need to find the probability that the Standard Normal Variable, Z, is greater than 0.62, $P(Z > 0.62)$. Begin by looking for the value of z, 0.62, to just one decimal place, i.e. 0.6, amongst the values listed in the column headed z on the left hand side. Once you have found 0.6 under z, look along the row to the right until you reach the figure in the column headed 0.02. The figure in the 0.6 row and the 0.02 column is the proportion of the distribution that lies to the right of 0.62, 0.2676. This area represents the probability that Z is greater than 0.62, so $P(Z > 0.62)$ is 0.2676 or 26.76%.

If you want the probability that Z is less than 1.04, $P(Z < 1.04)$, look first for 1.0 in the z column and then proceed to the right until you reach the figure in the column headed 0.04, 0.1492. This is the area to the right of 1.04 and represents the probability that Z is more than 1.04. To get the probability that Z is less than 1.04, subtract 0.1492 from 1:

$$P(Z < 1.04) = 1 - P(Z > 1.04) = 1 - 0.1492 = 0.8508 \text{ or } 85.08\%$$

In Example 13.1 you will find a further demonstration of the use of Table 5.

Example 13.1

Use Table 5 to find the following:

(a) The probability that Z is greater than 0.6, $P(Z > 0.6)$.
(b) The probability that Z is less than 0.6, $P(Z < 0.6)$.
(c) The probability that Z is greater than 2.24, $P(Z > 2.24)$.

(d) The probability that Z is greater than -1.37, $P(Z > -1.37)$.
(e) The probability that Z is less than -1.37, $P(Z < -1.37)$.
(f) The probability that Z is greater than 0.38 and less than 2.71, $P(0.38 < Z < 2.71)$.
(g) The probability that Z is less than -0.88 and more than -1.93, $P(-1.93 < Z < -0.88)$.
(h) The probability that Z is less than 1.59 and more than -0.76, $P(-0.76 < Z < 1.59)$.

Until you are used to dealing with the Standard Normal Distribution you may find it helpful to make a small sketch of the distribution and identify on the sketch the z value(s) of interest and the area that represents the probability you want.

(a) The probability that Z is greater than 0.6, $P(Z > 0.6)$.

The value of Z in this case is not specified to two places of decimals, so we take the figure to the immediate right of 0.6 in Table 5, in the column headed 0.00, which is 0.2743. This is the probability that Z is greater than 0.6. We could also say that 27.43% of z values are greater than 0.6.

This is represented by the shaded area in Figure 13.3.

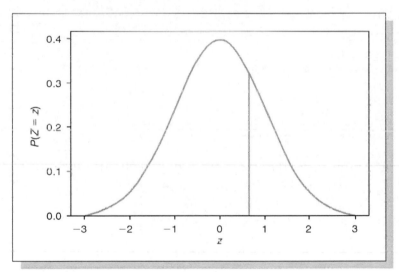

Figure 13.3
Example 13.1 (a): $P(Z > 0.6)$

(b) The probability that Z is less than 0.6, $P(Z < 0.6)$.

In part (a) we found that 27.43% of z values are bigger than 0.6. This implies that 72.57% of z values are less than 0.6, so the answer is $1 - 0.2743$ which is 0.7257.

This is represented by the unshaded area in Figure 13.3.

(c) The probability that Z is greater than 2.24, $P(Z > 2.24)$.

The figure in the row to the right of 2.2 and in the column headed 0.04 in Table 5 is 0.0125. This means that 1.25% of z values are bigger than 2.24. The probability that Z is bigger than 2.24 is therefore 0.0125.

    This is represented by the shaded area in Figure 13.4.

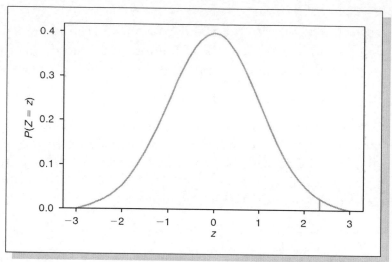

Figure 13.4
Example 13.1 (c): $P(Z > 2.24)$

(d) The probability that Z is greater than -1.37, $P(Z > -1.37)$.

The figure in the row to the right of -1.3 and the column headed 0.07 in Table 5 is 0.9147. This is the area of the distribution to the right of -1.37 and represents the probability that Z is greater than -1.37.

    This is shown as the shaded area in Figure 13.5.

(e) The probability that Z is less than -1.37, $P(Z < -1.37)$.

From part (d) we know that the probability that Z is greater than -1.37 is 0.9147, so the probability that Z is less than -1.37 (by which we mean -1.4, -1.5 and so on) is $1 - 0.9147$, which is 0.0853.

    This is represented by the unshaded area in Figure 13.5.

(f) The probability that Z is greater than 0.38 and less than 2.71, $P(0.38 < Z < 2.71)$.

The probability that Z is greater than 0.38, $P(Z > 0.38)$, is shown in Table 5 in the row for 0.3 and the column headed 0.08, 0.3520. You will find the probability that Z is

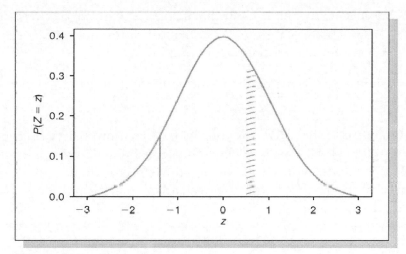

Figure 13.5
Example 13.1 (d): $P(Z > -1.37)$

greater than 2.71 in the row for 2.7 and the column headed 0.01, 0.0034. We can obtain the probability that Z is more than 0.38 and less than 2.71 by taking the probability that Z is more than 2.71 away from the probability that Z is more than 0.38:

$$P(0.38 < Z < 2.71) = P(Z > 0.38) - P(Z > 2.71) = 0.3520 - 0.0034 = 0.3486$$

This is represented by the shaded area in Figure 13.6.

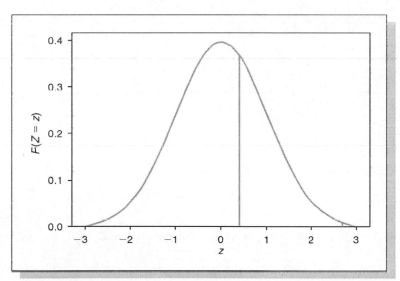

Figure 13.6
Example 13.1 (f): $P(0.38 < Z < 2.71)$

Another way of approaching this is to say that if 35.20% of the area is to the right of 0.38 and 0.34% of the area is to the right of 2.71, then the difference between these two percentages, 34.86%, is the area between 0.38 and 2.71.

(g) The probability that Z is greater than -1.93 and less than -0.88, $P(-1.93 < Z < -0.88)$.

In Table 5 the figure in the -1.9 row and the 0.03 column, 0.9732, is the probability that Z is more than -1.93, $P(Z > -1.93)$. The probability that Z is more than -0.88, $P(Z > -0.88)$ is the figure in the -0.8 row and the 0.08 column, 0.8106. The probability that Z is between -1.93 and -0.88 is the probability that Z is more than -1.93 minus the probability that Z is more than 0.88:

$$P(-1.93 < Z < -0.88) = P(Z > -1.93) - P(Z > -0.88)$$
$$= 0.9732 - 0.8106 = 0.1626$$

This is represented by the shaded area in Figure 13.7.

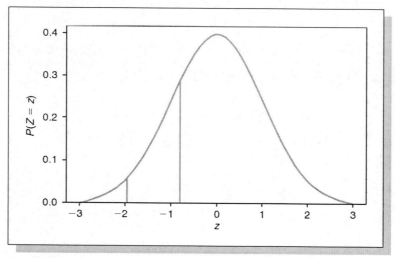

Figure 13.7
Example 13.1 (g): $P(-1.93 < Z < -0.88)$

(h) The probability that Z is greater than -0.76 and less than 1.59, $P(-0.76 < Z < 1.59)$.

The probability that Z is greater than -0.76, $P(Z > -0.76)$, is in the -0.7 row and the 0.06 column of Table 5, 0.7764. $P(Z > 1.59)$ is in the row for 1.5 and the column headed 0.09, 0.0559. The probability that Z is between -0.76 and 1.59 is the probability that Z is greater than -0.76 minus the probability that Z is greater than 1.59:

$$P(-0.79 < Z < 1.59) = P(Z > -0.79) - P(Z > 1.59) = 0.7764 - 0.0559 = 0.7205$$

This is represented by the shaded area in Figure 13.8.

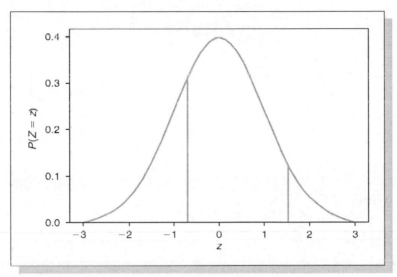

Figure 13.8
Example 13.1 (h): $P(-0.76 < Z < 1.59)$

Sometimes we need to use the Standard Normal Distribution in a rather different way. Instead of starting with a value of Z and finding a probability, we may have a probability and need to know the value of Z associated with it.

Example 13.2

Use Table 5 on pages 621–622 to find the specific value of Z, which we will call z_α, so that the area to the right of z_α, the probability that Z is greater than z_α, $P(Z > z_\alpha)$) is:

(a) 0.4207
(b) 0.0505
(c) 0.0250

(a) If you look carefully down the list of probabilities in Table 5, you will see that 0.4207 appears to the right of the z value 0.2, so in this case the value of z_α is 0.2. The probability that Z is greater than 0.2, $P(Z > 0.2)$, is 0.4207.

This is represented by the shaded area in Figure 13.9.

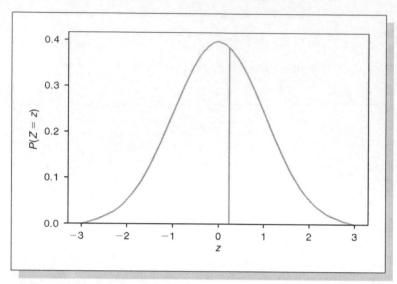

Figure 13.9
Example 13.2 (a): $0.4207 = P(Z > 0.2)$

(b) To find the value of Z that has an area of 0.0505 to the right of it you will have to look further down Table 5. The figure 0.0505 appears in the row for 1.6 and the column headed 0.04, 0.0505 is the probability that Z is more than 1.64, $P(Z > 1.64)$.

This is represented by the shaded area in Figure 13.10.

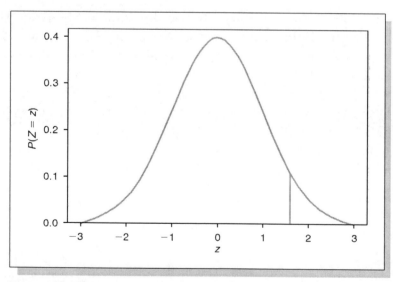

Figure 13.10
Example 13.2 (b): $0.0505 = P(Z > 1.64)$

(c) The value of Z that has an area of 0.0250, or 2.5% of the distribution, to the right of it, is 1.96 because the figure 0.0250 is in the row for 1.9 and the column headed 0.06 in Table 5. So 0.0250 is the probability that Z is more than 1.96, $P(Z > 1.96)$.

This is represented by the shaded area in Figure 13.11.

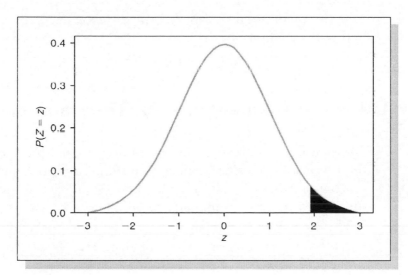

Figure 13.11
Example 13.2 (c): $0.0250 = P(Z > 1.96)$

The symbol we used in Example 13.2 to represent the value of Z we wanted to find, z_α, is a symbol that you will come across in later work. α represents the area of the distribution beyond z_α, in other words, the probability that z is beyond z_α.

$$P(Z > z_\alpha) = \alpha$$

In Example 13.2 (c), α is 0.0250 and z_α is 1.96, that is $P(Z > 1.96) = 0.0250$. 1.96 is the value of Z and 0.0250 or 2.5% is the area of the distribution beyond 1.96. As you can see from Figure 13.11, this is a small area in the right-hand tail of the distribution, so we sometimes refer to such as area as a *tail area*.

Sometimes it is convenient to represent a particular value of Z by the letter z followed by the tail area beyond it in the distribution in the form of a suffix. For instance, the z value 1.96 could be written as $z_{0.0250}$ because there is a tail of 0.0250 of the distribution beyond 1.96. We might say that the z value 1.96 'cuts off' a tail area of 0.0250 from the rest of the distribution.

In later work you will find that particular z values are often referred to in this style because it is the area of the tail that leads us to use a particular z value and we may want to emphasize the fact. Values of Z that cut off tails of 5%, 2.5%, 1% and ½% crop up in the topics we will look at in Chapter 16. The z values that cut off these tail areas, 1.64, 1.96, 2.33 and 2.58, are frequently referred to as $z_{0.05}$, $z_{0.025}$, $z_{0.01}$ and $z_{0.005}$ respectively.

At this point you may find it useful to try **Review Question 13.1** at the end of the chapter.

13.2.1 Using the Standard Normal Distribution

To use the Standard Normal Distribution to analyse other versions of the normal distribution we need to be able to express any value of the normal distribution that we want to investigate as a value of Z. This is sometimes known as finding its *Z-equivalent* or *Z score*.

The Z-equivalent of a particular value, x, of a normal variable, X, is the difference between x and the mean of X, μ, divided by the standard deviation of X, σ.

$$z = \frac{x - \mu}{\sigma}$$

Because we are dividing the difference between the value, x, and the mean of the distribution it belongs to, μ, by the standard deviation of the distribution, σ, to get it, the Z-equivalent of a value is really just the number of standard deviations the value is away from the mean.

Once we have found the Z-equivalent of a value of a normal distribution we can refer to the Standard Normal Distribution table, Table 5 on pages 621–622, to assess probabilities associated with it.

Example 13.3

The Plotoyani Restaurant offers a 10 oz Steak Special. The steaks they use for these meals have uncooked weights that are normally distributed with a mean of 9.8 oz and a standard deviation of 0.5 oz. Find the probability that a customer will get:

(a) a steak that has an uncooked weight of more than 10 oz?
(b) a steak that has an uncooked weight of more than 9.5 oz?
(c) a steak that has an uncooked weight of less than 10.5 oz?

If X represents the uncooked weights of the steaks, we want to find $P(X > 10)$. This is represented by the shaded area in Figure 13.12.

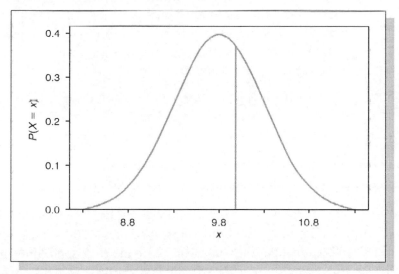

Figure 13.12
Example 13.3 (a), $P(X > 10)$

The Z-equivalent of $x = 10$ is

$$z = \frac{10 - 9.8}{0.5} = 0.4$$

So the probability that X is more than 10 is equivalent to the probability that Z is more than 0.4. From Table 5 on pages 621–622:

$$P(Z > 0.4) = 0.3446 \quad \text{or} \quad 34.46\%$$

(b) The Z-equivalent of 9.5, $z = \dfrac{9.5 - 9.8}{0.5} = -0.6$

So the probability that X is more than 9.5 is equivalent to the probability that Z is more than -0.6. From Table 5:

$$P(Z > -0.6) = 0.7257 \quad \text{or} \quad 72.57\%$$

(c) The Z-equivalent of 10.5, $z = \dfrac{10.5 - 9.8}{0.5} = 1.4$

The probability that X is less than 10.5 is the same as the probability that Z is less than 1.4. According to Table 5 the probability that Z is more than 1.4 is 0.0808, so the probability that Z is less than 1.4 is $1 - 0.0808$ which is 0.9192, or 91.92%.

In some situations you may need to find a specific point in the normal distribution that cuts off a particular tail area. To do this, you first have to select the value of Z that cuts off the same area in the Standard Normal Distribution. Once you have established this z value, find the point that number of standard deviations away from the mean. If the z value is positive, add that number of standard deviations to the mean, if it is negative, take them away.

Example 13.4

In the population of uncooked steaks in Example 13.3, what is:

(a) the minimum weight of the heaviest 20% of steaks?
(b) the maximum weight of the lightest 10% of steaks?

To answer (a), begin by looking at the probabilities in Table 5 on pages 621–622. Look down the table until you come to the figure closest to 0.2, 0.2005. This figure is in the row for 0.8 and the column headed 0.04, which means that the value of Z that cuts off a 20% tail on the right hand side of the distribution is 0.84. In other words $P(Z > 0.84)$ is 0.2005.

If 20% of the Standard Normal Distribution lies to the right of 0.84, 20% of any version of the normal distribution, including the one representing the distribution of uncooked weights of steaks in Example 13.3, lies to the right of a point 0.84 standard deviations above the mean. The mean of the distribution of uncooked weights of steaks is 9.8 oz and the standard deviation is 0.5 oz, so 20% of uncooked steaks weigh more than:

$$9.8 + (0.84 * 0.05) = 10.22 \, oz$$

We can conclude that the heaviest 20% of the steaks weigh more than 10.22 oz.

The figure for (b), the maximum weight of the lightest 10% of steaks, is also the minimum weight of the heaviest 90% of steaks. From Table 5 the value of Z that cuts off 90% of the area to the right of it is -1.28. If 90% of the Standard Normal Distribution is above -1.28 then 10% is below it. This means that the lowest 10% of any version of the normal distribution is 1.28 standard deviations below the mean, so the lightest 10% of steaks will weigh less than:

$$9.8 - (1.28 * 0.5) = 9.16 \, oz$$

The normal distribution is an important statistical distribution because it enables us to investigate the very many continuous variables that occur in business and many other fields, whose values are distributed in a normal pattern. What makes the normal distribution especially important, perhaps the most important distributions in Statistics, is that it enables us to understand how sample results vary. This is because many *sampling distributions* have a normal pattern.

At this point you may find it useful to try **Review Questions 13.2 to 13.11** at the end of the chapter.

13.3 The exponential distribution

The importance of the normal distribution and the attention rightly devoted to it in quantitative methods programmes often obscures the fact that it is not the only continuous probability distribution. The normal distribution is a symmetrical distribution and is therefore an entirely appropriate model for continuous random variables that vary in a symmetrical pattern. But not all continuous random variables that crop up in business analysis exhibit this characteristic.

Many business operations involve queues or waiting-lines; you have probably waited in a queue to pay for groceries, you may have waited in a queue for access to a telephone help-line. These are fairly obvious examples, but there are many others; you may have taken a flight in an aircraft that has had to wait in a queue in the airspace above an airport before it can land, when you post a letter in effect it joins a queue to be sorted by the postal service.

In the next section we shall consider a basic queuing model, but before we do so we will look at the exponential distribution. This is a continuous probability distribution that is important for analysing, among other things, service times in queuing processes.

The exponential distribution differs from the normal distribution in two respects; it describes variables whose variables can only be positive, and it is asymmetrical around its mean. The probability that an exponential random variable takes a particular value can be worked out using the formula:

$$P(X = x) = \frac{e^{-x/\mu}}{\mu}$$

where μ is the mean of the distribution and x is the value of interest. The letter e represents Euler's number, 2.7183 to four decimal places. Because the exponential distribution is a continuous probability distribution we are almost always interested in a cumulative probability such as the probability that the variable is greater than a particular value, which we can find using:

$$P(X > x) = e^{-x/\mu}$$

Or the probability that the variable is less than a particular value, which is:

$$P(X < x) = 1 - e^{-x/\mu}$$

To use these expressions for any specific distribution you need to know only the mean of the distribution and the specific value of interest.

Example 13.5

The times it takes to serve customers visiting a bus company office to renew their bus passes are exponentially distributed with a mean of 2 minutes. What is the probability that a customer has to wait more than 5 minutes?

If X represents the service times,

$$P(X > 5) = e^{-5/2} = e^{-2.5} = 2.7813^{-2.5} = 1/2.7183^{2.5} = 1/12.182 = 0.082$$

The calculation of the cumulative probability in Example 13.5 is shown in full, but you should be able to work out an expression like $e^{-2.5}$ on your calculator. Look for a key with e^x on or above it. It is unlikely to be the first function of the key so you may have to use a sequence like **SHIFT** then e^x then key in 2.5 then press $+/-$ then $=$. Your calculator may require a sequence that begins with the exponent, so you will have to key in 2.5 then press $+/-$ then **SHIFT** (or possibly **2nd** for second function) then e^x.

The exponential distribution for the service times in Example 13.5 is shown in Figure 13.13. The shaded area represents the probability that the service time exceeds 5 minutes.

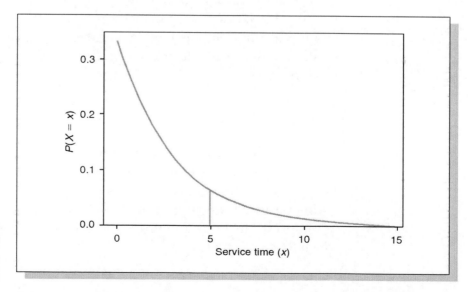

Figure 13.13
Distribution of
service times in
Example 13.5

You may recall that e, Euler's number appeared in the expression for the Poisson distribution that we looked at in section 12.3 of Chapter 12. The similarity is no accident; the two distributions are connected. The Poisson distribution is used to model incidents occurring over a period of time. If the number of accidents at a factory follows a Poisson distribution then the time interval between accidents will follow an exponential distribution with a mean that is the reciprocal of the mean of the Poisson distribution.

Example 13.6

The number of serious injuries occurring per month at the Appasney Engineering plant behaves according to the Poisson distribution with a mean of 2. What is the probability that the time between successive serious injuries exceeds a month?

If the mean number of serious injuries is 2, then the mean time interval between injuries is ½, 0.5. This is the mean of the exponential distribution of the times between serious injuries, X. The probability that the time between serious injuries is more than a month is:

$$P(X > 1) = e^{-1/0.5} = e^{-2} = 2.7813^{-2} = 1/2.7183^2 = 1/7.389 = 0.135$$

At this point you may find it useful to try **Review Questions 13.12 to 13.15** at the end of the chapter.

13.4 A simple queuing model

Queues are quite complex processes because they usually depend on the behaviour of random variables – the number of arrivals per unit of time and the time taken to deal with the people or things concerned. They can be difficult to manage because if for instance customers wait too long they may take their business elsewhere yet devoting too many staff to provide the service may result in their being unoccupied for significant periods of time.

Because of the importance of queuing systems in business operations, queuing theory is a substantial subject. Here we will look at one of the simpler models.

The point of any queuing theory model is to provide us with information about the operation of the queuing system it represents, specifically the average waiting time and the average length of the queue.

If we make certain assumptions about the behaviour of individuals in the queue and know the patterns of arrivals and service times we can do this.

The behaviour assumptions underlying the model we will consider are that having joined the queue an individual will stay in it until they have been served and that individuals in the queue are served on a FIFO (First In First Out) basis, in other words, first come first served. We will further assume that individuals join the queue according to the Poisson distribution with a mean of λ, and that service times are exponentially distributed according to the exponential distribution with a mean of μ.

The symbol λ, lambda, is the Greek letter l, which we will use to distinguish the mean of the Poisson arrivals distribution from the mean of the exponential service times distribution in keeping with the conventions of notation in queuing theory. Both means need to be expressed in the same style so we define λ, the mean of the arrivals distribution, as the mean arrival rate, and μ, the mean of the service times, as the mean service rate.

In queuing theory models are identified by the distributions of arrivals and service times, with M used to represent the Poisson and exponential distributions. In the simple model we shall study we assume there is just one service point. This model is known as the M/M/1, indicating Poisson arrivals, exponential service times and one server.

The ratio between the mean arrival rate and the mean service rate, λ/μ is the *traffic intensity* in the queuing system, represented by the Greek letter rho, ρ, the Greek r. For a queuing system to be viable the traffic intensity must be less than 1, in other words the mean arrival rate must be less than the mean service rate, otherwise the queue would simply continue to grow and the system would 'explode'.

By means of mathematical derivations involving probability and differentiation it is possible to determine a number of operating measures of an M/M/1 queuing system including:

> The probability that the server is idle $= 1 - \rho$
> The probability that there are more than r individuals in the queue $= \rho^{r+2}$
> The mean number in the queue, $L_q = \rho^2/(1 - \rho)$
> The mean waiting time in the queue, $W_q = \rho/(\mu - \lambda)$

Example 13.7

Between midnight and 6am there is one cashier on duty at a 24-hour service station. During this time customers arrive at the cash desk to pay for their fuel and other goods according to a Poisson distribution with a mean of 12 per hour and service times are exponentially distributed with a mean of 3 minutes.

The mean arrival rate, λ, is 12 per hour, the mean service rate, μ, is 20 per hour so ρ, the traffic intensity, is 12/20, 0.6.

The probability that the cashier is idle $= 1 - \rho = 1 - 0.6 = 0.4$

The probability that there is more than one person in the queue $= \rho^{2+1}$
$$= 0.6^3 = 0.216$$

The mean number in the queue $= \rho^2/(1 - \rho) = 0.6^2/(1 - 0.6) = 0.36/0.4 = 0.9$

The mean waiting time in the queue $= \rho/(\mu - \lambda) = 0.6/(20 - 12)$
$$= 0.6/8 = 0.075 \text{ hours or } 4 \text{ minutes}$$

At this point you may find it useful to try **Review Questions 13.16 to 13.19** at the end of the chapter.

This queuing model is only one of many models that constitute queuing theory. For more about the topic try Taha (1997) or Bronson and Naadimuthu (1997).

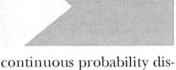

13.5 Using the technology: continuous probability distributions using EXCEL, MINITAB and SPSS

Statistical packages can analyse a variety of continuous probability distributions for you. In this section we will outline how to find probabilities for the distributions described in this chapter.

13.5.1 EXCEL

You can obtain a normal probability in EXCEL by clicking on an empty cell in the spreadsheet then

- Type = **NORMDIST(x,mean,standard deviation,TRUE)** in the Formula Bar. The number x is the value whose probability you want to find. The mean and the standard deviation are the parameters of the Normal distribution to which x belongs. **TRUE** denotes that we want a cumulative probability.
- To obtain the answer to Example 13.3 (a) type = **NORMDIST(10,9.8,0.5,TRUE)**.

▓ Click on the √ button to the left of the formula bar or press Enter. The probability that X is greater than x should appear in the cell you originally clicked. The probability shown for Example 13.3 (a) should be 0.655422, so the probability that X is greater than 10 is 0.344578.

13.5.2 MINITAB

For a normal probability

▓ Select the **Probability Distributions** option from the **Calc** menu.

▓ Pick the **Normal** option from the sub-menu. In the command window that appears choose to obtain a cumulative probability.

▓ Specify the **Mean** and the **Standard deviation** of the normal distribution you want to find out about. For the answer to Example 13.3 (a) these are 9.8 and 0.5 respectively.

▓ Click the button to the left of **Input constant** and in the space to the right type the x value whose probability you want. For Example 13.3 (a) this is 10.

▓ Click **OK** and you will see the cumulative probability that X is less than or equal to x appear in the session window. For Example 13.3 (a) the probability shown should be 0.6554. This is the probability that X is less than 10, so the probability that it is more than 10 is 0.3446.

For an exponential probability

▓ Select the **Probability Distributions** option from the **Calc** menu.

▓ Pick the **Exponential** option from the sub-menu. In the command window that appears choose to obtain a cumulative probability.

▓ Specify the **Mean** of the exponential distribution you want to investigate.

▓ Click the button to the left of **Input constant** and in the space to the right type the x value whose probability you want.

▓ Click **OK** and you will see the cumulative probability that X is less than or equal to x appear in the session window.

13.5.3 SPSS

To get cumulative probabilities of the normal distribution

- Choose the **Compute** option from the **Transform** pull-down menu.
- In the **Compute Variable** window click on **CDF.NORMAL (q,mean,stddev)** in the long list under **Functions:** on the right-hand side of the window, and click the ▲ button to the right of **Functions:** The command should now appear in the space under **Numeric Expression:** to the top right of the window with three question marks inside the brackets. Replace these question marks with the value of x whose cumulative probability you want (referred to as q in SPSS), and the mean and standard deviation of the normal distribution you wish to investigate, respectively.
- To use this facility to produce the probability in Example 13.3 (a) your command should be **CDF.NORMAL(10,9.8,0.5)**. You will need to enter the name of a column to store the answer in the space under **Target Variable:** this can be a default name like **var00001**.
- Click **OK** and the cumulative probability, 0.66, should appear in your target column. This is the probability that x is less than 10. The probability that x is more than 10 is therefore 0.34.

13.6 Road test: Do they really use the normal distribution?

In recent times companies have devoted more attention to the quality of their products, services and procedures. This has resulted in managers paying more attention to the variation in the quality of what they produce. In many cases this variation has followed a normal distribution and quality objectives have therefore been based on it, such as ensuring that the proportion of customers waiting more than a certain time at a supermarket checkout does not exceed a certain limit. Using the normal distribution, we could for instance say that if no more than 1% of customers should have to wait more than 5 minutes, then this waiting time should be at the point 2.33 standard deviations to the right of the mean of the distribution. This would lead us to ask what the mean and standard deviation of the distribution of waiting times would have to be in order to fulfil this objective, how do these parameters compare with current performance and by how much would we have to improve one or both in order to achieve the objective.

In this illustration 1% sounds an acceptably small proportion of customers, but if the store has on average 20,000 shoppers each day we would expect 200 of them to have to wait more than 5 minutes. For the store manager this may well be an unacceptably high number of shoppers to alienate and potentially lose.

This focus on the absolute numbers rather than the proportion resulted in quality experts developing an approach known as *six sigma*. The Greek letter sigma, σ, is the one we have used to represent the standard deviation of the normal distribution. The pioneers of six sigma argued that unacceptable performance should be restricted not to the proportion of the distribution beyond two or even three sigma, i.e. two or three standard deviations beyond the mean, but to six standard deviations beyond the mean. By doing this, unacceptable performance should only occur in a very small part of one per cent of cases.

Eckes (2001) describes the application of the six sigma strategy in one of the hotels in the Westin Hotel chain in the USA. One aspect of their operations that he deals with in some detail is the delivery of room service meals to guests' rooms. The manager in charge of room service ascertained through customer feedback that guests considered an interval of more than 30 minutes between phoning down their order and the meal being delivered to be unacceptable. Room service meal delivery times at the hotel were thought to be normally distributed with a mean of 26 minutes, which meant that the threshold of unacceptable service, 30 minutes, was roughly three sigmas (standard deviations) above the mean.

Looking at the process and introducing improvements in the communication and processing of customer orders reduced the mean to 23 minutes and meant that the unacceptable service threshold was more than four sigmas above the mean. The six sigma target could be reached either by reducing the mean further, which would probably prove difficult, or by reducing the value of sigma, the standard deviation, by making the delivery times more consistent (perhaps by rationalizing the room service menu), or by a combination of both.

Review questions

Answers to these questions, including fully worked solution to the Key questions marked with an asterisk (*), are on pages 662–663.

13.1   Find the areas of the Standard Normal Distribution that represent the following probabilities:
   (a) $P(Z > 1.44)$
   (b) $P(Z > -0.29)$
   (c) $P(Z < 2.06)$
   (d) $P(Z < -1.73)$
   (e) $P(0.52 < Z < 1.99)$
   (f) $P(-2.31 < Z < -1.08)$
   (g) $P(-0.97 < Z < 0.65)$

13.2*   A confectionery company produces 100 g 'Real Chocolate' bars that have a mean chocolate content of 70 g with a standard deviation of 0.8 g. The variation in chocolate content is normally distributed. What is the probability that a chocolate bar chosen at random contains:
   (a) more than 71 g?
   (b) more than 68 g?
   (c) less than 70 g?
   (d) between 69 and 72 g?

13.3   The colour dye used in the manufacture of certain garments fades after a mean of 96 machine washes, with a standard deviation of 7 washes. If the number of washes before fading follows a normal distribution, what proportion of the garments will first fade:
   (a) after 100 washes?
   (b) before 90 washes?
   (c) between 95 and 105 washes?

13.4   An automobile manufacturer produces a certain model of car. The fuel economy figures of these cars are normally distributed with a mean mileage per gallon (mpg) of 36.8 and a standard deviation of 1.3.
   (a) What is the probability that one of these cars will have an mpg of more than 37.5?
   (b) What is the probability that one of these cars will have an mpg of less than 35?
   (c) What is the probability that one of these cars will have an mpg of less than 40?
   (d) What is the probability that one of these cars will have an mpg of between 34 and 38 mpg?
   (e) What is the minimum mpg of the 15% most fuel efficient cars?
   (f) What is the maximum mpg of the 10% least fuel efficient cars?

13.5   A large company insists that all job applicants who are invited
        for interview take a psychometric test. The results of these tests
        follow a normal distribution with a mean of 61% and the stand-
        ard deviation of 7.2%.
        (a) What proportion of applicants would be expected to score
            over 70%?
        (b) What proportion of applicants would be expected to score
            under 40%?
        (c) What proportion of applicants would be expected to score
            between 50% and 65%?
        (d) What score is exceeded by 20% of applicants?
        (e) What is the highest score achieved by the 5% of applicants
            who do least well in the test?

13.6   A bed linen company manufactures duvets that have a mean
        TOG rating (a measure of thermal effectiveness) of 11.5 with a
        standard deviation of 0.18. If the TOG ratings are normally dis-
        tributed, what is the probability that a duvet selected at random
        has a TOG rating:
        (a) above 12?
        (b) above 11.3?
        (c) below 11.6?
        (d) below 11.1?
        (e) between 11.2 and 11.4?
        (f) between 11.5 and 11.9?

13.7   The weight losses that members of a slimming club can expect
        to achieve follow a normal distribution with a mean of 24.7 lb
        and a standard deviation of 5.2 lb.
        (a) What proportion of members can expect to lose more than
            25 lb?
        (b) What proportion of members can expect to lose more than
            20 lb?
        (c) What proportion of members can expect to lose less than
            35 lb?
        (d) What proportion of members can expect to lose less than
            15 lb?
        (e) What proportion of members can expect to lose between
            12 lbs and 30 lb?
        (f) What is the most weight that the least successful 40% of
            slimmers can expect to lose?
        (g) What is the least weight that the most successful 30% of
            slimmers can expect to lose?

13.8 The times taken by a traditional barber to cut hair are normally distributed with a mean of 15.6 minutes and a standard deviation of 3.4 minutes. What is the probability that he can cut a customer's hair in:

(a) less than 20 minutes?
(b) less than 10 minutes?
(c) between 8 and 14 minutes?
(d) between 17 and 22 minutes?
(e) between 12 and 18 minutes?

13.9 A drinks vending machine dispenses a variety of hot and cold beverages. The volumes of the drinks dispensed follow a normal pattern with a mean of 149.7 ml and a standard deviation of 1.2 ml.

(a) What proportion of drinks will be over 150 ml?
(b) What proportion of drinks will be over 147.5 ml?
(c) What proportion of drinks will be under 148 ml?
(d) What proportion of drinks will be under 152 ml?
(e) What proportion of drinks will be between 149 ml and 152.5 ml?
(f) What is the most that can be expected in the smallest 5% of drinks?
(g) What is the least that can be expected in the largest 25% of drinks?

13.10 The amount of time that visitors to a website browse the site is assumed to be normally distributed with a mean of 8.75 minutes and a standard deviation of 3.1 minutes. What is the probability that a randomly selected visitor browses the site for:

(a) less than 5 minutes?
(b) more than 10 minutes?
(c) less than 15 minutes?
(d) between 3 and 7 minutes?
(e) between 10 and 14 minutes?
(f) between 8 and 12 minutes?

13.11 The Doroga Motor Company offer a warranty of 60,000 miles on the cars they produce. Any part that fails before the car has attained that mileage is supplied and fitted at the company's expense. The lifetimes of the bearings they currently fit in their vehicles are normally distributed with a mean of 73,200 miles and a standard deviation of 7155 miles.

(a) What proportion of bearings will fail before the warranty mileage is reached?

(b) An alternative supplier offers the company bearings with a mean lifetime of 69,230 miles and a standard deviation of 4620 miles. What proportion of these bearings can be expected to fail before the warranty mileage is reached?

(c) Should the company change suppliers, and if so, why?

13.12* The times that elapse between the announcements of the winning numbers in a lottery and winners claiming their prizes are exponentially distributed with a mean of 20 hours. Work out the probability that the length of time a winner takes to claim their prize is:

(a) more than 24 hours

(b) less than 12 hours

(c) between 36 and 48 hours.

13.13 The delays in the departures of flights operated by Flotair follow an exponential distribution with a mean of 13 minutes. Find the probability that one of their flights:

(a) departs less than 10 minutes late

(b) departs more than 30 minutes late

(c) departs between 5 and 15 minutes late

13.14 In an office with a shared printer the time intervals between staff sending print instructions on their PCs and the jobs being printed form an exponential distribution with a mean of 1.4 minutes. What proportion of jobs sent to the printer take:

(a) over a minute

(b) less than 30 seconds

(c) between 3 and 5 minutes

13.15 A national vehicle breakdown and recovery service operates a website offering route planning guidance and maps to its members. The time it takes for users to get their directions and maps on screen has been a matter of complaint from many members. According to the available data the times to fulfil user requests are exponentially distributed, with a mean of 4.8 minutes.

(a) What is the probability that a user will have to wait

(i) more than 5 minutes

(ii) more than 10 minutes

(b) The website is being redesigned. Pilot runs suggest that under the new system service times will be exponentially distributed with a mean of 3.7 minutes. What is the probability that a user requesting route details from it will have to wait

(i) more than 5 minutes

(ii) more than 10 minutes

13.16* A large clothing store offers a 'no quibble' returns policy under which shoppers can return unwanted goods to the store and receive their money back. They have to take their unwanted goods to a returns desk where there is one server. Customers arrive at the desk according to a Poisson distribution with a mean of 24 per hour and service times at the desk are exponentially distributed with a mean of two minutes.

    (a) What is the traffic intensity in the returns system?

    (b) What is the probability that there are more than three customers queuing?

    (c) What is the mean waiting time?

    (d) What is the mean queue length?

13.17 There is only one pharmacist dispensing prescribed medicines in a small pharmacy. The pattern of customers arriving to obtain a prescription follows a Poisson distribution with a mean of six per hour. The times taken for the pharmacist to dispense the drugs are exponentially distributed with a mean of 7.5 minutes.

    (a)   (i) What is the traffic intensity of the system?

        (ii) What is the mean queue length?

        (iii) What is the mean waiting time in the queue?

    (b) If increasing the proportion of generic drugs in the pharmacy can reduce the mean service time to 6 minutes,

        (i) What is the traffic intensity of the system?

        (ii) What is the mean queue length?

        (iii) What is the mean waiting time in the queue?

13.18 A 'money shop' tax adviser operates a 'no appointments necessary' system whereby customers arrive at the shop when they wish and wait for a consultation. The adviser works alone and the times she takes to serve customers vary exponentially with a mean of 15 minutes. Customer arrivals are distributed according to the Poisson distribution with a mean of 2.5 per hour.

    (a) Work out the traffic intensity of the system.

    (b) There are four chairs that customers can sit on while waiting for a consultation. Find the probability that one or more customers will have to stand while they are waiting.

    (c) Calculate the mean length of the queue.

    (d) Determine the mean waiting time in the queue.

13.19 If an item of mail cannot be delivered it is returned to the local depot and a card sent to the addressee inviting them to come to the depot to collect it. At the depot the one postal worker deals with customers arriving according to a Poisson distribution with a mean of ten per hour. Service times are exponentially distributed with a mean of 4 minutes.

(a) What is the probability that the postal worker will be idle?

(b) What is the probability that there are more than two customers in the queue?

(c) What is the mean length of the queue?

(d) What is the mean waiting time in the queue?

13.20 Select the appropriate description for each term on the left-hand side from the list on the right-hand side.

(i) a z equivalent

(ii) mean waiting time in an M/M/1 queue

(iii) the normal distribution

(iv) mean length of an M/M/1 queue

(v) traffic intensity in an M/M/1 queue

(vi) FIFO

(vii) the Z distribution

(viii) the exponential distribution

(a) $L_q = \rho^2/(1 - \rho)$

(b) the Standard Normal Distribution

(c) first in first out discipline in queues

(d) $\rho = \lambda/\sigma$

(e) symmetrical and asymptotic

(f) $W_q = \rho/(\mu - \lambda)$

(g) asymmetrical and non-negative

(h) $(x - \mu)/\sigma$

CHAPTER 14

Getting from A to B — project planning using networks

This chapter will help you to:

- construct network diagrams
- apply critical path analysis (CPA)
- identify slack time available for project activities
- use the Program Evaluation and Review Technique (PERT)
- conduct cost analysis of projects using network diagrams
- become acquainted with business uses of CPA/PERT

Many business operations involve planning and coordinating a project – a series of interlinked tasks or activities all of which have to be performed in the correct sequence and within the least amount of time in order to achieve a successful conclusion to the venture. This is not only typical of large-scale projects such as you would find in industries like construction and shipbuilding, but also occurs on a more modest basis in administrative processes such as organizing events like conferences and concerts.

To help plan and execute projects successfully managers can turn to *network analysis*, a system of representing and linking the activities involved in a project. Once they have designed a network they can use *critical path analysis (CPA)* to establish the minimum duration of the project by identifying those tasks whose completion on time is essential, the *critical* activities. Beyond this they can bring into consideration the probability distributions that reflect the chances of the activities being completed by specific times using the *program evaluation and review technique (PERT)*. In this chapter we will look at these techniques.

14.1 Network analysis

We can apply network analysis to any project that consists of series of distinct activities provided that we know which activities must be completed before other activities can commence. This is called the precedence of the activities because it involves identifying the activities that must *precede* each activity. These are crucial because the point of a network diagram is to show how the activities in a project are linked.

The diagrams used for network analysis are built up using a single arrow for each activity. The arrow begins at a circle representing the point in time at which the activity begins and finishes at another circle that represents the completion of the activity. These circles are known as *event nodes*. We would represent a single activity as shown in Figure 14.1.

In Figure 14.1 the direction of the arrow tells us that the event node on the right marks the completion of the activity. The activity is labelled using a letter and the events nodes are numbered. Network diagrams consist of many arrows and many event nodes, so logical layout and labelling is important.

Networks should be set out so that the beginning of the project is represented by the event node on the extreme left of the diagram and the completion by the event node on the extreme right. In compiling them you should try to ensure that the event nodes are labelled sequentially from left to right from event number 1, the start of the project.

All the arrows should point from left to right either directly or at angle and certainly not from right to left. This is usually straightforward because the purpose of an arrow in a network is to represent the *position* of the activity in relation to other activities and not its *duration*. A network diagram is not intended to be to scale.

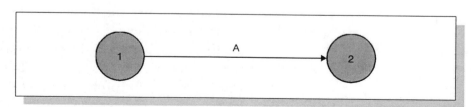

Figure 14.1
A single activity

Example 14.1

Avia Petitza is an independent airline flying short-haul routes in South America. The new general manager is keen to improve efficiency and believes that one aspect of their operations that can be improved is the time it takes to service planes between flights. She has identified the activities involved and their preceding activities and compiled the following table:

Activity	Description	Precedence
A	Drive service vehicles to plane	None
B	Attach stairway	A
C	Unload baggage	A
D	Refuel	A
E	Passengers disembark	B
F	Clean cabin	E
G	Load baggage	C
H	Load food and beverages	E
I	Stock up water tanks	A
J	Service toilets	I
K	Passengers embark	F, H
L	Detach stairway	K
M	Drive service vehicles from plane	D, G, J, L

Produce a network diagram to portray this project.

Activity A has no preceding activities so we can start the network with this as shown in Figure 14.2(a). Four subsequent activities, B, C, D and I depend on activity A being completed so we can extend the network as shown in Figure 14.2(b). Activity G must follow activity C and activity J follows activity I as depicted in Figure 14.2(c). Activity E follows activity B and activity F follows activity E as shown in Figure 14.2(d).

Before activity K can take place activity H must also have finished. This presents a problem because we cannot have two or more activities starting at the same event node and finishing at the same event node. If we did we would not be able to use the diagram for the sort of scheduling analysis you will meet in the next section of this chapter. To avoid activities F and H having the same event node marking their start and the same event node marking their completion we can introduce a *dummy activity*, an activity that takes no time nor uses any resources. Its role is merely to help us distinguish two activities that might otherwise be confused in later analysis. To distinguish between a dummy activity and real activities it is portrayed as a dotted line. You can see a dummy activity in Figure 14.2(e) used to ensure that the event node that marks the conclusion of activity H is not the same as that marking the end of activity F.

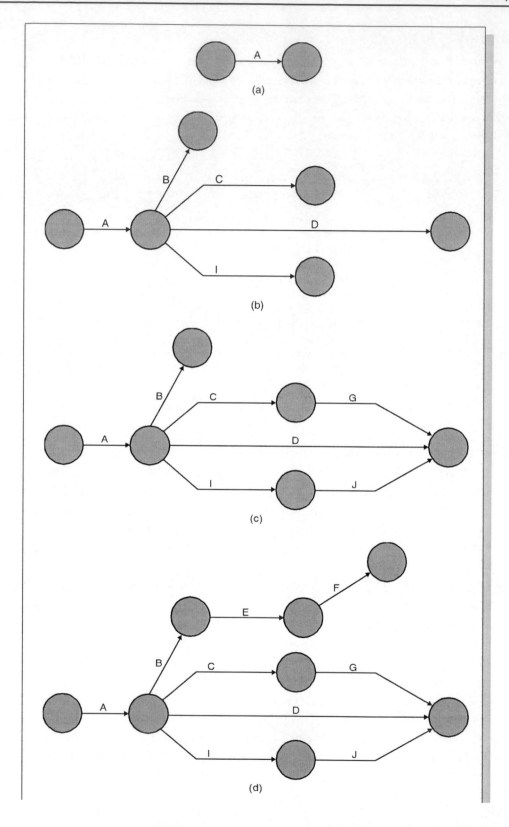

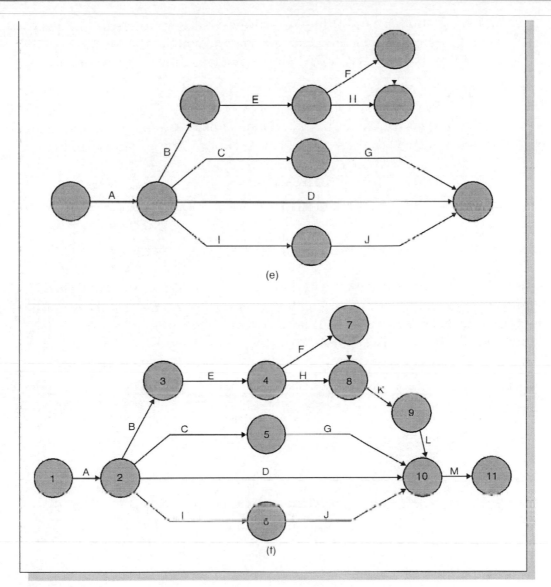

Figure 14.2
Stages in the compilation of the network diagram for aircraft servicing in Example 14.1

The final diagram, Figure 14.2(f), incorporates activities K, L and M. Activities K and L share the same finishing event as activities D and J. This event represents the beginning of activity M, whose closing event marks the conclusion of the project. We can also number the events now the diagram is complete.

The dummy activity in Figure 14.2(e) helps us to identify two separate activities. A dummy activity used in this way is an *identity dummy*. Dummy activities are also used to resolve logical difficulties that arise in some networks. A dummy activity used to do this is a *logical dummy*.

Both types of dummy activity serve only to clarify the network and avoid ambiguity. The important distinction between real and dummy activities is that the latter do not take time or use resources.

Example 14.2

Two building workers, Bru and Chai, like a mug of black tea in their morning break at work. Bru takes sugar, Chai does not. Making their tea involves four activities:

Activity	Description	Precedence
A	Put tea bags in the mugs	None
B	Put sugar in Bru's mug	None
C	Pour hot water in Chai's mug	A
D	Pour hot water in Bru's mug	A, B

It is tempting to represent these activities in the form of the network in Figure 14.3(a), but this implies that activity C, putting hot water in Chai's mug, depends on activity B, putting sugar in Bru's mug, which is not the case. To get around this we can include a dummy activity as shown in Figure 14.3 (b).

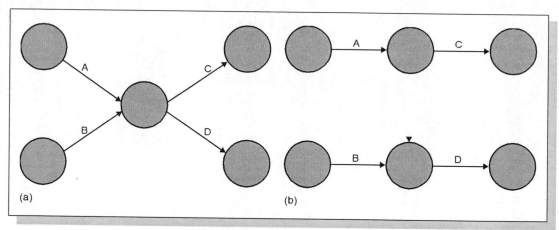

Figure 14.3
Incorrect (a) and correct (b) networks for Example 14.2

Compiling network diagrams often brings an understanding of the way in which activities that make up a project fit together. It enables you to clarify uncertainties about the planning of the project. This is something usually achieved by constructing drafts of the network before producing the final version.

Whilst an understanding of the sequence is important, there is much more to successful project planning. Ascertaining the minimum time in which the project can be completed and scheduling the activities over time are typically the central issues. The technique that enables us to do this is critical path analysis.

14.2 Critical path analysis

If we know the duration of each activity we can use a network diagram to find out the least amount of time it will take to finish the project.

A network diagram shows the way that activities are linked; in effect it portrays the project as a series of paths of activities. Since every activity must be finished for the project to be completed, the minimum duration of the project is the length of time required to carry out the most time-consuming path of activities. This path is known as the *critical path* since any delay in the completion of activities along it will prolong the entire project. Finishing those activities on the critical path on time is therefore *critical* for the project; they are known as *critical* activities.

Critical path analysis involves increasing the amount of information in the network by enhancing the role of the event nodes. In drawing a network diagram the event nodes are in effect the punctuation marks in the diagram; they bring order to the sequence of arrows. In critical path analysis they become distinct points in time. For each event node we assign an *earliest event time (EET)* and a *latest event time (LET)*. These are written in the circle that represents the event node beneath the event number, as illustrated in Figure 14.4.

The circle on the left in Figure 14.4 is the event node that marks the point in time when activity X begins. The number in the upper part of the circle is the event number, 20. The number below it to the left is the earliest event time and the number below it on the right is the latest event time. These numbers tell us that the earliest time that activity X can start is time period 9 and the latest time it can start is time period 11. From the equivalent figures in the event node to the right of activity X you can tell that the earliest time the activity can be completed is time period 13 and the latest time it can be completed is time period 15.

To work out the earliest and latest times for the events in a network we use the activity durations. Starting with the event node at the beginning

Figure 14.4
Earliest and latest
event times for a
single activity

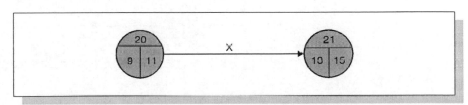

of the network and working through the network from left to right we write in the earliest time that each event node in the network can occur. This is referred to as making a *forward pass* through the network. When doing this you need to remember that where there are two or

Example 14.3

The durations of the activities undertaken during the ground servicing operation in Example 14.1 are given in the following table:

Activity	Description	Duration (minutes)
A	Drive service vehicles to plane	2
B	Attach stairway	3
C	Unload baggage	25
D	Refuel	15
E	Passengers disembark	8
F	Clean cabin	20
G	Load baggage	30
H	Load food and beverages	10
I	Stock up water tanks	5
J	Service toilets	5
K	Passengers embark	15
L	Detach stairway	3
M	Drive service vehicles from plane	2

Using these figures we can enter the earliest event times in the network. These are included in Figure 14.5.

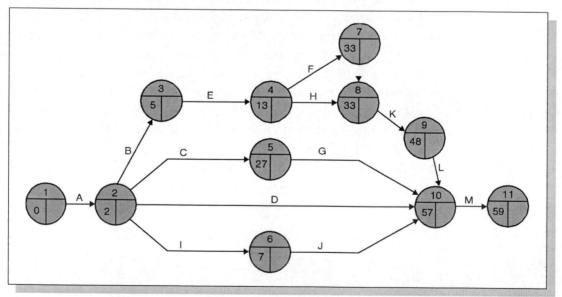

Figure 14.5
Network for ground servicing with earliest event times

more activities leading to the same event node it is the duration of the longest of the activities that determines the earliest time for the event since all the activities must be completed before the event is reached. We write the earliest event times in the lower left-hand side of the event nodes.

If you look carefully at Figure 14.5 you will see that the earliest event time for event 1 is 0 reflecting the fact that 0 minutes of project time have elapsed at the beginning of the project. The earliest event time for event 2 is 2, reflecting the 2 minutes needed for the completion of the only activity between event node 1 and event node 2, activity B, driving the service vehicles to the plane.

The earliest event time for event 8 is perhaps less obvious. The figure entered, 33, has been worked out based on the longest route to it. The activities leading to event node 8 are activity F, with its associated dummy activity between events 7 and 8, and activity H. The earliest time that activity F can start is the earliest event time on the event marking its beginning; the 13 in event 4. If we add the 20 minutes that activity F, cleaning the cabin, takes to the earliest event time for event 4 we get 33 minutes as the earliest time activity F can be completed. Event 4 also marks the beginning of activity H, loading the food and beverages. If we add the time this activity takes, 10 minutes, to the earliest event time of activity 4 we get 23 minutes. This would be the earliest event time for event 8 if we did not need to complete activity F, but since both activity F and activity H have to be completed before event 8 can occur, the earliest time we can get there must allow for the longer activity, activity F, to be concluded, hence the earliest event time for event 8 is 33 and not 23.

The event node indicating the completion of the project on the extreme right of the network has an earliest event time of 59 minutes. This is the minimum duration of the entire project; given the activity durations it cannot be completed in a lesser amount of time. We now need to turn our attention to the latest event times, as comparing these with the earliest event times will enable us to identify the critical path for the project.

Once we have established the minimum project duration, in the case of Example 14.3, 59 minutes, we assume that the project manager will want to complete it in that time. We now undertake the same sort of task to find the latest event times as we used to find the earliest event times, but this time we start on the right-hand side and work back through the network ascertaining the latest time each event can occur if the project is to be finished in the minimum time. This is referred to as making a *backward pass* through the network.

The latest event times for Example 14.3 are included in Figure 14.6. Each event now has a number entered in the lower right-hand side of its node.

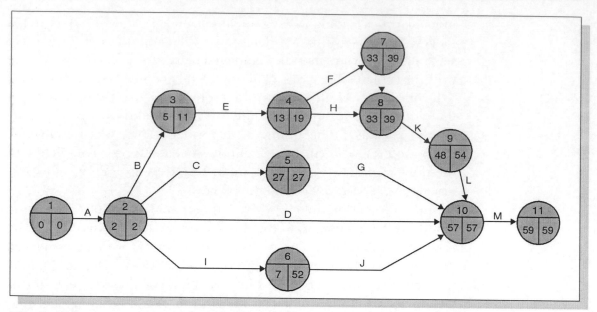

Figure 14.6
Network for ground servicing with latest event times

Looking at Figure 14.6 you can see that the latest event time for the last event, event 11, is 59 minutes. If the project is to be completed in 59 minutes then the latest time we must reach this point is 59 minutes. The latest event time of event 10 is 57 minutes, 59 minutes less the 2 minutes we must allow for activity M to be completed.

Several activities conclude at event 10, including activities G and L. Activity G begins at event 5. The latest time event time of event 5 is 27 minutes, sufficient to allow the 30 minutes necessary for the completion of activity G in time for event 10 to be reached in 57 minutes, which in turn allows for the 2 minutes to complete activity M and thus conclude the project in 59 minutes. Activity L begins at event 9. Since activity L, detaching the stairway, takes 3 minutes, the latest event time for event 9 is 54 minutes, sufficient to allow the 3 minutes for the completion of activity L so that event 10 can be reached in 57 minutes and thus leave 2 minutes for activity M to finish in time for completing the project in 59 minutes.

If you study Figure 14.6 carefully you will see that some events, such as event 5, have the same earliest and latest event times while other events, such as event 6, have different ones. In the case of event 6 the earliest event time is 7 minutes whereas the latest event time is 52 minutes. This implies that activity I can be completed by 7 minutes but it doesn't have to be finished until 52 minutes have elapsed. In other words, there is time to spare for the completion of activities I and J; they have what is called *slack* or *float*.

In contrast, the latest event time for event 5 is the same as its earliest event time, 27 minutes. In this case the earliest time event 5 can be reached is the same as the latest time it has to be reached if the project is to be completed in 59 minutes. This implies there is no slack or float for activities C and G; they must be undertaken at the earliest feasible opportunity as their completion on time is *critical* for the conclusion of the project, they are *critical activities*. If you look at the event nodes that have the same earliest and latest event times you will see that they connect activities A, C, G and M. These activities are driving service vehicles to the plane, unloading and loading baggage, and driving service vehicles from the plane. They form the longest or *critical* path through the network; a delay in the execution of any of them will result in the project being prolonged beyond 59 minutes. On the other hand, any reduction in the duration of any of them will reduce the duration of the project, but only up to a point; at some point another path will become critical.

By definition the critical activities in a network have no slack or float, but other activities will. A project manager is likely to be very interested in the float available for these activities, as it indicates the degree of latitude available in scheduling them.

To work out the total float for an activity we need to know the latest event time for the event that marks its completion, its *finishing event*, and the earliest event time for the event that represents its beginning, its *starting event*. If we subtract the duration of the activity from the difference between these times what is left over is the total float for the activity. We can summarize this procedure as:

$$\text{Total float} = \text{Latest event time (finishing event)}$$
$$- \text{earliest event time (starting event)}$$
$$- \text{activity duration}$$

Using abbreviations:

$$TF = LET\ (F) - EET\ (S) - AD$$

Look carefully at Table 14.1 in Example 14.4 and you will see that some activities have a zero float. These are the activities on the critical path – A, C, G and M. In contrast there is a float of 6 minutes in the path B–E–F–K–L, which is the uppermost path in Figure 14.6. This is float associated with the path rather than an individual activity; once used up by, say, taking 9 minutes rather than 3 minutes for activity B, attaching the stairway, it would not be available for the subsequent activities E, F, K and L, which as a consequence would become as critical as the activities on the critical path.

Example 14.4

Find the total floats for the ground servicing activities in Example 14.1.

Table 14.1
Total floats for activities in Example 14.1

Activity	LET (F) (1)	EET (S) (2)	AD(3)	TF(1)–(2)–(3)
A	2	0	2	0
B	11	2	3	6
C	27	2	25	0
D	57	2	15	40
E	19	5	8	6
F	39	13	20	6
G	57	27	30	0
H	39	13	10	16
I	52	2	5	45
J	57	7	5	45
K	54	33	15	6
L	57	48	3	6
M	59	57	2	0

Activity H, loading the food and beverages, has a total float of 16 minutes, 6 of which are shared with the other activities along its path; B, E , K and L. The remaining 10 minutes are specific to activity H; it must be completed by the same time as activity F, cleaning the cabin, if the project is to be finished in the minimum time, yet it takes 10 minutes less to perform.

Activity D, refuelling, has a float of 40 minutes, which cannot be shared with the other activities along its path, A and M, as they are both critical. The relatively large amount of float for this activity allows the project manager considerable flexibility in scheduling this activity. Similar flexibility exists for activities I and J, the water operations, which share a total float of 45 minutes.

At this point you may find it useful to try **Review Questions 14.1 to 14.11** at the end of the chapter.

14.3 The Program Evaluation and Review Technique (PERT)

So far we have assumed that the activities making up a project each have fixed durations. In reality this is unlikely to be the case. In the

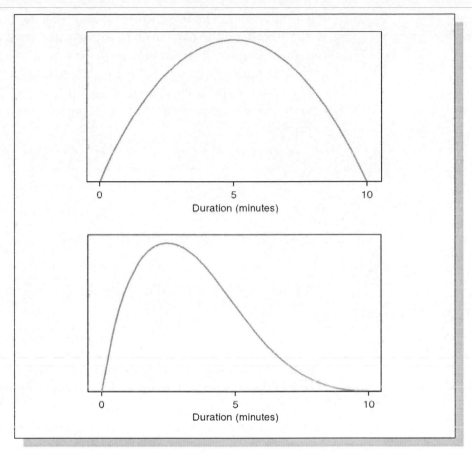

Figure 14.7
Examples of the
beta distribution

ground servicing project introduced in Example 14.1 factors such as the state of equipment, the time of the day or night, and weather conditions will influence the time it takes to complete the activities. Rather than being fixed, activity durations are more likely to be variable. PERT allows us to take this into account.

In using PERT we assume that the duration of an activity is a continuous variable that follows a continuous probability distribution. We looked at continuous probability distributions like the normal distribution in Chapter 13. The distribution used in PERT as the model for activity durations is the *beta distribution*. Like the normal distribution it is continuous, but unlike the normal distribution it can be skewed or symmetrical and it has a minimum and a maximum value. The key characteristics or parameters of the beta distribution are the minimum or *optimistic* duration, a, the maximum or *pessimistic* duration, b, and the *most likely* duration, m.

You can see two types of beta distribution in Figure 14.7. The upper diagram portrays a symmetrical distribution with a minimum of 0 and a maximum of 10. The most likely value of this distribution is 5 minutes, midway between the extremes. In the asymmetrical beta distribution in the lower diagram the minimum and maximum durations are the same as in the upper diagram but the most likely value is rather lower.

If you know the optimistic (a), most likely (m) and pessimistic (b) durations of an activity you can work out its mean duration using the expression:

$$\mu = \frac{a + 4m + b}{6}$$

The standard deviation of the activity duration is:

$$\sigma = \frac{(b - a)}{6}$$

The variance of the activity duration is the square of its standard deviation:

$$\sigma^2 = \frac{(b - a)}{6^2}$$

The mean duration of an entire project is the sum of the mean durations of the activities that are on the critical path, the critical activities. The variance of the project duration is the sum of the variances of the critical activities and the standard deviation of the project duration is the square root of its variance. Note that you cannot get the standard deviation of the project duration by adding together the standard deviations of the durations of the critical activities; it is the variances that sum, not the standard deviations.

Example 14.5

Using time sheets and airport records, the general manager in Example 14.1 has established the optimistic, most likely and pessimistic durations of the activities involved in the ground servicing of aircraft. They are set out in Table 14.2. Using appropriate figures from this table, work out the mean and standard deviation of the project duration.

The mean project duration is the sum of the mean durations of the critical activities. In this project the critical activities are A, C, G and M. The means of these activities are:

$$\mu_A = \frac{1 + (4 * 2) + 3}{6} = 2$$

$$\mu_C = \frac{22 + (4 * 25) + 31}{6} = 25.5$$

Table 14.2

Optimistic, most likely and pessimistic durations of ground operations

		Duration (minutes)		
Activity	Description	Optimistic (a)	Most likely (m)	Pessimistic (b)
A	Drive vehicles to plane	1	2	3
B	Attach stairway	2	3	5
C	Unload baggage	22	25	30
D	Refuel	14	15	17
E	Passengers disembark	6	8	12
F	Clean cabin	15	20	25
G	Load baggage	25	30	32
H	Load food and beverages	8	10	12
I	Stock up water tanks	4	5	7
J	Service toilets	3	5	10
K	Passengers embark	8	15	20
L	Detach stairway	2	3	4
M	Drive vehicles from plane	1	2	3

$$\mu_G = \frac{25 + (4 * 30) + 32}{6} = 29$$

$$\mu_M = \frac{1 + (4 * 2) + 3}{6} = 2$$

The mean duration of the critical path is the sum of these means:

$$\mu_{CP} = \mu_A + \mu_C + \mu_G + \mu_M = 2 + 25.5 + 29 + 2 = 58.5 \text{ minutes}$$

The standard deviation of the critical path is the square root of the variance of the critical path, which is the sum of the variances of the critical activities, A, C, G and M. The variances of these activities are:

$$\sigma_A^2 = ((3 - 1)/6)^2 = 4/36 = 1/9$$
$$\sigma_C^2 = ((31 - 22)/6)^2 = 81/36 = 9/4$$
$$\sigma_G^2 = ((32 - 25)/6)^2 = 49/36$$
$$\sigma_M^2 = ((3 - 1)/6)^2 = 4/36$$

The variance of the duration of the critical path is:

$$\sigma_{CP}^2 = \sigma_A^2 + \sigma_C^2 + \sigma_G^2 + \sigma_M^2 = \frac{4 + 81 + 49 + 4}{36} = \frac{138}{36} = 3.833$$

The standard deviation of the duration of the critical path is:

$$\sigma_{CP} = \sqrt{\sigma_{CP}^2} = \sqrt{3.833} = 1.958 \text{ minutes}$$

Unless there is clear evidence that the distributions of the durations of the individual activities are consistently skewed, we can assume that the distribution of the project duration is approximately normal. This means we can use the Standard Normal Distribution to work out the probability that the project is completed within a certain timescale or beyond a certain timescale.

Example 14.6

What is the probability that the ground servicing operation whose activity durations were detailed in Example 14.5 can be completed in one hour?

If X is the project duration, we want:

$$P(X < 60) = P\left(Z < \frac{60 - 58.5}{1.958}\right) = P(Z < 0.766)$$

If you check in Table 5 on pages 621–622 you will find that the probability that Z is more than 0.77 is 0.2206. The probability that Z is more than 0.77 is 1 less 0.2206, 0.7794, which is the probability that the ground servicing operation is completed within an hour.

We can also work out the timescale within which a certain proportion of ground operations should be completed using the Z distribution.

Example 14.7

What is the timescale within which 90% of ground servicing operations should be completed?

For this you will need the z value that cuts off a tail of 10%, $z_{0.10}$. You can find it by looking down the probabilities in Table 5 until you reach the figure closest to 10%, the 0.1003 in the row for 1.2 and the column headed 0.08, so $z_{0.10}$ is approximately 1.28. For a more precise figure for $z_{0.10}$ use the bottom row of the related Table 6 on page 623. The figure in this row and in the column headed 0.10 is 1.282 so 90% of the normal distribution is to the left of, or less than, 1.282 standard deviations above the mean. We can apply this to the distribution of the duration of the ground servicing operation; 90% of the operation will be completed in a time less than 1.282 standard deviations above the mean:

$$\mu_{CP} + 1.282\sigma_{CP} = 58.5 + 1.282 * 1.958 = 61.010 \text{ minutes}$$

At this point you may find it useful to try **Review Questions 14.12 to 14.16** at the end of the chapter.

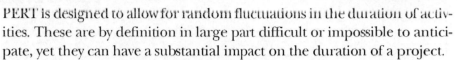

14.4 Cost analysis: crashing the project duration

PERT is designed to allow for random fluctuations in the duration of activities. These are by definition in large part difficult or impossible to anticipate, yet they can have a substantial impact on the duration of a project.

In contrast, it may be possible to reduce the project duration by cutting activity durations by intent. Typically this involves incurring extra cost, defined as the cost of *crashing* the duration of an activity below its anticipated duration.

In most projects there are at least some activities that can be performed more quickly, perhaps by providing more or better equipment, perhaps by allocating more staff, perhaps by hiring a sub-contractor. These contingencies will come at an additional cost, the *crash cost*, the cost of carrying out the activity in its *crash duration* rather than its normal duration.

Although there may be several activities in a project that can be crashed, it may not be worthwhile crashing all of them. The project duration is the critical path, the path of critical activities, whose completion on schedule is crucial for the minimum duration of the project to be achieved. If an activity is not on the critical path it is not worth crashing, or at least not until it might have become critical following the crashing of one or more critical activities. Crashing a non-critical activity will not reduce the duration of the critical path, but crashing a critical activity will always reduce the duration of the critical path. Having said that, there is a limit. Once the critical path activities have been crashed to the point that another path loses its float and becomes critical it is not worth crashing critical activities any further. Any further project reduction has to involve further crashing of the activities on the original critical path as well as crashing activities that have become critical after the initial crashing of the critical path activities.

There may be several critical activities than can be crashed. If this is the case the activities to be crashed should be selected on the basis of cost, with the cheapest options implemented first.

Example 14.8

The general manager in Example 14.1 has found that three of the activities that make up the ground servicing operation can be crashed; activities C, unloading the baggage, F, cleaning the cabin, and G, loading the baggage. The crash durations and crash costs of these activities are set out in Table 14.3.

Table 14.3

Crash durations and crash costs of operations C, F and G

Activity	Normal duration (minutes)	Crash duration (minutes)	Crash cost ($)	Crash cost per minute ($)
C	25	20	200	40
F	15	8	140	20
G	30	26	200	50

Although the cheapest activity to crash is activity F, cleaning the cabin, if you look back at Figure 14.6 you will see that it is not on the critical path, indeed if you check Example 14.4 you will find that there are 6 minutes of float available for activity F. Cutting its duration will merely add to its float and not reduce the minimum duration of the project.

Activities C and G are both on the critical path, so it is worth considering crashing them. The cheaper to crash is activity C, at $40 per minute compared to $50 per minute for crashing activity G.

To what extent should activity C be crashed? The answer is up to the point when the path with the least float becomes critical. The path B–E–F–K–L has 6 minutes of float, so it would be worth reducing the duration of activity C by 6 minutes. Since the crash duration of activity C is only 5 minutes, to achieve a reduction of 6 minutes in the project duration we would have to reduce the duration of activity G by 1 minute as well.

A greater reduction in the project duration would involve further crashing of activity G and crashing activity F. The possible stages in reducing the project duration and their associated costs are:

Stage 1:   Crash activity C by 5 minutes at a cost of $200 and reduce the project duration to 54 minutes.

Stage 2:   Crash activity G by 1 minute at a cost of $50 and reduce the project duration to 53 minutes. Total crashing cost $250.

Stage 3:   Crash activity G by a further 3 minutes and crash activity F by 3 minutes at a combined cost of $210 and reduce the project duration to 50 minutes. Total crashing cost $460.

Would it be worth incurring the extra costs of crashing in a case like Example 14.8? It depends on the circumstances. It may be that the normal duration of the ground servicing operation is longer than the allotted time slot at the airport and as a result the airline has to pay penalty costs to the airport authority. Alternatively, reducing the ground servicing time may enable the airline to schedule more flights and thus increase revenue. In either case, deciding how far to go in crashing the project will rest on balancing the costs of crashing and the financial, and possibly other, benefits of doing so.

At this point you may find it useful to try **Review Questions 14.17 to 14.19** at the end of the chapter.

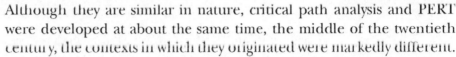

14.5 Road test: Do they really use critical path analysis and PERT?

Although they are similar in nature, critical path analysis and PERT were developed at about the same time, the middle of the twentieth century, the contexts in which they originated were markedly different.

Critical path analysis was originally known as the Kelly–Walker method after the two pioneers of the technique: J.E. Kelly of the Remington Rand Company and M.R. Walker of the Du Pont Company, the giant US chemicals corporation that developed Dynamite, Nylon, Teflon and Lycra as well as many other technological innovations. At the time, Remington Rand was the computer systems subsidiary of Du Pont. The initial application of the technique was in the construction of a major new chemical plant at Louisville, Kentucky.

While the origins of critical path analysis were civilian, the roots of PERT lie in the military. In the early phase of the Cold War the US military authorities were desperate to develop intercontinental ballistic missiles. They were concerned about the projections for the completion time of key projects: first the Atlas missile, then more prominently the Polaris system. To expedite matters a central coordinator was appointed to oversee the Polaris project. He assumed control of the entire project and under him PERT evolved as the means by which the myriad of activities involving hundreds of subcontractors were planned so that the Polaris programme was completed much sooner than the 10 years that was initially anticipated.

The success of the Polaris project meant that PERT became widely publicized. In telling the story of its development, Morris (1994, p. 31) notes that by 1964 there were almost 1000 overwhelmingly enthusiastic articles and books published about PERT. Whilst in retrospect this amounted to overselling the technique, like its close relation critical path analysis, it has become widely accepted as a key tool in successful project management.

In his study of the use made of quantitative methods in US businesses, Kathawala (1988) found that 54% of companies in his survey reported that they made moderate, frequent or extensive use of critical path analysis and PERT. More recently such planning tools have been used in projects like the expansion of the Kings Cross underground station in London (Lane, 2003).

Morris (1994) provides an interesting history of the techniques we have looked at in this chapter. For more on their capabilities try Klein (2001).

Answers to these questions, including fully worked solutions to the Key questions marked with an asterisk (*), are on pages 663–665.

14.1* Bibb and Tukka own and operate a successful chain of clothing stores. They plan to open a new outlet. The activities involved are listed below with the activities that must precede them and their durations.

Activity	Description	Precedence	Duration (days)
A	Negotiate the lease	—	10
B	Install the fixtures	A	8
C	Install the furnishings	B	3
D	Appoint the staff	A	2
E	Train the staff	D	10
F	Arrange the opening ceremony	D	7
G	Opening ceremony	C, E, F	1

(a) Compile a network diagram to represent this venture.
(b) Find the earliest and latest event times for the events in your network, and use them to identify the minimum duration of the project and the activities that are on its critical path.

14.2 Marsh and Root Construction have won the contract to widen and resurface a section of road. The site manager has identified the following tasks together with the tasks that must precede them and their anticipated durations:

Activity	Description	Precedence	Duration (days)
A	Relocate bus stop	—	2
B	Install temporary traffic lights	—	1
C	Install safety barriers	A, B	1
D	Plane road	C	2
E	Lift kerbstones	C	3

(*Continued*)

Activity	Description	Precedence	Duration (days)
F	Replace ironworks	D	3
G	Lay and roll tarmac	F	1
H	Replace kerbstones	E	4
I	Road painting	G	2
J	Remove safety barriers	I	1
K	Remove temporary traffic lights	J	1
L	Restore bus stop	H	2

(a) Construct a network to portray the project.

(b) Identify the critical path and hence ascertain the minimum duration for these roadworks.

14.3   The Raketa Racing Team are new entrants to motor racing. They have been practising their pit stop procedures and their performance is detailed below:

Activity	Description	Precedence	Duration (seconds)
A	Guide driver to pit	—	3
B	Jack up the car	A	2
C	Remove the old wheels	B	5
D	Fit the new wheels	C	5
E	Refuel the car	B	16
F	Wipe driver's visor	B	2
G	Release and clear jacks	D, F	2
H	Check all clear	E, G	2
I	Signal GO	H	1

(a) Draw a network for the pit stop procedure.

(b) Using your diagram work out the earliest and latest time for each event, find the minimum duration for the pit stop and identify the critical path.

14.4   Slattkey Sweets proposes to re-launch one of its mature brands, the Zubirot Bar. The brand manager has identified the tasks involved and produced the following information about them:

Activity	Description	Precedence	Duration (weeks)
A	Redesign the bar		8
B	Redesign the packaging	—	4

(*Continued*)

Activity	Description	Precedence	Duration (weeks)
C	Build pilot production line	A, B	13
D	Trial production run	C	1
E	Consumer panel tests	D	1
F	Main pilot production	E	6
G	Design promotional material	E	4
H	Test market redesigned product	F, G	10
I	Produce report for the Board	H	2

Draw a network to portray this enterprise and use it to find the minimum duration of the project and those activities that are on the critical path.

14.5   The renowned rock band Kamien have just completed a highly successful national tour. Tickets have sold so well that they would like to put on an extra concert. The tasks involved in organizing this, together with their preceding activities and expected durations, are:

Activity	Description	Precedence	Duration (days)
A	Agree the leasing of the hall	—	10
B	Engage the support acts	A	6
C	Hire security staff	A	8
D	Order and receive merchandising	B	14
E	Organize ticket sales	B	2
F	Early promotional work	E	4
G	Book hotels and transport	B	2
H	Final promotional work	F	5
I	Stage rehearsal/sound checks	G	1

(a) Create a network for this project.
(b) Find the minimum duration of the project and indicate the activities on the critical path.

14.6   Nat Chelnick has to go on an unexpected but urgent business trip to a city in Central Asia. The arrangements he has to make are:

Activity	Description	Precedence	Duration (days)
A	Renew his passport	—	8
B	Obtain a visa	A	10
C	Go for vaccination shots†	—	6
D	Order and receive currency	—	4
E	Order and receive tickets	B	1
F	Book accommodation	E	3
G	Book airport parking	E	2

† includes time to allow for side-effects of vaccine

Compile a network for this venture and using it, find how long Nat will have to wait before he can make the trip, and state which activities are critical.

14.7   Doris and Dennis Datcher, experts at DIY, want to build a summerhouse in their garden. They will start by drawing up a proper plan, which they can complete in 2 days. Once they have a plan they can prepare the site, which will take 6 days, order the timber, which will be delivered in 10 days from placing the order, and purchase the ironmongery, which will take 2 days. Once they have the timber and ironmongery they can construct the floor panels, which will take 4 days, make the frames for the walls, which will take 2 days, and construct the door, which will take 1 day. When they have made the wall frames they can board them up, which will take 2 days. When they have prepared the site and constructed the floor panels they can lay the floor, which will take 1 day. As soon as the floor is laid and the wall frames boarded they can erect the walls, which will take 1 day. Once the walls are erected the roof joists can be fixed, which will take 2 days. Having fixed the roof joists the roof can be boarded and weatherproofed, which will take 4 days. Once the door has been constructed and the walls erected they can hang the door, which will take 1 day.

(a) List the activities involved in building the summerhouse and identify the predecessor activities for each of them as well as their durations.

(b) Draw a network diagram for the building of the summerhouse and from it identify the critical path and the minimum duration of the project.

14.8   The Dom Stila fashion house intend to stage a fashion show to promote their autumn collection. Three designers, Mallover, Millasha and Mockry, have been commissioned to produce designs for the show. The tasks entailed in completing the project, together with their durations and tasks that must precede them, are:

Activity	Description	Precedence	Duration (days)
A	Mallover prepares designs	—	8
B	Millisha prepares designs	—	16
C	Mockry prepares designs	—	14
D	Select models	A, B, C	1
E	Make up Mallover designs	D	5
F	Make up Millisha designs	D	10
G	Make up Mockry designs	D	12
H	Design show (music, choreography and lighting etc.)	A, B, C	6
I	Construct the set	H	12
J	Obtain props and accessories	I	1
K	Design and print publicity	H	9
L	Distribute publicity	K	3
M	Rehearse show	E, F, G, J	2

Produce a network for this project, list the critical activities and ascertain the minimum duration of the project.

14.9   The new Raz Develka TV programme invites participants to design and re-decorate a room in a neighbour's house with the assistance of a designer and technical staff. One contestant has drawn up the following schedule for working on her neighbour's bedroom:

Activity	Description	Precedence	Duration (hours)
A	Clear the furniture	—	1
B	Remove the carpets	A	1

(*Continued*)

Activity	Description	Precedence	Duration (hours)
C	Sand the floor	B	3
D	Install multipoint lighting	B	2
E	Paint the ceiling	C, D	2
F	Paint the walls	E	4
G	Paint motifs on the walls	F	6
H	Build fitted wardrobes	F	4
I	Refurbish the bed	A	3
J	Make fabric blinds	—	5
K	Hang blinds	G, J	1
L	Acquire decorative ornaments	—	12
M	Lay out room	K, L	2

(a) Construct a network to represent this project and, using it, work out the minimum duration of the project and identify the activities on the critical path.

(b) The contestant ruins the bed after spending 2 hours refurbishing it. Building a new one will take 18 hours. Will this delay completion?

14.10 The Easkritsy Car Valet Service defines the standard car clean it offers as consisting of the following operations:

Activity	Description	Precedence	Duration (minutes)
A	External pre-wash	—	5
B	External main wash	A	8
C	External rinse	B	2
D	External wax and polish	C	12
E	Polish external windows	D	1
F	Enhance tyre wall black	D	4
G	Remove floor mats	—	2
H	Vacuum seats	G	4
I	Vacuum floor	H	6
J	Polish fascia and door panels	I	6
K	Apply air freshener	J	1

Draw a network to portray this enterprise and use it to find the minimum duration of the project and those activities that are on the critical path.

14.11 Members of the Keeshka Dining Club meet once a month to enjoy a meal with a set two-course menu at the club premises while listening to a string quartet. Planning the meal entails scheduling the activities listed below:

Activity	Description	Precedence	Duratio (minutes)
A	Lay table covers	—	10
B	Set out condiments and cutlery	A	5
C	Set out glasses	A	10
D	Set up musicians' equipment	—	40
E	Greet guests with aperitif	B, C	10
F	Seat guests	D, E	4
G	Take wine orders	F	6
H	Serve wine	G	8
I	Serve main course	H	5
J	Guests eat main course	I	30
K	Clear main course	J	5
L	Serve dessert	K	4
M	Guests eat dessert	L	15
N	Clear dessert	M	3
O	Serve coffee	M	6

(a) Prepare a network diagram for this procedure and from it ascertain the earliest time that the serving of coffee will be completed if the laying of the table covers begins at 11.30am.

(b) Identify the critical activities.

14.12* Bibb and Tukka from Question 14.1 have assembled further information about the completion times of the activities involved in their opening the new outlet:

		Duration (days)		
Activity	Description	Optimistic	Most likely	Pessimistic
A	Negotiate the lease	6	10	12
B	Install the fixtures	5	8	15
C	Install the furnishings	2	3	6

(Continued)

| | | Duration (days) | | |
Activity	Description	Optimistic	Most likely	Pessimistic
D	Appoint the staff	1	2	4
E	Train the staff	8	10	14
F	Arrange the opening ceremony	4	7	8
G	Opening ceremony	1	1	1

(a) Calculate the mean and the standard deviation of the project duration.

(b) The original plan was to complete everything, including the opening ceremony, in 22 days. What is the probability that this will be achieved?

(c) Within what time will there be a 95% chance of completing everything?

14.13 The head of the Raketa Racing Team from question 14.3 monitors the pit stop performances and presents the figures below:

| | | Duration (seconds) | | |
Activity	Description	Optimistic	Most likely	Pessimistic
A	Guide driver to pit	2	3	5
B	Jack up the car	1	2	4
C	Remove the old wheels	4	5	6
D	Fit the new wheels	5	5	7
E	Refuel the car	13	16	20
F	Wipe driver's visor	2	2	2
G	Release and clear jacks	2	2	4
H	Check all clear	2	2	3
I	Signal GO	1	1	2

(a) Calculate the mean and the standard deviation of the pit stop duration.

(b) The performance target for the team is 22 seconds. What is the probability that they will make it?

(c) Within how many seconds will 90% of pit stops be completed?

14.14   The brand manager at Slattkey Sweets in question 14.4 has more details of the tasks involved in the re-launch of the Zubirot bar:

		Duration (weeks)		
Activity	Description	Optimistic	Most likely	Pessimistic
A	Redesign the bar	5	8	10
B	Redesign the packaging	3	4	5
C	Build pilot production line	10	13	16
D	Trial production run	1	1	2
E	Consumer panel tests	1	1	1
F	Main pilot production	4	6	9
G	Design promotional material	2	4	5
H	Test market redesigned product	8	10	15
I	Produce report for the Board	2	2	3

(a) Determine the mean and the standard deviation for the product re-launch.

(b) Ascertain the probability that the project will be finished in 40 weeks.

(c) Within what number of weeks is there a 99% chance of completion?

14.15   Nat Chelnick the business traveller in question 14.6 has found out more about how long his preparations for the trip will take:

		Duration (days)		
Activity	Description	Optimistic	Most likely	Pessimistic
A	Renew his passport	5	8	12
B	Obtain a visa	6	10	20
C	Go for vaccination shots	6	6	8
D	Order and receive currency	3	4	6
E	Order and receive tickets	1	1	3
F	Book accommodation	1	3	4
G	Book airport parking	1	2	2

(a) Work out the mean and the standard deviation for these preparations.

(b) Nat would like to make the trip in within the next 30 days. What are the chances of his doing so?

(c) Within what timescale does he have an 80% chance making the trip?

14.16 The Easkritsy Car Valet Service in question 14.10 defines its standard car clean as its '30-minute valet'. Use the information below to ascertain the proportion of standard car cleans that are completed within 30 minutes:

		Duration (minutes)		
Activity	Description	Optimistic	Most likely	Pessimistic
A	External pre-wash	4	5	6
B	External main wash	5	8	12
C	External rinse	2	2	3
D	External wax and polish	9	12	15
E	Polish external windows	1	1	2
F	Enhance tyre wall black	3	4	5
G	Remove floor mats	1	2	3
H	Vacuum seats	3	4	6
I	Vacuum floor	5	6	7
J	Polish fascia and door panels	3	6	8
K	Apply air freshener	1	1	1

14.17* Bibb and Tukka from question 14.1 have identified the potential for crashing some of the tasks involved in opening their new outlet. The details are:

Activity	Normal duration (days)	Crash duration (days)	Crash cost (£)
B	8	4	800
C	3	1	300
E	10	8	600
F	7	5	400

(a) Use your network diagram for the project to work out the total float for each activity.

(b) Work out the crash cost per day for each activity that can be crashed. Outline what activities Bibb and Tukka should crash and in which order. Identify for each stage of crashing the reduction in the project duration and the total cost involved.

(c) If Bibb and Tukka make a net loss of £400 a day from lost business for every day the outlet is not open, what is their optimal crashing strategy?

14.18 Marsh and Root Construction in question 14.2 can earn a bonus of £1000 for every day less than 13 days the completion of the roadworks takes. They can crash the tasks listed below:

Activity	Normal duration (days)	Crash duration (days)	Crash cost (£)
D	2	1	600
E	3	2	200
F	3	2	300
H	4	2	500

Identify the activities that should be crashed and calculate the extra money they can make as a result.

14.19 In the light of information about a competitor's fashion show Dom Stila in question 14.8 want to reduce the time it takes to stage their show by three days, but at the least cost. A number of activities can be crashed:

Activity	Normal duration (days)	Crash duration (days)	Crash cost (£)
B	16	13	900
C	14	12	800
F	10	8	500
I	12	9	1500

Which activities should be crashed, by how much and at what total cost?

14.20 Select the appropriate description for each term on the left-hand side from the list on the right-hand side.

(i) network event node

(a) a continuous distribution used in PERT

(ii) minimum project duration

(b) paying more to reduce project duration

(iii) $(a + 4m + b)/6$

(c) the standard deviation of the beta distribution

(iv) network arrow

(d) represents the start or finish of an activity

(v) $(b - a)/6$

(e) slack time for the completion of an activity

(vi) beta distribution

(f) sum of the means of the critical activities

(vii) mean project duration

(g) mean of the beta distribution

(viii) float

(h) length of the critical path

(ix) crashing

(i) represents an activity

CHAPTER 15

Taking short cuts – sampling methods

This chapter will help you to:

- appreciate the reasons for sampling
- understand sampling bias and how to avoid it
- employ probabilistic sampling methods and be aware of their limitations
- use the technology: simple random sampling in MINITAB and SPSS
- become acquainted with business uses of sampling methods

A *population* is the entire set of items or people that form the subjects of study in an investigation and a *sample* is a subset of a population. Companies need to know about the populations they deal with: populations of customers, employees, suppliers, products and so on. Typically these populations are very large, so large that they are to all intents and purposes infinite.

Gathering data about such large populations is likely to be very expensive, time-consuming and to a certain extent impractical. The scale of expense can be immense; even governments of large countries only commit resources to survey their entire populations, that is, to conduct a census, about every ten years.

The amount of time involved in surveying the whole population means that it may be so long before the results are available that they are completely out of date. There may be some elements within the population that simply cannot be included in a survey of it; for instance, a car manufacturer may want to conduct a survey of all customers buying a certain model three years before in order to gauge customer satisfaction. Inevitably a number of those customers will have died in the period since buying their car and thus cannot be included in the survey.

To satisfy their need for data about the populations that matter to them without having to incur great expense or wait a long time for results companies turn to sampling, the process of taking a sample from a population in order to use the sample data to gain insight into the entire population. Although not as accurate as the results of a population survey, sample results can be precise enough to serve the purposes of the investigation.

The downside of sampling is that many different samples can be taken from the same population, even if the samples are the same size. You can work out the number of samples of n items that could be selected from a population of N items:

$$\text{Number of samples size } n = \frac{N!}{n!(N-n)!}$$

We can use this to work out the number of samples of size 6 that could be selected from a very small population of just 20 items.

$$\text{Number of samples size } 6 = \frac{20!}{6! \; 14!} = 38{,}760$$

You can imagine that the number of samples that could be selected from a much larger population will be so very large as to border on the infinite.

Each of the samples you could select from a population inevitably excludes much of the population, so sample results will not be precisely the same as those from the entire population. There will be differences known as *sampling errors* between sample results and the results of a population survey and furthermore different samples will yield different results and hence different sampling errors.

In this chapter you will find details of a variety of sampling methods, but before we look at them we need to consider what companies might look for in sampling, and what they would prefer to avoid.

15.1 Bias in sampling

The point of selecting a sample from a population is to study it and use the results to understand the population. To be effective a sample should therefore reflect the population as a whole. However, there is no guarantee that the elements of the population that are chosen for the sample will collectively reflect the population. Even if the population is quite small there will be an enormous number of combinations of elements that you could select in a sample. Inevitably some of these samples will represent the entire population better than others.

Although it is impossible to avoid the possibility of getting an unrepresentative sample, it is important to avoid using a sampling method that will almost invariably lead to your getting an unrepresentative sample. This means avoiding bias in selecting your sample.

Effective methods of sampling are those that minimize the chances of getting unrepresentative samples and allow you to anticipate the degree of sampling error using appropriate probability distributions. Such methods should give every element of the population the same chance of being selected in a sample as any other element of the population, and consequently every possible sample of a certain size the same chance of selection as every other sample of the same size.

If some elements of the population have a greater chance of being selected in a sample than others, then we have bias in our sampling method. Bias has to be avoided as the samples that can result will be extremely unlikely to reflect the population as a whole and such misleading results may have disastrous consequences.

Example 15.1

Packaged potato crisps are sold by the million every day of the week; it is a huge market. You might think that the company that pioneered the product would by now be a very large and successful one, but you would be wrong; after their initial success they ran into problems that eventually lead to their being taken over. Occasionally the company that now owns the brand re-launches it as a retro product, with the distinctive small blue paper twist of salt in the crisp packet.

A key factor in the decline of the potato crisp pioneers was product quality. The company received a consistent stream of complaints from customers about the number of charred and green-tinged crisps. The company directors knew of these complaints but were baffled by them; they knew their product was good because they tasted a sample taken from the production line every day with their morning coffee.

The problem for the directors was the method used to take the samples from the production line. The sample was selected by the shopfloor staff, who knew they were destined for the boardroom and quite understandably ensured that only the best were selected. The samples provided for the directors were therefore biased; the charred and green crisps that their customers wrote about had no chance of being selected in the samples taken for the directors.

The directors were reluctant to take action to deal with a problem they were convinced did not exist. This made it easier for competitors to enter the market and the initial advantage the pioneers enjoyed was lost.

In Example 15.1 the company directors were completely misled by the bias in the selection of their samples of potato crisps. Biased samples will mislead, no matter how large the samples are; in fact, the larger such samples are, the greater the danger of misrepresentation since it is always tempting to attach more credibility to a large sample.

Example 15.2

In the 1936 presidential election in the USA the incumbent Democrat, Franklin Roosevelt, faced the Republican governor of Kansas, Alfred Landon. Roosevelt was associated with the New Deal programme of large-scale public expenditure to alleviate the high level of unemployment in the depression of the time. Landon on the other hand wanted to end what he considered government profligacy.

The prominent US weekly magazine of the time, *The Literary Digest*, conducted one of the largest polls ever undertaken to predict the result of the election. After analysing the returns from over 2 million respondents, the *Digest* confidently predicted that Landon would win by a large margin, 56% to 44%. The actual result was that Roosevelt won by a large margin, obtaining 60% of the vote. How could the *Digest* poll have been so wrong?

The answer lay in the sampling method they used. They sent postcards to millions of people listed in telephone directories, car registration files and magazine subscription lists. The trouble was that in the USA of 1936 those who had telephones and cars and subscribed to magazines were the better-off citizens. In restricting the poll to such people, who largely supported Landon, the poll was biased against the poor and unemployed, who largely voted for Roosevelt.

The most effective way of avoiding bias in sample selection is to use probabilistic methods, which ensure that every element in the population has the same chance of being included in the sample. In the next section we will look at sampling methods that yield samples from which you can produce *unbiased estimators* of population measures, or *parameters* such as a mean or a proportion.

15.2 Probabilistic sampling methods

Perhaps the obvious way of giving every element in a population the same chance of being selected in sample is to use a random process such as those used to select winning numbers in lottery competitions. Lotteries are usually regarded as fair because every number in the population of lottery numbers has an equal chance of being picked as a winning number.

15.2.1 Simple random sampling

Selecting a set of winning numbers in a lottery is an example of simple random sampling, whether the process involves elaborate machines or simply picking the numbers from the proverbial hat. You can use the same approach in drawing samples from a population.

Before you can undertake simple random sampling you need to establish a clear definition of the population and compile a list of the elements in it. In the same way as all the numbers in a lottery must be included if the draw is to be fair, all the items in the population must be included for the sample we take to be random. The population list is the basis or framework of our sample selection so it is known as the *sampling frame*.

Once you have the sampling frame you need to number each element in it and then you can use random numbers to select your sample. If you have 100 elements in the population and you need a sample of 15 from it you can take a sequence of 15 two-digit random numbers from Table 4 on page 620 in Appendix 1 and select the elements for the sample accordingly; for instance if the first random number is 71 you take the 71st element on the sampling frame, if the second random number is 09 you take the ninth element and so on. If the random number 00 occurs in the sequence you take the 100th element.

Example 15.3

Strani Systems have 2000 employees in the UK. The HR director of the company wants to select a sample of 400 employees to answer questions about their experience of working for the company. How should she go about using simple random sampling?

The population in this case consists of all the Strani employees in the UK. The sampling frame would be a list of employees, perhaps the company payroll, with each employee numbered from 1 to 2000. The HR director should then take a sequence of four-digit random numbers such as those listed along row 7 of Table 4:

1426   7156   7651   0042   9537   2573   and so on

She does face a problem in that only two of the random numbers, 1426 and 0042, will enable her to select an employee from the list as the others are well above 2000. To get round this she could simply ignore the ones that are too high and continue until she has 400 random numbers that are in the appropriate range. This may take considerable time and she may prefer to replace the first digit in each number so that in every case they are either 0 or 1, making all the four-digit numbers in the range 0000 to 1999 (0000 would be used for the 2000th employee):

Change 0, 2, 4, 6, 8   to 0
Change 1, 3, 5, 7, 9   to 1

By applying this to the figures from row 7 of Table 4 she would get:

1426   1156   1651   0042   1537   0573

Now she can use every number in the sequence to select for the sample.

Simple random sampling has several advantages; it is straightforward and inexpensive. Because the probability of selection is known it is possible to assess the sampling error involved and ensure that estimates of population parameters based on the sample are unbiased.

A potential disadvantage of simple random sampling is that in a case such as Example 15.3 the sample may consist of elements all over the country, which will make data collection expensive. Another is that whilst it is an appropriate method for largely homogenous populations, if a population is subdivided by, for instance, gender and gender is an important aspect of the analysis, using simple random sampling will not ensure suitable representation of both genders.

15.2.2 Systematic random sampling

A faster alternative to simple random sampling is systematic sampling. This involves selecting a proportion of elements from the sampling frame by choosing elements at regular intervals through the list. The first element is selected using a random number.

Example 15.4

How can the HR director in Example 15.3 use systematic sampling to select her sample of 400 employees?

Since there are 2000 employees she needs to select every fifth employee in the list that constitutes the sampling frame. To decide whether she should start with the first, second, third, fourth or fifth employee on the list she could take a two-digit random number and if it is between 00 and 19 start with the first employee, between 20 and 39 the second, between 40 and 59 the third, between 60 and 79 the fourth, and between 80 and 99 the fifth. The first two-digit number at the top of column 9 of Table 4 is 47, so using this she should start with the third employee and proceed to take every fifth name after that.

As well as being cheap and simple, systematic sampling does yield samples with a definable sampling error and therefore able to produce unbiased estimates. This is true as long as the population list used to select the sample is not drawn up in such a way as to give rise to bias. In Example 15.4 a list of employees in alphabetical order should not result in bias but if most employees worked in teams of five, one of whom was the team leader and the list of employees was set out by teams rather than surnames, then the systematic sampling of every fifth employee would generate a sample with either all or none of the employees selected being team leaders.

Systematic sampling has the same disadvantages as simple random sampling; expensive data collection if the sample members are widely dispersed, and the possibility of sub-sections of the population being under-represented.

15.2.3 Stratified random sampling

One problem with both sampling methods we have looked at so far is that the samples they produce may not adequately reflect the balance of different constituencies within the population. In the long run this unevenness will be balanced out by other samples selected using the same methods, but this is little comfort if you only have the time or resources to take one sample.

To avoid sections of a population being under-, or for that matter over-represented you can use stratified random sampling. As the name implies, the sample selection is random, but it is structured using the sections or *strata* in the population. The starting point is to define the size of the sample and then decide what proportion of each section of the population needs to be selected for the sample. Once you have decided how many elements you need from each section, then use simple random sampling to choose them. This ensures that all the sections of the population are represented in the sample yet preserves the random nature of the selection and thus your ability to produce unbiased estimators of the population parameters from your sample data.

Example 15.5

The 2000 UK employees of Strani Systems are based at six locations; 400 work in Leeds, 800 in Manchester, 200 in Norwich, 300 in Oxford, 100 in Plymouth, and 200 in Reading. How can the HR director in Example 15.3 use stratified random sampling to choose her sample of 400 employees?

A sample of 400 constitutes 20% of the workforce of 2000. To stratify the sample in the same way as the population she should select 20% of the employees from each site; 80 from Leeds, 160 from Manchester, 40 from Norwich, 60 from Oxford, 20 from Plymouth and 40 from Reading. She should then use simple random sampling to choose the sample members from each site. For this she would need a sampling frame for each location.

The advantage of stratified random sampling is that it produces samples that yield unbiased estimators of population parameters whilst ensuring that the different sectors of the population are represented. The disadvantage in a case like Example 15.5 is that the sample consists of widely dispersed members and collecting data from them may be expensive, especially if face-to-face interviews are involved.

15.2.4 Cluster sampling

If the investigation for which you require a sample is based on a population that is widely scattered you may prefer to use cluster sampling. This method is appropriate if the population you wish to sample is composed of geographically distinct units or *clusters*. You simply take a complete list of the clusters that make up your population and take a random sample of clusters from it. The elements in your sample are *all* the individuals in each selected cluster.

Example 15.6

How can the HR director from Example 15.3 use cluster sampling to select a sample of employees?

She can make a random selection of two or maybe three locations by simply putting the names of the location in a hat and drawing two out. All the employees at these locations constitute her sample.

A rather more sophisticated approach would be to make the probability that a location is selected proportionate to its size by putting one ticket in the hat for every 100 employees at a location – four tickets for Leeds, eight for Manchester and so on.

As an alternative to drawing tickets from a hat, she could follow the approach we used in section 12.4 of Chapter 12 to simulate business processes and employ random numbers to make the selections in accordance with the following allocations:

Location	Random number allocation
Leeds	00–19
Manchester	20–59
Norwich	60–69
Oxford	70–84
Plymouth	85–89
Reading	90–99

The advantages of cluster sampling are that it is cheap, especially if the investigation involves face-to-face interviews, because the number of locations to visit is small and you only need sampling frames for the selected clusters rather than the entire population.

The disadvantages are that you may well end up with a larger sample than you need and there is a risk that some sections of the population may be under-represented. If Leeds and Manchester were the chosen clusters in Example 15.5, the sample size would be 1200 (the 400 employees at Leeds and the 800 at Manchester), a far larger sample than the HR director requires. If the overall gender balance of the company employees in Example 15.5 is 40% male and 60% females yet this balance was 90% male and 10% female at the Norwich and Reading sites there would be a serious imbalance in the sample if it consisted of employees at those two sites.

15.2.5 Multi-stage sampling

Multi-stage is a generic term for any combination of probabilistic sampling methods. It can be particularly useful for selecting samples from populations that are divided or layered in more than one way.

Example 15.6

The HR director from Example 15.3 likes the idea of cluster sampling as it will result in cost savings for her investigation, but she wants to avoid having a sample of more than 400 employees. How can she use multi-stage sampling to achieve this?

She can use cluster sampling to select her locations and then, rather than contact all the employees at each site, she could use stratified sampling to ensure that the sample size is 400. For instance, if Leeds and Manchester were selected the 1200 employees at those sites constitute three times as many as the HR director requires in her sample so she should select one-third of the employees at each site; 133 at Leeds and 267 at Manchester. She could use either systematic or simple random sampling to choose the sample members.

The advantage of multi-stage sampling is that you can customize your approach to selecting your sample; it enables you to benefit from the advantages of a particular method and use others alongside it to overcome its disadvantages. In Example 15.6 the HR director is able to preserve the cost advantage of cluster sampling and use the other methods to keep to her target sample size. Like other probabilistic methods it produces results that can be used as unbiased estimators of population parameters.

15.3 Other sampling methods

Wherever possible you should use probabilistic sampling methods, not because they are more likely to produce a representative sample (which is not always true) but because they allow you to make a statistical evaluation of the sampling error and hence you can use the results to make predictions about the population the sample comes from that are statistically valid. Doing this with samples obtained by other methods does not have the same validity.

Why then is it worth looking at other methods at all? There are several reasons: some populations that you might wish to investigate simply cannot be listed, such as the potential customers of a business, so it is impossible to draw up a sampling frame; secondly, some of these methods are attractive because they are convenient; and thirdly, they are used by companies and therefore it is a good idea to be aware of them and their limitations.

15.3.1 Quota sampling

In one respect quota sampling is similar to stratified random sampling: you start by working out what proportion of the population you want to include in your sample and then apply that proportion to the sections of the population to work out the *quota* of respondents needed from each section of the population. You then fill each quota by finding enough elements from each section of the population.

Example 15.7

How can the HR director from Example 15.3 use quota sampling to obtain a sample of 400 Strani employees?

Since she requires a sample that amounts to 20% of the workforce of 2000, she can set a quota of 20% of the employees at each location; 80 of the 400 at Leeds, 160 of the 800 at Manchester, 40 of the 200 at Norwich, 60 of the 300 at Oxford, 20 of the 100 at Plymouth and 40 of the 200 at Reading. She could then despatch her researchers to each site and they could approach employees as they were leaving the staff restaurant after their lunch. When the quota is filled they have completed the task, for instance, once the researchers at Leeds have data from 80 employees at the site they have finished.

The advantages of quota sampling are that the resulting sample should be representative, and that the process is cheaper and easier than using stratified sampling. In addition there is no need to find named individuals, who may, once found, decline to participate. Quota sampling is particularly useful for sampling from large populations for which an accurate sampling frame is unavailable, a situation that polling organizations typically face.

The disadvantages are that it is susceptible to bias and the results from quota samples are not unbiased estimators of population parameters as the sample selection process is not based on probability. The bias might arise inadvertently from the researcher; for instance in Example 15.7 a young male researcher may well be disposed to approach young female employees rather more than others.

15.3.2 Judgemental sampling

In judgemental sampling the selection of the sample is based entirely on the expertise of the investigator, who uses their judgement to select a sample they consider representative.

Example 15.8

The HR director from Example 15.3 knows that the Reading workforce consists almost entirely of younger women who have young children, whereas at other locations the workforce is largely composed of older males with grown-up families. Given this, she may judge that an appropriate sample would consist of all the employees at Reading and samples of the workforce at other locations.

The advantage of judgemental sampling is that it does allow you to customize your approach to sample selection. The disadvantage is that it is entirely subjective and non-random and as such does not yield results that can be used to predict the features of the population with any statistical rigour.

15.3.3 Snowball sampling

This method involves starting by finding a relatively few respondents who have a particular feature of interest to the investigator and using them to identify others who share the same feature. The sample 'snowballs' to include these others and perhaps yet more potential respondents whom they identify.

Example 15.9

The HR director from Example 15.3 is interested in promoting the health of their employees by opening gyms on their premises. She may wish to ascertain the interest in such a venture by obtaining a sample of employees who already use gyms. She could simply ask around her contacts to identify a 'starter' group of respondents and through them build up a sample.

Snowballing is a useful means of obtaining a sample of a population that may be difficult to access by other means, such as small-scale building contractors. It is open to bias because the initial respondents or contacts decide whose names to pass on to you and there is no valid way of assessing the sampling error so any generalization from the results is not statistically valid.

15.3.4 Convenience sampling

This method is very simple: samples are chosen purely on the basis of accessibility.

Example 15.10

The HR director from Example 15.3 is based at Strani's Manchester site. To select her sample she sends an email to all the employees in the building where her office is situated and invites them to a meeting where she asks them to complete a questionnaire.

Convenience sampling, as the name suggests, is easy and cheap. It can be a useful means of conducting an initial exploratory investigation but the sample is unlikely to be representative of the whole population and results from it should certainly not be used for estimating population parameters as they lack statistical validity.

15.3.5 Self-selection

This is sample selection by invitation; you might send an email or display a notice asking for people to participate in an interview or complete a questionnaire. The advantages are that it is cheap and easy, and what is more you are guaranteed to get willing respondents. Unfortunately this approach to sampling is almost invariably prone to bias; usually it is the people who have stronger feelings on the issues under investigation who put themselves forward and the sample composition is therefore biased against those with more neutral views.

15.4 Using the technology: random sample selection in MINITAB and SPSS

Random numbers play a key part in probabilistic sampling methods. You can use EXCEL to generate streams of random numbers as described in section 12.5.1 of Chapter 12. If you want a more direct approach to selecting random samples try the MINITAB and SPSS facilities described here.

15.4.1 MINITAB

Suppose you want to select a random sample of 15 of the 40 applications submitted for a job. If you number each of the applications 1 to 40 you can use this procedure to select your sample:

- Click the **Calc** button at the top of the screen and from the pull-down menu that appears select **Make Patterned Data**. Click **Simple Set of Numbers** on the sub-menu that comes up.
- In the command window that appears type C1 in the space to the right of **Store patterned data in:** then 1 in the space beside **From first value:** and 40 in the space beside **To last value:**. The default settings in the other spaces in the window (alongside **In steps of:**, **List each value**, and **List the whole sequence**) should be 1. If any are not, change them to 1. Click **OK** and you should see a list of numbers from 1 to 40 now located in column 1 of the worksheet.
- Click the **Calc** button again and choose **Random Data**. From the sub-menu that comes up pick **Sample From Columns**.
- In the command window that appears type 15 in the space between **Sample** and **rows from column(s):**, click in the space beneath and type C1. In the space below **Store samples in:** type C2 then click **OK**. The list of numbers that is now stored in column 2 of the worksheet is the random selection the package has produced and you can use it to select from the numbered applications; if the number 34 appears in column 2 then pick the 34th application and so on.

15.4.2 SPSS

If you want to use SPSS to help you select a random sample of 15 from 40 job applications use this procedure to select your sample:

- Type the applicants' names into a column of the worksheet.
- Click the **Data** button at the top of the screen then choose **Select Cases**.
- In the command window that appears click the button alongside **Random sample of cases**. Make sure that beneath **Unselected Cases Are** the button beside **Filtered** is the default selection, and if not choose it, then click the **Sample** button.

■ In the **Select Cases: Random Sample** window that comes up click the small button to the left of **Exactly** then type 15 and 40 respectively in the empty spaces in the phrase **Exactly— from the first—cases**. Click on **Continue** then **OK** in the **Select Cases** window. In the worksheet you should see a new column headed **filter** in which each cell has either 0 or 1. A 1 alongside an applicant indicates that that application should be included in the sample, a 0 that it should not. There should be as many ones in the column as the number of cases you asked to be selected.

15.5 Road test: Do they really use sampling?

In his survey of the extent to which US corporations used quantitative methods Kathawala (1988) found that 69% of companies reported that they made moderate, frequent or extensive use of statistical sampling. He found that life insurance companies and electrical utilities were among the heaviest users.

Million (1980) described the methods used to forecast future demand for water at the Thames Water Authority. He noted that forecasting the use of water by UK households was particularly difficult because relatively few had metered supplies. In order to get information about household use of water the Authority conducted sample surveys.

The MTV television channel undertakes a variety of sample investigations of the tastes, preferences and lifestyles of its subscribers. Wilson (2003) describes one of their surveys in which passages of music are played over the phone to a random sample of the MTV target audience who are asked whether or not they consider it suitable for the channel. Wilson also outlines how multi-stage sampling is used to conduct the UK National Readership survey, a key source of information for advertisers who want to know the size and nature of the readership of publications in which they might place advertisements, as well as for the publishers, who use the same information to set prices for the advertisements.

Hague and Jackson (1992) provide interesting accounts of a series of sample surveys conducted by a variety of companies seeking information about aspects of the markets in which they operate. They give real insight into the practical dilemmas and range of solutions used to overcome them.

The cases presented by Hague and Jackson include the research carried out by Philips Lighting to investigate the potential for its new Softone electric light bulb. The first stage of their research involved using quota sampling to assess the likely consumer response to the new bulb, which had a squarer shape than conventional bulbs and was to be produced in a range of pastel shades.

Another case they report is that of the attempt by British Gas to ascertain the future market prospects for gas wall heaters, sales of which had been declining. An important source of information was the National Domestic Establishment Survey conducted by the company every two years. The survey provided data gathered from a random sample of 45,000 households sub-divided in accordance with the 12 regions of British Gas. The company were able to use the results to study the potential market for gas wall heaters in relation to the ages of houses in which customers and prospective customers lived and the sales of rival products such as electric storage heaters.

CHAPTER 16

Test driving — sampling theory, estimation and hypothesis testing

This chapter will help you to:

- understand the theory behind the use of sample results for prediction
- make use of the *t* distribution and appreciate its importance
- construct and interpret interval estimates of population means and population proportions
- work out necessary sample sizes for interval estimation
- carry out tests of hypotheses about population means, proportions and medians, and draw appropriate conclusions from them
- use the technology; the t distribution, estimation and hypothesis testing in EXCEL, MINITAB and SPSS
- become acquainted with the business origins of the *t* distribution

In the previous chapter we reviewed the methods that can be used to select samples from populations in order to gain some understanding of those populations. In this chapter we will consider how sample results can be used to provide estimates of key features, or parameters, of the populations from which they were selected. It is important to note that the techniques described in this chapter, and the theory on which they are based, should only be used with results of samples selected using probabilistic or random sampling methods. The techniques are based on knowing, or at least having a reliable estimate of, the sampling error and this is not possible with non-random sampling methods.

In Chapter 13 we looked at the normal distribution, an important statistical distribution that enables you to investigate the very many continuous variables that occur in business and many other fields, whose values are distributed in a normal pattern. What makes the normal distribution especially important is that it enables us to anticipate how sample results vary. This is because many *sampling distributions* have a normal pattern.

16.1 Sampling distributions

Sampling distributions are distributions that show how sample results vary. They depict the 'populations' of sample results. Such distributions play a crucial role in quantitative work because they enable us to use data from a sample to make statistically valid predictions or judgements about a population. There are considerable advantages in using sample results in this way, especially when the population is too large to be accessible, or if investigating the population is too expensive or time-consuming.

A sample is a subset of a population, that is, it consists of some observations taken from the population. A random sample is a sample that consists of values taken at random from the population.

You can take many different random samples from the same population, even samples that consist of the same number of observations. Unless the population is very small the number of samples that you could take from it is to all intents and purposes infinite. A 'parent' population can produce an effectively infinite number of 'offspring' samples.

These samples will have different means, standard deviations and so on. So if we want to use, say, a sample mean to predict the value of the population mean we will be using something that varies from sample to sample, the sample mean ($\bar{x}$), to predict something that is fixed, the population mean.

To do this successfully we need to know how the sample means vary from one sample to another. We need to think of sample means as observations, $\bar{x}$s, of a variable, $\bar{X}$, and consider how they are distributed. What is more we need to relate the distribution of sample means to the parameters of the population the samples come from so that we can use sample statistics to predict population measures. The distribution of $\overline{X}$, the sample means, is a *sampling distribution*.

We will begin by considering the simplest case, in which we assume that the parent population is normally distributed. If this is the case, what will the sampling distributions of means of samples taken from the population be like?

If you were to take all possible random samples consisting of n observations from a population that is normal, with a mean μ and a standard deviation σ, and analyse them you would find that the sample means of all these samples will themselves be normally distributed.

You would find that the mean of the distribution of all these different sample means is exactly the same as the population mean, μ. You would also find that the standard deviation of all these sample means is the population standard deviation divided by the square root of the size of the samples, $\sigma/\sqrt{n}$.

So the sample means of all the samples size n that can be taken from a normal population with a mean μ and a standard deviation σ are distributed normally with a mean of μ and a standard deviation of $\sigma/\sqrt{n}$. In other words, the sample means are distributed around the same mean as the population itself but with a smaller spread.

We know that the sample means will be less spread out than the population because n will be more than one, so $\sigma/\sqrt{n}$ will be less than σ. For instance, if there are four observations in each sample, $\sigma/\sqrt{n}$ will be $\sigma/2$, that is the sampling distribution of means of samples which have four observations in them will have half the spread of the population distribution.

The larger the size of the samples, the less the spread in the values of their means, for instance if each sample consists of 100 observations the standard deviation of the sampling distribution will be $\sigma/10$, a tenth of the population distribution.

This is an important logical point. In taking samples we are 'averaging out' the differences between the individual values in the population. The larger the samples, the more this happens. For this reason it is better to use larger samples to make predictions about a population.

Next time you see an opinion poll look for the number of people that the pollsters have canvassed. It will probably be at least one thousand. The results of an opinion poll are a product that the polling organization wants to sell to media companies. In order to do this they have to persuade them that their poll results are likely to be reliable. They won't be able to do this if they only ask a very few people for their opinions!

The standard deviation of a sampling distribution, $\sigma/\sqrt{n}$, is also known as the *standard error* of the sampling distribution because it helps us anticipate the error we will have to deal with if we use a sample mean to predict the value of the population mean.

If we know the mean and standard deviation of the parent population distribution we can find the probabilities of ranges different sample means as we can do for any other normal distribution, by using the Standard Normal Distribution.

Example 16.1

Reebar Frozen Foods produces packs of four fish portions. On the packaging they claim that the average weight of the portions is 120 g. If the mean weight of the fish portions they buy is 124 g with a standard deviation of 4 g, what is the probability that the mean weight of a pack of four portions will be less than 120 g?

We will assume that the selection of the four portions to put in a pack is random. Imagine we took every possible sample of four portions from the population of fish portions purchased by Reebar (which we will assume for practical purposes to be infinite) and calculated the mean weight of each sample. We would find that the sampling distribution of all these means has a mean of 124 g and a standard error of $4/\sqrt{4}$, which is 2.

The probability that a sample of four portions has a mean of less than 120 g is the probability that a normal variable with a mean of 124 and a standard deviation of 2 is less than 120.

The z-equivalent of the value 120 in the sampling distribution is

$$z = \frac{\bar{x} - \mu}{\sigma/\sqrt{n}} = \frac{120 - 124}{4/\sqrt{4}} = -2.00$$

From Table 5 on pages 621–622 in Appendix 1 you will find that the probability that z is less than -2.00 is 0.0228 or 2.28%.

We can conclude that there is a less than one in forty chance that four portions in a pack chosen at random have a mean weight of less than 120 g. You might like to compare this with the probability of one fish portion selected at random weighing less than 120 g:

$$z = \frac{x - \mu}{\sigma} = \frac{120 - 124}{4} = -1.00$$

Using Table 5 you will find that the probability that Z is less than -1.00 is 0.1587 or 15.87%, approximately a one in six chance. This is rather greater than the chance of getting a pack of four whose mean weight is less than 120 g (2.28%); in general there is less variation among sample means than there is among single points of data.

The procedure we used in Example 16.1 can be applied whether we are dealing with small samples or with very much larger samples. As long as the population the samples come from is normal we can be sure that the sampling distribution will be distributed normally with a mean of μ and a standard deviation of $\sigma/\sqrt{n}$.

But what if the population is not normal? There are many distributions that are not normal, such as distributions of wealth of individuals or distributions of waiting times.

Fortunately, according to a mathematical finding known as the Central Limit Theorem, as long as n is large (which is usually interpreted to mean 30 or more) the sampling distribution of sample means will be normal in shape and have a mean of μ and a standard deviation of $\sigma/\sqrt{n}$. This is true *whatever* the shape of the population distribution.

Example 16.2

The times that passengers at a busy railway station have to wait to buy tickets during the rush hour follow a skewed distribution with a mean of 2 minutes 46 seconds and a standard deviation of 1 minute 20 seconds. What is the probability that a random sample of 100 passengers will, on average, have to wait more than 3 minutes?

The sample size, 100, is larger than 30 so the sampling distribution of the sample means will have a normal shape. It will have a mean of 2 minutes 46 seconds, or 166 seconds, and a standard error of $80/\sqrt{100}$ seconds.

$$P(\overline{X} > 180 \text{ seconds}) = P\left(\frac{Z > 180 - 166}{80/\sqrt{100}} \right)$$
$$= P(Z > 14/8) = P(Z > 1.75)$$

From Table 5 the probability that Z is more than 1.75 is 0.0401. So the probability that a random sample of 100 passengers will have to wait on average more than 3 minutes is 4.01%, or a little more than a one in twenty-five chance.

If the samples taken from a population that is not normal consist of fewer than 30 observations then the Central Limit Theorem does not apply. The sampling distributions of means of small samples taken from such populations do not have a normal pattern.

At this point you may find it useful to try **Review Questions 16.1 to 16.6** at the end of the chapter.

16.1.1 Estimating the standard error

The main reason for being interested in sampling distributions is to help us use samples to assess populations because studying the whole population is not possible or practicable. Typically we will be using a sample, which we do know about, to investigate a population, which we don't know about. We will have a sample mean and we will want to use it to assess the likely value of the population mean.

So far we have measured sampling distributions using the mean and the standard deviation of the population, μ and σ. But if we need to find out about the population using a sample, how can we possibly know the values of μ and σ?

The answer is that in practice we don't. In the case of the population mean, μ, this doesn't matter because typically it is something we are trying to assess. But without the population standard deviation, σ, we do need an alternative approach to measuring the spread of a sampling distribution.

Because we will have a sample, the obvious answer is to use the standard deviation, s, in place of the population standard deviation, σ. So instead of using the real standard error, $\sigma/\sqrt{n}$, we estimate the standard error of the sampling distribution with $s/\sqrt{n}$.

Using the estimated standard error, $s/\sqrt{n}$, is fine as long as the sample concerned is large (in practice, that n, the sample size, is at least 30). If we are dealing with a large sample we can use $s/\sqrt{n}$ as an approximation of $\sigma/\sqrt{n}$. The means of samples consisting of n observations will be normally distributed with a mean of μ and an estimated standard error of $s/\sqrt{n}$. The Central Limit Theorem allows us to do this even if the population the sample comes from is not itself normal in shape.

Example 16.3

The mean volume of draught beer served in pint glasses in the Nerry Ash Leavy Arms pub is known to be 0.538 litres. A consumer organization takes a random sample of 36 pints of draught beer and finds that the standard deviation of this sample is 0.066 litres. What is the probability that the mean volume of the sample will be less than a pint (0.568 litres)?

The population mean, μ, in this case is 0.538 and the sample standard deviation, s, is 0.042. We want the probability that $\bar{x}$ is less than 0.568, $P(\overline{X} < 0.568)$. The

z-equivalent of 0.568 is:

$$z = \frac{\bar{x} - \mu}{s/\sqrt{n}} = \frac{0.568 - 0.538}{0.066/\sqrt{36}}$$
$$= 2.73 \text{ to 2 decimal places}$$
$$\text{So } P(\bar{X} < 0.568) = P(Z < 2.73)$$

If you look at Table 5 you will find that the probability that Z is less than 2.73 is 0.9968, so the probability that the sample mean is more than a pint is 0.9968 or 99.68%.

It is important to remember that $s/\sqrt{n}$ is not the real standard error, it is the *estimated standard error*, but because the standard deviation of a large sample will be reasonably close to the population standard deviation the estimated standard error will be close to the actual standard error.

At this point you may find it useful to try **Review Question 16.7** at the end of the chapter.

16.1.2 The *t* distribution

In section 16.1.1 we looked at how you can analyse sampling distributions using the sample standard deviation, s, when you do not know the population standard deviation, σ. As long as the sample size, n, is 30 or more the estimated standard error will be a sufficiently consistent measure of the spread of the sampling distribution, whatever the shape of the parent population.

If, however, the sample size, n, is less than 30 the estimated standard error, $s/\sqrt{n}$, is generally not so close to the actual standard error, $\sigma/\sqrt{n}$, and the smaller the sample size, the greater will be the difference between the two. In this situation it is possible to model the sampling distribution using the estimated standard error, as long as the population the sample comes from is normal, but we have to use a modified normal distribution in order to do it.

This modified normal distribution is known as the *t distribution*. The development of the distribution was a real breakthrough because it made it possible to investigate populations using small sample results. Small samples are generally much cheaper and quicker to gather than a large sample so the *t* distribution broadened the scope for analysis based on sample data.

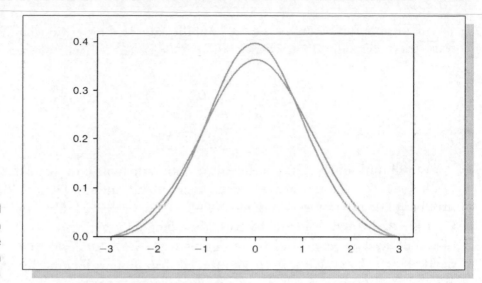

Figure 16.1
The Standard
Normal Distribution
(solid line) and the
t distribution
(dotted line)

The t distribution is a more spread out version of the normal distribution. The difference between the two is illustrated in Figure 16.1.

The greater spread is to compensate for the greater variation in sample standard deviations between small samples than between large samples.

The smaller the sample size, the more compensation is needed, so there are a number of versions of the t distribution. The one that should be used in a particular context depends on the number of degrees of freedom, represented by the symbol ν (nu, the Greek letter n), which is the sample size minus one, $n - 1$.

To work out the probability that the mean of a small sample taken from a normal population is more, or less, than a certain amount we first need to find its t equivalent, or t value. The procedure is very similar to the way we work out a z-equivalent.

$$t = \frac{\bar{x} - \mu}{s/\sqrt{n}}$$

Example 16.4

A customer visiting the pub in Example 16.3 purchases nine pints of draught beer. The precise volumes of the pints served are known to be normally distributed with a mean of 0.538 litres and the standard deviation of the volumes of the nine pints bought by the customer is 0.048 litres. What is the probability that the mean volume of each of the nine pints is less than a pint (0.568 litres)?

The population mean, μ, is 0.538 and the sample standard deviation, s, is 0.048. We want the probability that $\overline{X}$ is less than 0.568, $P\,(\overline{X} < 0.568)$. The t value equivalent to 0.568 is:

$$t = \frac{\overline{x} - \mu}{s/\sqrt{n}} = \frac{0.568 - 0.538}{0.048/\sqrt{9}} = 1.875$$

$$\text{So } P(\overline{X} < 0.568) = P(t < 1.875)$$

You will find some details of the t distribution in Table 6 on page 623 in Appendix 1. Look down the column headed ν on the left hand side until you see the figure 8, the number of degrees of freedom in this case (the sample size is 9). Look across the row to the right and you will see five figures that relate to the t distribution with eight degrees of freedom. The nearest of these figures to 1.875 is the 1.86 that is in the column headed 0.05. This means that 5% of the t distribution with eight degrees of freedom is above 1.86. In other words, the probability that t is more than 1.86 is 0.05. This means that the probability that the mean volume of nine pints will be less than 0.568 litres will be approximately 0.95.

The t value that we used in Example 16.4 could be written as $t_{0.05,8}$ because it is the value of t that cuts off a tail area of 5% in the t distribution that has 8 degrees of freedom. In the same way, $t_{0.01,15}$ represent the t value that cuts off a tail area of 1% in the t distribution that has 15 degrees of freedom.

You will find that the way the t distribution is used in further work depends on tail areas. For this reason, and also because the t distribution varies depending on the number of degrees of freedom, printed tables do not provide full details of the t distribution in the same way that Standard Normal Distribution tables give full details of the Standard Normal Distribution. Table 6 on page 623 gives selected values of t from the t distribution with different degrees of freedom for the most commonly used tail areas. If you need t distribution values that are not in Table 6 you can obtain them using computer software, as shown in section 16.4 later in this chapter.

Example 16.5

Use Table 6 to find:

(a) t with 4 degrees of freedom that cuts off a tail area of 0.10, $t_{0.10,4}$
(b) t with 10 degrees of freedom that cuts off a tail area of 0.01, $t_{0.01,10}$

(c) t with 17 degrees of freedom that cuts off a tail area of 0.025, $t_{0.025,17}$

(d) t with 100 degrees of freedom that cuts off a tail area of 0.005, $t_{0.005,100}$.

From Table 6:

(a) $t_{0.10,4}$ is in the row for 4 degrees of freedom and the column headed 0.10, 1.533. This means that the probability that t, with 4 degrees of freedom, is greater than 1.533 is 0.10 or 10%.

(b) $t_{0.01,10}$ is the figure in the row for 10 degrees of freedom and the column headed 0.01, 2.764.

(c) $t_{0.025,17}$ is in the row for 17 degrees of freedom and the 0.025 column, 2.110.

(d) $t_{0.005,100}$ is in the row for 100 degrees of freedom and the 0.005 column, 2.626.

At this point you may find it useful to try **Review Questions 16.8 and 16.9** at the end of the chapter.

16.1.3 Choosing the right model for a sampling distribution

The normal distribution and the t distribution are both models that you can use to model sampling distributions, but how can you be sure that you use the correct one? This section is intended to provide a brief guide to making the choice.

The first question to ask is, are the samples whose results make up the sampling distribution drawn from a population that is distributed normally? In other words, is the parent population normal? If the answer is yes then it is always possible to model the sampling distribution. If the answer is no then it is only possible to model the sampling distribution if the sample size, n, is 30 or more.

The second question is whether the population standard deviation, σ, is known. If the answer to this is yes then as long as the parent population is normal the sampling distribution can be modelled using the normal distribution whatever the sample size. If the answer is no the sampling distribution can be modelled using the normal distribution only if the sample size is 30 or more. In the absence of the population standard deviation, you have to use the sample standard deviation to approximate the standard error.

Finally, what if the parent population is normal, the population standard deviation is not known and the sample size is less than 30? In these circumstances you should use the t distribution and approximate the standard error using the sample standard deviation. Note that if the parent population is not normal *and* the sample size is less than 30 neither the normal distribution nor the *t* distribution can be used to model the sampling distribution, and this is true whether or not the population standard deviation is known.

16.2 Statistical inference: estimation

Businesses use statistical analysis to help them study and solve problems. In many cases the data they use in their analysis will be sample data. Usually it is too expensive, or too time-consuming or simply impossible to obtain population data.

So if there is a problem of customer dissatisfaction they will study data from a sample of customers, not all customers. If there is a problem with product quality they will study a sample of the products, not all of them. If a large organization has a problem with staff training they will study the experiences of a sample of their staff rather than all their staff.

Of course, they will want to analyse the sample data in order to draw general conclusions about the population. As long as the samples they use are random samples, in other words they consist of observed values chosen at random from the population, it is quite possible to do this.

The use of sample data in drawing conclusions, or making deductions, about populations is known as *statistical inference* from the word *infer* which means to deduce or conclude. Statistical inference that involves testing claims about population parameters is known as *statistical decision-making* because it can be used to help organizations and individuals take decisions.

In the last section we looked at sampling distributions. These distributions are the theoretical foundations on which statistical inference is built because they connect the behaviour of sample results to the distribution of the population the samples came from. Now we will consider the procedures involved in statistical inference.

There are two types of statistical inference technique that you will encounter in this chapter. The one we shall look at in this section is *estimation*, the using of sample data to predict population measures like means and proportions. The other is *hypothesis testing*, using sample data to verify or refute claims made about population measures, the subject of Section 16.3.

Collecting sample data can be time-consuming and expensive so in practice organizations don't like to gather more data than they need, but on the other hand they don't want to end up with too little in case they haven't enough for the sort of conclusive results they want. You will find a discussion of this aspect of planning statistical research in this section.

16.2.1 Statistical estimation

Statistical estimation is the use of sample measures such as means or proportions to estimate the values of their population counterparts. The easiest way of doing this is to simply take the sample measure and use it as it stands as a prediction of the population equivalent. So, we could take the mean of a sample and use it as our estimate of the population mean. This type of prediction is called *point estimation*. It is used to get a 'feel' for the population value and is a perfectly valid use of the sample result.

The main shortcoming of point estimation is given away by its name; it is a single point, a single shot at estimating one number using another. It is a crude way of estimating a population measure because not only is it uncertain whether it will be a good estimate, in other words close to the measure we want it to estimate, but we have no idea of the probability that it is a good estimate.

The best way of using sample information to predict population measures is to use what is known as *interval estimation*, which involves constructing a range or *interval* as the estimate. The aim is to be able to say how likely it is that the interval we construct is accurate, in other words, how *confident* we are that the interval does include within it the population measure. Because the probability that the interval includes the population measure, or the confidence we should have in the interval estimate, is an important issue, interval estimates are often called *confidence intervals*.

Before we look at how interval estimates are constructed and why they work, it will be helpful if we reiterate some key points about sampling distributions. For convenience we will concentrate on sample means for the time being.

- A sampling distribution of sample means shows how all the means of the different sample of a particular size, n, are distributed.
- Sampling distributions that describe the behaviour of means of samples of 30 or more are always approximately normal.
- The mean of the sampling distribution of sample means is the population mean, μ.
- The standard deviation of the sampling distribution of sample means, called the standard error, is the population standard deviation divided by the square root of the sample size, $\sigma/\sqrt{n}$.

The sampling distributions that are normal in shape, the ones that show how sample means of big samples vary, have the features of the normal distribution. One of these features is that if we take a point two standard deviations to the left of the mean and another point two standard deviations to the right of the mean, the area between the two points is roughly 95% of the distribution.

To be more precise, if these points were 1.96 standard deviations below and above the mean of the distribution the area would be exactly 95% of the distribution. In other words, 95% of the observations in the distribution are within 1.96 standard deviations from the mean.

This is also true for normal sampling distributions; 95% of the sample means in a sampling distribution that is normal will be between 1.96 standard errors below and 1.96 standard errors above the mean. You can see this illustrated in Figure 16.2.

The limits of this range or interval are:

$$\mu - 1.96\ \sigma/\sqrt{n} \text{ on the left-hand side}$$

$$\text{and}\quad \mu + 1.96\ \sigma/\sqrt{n} \text{ on the right-hand side.}$$

The greatest difference between any of the middle 95% of sample means and the population mean, μ, is 1.96 standard errors, $1.96\ \sigma\sqrt{n}$. The probability that any one sample mean is within 1.96 standard errors of the mean is:

$$P(\mu - 1.96\ \sigma/\sqrt{n} < \overline{X} < \mu + 1.96\ \sigma/\sqrt{n}) = 0.95$$

The sampling distribution allows us to predict values of sample means using the population mean. But in practice we wouldn't be interested in

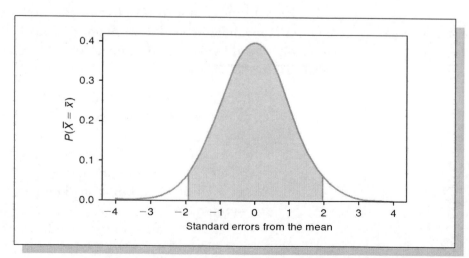

Figure 16.2
The middle 95% of
the area of a
sampling distribution

doing this because we don't know the population mean. Indeed, typically the population mean is the thing we want to find out about using a sample mean rather than the other way round. What makes sampling distributions so important is that we can use them to do this.

As we have seen, adding and subtracting 1.96 standard errors to and from the population mean creates an interval that contains 95% of the sample means in the distribution. But what if, instead of adding this amount to and subtracting it from the population mean, we add it to and subtract it from every sample mean in the distribution?

We would create an interval around every sample mean. In 95% of cases, the intervals based on the 95% of sample means closest to the population mean in the middle of the distribution, the interval would contain the population mean itself. In the other 5% of cases, those means furthest away from the population mean, the interval would not contain the population mean.

So, suppose we take the mean of a large sample and create a range around it by adding 1.96 standard errors to get an upper figure, and subtracting 1.96 standard errors to get a lower figure. There is a 95% chance that the range between the upper and lower figures will encompass the mean of the population. Such a range is called a *95% interval estimate* or a *95% confidence interval* because it is an interval that we are 95% confident, or certain, contains the population mean.

Example 16.6

The total bill sizes of shoppers at a supermarket have a mean of £50 and a standard deviation of £12.75. A group of researchers, who do not know that the population mean bill size is £50, finds the bill size of a random sample of 100 shoppers.

The sampling distribution that the mean of their sample belongs to is shown in Figure 16.3. The standard error of this distribution is $12.75/\sqrt{100} = 1.275$.

Ninety-five per cent of the sample means in this distribution will be between 1.96 standard errors below the mean, which is:

$$50 - (1.96 * 1.275) = 47.50$$

and 1.96 standard errors above the mean, which is:

$$50 + (1.96 * 1.275) = 52.50.$$

This is shown in Figure 16.4.

Suppose the researchers calculate the mean of their sample and it is £49.25, a figure inside the interval 47.50 to 52.50 that contains the 95% of sample means within

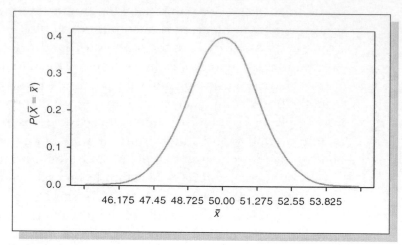

Figure 16.3
The sampling distribution in Example 16.6

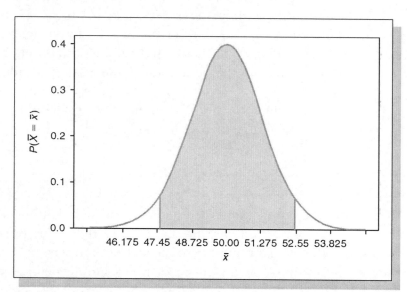

Figure 16.4
The middle 95% of the sampling distribution in Example 8.1

1.96 standard errors of the population mean. If they add and subtract the same 1.96 standard errors to and from their sample mean:

$$49.25 \pm (1.96 * 1.275) = 49.25 \pm 2.499 = £46.751 \text{ to } £51.749$$

The interval they create does contain the population mean, £50.

Notice the symbol '±' in the expression we have used. It represents the carrying out of two operations: both adding *and* subtracting the amount after it. The addition produces the higher figure, in this case 51.749, and the subtraction produces the lower figure, 46.751.

Imagine they take another random sample of 100 shoppers and find that the mean expenditure of this second sample is a little higher, but still within the central 95% of the sampling distribution, say £51.87. If they add and subtract 1.96 standard errors to and from this second mean:

$$51.87 \pm (1.96 * 1.275) = 51.87 \pm 2.499 = £49.371 \text{ to } £54.369$$

This interval also includes the population mean.

If the researchers in Example 16.6 took many samples and created an interval based on each one by adding and subtracting 1.96 standard errors they would find that only occasionally would the interval not include the population mean.

Example 16.7

The researchers in Example 16.6 take a random sample that yields a mean of £47.13. Calculate a 95% confidence interval using this sample mean.

$$47.13 \pm (1.96 * 1.275) = 47.13 \pm 2.499 = £44.631 \text{ to } £49.629$$

This interval does not include the population mean of £50.

How often will the researchers in Example 16.6 produce an interval that does not include the population mean? The answer is every time they have a sample mean that is among the lowest 2½% or the highest 2½% of sample means. If the sample mean is among the lowest 2½% the interval they produce will be too low, as in Example 16.7. If the sample mean is among the highest 2½% the interval will be too high.

As long as the sample mean is among the 95% of the distribution between the lowest 2½% and the highest 2½%, the interval they produce will include the population mean, in other words it will be an accurate estimate of the population mean.

Of course, usually when we carry out this sort of research we don't actually know what the population mean is, so we don't know whether the sample mean we have is among the 95% that will give us accurate interval estimates or whether it is among the 5% that will give us inaccurate interval estimates. The important point is that if we have a sample mean and we create an interval in this way there is a 95% chance that the interval will be accurate. To put it another way, on average

19 out of every 20 samples will produce an accurate estimate, and 1 out of 20 will not. That is why the interval is called a 95% interval estimate or a 95% confidence interval.

We can express the procedure for finding an interval estimate for a population measure as taking a sample result and adding and subtracting an *error*. This error reflects the uncertainties involved in using sample information to predict population measures.

$$\text{Population measure estimate} = \text{sample result} \pm \text{error}$$

The error is made up of two parts, the standard error and the number of standard errors. The number of standard errors depends on how confident we want to be in our estimation.

Suppose you want to estimate the population mean. If you know the population standard deviation, σ, and you want to be $(100 - \alpha)\%$ confident that your interval is accurate, then you can obtain your estimate of μ using:

$$\bar{x} \pm (z_{\alpha/2} * \sigma/\sqrt{n})$$

The letter 'z' appears because we are dealing with sampling distributions that are normal, so we can use the Standard Normal Distribution, the z distribution, to model them. You have to choose which z value to use on the basis of how sure you want or need to be that your estimate is accurate.

If you want to be 95% confident in your estimate, that is $(100 - \alpha)\% = 95\%$, then α is 5% and $\alpha/2$ is 2½% or 0.025. To produce your estimate you would use $z_{0.025}$, 1.96, the z value that cuts off a 2½% tail in the Standard Normal Distribution. This means that a point 1.96 standard errors away from the mean of a normal sampling distribution, the population mean, will cut off a tail area of 2½% of the distribution. So:

$$95\% \text{ interval estimate of } \mu = \bar{x} \pm (1.96 * \sigma/\sqrt{n})$$

This is the procedure we used in Example 16.6.

The most commonly used level of confidence interval is probably 95%, but what if you wanted to construct an interval based on a higher level of confidence, say 99%? A 99% level of confidence means we want 99% of the sample means in the sampling distribution to provide accurate interval estimates.

To obtain a 99% confidence interval the only adjustment we make is the z value that we use. If $(100 - \alpha)\% = 99\%$, then α is 1% and $\alpha/2$ is ½% or 0.005. To produce your estimate use $z_{0.005}$, 2.576, the z value

Table 16.1
Selected levels of confidence and associated z values

Level of confidence $(100 - \alpha)\%$	$\alpha/2$	$z_{\alpha/2}$
90%	0.050	1.645
95%	0.025	1.960
99%	0.005	2.576

that cuts off a ½% tail in the Standard Normal Distribution:

$$99\% \text{ interval estimate of } \mu = \bar{x} \pm (2.576 * \sigma/\sqrt{n})$$

The most commonly used confidence levels and the z values you need to construct them are given in Table 16.1.

Example 16.8

Use the sample result in Example 16.7, £47.13, to produce a 99% confidence interval for the population mean.

From Table 16.1 the z value that cuts off a 0.005 tail area is 2.576, so the 99% confidence interval is:

$$47.13 \pm (2.576 * 1.275) = 47.13 \pm 3.284 = £43.846 \text{ to } £50.414$$

Notice that the confidence interval in Example 16.8 includes the population mean, £50, unlike the 95% interval estimate produced in Example 16.7 using the same sample mean, £47.13. This is because this sample mean, £47.13, is not amongst the 95% closest to the population mean, but it is amongst the 99% closest to the population mean.

Changing the level of confidence to 99% has meant the interval is accurate, but it is also wider. The 95% interval estimate was £44.631 to £49.629, a width of £4.998. The 99% interval estimate is £43.846 to £50.414, a width of £6.568.

You can obtain the z values necessary for other levels of confidence by looking for the appropriate values of $\alpha/2$ in the body of Table 5 on pages 621–622 in Appendix 1 and finding the z values associated with them.

Example 16.9

Use the sample result in Example 16.7, £47.13, to produce a 98% confidence interval for the population mean.

From Table 5 the z value that cuts off a tail area of 0.01 is 2.33, so the 98% confidence interval is:

$$47.13 \pm (2.33 * 1.275) = 47.13 \pm 2.971 = £44.159 \text{ to } £50.101$$

At this point you may find it useful to try **Review Questions 16.10 and 16.11** at the end of the chapter.

16.2.2 Determining the sample size for estimating a population mean

All other things being equal, if we want to be more confident that our interval is accurate we have to accept that the interval will be wider, in other words less precise. If we want to be more confident and retain the same degree of precision, the only thing we can do is to take a larger sample.

In the examples we have looked at so far the size of the sample was already decided. But what if, before starting a sample investigation, you wanted to ensure that you had a big enough sample to enable you to produce a precise enough estimate with a certain level of confidence? To see how, we need to start with the expression we have used for the error of a confidence interval:

$$z_{\alpha/2} * \sigma/\sqrt{n}$$

Until now we have assumed that we know these three elements so we can work out the error. But what if we wanted to set the error and find the necessary sample size, *n*? We can change the expression for the error around so that it provides a definition of the sample size:

$$\text{error} = z_{\alpha/2} * \sigma/\sqrt{n}$$

Exchange error and $\sqrt{n}$: $\sqrt{n} = z_{\alpha/2} * \sigma/\text{error}$

So $n = (z_{\alpha/2} * \sigma/\text{error})^2$

This means that as long as you know the degree of precision you need (the error), the level of confidence (to find $z_{\alpha/2}$), and the population standard deviation (σ), you can find out what sample size you need to use.

Example 16.10

If the researchers in Example 16.6 want to construct 99% confidence intervals that are £5 wide, what sample size should they use?

If the estimates are to be £5 wide that means they will have to be produced by adding and subtracting £2.50 to and from the sample mean. In other words the error will be 2.50. If the level of confidence is to be 99% then the error will be 2.576 standard errors. We know that the population standard deviation, σ, is 12.75, so:

$$n = (2.576 * 12.75/2.50)^2$$

$$n = (13.1376)^2 = 172.6 \text{ to one decimal place.}$$

Since the size of a sample must be a whole number we should round this up to 173. When you are working out the necessary sample size you must round the calculated sample size up to the next whole number to achieve the specified confidence level. Here we would round up to 173 even if the result of the calculation was 172.01.

We should conclude that if the researchers want 99% interval estimates that are £5 wide they would have to take a sample of 173 shoppers.

At this point you may find it useful to try **Review Questions 16.12 and 16.13** at the end of the chapter.

16.2.3 Estimating without σ

Example 16.6 is artificial because we assumed that we knew the population mean, μ. This helped to explain how and why interval estimation works. In practice we wouldn't know the population mean, and we would probably not know the population standard deviation, σ, either.

Practical interval estimation is based on sample results alone, but it is very similar to the procedure we explored in Example 16.6. The main difference is that we have to use a sample standard deviation, s, to produce an estimate for the standard error of the sampling distribution the sample belongs to. Apart from this, as long as the sample we have is quite large, which we can define as containing 30 or more observations, we can follow exactly the same procedure as before.

That is, instead of

$$\text{estimate of } \mu = \bar{x} \pm (z_{\alpha/2} * \sigma/\sqrt{n})$$

we use

$$\text{estimate of } \mu = \bar{x} \pm (z_{\alpha/2} * s/\sqrt{n}).$$

Example 16.11

The mean weight of the cabin baggage checked in by a random sample of 40 passengers at an international airport departure terminal was 3.47 kg. The sample standard deviation was 0.82 kg. Construct a 90% confidence interval for the mean weight of cabin baggage checked in by passengers at the terminal.

In this case α is 10%, so $\alpha/2$ is 5% or 0.05 and according to Table 16.1 $z_{0.05}$ is 1.645.

$$\begin{aligned} 90\% \text{ interval estimate of } \mu &= \bar{x} \pm (1.645 * s/\sqrt{n}) \\ &= 3.47 \pm (1.645 * 0.82/\sqrt{40}) \\ &= 3.47 \pm 0.213 \\ &= 3.257 \text{ to } 3.683 \text{ kg} \end{aligned}$$

In Example 16.11 we are not told whether the population that the sample comes from is normal or not. This doesn't matter because the sample size is over 30. In fact, given that airlines tend to restrict cabin baggage to 5 kg per passenger the population distribution in this case would probably be skewed.

16.2.4 Estimating with small samples

If we want to produce an interval estimate based on a smaller sample, one with less than 30 observations in it, we have to be much more careful. First, for the procedures we will consider in this section to be valid, the population that the sample comes from must be normal. Second, because the sample standard deviation of a small sample is not a reliable enough estimate of the population standard deviation to enable us to use the z distribution, we must use the t distribution to find how many standard errors are to be added and subtracted to produce an interval estimate with a given level of confidence.

Instead of

$$\text{estimate of } \mu = x \pm (z_{\alpha/2} * \sigma/\sqrt{n})$$

we use

$$\text{estimate of } \mu = x \pm (t_{\alpha/2,\nu} * s/\sqrt{n}).$$

The form of the t distribution you use depends on ν, the number of degrees of freedom, which is the sample size less one ($n - 1$). You can find the values you need to produce interval estimates in Table 6 on page 623 of Appendix 1.

You may recall from section 16.1.2 that the t distribution is a modified form of the z distribution. If you compare the figures in the bottom row of the 0.05, 0.025 and 0.005 columns of Table 6 with the z values in Table 16.1, that is 1.645, 1.960 and 2.576, you can see that they are same. If, however, you compare these z values with the equivalent t values in the top row of Table 6, the ones for the t distribution with just one degree of freedom, which we would have to use for samples of only 2, you can see that the differences are substantial.

Example 16.12

A random sample of 15 employees of a call centre was taken and each employee took a competency test. The mean of the scores achieved by these employees was 56.3% with a standard deviation of 7.1%. Results of this test have been found to be normally distributed in the past. Construct a 95% confidence interval for the mean test score of all the employees of the call centre.

Here α is 5% so $\alpha/2$ is 2.5% or 0.025 and the number of degrees of freedom, ν, is $n - 1$, 14.

$$95\% \text{ estimate of } \mu = \bar{x} \pm (t_{0.025,14} * s/\sqrt{n})$$

From Table 6, $t_{0.025,14}$ is 2.145, so:

$$95\% \text{ estimate of } \mu = 56.3 \pm (2.145 * 7.1/\sqrt{15})$$

$$= 56.3 \pm 3.932 = 52.378\% \text{ to } 60.232\%$$

At this point you may find it useful to try **Review Questions 16.14 and 16.15** at the end of the chapter.

16.2.5 Estimating population proportions

Although so far we have concentrated on how to estimate population means, these are not the only population parameters that can be estimated. You will also come across estimates of population proportions, indeed almost certainly you already have.

If you have seen an opinion poll of voting intentions, you have seen an estimate of a population proportion. To produce the opinion poll result that you read in a newspaper pollsters have interviewed a sample of people and used the sample results to predict the voting intentions of the entire population.

In many ways estimating a population proportion is very similar to the estimation we have already considered. To start with you need a sample: you calculate a sample result around which your estimate will be constructed; you add and subtract an error based on the standard error of the relevant sampling distribution, and how confident you want to be that your estimate is accurate.

We have to adjust our approach because of the different nature of the data. When we estimate proportions we are usually dealing with qualitative variables. The values of these variables are characteristics, for instance people voting for party A or party B. If there are only two possible characteristics, or we decide to use only two categories in our analysis, the variable will have a binomial distribution.

As you will see, this is convenient as it means we only have to deal with one sample result, the sample proportion, but it also means that we cannot produce reliable estimates from small samples, those consisting of less than 30 observations. This is because the distribution of the population that the sample comes from must be normal if we are to use the t distribution, the device we have previously used to overcome the extra uncertainty involved in small sample estimation.

The sampling distribution of sample proportions is approximately normal in shape if the samples involved are large, that is, more than 30, as long as the sample proportion is not too small or too large. In practice, because we do not know the sample proportion before taking the sample it is best to use a sample size of over 100. If the samples are small, the sampling distribution of sample proportions is not normal.

Provided that you have a large sample, you can construct an interval estimate for the population proportion, π (pi, the Greek letter p), by taking the sample proportion, p, and adding and subtracting an error. The sample proportion is the number of items in the sample that possess the characteristic of interest, x, divided by the total number of items in the sample, n.

$$\text{Sample proportion,} \quad p = x/n$$

The error that you add to and subtract from the sample proportion is the z value appropriate for the level of confidence you want to use multiplied by the estimated standard error of the sampling distribution of the sample proportion. This estimated standard error is based on the sample proportion:

$$\text{estimated standard error} = \sqrt{\frac{p(1 - p)}{n}}$$

So the

$$\text{interval estimate of } \pi = p \pm z_{\alpha/2} * \sqrt{\frac{p(1-p)}{n}}$$

Example 16.13

A study of a sample of 110 supermarkets reveals that 31 offer trolleys suitable for shoppers with limited mobility. Construct a 95% interval estimate of the proportion of all supermarkets that have these trolleys.

$$p = 31/110 = 0.28$$
$$(100 - \alpha)\% = 95\%, \text{ so } z_{\alpha/2} = 1.96$$

$$\text{interval estimate of } \pi = 0.28 \pm 1.96 * \sqrt{\frac{0.28\,(1-0.28)}{110}}$$
$$= 0.28 \pm 1.96 * 0.043 = 0.28 \pm 0.084$$
$$= 0.196 \text{ to } 0.364$$

These results suggest that we can be 95% confident that the proportion of supermarkets with suitable trolleys for shoppers with limited mobility will be between 19.6% and 36.4%.

At this point you may find it useful to try **Review Questions 16.16 and 16.17** at the end of the chapter.

16.2.6 Determining the sample size for estimating a population proportion

If you know how confident you want to be that your interval estimate is accurate and you need your estimate to have a certain precision, in other words the error has to be a particular amount, you can work out the sample size you will need to use.

The precision of the test depends on the estimated standard error of the sample proportions, $\sqrt{p(1-p)/n}$. The value of this depends on p, the sample proportion. Clearly you won't know this until the sample data have been collected, but you can't collect the sample data until you have decided what sample size to use. You therefore need to make a prior assumption about the value of the sample proportion.

To be on the safe side we will assume the worst-case scenario, which is that the value of p will be the one that produces the highest value of

$p\,(1-p)$. The higher the value of $p\,(1-p)$ the wider the interval will be, for a given sample size. We need to avoid the situation where $p\,(1-p)$ turns out to be larger than we have assumed it is.

What is the largest value of $p\,(1-p)$? If you work out $p\,(1-p)$ when p is 0.1, you will get 0.09. If p is 0.2, $p\,(1-p)$ rises to 0.16. As you increase the value of p you will find that it keeps going up until p is 0.5, when $p\,(1-p)$ is 0.25, then it goes down again.

The error in an interval estimate of a population proportion is:

$$\text{error} = z_{\alpha/2} * \sqrt{\frac{p(1-p)}{n}}$$

If p is 0.5, in other words we assume the largest value of $p\,(1-p)$:

$$\text{error} = z_{\alpha/2} * \sqrt{\frac{0.5(1-0.5)}{n}}$$

$$= z_{\alpha/2} * \sqrt{\frac{0.5 * 0.5}{n}}$$

$$= z_{\alpha/2} * \frac{0.5}{\sqrt{n}}$$

This last expression can be re-arranged to obtain an expression for n:

$$\text{error} = z_{\alpha/2} * \frac{0.5}{\sqrt{n}}$$

$$\text{so} \quad \sqrt{n} = \frac{z_{\alpha/2} * 0.5}{\text{error}} \quad \text{and}$$

$$n = \left[\frac{z_{\alpha/2}}{2 * \text{error}}\right]^2$$

Example 16.14

How many supermarkets would have to be included in the sample in Example 16.13 if the confidence interval of the proportion of establishments with trolleys suitable for shoppers with limited mobility has to be within 5% of the actual population proportion with a 95% degree of confidence.

For the error to be 5%:

$$n = \left[\frac{1.96}{2 * 0.05}\right]^2 = 19.6^2 = 384.16$$

This has to be rounded up to 385 to meet the confidence requirement so a random sample of 385 supermarkets would have to be used.

At this point you may find it useful to try **Review Questions 16.18 and 16.19** at the end of the chapter.

16.3 Statistical inference: hypothesis testing

Usually when we construct interval estimates of population parameters we have no idea of the actual value of the parameter we are trying to estimate. Indeed the purpose of estimation using sample results is to tell us what the actual value is likely to be.

Sometimes we use sample results to deal with a different situation. This is where the population parameter is claimed to take a particular value and we want to see whether the claim is correct. Such a claim is known as a *hypothesis*, and the use of sample results to investigate whether it is true is called *hypothesis testing*. To begin with we will concentrate on testing hypotheses about population means using a single sample. Later in this section you will find hypothesis testing of population proportions and a way of testing hypotheses about population medians.

Hypothesis testing begins with a formal statement of the claim being made for the population parameter. This is known as the *null hypothesis* because it is the starting point in the investigation, and is represented by the symbol H_0, 'aitch-nought'.

We could find that a null hypothesis appears to be wrong, in which case we should reject it in favour of an *alternative hypothesis*, represented by the symbol H_1, 'aitch-one'. The alternative hypothesis is the collection of explanations that contradict the claim in the null hypothesis.

A null hypothesis may specify a single value for the population measure, in which case we would expect the alternative hypothesis to consist of other values both below and above it. Because of this 'dual' nature of the alternative hypothesis, the procedure to investigate such a null hypothesis is known as a *two-sided test*.

In other cases the null hypothesis might specify a minimum or a maximum value, in which case the alternative hypothesis consists of values below, or values above respectively. The procedure we use in these cases is called a *one-sided test*. Table 16.2 lists the three combinations of hypotheses.

In Table 16.2 μ_0 is used to represent the value of the population mean, μ, that is to be tested.

The type of null hypothesis that should be used depends on the context of the investigation and the perspective of the investigator.

Table 16.2

Types of hypotheses

Null hypothesis	Alternative hypothesis	Type of test
$H_0: \mu = \mu_0$	$H_1: \mu \neq \mu_0$ (not equal)	Two-sided
$H_0: \mu \leqslant \mu_0$	$H_1: \mu > \mu_0$ (greater than)	One-sided
$H_0: \mu \geqslant \mu_0$	$H_1: \mu < \mu_0$ (less than)	One-sided

Example 16.15

A bus company promotes a 'one-hour' tour of a city. Suggest suitable null and alternative hypotheses for an investigation by:

(a) a passenger who wants to know how long the journey will take.
(b) a journalist from a consumer magazine who wants to see whether passengers are being cheated.

In the first case we might assume that the passenger is as concerned about the tour taking too much time as too little time, so appropriate hypotheses would be that the population mean of the times of the tours is either equal to one hour or it is not.

$$H_0: \mu = 60 \text{ minutes} \qquad H_1: \mu \neq 60 \text{ minutes}$$

In the second case we can assume that the investigation is more focused. The journalist is more concerned that the trips might not take the full hour rather than taking longer than an hour, so appropriate hypotheses would be that the population mean tour time is either one hour or more, or it is less than an hour.

$$H_0: \mu \geqslant 60 \text{ minutes} \qquad H_1: \mu < 60 \text{ minutes}$$

After establishing the form of the hypotheses we can test them using the sample evidence we have. We need to decide if the sample evidence is compatible with the null hypothesis, in which case we cannot reject it. If the sample evidence contradicts the null hypothesis we reject it in favour of the alternative hypothesis.

To help us make this decision we need a *decision rule* to apply to our sample evidence. The decision rule is based on the assumption that the null hypothesis is true.

If the population mean really does take the value specified in the null hypothesis, then as long as we know the value of the population standard deviation, σ, and the size of our sample, n, we can identify the sampling distribution that our sample belongs to.

Example 16.16

The standard deviation of the bus tours in Example 16.15 is known to be 6 minutes. If the duration of a random sample of 50 tours is to be recorded in order to investigate the operation, what can we deduce about the sampling distribution the mean of the sample belongs to?

The null hypotheses in both sections of Example 16.15 specified a population mean, μ, of 60 minutes. If this is true the mean of the sampling distribution, the distribution of means of all samples consisting of 50 observations, is 60. The population standard deviation, σ, is 6 so the standard error of the sampling distribution, $\sigma/\sqrt{n}$, is $6/\sqrt{50}$, 0.849 minutes.

We can conclude that the sample mean of our sample will belong to a sampling distribution which is normal with a mean of 60 and a standard error of 0.849, if H_0 is true.

The next stage is to compare our sample mean to the sampling distribution it is supposed to come from if H_0 is true. If it seems to belong to the sampling distribution, in other words it is not too far away from the centre of the distribution, we consider the null hypothesis plausible. If, on the other hand, the sample mean is located on one of the extremes of the sampling distribution we consider the null hypothesis suspect.

We can make this comparison by working out the z equivalent of the sample mean and using it to find out the probability that a sample mean of the order of the one we have comes from the sampling distribution that is based on the null hypothesis being true. Because we are using a z-equivalent, this type of hypothesis test is called a z *test*.

Example 16.17

The mean of the random sample in Example 16.16 is 61.87 minutes. What is the z-equivalent of this sample mean, assuming it belongs to a sampling distribution with a mean of 60 and a standard error of 0.849? Use the z-equivalent to find the probability that a sample mean of this magnitude comes from such a sampling distribution.

$$z = \frac{\bar{x} - \mu}{\sigma/\sqrt{n}} = \frac{61.87 - 60}{0.849} = 2.203$$

Using Table 5 on pages 621–622 of Appendix 1:

$$P(z > 2.20) = 0.0139$$

This means $P(\bar{X} > 61.87) = 0.0139$ or 1.39%

This is shown in Figure 16.5 in the context of the sampling distribution.

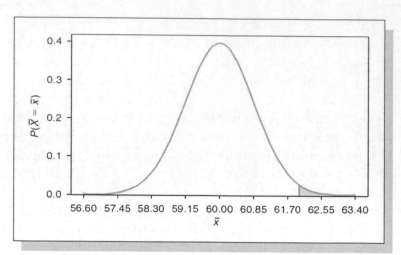

Figure 16.5
$P(\overline{X} > 61.87)$ in Example 16.17

Once we know how likely it is that a sample mean of this order belongs to the sampling distribution implied by the null hypothesis, we can make a judgement about the null hypothesis. We have to distinguish between 'acceptable' sample results, those that are compatible with the null hypothesis, and 'unacceptable' sample results, those that conflict with the null hypothesis.

If the probability that a sample mean of this order belongs to the sampling distribution that H_0 implies is quite high then it would be 'acceptable'. If it were quite low it would be 'unacceptable'. In Example 16.17 the probability that the sample mean (or a higher one) comes from the sampling distributions that H_0 suggests is only 1.39%, a low figure, so we may consider it to be 'unacceptable'.

But what exactly are 'quite high' and 'quite low' probabilities? When you get used to hypothesis testing you may well develop an intuitive 'feel' for what the appropriate dividing line is in a given situation, but until then you need to apply a decision rule.

In many practical applications this type of testing is a way of establishing that goods and services meet standards agreed between a supplier and a customer, or between a head office and local management. In these circumstances it is important that a decision rule that defines acceptable sample test results is agreed between the parties.

A decision rule should define how low the likelihood of a sample mean (or a more extreme sample mean in the sampling distribution) has to be before we consider it 'unacceptable'. 'Unacceptable' sample results are often described as *significant*, in the sense that they are significantly different to what the null hypothesis says they should be. The decision rule specifies what is called the *level of significance*.

If we say that we will use a 5% level of significance in our testing we are saying that if there is less than a 5% chance that a sample mean (or a more extreme one) belongs to the sampling distribution based on H_0 then we will consider it 'unacceptable'. We need to turn this around because it is really the null hypothesis that we would have found to be unacceptable in the light of the sample evidence. So if our sample result is 'unacceptable' we should reject the null hypothesis.

A 5% level of significance means that if the chance that the sample mean our investigation produces (or a more extreme one) does come from the sampling distribution H_0 implies is less than one in twenty, then it is such an unlikely result we believe that the sample evidence suggests the null hypothesis is wrong. Another way of putting it is to say that if our sample mean is amongst the 5% least likely to come from the sampling distribution that it should belong to if H_0 were true, then we will reject H_0.

The implication of rejecting H_0 is that the sample mean we have belongs to a different sampling distribution, because it is very unlikely to belong to the one that H_0 implies. It is very unlikely, but not impossible. The sort of sample mean that our decision rule says is significant, or 'unacceptable', could, just possibly, belong to the sampling distribution H_0 implies. In that case the decision to reject H_0 would be wrong, a mistake known as a Type I error (accepting H_0 when it is false is a Type II error). The level of significance that we specify in a decision rule is also therefore the risk we are prepared to take that we wrongly reject H_0.

When we apply our decision rule we need to take into account the type of null hypothesis we are dealing with. If it suggests that the population mean equals a particular figure we should conduct a two-sided test in order to assess it. That is, if the sample mean we produce is *either* too high *or* too low, then we should reject H_0.

In two-sided tests there are two types of 'unacceptable', or significant sample result. Because of this, if we use a 5% level of significance, the 5% least likely sample means that would lead us to reject the null hypothesis will consist of the lowest 2.5% of sample means and the highest 2.5% of sample means. If therefore the probability that our sample mean (or a more extreme one) belongs to the sampling distribution were less than 2.5%, or 0.025, we would reject H_0. But because the test is two-sided, we would say that we reject it *at the 5% level*.

These lowest and highest extremes of the sampling distribution are called the *rejection regions*, since we reject the null hypothesis if our sample mean is located in one of those parts of the distribution. Another

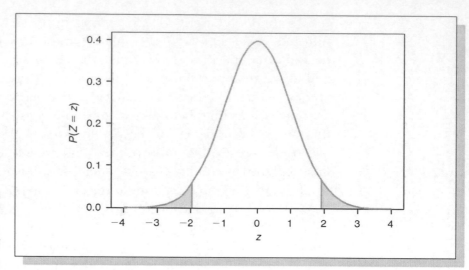

Figure 16.6
Rejection regions
for a two-tail test at
the 5% level of
significance

way of applying the decision rule is to use the z values that cut off the tails on the Standard Normal Distribution equivalent to the rejection regions as benchmarks that we compare to the z-equivalent of the sample mean. In this context the z-equivalent of the sample mean is called the *test statistic* and the z values that mark off the limits of the rejection regions are called the *critical values* of z.

In a two-sided, or *two-tail*, test using a 5% level of significance the rejection regions of the furthest 2.5% on the left and right sides of the sampling distribution are the areas of the Standard Normal Distribution beyond the critical z values, -1.96 and $+1.96$ respectively. If the z-equivalent of our sample mean, the test statistic, is either less than -1.96 or greater than $+1.96$, we should reject H_0. This is illustrated in Figure 16.6.

Example 16.18

Test the hypothesis that the population mean duration of the bus tours in Example 16.15 is 60 minutes, H_0: $\mu = 60$. Use the sample mean given in Example 16.17 and apply a 5% level of significance.

$$H_0\text{: } \mu = 60 \text{ minutes} \qquad H_1\text{: } \mu \neq 60 \text{ minutes}$$

The level of significance, $\alpha = 0.05$.

From Example 16.17 we know that the probability that the sample mean of 61.87 (or a larger one) belongs to a sampling distribution with a mean of 60 and a standard error of 0.85 is 0.0139 or 1.39%. Since this is less than 2.5% we can reject the null hypothesis at the 5% level.

Alternatively we can compare the test statistic, the z-equivalent of the sample mean, 2.20, to the critical values of z that cut off 2.5% tails of the Standard Normal Distribution, -1.96 and $+1.96$. Because it is larger than $+1.96$, we reject the null hypothesis; our sample evidence suggests that the tours take longer than 60 minutes.

If the null hypothesis suggests that the population mean is less than or equal to a particular figure we conduct a one-sided, or *one-tail*, test. If we do this using a 5% level of significance we reject the null hypothesis if our sample mean is amongst the highest 5% of samples in the sampling distribution that H_0 implies.

Since the null hypothesis includes the possibility that the population mean is lower than a particular value, a very low sample mean is compatible with the null hypothesis. It is only if the sample mean is very high that we would reject H_0.

The decision rule in this case means that if the probability that the sample mean (or a more extreme one) comes from the sampling distribution implied by H_0 is less than 5% or 0.05 *and* the sample mean is higher than the population mean specified in H_0, then we reject H_0. Alternatively, we could say that if the test statistic, the z-equivalent of our sample mean, is higher than 1.645, the z value that cuts off a tail of 5% on the right-hand side of the Standard Normal Distribution, we will reject H_0. This is illustrated in Figure 16.7.

If the null hypothesis states that the population mean is greater than or equal to a particular value, we would also conduct a one-tail test. But this

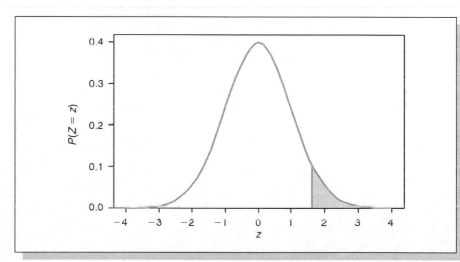

Figure 16.7
Rejection region for a one-tail test of a 'less than or equal' null hypothesis at the 5% level of significance

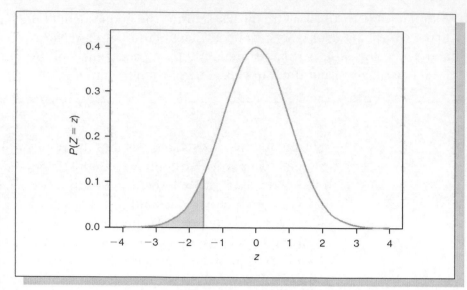

Figure 16.8
Rejection region for a one-tail test of a 'greater than or equal' null hypothesis at the 5% level of significance

time we would reject the null hypothesis if our sample mean were among the lowest 5% of samples in the sampling distribution that H_0 implies.

If the null hypothesis includes the possibility that the population mean is higher than a particular value, a very high sample mean is compatible with the null hypothesis. It is only if the sample mean is very low that we would reject H_0.

The decision rule is that if the probability that the sample mean (or a more extreme one) comes from the sampling distribution implied by H_0 is less than 5% or 0.05 *and* the sample mean is lower than the population mean specified in H_0, then we reject H_0. Alternatively we could say that if the test statistic were less than -1.645, the z value that cuts off a tail of 5% on the left-hand side of the Standard Normal Distribution, we would reject H_0. This is illustrated in Figure 16.8.

Example 16.19

Use the sample mean in Example 16.17 to test the hypothesis that the tours in Example 16.15 take at least 60 minutes, H_0: $\mu \geq 60$, at the 5% level of significance.

$$H_0: \mu \geq 60 \text{ minutes} \qquad H_1: \mu < 60 \text{ minutes}$$

The level of significance, $\alpha = 0.05$.

The sample mean is 61.87 and in Example 16.17 we found that the probability that it (or a larger one) comes from a sampling distribution with a mean of 60 and a standard error of 0.849 was 0.0139 or 1.39%, but because the null hypothesis includes the possibility that the population mean is larger than 60 we cannot reject it.

If we compare the test statistic, 2.20, with the z value that cuts off the 5% tail on the left-hand side of the Standard Normal Distribution, −1.645, we can see that 2.20 cannot be in the rejection region because it is not less than −1.645.

In the same way that you can use different levels of confidence in estimation, you can use different levels of significance in hypothesis testing. The most commonly used levels of significance are 10%, 5%, 1% and 0.1%. The lower the level of significance you use, the more rigorous the test. In circumstances where it is important that the result of a hypothesis test is robust, such as testing pharmaceutical products, it would be appropriate to use the 0.1% level of significance.

The level of significance you use determines the size of the rejection region and the critical value of z. Once you have decided which level of significance to use you can obtain the critical value by looking for the appropriate values of α (for a one-tail test) or $\alpha/2$ (for a two-tail test) in the body of Table 5 on pages 621–622 and finding the z values associated with them. Alternatively, you can find the probability that the sample result (or a more extreme one) occurs if the null hypothesis is true by working out its z-equivalent and then referring to Table 5 to find the critical value.

Example 16.20

According to the label on packets of mixed nuts there should be 25 g of cashew nuts in every packet. The standard deviation of the weight of cashew nuts per packet is known to be 2.2 g and the weights are normally distributed.

The mean weight of cashew nuts in a random sample of 15 packets is 23.5 g. Test the hypothesis that the information on the label is valid using a 1% level of confidence.

$$\text{H}_0: \mu = 25\,\text{g} \qquad \text{H}_1: \mu \neq 25\,\text{g}$$

$$\text{Level of significance, } \alpha = 0.01$$

$$z = \frac{(\bar{x} - \mu)}{\sigma/\sqrt{n}} = \frac{23.5 - 25}{2.2/\sqrt{15}} = -2.641$$

According to Table 5 the value of z that cuts off a tail area of 0.005, $z_{0.005}$, is between 2.57 and 2.58, so we will use −2.575 and +2.575 as the critical values for this test. The test statistic, −2.641, is beyond −2.575 on the left-hand side of the distribution and so falls in the rejection region. We should reject H_0 at the 1% level of significance.

Alternatively we can use Table 5 to find that $P(Z < -2.64) = 1 - 0.9959 = 0.0041$. This means that the probability a sample mean is less than 23.5, $P(\overline{X} < 23.5)$, is 0.0041. Because this is less than 0.005 (half of α; this is a two-tail test), reject H_0 at the 1% level of significance.

In Example 16.20 the sample size, 15, is small but we do not need to alter the procedure because the population the sample comes from is normal, which means that the sampling distribution for means of sample size 15 will also be normal.

Any sample result that leads to the rejection of a null hypothesis is referred to as significant. If the sample result allows us to reject a null hypothesis at an exacting level of significance like 1%, such as in Example 16.20, we refer to the sample result as highly significant.

You may find that at first the most difficult thing about hypothesis testing is the decision rule, and in particular making sure you use the appropriate critical value. It may help if you remember the connection between the type of null hypothesis and the critical value.

- If you are testing H_0: $\mu = \mu_0$, reject it if the test statistic is below $-z_{\alpha/2}$ or above $z_{\alpha/2}$.
- If you are testing H_0: $\mu \leq \mu_0$, reject it if the test statistic is above z_α.
- If you are testing H_0: $\mu \geq \mu_0$, reject it if the test statistic is below $-z_\alpha$.

At this point you may find it useful to try **Review Questions 16.20 to 16.22** at the end of the chapter.

16.3.1 Hypothesis testing without σ

In the hypothesis testing we have looked at so far we have assumed that we know the population standard deviation, σ. This could be the case, particularly if you are trying to find out whether a change had an effect by comparing sample data collected after the change with a previous situation that was well established and known. Perhaps a brewery wants to know if the refurbishment of a pub has had a significant effect on trade. In such a case the brewery records are likely to be comprehensive and they could be used to calculate the population standard deviation of the turnover per week. You could then use this figure to calculate the standard error of the sampling distribution that would provide the context for the test.

However, in many cases we won't know the population standard deviation. In these situations the sample size is the first key factor. If our sample evidence comes from a sample that consists of 30 or more observations, the sample standard deviation will be sufficiently close to the population standard deviation to allow us to use a z test; that is, to base our decision rule on the Standard Normal Distribution. We simply use the sample standard deviation in place of the population distribution when we calculate the estimated standard error; instead of $\sigma/\sqrt{n}$, we use $s/\sqrt{n}$.

Example 16.21

A hair products company claims that a hair colouring treatment it produces lasts for an average of 45 days before fading. The company wants to check that its claim is valid. The hair of a random sample of 40 customers who had applied the treatment was monitored and the time that elapsed until the colouring faded was recorded. The mean time it took for the hair colouring to fade on these customers was 46.1 days with a standard deviation of 2.9 days. Do these results support the claim that the mean time the colouring lasts is 45 days? Use a 10% level of significance.

We can assume that the company wants to ensure that the colouring lasts neither too short nor too long a period, so we will use a two-tail test.

$$H_0: \mu = 45 \qquad H_1: \mu \neq 45$$

Level of significance, $\alpha = 0.1$

If $\mu = 45$, the means of samples size 40 will form a sampling distribution that has a mean of 45 and an estimated standard error of $2.9/\sqrt{40}$. The test statistic is:

$$z = \frac{46.1 - 45}{2.9/\sqrt{40}} = 2.397$$

The probability that a z value is more than 2.40 is 0.0082, or 0.82%.

If we apply a 10% level of significance, this probability must be less than 0.05, or 5% in order to reject H_0. In this case we can reject H_0.

The z values that cut off tails of 5% are -1.645 and $+1.645$. H_0 should be rejected because the test statistic is outside these values.

At this point you may find it useful to try **Review Question 16.23** at the end of the chapter.

16.3.2 Hypothesis testing with small samples

Suppose we want to test a hypothesis using the mean of a sample that consists of less than 30 observations *and* we don't know the population standard deviation. We can do this but we have to be reasonably sure that the population that the sample comes from is normal.

We cannot rely on the sample standard deviation from a small sample being close enough to the population standard deviation to allow us to simply substitute *s* for σ as we could do with larger samples. This means we have to use the *t* distribution for benchmarks to use in comparing sample results to sampling distributions that null hypotheses imply. Because the *t* distribution is used hypothesis tests based on small samples are called *t tests*.

Example 16.22

On average 74.9 units of a brand of alco-pop drink are sold at a city centre pub each week. The manager puts on a special promotion to boost sales of the product. During the 5 weeks following the promotion the mean sales were 82.4 units per week with a standard deviation of 7.3 units. Test the hypothesis that the promotion has improved sales using a 5% level of significance.

We are only interested in investigating whether sales have improved, so we need to conduct a one-tail test. The null hypothesis assumes that the sales have not improved; the alternative hypothesis assumes that they have.

$$H_0: \mu \leq 74.9 \qquad H_1: \mu > 4.9$$

$$\text{Level of significance, } \alpha = 0.05$$

The test statistic is $\qquad t = \dfrac{(\bar{x} - \mu)}{s/\sqrt{n}} = \dfrac{82.4 - 74.9}{7.3/\sqrt{5}} = 2.301$

According to Table 6 on page 623 in Appendix 1, $t_{0.05,4}$ is 2.132, which means that the top 5% of values in the *t* distribution with 4 degrees of freedom will be greater than 2.132. Our test statistic is larger so we can conclude that there has been a significant increase in sales and H_0 should be rejected in favour of H_1.

At this point you may find it useful to try **Review Questions 16.24 to 16.28** at the end of the chapter.

16.3.3 Testing hypotheses about population proportions

The procedure for testing hypotheses about population proportions is similar to the way we test hypotheses about population means. We begin with a null hypothesis that specifies a population proportion to be tested, which we represent by the symbol π_0 (the Greek letter pi, π, is the symbol for the population proportion). If the null hypothesis is one of the 'equal to' type we conduct a two-tail test. If it is 'less than' or 'greater than', we conduct a one-tail test. The three possible combinations of hypotheses are listed in Table 16.3.

We calculate the test statistic from the sample proportion, represented by the symbol p, which comes from the sample data that we want to use to test the hypothesis. We assume that the sample proportion belongs to a sampling distribution that has a mean of π_0 and a standard error of:

$$\sqrt{\frac{\pi_0(1 - \pi_0)}{n}}$$

Note that we use the proportion from the null hypothesis to calculate the standard error, *not* the sample proportion.

The test statistic is:

$$z = \frac{p - \pi_0}{\sqrt{\pi_0(1 - \pi_0)/n}}$$

Sample proportions are distributed normally if they come from large samples. As long as the sample size is large, preferably over 100, we can use the Standard Normal Distribution as the benchmark for the test; in other words, it will be a z test.

As we have done before, we use a decision rule that specifies a level of significance in order to assess the validity of the null hypothesis.

Table 16.3

Types of hypotheses for the population proportion

Null hypothesis	Alternative hypothesis	Type of test
$H_0: \pi = \pi_0$	$H_1: \pi \neq \pi_0$ ('not equal')	Two-sided
$H_0: \pi \leqslant \pi_0$	$H_1: \pi > \pi_0$ ('greater than')	One-sided
$H_0: \pi \geqslant \pi_0$	$H_1: \pi < \pi_0$ ('less than')	One-sided

In this table π_0 represents the value of the population proportion that is to be tested.

Example 16.23

In her annual report the general manager of a car rental business observes that commercial bookings constituted 32% of the bookings received over the previous year. Out of a random sample of 146 bookings received for the current year, 40 are commercial bookings. Test the hypothesis that the proportion of commercial bookings in the current year is at least as high as the proportion received last year using a 5% level of significance.

We are interested in investigating whether the proportion is no lower than it was, so we will use a one-tail test. The hypotheses are:

$$H_0: \pi_0 \geq 0.32 \qquad H_1: \pi_0 < 0.32$$

$$\text{Level of significance, } \alpha = 0.05$$

The sample proportion, $p = 40/146 = 0.274$

$$\text{The test statistic, } z = \frac{p - \pi_0}{\sqrt{\pi_0(1 - \pi_0)/n}}$$

$$= \frac{0.274 - 0.32}{\sqrt{0.32(1 - 0.32)/146}}$$

$$= -1.191$$

From Table 5 on pages 621–622, the probability that z is -1.19 or less is 0.117, or 11.7%. Since this is more than 5% we cannot reject the null hypothesis.

Another way of assessing the test statistic is to compare it to the z value that cuts off a tail of 5% on the left-hand side of the distribution, -1.645. Because the test statistic is not less than this, the sample result is not significant. We can conclude that, although the sample proportion is lower than the proportion last year, it is not significantly lower.

At this point you may find it useful to try **Review Questions 16.29 and 16.31** at the end of the chapter.

16.3.4 A hypothesis test for the population median

For most of this section we have concentrated on testing population means. When sample sizes are large this is a generally applicable way of assessing the central tendency of populations. But as we have seen, it is not so straightforward when using small samples, samples that contain less than 30 items.

If you want to test a hypothesis about a mean using a small sample you have to be able to assume that the population that the sample comes from is normal. In many situations this is not a reasonable assumption; patterns of wealth and income, for instance, do not typically form a normal distribution.

When a distribution is skewed the sampling distributions for small samples based on it will also be skewed. You may recall that in the discussion about averages in section 6.1 of Chapter 6 we commented that the median was a more effective measure of location to use with skewed distributions. Here we will look at a test for the population median known as the *sign* test, which can be used with small samples drawn from non-normal populations.

The idea at the heart of the sign test is quite a simple one. The median is the midway point in the population. Exactly one-half of the values in the population are above the median and the other half are below it. This means that the probability a randomly selected value is less than the median is 0.5 and the probability it is more than the median is 0.5. If we have a random sample the values in it will be either above or below the median. The total number of values in the sample that are above and below the median can therefore be modelled using the binomial distribution, with say 'success' being defined as a value above the median, and *p*, the probability of success being 0.5.

You start with null and alternative hypotheses like those we have already looked at, except that they involve the population median. As before, the null hypothesis must identify the specific value of the population median to be tested. You then have to allocate a plus to each value in the sample that is above the median and a minus to each value that is below the median. In the unlikely event that your sample contains a value exactly the same as the null hypothesis population median, you can allocate a sign on the basis of the toss of a coin or simply ignore it.

Once every value has been assigned a plus or minus, you then count up the number of plus signs and the number of minus signs. Finally, use the appropriate binomial distribution to define the rejection region in keeping with the desired level of significance.

Example 16.24

The times taken to serve customers in Len's Liquor Store follow a skewed distribution. The service times, in minutes, for a random sample of 10 customers were:

$$2 \quad 6 \quad 1 \quad 4 \quad 2 \quad 5 \quad 1 \quad 1 \quad 3 \quad 2$$

Test the hypothesis that the population median service time is 2.5 minutes using a 5% level of significance.

$$H_0: \text{median} = 2.5 \qquad H_1: \text{median} \neq 2.5$$

First we allocate signs to each value, minus for a value below 2.5 and plus for a value above 2.5.

2	6	1	4	2	5	1	1	3	2
−	+	−	+	−	+	−	−	+	−

We have four plus signs and six minus signs. Table 2 on page 618 of Appendix 1 contains the probabilities for the binomial distribution for $n = 10$ and $p = 0.5$.

This is a two-tail test using a 5% level of significance so there are two parts of the rejection region, each with a tail area of 0.025. We will reject the null hypothesis if there are too many plusses (too many values above the suggested population median) or too few. But what are too many or too few?

We are dealing with discrete distributions so the tail areas will be approximate. From Table 2 we can see that the probability of 0 or 1 successes (in this context values above the median, plusses) is 0.011, and we can work out that the probability of 9 or 10 successes is also 0.11. This means that if the population median really were 2.5, the probability of getting 0, 1, 9 or 10 plusses is 0.022 or 2.2%. These numbers of plusses constitute the rejection region. As long as there are between 2 and 8 plusses inclusive, we cannot reject the null hypothesis.

In this case there are 4 plusses so we cannot reject H_0, the median could be 2.5.

Note that in effect we have used a 2.2% level of significance in this test. It is as near as we can get to 5% without exceeding it. If we were to include 2 and 8 in our rejection region the effective level of significance would be 11% (Table 2 gives the probability of 0, 1 or 2 successes as 0.055).

The sign test is one of a range of tests that can be applied in a broader range of contexts than the more traditional or classical methods we looked at earlier in the section. These tests are known as *nonparametric* tests because they are not generally based on the parameters used in the classical methods, the mean and the standard deviation. They are also referred to as *distribution-free* methods because they do not depend on assumptions about the population distribution.

Nonparametric methods are simpler to use and more widely applicable than classical methods, but they are not as efficient. Typically a nonparametric test requires more data than a classical test for the same degree of rigour. We have only considered one of the many nonparametric tests that are available. You can find out more about them in Sprent (1989).

At this point you may find it useful to try **Review Question 16.32** at the end of the chapter.

**16.4 Using the technology: the
t distribution, estimation and hypothesis
testing in EXCEL, MINITAB and SPSS**

Table 6 on page 623 of Appendix 1 offers limited information about the *t* distribution. In this section you will find guidance on using software to obtain more about the *t* distribution, as well as how to produce interval estimates and test hypotheses.

16.4.1 EXCEL

To find probabilities of the *t* distribution:

- Type **=TDIST(*x*, degrees of freedom, tails)** in the Formula Bar, where *x* is the *t* value you are interested in and 'tails' can be either one or two. Then press Enter.
- If you simply want the probability that *t* is bigger than a certain value, specify just one tail.
- In some circumstances it is useful to know the probability that *t* is more than a certain value or less than its negative equivalent, in which case we would specify two tails.

For interval estimates of the population mean:

- Find the error, that is the amount that needs to be added and subtracted to create the interval around the sample measure, by typing **=CONFIDENCE(alpha, standard deviation, size)** in the Formula Bar.
- Alpha is 100% minus the level of confidence expressed as a proportion, standard deviation is the population standard deviation, and size is the sample size.
- As long as your sample size is at least 30, you can type this in as the population standard deviation. To produce the error for Example 16.11 we would have to type **=CONFIDENCE (0.10, 0.82, 40)** and press Enter. This will produce the error to six places of decimals, in this case 0.213261.
- Apply this error to the sample mean as a separate numerical operation.

The **CONFIDENCE** command in EXCEL should only be used if you have a large sample. If you have a small sample you can't use it unless you know the population standard deviation, which is unlikely.

However, you could obtain the appropriate t value and sample measures using the other statistical tools available in the package, then assemble the interval yourself.

You can test a hypothesis about a population mean:

- Type **=ZTEST(array, *x*, sigma)** in the Formula Bar.
- The **array** is the sample data, which must be bracketed, *x* is the population mean that you want to test, and **sigma** is the population standard deviation.
- The result you get, described as a **P-value**, is the probability that the sample mean (or a more extreme one) belongs to the sampling distribution based on the population mean you are testing.

If you do not provide the population standard deviation the package will use the sample standard deviation instead. This is sound enough if the sample size is at least 30, but the results you get with smaller samples should be treated as rough approximations. There is a separate **TTEST** facility within EXCEL but it performs more complex tests, such as comparisons between sample means, than the simpler t tests we have considered in this chapter.

16.4.2 MINITAB

For cumulative probabilities of the t distribution:

- Choose **Probability Distributions** from the **Calc** menu, then t from the **Probability Distributions** sub-menu.
- In the command window you will have to select the **Cumulative probability** options and provide the number of **Degrees of freedom** (the sample size minus one) and the **Input column**, which is the column location of your t value(s).
- The result that you see in the Session window will be the probability that t is less than the value(s) in the **Input column**.

To construct an interval estimate of the population mean you need to have the sample data.

- Put your sample data into a worksheet column then select **Basic Statistics** from the **Stat** menu.
- Choose **1-Sample Z** from the **Basic Statistics** sub-menu.
- In the command window that appears you should specify the column location of the sample data, click the **Options** button and specify the level of confidence you require.

- You will also have to provide **Sigma**, the population standard deviation. If your sample consists of at least 30 observations you can type in the sample standard deviation instead.

If you want to obtain an interval estimate of the population mean using a small sample:

- Put the sample data into a worksheet column then select **Basic Statistics** from the **Stat** menu.
- Choose **1-Sample** *t* from the **Basic Statistics** sub-menu.
- In the command window that appears you should specify the column location of the sample data, click the **Options** button and specify the level of confidence you require.

Because you do not need to specify a standard deviation you may find **1-Sample** *t* easier whatever the size of your sample. Indeed, technically it is more correct to use a *t* distribution unless your sample consists of an infinite number of observations.

If you have access to EXCEL and MINITAB, use EXCEL when you need an interval using results from a large sample, rather than the original sample data, and MINITAB when you need an interval using small sample data.

To produce an interval estimate of a population proportion:

- Select **Basic Statistics** from the **Stat** menu.
- Pick the **1 Proportion** option from the **Basic Statistics** sub-menu.
- In the command window submit **Summarised data**. You need to provide the **Number of trials** and the **Number of successes**. In Example 16.13 these numbers were 110 and 31 respectively.

If you want to test hypotheses about a population mean you need to use the same commands as you use to produce estimates, either **1-Sample Z** or **1-Sample** *t* from the **Basic Statistics** sub-menu in **Stat**. Both of these commands assume that you have stored your sample data in a column in the worksheet.

- In the command window for **1-Sample Z** specify the column location of your data, then click the **Test mean** button and type into the box next to it the value of the population mean you want to test, i.e. the population mean featured in the null hypothesis.
- Click the **Options** button and in the space to the right of **Alternative** select the type of alternative hypothesis you want to use. The default is **not equal** but if you click the pull-down

menu you could select **less than** or **greater than** instead. Click **OK** to return to the command window.

- You will also have to type the value of the population standard deviation in the box next to **Sigma**.
- If you click the **Graphs** button the package will offer you a selection of diagrams that will portray your data and superimpose on the diagram the population mean being tested.
- The output that you will see in the session window includes the test statistic, **Z** and the probability that the test statistic (or a more extreme one) occurs if the null hypothesis is true, **P**.

The command window for **1-Sample** *t* is very similar to the **1-Sample Z**; the main difference is that you don't have to specify the population standard deviation.

To conduct a sign test:

- Pick **Nonparametrics** from the **Stat** menu then **1-Sample sign** from the sub-menu.
- Enter the column location of your data in the window below **Variables**.
- Click on the button beside **Test median** and enter the null hypothesis value of the median.
- Specify the form of the alternative hypothesis beside **Alternative** and click **OK**.
- The output that you will see in the session window includes counts of the numbers of values below, equal to and above the null hypothesis value of the population median, and the probability that the test statistic (or a more extreme one) occurs if the null hypothesis is true, **P**.

16.4.3 SPSS

To get cumulative probabilities of the *t* distribution:

- Choose the **Compute** option from the **Transform** pull-down menu.
- In the **Compute Variable** window click on **CDF.T(q, df)** in the long list under **Functions:** on the right-hand side of the window and click the ▲ button to the right of **Functions:**. The command should now appear in the space under **Numeric Expression:** to the top right of the window with two question marks inside the brackets. Replace these question marks with the value of *t* whose cumulative probability you want (referred

to as q in SPSS), and the number of degrees of freedom (df), respectively.

▨ To use this facility to produce the probability in Example 16.4 your command should be **CDF.T(1.875, 8)**. You will need to enter the name of a column to store the answer in the space under **Target Variable:**, this can be a default name like **var00001**.

▨ Click **OK** and the cumulative probability, 0.95, should appear in the column you have targeted. This is the probability that t is less than 1.875. To get the probability that t is more than 1.875 subtract it from one.

To produce a confidence interval for a population mean:

▨ Enter your data in a column of the worksheet.

▨ Click the **Analyze** pull-down menu and select **Descriptive Statistics** from it.

▨ Select **Explore** from the sub-menu.

▨ In the left hand side of the **Explore** dialogue box click on the variable name of the column where you have stored your data (this may be a default name like **var00001**) and click the ▶ button to the left of **Dependent List:**.

▨ Click the **Statistics** button at the bottom of the dialogue box and unless there is already a tick in it, click the box to the left of **Descriptive Statistics**. If the default level of confidence, 95%, is not the level you need, change it.

▨ Click **Continue** then **OK** in the **Explore** dialogue box. The information that appears in the output viewer should include a table headed **Descriptives** in which you should see the **Lower Bound** and **Upper Bound** of the **95% Confidence Interval for the Mean** that the package has produced using your sample data.

In producing confidence intervals the package uses the t distribution. If you have access to EXCEL and SPSS, use EXCEL when you need an interval using results from a large sample, rather than the original sample data, and SPSS when you need an interval using small sample data.

To test a hypothesis about a population mean:

▨ Enter your data in a worksheet column.

▨ Click the **Analyze** pull-down menu and select **Compare Means**.

▨ Select **One-Sample T Test** from the sub-menu.

▨ In the window to the left of the dialogue box click on the variable name of the column where you have stored your data

(this may be a default name like **var00001**) and click the ▶
button to the left of **Test Variable(s):**.

- ■ Enter the value of the population mean you want to test in the
  space to the right of **Test Value:** then Click **OK**.
- ■ There should be a table headed **One-Sample Test** in the output viewer. In it you should see a figure under *t*, which is the
  test statistic, and a figure under **Sig (2-tailed)**, which is the
  area of the *t* distribution beyond the test statistic and its equivalent on the other side of the distribution. It is the probability
  that the population mean is indeed the value that you specified as the **Test value** given your sample results.

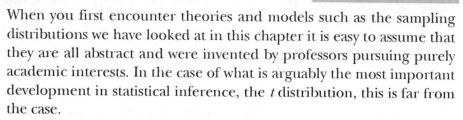

16.5 Road test: Do they really use small sample inference?: the business origins of the *t* distribution

When you first encounter theories and models such as the sampling
distributions we have looked at in this chapter it is easy to assume that
they are all abstract and were invented by professors pursuing purely
academic interests. In the case of what is arguably the most important
development in statistical inference, the *t* distribution, this is far from
the case.

The *t* distribution was a key step forward in quantitative methods
because it offered a framework within which results from a small sample
could be used to make predictions and assessments of populations with
a known probability of error. Small samples are cheaper to collect and
quicker to process than large samples, so the *t* distribution is invaluable
for companies looking for economy and speed in any quantitative
analysis they conduct.

The original name of the *t* distribution was 'Student's *t* distribution'.
'Student' was the pseudonym of William Sealy Gosset (1876–1937), an
Oxford science graduate, who worked for Guinness from 1899 until his
death. He was employed by Guinness initially as a brewer, ultimately
becoming the manager of the Guinness brewery in London.

Guinness was a long-established company even in Gosset's day. By
the late nineteenth century their demand for barley dominated the
Irish economy and the beer they produced was successful both in
Ireland and abroad. They specialized in a type of dark beer known as
porter. Like any producer of a generic product the company was keen
to establish the distinctiveness of its own beer and cement the brand
loyalty of its customers. One way it sought to do this was naming its

product 'stout' rather than porter. Another was to recruit scientists like Gosset to help them manage the production process more effectively and hence make the quality of the product more consistent.

The difficulty that Gosset faced was that brewing beer was a very erratic affair; the quality of the key ingredients like barley and yeast varied, and the process was notoriously susceptible to temperature changes. Brewers took samples to try to monitor and control the process and the quality of the ingredients, but given the number of changing factors such samples were inevitably small and it was impossible to calculate the likely error in using the results from them to draw general conclusions.

In the late nineteenth century the subject of Statistics in the British Isles was dominated by the biometric school. Biometry was the study of human measurements and characteristics, a field that developed in the aftermath of Charles Darwin's work on heredity. The biometricians dealt with large samples, typically running to thousands of elements, and automatically assumed that sample statistics from such large samples differed little from the parameters of the populations from which they were drawn. They found it difficult to conceive that anyone would want to draw conclusions with a known probable error about populations using small samples. Indeed the contrast between their practice and Gosset's objectives meant that in one work on the period he is referred to as 'The Outsider' (MacKenzie, 1981, p. 111).

Gosset created an approach, encapsulated in the *t* distribution, that enabled him use small samples to make inferences about populations with known levels of probable error, or confidence. He took great interest in applying his work to the improvement of the yield from barley crops in Ireland as well as in the growth of yeast. You can read more about Gosset in McMullen (1970) and the development of his ideas in Pearson (1970).

Review questions

Answers to these questions, including full worked solution to the key questions marked with an asterisk (*), are on pages 665–669.

16.1*   The population mean legal lifetime (the number of miles travelled before the tyre is worn down to the legal limit) of car tyres of a certain brand is 23,450 miles. The standard deviation is 1260 miles. If the lifetimes of the tyres are normally distributed, what is the probability that a random sample of four tyres fitted to a vehicle will have a mean legal lifetime of:

(a) more than 25,000 miles?

(b) more than 22,000 miles?

(c) less than 24,000 miles ?

(d) less than 23,000 miles?

(e) between 22,500 and 24,500 miles?

(f) between 23,400 and 24,200 miles?

16.2   The playing time of C180 videocassettes produced by one manufacturer varies normally with a mean of 182.4 minutes and a
standard deviation of 1.3 minutes. What proportion of packs of
5 of these videocassettes will have a mean playing time of:

(a) longer than 183 minutes?

(b) longer than 182 minutes?

(c) shorter than 184 minutes?

(d) shorter than 181 minutes?

(e) between 181.5 and 182.5 minutes?

(f) between 181.3 and 182.3 minutes?

16.3   As part of a charity event a radio DJ plans to broadcast a selection of 12 tracks chosen at random from the very large stock of
music CDs stored at the radio station. The lengths of the tracks
on these CDs are normally distributed with a mean of 3 minutes
9 seconds and a standard deviation of 43 seconds.

(a) What is the probability that the mean track length of the
selected sample is longer than 3 minutes?

(b) What is the probability that the mean track length of
the sample of tracks selected is shorter than 2 minutes
50 seconds?

(c) What is the probability that the mean track length of the
sample of tracks selected is longer than three and a half
minutes?

(d) What is the probability that the mean track length of the
sample of tracks selected is between 2 minutes 45 seconds
and 3 minutes 15 seconds?

(e) If the DJ has a hour for the show and 20 minutes are
required for advertising slots and messages, what is the
probability that the show will run over time?

16.4   A large administrative centre is replacing its IT facilities. As
part of this operation all standard client files are to be stored
temporarily on floppy disks as a precaution. The disk spaces
that these files require are normally distributed with a mean
of 0.20 Mb and a standard deviation of 0.085 Mb. The capacity
of the floppy disks that are to be used is 1.44 Mb. Staff are

instructed to save six files on to each disk. Assuming that the selection of files will be random:

(a) Work out the maximum mean disk space per file that is available and find the probability that there is insufficient disk space on a disk for six files.

(b) What is the probability that there is insufficient disk space if only five files are stored per disk?

16.5   Multi-Passenger Vehicles (MPVs) produced by a manufacturer can accommodate seven adults. The load capacity of the passenger compartment is 1240 lb. If the weights of adults are distributed normally with a mean of 170 lb and a standard deviation of 18 lb, what is the probability that the mean weight of a sample of seven adults will exceed the maximum average weight that the load capacity permits?

16.6   The delays to scheduled airline departures at an international airport are known to follow a skewed distribution with a mean of 11 minutes and a standard deviation of 7 minutes. What is the probability that the mean delay of a random sample of 40 flights is:

(a) more than 12 minutes?

(b) more than 10 minutes?

(c) less than 8 minutes?

(d) less than 11 minutes?

(e) between 9 minutes and 10.5 minutes?

(f) between 11.5 and 12.5 minutes?

(g) between 9.5 and 14 minutes?

16.7   The amount of analgesic per pill in a proprietary brand of painkiller follows a normal distribution with a mean of 7.5 mg. The pills are sold in bottles of 50. If the standard deviation of the analgesic content of the 50 pills in one bottle is 0.4 mg, what is the probability that the mean analgesic content of 50 pills is:

(a) above 7.35 mg?

(b) above 7.6 mg?

(c) below 7.55 mg?

(d) below 7.45 mg?

(e) between 7.4 and 7.65 mg?

16.8* The contents of pots of a certain brand of yoghurt are normally distributed with a mean of 101.4 g. The yoghurts are sold in packs of four. The contents of each pot in one pack of four were measured and the standard deviation was found to be 3.1 g.

(a) What mean amount of content will be exceeded by 10% of packs?

      (b) What mean amount of content will be exceeded by 5% of packs?

      (c) What mean amount of content will be exceeded by 1% of packs?

16.9   The times taken by buses to travel between two stops on a route follow a normal pattern of variation with a mean of 13.9 minutes. A commuter makes this journey ten times each week. One week she times the ten journeys and works out that the standard deviation of them is 1.7 minutes. Treating the ten journeys in a week as a random sample:

      (a) what mean journey time will be exceeded one week in twenty?

      (b) what mean journey time will be exceeded one week in forty?

      (c) what mean journey time will not be exceeded 90% of the time?

16.10*   The standard deviation of the fat content of a brand of flapjack is known to be 0.8 g per 100 g bar. The mean fat content of a random sample of 33 bars is 24.7 g.

      (a) Construct a 95% confidence interval for the population mean fat content of the bars of flapjack.

      (b) Construct a 99% confidence interval for the population mean fat content of the bars of flapjack.

16.11   The burning times of aromatherapy candles are known to be normally distributed with a standard deviation of 6 minutes. The mean burning time of a random sample of 18 candles was 3 hours 51 minutes. Set up:

      (a) a 95% confidence interval for the mean burning time of the candles.

      (b) a 99% confidence interval for the mean burning time of the candles.

16.12   To help shape her promotional strategy, the general manager of a regional airport wants to know how far passengers travel to use the airport. The mean and standard deviation of the distances travelled by a random sample of 61 passengers were 24.1 miles and 5.8 miles respectively.

      (a) Find a 90% confidence interval for the mean distance travelled by passengers.

      (b) If the population standard deviation were later found to be 6.3 miles, what size sample would be needed in order to estimate the mean distance travelled by passengers for the error to be one mile with a 90% level of confidence?

16.13   The distribution of rents of two-bedroom flats in the central district of a city is known to follow a skewed distribution with most flats being relatively cheap to rent but some, in prestige blocks, are very expensive. The mean rent of a sample of 48 flats was £403 per month with a standard deviation of £65.

(a)   Construct a 90% interval estimate of the mean rent of two-bedroom flats in the area.

(b)   The population standard deviation turns out to be £59. In the light of this new information, determine the size of sample necessary to enable the mean rent to be estimated to within £10, in other words for the error to be £10, with a 90% level of confidence.

16.14   The weights of bags of pears sold to customers asking for one pound of pears at a market stall are known to be normally distributed. The weights of a sample of 15 bags were measured. The sample mean weight was 1.06 lb with a standard deviation of 0.11 lb.

(a)   Produce a 95% confidence interval for the weight of 'one pound' bags of pears.

(b)   Produce a 99% confidence interval for the weight of 'one pound' bags of pears.

16.15   A waste management consultant is investigating the waste generated by households. She is certain that the weights of household waste are distributed normally. She selects a random sample of 12 households and measures the weight of the waste they put in their 'wheelie bin' one week. The results (to the nearest kilogram) are as follows:

28   41   36   50   17   39   21   64   26   30   42   12

(a)   Use these figures to construct a 99% confidence interval for the mean weight of waste in 'wheelie bins'.

(b)   Does the interval suggest that the mean weight of the contents of all 'wheelie bins' can be assumed to be less than 40 kg?

16.16* In a UK survey of a random sample of 281 working women who had children, 175 reported that they felt that having children had held back their career prospects. In a similar study of 138 women in Denmark, 65 reported that having children had held back their career.

(a)   Produce a 95% confidence interval for the proportion of women in the UK who consider that having children held back their career prospects.

(b) Produce a 95% confidence interval for the proportion of women in Denmark who consider that having children held back their career prospects.

(c) How do the two confidence intervals compare?

16.17   As part of a survey of a random sample of students, respondents were asked whether they were satisfied with the Students' Union Entertainments programme. Of the 109 respondents from the Arts Faculty 83 reported that they were satisfied with the Entertainments programme. Of the 116 respondents from the Business Faculty 97 reported that they were satisfied with the Entertainments programme.

(a) Construct a 90% confidence interval for the proportion of students in the Arts Faculty who are satisfied with the Entertainments programme.

(b) Construct a 90% confidence interval for the proportion of students in the Business Faculty who are satisfied with the Entertainments programme.

(c) Contrast the two confidence intervals.

16.18   A major grocery retailer is interested in developing an Internet ordering service as it believes that the prospects for the service have improved. Five years ago they asked each of a random sample of 431 shoppers if they would use such a service and 87 said they would. On the basis of these results the company did not pursue the venture. In a recent survey of a random sample of 256 shoppers 71 said they would use such a service.

(a) Produce a 99% confidence interval for the population proportion of shoppers that would use the Internet service five years ago.

(b) Use the results of the recent survey to produce another 99% confidence interval for the population proportion of shoppers that would use the service today.

(c) Assess whether the prospects for the Internet service have improved by comparing the two confidence intervals.

16.19   A television audience research company intends to install monitoring devices in a random sample of households in order to produce 95% interval estimates of the proportion of households watching specific programmes. If the company wants to estimate to within 2% of the real figure, in other words so that the error is 2%, in how many households will it have to install monitoring devices?

16.20* The standard deviation of the recovery times of young adults who contract a strain of influenza is known to be 1.3 days.

The sample mean recovery time of a random sample of 40 young adults is 12.9 days. Use this result to test the hypothesis that the mean duration of the illness is 12 days with a 5% level of significance.

16.21   The alcohol content of bottles of an imported brand of flavoured vodka is presumed to be normally distributed with a standard deviation of 0.83%. The mean alcohol content of a random sample of 12 bottles is 64.6%. Test the validity of the claim made by the importer that the average alcohol content is at least 65%. Use a 5% level of significance.

16.22   The Hot Shots Beverage Co. has developed a self-heating alcoholic beverage, the Winter Warmer. To test the effectiveness of the exothermic reaction that heats the drink the maximum temperature reached during the heating of a random sample of 15 Winter Warmers was measured. The mean temperature of this sample was 47° Celsius. The population standard deviation of the maximum temperatures reached during this process is known to be 3.2° Celsius. According to the product specifications, the mean maximum temperature reached should be no more than 45° Celsius. Formulate the latter as a null hypothesis and test it using a 1% level of significance.

16.23   Office workers at a large organization are told that they should not work for more than one and a half hours at their PCs before taking a break. A survey of a random sample of 37 employees found that the mean time that they worked at their PCs before taking a break one morning was 1 hour 43 minutes with a standard deviation of 18 minutes. Test the hypothesis that on average the employees of this organization are working for no more than one and a half hours before taking a break using a 1% level of significance.

16.24   In an advertisement it is claimed that a brand of domestic air freshener will last on average at least 70 days. The mean and standard deviation of the lifetimes of a sample of 19 air fresheners were 69.3 days and 2.9 days respectively.

   (a) Test the claim made for the product using a 5% level of significance.

   (b) What assumption must be made for the test to be valid?

16.25   An oil company has developed a new petroleum product designed to improve the fuel efficiency of vehicles with petrol engines. In tests the fuel efficiency of a random sample of 10 cars of the same make and model were driven at fixed speed on a gallon of the new fuel and the miles travelled recorded. The following figures were recorded:

37   38   40   35   36   35   39   37   40   37

The manufacture of the car claims that the mean mileage per gallon for these vehicles (driven at the same speed as in these tests) was 36. Test the hypothesis that the mean mileage per gallon is greater with the new fuel using a 1% level of significance and comment on your results.

16.26   An IT manager considers that the average number of hits per week on the company intranet pages should be 75. The mean number of hits per week on a random sample of 38 pages is 71.4 with a standard deviation of 31.9.

(a) Test a suitable hypothesis at the 10% level of significance to assess the plausibility of the IT manager's assertion.

(b) It later emerges that 18 of these pages are often visited by non-company users, and should therefore not be included in the sample. The mean and standard deviation of the remaining 20 pages are 65.8 and 28.3 respectively. Test the same hypothesis again at the 10% level. What assumption must you make for the test to be valid?

16.27   A bus company claims that the mean journey time for the service from Paglashonny to Gorley is 53 minutes. A random sample of 35 journeys was chosen and each journey timed. The mean journey time of these journeys was 57 minutes with a standard deviation of 4.6 minutes.

(a) Test the bus company's claim at the 5% level of significance and comment on the result.

(b) It appears that for 14 of these journeys the regular driver was absent from work through illness and relief drivers, who were unfamiliar with the route, had to be used. The mean journey time for the remaining journeys was 55 minutes with a standard deviation of 3.1 minutes. Test the bus company's claim again at the 5% level of significance using these figures and comment on the result.

(c) What do you need to assume about the population of journey times for the results from the second test to be valid?

16.28   A high street chemist has installed a new stock control system to expedite the delivery of prescription medicines to its customers. Prior to the installation of this system the mean time interval between customers presenting prescriptions and the medicines being dispensed to them was 15.8 minutes. Since the introduction of the new system the manager measured the time taken to dispense prescriptions to a random sample of 41 customers. The mean time taken to dispense prescriptions to this sample of customers was 14.6 minutes with a standard deviation of 5.3 minutes.

(a) Test the hypothesis that the new stock control system has resulted in a faster average dispensing time using a 5% level of significance.

(b) Later it emerges that 25 of the prescriptions out of the sample of 41 were dispensed by an employee who had received no training in the use of the system. If these results are removed the mean and standard deviation of the dispensing times of the remaining prescriptions were 13.1 and 4.6 respectively. Test the hypothesis that the new stock control system has yielded a faster average dispensing time using these sample results and a 5% level of significance.

(c) Contrast the results of the two tests and identify the assumption that must be made for the second test to be valid.

16.29 Last year 61% of total job applications received by a national recruitment agency were from female applicants. Out of a random sample of 192 applications received this year 105 were from females. Test the hypothesis that the proportion of applications from females has not changed using a 10% level of significance.

16.30 A cinema manager claims that at least 25% of customers buy popcorn during their visit to the cinema. If 38 out of a random sample of 176 customers buy popcorn, is the manager right? Use a 5% level of significance.

16.31 The View4U bookings agency rents out self-catering holiday accommodation. The Managing Director believes that one-third of current bookings are made through the Internet. Out of a random sample of 379 recent bookings 101 were made through the company Internet pages. Establish whether the Managing Director's assessment is correct by testing an appropriate hypothesis using the 5% level of significance.

16.32 The number of pairs of shoes owned by adult women is assumed to follow a skewed distribution. A random sample of 10 women was taken and each woman was asked how many pairs of shoes she owned. Their responses were:

7   24   15   7   18   15   9   13   8   14

Using these data test the hypothesis that the median number of pairs of shoes owned by adult women is 12. Apply the sign test with a 5% level of significance.

16.33   Select the appropriate definition from the list on the right-hand side for the terms listed on the left-hand side.

(i)	sampling distributions	(a)	a single figure estimate
(ii)	$\sigma/\sqrt{n}$	(b)	what to add and subtract to create an interval estimate
(iii)	$s/\sqrt{n}$	(c)	a result that refutes a null hypothesis
(iv)	the t distribution	(d)	show how sample results vary
(v)	a point estimate	(e)	the likelihood that an estimate is accurate
(vi)	a z interval	(f)	the standard error of the sample mean
(vii)	the error	(g)	another name for an interval estimate
(viii)	confidence	(h)	an interval estimate based on a small sample
(ix)	a t interval	(i)	the estimated standard error of the sample mean
(x)	a confidence interval	(j)	an interval estimate based on a large sample
(xi)	a null hypothesis	(k)	a model distribution used for small samples
(xii)	significant	(l)	a claim, to be tested, about a population measure

High performance — statistical inference for comparing population means and bivariate data

This chapter will help you to:

- test hypotheses on the difference between two population means using independent samples and draw appropriate conclusions
- carry out tests of hypotheses about the difference between two population means using paired data and draw appropriate conclusions
- test differences between population means using analysis of variance analysis (ANOVA) and draw appropriate conclusions

▪ conduct hypothesis tests about population correlation coefficients and draw appropriate conclusions

▪ produce interval estimates using simple linear regression models

▪ perform contingency analysis and interpret the results

▪ use the technology; test differences between sample means, apply correlation and regression inference, and contingency analysis in EXCEL, MINITAB and SPSS

▪ become acquainted with the business use of contingency analysis

In the previous chapter we looked at statistical inference in relation to univariate data, estimating and testing single population parameters like the mean using single sample results. In this chapter we will consider statistical inference methods that enable us to compare means of two or more populations, to test population correlation coefficients, to make predictions from simple linear regression models and to test for association in qualitative data.

17.1 Testing hypotheses about two population means

In section 16.3 of the previous chapter we looked at tests of the population mean based on a single sample mean. In this section we will consider tests designed to assess the difference between two population means. In businesses these tests are used to investigate whether, for instance, the introduction of a new logo improves sales.

To use these tests you need to have a sample from each of the two populations. For the tests to be valid the samples must be random, but they can be *independent* or *dependent*.

Independent samples are selected from each population separately. Suppose a domestic gas supplier wanted to assess the impact of a new charging system on customers' bills. The company could take a random sample of customers and record the size of their bills under the existing charging system then, after the new system is introduced, take another random sample of customers and record the size of their bills. These samples would be independent.

Dependent samples consist of matched or paired values. If the gas supplier took a random sample of customers and recorded the size of their bills both before and after the introduction of the new charging system they would be using a paired or dependent sample.

The choice of independent or dependent samples depends on the context of the test. Unless there is a good reason for using paired data it is better to use independent samples. We will begin by looking at tests for use with independent samples and deal with paired samples later in this section.

As with single sample tests, the size of the samples is important because it determines the nature of the sampling distribution. In this section we will assume that the population standard deviations are not known.

17.1.1 Large independent samples

The null hypothesis we use in comparing population means is based on the difference between the means of the two populations, $\mu_1 - \mu_2$. The possible combinations of null and alternative hypotheses are shown in Table 17.1.

The hypotheses listed in Table 17.1 all assume that the focus of the test is that there is no difference between the population means. This is very common but the same formats can be used to test whether the difference between two population means is a non-zero constant, e.g. $H_0: \mu_1 - \mu_2 = 6$.

If both samples contain 30 or more items the difference between their means, $\bar{x}_1 - \bar{x}_2$, belongs to the sampling distribution of $\bar{X}_1 - \bar{X}_2$. This sampling distribution is normally distributed with a mean of $\mu_1 - \mu_2$, and a standard error of:

$$\sqrt{\frac{\sigma_1^2}{n_1} + \frac{\sigma_2^2}{n_2}}$$

where σ_1 and σ_2 are the standard deviations of the first and second populations, and n_1 and n_2 are the sizes of the samples from the first and second populations.

Table 17.1

Types of hypotheses for comparing population means

Null hypothesis	Alternative hypothesis	Type of test
$H_0: \mu_1 - \mu_2 = 0$	$H_1: \mu_1 - \mu_2 \neq 0$	Two-sided
$H_0: \mu_1 - \mu_2 \leqslant 0$	$H_1: \mu_1 - \mu_2 > 0$	One-sided
$H_0: \mu_1 - \mu_2 \geqslant 0$	$H_1: \mu_1 - \mu_2 < 0$	One-sided

We will assume that the population standard deviations are not known, in which case the estimated standard error of the sampling distribution is:

$$\sqrt{\frac{s_1^2}{n_1} + \frac{s_2^2}{n_2}}$$

The test statistic is:

$$z = \frac{(\bar{x}_1 - \bar{x}_2) - (\mu_1 - \mu_2)}{\sqrt{\frac{s_1^2}{n_1} + \frac{s_2^2}{n_2}}}$$

If the null hypothesis suggests that the difference between the population means is zero, we can simplify this to:

$$z = \frac{(\bar{x}_1 - \bar{x}_2)}{\sqrt{\frac{s_1^2}{n_1} + \frac{s_2^2}{n_2}}}$$

Once we have calculated the test statistic we need to compare it to the appropriate critical value from the Standard Normal Distribution.

Example 17.1

A national breakdown recovery service has depots at Oxford and Portsmouth. The mean and standard deviation of the times that it took for the staff at the Oxford depot to assist each of a random sample of 47 motorists were 51 minutes and 7 minutes respectively. The mean and standard deviation of the response times recorded by the staff at the Portsmouth depot in assisting a random sample of 39 customers were 49 minutes and 5 minutes respectively. Test the hypothesis that there is no difference between the mean response times of the two depots. Use a 5% level of significance.

$$H_0: \mu_1 - \mu_2 = 0 \qquad H_1: \mu_1 - \mu_2 \neq 0$$

$$\text{Test statistic,} \quad z = \frac{51 - 49}{\sqrt{\frac{7^2}{47} + \frac{5^2}{39}}}$$

$$= 2/1.298 = 1.541$$

This is a two-tail test using a 5% level of confidence so the critical values are $\pm z_{0.025}$. Unless the test statistic is below -1.96 or above $+1.96$ the null hypothesis cannot be rejected. The test statistic, 1.541, is within ± 1.96 so we cannot reject H_0. The population mean response times of the two breakdown services could be equal.

Notice that in Example 17.1 we have not said anything about the distributions of response times. The Central Limit Theorem allows us to use the same two-sample z test whatever the shape of the populations from which the samples were drawn as long as the size of both samples is 30 or more.

At this point you may find it useful to try **Review Questions 17.1 to 17.3** at the end of the chapter.

17.1.2 Small independent samples

If the size of the samples you want to use to compare population means is small, less than 30, you can only follow the procedure outlined in the previous section if both populations are normal and both population standard deviations known. In the absence of the latter it is possible to test the difference between two population means using small independent samples but only under certain circumstances.

If both populations are normal and their standard deviations can be assumed to be the same, that is $\sigma_1 = \sigma_2$, we can conduct a two-sample t test. We use the sample standard deviations to produce a pooled estimate of the standard error of the sampling distribution of $\overline{X}_1 - \overline{X}_2$, s_p.

$$s_p = \sqrt{\frac{(n_1-1)s_1^2 + (n_2-1)s_2^2}{n_1 + n_2 - 2}}$$

The test statistic is

$$t = \frac{(\overline{x}_1 - \overline{x}_2)}{s_p * \sqrt{\dfrac{1}{n_1} + \dfrac{1}{n_2}}}$$

We then compare the test statistic to the appropriate critical value from the t distribution. The number of degrees of freedom for this test is $n_1 + n_2 - 2$, one degree of freedom is lost for each of the sample means.

Example 17.2

A cereal manufacturer claims to use no more oats, the cheapest ingredient, in producing packets of 'own-brand' muesli for a supermarket chain than they use to produce their own premium brand. The mean and standard deviation of the oat content by weight of a random sample of 14 'own-brand' packets are 34.9% and 1.4% respectively. The mean and standard deviation of the oat content of a random sample of 17 premium brand packets are 33.4% and 1.1% respectively. Test the hypothesis that the mean oat content of the premium brand is no greater than the mean oat content of the 'own-brand' muesli using a 1% level of significance.

We will define μ_1 as the population mean of the 'own-brand' and μ_2 as the population mean of the premium product.

$$H_0: \mu_1 - \mu_2 \leq 0 \qquad H_1: \mu_1 - \mu_2 > 0$$

First we need the pooled estimate of the standard error:

$$s_p = \sqrt{\frac{(14-1)1.4^2 + (17-1)1.1^2}{14 + 17 - 2}}$$
$$= 1.243$$

Now we can calculate the test statistic:

$$t = \frac{34.9 - 33.4}{1.243 * \sqrt{\frac{1}{14} + \frac{1}{17}}}$$
$$= 3.344$$

This is a one-tail test so the null hypothesis will only be rejected if the test statistic exceeds the critical value. From Table 6 on page 623 in Appendix 1, $t_{0.01,29}$ is 2.462. Since the test statistic is greater than the critical value we can reject the null hypothesis at the 1% level. The difference between the sample means is very significant.

At this point you may find it useful to try **Review Questions 17.4 to 17.6** at the end of the chapter.

17.1.3 Paired samples

If you want to test the difference between population means using dependent or paired samples the nature of the data enables you to test the mean of the differences between all the paired values in the population, μ_d. This approach contrasts with the methods described in the earlier parts of this section where we have tested the difference between population means, $\mu_1 - \mu_2$.

The procedure involved in testing hypotheses using paired samples is very similar to the one-sample hypothesis testing we discussed in section 16.3 of Chapter 16. We have to assume that the differences between the paired values are normally distributed with a mean of μ_d, and a standard deviation of σ_d. The sampling distribution of sample mean

Table 17.2

Types of hypotheses for the mean of the population of differences

Null hypothesis	Alternative hypothesis	Type of test
$H_0: \mu_d = \mu_{d0}$	$H_1: \mu_d \neq \mu_{d0}$ (not equal)	Two-sided
$H_0: \mu_d \leq \mu_{d0}$	$H_1: \mu_d > \mu_{d0}$ (greater than)	One-sided
$H_0: \mu_d \geq \mu_{d0}$	$H_1: \mu_d < \mu_{d0}$ (less than)	One-sided

In this table μ_{d0} represents the value of the population mean that is to be tested.

differences will also be normally distributed with a mean of μ_d and a standard error of $\sigma_d/\sqrt{n}$, where n is the number of differences in the sample. Since we assume that σ_d is unknown we have to use the estimated standard error $s_d/\sqrt{n}$, where s_d is the standard deviation of the sample differences.

Typically samples of paired data tend to be small so the benchmark distribution for the test is the t distribution. The test is therefore called the *paired t* test. Table 17.2 lists the three possible combinations of hypotheses.

The test statistic is:

$$t = \frac{\bar{x}_d - \mu_{d0}}{s_d/\sqrt{n}}$$

where $\bar{x}_d$ is the mean of the sample differences.

We then compare the test statistic to the appropriate critical value from the t distribution with $n - 1$ degrees of freedom.

Example 17.3

A Business School claims that, on average, people who take their MBA programme will enhance their annual salary by at least £8000. Each of a random sample of 12 graduates of the programme were asked for their annual salary prior to beginning the programme and their current annual salary. Use the sample data to test whether the mean difference in annual earnings is £8000 or more using a 10% level of significance.

$$H_0: \mu_d \geq 8.00 \qquad H_1: \mu_d < 8.00$$

To conduct the test we first need to find the mean and standard deviation of the salary differences in the sample.

Graduate	1	2	3	4	5	6	7	8	9	10	11	12
Prior salary (£000)	22	29	29	23	33	20	26	21	25	27	27	29
Current salary (£000)	31	38	40	29	41	25	29	26	31	37	41	36
Salary difference (£000)	9	9	11	6	8	5	3	5	6	10	14	7

The mean and standard deviation of the sample differences are 7.75 and 3.05, to 2 decimal places. The test statistic is:

$$t = \frac{7.75 - 8.00}{3.05/\sqrt{12}} = \frac{-0.25}{0.88} = -0.284$$

From Table 6 on page 623, $t_{0.10,11}$ is 1.363. The alternative hypothesis is that the population mean salary difference is less than £8000 so the critical value is -1.363. A sample mean that produces a test statistic this low or lower would lead us to reject the null hypothesis. In this case, although the sample mean is less than £8000, the test statistic, -0.28, is not less than the critical value and the null hypothesis cannot be rejected. The population mean of the salary differences could well be £8000.

At this point you may find it useful to try **Review Questions 17.7 to 17.9** at the end of the chapter.

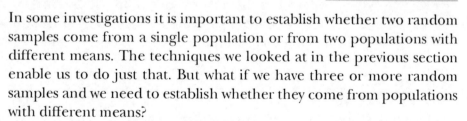

17.2 Testing hypotheses about more than two population means – one-way ANOVA

In some investigations it is important to establish whether two random samples come from a single population or from two populations with different means. The techniques we looked at in the previous section enable us to do just that. But what if we have three or more random samples and we need to establish whether they come from populations with different means?

You might think that the obvious answer is to run t tests using each pair of random samples to establish whether the first sample came from the same population as the second, the first sample came from the same population as the third and the second sample came from the same population as the third and so on. In doing this you would be testing the hypotheses:

$$H_0: \mu_1 = \mu_2 \qquad H_0: \mu_1 = \mu_3 \qquad H_0: \mu_2 = \mu_3 \text{ etc.}$$

Although feasible, this is not the best way to approach the investigation. For one thing the more random samples that are involved the greater the chance that you miss out one or more possible pairings. For another, each test you conduct carries a risk of making a type 1 error, wrongly rejecting a null hypothesis because you happen to have a sample result from an extreme end of its sampling distribution. The chance of this occurring is the level of significance you use in conducting the test. The problem when you conduct a series of related tests is that the probability of making a type 1 error increases; if you use a 5% level of significance then the probability of not making a type 1 error in a sequence of three tests is, using the multiplication rule of probability, 0.95 * 0.95 * 0.95 or 0.857. This means the effective level of significance is 14.3%, considerably greater than you might have assumed.

To establish whether more than two samples come from populations with different means we use an alternative approach, *analysis of variance*, usually abbreviated to *ANOVA (analysis of variance)*. At first sight it seems rather odd to be using a technique based on variance, a measure of *spread*, to assess hypotheses about means, which are measures of *location*. The reason for doing this is that it enables us to focus on the spread of the sample means, after all the greater the differences between the sample means the greater the chance that they come from populations with different means. However, we have to be careful to put these differences into context because, after all, we can get different samples from the *same* population. Using ANOVA involves looking at the balance between the variance of the sample means and the variance in the sample data overall. Example 17.4 illustrates why this is important.

Example 17.4

The Kranilisha Bank operates cash dispensing machines in Gloucester, Huddersfield and Ipswich. The amounts of cash dispensed (in £000s) at a random sample of machines during a specific period were:

Gloucester	25	30	32	39	44
Huddersfield	17	25	27	31	
Ipswich	29	34	44	47	51

These are independent samples and so the fact that one sample (Huddersfield) contains fewer values does not matter. The sample data are shown in the form of boxplots in Figure 17.1.

The distributions in Figure 17.1 suggest that there are differences between the amounts of cash dispensed at the machines, with those in Ipswich having the largest turnover and those in Huddersfield having the smallest. The sample means, which are represented by the dots, bear out this impression: 34 for Gloucester, 25 for Huddersfield and 41 for Ipswich.

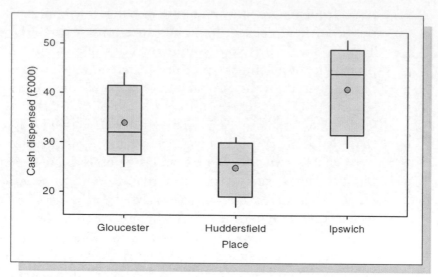

Figure 17.1
Cash dispensed at machines in Gloucester, Huddersfield and Ipswich

In Example 17.4 the sample means are diverse enough and the distributions shown in Figure 17.1 distinct enough to indicate differences between the locations, but is it enough to merely compare the sample means?

Example 17.5

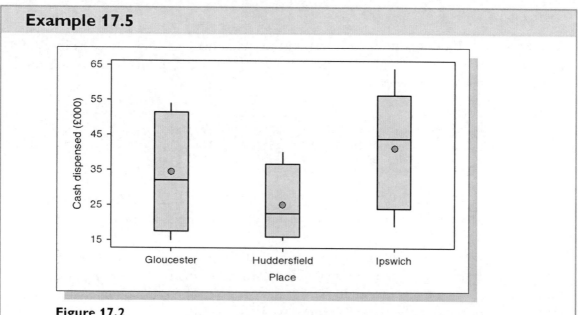

Figure 17.2
Revised amounts of cash dispensed at machines in Gloucester, Huddersfield and Ipswich

Many of the figures for the cash dispensing machines in Example 17.4 were recorded incorrectly, although the means are correct. The amended figures are:

Gloucester	14	21	32	49	54
Huddersfield	15	18	27	40	
Ipswich	19	29	44	49	64

These revised figures are depicted in Figure 17.2.

In Figure 17.2 the considerable overlaps between the data from the three locations suggest that despite the contrasts in the means it is more likely that the three samples come from the same population. Concentrating on the means alone in this case would have led us to the wrong conclusion.

So how we can test whether the three samples all come from the same population, in other words that there is no difference between the population mean amounts of cash dispensed per period in the three towns? For convenience we will use μ_G, μ_H and μ_I to represent the population means for Gloucester, Huddersfield and Ipswich respectively. The hypothesis we need to test is:

$$H_0: \mu_G = \mu_H = \mu_I$$

The alternative hypothesis is that there is a difference between at least two of the population means for the three towns.

If the null hypothesis is true and the three samples all come from a single population the best estimate of the mean of that population is the mean of the values in all three samples, the *overall mean*. Since we already know the three sample means we can work this out by taking the mean of the sample means, being careful to weight each mean by the number of observations in the sample. In the first instance we will use the original data from Example 17.4:

$$\bar{x} = \frac{(5 * 34) + (4 * 25) + (5 * 41)}{14} = \frac{475}{14} = 33.929$$

The test statistic we will use is based on comparing the variation between the sample means with the variation within the samples. One of the measures of variation or spread that we looked at in Chapter 6 was the sample variance, the square of the sample standard deviation:

$$s^2 = \frac{\sum_{i=1}^{n} (x_i - \bar{x})^2}{n-1}$$

The basis of the variance is the sum of the squared deviations between each observation and the sample mean. This amount, which is usually abbreviated to the *sum of squares*, is used to measure variation in analysis of variance. The sum of squares for the Gloucester sample, which we will denote as SS_G, is:

$$SS_G = \sum_{i=1}^{n} (x_i - \bar{x}_G)^2 = (25 - 34)^2 + (30 - 34)^2$$
$$+ (32 - 34)^2 + (39 - 34)^2 + (44 - 34)^2$$
$$= 81 + 16 + 4 + 25 + 100 = 226$$

We can work out the equivalent figures for the Huddersfield and Ipswich samples:

$$SS_H = \sum_{i=1}^{n} (x_i - \bar{x}_H)^2 = (17 - 25)^2 + (25 - 25)^2$$
$$+ (27 - 25)^2 + (31 - 25)^2 = 104$$

$$SS_I = \sum_{i=1}^{n} (x_i - \bar{x}_I)^2 = (29 - 41)^2 + (34 - 41)^2$$
$$+ (44 - 41)^2 + (47 - 41)^2 + (51 - 41)^2 = 338$$

The sum of these three sums of squares is the sum of the squares *within* the samples, SSW:

$$SSW = SS_G + SS_H + SS_I = 226 + 104 + 338 = 668$$

The measure we need for the variation between the sample means is the sum of the squared deviations between the sample means and the mean of all the observations in the three samples. This is the sum of the squares *between* the samples, SSB. In calculating it we have to weight each squared deviation by the sample size:

$$SSB = (n_G)*(\bar{x}_G - \bar{x})^2 + (n_H)*(\bar{x}_H - \bar{x})^2 + (n_I)*(\bar{x}_I - \bar{x}_I)^2$$
$$= 5*(34 - 33.929)^2 + 4*(25 - 33.929)^2 + 5*(41 - 33.929)^2$$
$$= 568.929$$

If we add the sum of squares within the samples, SSW, to the sum of squares between the samples, SSB, the result is the total sum of squares in the data, denoted by SST. The total sum of squares is also the sum of the squared deviations between each observation in the set of three samples and the mean of the combined data:

$$SST = (25 - 33.929)^2 + (30 - 33.929)^2 + (32 - 33.929)^2$$
$$+ (39 - 33.929)^2 + (44 - 33.929)^2$$
$$+ (17 - 33.929)^2 + (25 - 33.929)^2 + (27 - 33.929)^2$$
$$+ (31 - 33.929)^2$$
$$+ (29 - 33.929)^2 + (34 - 33.929)^2 + (44 - 33.929)^2$$
$$+ (47 - 33.929)^2 + (51 - 33.929)^2$$
$$= \quad 79.719 + \quad 15.434 + \quad 3.719 + \quad 25.719 + 101.434$$
$$+ 286.577 + \quad 79.719 + \quad 48.005 + \quad 8.577$$
$$+ \quad 24.291 + \quad 0.005 + 101.434 + 170.862 + 291.434$$
$$= 1236.929$$
$$= SSW + SSB = 668 + 568.929 = 1236.929$$

When you calculate a sample variance you have to divide the sum of squared deviations by the sample size less one, $n - 1$. This is the number of degrees of freedom left in the data; we lose one degree of freedom because we use the mean in working out the deviations from it. Before we can use the sums of squares we have determined above to test the hypothesis of no difference between the population means we need to incorporate the degrees of freedom associated with each sum of squares by working out the mean sum of squares. This makes the variation within the samples directly comparable to the variation between samples.

The mean sum of squares within the samples, *MSW*, is the sum of squares within the samples divided by the number of observations in all three samples, in this case 14, less the number of samples we have, 3. You may like to think of subtracting three as reflecting our using the three sample means in working out the sum of squares within the samples. If we use k to represent the number of samples we have:

$$MSW = \frac{SSW}{n - k} = \frac{668}{14 - 3} = 60.727$$

The mean sum of squares between the samples, MSB, is the sum of squares between the samples divided by the number of samples, k minus one. We lose one degree of freedom because we have used the overall mean to find the sum of squares between the samples.

$$MSB = \frac{SSB}{k - 1} = \frac{568.929}{3 - 1} = 284.465$$

The test statistic used to decide the validity of the null hypothesis is the ratio of the mean sum of squares between samples to the mean sum of squares within the sample. Because the benchmark distribution we shall use to assess it is the F distribution after its inventor, R. A. Fisher, the test statistic is represented by the letter F:

$$F = \frac{MSB}{MSW} = \frac{284.465}{60.727} = 4.684$$

Before comparing this to the F distribution it is worth pausing to consider the meaning of the test statistic. If the three samples came from a single population, in other words the null hypothesis is true, both the MSB above the line, the numerator, and the MSW below the line, the denominator, would both be unbiased estimators of the variance of that population. If this were the case, the test statistic would be close to one.

If on the other hand the samples do come from populations with different means, in other words the null hypothesis is not true, we would expect the MSB, the numerator, to be much larger than the denominator. Under these circumstances the test statistic would be greater than one.

In order to gauge how large the test statistic would have to be to lead us to reject the null hypothesis we have to look at it in the context of the F distribution. This distribution portrays the variety of test statistics we would get if we compared all conceivable sets of samples from a single population and worked out the ratio of MSB to MSW. Since neither the MSB nor the MSW can be negative, as they are derived from *squared* deviations, the F distribution consists of entirely positive values.

The version of the F distribution you use depends on the numbers of degrees of freedom you use to work out the MSB and the MSW, respectively the nominator and denominator of the test statistic. The F distribution with 2 degrees of freedom in the numerator and 11 degrees of freedom in the denominator, which is the appropriate version for the bank data from Example 17.4, is shown in Figure 17.3.

We can assess the value of the test statistic for the data from Example 17.4 by comparing it with a benchmark figure or *critical value* from the distribution shown in Figure 17.3. The critical value you use depends on the level of significance you require. Typically this is 5% or 0.05. The shaded area in Figure 17.3 is the 5% of the distribution beyond 3.98. If the null hypothesis really were true we would only expect to have test statistics greater than 3.98 in 5% of cases. In the case of Example 17.4 the test statistic is rather higher, 4.684, so the null hypothesis should be rejected at the 5% level. At least two of the means are different.

In general, reject the null hypothesis if the test statistic is greater than $F_{k-1,\, n-k,\, \alpha}$, where k is the number of samples, n is the number of values in the samples overall and α is the level of significance. Note that this is a

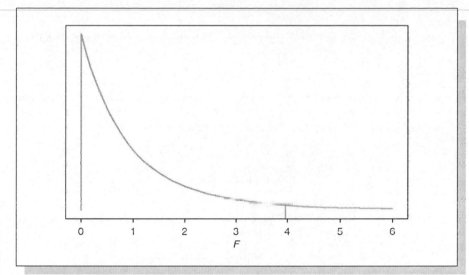

Figure 17.3
The *F* distribution
with 2 (numerator)
and 11 (denominator)
degrees of freedom

one-tail test; it is only possible to reject the hypothesis if the test statistic is larger than the critical value you use. Values of the test statistic from the left-hand side of the distribution are consistent with the null hypothesis.

Table 7 on page 624 in Appendix 1 contains details of the *F* distribution. You may like to check it to locate $F_{2, 11, 0.01}$ which is the value of *F* with 2 numerator degrees of freedom and 11 denominator degrees of freedom that cuts off a right-hand tail area of 1%, 7.21. This value is greater than the test statistic for the data from Example 17.4 so we cannot reject the null hypothesis at the 1% level of significance.

Example 17.6

Use the revised bank data from Example 17.5 to test whether there are differences between the population means of the amounts of cash dispensed in Gloucester, Huddersfield and Ipswich.

The overall mean and the three sample means are exactly the same as those derived from the data in Example 17.4 so the mean sum of squares between the samples is unchanged, 284.465.

We need to calculate the sum of squares within the samples for the amended data:

$$SS_G = \sum_{i=1}^{n} (x_i - \bar{x}_G)^2 = (14 - 34)^2 + (21 - 34)^2 + (32 - 34)^2 + (49 - 34)^2 + (54 - 34)^2$$
$$= 1198$$

$$SS_H = \sum_{i=1}^{n} (x_i - x_H)^2 = (15 - 25.0)^2 + (18 - 25.0)^2 + (27 - 25.0)^2 + (40 - 25.0)^2 = 378$$

$$SS_I = \sum_{i=1}^{n}(x_i - \bar{x}_I)^2 = (19 - 41)^2 + (29 - 41)^2 + (44 - 41)^2 + (49 - 41)^2 + (64 - 41)^2$$
$$= 1230$$

$$SSW = SS_G + SS_H + SS_I = 1198 + 378 + 1230 = 2806$$

$$MSW = \frac{2806}{11} = 255.091$$

$$\text{The test statistic,} \quad F = \frac{284.465}{255.091} = 1.115$$

In this case the test statistic is much lower than the critical value for a 5% level of significance, 3.98, and the null hypothesis should not be rejected; it is a reasonable assumption that these three samples come from a single population, confirming the impression from Figure 17.2.

There are several assumptions that apply when we use analysis of variance to test differences between population means. To begin with the populations from which the samples are drawn should be normal and the populations should have the same variance. Furthermore, the samples must be random and independent.

In this section we have used *one-way* analysis of variance; one-way because we have only considered one factor, geographical location, in our investigation. There may be other factors that may be pertinent to our analysis, such as the type of location of the cash dispensers in Example 17.4, i.e. town centre, supermarket, or garage. ANOVA is a flexible technique that can be used to take more than one factor into account. For more on its capabilities and applications see Roberts and Russo (1999).

At this point you may find it useful to try **Review Questions 17.10 to 17.12** at the end of the chapter.

17.3 Testing hypotheses and producing interval estimates for quantitative bivariate data

In this section we will look at statistical inference techniques that enable you to estimate and test relationships between variables in populations based on sample data. The sample data we use to do this is called *bivariate* data because it consists of observed values of *two* variables. This sort of data is usually collected in order to establish whether there is a relationship between the two variables, and if so, what sort of relationship it is.

Many organizations use this type of analysis to study consumer behaviour, patterns of costs and revenues, and other aspects of their operations. Sometimes the results of such analysis have far-reaching consequences. For example, if you look at a tobacco product you will see a health warning prominently displayed. It is there because some years ago researchers used these types of statistical methods to establish that there was a relationship between tobacco consumption and certain medical conditions.

The quantitative bivariate analysis that we considered in Chapter 7 consisted of two related techniques: correlation and regression. Correlation analysis, which is about calculating and evaluating the correlation coefficient, enables you to tell whether there is a relationship between the observed values of two variables and how strong it is. Regression analysis, which is about finding lines of best fit, enables you to find the equation of the line that is most appropriate for the data, the *regression model.*

Here we will address how the results from applying correlation and regression to sample data can be used to test hypotheses and make estimates for the populations the sets of sample data belong to.

17.3.1 Testing the population correlation coefficient

The sample correlation coefficient, represented by the letter r, measures the extent of the linear association between a sample of observations of two variables, X and Y. You can find the sample correlation coefficient of a set of bivariate data using the formula:

$$r = \frac{\mathrm{Cov}_{XY}}{(s_x * s_y)}$$

where $\mathrm{Cov}_{XY} = \dfrac{\Sigma(x - \bar{x})(y - \bar{y})}{(n - 1)}$

and s_x and s_y are the standard deviations of the x and y values respectively.

If we select a random sample from populations of X and Y that are *both* normal in shape, the sample correlation coefficient will be an unbiased estimate of the population coefficient, represented by the Greek r, the letter rho, ρ. In fact the main reason for calculating the sample correlation coefficient is to assess the linear association, if any, between the X and Y populations.

The value of the sample correlation coefficient alone is some help in assessing correlation between the populations, but a more thorough approach is to test the null hypothesis that the population correlation coefficient is zero:

$$H_0: \rho = 0$$

The alternative hypothesis you use depends on what you would like to show. If you are interested in demonstrating that there is significant correlation in the population, then use:

$$H_1: \rho \neq 0$$

If you want to test for significant positive correlation in the population then:

$$H_1: \rho > 0$$

If you want to test for significant negative correlation in the population then:

$$H_1: \rho < 0$$

If we adopt the first of these, $H_1: \rho \neq 0$, we will need to use a two-tail test, if we use one of the other forms we will conduct a one-tail test. In practice it is more usual to test for either positive or negative correlation rather than for both.

Once we have established the nature of our alternative hypothesis we need to calculate the test statistic from our sample data. The test statistic is:

$$t = \frac{r\sqrt{n-2}}{\sqrt{1-r^2}}$$

Here r is the sample correlation coefficient and n is the number of *pairs* of observations in the sample.

As long as the populations of X and Y are normal the test statistic will belong to a t distribution with $n - 2$ degrees of freedom and a mean of zero, *if* the null hypothesis is true and there is no linear association between the populations of X and Y.

Example 17.7

A shopkeeper wants to investigate the relationship between the temperature and the number of cans of soft drinks she sells. The maximum daytime temperature (in degrees Celsius) and the soft drinks sales on 10 working days chosen at random are:

Temperature	Cans sold
14	19
11	29
17	47
8	12
20	45
13	41
24	67
3	10
16	28
5	21

The sample correlation coefficient is 0.871. Test the hypothesis of no correlation between temperature and sales against the alternative that there is positive correlation using a 5% level of significance.

$$\text{The test statistic, } \quad t = \frac{r\sqrt{n-2}}{\sqrt{1-r^2}} = \frac{0.871*\sqrt{10-2}}{\sqrt{1-0.871^2}}$$
$$= 5.02$$

We need to compare this test statistic to the t distribution with $n-2$, in this case 8, degrees of freedom. According to Table 6 on page 623 in Appendix 1 the value of t with 8 degrees of freedom that cuts off a 5% tail on the right-hand side of the distribution, $t_{0.05,8}$, is 1.860. Since the test statistic is larger than 1.860 we can reject the null hypothesis at the 5% level of significance. The sample evidence strongly suggests positive correlation between temperature and sales in the population.

At this point you may find it useful to try **Review Questions 17.13 to 17.15** at the end of the chapter.

17.3.2 Testing regression models

The second bivariate quantitative technique we looked at in Chapter 7 was simple linear regression analysis. This allows you to find the equation of the line of best fit between two variables, X and Y. Such a line has two distinguishing features, its *intercept* and its *slope*. In the standard formula we used the intercept is represented by the letter *a* and the slope by the letter *b*:

$$Y = a + bX$$

The line that this equation describes is the best way of representing the relationship between the dependent variable, *Y*, and the independent variable, *X*. In practice it is almost always the result of a sample investigation that is intended to shed light on the relationship between the populations of *X* and *Y*. That is why we have used ordinary rather than Greek letters in the equation.

The results of a sample investigation can provide you with an understanding of the relationship between the populations. The intercept and slope of the line of best fit for the sample are point estimates for the intercept and slope of the line of best fit for the populations, which are represented by the Greek equivalents of *a* and *b*, α and β:

$$Y = \alpha + \beta X$$

The intercept and slope from the sample regression line can be used to test hypotheses about the equivalent figures for the populations. Typically we use null hypotheses that suggest that the population values are zero:

$$H_0: \alpha = 0 \text{ for the intercept}$$

and

$$H_0: \beta = 0 \text{ for the slope.}$$

If the population intercept is zero, the population line of best fit will be represented by the equation $Y = 0 + \beta X$, and the line will begin at the origin of the graph. You can see this type of line in Figure 17.4.

If we wanted to see whether the population intercept is likely to be zero, we would test the null hypothesis $H_0: \alpha = 0$ against the alternative hypothesis:

$$H_1: \alpha \neq 0$$

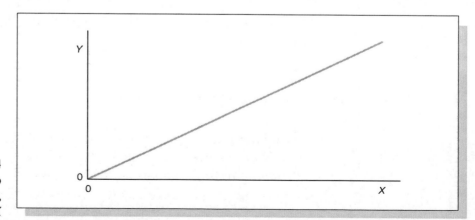

Figure 17.4
Line with zero
intercept,
$Y = 0 + \beta X$

When you use regression analysis you will find that investigating the value of the intercept is rarely important. Occasionally it is of interest, for instance if we are looking at the relationship between an organization's levels of operational activity and its total costs at different periods of time then the intercept of the line of best fit represents the organization's fixed costs.

Typically we are much more interested in evaluating the slope of the regression line. The slope is pivotal; it tells us how the dependent variable responds to changes in the independent variable. For this reason the slope is also known as the *coefficient* of the independent variable.

If the population slope turns out to be zero, it tells you that the dependent variable does not respond to the independent variable. The implication of this is that your independent variable is of no use in explaining how your dependent variable behaves and there would be no point in using it to make predictions of the dependent variable.

If the slope of the line of best fit is zero, the equation of the line would be $Y = \alpha + 0X$, and the line would be perfectly horizontal. You can see this illustrated in Figure 17.5.

The line in Figure 17.5 shows that whatever the value of X, whether it is small and to the left of the horizontal axis or large and to the right of it, the value of Y remains the same. The size of the x value has no impact whatsoever on Y, and the regression model is useless.

We usually want to use regression analysis to find useful rather than useless models – regression models that help us understand and anticipate the behaviour of dependent variables. In order to demonstrate that a model is valid, it is important that you test the null hypothesis that the slope is zero. Hopefully the sample evidence will enable you to reject the null hypothesis in favour of the alternative, that the slope is not zero.

The test statistic used to test the hypothesis is:

$$t = \frac{b - 0}{s_b}$$

Figure 17.5
Line with zero
slope, $Y = \alpha + 0X$

Where b is the sample slope, 0 is the zero population slope that the null hypothesis suggests, and s_b is the estimated standard error of the sampling distribution of the sample slopes.

To calculate the estimated standard error, s_b, divide s, the standard deviation of the sample residuals, the parts of the y values that the line of best fit does not explain, by the square root of the sum of the squared deviations between the x values and their mean, $\bar{x}$.

$$s_b = \frac{s}{\sqrt{\Sigma(x - \bar{x})^2}}$$

Once we have the test statistic we can assess it by comparing it to the t distribution with $n - 2$ degrees of freedom, two fewer than the number of pairs of x and y values in our sample data.

Example 17.8

The equation of the line of best fit for the sample data in Example 17.7 is:

Sales $= 0.74 + 2.38$ Temperature

Test the hypothesis that the population slope is zero using a 5% level of significance.

$$H_0: \beta = 0 \qquad H_1: \beta \neq 0$$

To find the test statistic we first need to calculate the standard deviation of the residuals. We can identify the residuals by taking each x value, putting it into the equation of the line of best fit and then working out what Y 'should' be, according to the model. The difference between the y value that the equation says should be associated with the x value and the y value that is actually associated with the x value is the residual.

To illustrate this, we will look at the first pair of values in our sample data, a day when the temperature was 14° and 19 cans of soft drink were sold. If we insert the temperature into the equation of the line of best fit we can use the equation to estimate the number of cans that 'should' have been sold on that day:

Sales $= 0.74 + (2.38 * 14) = 34.06$

The residual is the difference between the actual sales level, 19, and this estimate:

residual $= 19 - 34.06 = -15.04$

The standard deviation of the residuals is based on the squared residuals. The residuals and their squares are:

Temperature	Sales	Residuals	Squared residuals
14	19	−15.04	226.23
11	29	2.10	4.39

(Continued)

Temperature	Sales	Residuals	Squared residuals
17	47	5.82	33.91
8	12	−7.77	60.35
20	45	−3.31	10.98
13	11	9.34	87.20
24	67	9.17	84.12
3	10	2.13	4.52
16	28	−10.80	116.61
5	21	8.37	70.02
			698.33

We find the standard deviation of the residuals by taking the square root of the sum of the squared residuals divided by n, the number of residuals, minus 2. (We have to subtract two because we have 'lost' 2 degrees of freedom in using the intercept and slope to calculate the residuals.)

$$s = \sqrt{698.33/(n-2)} = \sqrt{698.33/8} = 9.343$$

To get the estimated standard error we divide this by the sum of squared differences between the temperature figures and their mean.

Temperature (x)	$\bar{x}$	$x - \bar{x}$	$(x - \bar{x})^2$
14	13.1	0.9	0.81
11	13.1	−2.1	4.41
17	13.1	3.9	15.21
8	13.1	−5.1	26.01
20	13.1	6.9	47.61
13	13.1	−0.1	0.01
24	13.1	10.9	118.81
3	13.1	−10.1	102.01
16	13.1	2.9	8.41
5	13.1	−8.1	65.61
			388.90

The estimated standard error is:

$$s_b = s / \sqrt{\Sigma(x - \bar{x})^2} = 9.343 / \sqrt{388.90} = 0.4738$$

and the test statistic $t = (b - 0)/s_b = 2.38/0.4738 = 5.02$

From Table 6, the t value with 8 degrees of freedom that cuts off a tail area of 2.5%, $t_{8,0.025}$, is 2.306. If the null hypothesis is true and the population slope is zero only 2.5% of test statistics will be more than 2.306 and only 2.5% will be less than −2.306. The level of significance is 5% so our decision rule is therefore to reject the null hypothesis if the test statistic is outside ±2.306. Since the test statistic in this case is 5.02 we should reject H_0 and conclude that the evidence suggests that the population slope is not zero.

The implication of the sort of result we arrived at in Example 17.8 is that the model, represented by the equation, is sufficiently sound to enable the temperature variable to be used to predict sales.

If you compare the test statistic for the sample slope in Example 17.8 with the test statistic for the sample correlation coefficient in Example 17.7, you will see that they are both 5.02. This is no coincidence; the two tests are equivalent. The slope represents the form of the association between the variables whereas the correlation coefficient measures its strength. We use the same data in the same sort of way to test both of them.

17.3.3 Constructing interval predictions

When you use a regression model to make a prediction, as we did in Example 17.8 to obtain the residuals, you get a single figure that is the value of Y that the model suggests is associated with the value of X that you specify.

Example 17.9

Use the regression model in Example 17.8 to predict the sales that will be achieved on a day when the temperature is 22° Celsius.

If temperature = 22, according to the regression equation:

$$\text{Sales} = 0.74 + 2.38\,(22) = 53.1.$$

Since the number of cans sold is discrete, we can round this to 53 cans.

The problem with single-figure predictions is that we do not know how likely they are to be accurate. It is far better to have an interval that we know, with a given level of confidence, will be accurate.

Before looking at how to produce such intervals, we need to clarify exactly what we want to find. The figure we produced in Example 17.9 we described as a *prediction* of sales on a day when the temperature is 22°. In fact, it can also be used as an *estimate* of the mean level of sales that occur on days when the temperature is 22°. Because it is a single figure it is a point estimate of the mean sales levels on such days.

We can construct an interval estimate, or confidence interval, of the mean level of sales on days when the temperature is at a particular level by taking the point estimate and adding and subtracting an error. The error is the product of the standard error of the sampling distribution of the point estimates and a figure from the t distribution. The t distribution should have $n - 2$ degrees of freedom, n being the number of pairs of data in our sample, and the t value we select from it is based on the level of confidence we want to have that our estimate will be accurate.

We can express this procedure using the formula:

$$\text{Confidence interval} = \hat{y} \pm t_{\alpha/2,\, n-2} * s\sqrt{\frac{1}{n} + \frac{(x_0 - \bar{x})^2}{\Sigma(x - \bar{x})^2}}$$

Here $\hat{y}$ is the point estimate of the mean of the y values associated with the x value of interest, x_0, and s is the standard deviation of the sample residuals.

Example 17.10

Construct a 95% confidence interval for the mean sales of soft drinks that the shopkeeper in Example 17.7 can expect on days when the temperature is 22° Celsius.

From Example 17.9 the point estimate for the mean, $\hat{y}$, is 53.1 cans. We can use the precise figure because the mean, unlike sales on a particular day, does not have to be discrete. We also know from Example 17.9 that s, the standard deviation of the sample residuals, is 9.343, $\bar{x}$ is 13.1 and $\Sigma(x - \bar{x})^2$ is 388.90.

The t value we need is 2.306, the value that cuts off a tail of 2.5% in the t distribution with $10 - 2 = 8$ degrees of freedom. The value of x_0, the temperature on the days whose mean sales figure we want to estimate, is 22.

$$\begin{aligned}
\text{Confidence interval} &= \hat{y} \pm t_{\alpha/2,\, n-2} * s\sqrt{\frac{1}{n} + \frac{(x_0 - \bar{x})^2}{\Sigma(x - \bar{x})^2}} \\
&= 53.1 \pm 2.306 * 9.343 \sqrt{[(1/10 + (22 - 13.1)^2/388.90)]} \\
&= 53.1 \pm 11.873 = 41.227 \text{ to } 64.973
\end{aligned}$$

The confidence interval we produced in Example 17.10 is a reliable guide to what the mean sales are on days when the temperature is 22°. This is because, although this level of temperature is not amongst the temperature values in our sample data, it is within the range of the temperatures in our sample data, which is from 3° to 24°.

If we produce a confidence interval for the mean of the y values associated with an x value outside the range of x values in the sample it will be both wide and unreliable.

Example 17.11

Construct a 95% confidence interval for the mean sales of cans of soft drinks which the shopkeeper in Example 17.7 can expect on days when the temperature is 35°.

The point estimate for the mean, $\hat{y} = 0.74 + 2.38 (35) = 84.04$

$$\text{Confidence interval} = \hat{y} \pm t_{\alpha/2,\ n-2} * s \sqrt{\frac{1}{n} + \frac{(x_0 - \bar{x})^2}{\Sigma(x - \bar{x})^2}}$$

$$= 84.04 \pm 2.306 * 9.343 \ \sqrt{[(1/10 + (35 - 13.1)^2/388.90)]}$$

$$= 84.04 \pm 24.88 = 59.16 \text{ to } 108.92$$

The confidence interval we produced in Example 17.11 is of no real use because the temperature on which it is based, 35°, is well beyond the range of temperatures in our sample. Confidence intervals produced from regression lines will be wider when they are based on *x* values further away from the mean of the *x* values. This is shown in Figure 17.6.

If you want to produce a prediction of an individual *y* value associated with a particular *x* value rather than an estimate of the mean *y* value associated with the *x* value, with a given level of confidence, you can produce what is called a prediction interval. This is to distinguish this type of forecast from a confidence interval, which is a term reserved for estimates of population measures like means.

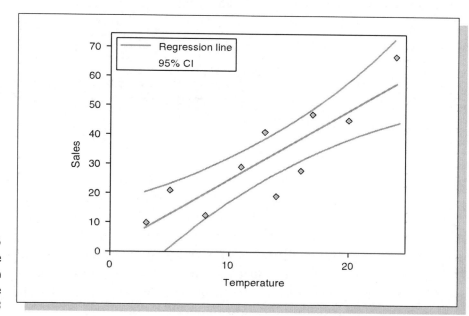

Figure 17.6
95% confidence intervals based on the regression line in Example 17.8

The procedure used to produce prediction intervals is very similar to the one we used to produce confidence intervals for means of values of dependent variables. It is represented by the formula:

$$\text{Prediction interval} = \hat{y} \pm t_{\alpha/2,\ n-2} * s\sqrt{1 + \frac{1}{n} + \frac{(x_0 - \bar{x})^2}{\Sigma(x - \bar{x})^2}}$$

If you look carefully you can see that the difference between this and the formula for a confidence interval is that we have added one to the expression beneath the square root sign. The effect of this will be to widen the interval considerably. This is to reflect the fact that individual values vary more than statistical measures like means, which are based on sets of values.

Example 17.12

Construct a 95% prediction interval for the sales of cans of soft drinks which the shop-keeper in Example 17.7 can expect on a day when the temperature is 22° Celsius.

$$\text{Prediction interval} = \hat{y} \pm t_{\alpha/2,\ n-2} * s\sqrt{1 + \frac{1}{n} + \frac{(x_0 - \bar{x})^2}{\Sigma(x - \bar{x})^2}}$$

$$= 53.1 \pm 2.306 * 9.343 \sqrt{[(1/10 + (22 - 13.1)^2/388.90)]}$$

$$= 53.1 \pm 24.60 = 28.50 \text{ to } 77.70$$

If you compare the prediction interval in Example 17.12 to the confidence interval in Example 17.10 you will see that the prediction interval is much wider, although the level of confidence involved, 95%, is the same.

Just like confidence intervals produced using regression models, prediction intervals are more dependable if they are based on x values nearer the mean of the x values. Prediction intervals based on x values that are well outside the range of the sample data are of very little value.

The usefulness of the estimates that you produce from a regression model depends to a large extent on the size of the sample that you have. The larger the sample on which your regression model is based, the more precise and confident your predictions and estimates will be.

As we have seen, the width of the intervals increases the further the x value is away from the mean of the x values, and estimates and predictions based on x values outside the range of x values in our sample are useless. So, if you know that you want to construct intervals based on specific values of x, try to ensure that these values are within the range of x values in your sample.

At this point you may find it useful to try **Review Questions 17.16 to 17.20** at the end of the chapter.

17.3.4 When simple linear models won't do the job

So far we have concentrated on the simple linear regression model. Although it is used extensively and is the appropriate model in many cases, some sets of quantitative bivariate data show patterns that cannot be represented adequately by a simple linear model. If you use such data to test hypotheses about the slopes of linear models you will probably find that the slopes are not significant. This may be because the relationship between the variables is non-linear and therefore the best-fit model will be some form of curve.

Example 17.13

A retail analyst wants to investigate the efficiency of the operations of a large supermarket chain. She takes a random sample of 22 of their stores and produced the following plot of the weekly sales per square foot of selling area (in £s) against the sales area of the store (in 000s sq ft).

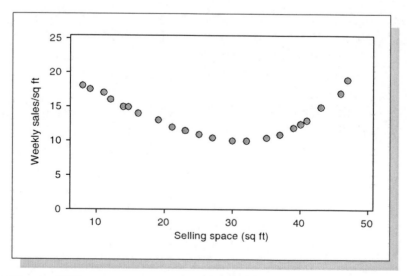

Figure 17.7
Sales per square foot and sales area

It is clear from Figure 17.7 that the relationship between the two variables does not seem to be linear. In this case to find an appropriate model you would have to look to the methods of non-linear regression. The variety of non-linear models is wide and it is not possible to discuss them here, but they are covered in Bates and Watts (1988) and Seber and Wild (1989). Non-linear models themselves can look daunting but in essence using them may involve merely transforming the data so that the simple linear regression technique can be applied; in effect you 'straighten' the data to use the straight-line model.

The simple linear regression model you produce for a set of data may not be effective because the true relationship is non-linear. But it might be that the two variables that you are trying to relate are not the whole story; perhaps there are other factors that should be taken into account. One way of looking into this is to use residual plots. You can obtain them from MINITAB. You will find guidance on doing this in section 17.5.2 below.

One type of *residual plot* is a plot of the residuals against the fits (the values of the *Y* variable that should, according to the line, have occurred). It can be particularly useful because it can show you whether there is some systematic variation in your data that is not explained by the model.

Example 17.14

Produce a plot of the residuals against fits for the best-fit simple linear regression model for the data in Example 17.7 (temperature and cans of soft drinks sold).

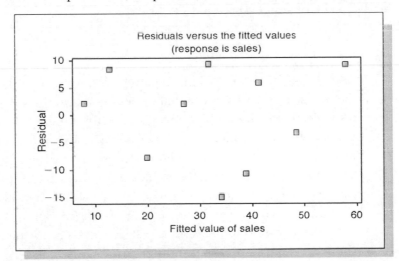

Figure 17.8
A residual plot for the model in Example 17.8

There is no apparent systematic pattern to the scatter in Figure 17.8 so we would conclude that there is no case for looking for another variable to include in the model; the simple linear model appears to be sufficient.

Example 17.15

Produce a plot of the residuals against fits for the best-fit simple linear regression model for the data in Example 17.13.

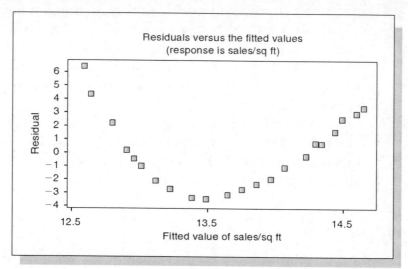

Figure 17.9
A residual plot for the model in Example 17.13

In Figure 17.9 there is clearly a pattern of variation in the residuals. It appears that the stores with smaller sales areas and the stores with larger sales areas seem to have higher sales rates than medium-sized stores. If this company has modern smaller stores in prime city-centre locations that perform well and modern large stores on new retail parks that also perform well, yet also has stores that were constructed in the 1970s in locations where the income of the local population has fallen, then it is clear that other factors such as the age of the store should be included. We should consider regressing the sales variable not just against one variable, the sales area, but another variable as well. The appropriate technique for this is multiple regression, a technique that is outside the scope of this book, but covered in Dielman (1996), Draper and Smith (1998), and Mendenhall and Sincich (1989).

17.4 Contingency analysis

To investigate association involving qualitative variables, which consists of different categories of attributes or characteristics, you can apply contingency analysis. This tests whether one characteristic is associated with, or *contingent* upon, another. It can also be used with quantitative data as long as the data are discrete and have only a very few values or are sorted into relatively few categories.

If you have to analyse the results of questionnaire research, you may want to find out how different characteristics are related to each other. For instance, you may want to assess the possible connection between the socio-economic class of respondents and the newspapers they buy. You would need to conduct a contingency test in order to ascertain whether a connection you might find in your sample results is strong enough to enable you to conclude that there is a connection in the population at large, in other words to see if the sample results are *significant*.

Contingency tests are conducted in the same way as the hypothesis tests we looked at previously. You begin with a null hypothesis, H_0, which in contingency analysis is always that there is no association between the characteristics, and an alternative hypothesis, H_1, which is that there is an association between them.

The next stage is to analyse the sample results that we want to use to decide which hypothesis is the more plausible. The first step is to put the data into a *contingency table*.

Example 17.16

In a TV audience survey, a random sample of 100 respondents were asked if they considered there was too much or not enough sport on TV. Of the 40 men in the sample, 15 said too much. Of the 60 women in the sample, 35 said too much. Do these results suggest there a significant connection between gender and attitude to the amount of sport on TV?

The hypotheses are:

H_0: There is no association between gender and attitude.
H_1: There is association between gender and attitude.

Start by arranging the sample data in a contingency table.

	Men	Women	Total
Too much sport	15	35	50
Not enough sport	25	25	50
Total	40	60	100

To test the hypotheses the sample results must be consolidated into a test statistic in the form of a measure of contingency. This test statistic is known as *chi-square* after the Greek letter chi, χ, and the benchmark distribution used to assess its value is the *chi-square (χ^2) distribution*.

You find the value of chi-square by comparing the sample results, referred to as the *observed* frequencies and represented by the letter O, to the results that you would expect if the null hypothesis were true. These values, which you have to work out, are known as the *expected* frequencies and are represented by the letter E.

Example 17.17

What results would we expect to see in the contingency table in Example 17.16 if there were no association between gender and attitude to sport on TV?

We know from the totals in the contingency table in Example 17.16 that the respondents are split equally between the 50 who think there is too much sport and the 50 who think there is not enough. If there is no association between the attitudes that people have towards the amount of sport on television and gender we would therefore expect men and women to be evenly split on the issue. In other words, if gender makes no difference to whether people think there is too much sport on TV, we would expect the same proportion of men as women to say so, and the same proportion of men as women to say there is not enough.

The contingency table would look like this:

	Men	Women	Total
Too much sport	20	30	50
Not enough sport	20	30	50
Total	40	60	100

In this table each group, men and women, has been divided equally between the opposing viewpoints. These figures are the expected figures we need to work out the test statistic.

Note that although the figures within the table are different, the row and column totals are unchanged.

The formal way of finding expected frequencies is to multiply the row total by the column total and divide the product by the overall total. So to find how many men in Example 17.17 we would expect to say there is too much sport on TV, assuming there is no association, multiply the total number of men by the total number saying there is too much sport on television and divide the result by 100, the total number of respondents in the sample:

$$\text{expected frequency} = \frac{\text{row total * column total}}{\text{overall total}} = \frac{50 * 40}{100} = 20$$

We compare the expected frequencies to the observed frequencies, the actual sample results, by putting them together in a single table.

Example 17.18

Produce a contingency table showing the observed frequencies from Example 17.16 alongside the expected frequencies from Example 17.17 and compare the two sets of frequencies.

In the following table the expected frequencies are shown in brackets:

	Men	Women	Total
Too much sport	15 (20)	35 (30)	50
Not enough sport	25 (20)	25 (30)	50
Total	40	60	100

Note that fewer men than we would expect if there were no association say there is too much sport and more women than we would expect if there were no association say there is too much.

The conclusions in Example 17.18 suggest that there is some association in the sample results but is the association strong enough to be significant, in other words does the evidence point to association in the entire population? To find out we need to calculate the test statistic, χ^2.

To do this we subtract each expected frequency from its corresponding observed frequency and then square the result. We will be adding these differences between observed and expected frequencies, so we have to square them otherwise the positive and negative differences will cancel each other out and the test statistic will be useless. We then divide each squared difference by its expected frequency. This is to standardize the test statistic, in other words to enable us to compare it to a standard χ^2 distribution. Finally we add together the standardized squared differences, one for each section or cell of the contingency table. The total we get is the test statistic, χ^2, for the sample results.

The procedure can be represented using the following formula.

$$\chi^2 = \Sigma(O - E)^2/E$$

Example 17.19

Find the value of χ^2 for the sample data in Example 17.16.
We can work from the contingency table produced in Example 17.18.

	Men	Women
Too much sport	15 (20)	35 (30)
Not enough sport	25 (20)	25 (30)

Start with men who say there is too much sport on TV. The observed frequency, O, is 15 and the expected frequency, E, is 20, so:

$$(O - E)^2/E = (15 - 20)^2/20 = 25/20 = 1.250$$

Next the women who say there is too much sport on TV.

$$(O - E)^2/E = (35 - 30)^2/30 = 25/30 = 0.833$$

Then the men who say there is not enough sport on TV.

$$(O - E)^2/E = (25 - 20)^2/20 = 1.250$$

Finally the women who say there is not enough sport on TV.

$$(O - E)^2/E = (25 - 30)^2/30 = 0.833$$

The test statistic, χ^2, is the sum of these four results:

$$\chi^2 = 1.250 + 0.833 + 1.250 + 0.833 = 4.166$$

Does the test statistic in Example 17.19 suggest that there is association between gender and attitude to the amount of sport on TV in the entire population? We can only establish this by comparing the test statistic to the benchmark distribution.

The distribution we use to assess the test statistic is the *chi-square* distribution, and the procedure is referred to as a *chi-square test*. This distribution describes the behaviour of the measure of contingency that we have used. The shape of the chi-square distribution is shown in Figure 17.10.

There are different versions of the chi-square distributions. The one to use depends on the number degrees of freedom you have in your sample results. You can work this out by taking the number of rows in the contingency table, subtracting one, and then multiplying by the number of columns in the contingency table minus one. If we use r to represent the number of rows and c to represent the number of columns:

$$\text{degrees of freedom} = (r - 1) * (c - 1)$$

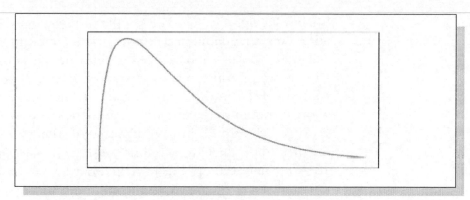

Figure 17.10
The chi-square
distribution

The contingency table in Example 17.19 has two rows and two columns, so the benchmark version of the chi-square distribution has one degree of freedom. This describes the pattern of chi-square values we would get if we took all the samples we possibly could from a population that had no association between two characteristics, each of which had only two categories, and calculated a chi-square value from each set of sample results.

Once you specify a level of significance for the contingency test you need to find the appropriate critical value from the chi-square distribution. The test is a one-tail test; if your test statistic is greater than the critical value then it is less likely to arise from a population with no association than your level of significance.

Table 8 on page 625 in Appendix 1 provides information about chi-square distributions, with up to 10 degrees of freedom. In it the figure in the first row, the row for 1 degree of freedom, and the column headed 0.10 is 2.706. This means that 10% of the distribution is to the right of 2.706. If we wanted to test the null hypothesis of no association at a 10% level of significance, then the test statistic from our sample results would need to be larger than 2.706 in order to reject the null hypothesis.

From Table 8 we also find that 5% of the distribution is to the right of 3.841. If the test statistic is more than this we can reject the null hypothesis at the 5% level of significance. Similarly, in order to reject the null hypothesis at the 1% level the test statistic would have to be larger than 6.635.

Notice that the larger our test statistic is, the stronger the evidence of association will be. Rejecting the null hypothesis at 1% is far more conclusive than rejecting it at 10%. This is not surprising because the test statistic, χ^2, is based on differences between the observed frequencies and those we would expect if there were no association. If there were association then we would anticipate large differences between observed and expected frequencies. If there were no association we would expect small differences.

The test statistic in Example 17.19 was 4.166, which is large enough (larger than 3.841) to lead us to reject the null hypothesis at the

5% level of significance. The sample results suggest that there is association between gender and attitude to the amount of sport on TV.

The set of data we have used to illustrate chi-square tests for association is a simple one. In practice you are likely to have more rows and/or columns. Even in the example data, we might have had another category of response to cope with – perhaps the view that the amount of sport on television is just right. Although the table is more elaborate, the procedure you have to follow is essentially the same. However, there are some important points to remember.

The first is that more rows and columns mean more degrees of freedom, so you must use the correct version of the χ^2 distribution. The second point concerns the amount of data. Like other types of statistical testing the more data you have the firmer your conclusions will be. We should have enough data to ensure that none of the expected frequencies is less than 5; otherwise our results may be unreliable. If any expected frequencies are less than 1, the results of the test will be useless.

If one or more expected frequencies are too low there are two possible solutions; obtain more data or merge categories so that there are fewer rows and columns. If you are managing the project yourself you can avoid the problem by planning the research carefully.

Example 17.20

In a survey a random sample of 135 motorists were each asked their age and the type of car they drove. The results are shown in the following contingency table:

Age group	Car type Performance	Sports	Super-mini	Family car	Total
40 or over	4	26	12	28	70
Under 40	3	24	18	20	65
Total	7	50	30	48	135

Use these sample results to test for association between age group and type of car using a 5% level of significance.

H_0: There is no association between age group and type of car.
H_1: There is association between age group and type of car.

To test the null hypothesis we need the expected frequencies for each cell, but when we calculate the expected frequencies for the drivers with performance cars we find that for both age groups the figures are less than 5:

Expected number of drivers 40 or over with performance cars $= (70 * 7)/135$
$$= 3.630$$

Expected number of drivers under 40 with performance cars = $(65 * 7)/135 = 3.370$

These low expected frequencies would weaken the test. We can overcome this by merging the performance and sports categories:

	Performance/Sports	Super-mini	Family car	Total
40 or over	30	12	28	70
Under 40	27	18	20	65
Total	57	30	48	135

The expected values are now:

40 or over with Performance/Sports cars = $(70 * 57)/135 = 29.556$
Under 40 with Performance/Sports cars = $(65 * 57)/135 = 27.444$
40 or over with super-minis = $(70 * 30)/135 = 15.556$
Under 40 with super-minis = $(65 * 30)/135 = 14.444$
40 or over with family cars = $(70 * 48)/135 = 24.889$
Under 40 with family cars = $(65 * 48)/135 = 23.111$

These can now be inserted in the contingency table.

	Performance/Sports	Super-minis	Family cars	Total
40 or over	30 (29.56)	12 (15.56)	28 (24.88)	70
Under 40	27 (27.44)	18 (14.44)	20 (23.12)	65
Total	57	30	48	135

The test statistic is:

$$\chi^2 = [(30 - 29.56)^2/29.56] + [(12 - 15.56)^2/15.56] + [(28 - 24.88)^2/24.88]$$
$$+ [(27 - 27.44)^2/27.44] + [(18 - 14.44)^2/14.44] + [(20 - 23.12)^2/23.12]$$
$$= 0.0066 + 0.8145 + 0.3913$$
$$+ 0.0071 + 0.8777 + 0.4210 = 2.5182$$

The degrees of freedom = (rows − 1) * (columns − 1) = $(2 - 1) * (3 - 1) = 2$.

According to Table 8, the value of χ^2 that cuts off a 5% area in the right-hand side of the χ^2 distribution that has two degrees of freedom is 5.991. This is the critical value of χ^2 at the 5% level. Since the test statistic, 2.5182, is less than the critical value we cannot reject the null hypothesis. The evidence suggests there is no significant association between age group and type of car. However, it is worth noting that the largest two of the six components of the test statistic, 0.8145 and 0.8777, both relate to super-minis. Fewer drivers 40 or over and more drivers under 40 drive this type of car than we would expect.

At this point you may find it useful to try **Review Questions 17.21 to 17.29** at the end of the chapter.

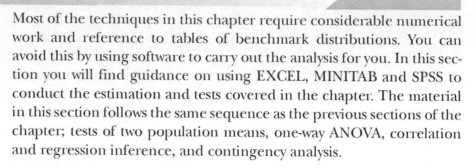

17.5 Using the technology: testing differences between population means and inference with bivariate data in EXCEL, MINITAB and SPSS

Most of the techniques in this chapter require considerable numerical work and reference to tables of benchmark distributions. You can avoid this by using software to carry out the analysis for you. In this section you will find guidance on using EXCEL, MINITAB and SPSS to conduct the estimation and tests covered in the chapter. The material in this section follows the same sequence as the previous sections of the chapter; tests of two population means, one-way ANOVA, correlation and regression inference, and contingency analysis.

17.5.1 EXCEL

To test differences between two population means using independent samples:

- Enter your first sample data into one column of the spreadsheet and your second sample data into another.
- Select **Data Analysis** from the **Tools** pull-down menu.
- In the **Data Analysis** window choose **t-Test: Two-Sample Assuming Equal Variances** and click **OK**. As the title suggests, this assumes the populations from which the samples are taken have the same, or at least similar variances and hence a pooled estimate of the standard error can be used. If this is not the case, choose **t-Test: Two-Sample Assuming Unequal Variances** instead. With small samples, say less than 30, it is better to assume equal variances as otherwise the test is not so robust.
- In the command window the cursor will be positioned in the space to the right of **Variable 1 Range**. Click and drag over the spreadsheet cells containing the first sample data then click the space to the right of **Variable 2 Range** and click and drag over the spreadsheet cells containing the second sample data. Enter the appropriate value in the space to the right of **Hypothesized Mean Difference** and check that the value of **Alpha:**, 0.05, is the level of significance you want to use then click **OK**.
- The output that appears includes the test statistic, **t Stat**. Below it is the probability that the test statistic (or a more extreme one) arises if the null hypothesis of no difference

between the population means is true, assuming a one-tail test, $P(T<=t)$ **one-tail**, and a two-tail test, $P(T<=t)$ **two-tail**. There are also critical values for the one- and two-tail tests at the level of confidence, **Alpha:**.

To test differences between population means using paired data:

- Enter the observations of the two samples into two columns of the spreadsheet.
- Select **Data Analysis** from the **Tools** pull-down menu.
- In the **Data Analysis** window choose **t-Test: Paired Two Sample for Means** and click **OK.**
- In the command window the cursor will be in the space to the right of **Variable 1 Range.** Click and drag over the cells containing the first sample data then click the space to the right of **Variable 2 Range** and click and drag over the cells containing the second sample data. Enter the appropriate value in the space to the right of **Hypothesized Mean Difference** and check that the value of **Alpha:**, 0.05, is the level of significance you want then click **OK.**
- The output includes the test statistic, **t Stat**, and the probabilities that the test statistic (or a more extreme one) arises if the null hypothesis of no difference between the population means is true under a one-tail and a two-tail test, $P(T<=t)$ **one-tail** and $P(T<=t)$ **two-tail** respectively. You will also see the critical values of t for the one- and two-tail tests at the level of confidence, **Alpha:**.

To test for differences between population means using analysis of variance:

- Enter the data from your samples into the spreadsheet using a separate column for each sample.
- Select **Data Analysis** from the **Tools** pull-down menu.
- In the **Data Analysis** window click on the very first tool on the list, **Anova: Single Factor** then click **OK.**
- In the command window that appears make sure the cursor is positioned in the space to the right of **Input Range** then click and drag the mouse over the cells where your data are stored.
- Check that the **Columns** option to the right of **Grouped By:** is selected and that the default value in the box beside **Alpha:** 0.05 is the level of significance that you want to use then click **OK.**
- The upper section of the output that appears contains summary measures for your samples, the lower part includes the test statistic, F, and the probability of getting that test statistic (or a more extreme one) if the null hypothesis of no difference

between the population means is true, the **P-value**. The **F crit** is the critical F value at the level of significance given as **Alpha:**.

To test hypotheses about bivariate regression model components:

- Enter your *x* values in one column of the spreadsheet and your *y* values in another.
- Select **Data Analysis** from the **Tools** menu and pick the **Regression** option from the sub-menu then click **OK**.
- Enter the cell locations of your values of *X* and *Y* in the appropriate spaces of the command window then click **OK**.
- The output that appears will include a table listing the test statistics of the sample regression intercept and slope in a column headed **t Stat**, and the associated **P-value** of each. If you use this procedure to analyse the data from Example 17.7 you should see the following table in the spreadsheet:

	Coefficients	Standard error	t Stat	P-value
Intercept	0.738236	6.873624	0.107401	0.917115
X variable	2.378761	0.473761	5.021009	0.001026

- The upper **P-value**, 0.917115, is the probability of getting a sample intercept of 0.738236 (or a larger one) if the population intercept is zero. The lower, 0.001026, is the probability of getting a sample slope of 2.3788 (or a larger one) if the population slope is zero. The first probability suggests there is a strong possibility that the population intercept is zero whereas the second is below 0.01 so we can reject the null hypothesis that the population slope is zero at the 1% level. You might like to compare these results with those in Example 17.8.

To run a contingency test on tabulated data:

- Store the table of observed frequencies, referred to in EXCEL as the 'actual range', in one set of spreadsheet cells, and the table of expected frequencies, the 'expected range' in another. Note that you will have to work these out before using this procedure.
- Move the cursor to an empty cell.
- Type **=CHITEST(actual range,expected range)** in the Formula bar. Click and drag over the actual and expected ranges or type in their cell locations. Press the **Enter** key.
- The probability that the test statistic (or a more extreme one) occurs if the null hypothesis of no association is true should appear in the cell.

17.5.2 MINITAB

To test differences between two population means using independent samples:

- Enter your sample data into the worksheet, one sample in one column, the second in another.
- Choose **Basic Statistics** from the **Stat** pull-down menu and pick **2-Sample** *t* from the sub-menu that appears.
- In the command window click the box beside **Samples in different columns** and enter the column locations of your first and second samples.
- If you want to use a pooled estimate of the standard error click the box beside **Assume equal variances**.
- Click the **Options** button. The default for the null hypothesis value of the difference between the population means beside **Test mean** is zero; change it if you want to test another figure for the difference between the means. Select the form of the alternative hypothesis from the list under **Alternative**.
- Click **OK** in the **Options window** then **OK** in the command window.
- The output that appears in the session window includes the test statistic, the **T-value**, and the probability of the test statistic (or a more extreme one) arising if the null hypothesis is true, the **P-value**.

If your samples are small, say less than 30 observations in each, you should use a pooled estimate of the standard error variance. The distribution of differences between the means of small samples only approximately fits the *t* distribution, which means that unless you do so the test is not entirely robust.

To test differences between population means using paired data:

- Enter the observations of the two samples into two columns of the worksheet.
- Choose **Basic Statistics** from the **Stat** pull-down menu and pick **Paired** *t* from the sub-menu that appears.
- In the command window enter the column locations of the sample data then click the **Options** button.
- In the **Options** window the default for the null hypothesis value of the difference between the population means beside **Test mean** is zero; change it if you want to test another figure for the difference between the means. Select the form of the alternative hypothesis from the list under **Alternative**.

- Click **OK** in the **Options window** then **OK** in the command window.
- The output that appears in the session window includes the test statistic, the **T-value**, and the probability of the test statistic (or a more extreme one) arising if the null hypothesis is true, the **P-value**.

To test differences between population means using analysis of variance:

- Enter the data from your samples into the worksheet. Use one column for each sample.
- Choose **ANOVA** from the **Stat** pull-down menu and pick **One-way (Unstacked)** from the sub-menu.
- In the command window type the column locations of your data into the space beneath **Responses.** If you click the **Graphs** button you can opt to have either **Dotplots of data** or **Boxplots of data**, or both, to accompany your output. Click **OK** in the **Graphs** window then **OK** in the command window.
- The upper part of the output that appears in the session window includes the test statistic, **F**, and the probability that the test statistic (or a larger one) occurs if the null hypothesis of no difference between the population means is true, **P**. The lower part of the output contains summary statistics of your sample data.

To test hypotheses about population correlation coefficients:

- Enter the observations of your X and Y variables in two columns of the worksheet.
- Select **Basic Statistics** from the **Stat** pull-down menu.
- Pick **Correlation** from the **Basic Statistics** sub-menu and specify the column locations of your data in the command window, checking that there is a cross in the box next to **Display *p*-values.**
- In the session window you should see the sample correlation coefficient and a **P-value**. This is the probability of the sample correlation coefficient (or a larger one) arising if there is no correlation in the population.

Note that the **P-value** is based on the assumption that the alternative hypothesis is $H_1: \rho \neq 0$ and therefore the test is a two-tail test. If you want to use a one-tail form of the alternative hypothesis, divide the **P**-value by two.

To test hypotheses about bivariate regression model components:

- Enter the observations of your X and Y variables in two columns of the worksheet.
- Select **Regression** from the **Stat** menu and **Regression** from the **Regression** sub-menu.

■ Specify in the command window the column location of your *y* values in the box beside **Response** and the column location of your *x* values in the box beside **Predictor**. Click **OK**.

■ If you use this procedure to analyse the data from Example 17.7 in the session window you should see an analysis that includes:

The regression equation is
Sales = 0.74 + 2.38 Temperature

Predictor	Coef	SE Coef	T	P
Constant	0.738	6.874	0.11	0.917
Temperature	2.3788	0.4738	5.02	0.001

S = 9.343

■ Below the regression equation the column headed 'Predictor' contains the components of the model we can use to predict sales using temperature, the **Constant** (the intercept) and the Temperature variable. The sample intercept and slope are in the **Coef** column and the estimated standard errors of these are in the **SE Coef** column.

■ The figures in the *T* column are the test statistics for the sample intercept and the sample slope. The upper figure in the *P* column, 0.917, is the probability of getting a sample intercept of 0.738 (or a larger one) if the population intercept is zero, the lower, 0.001 is the probability of getting a sample slope of 2.3788 (or a larger one) if the population slope is zero. The first of these suggests that the population intercept is zero. The second is under 0.01 so we can reject the null hypothesis that the population slope is zero at the 1% level.

■ *S* is the standard deviation of the residuals. You may like to compare this and the other figures here with the results in Example 17.8.

As part of its **Regression** facility MINITAB will identify any unusual observations in the data. These will be listed below the analysis of the model and will be tagged **R** if they are unusual because they are a long way from the line of best fit and **X** if they are a long way from the rest of the data but not significantly distant from the line of best fit. If you have unusual observations check that they have been recorded correctly and, if so, try to find out why they are unusual. It is well worth spending time studying outliers; they do make the model less effective but they can help you think of ways of improving the model, perhaps by measuring the variables in different ways.

To produce interval estimates from bivariate regression models:

▪ Enter the observations of your X and Y variables in two columns of the worksheet.

▪ Select **Regression** from the **Stat** menu then **Regression** from the sub-menu.

▪ In the command window specify the column locations of the **Response** (Y) and **Predictor** (X) variables.

▪ Click the **Options** button. In the **Options** window there is a box labelled **Prediction intervals for new observations**. Type the x value that you want the package to use to produce the intervals in the box, then **OK** and **OK** in the command window. (If you want intervals based on several different x values, put them in a column in the worksheet and type the column location in the **Prediction intervals for new observations** box.)

▪ The confidence and prediction intervals, labelled 'CI' and 'PI' respectively, will appear at the end of the regression analysis.

If you want a residuals plot like those shown in Figures 17.8 and 17.9:

▪ Enter your data in two columns of the worksheet.

▪ Select **Regression** from the **Stat** menu and specify the column locations of the **Response** and **Predictor** variables in the command window.

▪ Click the **Graphs** button and in the **Graphs** window, click next to **Residuals versus fits** then click **OK** and **OK** on the **Regression** command window.

▪ The graph that appears is the plot of the residuals against the fits (the values of the Y variable that fit the line). This will show up any systematic variation in the data that is not explained by the model.

To run a contingency test on tabulated data:

▪ Store the tabulated data in the worksheet. For instance the data in Example 17.6 the data should be entered in the following fashion:

C1	C2
Men	Women
15	35
25	25

▪ Select the **Tables** option from the **Stat** pull-down menu and pick the **Chi-Square Test** option from the **Tables** sub-menu.

▪ Specify the column locations of the tabulated data and click **OK**.

▪ The output that you should see in the session window includes the test statistic (Chi-Sq), the degrees of freedom (DF), and the probability of getting the test statistic (or a larger one) if there were no association (*P*-Value).

17.5.3 SPSS

To test differences between two population means using independent samples:

- Enter your sample data into a single column of the worksheet, the data from the first sample then the data from the second.
- Enter a code for each value in an adjacent column to indicate to which sample it belongs, for instance a '1' next to each observation from the first sample and a '2' next to each observation from the second.
- Choose **Compare means** from the **Analyze** pull-down menu and pick **Independent-Samples *T* Test** from the sub-menu that appears.
- In the command window position click the column location of your sample data in the space on the left of the window then click ▶ beside **Test Variable(s):**. The column location should now appear in the space below **Test variable(s):**.
- Click on the column location of your codes in the space on the left of the window then click ▶ beside **Grouping Variable:** and the column location should now appear in the space below **Grouping Variable:**.
- Click the **Define Groups** button and in the **Define Groups** window type 1 in the space beside **Group 1:** and 2 in the space beside **Group 2:**. Click the **Continue** button then **OK** in the command window.
- The output that appears includes an **Independent Samples Test** table. In this table there are two rows of output. The results in the upper row are based on the assumption that the population variances are equal, those in the lower row on the assumption that they are not. In both rows there is a test statistic in the column headed **t** and a probability in the column under **Sig. (2-tailed)**. In order to help you choose which row of results you should use, the package provides a test statistic, *F* for the null hypothesis of no difference between the population variances based on the sample variances. If the **Sig.** figure to the right of the test statistic is less than say 0.05 the evidence suggests there is a significant difference between the variances of the populations and you should use the lower row of results, otherwise use the upper row.

To test differences between population means using paired data:

- Enter the observations of the two samples into two columns of the worksheet.
- Choose **Compare Means** from the **Analyze** pull-down menu and pick **Paired-Samples T Test** from the sub-menu.
- In the command window click on both of the column locations of the sample data then click ▶ to bring them into the space below **Paired Variables** and click **OK**.
- The output that appears in the **Paired Samples Test** table includes the test statistic, **t**, and the probability of the test statistic (or a more extreme one) arising if the null hypothesis is true, the **sig. (2-tailed)**. Note that the null hypothesis the package uses is that the difference between the population means is zero.

To test differences between population means using analysis of variance:

- Enter your sample data into a single column of the worksheet, the data from the first sample then the data from the second, then the data from the third and so on.
- Enter a code for each value in an adjacent column according to which sample it belongs, for instance a '1' next to each observation from the first sample and a '2' next to each observation from the second and so on.
- Choose **Compare means** from the **Analyze** pull-down menu and pick **One-Way ANOVA** from the sub-menu.
- In the command window position click the column location of your sample data in the space on the left of the window then click ▶ beside **Dependent List:**. The column location should now appear in the space below **Dependent List:**.
- Click on the column location of your codes in the space on the left of the window then click ▶ beside **Factor:** and the column location should now appear in the space below **Factor:**. Click the **Options** button and in the window that appears click the button to the left of **Descriptive**, to request summary statistics for your samples, then click the **Continue** button and **OK** in the command window.
- In the **ANOVA** table that appears in the output viewer you should see the **Sum of Squares**, the test statistic, **F**, and the probability that the test statistic (or a larger one) occurs if the null hypothesis of no differences between the population means is true, **Sig**.

To test hypotheses about bivariate regression model components:

- Enter the observations of your *X* and *Y* variables in two columns of the worksheet.

- Select **Regression** from the **Analyze** pull-down menu and **Linear** from the **Regression** sub-menu.
- In the command window click the column location of your *y* values and then the ▶ pointing to the space under **Dependent:** then click the column location of your *x* values and click the ▶ pointing to the space under **Independent(s):**.
- Click on the **Statistics** button and in the window that appears click the space to the left of **Estimates**. Click the **Continue** button then **OK** in the command window.
- In the output viewer you will see a **Coefficients** table with an upper row of results relating to the (**Constant**) or intercept and a lower row of results relating to the coefficient on the independent variable, the slope. The upper value in the **t** column is the test statistic of the sample intercept and the figure to its left under **Sig.** is the probability of obtaining the sample intercept (or a larger one) if the population intercept is zero. The lower **t** figure is the test statistic of the sample slope and the adjacent **Sig.** figure is the probability of the sample slope (or a larger one) occurring if the population slope is zero. If you use this procedure to analyse the data from Example 17.7 you should see the following **Coefficients** table:

Model	Unstandardized coefficients		Standardized coefficients	t	Sig.
1	**B**	**St Error**	**Beta**		
(Constant)	738	6.874	.871	.107	.917
Temperature	2.379	.474		5.021	.001

You might like to compare these with the results in Example 17.8. The upper **Sig.** value, 0.917, suggests that the population intercept could well be zero, the lower figure, 0.001 suggests that the population slope is very unlikely to be zero.

To run a contingency test on data that is already tabulated:

- Enter your data into three columns of the worksheet; the row numbers in the first column, the column numbers in the second and the observed values in the third. To analyse the merged data from Example 17.20 you should enter the following:

1	1	30
1	2	12
1	3	28
2	1	27
2	2	18
2	3	20

- Choose **Weight Cases** from the **Data** pull-down menu and click the button to the left of **Weight cases by** in the command window.
- In the space to the left of the command window click on the column location of your observed values and then click the ▶ pointing to the space under **Frequency Variable:**. then click **OK**.
- Choose **Descriptive Statistics** from the **Analyze** pull-down menu and select **Crosstabs** from the sub-menu.
- In the space to the left of the command window click the column location of your row numbers and then the ▶ pointing to the space under **Row(s):** then click the column location of your column numbers and click the ▶ pointing to the space under **Column(s):**.
- Click the **Statistics** button and in the window that appears click the space to the left of **Chi-square** then click the **Continue** button.
- Click the **Cells** button in the command window and click the spaces to the left of **Observed** and **Expected** in the **Counts** section to the top left of the window. Click the **Continue** button then **OK** in the command window.
- In the output viewer you should see the contingency table headed **Crosstabulation**, and below it a table of **Chi-Square Tests** that includes the **Value** of the **Pearson Chi-Square**, the test statistic, the **df**, the number of degrees of freedom, and a figure for **Asymp. Sig. (2-sided)**, which is the probability that the test statistic (or a larger one) occurs if there is no association in the population.

17.6 Road test: Do they really use contingency analysis?

The chi-square hypothesis tests based on contingency tables that we considered in section 17.4 are widely used in analysing the results of questionnaire research. This type of research is very common in investigations of consumer preferences and behaviour.

Schimmel and Nicholls (2003) report the findings of a survey of Internet users undertaken for an Internet retailer to assess the influence of gender on inclination to shop on the Internet. Their analysis includes the application of chi-square tests to assess the association between gender and the frequency with which respondents made purchases and between gender and the amounts respondents spent on Internet shopping. In contrast to earlier studies, which according to the authors suggested that males exhibited a greater propensity to shop on the Internet, the conclusions arising from these chi-square tests were that there were no significant associations between gender and the number of purchases or the amount spent.

Retailers pay a lot of attention to how intangible factors, or 'atmospherics' influence the behaviour of customers visiting their stores. Areni and Kim (1993) undertook a study of the effect that different types of background music had on the inclination of visitors to browse and make purchases in a US wine store. Their field research consisted of observing the behaviour of customers and analysing till records on a series of Friday and Saturday evenings over a three month period. On some of these evenings 'classical' background music was played, on others 'Top-Forty' top-selling recordings were used. Much of their analysis involved ANOVA but they also used chi-square contingency analysis to investigate association between age group and influence of music type, and customer type (gender, single or couple or group) and influence of music type. Their results suggested that classical music influenced customers to spend more, but by buying more expensive wines rather than greater quantities.

Baysan (2001) presents the results of a survey of attitudes of tourists towards environmental issues related to tourism intended to ascertain whether attitude was associated with the nationality of tourists, their levels of education and their occupations. His respondents were German, Russian and Turkish holiday-makers staying at a resort in the Antalya region of Turkey. Using chi-square analysis he found that there was a stronger association between nationality and attitudes than between either education level or occupation. German tourists exhibited a distinctly more sensitive attitude towards environmental issues that their Russian and Turkish counterparts when asked, among other things, about their inclination to engage in motorboat sports or use oil-based sun-creams.

In employment law in the USA there are landmark cases in which statistical evidence was of central importance. Meier, Sacks and Zabell (1986) discuss a number of cases in which statistical analysis, including chi-square tests on contingency tables, was used as evidence of racial discrimination in employment. This analysis was applied in cases involving the fairness of written tests used in recruitment and promotion procedures.

Answers to these questions, including fully worked solutions to those questions marked with an asterisk (*), are on pages 669–672.

17.1*   Professor Soyuz, adviser to a trade union, has been asked to ascertain whether the mean hours worked per week are higher in the Deshovy region than in the Bugatty region. The mean and standard deviation of hours worked per week by a random sample of 62 workers in Deshovy are 43.7 and 4.1 respectively. The mean and standard deviation of hours worked by a random sample of 55 workers in Bugatty are 41.9 and 3.2 respectively. Test the hypothesis that on average workers in Deshovy work no more hours per week than workers in Bugatty. Use a 5% level of significance.

17.2   The mean number of Internet sessions undertaken by a random sample of 38 subscribers to the Sietka service provider in a month was 36.6 with a standard deviation of 7.0. The mean and standard deviation of the number of sessions undertaken in a month by a random sample of 46 subscribers to the Preeboy service were 33.2 and 10.7 respectively. Test the hypothesis that the population mean number of sessions per month is higher for the Sietka subscribers using a 1% level of significance.

17.3   Brod Automotive manufactures a range of popular motor cars. A research project initiated by its Marketing Department reveals that a random sample of 71 males who each purchased a particular model new sold them after an average of 32.9 months with a standard deviation of 13.4 months, whereas a random sample of 58 females who purchased the same model new sold their cars after an average of 36.2 months with a standard deviation of 10.7 months. Test the hypothesis that there is no difference between the average time that men and women who buy this model new keep the car before selling it. Use a 10% level of significance.

17.4*   The speeds of a random sample of 28 cars travelling through a residential area were recorded. The mean speed of these cars was 31.7 mph with a standard deviation of 4.1 mph. After a major poster campaign urging motorists to reduce speed when driving through the area the speeds travelled by a random sample of 24 cars were recorded. The mean speed of this second sample was 29.5 mph with a standard deviation of 3.2. Test the hypothesis that the poster campaign resulted in no reduction of speed in the area using a 5% level of significance and a pooled estimate of the standard error.

17.5   In an attempt to increase turnover by reducing the time customers occupy their seats while consuming the food and beverages they purchase the proprietor of the Kusocheck Cafe has removed the amusement machine and banned smoking. Before the changes she discovered that the mean time that a random sample of 15 customers spent consuming their purchases was 24.3 minutes with a standard deviation of 5.9 minutes. After the changes she found that the mean time that a random sample of 17 customers spent consuming their purchases was 19.6 minutes with a standard deviation of 7.1 minutes. Test the hypothesis that the changes have resulted in a reduction in the mean time that customers spend consuming their purchases using a 1% level of significance.

17.6   The mean number of shirts owned by a random sample of 14 males aged over 40 is 35.8 with a standard deviation of 4.7. The mean number of shirts owned by a random sample of 18 males aged between 25 and 34 was 27.2 with a standard deviation of 6.3. Use a 10% level of significance to test the hypothesis that there is no difference between the mean number of shirts owned by males over 40 and the mean number of shirts owned by males between 25 and 34.

17.7*   The Zilioni-Meer garage offers a 'clean and green engine makeover', which it promises will reduce the amount of CO_2 emissions from cars. A random sample of ten cars was tested for CO_2 emissions before and after the service. The emission figures (in grams of CO_2 per kilometre travelled) were:

					Car					
	1	2	3	4	5	6	7	8	9	10
Before	174	160	196	214	219	149	292	158	186	200
After	169	158	183	210	204	148	285	155	179	183

Test the hypothesis that after the service emission levels are at least as high as before against the alternative that emission levels are lower. Use a 1% level of significance.

17.8   Following newspaper revelations about contamination of a certain brand of meat paste the manufacturer of a rival product wants to establish whether demand for their product has been affected. The Sales Director contacts a random sample of stockists and asks them how many units were sold in the week before the publicity and how many were sold in the week following it. The results are, in thousands of units:

		Stockist								
	1	2	3	4	5	6	7	8	9
Sales before	137	152	217	279	294	299	313	351	379
Sales after	130	149	153	265	210	272	236	317	357

Using a 5% level of significance test the hypothesis that on average sales have not decreased in the week following the publicity.

17.9   Every sales agent at Prodagia plc attends an annual sales conference designed to boost their motivation and enhance their performance. The numbers of new sales contracts generated by each of a random sample of 12 sales agents were recorded for the month before the conference and the month after:

		Agent										
	1	2	3	4	5	6	7	8	9	10	11	12
Contracts before	15	23	26	30	31	34	35	37	38	41	43	48
Contracts after	24	29	30	30	31	32	42	42	46	49	49	52

Test the hypothesis that attending the sales conference has resulted in an increase in the mean number of contracts per month using a 1% level of significance.

17.10* Truba Construction has a major contract to lay pipelines for the oil industry in the Caucasus. The necessary steel pipes are unavailable locally and must be transported from a railhead in the Ukraine. There are three ways the company can get these supplies from there to their destination; on barges through the canals, by rail and using convoys of trucks. All of these take considerable time, and whilst in transit the cargo is subject to loss through accidental damage and theft. The company has tried all three modes of transport a number of times and recorded the percentage of the cargo lost each time:

Canal	17%	1%	10%	19%	4%	18%
Rail	0%	20%	25%	15%	2%	
Truck	19%	15%	12%	15%	10%	

Use one-way ANOVA and a 5% level of significance to test for differences between the population mean percentage losses for the three modes of transport.

17.11   Book-Galtier-Ritzar (BGR) is a large international accounting firm that recruits graduate trainees. Recently the firm recruited 15 graduates who have now taken their professional examinations. Their overall mark in these examinations by the universities from which they graduated are:

Neesky University graduates	38	33	58	51	50	
Seredina University graduates	62	48	59	44	63	58
Visocky University graduates	52	84	77	77		

Test the hypothesis that there is no difference between the mean professional examination marks achieved by graduates of these universities using a 1% level of significance.

17.12   A water company supplies the city of Sukoy from three reservoirs, all of which are prone to low level pollution from the local metal-processing industry. The company takes samples from each reservoir in order to monitor levels of pollution. Chemical analysis of the most recent samples has yielded the following results:

Reservoir	*Pollution level (parts per million)*				
Cheesty	5.2	10.6	7.0	10.4	3.9
Griazny	12.7	21.2	17.8	8.0	15.0
Mussor	9.0	8.0	10.8	12.4	10.9

The company believe that there is no difference between the pollution levels of the three reservoirs. Test this hypothesis at both the 5% and 1% levels of significance.

17.13* In an investigation into household expenditure on home entertainment products commissioned by Zabavar Electrical researchers studied a random sample of 28 households. They found that there was a correlation coefficient of +0.683 between the amount spent on home entertainment products and household income. Test the hypothesis that there is no positive correlation between household income and expenditure on home entertainment products using a 5% level of significance.

17.14   The correlation coefficient between the percentage increase in profits and the percentage increase in share price on the day the profits were announced for a random sample of 19 publicly quoted companies was +0.490. Test the hypothesis of no positive correlation at the 5% level of significance.

17.15   An HR consultant undertook a survey of a random sample of 52 employees of the D N Ghee International Bank. She found a correlation coefficient of -0.377 between the satisfaction levels reported by employees and the length of service they had achieved. Test the hypothesis that there is significant negative correlation at the 1% level.

17.16* Ken Kamien stages 'retro rock nights' on an occasional basis at a large city centre venue. Teams of casual employees hand out 'discount' ticket cards at colleges and music venues to advertise these events. The number of cards handed out before each of the nine events staged so far, and the audience they attracted are given below.

Number of cards	3750	4100	4500	4750	4800	5250	4600	4800	4320
Audience	925	1000	1150	1200	1100	1680	1480	1370	860

(a) Find the least squares regression equation and test the hypothesis, at the 5% level of significance, that the population slope is zero.

(b) Construct a 95% confidence interval for the mean number of people attracted to an event when 4400 cards have been distributed.

17.17 The number of cash machines in a random sample of eight towns, and the population of the towns are:

Cash machines	20	23	28	41	53	46	82	126
Population (000s)	37	51	69	72	90	105	163	227

(a) Regress the number of cash machines against population and test the hypothesis that the population slope is zero at the 5% level of significance.

(b) Produce a 95% confidence interval for the mean number of cash machines in towns with a population of 80,000 people.

17.18 Komnatar Estates are building a commercial development 15 miles from the location of an international financial centre. A study of the number of enquiries from prospective tenants received by a random sample of nine similar developments in the area that have recently been let revealed that the number of enquiries and the distances, in miles, between the developments and the financial centre were:

Enquiries	35	61	74	92	113	159	188	217	328
Distance	28	20	17	12	16	8	2	3	1

(a) Find the regression equation and test the hypothesis, at the 5% level of significance, that the population slope is zero.

(b) Produce a 95% confidence interval for the mean number of enquiries that could be expected from prospective tenants for office blocks 15 miles from the financial centre.

(c) Produce a 95% prediction interval for the number of enquiries that could be expected for a single office block 15 miles from the financial centre.

17.19   The engine capacity (in litres) and the fuel efficiency (in miles per gallon) of a random sample of 10 petrol-driven cars are:

Capacity	1.0	1.2	1.4	1.6	2.0	2.4	2.5	2.8	3.2	4.0
Fuel efficiency	44	47	41	37	33	30	25	26	23	21

(a) Determine the regression equation and test the hypothesis that the population slope is zero using a 1% level of significance.

(b) Construct a 99% confidence interval for the mean fuel efficiency of cars with an engine capacity of 1.8 litres.

(c) Construct a 99% prediction interval for the fuel efficiency of a single car with an engine capacity of 1.8 litres.

17.20   The ages and annual expenditure on traditional suits by a random sample of eight males belonging to the AB socio-economic class were:

Age	27	29	33	34	39	42	49	56
Expenditure (£)	280	400	650	800	1200	1100	1250	1800

(a) Regress expenditure against age and test the hypothesis of a zero population slope at the 10% level of significance.

(b) Produce a 90% confidence interval for 35-year-old AB class males' mean annual expenditure on suits.

(c) Produce a 90% confidence interval for 75-year-old AB class males' mean annual expenditure on suits.

(d) Compare your answers to (b) and (c). Which is the more valid, and why?

17.21   As part of a survey of commuting patterns a random sample of 120 employees at the Stavka Finance headquarters complex were asked how they travelled to work and whether they considered there were enough car parking spaces at the complex.

	Mode of travel	
	Car	*Other*
Enough parking spaces	27	23
Not enough parking spaces	53	17

Test the hypothesis that there is no association between mode of travel and opinion on parking places:
(a) at the 5% level of significance
(b) at the 1% level of significance

17.22* The Potchtar Direct Supplies mail order company has commissioned market research in an attempt to find whether there is a connection between the type of area that people live in and whether they buy from mail order companies. The following table gives the results from a random sample of 150 people:

	Area		
	Urban	Suburban	Rural
Use mail order	14	33	31
Don't use mail order	26	37	9

Test the hypothesis that there is no association between the area people live in and their use of mail order companies using a 1% level of significance.

17.23 A leak of a hazardous substance at the Apassney Engineering factory threatens the health of the workforce. A random sample of 80 employees had their contamination levels checked. The results were:

Level of contamination	Department	
	Production	Administration
High	11	4
Medium	24	10
Low	15	16

Test the hypothesis that there is no association between department and contamination level. Use a 5% level of significance.

17.24 Plattia Fashions operates a 'no-questions' returns policy that enables customers to return goods and get their money back as long as they have proof of purchase. A random sample of 500 transactions were tracked in order to find out whether there is a connection between type of garment and the likelihood of returns.

	Garment type		
	Ladies'	Men's	Children's
Returned	37	14	19
Not returned	163	106	161

Test for association between garment type and whether or not a garment is returned using a 5% level of significance.

17.25 In a survey, a random sample of 200 adults were asked whether they preferred talk or music radio. The results, broken down by socio-economic class, were:

	Talk	Music
AB	16	24
C1C2	27	43
DE	41	49

Does this set of data suggest there is significant association between socio economic class and listening preference at the 10% level of significance?

17.26 Meer Manufacturing owns four plants in the UK. The HR Director has produced the following table, based on data about a random sample of 250 employees, as part of an analysis of union membership patterns:

	Plant location			
	Bolton	Cardiff	Derby	Edinburgh
Members of a union	26	62	41	37
Not members of a union	14	18	29	23

Is there evidence of association between union membership and plant location
(a) at the 10% level of significance?
(b) at the 5% level of significance?

17.27 A survey of a random sample of 320 pet owners undertaken by Patrocka Petfoods yielded the following data about type of pet and size of household:

	Type of household		
Pet	Single person	Couple	Family
Dog	31	40	55
Cat	67	17	12
Other	52	13	33

(a) Using a 1% level of significance test for association between type of pet and type of household.
(b) Examine the components of the test statistic and comment on the patterns they reveal.

17.28 In a survey a random sample of 140 male teenagers from different cities in the UK were each asked to name their favourite sport. The responses are given in the following table:

Favourite sport	City		
	Birmingham	Newcastle	Bristol
Cricket	12	7	16
Football	19	25	27
Rugby	9	8	17

Test for association between city and preferred sport using a 10% level of significance, and comment on any prominent component of the test statistic.

17.29   A survey of the cinema-going habits of a random sample of 500 children, adults of working age and retirees produced the follow responses to the question 'How often do you go to the cinema?':

	Never	Rarely	Sometimes	Frequently
Children	8	15	56	21
Adults	19	83	111	37
Retirees	47	39	30	34

Test the hypothesis that there is no association at the 1% level of significance and interpret any particularly large components of the test statistic.

17.30   Select the appropriate definition from the list on the right-hand side for the terms and symbols listed on the left-hand side:

(i) dependent sample	(a) the intercept of the population regression line
(ii) s_p	(b) an interval estimate of a population measure
(iii) F	(c) the benchmark distribution in contingency analysis
(iv) ρ	(d) a sample consisting of paired values
(v) α	(e) the slope of the population regression line
(vi) β	(f) the population correlation coefficient
(vii) chi-square	(g) an interval estimate of an individual value
(viii) confidence interval	(h) a test of association between characteristics
(ix) prediction interval	(i) the benchmark distribution in ANOVA
(x) contingency test	(j) the pooled estimate of the standard error

CHAPTER 18

Going off-road — managing quantitative research for projects and dissertations

This chapter will help you to:

- plan quantitative research work
- identify data requirements for a project
- gather and use secondary data
- design and implement questionnaire research
- present your results effectively

As you approach the final stage of your course you will probably be told that one of the course requirements is a final year project or dissertation. This typically means that you have to identify a project idea, write a project proposal, undertake research to investigate your project idea, and then produce a substantial written document to deliver your findings.

You may see this as a daunting task, particularly when you are trying to think of ideas for a project, but if you approach it positively and manage the task well you can get a great deal out of it. A good final year project could improve the grade of the qualification you receive. It could also be a useful document to show potential employers as an example of your work.

Your project is probably the first, if not the only, time during your course when your tutors offer you the opportunity to decide what topic to study. Those parts of your course that you have done so far have probably consisted of studying things that somebody else has decided you should do. Your project is different; it is 'your baby'.

It is very hard to produce a good project if you are not committed to it, so it is worth putting time and effort into thinking up three or four possible ideas at a very early stage. But how can you generate project ideas? It may help if you ask yourself these questions:

- Which parts of the course have I enjoyed most?
- Were there any particularly interesting aspects of my experience of work? (Perhaps a placement, part-time jobs, or work before beginning the course.)
- What interests do I have outside my studies?
- What are my academic strengths?
- Do I have any special contacts and resources at my disposal?

Make a list of your responses to these questions. Look at the responses in relation to one another; perhaps there are some interesting combinations? You may have enjoyed Marketing as a subject, you may have worked at a football ground on a part-time basis, and you may have a strong interest in football. If all this is true then perhaps a project that looks into how football clubs market season tickets is a possibility?

If you have thought about your responses and no project ideas come to mind, try talking through your responses with somebody else, perhaps a friend or a tutor. It doesn't matter too much if that person is not involved with your course; simply explaining your thinking to somebody else may prompt some excellent project ideas.

Once you have established at least one viable project idea you will probably have to shape your outline ideas into a formal proposal and carry out some sort of literature survey. A good proposal will identify specific propositions and hypotheses that your project is intended to investigate. A good literature survey will find what published material is available through your college library or electronically on the subject you have chosen. This is important because it will influence the nature and scope of the research you will have to undertake.

At this stage you need to consider the data that you will need for your investigation. Perhaps the data are available from published or electronic sources, if not, you will have to consider how you can obtain them yourself. In fact you will probably find that some of the data you need are already available but other data will need to be collected.

Data that are already available, perhaps in a publication in a library or on the Internet, are there because somebody else collected and analysed it. As far as you are concerned they are secondary data, in other words 'second hand'. Whoever has produced them did so to fulfil their own requirements rather than yours, so assess the value of the data to your project carefully.

As we shall see later on in this chapter, when you collect data yourself, that is when you gather primary or first-hand data, you will have to decide what to ask, whom to ask and so on. These are issues that require careful thought.

Whether the data you analyse in your work are primary or secondary, you will have to consider how to present the analysis in your final document. This is something we will consider in the last section of the chapter.

18.1 Using secondary data

If you use secondary data it is the person or agency that collected the data that has decided how the data were collected. You have had no control over this or over the way in which the data are presented to you. It may be that the secondary data that you have found are exactly what you require for your investigation, and they could be already presented in a form that will suit your purposes. But you need to look into both of these issues.

There are a number of questions you should consider about the collection of secondary data. First, exactly when were the data collected? Published results are by definition historic, they relate to the past. This is inevitable because publication takes time. The data may be fairly recent if they are in a journal or on a website, but may be much older if they are in a book.

If you are researching a field that has changed relatively little since the publication of the secondary data that you have found then they may still be useful. However, if your field of research is rapidly changing then ageing secondary data are likely to be of limited value. If you decide to use them you will have to caution your readers about their validity for the present and explain how what has happened since the data were collected has reduced their usefulness.

If you want to use the data as the basis of a comparison between then and now, the age of the data is what makes them useful. You will of course need to make sure that if you collect data as part of your investigation of the current situation, you generate data that can be compared to the secondary data. This means you will have to ask or measure the same sort of things about the same sort of sample.

A second issue to consider is how the secondary data were collected. Unless the results are from all the elements of a population, they are sample data. So, how large was the sample? How were the people or items in the sample selected? Was it a random sample of the population to which it belonged?

If the population consisted of things, how were the items in the sample measured or counted? If the population consisted of people, how and when were they asked for the data they provided?

You will probably have to study the source in which you found the secondary data very carefully to find the answers to these questions. Look for a section called 'Methodology', which should explain the methods used to gather the data. Look through any footnotes or notes at the end of the source for information about how the data were collected, any difficulties the researchers had, and any warnings they give about the validity of the results.

You may be fortunate in finding secondary data that are sufficiently up to date and collected without bias. If this is the case the next thing you have to think about is the way in which the secondary data are presented in the secondary source.

The author or authors who prepared the secondary source may have included their original data in their publication, perhaps in an appendix, so check the source carefully. If the original data are included you will be able to consider various ways in which you can present their data in your report. You can decide which form of presentation will be most appropriate for your discussion of the data.

However, it is more likely that the researchers who collected the original data have not included them in their published results. This is almost inevitable if the study was large. The data will probably be presented in the form of statistical measures and diagrams. You may find that although the forms of presentation that have been used in the secondary source may not be the ones that you would have chosen, they are appropriate for your discussion.

If the form of presentation used in the published source is not appropriate for your report the first thing to consider is alternative ways of presenting the data, which can be based on the form in which it is published. If the secondary source contains a grouped frequency distribution, you can produce a histogram or an approximation of the mean from it. If they have used a contingency table, you can produce a bar chart, and so on.

You may not be able to present the data as you would like using the forms that appear in the secondary source. This may be a problem if you are trying to compare two or more studies from different points in time or locations.

If you really would like to present the data in a way that cannot be based on the data as they are published, then try contacting the authors of the study directly to ask if you can access the original data. If this seems rude, remember that the secondary source you have found has been produced by people who have spent considerable time and effort in carrying out their research and are quite justifiably proud of it. They would probably welcome any inquiry about their work, particularly from somebody like you, who is undertaking their own research and may well introduce the original work to a new audience. Authors of published articles often provide details of the place they work or an email address so that interested readers can contact them. At the very worst they can only turn down your request or ignore it.

It is also worth contacting authors of secondary sources if you have any questions about their research, or if they know of any follow-up work that has been done on it. However, you must give them time to respond to your request. Perhaps they have changed jobs, or are simply too busy to reply to you right away. Try to contact them at least a month or so before the latest time you would need to have their response in order to make use of it.

When you prepare your project report for submission you must acknowledge the sources of all secondary data that you use, even if the form in which it is presented in your report is your own work. There is nothing at all wrong with quoting data or text from other publications in your report as long as you cite the reference, in other words, indicate clearly where it came from using a recognized style, such as the Harvard system.

18.2 Collecting primary data

Often the main difficulty in using secondary data for a project is that they may not fit your requirements. They may not be the data that you would like to have to support the arguments and discussion that you want to develop in your project. You can get around this by gathering primary data. The advantages of doing this are that the data will be up to date and should be exactly what you want for your project. The disadvantage is that collecting primary data requires careful thought, detailed planning and plenty of time.

You will have to decide whether you are going to collect primary data as early as possible. Try to identify your data requirements at the same stage as you produce your literature survey. Successful primary data collection is very difficult to do successfully in a short period of time.

After you have identified your data requirements you will need to address two questions: first, who can provide you with the data, and secondly, how can you obtain them?

If the data you need can be collected by undertaking experiments in a particular place such as a laboratory, or by making direct observations then the first of these questions is answered. You will next need to consider the second question; you will have to identify the method of investigation or the means of observation, define the population, decide how large the sample needs to be and how you will select it.

However, a lot of business research involves getting data from individuals or organizations. If this is true in your case then you will need to define the types of people or organizations carefully. If the number of people or organizations that fit your definition is quite small then you might carry out a survey of the whole population otherwise you will have to take a sample from the population.

The method you use to select your sample depends on whether you can compile a *sampling frame*, a list all the things, people or organizations that make up the population that you want to investigate. If you can do this, which is possible if you are looking, for instance, at league football clubs in the UK, then depending on the structure of the population you can use the random selection procedures described in section 15.2 of Chapter 15. The advantage of these methods is that you can produce statistically sound estimates about the population from them. If you cannot draw up a sampling frame, which may well be the case if you want to investigate small-scale building contractors, then you will have to consider the alternative selection methods outlined in section 15.3 of Chapter 15.

18.2.1 Choosing the right sample size

As well as deciding how you will select your sample you need to decide how large it should be. Basically, the larger the sample the better, but also the larger the sample the more time and resources will be required to collect the data. There are two issues that you have to consider: how much data you will need in order to use the techniques you would like to use to analyse them, and what is the likely *response rate*, the proportion of inquiries that will be successful.

Although we can say that the larger the sample the better, we should add that the larger the sample the less the marginal advantage of a large sample tends to be. For instance, a sample that consists of 30 elements means you would be able to use the Standard Normal Distribution in any statistical decision-making based on the sample data and the sample doesn't have to come from a normal population. So having a sample that consists of at least 30 elements is to your advantage. The extra advantage of having a very large sample, of say 200 elements, rather than a sample of say 100 elements is not great, in fact so little that it may be difficult to justify the extra time involved.

If you need to produce inference results to a particular degree of precision and level of confidence then you need to calculate the minimum sample size you should use. Sections 16.2.2 and 16.2.6 in Chapter 16 illustrate how you can do this.

If you plan to carry out the contingency analysis we considered in section 17.4 of Chapter 17 on your sample data to test for association between characteristics, then you have to take into account the number of categories in each of the characteristics. Suppose you want to ask a sample of respondents from five different geographical regions their opinion of five different types of leisure activity, then the contingency table you will be using for your results will have five rows and five columns, making 25 cells in all. If your sample consists of 100 respondents then the sample data will be spread around these cells far too thinly, on average only four per cell. If you cannot reduce the number of categories you will have to increase the sample size to ensure that your results are substantial enough to make your conclusions valid.

You should also consider that the sample size is not necessarily the same as the number of people or organizations that you will need to approach for data. The reason is that some of them will be disinclined or unable to respond to your request. The proportion of responses that are successful is the response rate.

The response rate you achieve will depend partly on the method you use to collect your data and there are a number of things that you can do to make the response rate higher. We will look at these in the next section. However, when you are planning your data collection you need to build a figure for the response rate into your calculations.

Response rates vary widely, but in most investigations like the one you may be considering a response rate of more than 40%, which means that more than 40% of requests made are successful, would be considered good whereas a response rate of less than 20% would be considered poor.

To make sure that you get enough responses to satisfy your sample size requirements multiply the sample size you need by a factor of three, or even four if your requests will be difficult for your respondents to meet. This means that if, for the purposes of your analysis you need a sample of 30, then you should plan to approach a sample of 90, or even 120.

18.2.2 Methods of collecting primary data

If the primary data that you require will be collected as a result of experiments you will be carrying out in laboratory-style conditions, planning the process of collection involves allocating your time and making sure you have access to the appropriate facilities when you need to use them. The process of collection is under your control. You should allow sufficient time for conducting the experiments and an extra margin of time in case something goes wrong. Even if things go badly wrong there is every chance that you will be able to reschedule your other work in order to complete your research in time to be able to use the data.

Although there are areas of research in the field of business that do involve this sort of work, for instance research into workplace ergonomics, it is much more likely that your project will involve seeking information from other people or organizations. If your project involves collecting data from others, you need to take into account that you do not control their actions. You will have to consider how and when to make your requests very carefully and allow time in your schedule for people who you will ask for data to make their response.

Start by being absolutely clear about the information you want from them. If you do not understand this, how can you expect them to understand your request? Probably the least effective approach that you could make is to write to them, tell them what your project is about and ask them if they can supply you with any relevant information. At best they will send you a leaflet about their business that will probably be of little value to you. Most likely they will not respond to your request at all. After all, if you don't take the trouble to be clear about your information needs, why should they take the trouble to help you?

So, you have to be absolutely clear about what you want to know, who will be able to give you the information you need, and how you plan to ask them for it. Be precise about your requirements, make sure you are approaching the right people and ask them for what you need in such a way that they will find it as easy as possible to help you.

If your respondents are individuals, make sure that you have the correct name and address for every one of them. If your respondents are people who hold certain types of posts within organizations, make sure you have the correct name, job title and business address for every one of them. Getting these details right will improve your response rate. The fastest way that anything you send gets binned or deleted is if it isn't directed to a named individual.

Your request for information should be made in the form of a business letter. It must be word-processed and you should use appropriate opening and closing formalities. The letter should explain clearly to the recipient who you are, what research you are undertaking, and how they can help you. The final paragraph should thank them in anticipation of their help.

You may prefer to send out your request electronically. The advantage is that it is usually quicker and cheaper. The disadvantage is that the recipient can dismiss it as yet another piece of junk email and delete it. To reduce the risk of this happening it is even more important to express the request in a suitably polite and formal style, and to ensure that your questions are as concise as possible.

On balance, unless you have a particular reason for using email to send your request, for instance you may want to survey respondents abroad, it is probably better to use the postal service. The amount of postal junk mail that your recipients receive is probably less than the amount of junk email they receive. In addition, many older respondents will treat a request by letter much more seriously than they will an email message.

What you ask your respondents to do depends on the depth and breadth of the information that you are seeking. If you only want one or two pieces of data, then simply ask for this in your letter, making sure that you are as precise as possible about your requirements. For instance, if you want a figure relating to a particular year or location, then say so.

If you need information in depth, such as opinion and comment on particular issues, then consider requesting an interview with each of your respondents. If you decide to do this, ask for an interview in your letter and explain in the letter what sort of issues you would like to ask them about. To make it easy to compare the results from the different respondents, conduct *structured interviews*, interviews that consist of the same framework of primary and supplementary questions.

If you need a broad range of information, then you will probably have to design and use a questionnaire. This is a standard document that consists of a series of questions and spaces for the respondents to provide their responses.

Before you start compiling a questionnaire, make sure that it is the most appropriate method of collecting the data you need. Good questionnaire research is not easy to conduct, so explore all other ways of assembling the data you need first.

Unfortunately, there are many final year students who have launched themselves straight into collecting data using questionnaires without thinking things through. One student studying the effectiveness of special hospitality events in boosting sales sent a questionnaire to every member of the Marketing Department of a large IT company. She asked each respondent to say how many new sales leads had come from special events over the previous year. The Administrative Officer in the Marketing Department had this information at her fingertips. In that case one well-directed letter would have produced better results more quickly than the 50 or so questionnaires she sent out.

However, if you want responses to many precise questions from many respondents, then a questionnaire is probably the best way of getting them. If you do it properly, questionnaire research will give you the data you need at relatively modest cost and in a form that makes data contributed by different respondents comparable. But done badly, questionnaire research can result in poor response rates and inappropriate data.

So, how can we undertake questionnaire research to maximize the chances of good results? The key is to design the questionnaire carefully and to test it before sending it out to all the respondents in your sample. If you make the effort to produce a questionnaire that is straightforward for your respondents to complete, you will get a higher response rate.

You should send the questionnaire out with a covering letter requesting help from your respondents. If you do not send it out with such a letter, perhaps because you will be distributing it personally, insert a message thanking your respondents for their help at the top of the questionnaire. If you want your respondents to return the completed questionnaires by post, you can improve the chances of them doing so by enclosing a self-addressed envelope with the questionnaire.

You may also be able to improve the chances of getting a good response rate if you offer 'lures' for respondents who return completed questionnaires such as entry into a raffle for a prize, or a copy of your results when they are available. The effectiveness of these depends largely on the respondents you are targeting. The raffle prize is probably a better bet if you are contacting individuals, whereas your results may be more useful when your respondents have a specific type of role within organizations and may well have a specialist interest in your field of research.

Aim to restrict the length of the questionnaire to two sides. This will mean the task of completing it will feel less onerous to your respondents and make it easier for you to collate the results at a later stage. Think carefully about how to lay out the document – the font, spacing, indentation and so on. Make the document as simple, clear and uncluttered as possible so that your respondents are not sidetracked by over-elaborate or poorly organized text.

The sequence in which you pose the questions needs careful thought. You may want to know some details about the respondents, such as the time they have worked in their current post, or their qualifications. It is probably best to ask these sorts of questions first, because they will be easy for your respondents to answer, and once they have started filling in your questionnaire they are likely to finish it.

Sometimes researchers will put questions that seek personal information at the very end of the questionnaire. They do this because they are concerned that putting requests for personal information first makes the questionnaire seem too intrusive and respondents will be wary about completing it. This is a matter of judgement. Unless the questions you use to request personal information are invasive, it is probably better to put them first.

Arrange the questions that you want to put in your questionnaire in a logical sequence. Avoid jumping from one topic to another. You may find it useful to arrange the questionnaire in sections, with each section containing a set of questions about a particular topic or theme.

Design the questions so that they will be easy for your respondents to answer and so that the answers will be easy for you to collate. Avoid open-ended questions like 'What do you think about Internet marketing?' Many respondents will be deterred from answering questions like this because they feel they have to write a sentence or a paragraph to respond to them. You will find the responses difficult to analyse because there will probably be no obvious way of segregating and arranging them. At best you will be able to put them into broad categories of response.

You will find the results far easier to analyse if you build the categories into the questions. In some cases these categories are obvious, such as female and male for gender. In other cases you may need to establish the categories yourself, for instance types of qualification.

There are standard types of question that are used by organizations like market research agencies, which use questionnaires for commercial purposes. Sometimes they will use open-ended questions, especially for exploratory purposes, when they are trying to formulate alternatives to offer respondents by piloting the questionnaire before proceeding to the full survey. More generally they use closed or *closed-ended* questions of three types: dichotomous, multichotomous and scaled.

Dichotomous questions, so-called from the word dichotomy meaning a division into two, offer a simple choice between two alternative mutually exclusive responses. An example is:

Do you have a current driving licence?   Yes ___   No ___

These types of question are often used as *filter* questions. Depending on the answer the respondent gives they may be directed to proceed straight to a subsequent section of the questionnaire.

Multichotomous questions offer more than two alternative responses, either where only one is required or where more than one is possible. An example of the former is:

Which party did you vote for in the last general election?

Conservative ____   Labour ____   Liberal ____
Other ____   None ____

An example of a question which allows for more than one response is:

Which of the following types of places of entertainment have you visited in the past seven days?

Cinema ___   Concert Hall ___   Night Club ___

Public House ___   Restaurant ___   Theatre ___

When you use a multichotomous question you should indicate that the respondent should select only one, or all that apply, as appropriate.

Scaled questions are designed to assist respondents to record their attitudes in a form that you can analyse systematically. One form of scaled question invites respondents to rank a number of factors in relation to each other. An example is:

When choosing a holiday destination which criteria matter to you? Please rank the following in order of importance to you with 1 as the most important and 4 as the least important:

Cost ____   Sunshine ____   Scenery ____   Nightlife ____

Questions like these enable you to compare the rankings of different respondents quite easily, but do be careful not to ask your respondents to rank too many factors. Beyond six or so the respondent will reach the point of indifference between factors, if not about completing your questionnaire!

Likert scales offer a standard set of responses to a statement making an assertion, for instance:

The Internet will become increasingly important for our business.

| Strongly agree | Agree | Neither agree nor disagree | Disagree | Strongly disagree |

A variation of this is to ask them to indicate their opinion by giving us a rating on a scale of 1 to 5, where 1 is strong agreement with the statement and 5 is strong disagreement with the statement. When you use this style of question try to make the statement as clear as possible otherwise you may get respondents who register indifference but actually are giving that response because they do not fully understand the statement.

Semantic differential questions offer respondents a linear scale between two polar positions on which to indicate their attitude to a statement. An example is:

The prospect of a new type of cricket tournament is

Interesting _ _ _ _ _ _ Boring

Stapel scale questions ask respondents to make an assessment of a statement by indicating how strongly the adjective describes their attitude. For instance:

I think the promotion procedures in my company are

+3

+2

+1

FAIR

−1

−2

−3

The data from questions that use rating scales can be described as 'soft', to suggest that they are likely to be a little vague or erratic. The adjectives 'firm' or 'hard' on the other hand describe data that are clear and consistent. The reason that data collected by means of rating scales are 'soft' is that the scales are subject to the interpretation of the respondents. Different respondents will have different perceptions of 'Strongly agree'. Two people may have identical viewpoints but one may consider they 'Strongly agree' whereas the other may consider they 'Agree'. We would not have the same difficulty with a question like 'How long, to the nearest year, have you worked for this organization?' which would generate hard data.

It is better to ask questions that will provide hard data if you can. For instance, instead of the request for an opinion on a statement about Internet marketing, it would be better to ask if the organization uses the Internet in its marketing activities, how much business has been generated through it, and so on.

If you do use scaled questions, bear in mind that the results they generate are *ordinal* data, data whose order of responses are consistent, for instance 'Strongly agree' is more forceful than 'Agree', but there is no consistent unit of measurement. There is no basis for saying that the interval on the scale between say 'Strongly agree' and 'Agree' is larger or smaller than the interval between 'Agree' and 'Neither agree nor disagree'. This is true even if you use numerical scales, for instance where respondents are asked to make a selection between '1' for strong agreement and '5' for strong disagreement. You might be tempted to employ arithmetic measures such as the mean to summarize the results, but this would be quite wrong because even though the results are numerical the scale on which they are based is not arithmetically consistent. You may like to refer back to section 4.3 of Chapter 4 for more on types of data and the analytical tools that are appropriate for each.

We have assumed so far that any questionnaire you design will be sent to the respondents either electronically or by post. As an alternative you might consider asking your questions more directly, either by means of face-to-face interviews or by telephone. The advantages are that you can clarify misunderstandings and the response rate will probably be improved because you have the attention of the respondent and you don't have to rely on their sending the document back to you. The disadvantage is that it is easy to unwittingly introduce bias by the way in which you ask the questions and put the responses.

There are a number of good specialist texts on questionnaire design. For more guidance on the subject, try Converse and Presser (1986), Hague (1993), or Oppenheim (1992).

When you have designed your questionnaire it is absolutely vital that you try it out before you send it out to your respondents. You need to make sure that somebody who is reading it for the first time will understand it completely and be able to respond to the questions asked. This is something you simply cannot do yourself. You have written and designed it, so of course it makes sense to you, but the key question is will it make sense to the people that you want to complete it?

Try to test or 'pilot' your questionnaire by asking a number of people to complete it. Ideally these people should be the same sort of people as the respondents in your sample, the same sort of age, occupation etc. If you can't find such people then ask friends. Whoever you get to test the questionnaire for you, talk to them about it after they have completed it. You need to know which questions were difficult to understand, which ones difficult to answer, was the sequence logical, and so on. If necessary, modify the questionnaire in the light of their criticisms. Then test it again, preferably on different people. Keep testing it until it is as easy for respondents to use as possible, yet it will still enable you to get the information you need.

Testing a questionnaire can be a tedious and annoying process, not least because you are convinced that your questionnaire is something that even a complete idiot can understand. The point is that it is not your assessment of the questionnaire that matters. It is whether the respondents who can provide you with the information you want will understand it. If they can't, the whole exercise will turn into a waste of time. So, be patient and learn from the people who test your questionnaire. Their advice can improve your response rate and the quality of information you get.

18.3 Presenting your analysis

When you have completed your investigations and analysed your results you will need to think about how you will incorporate your analysis into your report. The key editorial questions that you have to address are what to include, how to present it and where to put it. You will have to think about these issues when you plan the structure of your final document.

If you have collected primary data you will need to explain how you collected them. You should do this in a section called 'Methodology' that ought to be located amongst the early sections of the report, probably after the introductory sections. Your reader should be able to find out from your methodology section how you selected your sample, and what process you used to gather your data.

You shouldn't need to include the raw data in your report. Your reader is unlikely to want to comb through completed letters, completed questionnaires, or record sheets. However it may be wise to put a single example in an appendix and make reference to that appendix in the methodology section, to help your reader understand how the data were collected.

Unless you have a very modest amount of data, use a suitable computer package to produce your analysis. If you have a set of completed questionnaires make sure you number each one before you store data from them in the package. Put the data from questionnaire number one into row one of the worksheet or spreadsheet and so on. If you do this you will find it much easier to rectify any mistakes that you make when you enter your data. You will also find it convenient if you need to check specific responses when you come to examine the analysis.

The package you use to analyse your data may provide ways of saving you time when you enter your data. For instance, you may have data about business locations in the UK that consists of replies that are

'England', 'Scotland', or 'Wales'. Typing these words repeatedly is laborious. If you use MINITAB you can use the coding facility to change labels like 'E' for England and 'S' for Scotland, which are much easier to enter, to the full country name. Select **Code** from the **Manip** menu then **Text to Text** from the sub-menu (or **Numeric to Text** if you use numeric labels). In the command window you will have to specify the location of the data you want to change, where you want the changed data stored, and exactly how you want the data changed.

If your data has been generated by a questionnaire that includes scores respondents have given in answer to scaled questions you may be advised to include an assessment of the reliability of your data. One measure of this that you may hear of is Cronbach's Alpha. Lee Cronbach was an eminent American education professor who specialized in psychological testing. He developed what he called the Coefficient Alpha, which is based on measuring correlation, to measure the internal consistency of responses to separate questions designed to generate scores that could be combined to give an overall assessment of the respondents' abilities or attitudes. In his original work (Cronbach, 1951) he gives examples of tests of mechanical reasoning and morale. Researchers are often tempted to use Cronbach's Alpha because it appears to give an overall and easily understandable reliability check on an entire data set – on a scale of zero to one, perfect reliability yields an alpha value of one. However, be wary of employing the coefficient; it is only of any use if you have reason to expect reliability between sets of responses in the first place. If you decide to use it, SPSS can produce it for you: select **Scale** from the **Analyze** menu, then **Reliability Analysis** and **Alpha** as the model.

The results that you do eventually include in your report should be those that have proved useful. There may be data that you tried to collect, but were unable to. Perhaps your respondents simply didn't have the information; perhaps they supplied the wrong data. For a variety of reasons collecting primary data can produce disappointment.

If part of your data collection activity has not borne fruit, there's not a lot you can do about it. Don't be tempted to include inappropriate data purely because you have collected them. The results you include in the report should be the ones that have a part to play within your report, not ones for which you have to create an artificial role.

You may well need to discuss the reasons for the failure of part of your quest for information in your report, particularly if it relates to an important aspect of your project. Others could use your work and you will be making a valid contribution to knowledge if your unfortunate experience is something they can learn from.

The structural plan of your final report should help you decide what results you will need to include, but you will also have to decide how to present them. You need to remember that your reader will be looking at your final report without experiencing the process of carrying out the project. You will have to introduce the results to them gradually, starting with the more basic forms of presentation before showing them more elaborate types of analysis.

In the early parts of the discussion of your results you should explain the composition of your sample. You can do this effectively by using simple tables and diagrams. Further on you may want to show what your respondents said in response to the questions you asked them. Again there is scope here for using simple tables and diagrams. If the results you are reporting consist of quantitative data, use summary measures to give your reader an overview of them.

Later on in your report you will probably want to explore connections between the characteristics of your respondents, or the organizations they work for, and the facts or opinions they have provided. Here you can make use of bivariate techniques: contingency tables for qualitative data, and scatter diagrams, regression and correlation for quantitative data.

At the heart of most good projects is at least one proposition or hypothesis that the project is designed to evaluate. You should be able to put your hypothesis to the test by using statistical decision-making techniques, the methods of statistical inference that feature in Chapters 16 and 17. These techniques will enable you to make judgements about the population from which your sample is drawn using your sample results.

For instance, suppose the proposition that your project is intended to assess is that successful clothing retailers use Internet marketing. You could use a contingency test to test for association between whether or not clothing retailers use Internet marketing and whether or not they recorded an increase in turnover in their most recent accounts. If your proposition is that hours worked in the road haulage industry exceed those specified in working time regulations you could test the hypothesis using data from a random sample of haulage contractors.

If you want to produce estimates or test hypotheses and your sample results come from a small population you may have to make a small adjustment when you calculate the estimated standard error. You need to multiply it by the *finite population correction factor*. If we use n to represent the size of the sample and N to represent the size of the population, we can express the correction factor as:

$$\frac{(N-n)}{N}$$

Example 18.1

A random sample of 40 car dealers is taken from the 160 dealers franchised to a particular manufacturer. The standard deviation of the number of cars sold per month by these 40 dealers is 25. Calculate the estimated standard error using the appropriate finite population correction factor.

$$\text{Estimated standard error} = \frac{s}{\sqrt{n}} * \frac{(N-n)}{N}$$

$$= \frac{25}{\sqrt{40}} * \frac{(160-40)}{160}$$

$$= 2.965$$

The adjustment is important if the sample constitutes a large proportion of a population, as in Example 18.1. However, if the sample constitutes less than 5% of the population it is not necessary to make the adjustment.

Once you have decided which analysis to include in your final report and the form in which you will present it, you must consider exactly where the various tables, diagrams and numerical results will be located within your report. You will have gone to a lot of trouble to collect your data and analyse them so it is worth making sure that you use them in the most effective way.

Your guiding principle should be to make it as easy as possible for your readers to find the pieces of your analysis that you want them to consult. If the piece of analysis is a diagram or a table you have two options: you can insert it within the text of your report or you can put it in an appendix. If the piece of analysis is a numerical result you have a third option; you can weave it into the text itself.

In order to decide where to put a piece of analysis, consider how important it is that your readers look at it. If it is something that readers must see in order to follow your discussion, then it really should be inserted within the text. Avoid full-page inserts and make sure that the analysis is positioned as closely as possible to the section of the text that first refers to it. It will be very frustrating for your readers if they have to comb through the whole report to look for something that you refer to pages away from it. Every insert you place within the text must be labelled, for instance 'Figure 1' or 'Table 3', and you should always refer to it using the label, for instance '... the distribution of hours worked is shown in Figure 1'.

If you have some analysis that you consider your readers may want to refer to, but don't need to look at, put it in an appendix. Make sure that the appendix is numbered, and that you use the appendix number whenever you refer to the analysis in it. Arrange your appendices so that the first one that readers find referred to in your text is Appendix 1, and so on. Don't be tempted to use appendices as a 'dustbin' for every piece of analysis that you have produced, whether you refer to it or not. Any analysis that you do not refer to directly will be superfluous as far as your readers are concerned and may distract them from what you want them to concentrate on.

Single numerical results such as means and standard deviations can be reported directly as part of you text. However, you may want to draw your readers' attention to the way in which it has been produced. If so, you can put the derivation of the result in an appendix and refer your readers to it. This is a particularly good idea if you have had to adjust the procedure that your readers would expect you to use to produce such a result, for instance if you have to use the finite population correction factor that we looked at in Example 18.1.

Allow yourself time in your schedule to read through your final report carefully before submitting it. Make sure that all your inserts are labelled, all your appendices numbered and all your sources acknowledged. If you have time, ask a friend to read through in case there are any mistakes that you have overlooked. Ask them how easy it was to find the inserts and appendices when they were referred to them.

Checking the draft and the final version can be tedious and time-consuming, but it is time and effort well spent. When your tutors read it in order to assess it you want to make sure that the version they read is as polished and professional as possible.

Statistical and accounting tables

Table 1 Present values

This table provides the present value of one unit of currency received in *n* years' time when the rate of interest is *r*%. To use this table to discount a future flow of cash find the figure in the row for the appropriate number of years until the cash flow takes place and in the column for the appropriate rate of interest, the discount rate. Multiply this figure by the sum of money involved.

Example

Using a discount rate of 4%, find the present value of $5000 received in three years' time. The figure in the row for 3 years and the column for 4% is 0.889. $5000 multiplied by 0.889 is $4445, which is the present value of $5000 at a discount rate of 4%.

	Discount rate (*r*)									
Year (*n*)	1%	2%	3%	4%	5%	6%	7%	8%	9%	10%
1	0.990	0.980	0.971	0.962	0.952	0.943	0.935	0.926	0.917	0.909
2	0.980	0.961	0.943	0.925	0.907	0.890	0.873	0.857	0.842	0.826
3	0.971	0.942	0.915	0.889	0.864	0.840	0.816	0.794	0.772	0.751
4	0.961	0.924	0.888	0.855	0.823	0.792	0.763	0.735	0.708	0.683
5	0.951	0.906	0.863	0.822	0.784	0.747	0.713	0.681	0.650	0.621
6	0.942	0.888	0.837	0.790	0.746	0.705	0.666	0.630	0.596	0.564
7	0.933	0.871	0.813	0.760	0.711	0.665	0.623	0.583	0.547	0.513
8	0.923	0.853	0.789	0.731	0.677	0.627	0.582	0.540	0.502	0.467
9	0.914	0.837	0.766	0.703	0.645	0.592	0.544	0.500	0.460	0.424
10	0.905	0.820	0.744	0.676	0.614	0.558	0.508	0.463	0.422	0.386
11	0.896	0.804	0.722	0.650	0.585	0.527	0.475	0.429	0.388	0.350
12	0.887	0.788	0.701	0.625	0.557	0.497	0.444	0.397	0.356	0.319
13	0.879	0.773	0.681	0.601	0.530	0.469	0.415	0.368	0.326	0.290
14	0.870	0.758	0.661	0.577	0.505	0.442	0.388	0.340	0.299	0.263
15	0.861	0.743	0.642	0.555	0.481	0.417	0.362	0.315	0.275	0.239

	Discount rate (*r*)									
Year (*n*)	11%	12%	13%	14%	15%	16%	17%	18%	19%	20%
1	0.901	0.893	0.885	0.877	0.870	0.862	0.855	0.847	0.840	0.833
2	0.812	0.797	0.783	0.769	0.756	0.743	0.731	0.718	0.706	0.694
3	0.731	0.712	0.693	0.675	0.658	0.641	0.624	0.609	0.593	0.597
4	0.659	0.636	0.613	0.592	0.572	0.552	0.534	0.516	0.499	0.482
5	0.593	0.567	0.543	0.519	0.497	0.476	0.456	0.437	0.419	0.402
6	0.535	0.507	0.480	0.456	0.432	0.410	0.390	0.370	0.352	0.335
7	0.482	0.452	0.425	0.400	0.376	0.354	0.333	0.314	0.296	0.279
8	0.434	0.404	0.376	0.351	0.327	0.305	0.285	0.266	0.249	0.233
9	0.391	0.361	0.333	0.308	0.284	0.263	0.243	0.225	0.209	0.194
10	0.352	0.322	0.295	0.270	0.247	0.227	0.208	0.191	0.176	0.162
11	0.317	0.287	0.261	0.237	0.215	0.195	0.178	0.162	0.148	0.135
12	0.286	0.257	0.231	0.208	0.187	0.168	0.152	0.137	0.124	0.112
13	0.258	0.229	0.204	0.182	0.163	0.145	0.130	0.116	0.104	0.093
14	0.232	0.205	0.181	0.160	0.141	0.125	0.111	0.099	0.088	0.078
15	0.209	0.183	0.160	0.140	0.123	0.108	0.095	0.084	0.074	0.065

Table 2 Binomial probabilities and cumulative binomial probabilities

Use this table to solve problems involving a series of n trials each of which can result in 'success' or 'failure'. Begin by finding the section of the table for the appropriate values of n (the number of trials) and p (the probability of success in any one trial). You can then use the table in three ways:

1. To find the probability that there are exactly x 'successes' in n trials look for the entry in the $P(x)$ column and the row for x.
2. To find the probability that there are x or fewer 'successes' in n trials look for the entry in the $P(X \leqslant x)$ column and the row for x.
3. To find the probability that there are more than x 'successes' in n trials, $P(X > x)$, look for the entry in the $P(X \leqslant x)$ column and the row for x. Subtract the figure you find from one. The result, $1 - P(X \leqslant x)$ is $P(X > x)$.

Example

The probability of success in a trial is 0.3 and there are 5 trials. The probability that there are exactly 2 successes, $P(2)$, is 0.309. The probability that there are two or fewer successes, $P(X \leqslant 2)$ is 0.837. The probability that there are more than two successes, $P(X > 2)$, is $1 - 0.837, 0.163$.

FOR 5 TRIALS ($n = 5$)

	$p = 0.1$		$p = 0.2$		$p = 0.3$		$p = 0.4$		$p = 0.5$	
	$P(x)$	$P(X \leqslant x)$	$P(x)$	$P(X \leqslant x)$	$P(x)$	$P(X \leqslant x)$	$P(x)$	$P(X \leqslant x)$	$P(x)$	$P(X \leqslant x)$
$x{:}0$	0.590	0.590	0.328	0.328	0.168	0.168	0.078	0.078	0.031	0.031
$x{:}1$	0.328	0.919	0.410	0.737	0.360	0.528	0.259	0.337	0.156	0.187
$x{:}2$	0.073	0.991	0.205	0.942	0.309	0.837	0.346	0.683	0.313	0.500
$x{:}3$	0.008	1.000	0.051	0.993	0.132	0.969	0.230	0.913	0.313	0.813
$x{:}4$	0.000	1.000	0.006	1.000	0.028	0.998	0.077	0.990	0.156	0.969
$x{:}5$	0.000	1.000	0.000	1.000	0.002	1.000	0.010	1.000	0.031	1.000

FOR 10 TRIALS ($n = 10$)

	$p = 0.1$		$p = 0.2$		$p = 0.3$		$p = 0.4$		$p = 0.5$	
	$P(x)$	$P(X \leqslant x)$	$P(x)$	$P(X \leqslant x)$	$P(x)$	$P(X \leqslant x)$	$P(x)$	$P(X \leqslant x)$	$P(x)$	$P(X \leqslant x)$
$x{:}\ 0$	0.349	0.349	0.107	0.107	0.028	0.028	0.006	0.006	0.001	0.001
$x{:}\ 1$	0.387	0.736	0.268	0.376	0.121	0.149	0.040	0.046	0.010	0.011
$x{:}\ 2$	0.194	0.930	0.302	0.678	0.233	0.383	0.121	0.167	0.044	0.055
$x{:}\ 3$	0.057	0.987	0.201	0.879	0.267	0.650	0.215	0.382	0.117	0.172
$x{:}\ 4$	0.011	0.998	0.088	0.967	0.200	0.850	0.251	0.633	0.205	0.377
$x{:}\ 5$	0.001	1.000	0.026	0.994	0.103	0.953	0.201	0.834	0.246	0.623
$x{:}\ 6$	0.000	1.000	0.006	0.999	0.037	0.989	0.111	0.945	0.205	0.828
$x{:}\ 7$	0.000	1.000	0.001	1.000	0.009	0.998	0.042	0.988	0.117	0.945
$x{:}\ 8$	0.000	1.000	0.000	1.000	0.001	1.000	0.011	0.998	0.044	0.989
$x{:}\ 9$	0.000	1.000	0.000	1.000	0.000	1.000	0.002	1.000	0.010	0.999
$x{:}10$	0.000	1.000	0.000	1.000	0.000	1.000	0.000	1.000	0.001	1.000

Table 3 Poisson probabilities and cumulative Poisson probabilities

Use this table to solve problems involving the number of incidents, *x*, that occurs during a period of time or over an area. Begin by finding the section of the table for the mean number of incidents per unit of time or space, μ. You can then use the table in three ways:

1. To find the probability that exactly *x* incidents occur look for the entry in the *P(x)* column and the row for *x*.
2. To find the probability that there are *x* or fewer incidents look for the entry in the $P(X \leqslant x)$ column and the row for *x*.
3. To find the probability that there are more than *x* incidents, $P(X > x)$, look for the entry in the $P(X \leqslant x)$ column and the row for *x*. Subtract the figure you find from one. The result, $1 - P(X \leqslant x)$ is $P(X > x)$.

Example

The mean number of incidents is 4. The probability that there are exactly 2 incidents, P(2), is 0.147. The probability that there are two or fewer incidents, $P(X \leqslant 2)$ is 0.238. The probability that there are more than two successes, $P(X > 2)$, is $1 - 0.238, 0.762$.

	$\mu = 1.0$		$\mu = 2.0$		$\mu = 3.0$		$\mu = 4.0$		$\mu = 5.0$	
	P(x)	P(X ⩽ x)	P(x)	P(X ⩽ x)	P(x)	P(X ⩽ x)	P(x)	P(X ⩽ x)	P(x)	P(X ⩽ x)
x: 0	0.368	0.368	0.135	0.135	0.050	0.050	0.018	0.018	0.007	0.007
x: 1	0.368	0.736	0.271	0.406	0.149	0.199	0.073	0.092	0.034	0.040
x: 2	0.184	0.920	0.271	0.677	0.224	0.423	0.147	0.238	0.084	0.125
x: 3	0.061	0.981	0.180	0.857	0.224	0.647	0.195	0.433	0.140	0.265
x: 4	0.015	0.996	0.090	0.947	0.168	0.815	0.195	0.629	0.175	0.440
x: 5	0.003	0.999	0.036	0.983	0.101	0.916	0.156	0.785	0.175	0.616
x: 6	0.001	1.000	0.012	0.995	0.050	0.966	0.104	0.889	0.146	0.762
x: 7	0.000	1.000	0.003	0.999	0.022	0.988	0.060	0.949	0.104	0.867
x: 8	0.000	1.000	0.001	1.000	0.008	0.996	0.030	0.979	0.065	0.932
x: 9	0.000	1.000	0.000	1.000	0.003	0.999	0.013	0.992	0.036	0.968
x: 10	0.000	1.000	0.000	1.000	0.001	1.000	0.005	0.997	0.018	0.986
x: 11	0.000	1.000	0.000	1.000	0.000	1.000	0.002	0.999	0.008	0.995
x: 12	0.000	1.000	0.000	1.000	0.000	1.000	0.001	1.000	0.003	0.998
x: 13	0.000	1.000	0.000	1.000	0.000	1.000	0.000	1.000	0.001	0.999
x: 14	0.000	1.000	0.000	1.000	0.000	1.000	0.000	1.000	0.000	1.000
x: 15	0.000	1.000	0.000	1.000	0.000	1.000	0.000	1.000	0.000	1.000

Table 4 Random numbers

Use this table by starting from some point in the table (you could choose this by putting your finger down somewhere on the table without looking at the table). Use the random numbers in strict sequence from that point either down from it, up from it, to the right of it or to the left of it.

Example

Suppose we start from the seventh entry in the tenth column and decide to go down from that point. The sequence of numbers we would use are: 37 58 52 01 etc.

1	2	3	4	5	6	7	8	9	10	11	12	13	14	15
42	25	33	31	02	09	45	22	47	43	82	42	00	93	54
45	19	83	72	21	31	13	13	98	52	69	96	85	66	10
77	97	33	52	62	74	22	88	53	91	52	34	54	82	81
38	03	38	43	40	71	31	13	90	95	55	16	44	75	60
98	28	37	30	52	41	79	75	95	25	31	97	72	82	23
59	01	27	34	52	61	33	75	64	88	87	79	40	94	91
14	26	71	56	76	51	00	42	95	37	25	73	74	42	18
92	16	76	70	23	98	06	69	76	58	89	43	58	29	23
35	34	09	18	17	34	11	32	78	52	07	05	39	98	25
84	22	97	30	02	34	93	15	59	01	97	43	10	90	66
07	72	31	79	66	18	01	80	90	84	93	85	61	46	17
50	37	30	61	42	01	53	02	93	82	59	25	90	81	51
30	39	71	29	65	19	95	34	61	91	00	92	35	55	92
36	54	68	01	91	97	95	89	82	75	68	95	40	58	37
15	75	66	52	73	69	32	100	25	89	44	56	60	42	58
28	30	77	44	16	16	90	76	32	38	86	55	81	00	04
03	41	28	95	96	19	71	56	86	99	59	10	61	31	81
20	83	85	13	43	03	09	41	69	31	08	66	01	78	23
06	51	04	97	18	68	73	25	76	94	57	04	08	53	13
39	77	12	45	53	48	52	69	72	05	02	77	88	37	16
81	35	60	28	48	21	75	17	50	88	96	78	01	65	01
72	50	45	71	90	99	67	01	12	37	05	43	44	24	77
83	15	08	28	66	16	72	13	10	68	26	61	59	06	92
66	46	23	38	37	08	71	76	22	79	79	11	68	25	08
09	02	24	39	40	77	71	97	70	50	13	98	32	46	02
94	82	36	40	08	12	08	98	41	99	87	54	54	71	73
64	95	39	07	49	32	12	51	84	75	96	44	64	55	94
76	39	06	67	66	36	61	66	46	95	08	26	04	36	78
54	15	15	22	37	25	63	62	61	79	33	52	98	45	15
61	45	16	62	79	84	18	12	25	90	98	12	05	93	91
21	74	66	52	01	96	26	29	04	58	14	97	89	06	75
13	12	32	82	23	99	19	57	73	94	69	31	03	89	00
60	19	52	31	55	90	92	27	61	75	24	26	10	22	96
08	78	10	09	73	45	00	51	13	00	74	76	35	23	50
01	01	19	39	72	27	49	78	62	14	72	45	39	66	18
09	09	58	93	31	33	33	85	79	93	02	30	27	39	51
45	67	71	94	64	80	24	35	39	41	37	48	05	48	54
44	03	31	59	42	84	09	23	09	60	89	38	69	98	60
47	19	04	04	43	65	21	36	19	88	35	54	04	29	08
48	36	42	24	17	96	09	03	77	43	74	78	41	35	39
73	60	54	56	80	79	97	78	62	32	16	00	32	40	54
69	32	50	14	43	38	04	66	17	53	26	59	77	52	77
38	81	23	56	78	59	43	98	08	87	30	54	87	66	85
09	36	85	37	60	80	54	74	16	98	67	21	03	22	88
60	67	85	05	80	22	59	89	12	43	46	04	53	52	12
55	11	45	15	35	41	25	45	40	12	73	04	65	95	77
86	23	12	64	73	37	37	43	51	19	12	46	30	84	03
02	61	75	96	96	84	06	92	14	46	83	77	24	32	76
78	40	58	13	07	36	48	38	81	21	71	39	23	88	10
30	10	85	02	44	44	48	91	20	34	59	79	36	03	98

Table 5 Cumulative probabilities for the Standard Normal Distribution

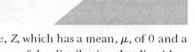

This table describes the pattern of variation of the Standard Normal Variable, Z, which has a mean, μ, of 0 and a standard deviation, σ, of 1. You can use this table to find proportions of the area of the distribution that lie either to the right or to the left of a particular value of Z, z.

To find the proportion of the area to the right of z, which represents the probability that Z is greater than z, $P(Z > z)$, find the row for the value of z to the first decimal place and then look across the columns until you reach the column associated with the second figure after the decimal place.

Example 1

The probability that Z is greater than -1.62 is in the row for -1.6 and in the column labelled 0.02. $P(Z > -1.62) = 0.9474$.

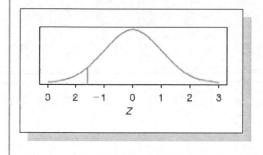

Example 3

To obtain the probability that Z is less than -0.85, first find the figure in the row for -0.8 and in the column labelled 0.05. This is $P(Z > -0.85)$, 0.8023. $P(Z < -0.85) = 1 - 0.8023 = 0.1977$.

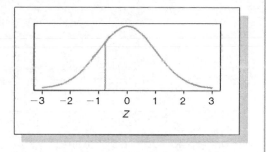

Example 2

The probability that Z is greater than 0.57 is in the row for 0.5 in the column labelled 0.07. $P(Z > 0.57) = 0.2843$.

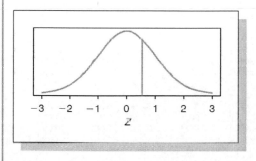

Example 4

To obtain the probability that Z is less than 2.10, first find the figure in the row for 2.1 and in the column labelled 0.00. This is $P(Z > 2.1)$, 0.0179. $P(Z < 2.1) = 1 - 0.0179 = 0.9821$.

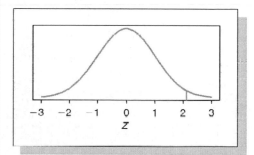

z	0.00	0.01	0.02	0.03	0.04	0.05	0.06	0.07	0.08	0.09
−2.9	0.9981	0.9982	0.9982	0.9983	0.9984	0.9984	0.9985	0.9985	0.9986	0.9986
−2.8	0.9974	0.9975	0.9976	0.9977	0.9977	0.9978	0.9979	0.9979	0.9980	0.9981
−2.7	0.9965	0.9966	0.9967	0.9968	0.9969	0.9970	0.9971	0.9972	0.9973	0.9974
−2.6	0.9953	0.9955	0.9956	0.9957	0.9959	0.9960	0.9961	0.9962	0.9963	0.9964
−2.5	0.9938	0.9940	0.9941	0.9943	0.9945	0.9946	0.9948	0.9949	0.9951	0.9952
−2.4	0.9918	0.9920	0.9922	0.9925	0.9927	0.9929	0.9931	0.9932	0.9934	0.9936
−2.3	0.9893	0.9896	0.9898	0.9901	0.9904	0.9906	0.9909	0.9911	0.9913	0.9916
−2.2	0.9861	0.9864	0.9868	0.9871	0.9875	0.9878	0.9881	0.9884	0.9887	0.9890
−2.1	0.9821	0.9826	0.9830	0.9834	0.9838	0.9842	0.9846	0.9850	0.9854	0.9857
−2.0	0.9772	0.9778	0.9783	0.9788	0.9793	0.9798	0.9803	0.9808	0.9812	0.9817
−1.9	0.9713	0.9719	0.9726	0.9732	0.9738	0.9744	0.9750	0.9756	0.9761	0.9767
−1.8	0.9641	0.9649	0.9656	0.9664	0.9671	0.9678	0.9686	0.9693	0.9699	0.9706
−1.7	0.9554	0.9564	0.9573	0.9582	0.9591	0.9599	0.9608	0.9616	0.9625	0.9633
−1.6	0.9452	0.9463	0.9474	0.9484	0.9495	0.9505	0.9515	0.9525	0.9535	0.9545
−1.5	0.9332	0.9345	0.9357	0.9370	0.9382	0.9394	0.9406	0.9418	0.9429	0.9441
−1.4	0.9192	0.9207	0.9222	0.9236	0.9251	0.9265	0.9279	0.9292	0.9306	0.9319
−1.3	0.9032	0.9049	0.9066	0.9082	0.9099	0.9115	0.9131	0.9147	0.9162	0.9177
−1.2	0.8849	0.8869	0.8888	0.8907	0.8925	0.8944	0.8962	0.8980	0.8997	0.9015
−1.1	0.8643	0.8665	0.8686	0.8708	0.8729	0.8749	0.8770	0.8790	0.8810	0.8830
−1.0	0.8413	0.8438	0.8461	0.8485	0.8508	0.8531	0.8554	0.8577	0.8599	0.8621
−0.9	0.8159	0.8186	0.8212	0.8238	0.8264	0.8289	0.8315	0.8340	0.8365	0.8389
−0.8	0.7881	0.7910	0.7939	0.7967	0.7995	0.8023	0.8051	0.8078	0.8106	0.8133
−0.7	0.7580	0.7611	0.7642	0.7673	0.7703	0.7734	0.7764	0.7794	0.7823	0.7852
−0.6	0.7257	0.7291	0.7324	0.7357	0.7389	0.7422	0.7454	0.7486	0.7517	0.7549
−0.5	0.6915	0.6950	0.6985	0.7019	0.7054	0.7088	0.7123	0.7157	0.7190	0.7224
−0.4	0.6554	0.6591	0.6628	0.6664	0.6700	0.6736	0.6772	0.6808	0.6844	0.6879
−0.3	0.6179	0.6217	0.6255	0.6293	0.6331	0.6368	0.6406	0.6443	0.6480	0.6517
−0.2	0.5793	0.5832	0.5871	0.5910	0.5948	0.5987	0.6026	0.6064	0.6103	0.6141
−0.1	0.5398	0.5438	0.5478	0.5517	0.5557	0.5596	0.5636	0.5675	0.5714	0.5753
−0.0	0.5000	0.5040	0.5080	0.5120	0.5160	0.5199	0.5239	0.5279	0.5319	0.5359
0.0	0.5000	0.4960	0.4920	0.4880	0.4840	0.4801	0.4761	0.4721	0.4681	0.4641
0.1	0.4602	0.4562	0.4522	0.4483	0.4443	0.4404	0.4364	0.4325	0.4286	0.4247
0.2	0.4207	0.4168	0.4129	0.4090	0.4052	0.4013	0.3974	0.3936	0.3897	0.3859
0.3	0.3821	0.3783	0.3745	0.3707	0.3669	0.3632	0.3594	0.3557	0.3520	0.3483
0.4	0.3446	0.3409	0.3372	0.3336	0.3300	0.3264	0.3228	0.3192	0.3156	0.3121
0.5	0.3085	0.3050	0.3015	0.2981	0.2946	0.2912	0.2877	0.2843	0.2810	0.2776
0.6	0.2743	0.2709	0.2676	0.2643	0.2611	0.2578	0.2546	0.2514	0.2483	0.2451
0.7	0.2420	0.2389	0.2358	0.2327	0.2297	0.2266	0.2236	0.2206	0.2177	0.2148
0.8	0.2119	0.2090	0.2061	0.2033	0.2005	0.1977	0.1949	0.1922	0.1894	0.1867
0.9	0.1841	0.1814	0.1788	0.1762	0.1736	0.1711	0.1685	0.1660	0.1635	0.1611
1.0	0.1587	0.1562	0.1539	0.1515	0.1492	0.1469	0.1446	0.1423	0.1401	0.1379
1.1	0.1357	0.1335	0.1314	0.1292	0.1271	0.1251	0.1230	0.1210	0.1190	0.1170
1.2	0.1151	0.1131	0.1112	0.1093	0.1075	0.1056	0.1038	0.1020	0.1003	0.0985
1.3	0.0968	0.0951	0.0934	0.0918	0.0901	0.0885	0.0869	0.0853	0.0838	0.0823
1.4	0.0808	0.0793	0.0778	0.0764	0.0749	0.0735	0.0721	0.0708	0.0694	0.0681
1.5	0.0668	0.0655	0.0643	0.0630	0.0618	0.0606	0.0594	0.0582	0.0571	0.0559
1.6	0.0548	0.0537	0.0526	0.0516	0.0505	0.0495	0.0485	0.0475	0.0465	0.0455
1.7	0.0446	0.0436	0.0427	0.0418	0.0409	0.0401	0.0392	0.0384	0.0375	0.0367
1.8	0.0359	0.0351	0.0344	0.0336	0.0329	0.0322	0.0314	0.0307	0.0301	0.0294
1.9	0.0287	0.0281	0.0274	0.0268	0.0262	0.0256	0.0250	0.0244	0.0239	0.0233
2.0	0.0228	0.0222	0.0217	0.0212	0.0207	0.0202	0.0197	0.0192	0.0188	0.0183
2.1	0.0179	0.0174	0.0170	0.0166	0.0162	0.0158	0.0154	0.0150	0.0146	0.0143
2.2	0.0139	0.0136	0.0132	0.0129	0.0125	0.0122	0.0119	0.0116	0.0113	0.0110
2.3	0.0107	0.0104	0.0102	0.0099	0.0096	0.0094	0.0091	0.0089	0.0087	0.0084
2.4	0.0082	0.0080	0.0078	0.0075	0.0073	0.0071	0.0069	0.0068	0.0066	0.0064
2.5	0.0062	0.0060	0.0059	0.0057	0.0055	0.0054	0.0052	0.0051	0.0049	0.0048
2.6	0.0047	0.0045	0.0044	0.0043	0.0041	0.0040	0.0039	0.0038	0.0037	0.0036
2.7	0.0035	0.0034	0.0033	0.0032	0.0031	0.0030	0.0029	0.0028	0.0027	0.0026
2.8	0.0026	0.0025	0.0024	0.0023	0.0023	0.0022	0.0021	0.0021	0.0020	0.0019
2.9	0.0019	0.0018	0.0018	0.0017	0.0016	0.0016	0.0015	0.0015	0.0014	0.0014

Table 6 Selected points of the *t* distribution

This table provides values of the *t* distribution, with different numbers of degrees of freedom, which cut off certain tail areas to the right of the distribution, $t_{\alpha, \nu}$. To use it you will need to know the number of degrees of freedom, ν, and the size of the tail area, α. Find the row for the number of degrees of freedom and then look to the right along the row until you come to the figure in the column for the appropriate tail area.

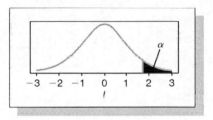

Example

The value in the *t* distribution with 7 degrees of freedom that cuts off a tail area of 0.05, $t_{0.05,7}$ is in the row for 7 degrees of freedom and the column headed 0.05, 1.895.

ν	0.10	0.05	0.025	0.01	0.005
1	3.078	6.314	12.706	31.821	63.657
2	1.886	2.920	4.303	6.965	9.925
3	1.638	2.353	3.182	4.541	5.841
4	1.533	2.132	2.776	3.747	4.604
5	1.476	2.015	2.571	3.365	4.032
6	1.440	1.943	2.447	3.143	3.707
7	1.415	1.895	2.365	2.998	3.499
8	1.397	1.860	2.306	2.896	3.355
9	1.383	1.833	2.262	2.821	3.250
10	1.372	1.812	2.228	2.764	3.169
11	1.363	1.796	2.201	2.718	3.106
12	1.356	1.782	2.179	2.681	3.055
13	1.350	1.771	2.160	2.650	3.012
14	1.345	1.761	2.145	2.624	2.977
15	1.341	1.753	2.131	2.602	2.947
16	1.337	1.746	2.120	2.583	2.921
17	1.333	1.740	2.110	2.567	2.898
18	1.330	1.734	2.101	2.552	2.878
19	1.328	1.729	2.093	2.539	2.861
20	1.325	1.725	2.086	2.528	2.845
21	1.323	1.721	2.080	2.518	2.831
22	1.321	1.717	2.074	2.508	2.819
23	1.319	1.714	2.069	2.500	2.807
24	1.318	1.711	2.064	2.492	2.797
25	1.316	1.708	2.060	2.485	2.787
26	1.315	1.706	2.056	2.479	2.779
27	1.314	1.703	2.052	2.473	2.771
28	1.313	1.701	2.048	2.467	2.763
29	1.311	1.699	2.045	2.462	2.756
30	1.310	1.697	2.042	2.457	2.750
50	1.299	1.676	2.009	2.403	2.678
100	1.290	1.660	1.984	2.364	2.626
∞	1.282	1.645	1.960	2.326	2.576

Note that as the number of degrees of freedom increases, the *t* distribution becomes more like the Standard Normal Distribution. Look at the bottom row of this table and you will see a row of *t* values that are from the *t* distribution that has an infinite (∞) number of degrees of freedom. This 'extreme' *t* distribution is the Standard Normal Distribution, and the figures along the bottom row here can also be found in Table 5, for example, look up the *z* value 1.96 in Table 5 and you will see the probability that *Z* is more than 1.96 is 0.025. In this Table 1.96 is listed as the value of *t* with infinite degrees of freedom that cuts off a tail area of 0.025.

Table 7 Selected points of the *F* distribution

This table provides values of the *F* distribution, with different numbers of degrees of freedom for the numerator and denominator, which cut off tail areas of 0.05 and 0.01 to the right of the distribution, $F_{\nu 1, \nu 2, \alpha}$. To use it you will need to know the degrees of freedom of the numerator, ν_1, the degrees of freedom of the denominator, ν_2, and the size of the tail area, α. Find the column for the degrees of freedom for the numerator and the row for the degrees of freedom for the denominator. The upper figure in the cell you have located is the *F* value that cuts off a tail area of 0.05, the lower figure, in italics, is the *F* value that cuts off a tail area of 0.01.

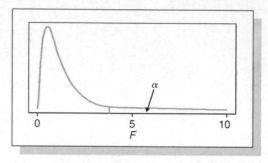

Example

The value in the *F* distribution with 3 numerator degrees of freedom and 7 denominator degrees of freedom that cuts off a tail area of 0.05, $F_{3,7,0.05}$ is the upper figure in the column for 3 degrees of freedom and the row for 7 degrees of freedom, 4.35. The figure below it, 8.45, is $F_{3,7,0.01}$.

ν_2	ν_1 1	2	3	4	5
1	161.45	199.50	215.71	224.58	230.16
	4050.00	*5000.00*	*5040.00*	*5620.00*	*5760.00*
2	18.51	19.00	19.16	19.25	19.30
	98.50	*99.00*	*99.17*	*99.25*	*99.30*
3	10.13	9.55	9.28	9.12	9.01
	34.12	*30.82*	*29.46*	*28.71*	*28.24*
4	7.71	6.94	6.59	6.39	6.26
	21.20	*18.00*	*16.69*	*15.98*	*15.52*
5	6.61	5.79	5.41	5.19	5.05
	16.26	*13.27*	*12.06*	*11.39*	*10.97*
6	5.99	5.14	4.76	4.53	4.39
	13.75	*10.92*	*9.78*	*9.15*	*8.75*
7	5.59	4.74	4.35	4.12	3.97
	12.25	*9.55*	*8.45*	*7.85*	*7.46*
8	5.32	4.46	4.07	3.84	3.69
	11.26	*8.65*	*7.59*	*7.01*	*6.63*
9	5.12	4.26	3.86	3.63	3.48
	10.56	*8.02*	*6.99*	*6.42*	*6.06*
10	4.96	4.10	3.71	3.48	3.33
	10.04	*7.56*	*6.55*	*5.99*	*5.64*
11	4.84	3.98	3.59	3.36	3.20
	9.65	*7.21*	*6.22*	*5.95*	*5.32*
12	4.75	3.89	3.49	3.26	3.11
	9.33	*6.93*	*5.95*	*5.41*	*5.06*
13	4.67	3.81	3.41	3.18	3.03
	9.07	*6.70*	*5.74*	*5.21*	*4.86*
14	4.60	3.74	3.34	3.11	2.96
	8.86	*6.51*	*5.56*	*5.04*	*4.70*
15	4.54	3.68	3.29	3.06	2.90
	8.68	*6.36*	*5.42*	*4.89*	*4.56*

Table 8 Selected points of the chi-square distribution

This table provides values of the χ^2 distribution, with different numbers of degrees of freedom, which cut off certain tail areas to the right of the distribution, $\chi^2_{\alpha,\nu}$. To use it you will need to know the number of degrees of freedom, ν, and the size of the tail area, α. Find the row for the number of degrees of freedom and then look to the right along the row until you come to the figure in the column for the appropriate tail area.

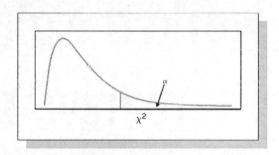

Example

The value in the χ^2 distribution with 3 degrees of freedom that cuts off a tail area of 0.05, $\chi^2_{0.05,3}$, is in the row for 3 degrees of freedom and the column headed 0.05, 7.815.

ν	0.10	0.05	0.01
1	2.706	3.841	6.635
2	4.605	5.991	9.210
3	6.251	7.815	11.345
4	7.779	9.488	13.277
5	9.236	11.070	15.086
6	10.645	12.592	16.812
7	12.017	14.067	18.475
8	13.362	15.507	20.090
9	14.684	16.919	21.666
10	15.987	18.307	23.209

Answers and selected worked solutions to review questions

The solutions to Key review questions are given in full, all the numerical and some of the verbal answers to the rest are provided. Where the full solution is not given, you will find the chapter Example that most closely resembles the question in square brackets to the right of the question number.

All numerical answers are either precise or accurate to at least 3 decimal places unless stated otherwise.

Chapter 1

1.1
    (i) $4 + 3 + 8 * 2 - 5 = 4 + 3 + 16 - 5$
$$= 23 - 5 = 18 \qquad \text{answer (g)}$$

    (ii) $15/3 * 2 - 4 + 6 = 5 * 2 - 4 + 6$
$$= 10 - 4 + 6$$
$$= 6 + 6 = 12 \qquad \text{answer (h)}$$

    (iii) $3 * 8/6 + 1 - 5 = 24/6 + 1 - 5$
$$= 4 + 1 - 5 = 5 - 5 = 0 \qquad \text{answer (f)}$$

    (iv) $(4 + 3 + 8) * 2 - 10 = 15 * 2 - 10$
$$= 30 - 10 = 20 \qquad \text{answer (e)}$$

(v) $(2 * 8) + (3 - 5) = 16 + (-2)$
$= 16 - 2 = 14$ answer (a)

(vi) $(((5 - 2) + 7) * 4) = ((3 + 7) * 4)$
$= (10 * 4) = 40$ answer (j)

(vii) $(6 - 2)^2 * 3 = 4^2 * 3 = 16 * 3 = 48$ answer (d)

(viii) $\sqrt{64} = 8$ or -8 answer (b)

(ix) $\sqrt{36}/4 = 6/4 = 1.5$
or $\sqrt{36}/4 = -6/4 = -1.5$ answer (c)

(x) $\sqrt{(36/4)} - \sqrt{9} = 3$ or -3 answer (i)

1.2   (i) (b), (ii) (c), (iii) (h), (iv) (f), (v) (g),
(vi) (a), (vii) (e), (viii) (d)

1.3   (i) 40% of $200 = 0.4 * 200 = 80$ answer (e)

(ii) $\dfrac{2}{3} * \dfrac{3}{5} = \dfrac{2*3}{3*5} = \dfrac{6}{15} = \dfrac{2}{5}$ answer (g)

(iii) 120% of $100 = 1.2 * 100 = 120$ answer (a)

(iv) $\dfrac{5}{4} \div \dfrac{3}{4} = \dfrac{5}{4} * \dfrac{4}{3} = \dfrac{5*4}{4*3} = \dfrac{20}{12} = \dfrac{5}{3}$ answer (c)

(v) $\dfrac{1}{5} + \dfrac{1}{4} = \dfrac{4+5}{20} = \dfrac{9}{20}$ answer (f)

(vi) $\dfrac{1}{3} - \dfrac{1}{5} = \dfrac{5-3}{15} = \dfrac{2}{15}$ answer (b)

(vii) 20% of $40\% = 0.2 * 0.4 = 0.08$ or 8% answer (d)

1.4   (a) (i) Italy 1,440,000   USA 543,400
Australia 197,000   [1.19]
(ii) Italy 1,400,000   USA 540,000
Australia 200,000   [1.19]

(b) Italy 0.209
USA 0.079
Australia 0.029   [1.20]

1.5   (a) $17.30 - 1.15 - 0.30 - 2.00 = 17.30 - 3.45$
$= 13.45$ or 1.45pm

(b) $17.30 + 11.30 + 1.00 + 9.00 = 17.30 + 21.30$
$= 15.00$ or 3pm the next day

1.6   Alexander $0.4 * 57 + 0.6 * 47 = 51\%$ Pass
Bukhtar $0.4 * 68 + 0.6 * 38 = 50\%$ Pass
Ciani $0.4 * 43 + 0.6 * 36 = 38.8\%$ Fail (less than 40%)
Dalkiro $0.4 * 65 + 0.6 * 33 = 45.8\%$ Fail (exam less than 35%)

          Elchin $0.4 * 51 + 0.6 * 39 = 43.8\%$ Pass

          Franklin $0.4 * 40 + 0.6 * 37 = 38.2\%$ Fail (less

                                                    than 40%)

1.7   (a) $5 + 8 + 3 + 6 + 4 = 26$

        (b) $8 + 3 + 6 = 17$ the number of sales operatives

        (c) $5 * 230 + 8 * 310 + 3 * 300 + 6 * 280 + 4 * 200$

              $= 1150 + 2480 + 900 + 1680 + 800$

              $= £7010$

1.8   (a)   1225   [1.12]

        (b)   33 m long by 33 m wide   [1.15]

1.9   324   [1.16]

1.10   Net cost of supermarket deal $= £12,500 - £1700 = £10,800$

       Dealer price $= £14,995$

       Discount $= £14,995 * 0.08 = £1199.60$

       Dealer price less discount

          $= £14,995.00 - £1199.60$

          $= £13,795.40$

       less net cost of supermarket deal

          $= £13,795.40 - £10,800$

          $= £2995.40$

       Trade-in of at least £2995.40 required

1.11   425   [1.21]

1.12   (a)   £12,155   [1.21]

       (b)   £17,875   [1.21]

1.13   £56.77 to the nearest penny   [1.21]

1.14   £297.85 to the nearest penny   [1.21]

1.15   £1293.81 to the nearest penny   [1.21]

1.16   £1974   [1.16]

1.17   (a)   £2520   [1.21]

       (b)   £1890   [1.21]

1.18   (a)   £559.32   [1.21]

       (b)   £27.97 to the nearest penny   [1.21]

1.19   0.625 litres of gin, 0.5 litres of red wine and 1 litre of lemonade

1.20

Operator	% over an hour	Label	
CC	7.391	Poor	
HH	15.470	Very poor	
RAP	4.980	None	
RR	12.857	Poor	
WR	13.268	Poor	[1.16]

1.21   34.456 mpg   [1.9, 1.11]

Chapter 2

2.1   (a) Budget $= 35000 + 500x$ where x is the number of corporate clients

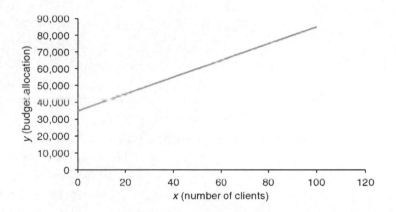

(b)   (i) Budget for A $= 35000 + 500 * 43$
$$= 35000 + 21500 = £56,500$$
(ii) Budget for B $= 35000 + 500 * 29$
$$= 35000 + 14500 = £49,500$$
(iii) Budget for C $= 35000 + 500 * 66$
$$= 35000 + 33000 = £68,000$$

(c) New model: Budget $= 20000 + 800x$
New budget for A $= 20000 + 800 * 43$
$$= 20000 + 34400 = £54,400$$
New budget for B $= 20000 + 800 * 29$
$$= 20000 + 23200 = £43,200$$
New budget for C $= 20000 + 800 * 66$
$$= 20000 + 52800 = £72,800$$
A down by £2100, B down by £6300, C up by £4800

2.2   First payment method cost: $8 * 32 = £256$
Second payment method cost: $20 + 0.08x$
where x is water used in m^3

Second method is economical
when $20 + 0.08x < 256$
Solve $20 + 0.08x = 256$
$$0.08x = 256 - 20 = 236$$
$$x = 236/0.08 = 2950$$

The second method is more economical if water used is less than $2950\,m^3$

2.3   (a) $x = 1$ $y = 2$ (b) $x = 2$ $y = 3$
        (c) $x = 5$ $y = -1$ (d) $x = 0.5$ $y = 4$
        (e) $x = 6$ $y = 5$ (f) $x = 0.1$ $y = 0.2$ [2.10]

2.4   Diesel is cheaper if more than 25,000 miles
        are travelled   [2.10]

2.5   TR = 90Q   TC = 319000 + 35Q
        (a) Break even when   TR = TC
                                  90Q = 319000 + 35Q
                          90Q $-$ 35Q = 319000
                                  55Q = 319000
                                    Q = 319000/55 = 5800 sets

        (b) Profit = TR $-$ TC
             At sales of 6000,
                    TR $-$ TC = (90 * 6000) $-$ (319000 + 35 * 6000)
                              = 540000 $-$ (319000 + 210000)
                              = 540000 $-$ 529000 = £11,000
             Margin of safety = (6000 $-$ 5800)/6000 * 100 = 3.333%

2.6   (a) 32,000 scooters
        (b) 40,000 scooters   [2.11]

2.7   (a) 800 days
        (b) 960 days   [2.11]

2.8   (a) 1400 hot dogs
        (b) 1120 hot dogs   [2.11]

2.9   (a) 800,000 ovens
        (b) 960,000 ovens   [2.11]

2.10   Let x = 10-litre lots of Zombie produced
               y = 10-litre lots of Skyjack produced
               Maximize: $15x + 20y$
               Subject to: $3x + 5y \leqslant 1500$ (vodka)
                                $6x + 3y \leqslant 1500$ (vermouth)
                                 $x + 2y \leqslant 400$ (ginger)

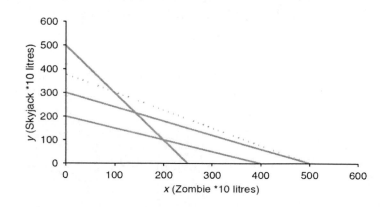

Optimal solution

where: (1) $6x + 3y = 1500$ (vermouth)

and: (2) $x + 2y = 400$ (ginger)

(3) = (2) * 6 $6x + 12y = 2400$

(1) $6x + 3y = 1500$

(3) − (1) $9y = 900$

$y = 100$

Sub in (1) $6x + 3 * 100 = 1500$

$6x + 300 = 1500$

$6x = 1500 − 300 = 1200$

$x = 1200/6 = 200$

Make 200 lots of Zombie and 100 lots of Skyjack.

Profit = 200 * 15 + 100 * 20 = 3000 + 2000 = £5000

Vermouth and ginger are tight constraints, vodka is slack

2.11   110 litres of Smazka and 70 litres of Neftianikov.

Profit = £830   [2.13–2.22]

2.12   16,000 standard and no executive portions.

Revenue = £25,600   [2.13–2.22]

2.13   50 2-bedroom and 30 4-bedroom houses.

Profit = £2,250,000   [2.13–2.22]

2.14   (a) 60,000 bottles of Volossy and 60,000 bottles of
Sedina. Profit = £36,000

(b) Solidifier and licence are tight, colourant and
commitments slack   [2.13–2.22]

2.15   1500 Soap Dishes and no Houstons.

Profit = £24,000   [2.13–2.22]

2.16   (a) Buy 12 peak and 24 off-peak slots.
Audience = 264 m

(b) Yes. 60 off-peak and no peak slots.
Audience = 300 m   [2.13–2.22]

2.17   No pairs of Nelson and 200 pairs of Oldham.

Profit = £2400   [2.13–2.22]

2.18   (a)

	Standard	Luxury	
Selling price	80	145	
Less			
Direct materials		25	45
Cutting		10	15
Machining		20	50
Packing		15	15
		70	125
Profit		10	20

(b) Let x = packs of Standard produced
and y = packs of Luxury produced

Maximize: $10x + 20y$

Subject to: $0.25x + 0.375y \leqslant 375$ (cutting)

$2.5x + 6.25y \leqslant 5625$ (machining)

$1.25x + 1.25y \leqslant 1500$ (packing)

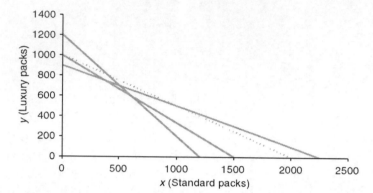

Optimal solution

where: (1) $0.25x + 0.375y = 375$ (cutting)

and: (2) $2.5x + 6.25y = 5625$ (machining)

(3) = (1) * 10 $2.5x + 3.75y = 3750$

(2) − (3) $2.5y = 1875$

$y = 1875/2.5 = 750$

Sub in (2) $2.5x + 6.25 * 7500 = 5625$

$2.5x + 4687.5 = 5625$

$2.5x = 5625 - 4687.5 = 937.5$

$x = 937.5/2.5 = 375$

Make 375 packs of Standard and 750 packs of Luxury

Profit = $10 * 375 + 20 * 750 = 3750 + 15000 = £18,750$

(c) Cutting and machining are tight, packing is slack

2.19   (a) 350 pairs of Cosmic and 225 pairs of Celestial.
Revenue = £55,475

(b) £10 per pair of Cosmic and £25 per pair of Celestial

(c) 200 pairs of Cosmic and 300 pairs of Celestial.
Profit = £9500

(d) 400 pairs of Celestial. Profit = £10,000,
£500 more.   [2.13–2.22]

2.20   Let x = kilograms of Seelni-swine bought, and y = kilograms
of Vita-sosiska bought

Minimize: $20x + 15y$

Subject to: $0.6x + 0.9y \geqslant 36$ (protein)

$0.4x + 0.1y \geqslant 10$ (vitamin)

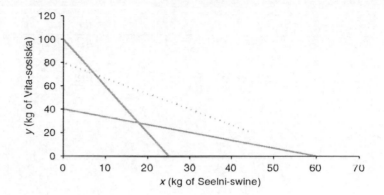

Optimal solution

where: (1) $0.6x + 0.9y = 36$ (protein)
and: (2) $0.4x + 0.1y = 10$ (vitamin)
                (3) = (2) * 9 $3.6x + 0.9y = 90$
                (1) $0.6x + 0.9y = 36$
                (3) − (1) $3x = 54$
                                  $x = 54/3 = 18$

Sub in (1) $0.6 * 18 + 0.9y = 36$
             $10.8 + 0.9y = 36$
             $0.9y = 36 - 10.8 = 25.2$
             $y = 25.2/0.9 = 28$

Buy 18 kg of Seelni-swine and 28 kg of Vita-sosiska
Cost = $20 * 18 + 15 * 28 = 360 + 420 = £780$

2.21   Buy 5 kg of Great Grit and 10 kg of A1 Aggregate.
        Cost = £12.50   [2.23]

Chapter 3

3.1   (i) $y = 3x = 3x^1$ $\dfrac{dy}{dx} = 3x^{1-1} = 3x^0 = 3$ answer (f)

        (ii) $\dfrac{dy}{dx} = 2 * 4x^{2-1} = 8x^1 = 8x$ answer (c)

        (iii) $\dfrac{dy}{dx} = 3 * 2x^{3-1} = 6x^2$ answer (g)

        (iv) $y = \dfrac{1}{x} = x^{-1}$ $\dfrac{dy}{dx} = -1 * x^{-1-1} = -x^{-2}$

                          $= \dfrac{-1}{x^2}$ answer (a)

(v) $y = \dfrac{x^4}{2} = \dfrac{1}{2}x^4$ $\dfrac{dy}{dx} = 4 * \dfrac{1}{2}x^{4-1} = 2x^3$ answer (b)

(vi) $\dfrac{dy}{dx} = 3 * 3x^{3-1} = 9x^2$ answer (j)

(vii) $\dfrac{dy}{dx} = 2x^{2-1} + 4x^{1-1} = 2x + 4x^0 = 2x + 4$ answer (d)

(viii) $y = \dfrac{5}{x^2} - x = 5x^{-2} - x$ $\dfrac{dy}{dx} = -2 * 5x^{-2-1} - x^{1-1}$

$$= -\dfrac{10}{x^3} - 1$$ answer (e)

(ix) $y = \dfrac{2}{3x} + 5x^2 = \dfrac{2}{3}x^{-1} + 5x^2$

$$\dfrac{dy}{dx} = -1 * \dfrac{2}{3}x^{-1-1} + 2 * 5x^{2-1}$$

$$= \dfrac{-2}{3x^2} + 10x$$ answer (h)

(x) $\dfrac{dy}{dx} = 4 * 4x^{4-1} + 3 * 3x^{3-1} = 16x^3 + 9x^2$ answer (i)

3.2   (a) $\dfrac{dy}{dx} = 4x - 280$ When $4x - 280 = 0$

$$4x = 280$$
$$x = 70$$

To minimize the cost make 70 conservatories per month

(b) $\dfrac{d^2y}{dx^2} = 4$ which is positive so cost is at a minimum when $x = 70$

(c) $y = 2 * 70^2 - 280 * 70 + 16000$
$$= 9800 - 19600 + 16000$$
$$= £25,800$$

3.3   (a) 36   [3.6]

(b) positive (1), so a minimum   [3.8]

(c) £652   [3.7]

3.4   (a) 10   [3.6]

(b) positive (1.6), so a minimum   [3.8]

(c) £70   [3.7]

3.5   (a) $\dfrac{dy}{dx} = -8x + 960$ When $-8x + 960 = 0$

$$8x = 960$$
$$x = 120$$

To maximize revenue the price should be £120

(b) $\dfrac{d^2y}{dx^2} = -8$　　Negative so revenue is at a maximum when the price is £120

(c) $y = -4 * 120^2 + 960 * 120 = -57600 + 115200$
$$= £57,600$$

3.6　(a) £500　　　　　　　　　　　　　　　　　　　　　[3.9]
　　　(b) Negative (-6), so a maximum
　　　(c) £750,000

3.7　(a) £25　　　　　　　　　　　　　　　　　　　　　　[3.9]
　　　(b) Negative $(-2/5)$, so a maximum
　　　(c) £35,000

3.8　(a) Revenue = Price $* x = (500 - 3x) * x = 500x - 3x^2$
　　　　　Profit = Revenue − Cost
$$= 500x - 3x^2 - (150 + 20x + x^2)$$
$$= 500x - 3x^2 - 150 - 20x - x^2$$
$$= 480x - 4x^2 - 150$$

　　　(b) $\dfrac{d\text{Profit}}{dx} = 480 - 8x$　　When $480 - 8x = 0$
$$480 = 8x$$
$$x = 60$$

　　　Produce 60 amplifiers
　　　At this output level,
　　　　　Price $= 500 - 3 * 60 = 500 - 180 = £320$
　　　　　Profit $= 480 * 60 - 4 * 60^2 - 150$
$$= 2880 - 14400 - 150 = £14,250$$

　　　(c) $\dfrac{d^2\text{Profit}}{dx} = -8$　　Negative so profit is at a maximum when output is 60.

3.9　(a) Profit $= 54x - 3x^2 - 80$
　　　(b) 9000 clients, price = £51, profit = £163,000　　　　[3.9]
　　　(c) Negative (-6), so a maximum

3.10　(a) Profit $= 630x - 3.5x^2 - 450$
　　　(b) Sell 90, price = £365, profit = £27,900　　　　　[3.9]
　　　(c) Negative (-7), so a maximum

3.11　(a) Profit $= 240x - 0.5x^2 - 300$
　　　(b) Produce 240, price = £146, profit = £28,500
　　　(c) Negative (-1), so a maximum

3.12　$Q - \sqrt{[(2 * 20 * 2000)/50]} = 40$ litres

3.13　130 kg　　　　　　　　　　　　　　　　　　　　　[3.11]

3.14　200 packs　　　　　　　　　　　　　　　　　　　　[3.11]

3.15　75 litres　　　　　　　　　　　　　　　　　　　　[3.11]

3.16   (a) 28 kg   [3.11]
        (b) 2
3.17   (a) 210 kg   [3.11]
        (b) £1050
3.18   (a) 400 bags   [3.11]
        (b) 200 bags
        (c) Questionable – likely seasonal variation in
             demand for this product
3.19   (a) 320 kg   [3.11]
        (b) Yes. Maximum stock will be 320 kg
        (c) 267.731 kg
3.20   (a) 208 litres   [3.11]
        (b) Not at all

Chapter 4

4.1   (a) (v), (b) (vi), (c) (i), (d) (ii), (e) (iii), (f) (iv)
4.2   (a) ordinal, (b) ratio, (c) ordinal, (d) nominal, (e) ratio,
        (f) ordinal, (g) nominal, (h) ordinal, (i) interval
4.3   Discrete: (b) (e) (f) (h)   Continuous: (a) (c) (d) (g)
4.4   Qualitative: (b) (e)   Discrete quantitative: (d) (f)
        Continuous quantitative: (a) (c)
4.5   (a) (iv), (b) (vii), (c) (v), (d) (ii), (e) (viii), (f) (iii), (g) (i),
             (h) (vi)
4.6

	Bus pass	Cash	Total
East	35,000	43,000	78,000
North	43,000	81,000	124,000
South	29,000	34,000	63,000
West	51,000	114,000	165,000
Total	158,000	272,000	430,000

4.7   [4.5]
4.8   [4.5]
4.9

Passengers	Frequency
1	20
2	7
3	3
4	4
5	1
Total	35

4.10   [4.6]

4.11   [4.6]

4.12   (a)   [4.6]

        (b)   [4.7]

4.13   *Speed (mph)*   *Frequency*

        20 and under 25   4

        25 and under 30   6

        30 and under 35   6

        35 and under 40   7

        40 and under 45   1

        Total   24

4.14   [4.7]

4.15   [4.8]

4.16   [4.7]

4.17   [4.8]

4.18   (a) and (b)

Fees (£)	*Frequency (clubs)*	*Relative frequency (clubs)*	*Frequency (leisure centres)*	*Relative frequency (leisure centres)*
20 and under 30	2	9.1%	4	23.5%
30 and under 40	3	13.6%	5	29.4%
40 and under 50	6	27.3%	2	11.8%
50 and under 60	1	4.6%	6	35.3%
60 and under 70	7	31.8%	0	0.0%
70 and under 80	3	13.6%	0	0.0%
Total	22	100.0%	17	100.0%

        (c) (4.6% + 31.8% + 13.6%) = 50% of clubs charge
             £50 or more compared to 35.3% of leisure centres

4.19   (a)   [4.7]

        (b)   [4.9]

        (c) 16.7% of staff from Manchester and (16.7% + 8.3% =)
             25% of staff from Southampton achieved
             unsatisfactory marks   [4.9]

4.20   (a)   [4.7]

        (b)   [4.9]

        (c) 90.5% of visits in Redcar, 88.9% of visits to
             Skegness, and 15% of visits in Torquay last
             at least 20 minutes   [4.9]

Chapter 5

5.1 (a)

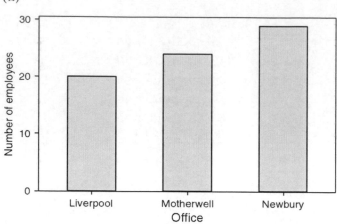

(b)

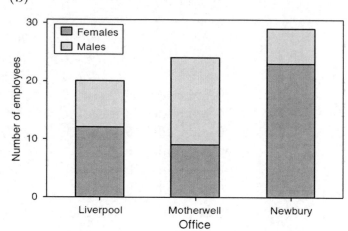

(c)

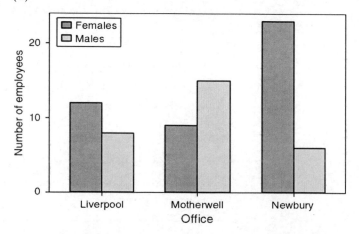

5.2   (a)   [5.3]
        (b)   [5.4]
        (c)   [5.5]
5.3   (a)   [5.3]
        (b)   [5.4]
        (c)   [5.5]
5.4   [5.7]
5.5   (a)

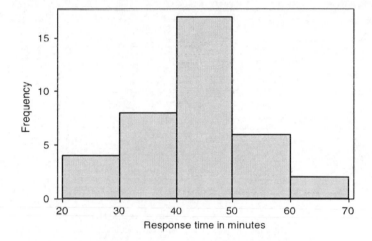

The distribution is broadly symmetrical.

(b) | *Response time (minutes)* | *Cumulative frequency* |
     |---|---|
     | 20 and under 30 | 4 |
     | 30 and under 40 | 12 |
     | 40 and under 50 | 29 |
     | 50 and under 60 | 35 |
     | 60 and under 70 | 37 |

(c)

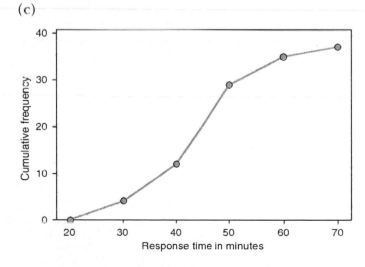

5.6   (a)   [5.8]

       (b)   [5.11]

       (c)   [5.12]

5.7   (a)   [5.8]

       (b)   [5.11]

       (c)   [5.12]

5.8   (a)   [5.8]

       (b)   [5.14]

       (c)   [5.14]

5.9   (a)   [5.8]

       (b)   [5.14]

       (c)   [5.14]

5.10   *Stem*   *Leaves*

       2   **2** 7

       3   **2** 3 4

       4   1 **3** 4 **8 8**

       5   6

       6   0 3 5 7 7 7 9

       7   3 7 8

                      Leaf unit = £1

5.11   (a)   [5.17]

       (b) Health clubs have more varied fees   [5.17]

5.12   (a)   [5.15]

       (b)   [5.18]

5.13   (a)   [5.15]

       (b)   [5.18]

       (c)   [5.20]

5.14   (a) Expenditure

       (b)

       (c) Direct

5.15   (a) Price   [5.21]

             (b)   [5.21]

             (c) Inverse   [5.21]

5.16   (a) Engine size   [5.21]

             (b)   [5.21]

             (c) Direct   [5.21]

5.17

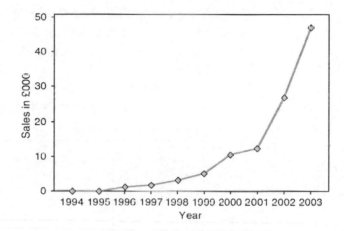

5.18   [5.23]

5.19   [5.23]

5.20   (i) (e), (ii) (f), (iii) (g), (iv) (a), (v) (d), (vi) (c), (vii) (b)

Chapter 6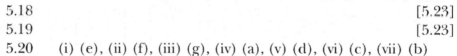

6.1   (a) Array   7 7 7 7 8 8 8 8 8 8 9 9 9 9 9 9 9 10 10 10 10

             Mode = 9   Median = (21 + 1)/2 = 11th value,

             9 (in bold)

             Mean = $(7 + 7 + 7 + \cdots + 10)/21 = 179/21 = 8.524$

       (b) Close so fairly symmetrical distribution

       (c)

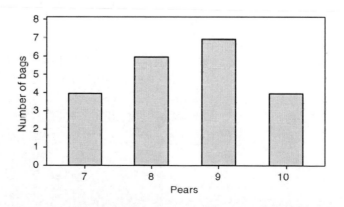

6.2   (a) Mode = 1 Median   [6.1, 6.3]
           (b) Mean = 2.8 – higher, suggesting positive skew   [6.5, 6.8]
6.3   (a) Mode = 2, Median = 2, Mean = 1.923   [6.1, 6.4, 6.5]
           (b) Symmetrical distribution   [6.9]
6.4   (a) Mode = 10, Median = 9, Mean = 8.737   [6.1, 6.3, 6.5]
           (b) Mean lowest suggesting negative skew   [6.8]
6.5   (a) Mode = 1

Median position = (28 + 1)/2 = 14.5th position, midway between the 14th and 15th values. 1st to 10th values are 1, 11th to 18th are 2, so median is 2
Mean

= [(10 * 1) + (8 * 2) + (4 * 3) + (3 * 4) + (3 * 5)]/28
= (10 + 16 + 12 + 12 + 15)/28 = 65/28 = 2.321

(b)

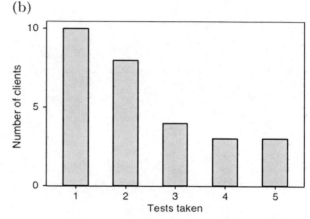

6.6   F: Mode = 2, Median = 2, Mean = 2.03
               M: Mode = 1, Median = 2, Mean = 2.144   [6.11]
6.7   (a) Mode = 13   Range = 33 − 5 = 28
           (b) Array: 5 6 7 8 8 9 9 10 11 12 12 12 13 13 **13** 13 15 17 18 18
                   19 19 20 20 21 22 22 22 33
               Median = (29 + 1)/2 = 15th value, 13 (in bold)
           (c) Quartile position = (15 + 1)/2 = 8th value, lower quartile = 10, upper quartile = 19
           (d) SIQR = (19 − 10)/2 = 9/2 = 4.5
6.8   (a) AA: Median = 1781.5, SIQR = 206
               RSR: Median = 1992, SIQR = 109.5   [6.4, 6.17, 6.18]
           (b) AA has lower median and more spread   [6.19]
6.9   Mean = (11 + 31 + 27 + ⋯ + 20)/17 = 427/17 = 25.118

$$\text{Standard deviation} = \sqrt{1/16 * [(11^2 + 31^2 + \cdots + 20^2) - (427)^2/17]}$$
$$= \sqrt{1/16 * (11391 - 182329/17)}$$
$$= \sqrt{1/16 * (11391 - 10725.235)}$$
$$= \sqrt{1/16 * 665.765} = \sqrt{41.610} = 6.451$$

6.10   Bus: Mean = 35.75, Standard deviation = 5.148

Cycle: Mean = 28.75, Standard deviation = 3.1   [6.5, 6.26]

6.11   (a)   False (Dolg bills vary less than Akula)

(b)   False (Bremia bills vary less than the other companies)

(c)   True

(d)   False (Akula bills vary more than Dolg)

(e)   False (Bremia bills vary less than Dolg)

(f)   True

6.12

Class	Midpoint (x)	Frequency (f)	fx	x²	fx²
80 a.u. 120	100	3	300	10000	30000
120 a.u. 160	140	11	1540	19600	215600
160 a.u. 200	180	9	1620	32400	291600
200 a.u. 240	220	7	1540	48400	338800
240 a.u. 280	260	2	520	67600	135200

$\Sigma f = 32$ $\Sigma fx = 5520$ $\Sigma fx^2 = 1011200$

(a)   Median position = (32 + 1)/2 = 16.5th

Median class is 160 a.u. 200

Approximate median

= 160 + [(16.5 − 14)/9 * 40] = 171.111

(b)   Approximate mean = 5520/32 − 172.5

Approximate

standard deviation = $\sqrt{1/31} * [1011200 − (5520)^2/32]$

= $\sqrt{1/31} * (1011200 − 30470400/32)$

= $\sqrt{1/31} * (1011200 − 952200)$

= $\sqrt{1/31} * 59000 = \sqrt{1903.226} = 43.626$

6.13   (a)   C: Median = 47.045, Mean = 46.974

R: Median = 43.382, Mean = 42.917   [6.13, 6.15]

(b)   Standard deviations: 5.801 (C) and 5.242 (R)   [6.29]

6.14   (a)   Before: Mean = 29.937, Median = 30

After: Mean = 20.410, Median = 21.613   [6.13, 6.15]

(b)   Standard deviations: 11.753 (Before), 8.281

(After)   [6.29]

6.15   (a)   Peeshar: Mean = 48.182, S.D. = 23.702

Peevar: Mean = 32.031, S.D. = 19.088   [6.15, 6.29]

6.16   Median position = (31 + 1)/2 = 16th value

Median = £12

Quartile position = (16 + 1)/2 = 8.5th

= (8th value + 9th value)/2

Q1   = (07 + 07)/2 = £7   Q3 = (15 + 15)/2 = £15

SIQR = (15 − 7)/2 = 8/2 = £4

6.17   Median = 289, Q1 = 230, Q3 = 408   [6.10]

(*Continued*)

6.18   (a)   *Balance (£)*   *Cumulative relative frequency*

Balance (£)	Cumulative relative frequency
0 and under 500	0.12
500 and under 1000	0.41
1000 and under 1500	0.67
1500 and under 2000	0.86
2000 and under 2500	0.95
2500 and under 3000	1.00

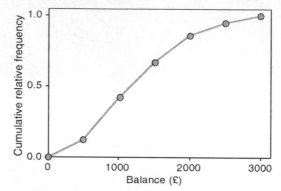

Approximate values: median = 1175   Q1 = 725
Q3 = 1710   SIQR = (1710 − 725)/2 = 492.5

6.19   Median = 720, Q1 = 425, Q3 = 1060, SIQR = 317.51

                                                    [6.14, 6.30]

6.20   (a) False, (b) True, (c) True, (d) True, (e) False, (f) True,
           (g) True

6.21   Only the last value (3.5) is outside the control limits   [6.31]

6.22   (i) (e), (ii) (d), (iii) (a), (iv) (b), (v) (f), (vi) (c)

Chapter 7

7.1   (a) positive, (b) negative, (c) negative, (d) negative,
           (e) positive, (f) positive, (g) negative

7.2   (a)

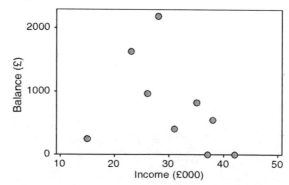

(b)

Income (x)	Balance (y)	x^2	y^2	xy
15	250	225	62500	3750
23	1630	529	2656900	37490
26	970	676	940900	25220
28	2190	784	4796100	61320
31	410	961	168100	12710
35	830	1225	688900	29050
37	0	1369	0	0
38	550	1444	302500	20900
42	0	1764	0	0
275	6830	8977	9615900	190440	$n-9$

$$r = \frac{9*190440 - 275*6830}{\sqrt{(9*8977 - 275^2)*(9*9615900 - 6830^2)}}$$

$$= \frac{1713960 - 1878250}{\sqrt{(80793 - 75625)*(86543100 - 46648900)}}$$

$$= \frac{-164290}{\sqrt{5138*39894200}} = \frac{-164290}{\sqrt{204976399600}}$$

$$= \frac{-164290}{452743.194} = -0.363 \qquad \text{weak, negative}$$

7.3   (b) -0.964 strong, negative   [7.3]

7.4   (a) Turnover

    (c) 0.943 strong, positive   [7.3]

7.5   (a) Cost

    (c) 0.907 strong, positive   [7.3]

7.6

Critics' rank	Takings rank	d	d^2
1	2	−1	1
2	5	−3	9
3	1	2	4
4	3	1	1
5	4	1	1
6	6	0	0
		16	$n-6$

$$r_s = 1 - \frac{6*16}{6(6^2 - 1)} = 1 - \frac{96}{6(36 - 1)} = 1 - \frac{96}{6*35}$$

$$= 1 - \frac{96}{210} = 1 - 0.457 = 0.543$$

weak, positive

7.7	-0.762 fair, negative	[7.5]
7.8	0.624 fair, positive	[7.5]
7.9	(a) 0.952	[7.5]
7.10	(a)	

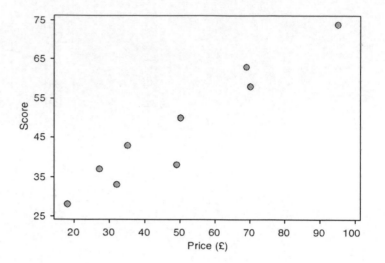

(b)

Price (£)	Score	x^2	xy	
95	74	9025	7030	
69	63	4761	4347	
18	28	324	504	
32	33	1024	1056	
27	37	729	999	
70	58	4900	4060	
49	38	2401	1862	
35	43	1225	1505	
50	50	2500	2500	
445	424	26889	23863	$n = 9$

$$b = \frac{23863 - (455 * 424)/9}{26889 - (445)^2/9} = \frac{23863 - 188680/9}{26889 - 198025/9}$$

$$= \frac{23863 - 20964.444}{26889 - 22002.778} = \frac{2898.556}{4886.222} = 0.593$$

$$a = (424 - 0.593 * 445)/9 = (424 - 263.885)/9$$
$$= 160.115/9 = 17.791$$

Score $= 17.791 + 0.593$ Price

(c)

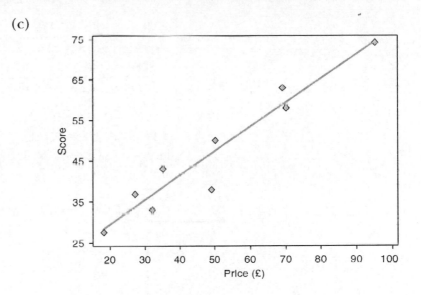

(d) Score − 17.791 + 0.593(45) = 17.791 + 26.685 = 44.476

7.11 (b) Position = 31.264 − 0.381 Goals   [7.8]
      (c) 12.214 (12th position)   [7.9]

7.12 (a) Mean journey time
      (c) Mean journey time = 1.204 + 4.781 Distance   [7.8]
      (d) Mean journey time = 1.204 + 4.781 * 9
                            = 44.233 minutes   [7.9]

7.13 (a) Mileage
      (c) Price = 7.049 − 0.089 Mileage   [7.8]
      (d) Price = 7.049 − 0.089 * 25 = 4,824 (£4824)   [7.9]

7.14 (a) Experience
      (b) and (c)

Experience (x)	Salary (y)	x^2	xy	y^2	
1	13	1	13	169	
4	18	16	72	324	
3	19	9	57	361	
2	22	4	44	484	
7	25	49	175	625	
8	27	64	216	729	
5	31	25	155	961	
13	36	169	468	1296	
20	38	400	760	1444	
22	42	484	924	1764	
85	271	1221	2884	8157	$n = 10$

$$b = \frac{2884 - (85 * 271)/10}{1221 - (85)^2/10} = \frac{2884 - 23035/10}{1221 - 7225/10}$$

$$= \frac{2884 - 2303.5}{1221 - 722.5} = \frac{580.5}{498.5} = 1.164$$

$a = (271 - 1.164 * 85)/10 = (271 - 98.982)/10$
$\quad = 172.018/10 = 17.202$

Salary $= 17.202 + 1.164$ Experience

(d) $$r = \frac{10*2884 - 85*271}{\sqrt{(10*1221 - 85^2)*(10*8157 - 271^2)}}$$

$$= \frac{28840 - 23035}{\sqrt{(12210 - 7225)*(81570 - 73441)}}$$

$$= \frac{5805}{\sqrt{4985*8129}} = \frac{5805}{\sqrt{40523065}}$$

$$= \frac{5805}{6365.773} = 0.912$$

$R^2 = 0.912^2 = 0.832$

83.2% of the variation in salary can be explained by the variation in experience

7.15   (a) Mean hourly wage

(c) Mean hourly wage ($) $= 10.333 + 0.338$ Union
membership (%)   [7.8]

(d) 0.713 (71.3%)   [7.3, 7.4]

7.16   (a)   Turnover

        (c)   Turnover $= -0.027 + 0.113$ Employees   [7.8]

        (d)   0.804 (80.4%)   [7.3, 7.4]

7.17   (a)   Contamination level – depends on hours worked

        (c)   Contamination level $= 0.229 + 9.705$ Hours worked   [7.8]

        (d)   0.985 (98.5%)   [7.3, 7.4]

7.18   (b)   Motorway network $= 219.924 + 17.729$ Land area   [7.8]

        (c)   0.542 (54.2%)   [7.3, 7.4]

7.19   (a)   4,320

        (b)   6,690

        (c)   0.805

7.20   (i) (e), (ii) (f), (iii) (d), (iv) (g), (v) (h), (vi) (a), (vii) (b), (viii) (c)

Chapter 8

8.1   (a)   (i) 113.636, (ii) 127.273, (iii) 192.308, (iv) 215.385   [8.1]

        (b)   Low price in 1999 so rises are more dramatic when 1999 is the base year

8.2 $2002 \quad \dfrac{11.99 + 48.99}{9.99 + 44.99} * 100 = \dfrac{60.98}{54.98} * 100 = 110.913$

       $2003 \quad \dfrac{12.99 + 49.99}{9.99 + 44.99} * 100 = \dfrac{62.98}{54.98} * 100 = 114.551$

8.3   (a)   2001 index: 143.913   2003 index: 173.913   [8.2]

        (b)   The amounts used.

8.4   (a) $\dfrac{(23000 * 0.45) + (1500 * 0.60)}{(23000 * 0.25) + (1500 * 0.50)} * 100 = \dfrac{10350 + 900}{5750 + 750} * 100$

$$= \dfrac{11250}{6500} * 100$$

$$= 173.077$$

        (b) $\dfrac{(12000 * 0.45) + (15000 * 0.60)}{(12000 * 0.25) + (15000 * 0.50)} * 100 = \dfrac{5400 + 9000}{4000 + 7500} * 100$

$$= \dfrac{14400}{11500} * 100$$

$$= 125.217$$

(c) Answer (b) is much lower. Use Paasche as usage rates have changed so much

8.5   (a) 154.5   [8.3]
       (b) 154.433   [8.4]
       (c) Little change in consumption so historic figures are adequate.
8.6   (a) 2002 index: 109.790   2003 index: 118.509   [8.3]
       (b) 2002 index: 109.829   2003 index: 119.565   [8.4]
8.7   (a) 2000 index: 118.643   2003 index: 132.072   [8.3]
       (b) 2000 index: 117.773   2003 index: 127.666   [8.4]

8.8   1998: 7022   1999: $7101 * \dfrac{162.9}{165.4} = 6993.669$

       2000: $7350 * \dfrac{162.9}{170.3} = 7030.622$

       2001: $7844 * \dfrac{162.9}{173.3} = 7373.269$

       2002: $8249 * \dfrac{162.9}{176.2} = 7626.346$

       2003: $8598 * \dfrac{162.9}{181.3} = 7725.395$

8.9   1993: 5000   1995: 5473.239   1997: 4645.333
       1999: 4678.658   2001: 5033.699   2003: 4656.371   [8.5]
8.10   (a) 72.971   [8.5]
       (b) 27.638
8.11   (i) (d), (ii) (f), (iii) (g), (iv) (e), (v) (a), (vi) (c), (vii) (b)
8.12   (a) 50%   [8.6]
       (b) Half-way through the third year   [8.7]
8.13   (a)

End of year	Net cash flow (£)	Cumulative cash flow (£)
0	−15000	−15000
1	4000	−11000
2	4000	−7000
3	4000	−3000
4	4000	+1000
5	4000	+5000

Payback period is $3 + 3000/4000 = 3.75$ years.

(b)

End of year	Net cash flow (£)	Discount factor	Present value (£)
0	−15000	1.000	−15000
1	4000	0.952	3808
2	4000	0.907	3628
3	4000	0.864	3456
4	4000	0.823	3292
5	4000	0.784	3136

Net present value = 2320

(c)

End of year	Net cash flow (£)	Discount factor	Present value (£)
0	−15000	1.000	−15000
1	3000	0.952	2856
2	3000	0.907	2721
3	3000	0.864	2592
4	3000	0.823	2469
5	3000	0.784	2352

Net present value = −2010

8.14	(a)	Six years	[8.7]
	(b)	£605	[8.12]
8.15	(a)	−£7330	[8.12]
	(b)	NPV = £11,180. IRR is about 13%	[8.13]
8.16	(a)	−$4.903 m	[8.12]
	(b)	NPV = $3.632 m. IRR is about 17%	[8.13]
8.17	(a)	3 + 15/75 = 3.2 years for the cafe bar, 3 years for the family pub	[8.7]
	(b)	£58,010 for the cafe bar, £37,730 for the family pub	[8.12]
8.18	(a)	4.111 years (Markets), 4.0 (Riverside)	[8.7]
	(b)	+51.78 (Markets), +17.87(Riverside)	[8.12]
	(c)	Markets. The payback is marginally longer but the NPV is much higher	
8.19		$0.328 m (thriller), −$0.358 m (comedy), $0.001 m (science fiction)	[8.12]
		The thriller	
		The science fiction film is marginal	
8.20		£7340 (e-mergency), −£1245 (e-ssential), −£70 (e-xpeditious)	[8.12]
		Purchase the e-mergency design.	

Chapter 9

9.1

Day	Time	Revenue (£)	3-point MA
1	am	320	
1	pm	92	210
1	eve	218	217
2	am	341	220
2	pm	101	222
2	eve	224	228
3	am	359	233
3	pm	116	249
3	eve	272	

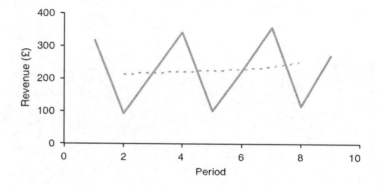

9.2 (b) 531   550   553   592   610   631   650   [9.2]

9.3 (b) 14.8   14.6   14.6   15.0   15.8   16.8   17.4
        17.6   18.2   18.0   18.6   [9.2]

9.4 (b) 17.375   17.500   17.750   17.875   18.125
        18.125   17.875   17.750   [9.3]

9.5 (b) 32.000   33.750   34.875   34.250   34.375
        35.250   36.750   38.000   [9.3]

9.6 (b) 14.0375   14.3625   14.3750   14.6500
        15.3125   15.8500   16.0125   16.1375   [9.3]

9.7

Day	Time	Revenue (£)	3-point MA	Revenue − MA
1	am	320		
1	pm	92	210	−118
1	eve	218	217	1
2	am	341	220	121
2	pm	101	222	−121
2	eve	224	228	−4
3	am	359	233	126
3	pm	116	249	−133
3	eve	272		

	Morning	Afternoon	Evening
Day 1		−118	1
Day 2	121	−121	−4
Day 3	126	−133	
Total	247	−372	−3
Mean	123.5	−124	−1.5

$[123.5 + (−124) + (−1.5) = −2]$

| Adjustment | +0.667 | +0.667 | +0.667 |
| Component | 124.167 | −123.333 | −0.833 |

Day	Time	Revenue	MA	Component	Predicted	Error	Error^2
1	am	320					
1	pm	92	210	−123.333	86.667	5.333	28.441
1	eve	218	217	−0.833	216.167	1.833	3.360
2	am	341	220	124.167	344.167	−3.167	10.030
2	pm	101	222	−123.333	98.667	2.333	5.443
2	eve	224	228	−0.833	227.167	−3.167	10.030
3	am	359	233	124.167	357.167	−1.833	3.360
3	pm	116	249	−123.333	125.667	−9.667	93.451
3	eve	272					

Total squared deviation 154.115

Mean squared deviation 22.016

9.8 (a) Winter 9.609   Spring −4.391   Summer −10.828

Autumn 5.609   [9.4, 9.5]

(b) 0.146   [9.8]

9.9 (a) Winter −21.906   Spring 14.281

Summer 25.719   Autumn −18.094   [9.4, 9.5]

(b) 3.006   [9.8]

9.10 (a)

Day	Time	Revenue (£)	3-point MA	Revenue/MA
1	am	320		
1	pm	92	210	0.438
1	eve	218	217	1.005
2	am	341	220	1.550
2	pm	101	222	0.455
2	eve	224	228	0.982
3	am	359	233	1.541
3	pm	116	249	0.466
3	eve	272		

	Morning	Afternoon	Evening
Day 1		0.438	1.005
Day 2	1.550	0.455	0.982
Day 3	1.541	0.466	
Total	3.091	1.359	1.987
Mean	1.5455	0.453	0.994

[1.5455 + 0.453 + 0.994 = 2.9925]

Adjustment	+0.0025	+0.0025	+0.0025
Factor	1.548	0.4555	0.9965

(b)

Day	Time	Revenue	MA	Factor	Predicted	Error	Error^2
1	am	320					
1	pm	92	210	0.4555	95.655	−3.655	13.359
1	eve	218	217	0.9965	216.2405	1.7595	3.096
2	am	341	220	1.548	340.560	0.440	0.194
2	pm	101	222	0.4555	101.121	−0.121	0.015
2	eve	224	228	0.9965	227.202	−3.202	10.253
3	am	359	233	1.548	360.684	−1.684	2.836
3	pm	116	249	0.4555	113.4195	2.5805	6.659
3	eve	272					

Total squared deviation   36.412

Mean squared deviation   5.202

(c) MSD of 5.202 is lower than the MSD for the additive model (22.016) so the multiplicative model is more appropriate

9.11 (a) Winter 1.540, Spring 0.754, Summer 0.391, Autumn 1.315   [9.9]

(b) 0.104   [9.9]

(c) Multiplicative   [9.9]

9.12 (a) Winter 0.377, Spring 1.386, Summer 1.770, Autumn 0.467   [9.9]

(b) 4.922   [9.9]

(c) Additive   [9.9]

9.13 Use multiplicative model

Trend change per period = $(249 - 210)/6 = 6.5$

Forecast for morning of day 4 $= [249 + (2 * 6.5)] * 1.548$
$= 405.576$

Forecast for afternoon of day 4 $= [249 + (3 * 6.5)] * 0.4555$
$= 122.302$

Forecast for evening of day 4 = [249 + (4 * 6.5)] * 0.9965

= 274.038

9.14   Multiplicative. Winter 27.585, Spring 13.546,
Summer 7.046, Autumn 23.767   [9.10]

9.15   Additive. Winter 18.665, Spring 55.709,
Summer 68.004, Autumn 25.049   [9.10]

9.16   (a)

Items stolen	Prediction	Error	Error^2
63			
56	63.0000	−7.0000	49.000
49	57.4000	−8.4000	70.560
45	50.6800	−5.6800	32.262
51	46.1360	4.8640	23.659
36	50.0272	−14.0272	196.762
42	38.8054	3.1946	10.206
37	41.3611	−4.3611	19.019
	37.8722		

Total   401.468

Mean squared deviation   57.353

(c)

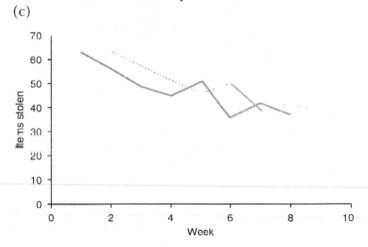

9.17   (a) Month 10 = 273.809   [9.11]
(c) 1189.48   [9.11]

9.18   (a) Day 9 = 140.397   MSD = 2986.376   [9.11]
(b) Day 9 = 180.466   MSD = 1919.384   Better   [9.11]

9.19   (a) Week 10 = 405.547   MSD = 8307.63   [9.11]
(b) Week 10 = 349.935   MSD = 8648.838
Model (a) is better   [9.11]

9.20   (i) (h), (ii) (d), (iii) (e), (iv) (g), (v) (h), (vi) (a),
(vii) (f), (viii) (c)

Chapter 10

10.1   (a) 0.427   (b) 0.573   [10.2]
10.2   (a) 0.915   (b) 0.085   [10.2]
10.3   (a) 0.054   (b) 0.027   [10.2]
10.4   (a) Total days = 68 + 103 + 145 + 37 + 12 = 365
             2 call-outs on 145 days so P(2 call-outs)
                        = 145/365 = 0.397
        (b) P(2 or fewer) = P(2 or 1 or 0)
                        = P(2) + P(1) + P(0)
                        = 145/365 + 103/365 + 68/365 = 0.866
        (c) P(1 or more) = P(1 or 2 or 3 or 4)
                        = P(1) + P(2) + P(3) + P(4)
                        = 103/365 + 145/365 + 37/365 + 12/365
                        = 0.814
        (d) P(less than 4) = P(3 or 2 or 1 or 0)
                        = P(3) + P(2) + P(1) + P(0)
                        = 37/365 + 145/365 + 103/365 + 68/365
                        = 0.967
        (e) P(more than 2) = P(3 or 4) = 37/365 + 12/365 = 0.134
10.5   (a) 0.313   (b) 0.277   (c) 0.723   [10.5]
10.6   (a) P(more respect)
                = P(manual and more respect) + P(clerical and more
                  respect) + P(managerial and more respect)
                = 7/120 + 6/120 + 6/120 = (7 + 6 + 6)/120
                = 19/120 = 0.158
        (b) P(clerical or better promotion)
                = P(clerical) + P(better promotion)
                  − P(clerical and better promotion)
                = (12 + 19 + 6)/120 + (12 + 12 + 3)/120 − 12/120
                = 37/120 + 27/120 − 12/120 = 52/120 = 0.433
        (c) P(higher pay | manual)
                = P(higher pay and manual)/P(manual)
                = 53/120 ÷ (12 + 53 + 7)120 = 53/120 ÷ 72/120
                = 53/120 * 120/72 = 53/72 = 0.736
        (d) P(more respect | managerial) = 6/120 = 0.05
        (e) P(higher pay | managerial)
                = P(higher pay and managerial)/P(managerial)
                = 2/120 ÷ (3 + 2 + 6)/120 = 2/120 ÷ 11/120
                = 2/120 * 120/11 = 2/11 = 0.182
10.7   (a) 0.733   (b) 0.272   [10.3]
        (c) 0.121   [10.4]

(d) 0.868   [10.6]

(e) Country and recognition are dependent   [10.12]

10.8 (a) 0.129   (b) 0.1   [10.3]

(c) 0.686   [10.5]

(d) 0.181   [10.4]

(e) 0.190 Higher than (a) so not independent   [10.6]

10.9 (a) 0.216   (b) 0.256   [10.3]

(c) 0.464   (d) 0.572   [10.5]

(e) 0.1   (f) 0.116   [10.4]

(g) 0.093   (h) 0.481   [10.6]

(i) No   [10.12]

10.10 0.008   [10.11]

10.11 (a) 0.795   [10.14]

(b) 0.205   [10.10]

(c) 0.060   [10.14]

10.12 Let D represent Declan succeeds and D′ represent Declan fails

Let E represent Emily succeeds and E′ represent Emily fails

Let F represent Farid succeeds and F′ represent Farid fails

(a) P(D and E and F) = P(D) * P(E) * P(F) (independent outcomes)

P(D) = 1 P(D′) = 1 − 0.6 = 0.4

P(E) = 1 − P(E′) = 1 − 0.75 = 0.25

P(F) = 1 − P(F′) = 1 − 0.8 = 0.2

P(D and E and F) = 0.4 * 0.25 * 0.2 = 0.02

(b) P(two succeed)

= P(D and E and F′) + P(D and E′ and F) + P(D′ and E and F)

= (0.4 * 0.25 * 0.8) + (0.4 * 0.75 * 0.2)

+ (0.6 * 0.25 * 0.2) = 0.08 + 0.06 + 0.03 = 0.17

(c) P(D′ and E′ and F′) = P(D′) and P(E′) and P(F′)

= 0.6 * 0.75 * 0.8 = 0.36

10.13 (a) 0.074   (b) 0.601   (c) 0.681   [10.15]

10.14 (a) 0.3   (b) 0.4   (c) 0.3   [10.15]

10.15 (a) 0.857   (b) 0.064   (c) 0.422   (d) 0.189   (e) 0.2685 [10.11]

10.16 0.417   [10.16]

10.17 0.597, pay 59.7% of costs   [10.16]

10.18 (a) 0.36176   (b) 0.11424   (c) 0.43952

(d) 0.07296   (e) 0.17568   [10.18]

10.19 (a) 0.315   (b) 0.450   (c) 0.235   [10.18]

10.20 (i) (i), (ii) (c), (iii) (f), (iv) (h), (v) (a), (vi) (d), (vii) (b), (viii) (j), (ix) (g), (x) (e)

Chapter 11

11.1 P(no side effect) = 0.85, P(minor side effect) = 0.11,
P(major side effect) = 0.04
Expected value of compensation = (0.85 * £0) + (0.11 * £2500)
+ (0.04 * £20000)
= 0 + £275 + £800 = £1075

11.2   £30,824   [11.2]

11.3   £415   [11.2]

11.4 $200,000   [11.2]

11.5   Pay-off table:

	Win	*Lose*
Standard fee	13,500	−1500
No win no fee	10,000	0

(a) Maximum returns: 13,500 (standard fee), 10,000 (no win no fee) Choose standard fee.

(b) Minimum returns: −1500 (standard fee), 0 (no win no fee) Choose no win no fee.

(c) Opportunity losses:

	Win	*Lose*
Standard fee	0	1500
No win no fee	3500	0

Maximum regrets: 1500 (standard fee), 3500 (no win no fee) Choose standard fee

(d) P(win) = P(lose) = 0.5
EMV(standard fee) = 0.5 * 13,500 + 0.5 * (−1500) = 6000
EMV(no win no fee) = 0.5 * 10,000 + 0.5 * 0 = 5000
Choose standard fee.

11.6   (a) Ice cream   (b) Mix   (c) Mix   (d) Mix   [11.3–11.7]

11.7   (a) Don't vaccinate   (b) Vaccinate   (c) Vaccinate
(d) Vaccinate   [11.3–11.7]

11.8   (a) Don't discount   (b) Discount   (c) Don't discount
(d) Don't discount   [11.3–11.7]

11.9   (a) Increase   (b) Decrease   (c) Same   (d) Same
                              [11.3–11.7]

11.10   (a)

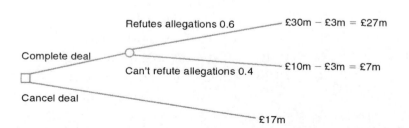

EMV(Complete deal) = (0.6 * £27m) + (0.4 * £7m)
                   = £16.2m + £2.8m = £19m

This is higher than the return from cancelling the deal, £17m, so complete

(b)   EMV (Complete deal) − (0.4 * £27m) + (0.6 * £7m)
                   = £10.8m + £4.2m = £15m

This is lower than the return from cancelling the deal, £17m, so cancel

11.11   (a)   EMV(A) = 6400   EMV(B) = 3750   Choose A   [11.8]
          (b)   EMV(A) = 3800   Choose A

11.12   EMV (stay) = 1.26   EMV (go) = 1.00
               Choose to stay   [11.8]

11.13   (b)   EMV(S) = 2.05, EMV(P) = 4.5
               Choose Parooka   [11.8]
          (c)   New EMV(S) = 4.6 > EMV(P), so now
               Choose Sloochai   [11.8]

11.14   (a)   EMV(Modified crop)   = £58000,
               EMV(Unmodified crop) = £50000
               Sow modified crop   [11.8]
          (b)   EMV(Modified crop) = £49500. Sow unmodified crop.

11.15   (a)

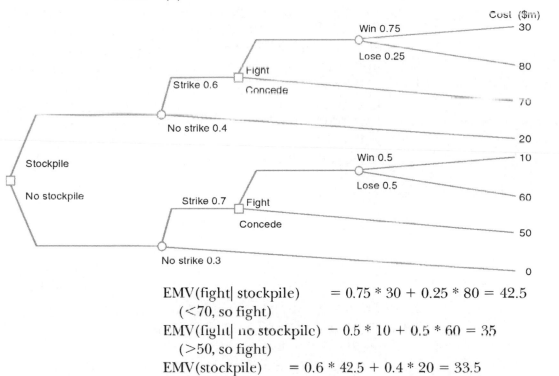

EMV(fight| stockpile)   = 0.75 * 30 + 0.25 * 80 = 42.5
     (<70, so fight)
EMV(fight| no stockpile) − 0.5 * 10 + 0.5 * 60 = 35
     (>50, so fight)
EMV(stockpile)   = 0.6 * 42.5 + 0.4 * 20 = 33.5

EMV(no stockpile) = 0.7 * 35 + 0.3 * 0 = 24.5
Build a stockpile and fight if the strike goes ahead

(b) Let p = probability management wins if they have built a stockpile

Fight and Concede options have equal value when

$$p * 30 + (1 - p) * 80 = 70$$
$$30p + 80 - 80p = 70$$
$$80 - 50p = 70$$
$$80 - 70 = 50p$$
$$10 = 50p$$
$$10/50 = p = 0.2$$

If the probability of winning falls below 0.2 management should concede

11.16 (a) EMV(star) = 1, EMV(no star) = −2, EMV(bid) = 0.85
Bid for the rights and hire a star   [11.10–11.12]

(b) If P(success without a star) > 0.275, don't hire a star   [11.13]

11.17 (a) EMV(large-scale) = 0, EMV(small-scale) = 11, EMV (develop) = 7.75
Develop and start small-scale production if the tests are passed.   [11.10–11.12]

(b) Choose large-scale production if P(approval) > 0.529   [11.13]

11.18 EMV(5MW) = 433, EMV(2MW) = 188, EMV(build) = 156.5
Start building the 5MW reactor if the government is unchanged   [11.10–11.12]

11.19 EMV (build if expert predicts failure) = 5.8, so sell
EMV (build if expert predicts success) = 20.2, so build
EMV (build if no advice is sought) = 13
EMV (seek expert advice) = 14.1
Get expert advice, build if prediction is success, sell if it is failure   [11.14]

11.20 (i) (d), (ii) (f), (iii) (g), (iv) (b), (v) (a), (vi) (e), (vii) (c)

Chapter 12

12.1 (a) 0.512   (b) 0.384   (c) 0.096   (d) 0.008   [12.1]

12.2 Using I for Internet booker and N for non-Internet booker, P(I) = 0.3 and P(N) = 0.7

(a) P(NNNN) = 0.7 * 0.7 * 0.7 * 0.7 = 0.2401

(b) P(INNN or NINN or NNIN or NNNI)

  $= P$(INNN) $+ P$(NINN) $+ P$(NNIN) $+ P$(NNNI)

  $= 4 * (0.3 * 0.7^3) = 0.4116$

(c) P(IINN or ININ or INNI or NIIN or NINI or NNII)

  $= 6 * (0.3^2 * 0.7^2) = 0.2646$

(d) P(IIIN or IINI or INII or NIII) $= 4 * (0.3^3 * 0.7) = 0.0756$

(e) P(IIII) $= 0.3^4 = 0.0081$

12.3 (a) 0.590   (b) 0.991   (c) 0.081   (d) 0.009   [12.5]

12.4 (a) 0.328   (b) 0.672   (c) 0.006   [12.5]

12.5 (a) 0.107   (b) 0.879   (c) 0.624   (d) 0.967   (e) 0.006 [12.5]

12.6 (a) 0.028   (b) 0.121   (c) 0.650   (d) 0.150   (e) 0.047 [12.5]

12.7 (a) 0.349   (b) 0.070   (c) 0.001   (d) 0.736   [12.5]

12.8 (a) 0.006   (b) 0.633   (c) 0.111   (d) 0.055   [12.5]

12.9 Poisson distribution: $\mu = 1.0$

  (a) $P(X = 0) = 0.368$ (b) $P(X = 2) = 0.184$

  (c) $P(X \leq 4) = 0.996$ (d) $P(X > 3) = 1 - P(X \leq 3)$

    $= 1 - 0.981 = 0.019$

12.10 (a) 0.007   (b) 0.265   (c) 0.616   (d) 0.133   [12.7]

12.11 (a) 0.050   (b) 0.149   (c) 0.423   (d) 0.185   [12.7]

12.12 (a) 0.135   (b) 0.406   (c) 0.018   (d) 0.908   [12.7]

12.13 (a) 0.050   (b) 0.224   (c) 0.647   (d) 0.950   [12.7]

12.14 (a) 0.368   (b) 0.920   (c) 0.264   [12.7]

12.15

Demand	Probability	Cumulative probability	Random numbers
0	0.05	0.05	00–04
1	0.05	0.10	05–09
2	0.10	0.20	10–19
3	0.15	0.35	20–34
4	0.20	0.55	35–54
5	0.20	0.75	55–74
6	0.15	0.90	75–89
7	0.05	0.95	90–94
8	0.05	1.00	95–99

Day	Random number	Demand	Unsatisfied customers
1	43	4	0
2	52	4	0
3	91	7	2
4	95	8	3
5	25	3	0
6	88	6	1
7	37	4	0

(*Continued*)

Day	Random number	Demand	Unsatisfied customers
8	58	5	0
9	52	4	0
10	01	0	0
			6

Average number of unsatisfied customer per day = 6/10 = 0.6

12.16 (a) 375   (b) 20, cope with capacity to spare
                            on several days   [12.8–12.11]

12.17 £5920   [12.8–12.11]

12.18 £10,790   [12.8–12.11]

12.19 £18,400   [12.8–12.11]

12.20 (i) (e), (ii) (g), (iii) (d), (iv) (a), (v) (c), (vi) (b), (vii) (f)

Chapter 13

13.1   (a) 0.0749   (b) 0.6141   (c) 0.9803   (d) 0.0418
        (e) 0.2782   (f) 0.1297   (g) 0.5762   [13.1]

13.2 $\mu = 70$ grams $\sigma = 0.8$ grams. Use Table 5 on
        pages 621–622 in Appendix 1.

        (a) $P(x > 71) = P\left(Z > \dfrac{71 - 70}{0.8}\right) = P(Z > 1.25) = 0.1056$

        (b) $P(x > 68) = P\left(Z > \dfrac{68 - 70}{0.8}\right) = P(Z > -2.5) = 0.9938$

        (c) $P(x < 70) = P\left(Z < \dfrac{70 - 70}{0.8}\right) = P(Z < 0) = 0.5$

        (d) $P(69 < x < 72) = P\left(\dfrac{69 - 70}{0.8} < Z < \dfrac{72 - 70}{0.8}\right)$

                    $= P(-1.25 < Z < 2.5)$
                    $= 0.8944 - 0.0062 = 0.8882$

13.3   (a) 0.2843   (b) 0.1949   (c) 0.4572   [13.3]

13.4   (a) 0.2946   (b) 0.0838   (c) 0.9931   (d) 0.8054 [13.3]
        (e) 38.152   (f) 35.136   [13.4]

13.5   (a) 0.1056   (b) 0.0018   (c) 0.6493   [13.3]
        (d) 67.048   (e) 49.192   [13.4]

13.6   (a) 0.0027   (b) 0.8665   (c) 0.7123   (d) 0.0132
        (e) 0.2402   (f) 0.4868   [13.3]

13.7   (a) 0.4761   (b) 0.8159   (c) 0.9761   (d) 0.0307
        (e) 0.8388   [13.3]
        (f) 23.400   (g) 27.404   [13.4]

13.8   (a) 0.9015   (b) 0.0495   (c) 0.3067   (d) 0.3108   (e) 0.6165
13.9   (a) 0.4013   (b) 0.9664   (c) 0.0778   (d) 0.9726
       (e) 0.7091   [13.3]
       (f) 147.732 (g) 150.504   [13.4]
13.10 (a) 0.1131   (b) 0.3446   (c) 0.9783   (d) 0.2555
       (e) 0.2991   (f) 0.4479   [13.3]
13.11 (a) 0.0329   (b) 0.0228
       (c) Yes – fewer fail < 60,000 miles   [13.3]
13.12 (a) $P(X > 24) = e^{-24/20} - 0.301$
       (b) $P(X < 12) = 1 - e^{-12/20} = 1 - 0.549 = 0.451$
       (c) $P(36 < X < 48) - P(X > 36) - P(X > 48)$
                    $= e^{-36/20} - e^{-48/20} = 0.165 - 0.091 = 0.074$
13.13 (a) 0.537   (b) 0.099   (c) 0.365   [13.5]
13.14 (a) 0.490   (b) 0.300   (c) 0.089   [13.5]
13.15 (a) (i) 0.353   (ii) 0.125   (b) (i) 0.259   (ii) 0.067 [13.5]
13.16 (a) $\lambda = 24$ $\mu = 30$ $\rho = 24/30 = 0.8$
       (b) $P(r > 3) = 0.8^{3+2} = 0.328$
       (c) $W_q = 0.8/(30 - 24) = 0.133$ hours – 8 minutes
       (d) $L_q = 0.8^2/(1 - 0.8) = 0.64/0.2 = 3.2$
13.17 (a) (i) 0.75   (ii) 2.25   (iii) 0.375 hr = 22.5 minutes [13.7]
       (b) (i) 0.6   (ii) 0.9   (iii) 0.15 hr = 9 minutes   [13.7]
13.18 (a) 0.625   (b) 0.060   (c) 1.042
       (d) 0.417 hr – 25 minutes   [13.7]
13.19 (a) 0.333   (b) 0.198   (c) 1.333
       (d) 0.133 hr = 8 minutes   [13.7]
13.20 (i) (h), (ii) (f), (iii) (e), (iv) (a), (v) (d), (vi) (c),
       (vii) (b), (viii) (g)

Chapter 14

14.1   (a)

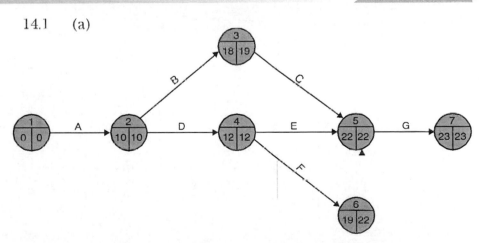

(b) Critical path: A, D, E, G. Minimum duration
is 23 days.

14.2   (b) A–C–D–F–G–I–J–K, 13 days   [14.1, 14.3]

14.3   (b) A–B–E–H–I, 24 seconds   [14.1, 14.3]

14.4   41 weeks, A–C–D–E–F–H–I   [14.1, 14.3]

14.5   (b) 30 days, A–B–D   [14.1, 14.3]

14.6   22 days, A–B–E–F   [14.1, 14.3]

14.7   (b) Draw plan, order timber, make floor panels,
lay floor, erect walls, fix roof joists, board and
weatherproof roof. 24 days   [14.1, 14.3]

14.8   (a) B–H–I–J–M, 37 days   [14.1, 14.3]

14.9   (a) 20 hours, A–B–C–E–F–G–K–M

(b) Yes – by 1 hour   [14.1, 14.3]

14.10   31 minutes, A–B–C–D–F   [14.1, 14.3]

14.11   (a) 1.33 pm   (b) D–F–G–H–I–J–K–L–M–O   [14.1, 14.3]

14.12   (a)

$$\mu_A = \frac{6 + (4*10) + 12}{6} = 9.667$$

$$\mu_D = \frac{1 + (4*2) + 4}{6} = 2.167$$

$$\mu_E = \frac{8 + (4*10) + 14}{6} = 10.333$$

$$\mu_G = \frac{1 + (4*1) + 1}{6} = 1.000$$

$\mu_{CP} = 9.667 + 2.167 + 10.333 + 1.000 = 23.167$ days

$\sigma_A^2 = ((12 - 6)/6)^2 = 1.000$

$\sigma_D^2 = ((4 - 1)/6)^2 = 0.250$

$\sigma_E^2 = ((14 - 8)/6)^2 = 1.000$

$\sigma_G^2 = ((1 - 1)/6)^2 = 0.000$

$\sigma_{CP}^2 = 1.000 + 1.000 + 0.250 + 0.000 = 2.250$

$\sigma_{CP} = \sqrt{2.25} = 1.5$ days

(b) $P(X < 22) = P(Z < ((22 - 23.167)/1.5)$
$= P(Z < -0.78) = 0.2177$

(c) 95% of durations less than 1.645 standard deviations
above the mean, $23.167 + (1.645 * 1.5) = 25.635$

14.13   (a) 24.833 seconds, 1.384 seconds   (b) 0.0202

(c) 26.607   [14.5–14.7]

14.14   (a) 41.833, 1.951   (b) 0.1736   (c) 46.371   [14.5–14.7]

14.15   (a) 23.333, 2.677   (b) 0.9936   (c) 25.582   [14.5–14.7]

14.16   0.2033   [14.5–14.7]

14.17 (a)

Activity	Latest event time	Earliest event time	Activity duration	Total float
A	10	0	10	0
B	19	10	8	1
C	22	18	3	1
D	12	10	2	0
E	22	12	10	0
F	22	12	7	3

(b) Crash costs per day: £200 for B, £150 for C, £300 for E and £200 for F

Stage 1: crash E by 1 day, cost £300, project duration 22 days

Stage 2: crash E by a further day and C by 1 day, cost £450, project duration 21 days

(c) Crashing to 22 days is worthwhile as cost (£300) < net loss (£400)

Crashing to 21 days costs more (£450) than the net loss (£400)

14.18 Crash D and F: £1100   [14.8]

14.19 Crash B (2 days) and I (1 day): £1100   [14.8]

14.20 (i) (d), (ii) (h), (iii) (g), (iv) (i), (v) (c), (vi) (a), (vii) (f), (viii) (e), (ix) (b)

Chapter 16

16.1 $\mu = 23{,}450$ miles, $\sigma = 1260$ miles, $n = 4$. Use Table 5 on pages 621–622 in Appendix 1.

(a)

$$P(\bar{x} > 25000) = P\left(Z > \frac{25000 - 23450}{1260/\sqrt{4}}\right) = P\left(Z > \frac{1655}{630}\right)$$
$$= P(Z > 2.46) = 0.0069$$

(b)

$$P(\bar{x} > 22000) = P\left(Z > \frac{22000 - 23450}{1260/\sqrt{4}}\right) = P\left(Z > \frac{-1450}{630}\right)$$
$$= P(Z > -2.30) = 0.9893$$

(c)

$$P(\bar{x} < 24000) = P\left(Z < \frac{24000 - 23450}{1260/\sqrt{4}}\right) = P\left(Z < \frac{550}{630}\right)$$

$$= P(Z < 0.87) = 1 - P(Z > 0.87)$$
$$= 1 - 0.1922 = 0.8078$$

(d) $\quad P(\bar{x} < 23000) = P\left(Z < \dfrac{23000 - 23450}{1260/\sqrt{4}}\right)$

$$= P\left(Z < \dfrac{-450}{630}\right)$$

$$= P(Z < -0.71)$$
$$= 1 - P(Z > -0.71)$$
$$= 1 - 0.7611 = 0.2389$$

(e) $\quad P(22500 < \bar{x} < 24500)$

$$= P\left(\dfrac{22500 - 23450}{1260/\sqrt{4}} < Z < \dfrac{24500 - 23450}{1260/\sqrt{4}}\right)$$

$$= P\left(\dfrac{-950}{630} < Z < \dfrac{1050}{630}\right) = P(-1.51 < Z < 1.67)$$

$$P(Z > -1.51) = 0.9345$$
$$P(Z > 1.67) = 0.0475$$
$$P(-1.51 < Z < 1.67) = 0.9345 - 0.0475 = 0.8870$$

(f) $\quad P(23400 < \bar{x} < 24200)$

$$= P\left(\dfrac{23400 - 23450}{1260/\sqrt{4}} < Z < \dfrac{24200 - 23450}{1260/\sqrt{4}}\right)$$

$$= P\left(\dfrac{-50}{630} < Z < \dfrac{750}{630}\right) = P(-0.08 < Z < 1.19)$$

$$P(Z > -0.08) = 0.5319 \text{ and } P(Z > 1.19) = 0.1170$$
$$P(-0.08 < Z < 1.19) = 0.5319 - 0.1170 = 0.4149$$

16.2   (a) 0.1515   (b) 0.7549   (c) 0.9970   (d) 0.0080
      (e) 0.5069   (f) 0.4031   [16.1]

16.3   (a) 0.7673   (b) 0.0630   (c) 0.0455   (d) 0.6576
      (e) 0.1867   [16.1]

16.4   (a) 0.1251   (b) 0.0104   [16.1]

16.5   0.1469   [16.1]

16.6   (a) 0.1841   (b) 0.8159   (c) 0.0034   (d) 0.5
      (e) 0.2913   (f) 0.2395   (g) 0.9097   [16.2]

16.7   (a) 0.9960   (b) 0.0384   (c) 0.8106   (d) 0.1894
      (e) 0.9576   [16.3]

16.8 $\mu = 101.4$ grams, $s = 3.1$ grams, $n = 4$, $\nu = 3$. Use Table 6 on
    page 623.

(a) $t_{0.10,3} = 1.638$

heaviest 10% will weigh $> 101.4 + \left(1.638 * \dfrac{3.1}{\sqrt{4}}\right)$

$$= 101.4 + (1.638 * 1.55)$$
$$= 101.4 + 2.539 = 103.939$$

(b) $t_{0.05,3} = 2.353$

heaviest 5% will weigh $> 101.4 + \left(2.353 * \dfrac{3.1}{\sqrt{4}}\right)$

$$= 101.4 + (2.353 * 1.55)$$
$$= 101.4 + 3.647 = 105.047$$

(c) $t_{0.01,3} = 4.541$

heaviest 1% will weigh $> 101.4 + \left(4.541 * \dfrac{3.1}{\sqrt{4}}\right)$

$$= 101.4 + (4.541 * 1.55)$$
$$= 101.4 + 7.039 = 108.439$$

16.9   (a) 14.885   (b) 15.116   (c) 14.643   [16.5]

16.10 $\sigma = 0.8$, $\bar{x} = 24.7$, $n = 33$

(a) $\alpha = 5\%$, $Z_{\alpha/2} = Z_{0.025} = 1.96$

$$95\% \text{ CI} = 24.7 \pm 1.96 * \dfrac{0.8}{\sqrt{33}}$$
$$= 24.7 \pm 1.96 * 0.139$$
$$= 24.7 \pm 0.273$$
$$= 24.427 \text{ to } 24.973 \text{ g}$$

(b) $\alpha = 1\%$, $Z_{\alpha/2} = Z_{0.005} = 2.576$

$$99\% \text{ CI} = 24.7 \pm 2.576 * \dfrac{0.8}{\sqrt{33}}$$
$$= 24.7 \pm 2.576 * 0.139$$
$$= 24.7 \pm 0.359$$
$$= 24.341 \text{ to } 25.059 \text{ g}$$

16.11   (a)   228.228 minutes to 233.772 minutes   [16.7]

         (b)   227.357 minutes to 234.643 minutes   [16.8]

16.12   (a)   22.878 miles to 25.322 miles   [16.8]

         (b)   108   [16.10]

16.13   (a)   £387.567 to £418.433   [16.7]

         (b)   95   [16.10]

16.14   (a)   0.999 lb to 1.121 lb   (b) 0.975 lb to 1.145 lb   [16.12]

16.15   (a)   20.712 kg to 46.954 kg   [16 12]

         (b)   No. Confidence interval includes 40 kg.

16.16   (a) $p = 175/281 = 0.623$ $\alpha = 5\%$ $Z_{\alpha/2} = Z_{0.025} = 1.96$

$$95\% \ CI = 0.623 \pm 1.96 * \sqrt{\frac{0.623 * (1 - 0.623)}{281}}$$

$$= 0.623 \pm 1.96 * \sqrt{\frac{0.235}{281}} = 0.623 \pm 1.96 * 0.029$$

$$= 0.623 \pm 0.057 = 0.566 \ to \ 0.680 \quad 56.6\% \ to \ 68.0\%$$

    (b) $p = 65/138 = 0.471$ $\alpha = 5\%$ $Z_{\alpha/2} = Z_{0.025} = 1.96$

$$95\% \ CI = 0.471 \pm 1.96 * \sqrt{\frac{0.471 * (1 - 0.471)}{138}}$$

$$= 0.471 \pm 1.96 * \sqrt{\frac{0.249}{138}} = 0.471 \pm 1.96 * 0.0425$$

$$= 0.471 \pm 0.083 = 0.388 \ to \ 0.554 \quad 38.8\% \ to \ 55.4\%$$

    (c)   UK proportion significantly higher

16.17   (a)   0.694 to 0.828   (b)   0.779 to 0.893   [16.13]

    (c)   Some overlap. Business students seem more
          appreciative

16.18   (a)   0.152 to 0.252   (b)   0.205 to 0.349   [16.13]

    (c)   Recent prospects seem better, although there is some
          overlap

16.19   2401   [16.14]

16.20 $\sigma = 1.3$, $\bar{x} = 12.9$, $n = 40$

    $H_0: \mu = 12$ $H_1: \mu \neq 12$ $\alpha = 0.05$ two-sided test

$$\text{Test statistic} = \frac{12.9 - 12}{1.3/\sqrt{40}} = \frac{0.9}{0.2055} = 4.379$$

    Critical values $= \pm Z_{0.025} = \pm 1.96$

    Reject H_0 because the test statistic, 4.379, > 1.96

16.21   Test statistic $= -1.669$. Reject H_0 at the 5% level   [16.17, 16.19]

16.22   Test statistic $= 2.421$. Reject H_0 at the 1% level   [16.19]

16.23   Test statistic $= 4.393$. Reject H_0 at the 1% level   [16.21]

16.24   (a)   Test statistic $= -1.052$. Can't reject H_0 at the
          5% level   [16.22]

    (b)   Lifetimes of air fresheners are normally distributed

16.25   Test statistic $= 2.409$. Can't reject H_0 at the 1% level   [16.22]

16.26   (a)   Test statistic $= -0.696$. Can't reject H_0 at the
          10% level   [16.21]

    (b)   Test statistic $= -1.454$. Can't reject H_0 at the
          10% level   [16.22]

16.27   (a)   Test statistic $= 5.144$. Reject H_0 at the 5%
          level   [16.21]

    (b)   Test statistic $= 2.957$. Reject H_0 at the 5% level   [16.22]

    (c)   It is normally distributed

16.28 (a) Test statistic $= -1.450$. Can't reject H_0 at the
            5% level   [16.21]
       (b) Test statistic $= -2.348$. Reject H_0 at the 5% level [16.22]
       (c) New system seems to be significantly faster when
            the sample is adjusted. Dispensing times should be
            normally distributed

16.29 Test statistic $= -1.793$. Reject H_0 at the 10% level   [16.23]
16.30 Test statistic $= -1.044$. Can't reject H_0 at the 5% level [16.23]
16.31 Test statistic $= -2.760$. Reject H_0 at the 5% level   [16.23]
16.32 $6 + s$ and $4 - s$. Can't reject H_0 at the 5% level   [16.24]
16.33 (i) (d), (ii) (f), (iii) (i), (iv) (k), (v) (a), (vi) (j),
       (vii) (b), (viii) (e), (ix) (h), (x) (g), (xi) (l), (xii) (c)

Chapter 17

17.1 Let D represent Deshovy and B represent Bugatty
      $s_D = 4.1 \quad s_B = 3.2 \quad \bar{x}_D = 43.7 \quad \bar{x}_B = 41.9 \quad n_D = 62 \quad n_B = 55$
      $H_0: \mu_D \leqslant \mu_B \quad H_1: \mu_D > \mu_B \quad \alpha = 5\% \quad$ one sided test

$$\text{Test statistic} = \frac{43.7 - 41.9}{\sqrt{(4.1^2/62 + 3.2^2/55)}} = \frac{1.8}{0.676} = 2.663$$

      Critical value $= z_{0.05} = 1.645$
      $2.663 > 1.645$ so reject H_0

17.2 Test statistic -1.749. Can't reject H_0 at the 1% level   [17.1]
17.3 Test statistic $= -1.555$. Can't reject H_0 at the 10% level [17.1]
17.4 Let B represent before the campaign and A represent after
      $s_B = 4.1 \quad s_A = 3.2 \quad \bar{x}_B = 31.7 \quad \bar{x}_A = 29.5 \quad n_B = 28 \quad n_A = 24$
      $H_0: \mu_A \geqslant \mu_B \quad H_1: \mu_A < \mu_B \quad \alpha = 5\% \quad$ one-sided test
      Pooled estimated standard error

$$= \sqrt{\frac{[(24 - 1) * 3.2^2] + [(28 - 1) * 4.1^2]}{24 + 28 - 2}} = 3.713$$

$$\text{Test statistic} = \frac{29.5 - 31.7}{3.713 * \sqrt{(1/24 + 1/28)}}$$

$$= \frac{-2.2}{1.033} = -2.130$$

      $\nu = 24 + 28 - 2 - 50$
      Critical value $= -t_{0.05,50} = -1.676$
      $-2.130 < -1.676$ so reject H_0

17.5   Test statistic $= -2.020$. Can't reject H_0 at the 1% level   [17.2]

17.6   Test statistic $= 4.262$. Reject H_0 at the 5% level   [17.2]

17.7   Differences $= -5 \ -2 \ -13 \ -4 \ -15 \ -1 \ -7 \ -3 \ -7 \ -17$
       $s_d = 5.661 \quad \bar{x}_d = -7.4 \quad n = 10 \quad \nu = 9$
       $H_0: \mu_d \geqslant 0 \quad H_1: \mu_d < 0 \quad \alpha = 1\% \quad$ one-sided test

$$\text{Test statistic} = \frac{-7.4 - 0}{5.661/\sqrt{10}} = -4.134$$

Critical value $= -t_{0.01,\,9} = -2.821$
$-4.134 < -2.821$ so reject H_0

17.8   Test statistic $= -3.625$. Reject H_0 at the 5% level   [17.3]

17.9   Test statistic $= 4.467$. Reject H_0 at the 1% level   [17.3]

17.10 Let C represent Canal, R Rail and T Truck
       $H_0: \mu_C = \mu_R = \mu_T$
       Sample means: 11.5 (C), 12.4 (R), 14.2 (T).
       Overall mean $= 12.625$
       $\begin{aligned} SS_C &= (17 - 11.5)^2 + (1 - 11.5)^2 + (10 - 11.5)^2 \\ &\quad + (19 - 11.5)^2 + (4 - 11.5)^2 + (18 - 11.5)^2 = 297.5 \end{aligned}$
       $\begin{aligned} SS_R &= (0 - 12.4)^2 + (20 - 12.4)^2 + (25 - 12.4)^2 \\ &\quad + (15 - 12.4)^2 + (2 - 12.4)^2 = 485.2 \end{aligned}$
       $\begin{aligned} SS_T &= (19 - 14.2)^2 + (15 - 14.2)^2 + (12 - 14.2)^2 \\ &\quad + (15 - 14.2)^2 + (10 - 14.2)^2 = 46.8 \end{aligned}$
       $SSW = 297.5 + 485.2 + 46.8 = 829.5$
       $\begin{aligned} SSB &= 6 * (11.5 - 12.625)^2 + 5 * (12.4 - 12.625)^2 + 5 * \\ &\quad (14.2 - 12.625)^2 = 20.25 \end{aligned}$
       $MSW = 829.5/(16 - 3) = 63.808$
       $\quad MSB = 20.25/(3 - 1) = 10.125$
       Test statistic, $F = 10.125/63.808 = 0.159 \quad F_{2,13,0.05} = 3.81$
       $0.159 < 3.81$ so can't reject H_0

17.11 Test statistic $= 7.186$. Reject H_0 at the 1% level   [17.6]

17.12 Test statistic $= 5.817$. Reject H_0 at the 5% level but
       not at the 1% level   [17.6]

17.13 $H_0: \rho = 0 \quad H_1: \rho > 0 \quad \alpha = 0.05 \quad$ one-sided test
       $r = 0.683 \quad n = 28 \quad$ degrees of freedom, $\nu = n - 2 = 26$

$$\text{Test statistic} = \frac{0.683 * \sqrt{28 - 2}}{\sqrt{1 - 0.683^2}} = 4.768$$

Critical value, $t_{0.05,26} = 1.706$
Reject H_0 because $4.768 > 1.706$

17.14 Test statistic $= 2.318$. Reject H_0 at the 5% level   [17.7]

17.15 Test statistic $= -2.878$. Reject H_0 at the 1% level   [17.7]

17.16   (a) The regression equation: Audience $= -1018 + 0.487$ Cards
        $H_0: \beta = 0$ $H_1: \beta \neq 0$

Cards (x)	Audience (y)	Residuals	Squared residuals
3750	925	114.544	13120
4100	1000	18.924	358
4500	1150	−26.070	680
4750	1200	−97.941	9593
4800	1100	−222.316	49424
5250	1680	138.316	19131
4600	1480	255.181	65118
4800	1370	47.684	2274
4320	860	−228.323	52131
			211829

Standard deviation of the residuals, $s = \sqrt{211829/7} = 173.958$

Cards (x)	$\bar{x}$	$(x - \bar{x})$	$(x - \bar{x})^2$
3750	4541.1	−791.1	625839
4100	4541.1	−441.1	194569
4500	4541.1	−41.1	1689
4750	4541.1	208.9	43639
4800	4541.1	258.9	67029
5250	4541.1	708.9	502539
4600	4541.1	58.9	3469
4800	4541.1	258.9	67029
4320	4541.1	−221.1	48885
			1554689

Estimated standard error, $s_b = 173.958 / \sqrt{1554689} = 0.140$

Test statistic, $t = \dfrac{0.487 \quad 0}{0.140} = 3.479$

This is higher than $t_{0.025,7}$, 2.365, so reject H_0
(b) $\hat{y} = -1018 + 0.487 (4400) = 1124.8$

$\qquad$ 95% CI $= 1124.8 \pm 2.365 * 173.958$

$$* \sqrt{[1/9 + (4400 - 4541.111)^2 / 1554689]}$$
$$= 1124.8 + 144.825 = 979.975 \text{ to } 1269.625$$

17.17   (a) Test statistic $= 15.005$. Reject H_0 at the 5% level   [17.8]
        (b) 34.581 to 46.059   [17.9, 17.10]
17.18   (a) Test statistic $= -5.136$. Reject H_0 at the 5% level   [17.8]
        (b) 75.005 to 150.935   [17.9, 17.10]
        (c) −0.756 to 226.696   [17.12]
17.19   (a) Test statistic $= -8.198$. Reject H_0 at the 1% level   [17.8]
        (b) 32.728 to 40.142   [17.9, 17.10]
        (c) 25.131 to 47.739   [17.12]

17.20   (a) Test statistic = 9.141. Reject H_0 at the 10% level   [17.8]
        (b) £656.475 to £862.935   [17.9, 17.10]
        (c) £2307.997 to £3080.453   [17.9, 17.10]
        (d) 75 is beyond the range of the data so answer
        (c) is not valid

17.21   Test statistic = 6.189. Reject H_0 at the 5% level but not at 1%
                                                                        [17.16–17.19]

17.22 H_0: No association H_1: Association
        Expected frequencies:

$$\frac{78 * 40}{150} = 20.8 \qquad \frac{78 * 70}{150} = 36.4 \qquad \frac{78 * 40}{150} = 20.8$$

$$\frac{72 * 40}{150} = 19.2 \qquad \frac{72 * 70}{150} = 33.6 \qquad \frac{72 * 40}{150} = 19.2$$

Test statistic

$$= \frac{(14 - 20.8)^2}{20.8} + \frac{(33 - 36.4)^2}{36.4} + \frac{(31 - 20.8)^2}{20.8}$$
$$+ \frac{(26 - 19.2)^2}{19.2} + \frac{(37 - 33.6)^2}{33.6} + \frac{(9 - 19.2)^2}{19.2}$$

$$= 2.223 + 0.318 + 5.002$$
$$+ 2.408 + 0.344 + 5.419$$
$$= 15.714$$

Degrees of freedom, $\nu = (2 - 1) * (3 - 1) = 2$ $\alpha = 0.01$
Critical value, $\chi^2_{0.01,2} = 9.210$
Test statistic > critical value, so reject H_0

17.23   Test statistic = 4.335. Can't reject H_0 at the 5% level   [17.20]
17.24   Test statistic = 5.680. Can't reject H_0 at the 5% level   [17.20]
17.25   Test statistic = 0.871. Can't reject H_0 at the 10% level   [17.20]
17.26   Test statistic = 6.979. Reject H_0 at the 10% level but
        not at 5%   [17.20]
17.27   (a) Test statistic = 51.769. Reject H_0 at the 1% level   [17.20]
        (b) Large components for Single/Dog, Single/Cat,
             and Family/Cat
17.28   Test statistic = 3.690. Can't reject H_0 at the 10% level   [17.20]
        Largest components are Newcastle/Cricket and
        Newcastle/Football
17.29   Test statistic = 74.895. Reject H_0 at the 1% level   [17.20]
        Largest components are Retirees/Never and Retirees/
        Sometimes
17.30   (i) (d), (ii) (j), (iii) (i), (iv) (f), (v) (a), (vi) (e), (vii) (c),
        (viii) (b), (ix) (g), (x) (h)

References

Areni, C.S. and Kim, D. (1993) The influence of background music on shopping behaviour: classical versus top-forty music in a wine store. *Advances in Consumer Research*, **20**: 336–340.

Bates, D.M. and Watts, D.G. (1988) *Nonlinear Regression Analysis and Its Applications*. New York: Wiley.

Baysan, S. (2001) Perceptions of the environmental impacts of tourism: a comparative study of the attitudes of German, Russian and Turkish tourists in Kemer, Antalya. *Tourism Geographies*, **3**(2): 218–235.

Beattie, D.W. (1969) Marketing a new product. *Operational Research Quarterly*, **20**: 429–435. Also in S. French (ed.), *Readings in Decision Analysis*. London: Chapman and Hall, 1989, pp. 64–70.

Berk, J. and Berk, S. (1993) *Total Quality Management*. New York: Sterling.

Boghani, A.B. (1990) Are special trains really safer? In: L.A. Cox, Jr and P.F. Ricci (eds), *New Risks: Issues and Management*. New York: Plenum Press, pp. 681–692.

Boyer, C.B. (1968) *A History of Mathematics*. New York: Wiley.

Bronson, R. and Naadimuthu, G. (1997) *Operations Research*, 2nd edn. New York: McGraw–Hill.

Brooks, R. and Robinson, S. (2001) *Simulation*. Basingstoke: Palgrave.

Brown, R.V., Kahr, A.S. and Peterson, C.R. (1974) *Decision Analysis for the Manager*. New York: Holt Rinehart and Winston.

Chatfield, C. (1996) *The Analysis of Time Series*, 5th edn. London: Chapman and Hall.

Chvatal, V. (1983) *Linear Programming*. New York: W.H. Freeman.

Converse, J.M. and Presser, S. (1986) *Survey Questions: Handcrafting the Standardised Questionnaire*. London: Sage.

Conway, D.A. and Roberts, H.V. (1986) Regression analyses in employment discrimination cases. In: M.H. Degroot and S.E. Fienberg (eds), *Statistics and the Law*. New York: Wiley, pp. 107–195.

Coopersmith, E., Dean, G., McVean, J. and Storaune, E. (2000) Making decisions in the oil and gas industry. *Oilfield Review*, Winter 2000/2001: 2–9.

Cravens, D.W., Woodruff, R.B. and Stamper, J.C. (1972) An analytical approach for evaluating sales territory performance. *Journal of Marketing*, **36**: 31–37.

Croft, A. and Davison, R. (2003) *Foundation Maths*, 3rd edn. Harlow: Prentice Hall.

Cronbach, L.J. (1951) Coefficient alpha and the internal structure of tests. *Psychometrika*, **16**(3): 297–334.

Cryer, J.D. (1986) *Time Series Analysis*. Boston: Duxbury Press.

Curwin, J. and Slater, R. (2000) *Improve Your Maths: A Refresher Course*. London: International Thomson Business Press.

Dantzig, G.B. (1999) *Linear Programming and Extensions*. Princeton, NJ: Princeton University Press.

Daykin, C.D., Pentikäinen, T. and Pesonen, M. (1994) *Practical Risk Theory for Actuaries*. London: Chapman and Hall.

Dielman, T.E. (1996) *Applied Regression Analysis for Business and Economics*, 2nd edn. California: Duxbury Press.

Draper, N.R. and Smith, H. (1998) *Applied Regression Analysis*, 3rd edn. New York: Wiley.

Drury, C. (2000) *Management and Cost Accounting*, 5th edn. London: Business Press.

Eckes, G. (2001) *The Six Sigma Revolution: How General Electric and Others Turned Process into Profits*. New York: Wiley.

Frankel, S.H. (1967) *Investment and the Return to Equity Capital in the South African Gold Mining Industry, 1887–1965*. Oxford: Basil Blackwell.

Gass, S.I. (1970) *Illustrated Guide to Linear Programming*. New York: McGraw–Hill.

Gorman, J. (1988) Manufacturing with robots. In: J. Szymankiewicz, J. McDonald and K. Turner(eds), *Solving Business Problems by Simulation*, 2nd edn. London: McGraw–Hill, pp. 353–360.

Hague, P. and Jackson, P. (1992) *Marketing Research in Practice*. London: Kogan Page.

Hague, P.N. (1993) *Questionnaire Design*. London: Kogan Page.

Hall, R.W. (1987) Kawasaki USA. In: C.A. Voss(ed.), *Just-in-time Manufacture*. Bedford: IFS, pp. 339–364.

Harris, F.W. (1990) How many parts to make at once. *Operations Research*, **38**(6): 947–950.

Heroux, R.L. and Wallace, W.L. (1975) New community development with the aid of linear programming. In: H.M. Salkin and J. Saha (eds), *Studies in Linear Programming*. Amsterdam: North-Holland, pp. 309–322.

Hobsons (2002) *The Hobsons Graduate career directory 2003*. London: Hobsons plc.

Holmes, N. (1991) *Designers Guide to Creating Charts and Diagrams*. New York: Watson–Guptill.

Huish, M., Woodhouse, H. and Watkin, E. (1853) Report to the Permanent Way Committee on the Renewal Fund. In: J.R. Edwards (ed.), *Reporting Fixed Assets in Nineteenth Century Company Accounts*. New York: Garland Publishing, 1986, pp. 269–286.

Huss, W.R. (1987) Forecasting in the electric utility supply industry. In: S. Makridakis and S.C. Wheelwright(eds), *The Handbook of Forecasting: A Manager's Guide*. New York: Wiley, pp. 87–117.

Jennings, D.R. and Wattam, S. (1998) *Decision Making: An Integrated Approach*, 2nd edn. London: Pitman Publishing.

Johnson, H.T. and Kaplan, R.S. (1991) *Relevance Lost – The Rise and Fall of Management Accounting*. Boston: Harvard Business School Press.

Juran, J.M. (1995) The history of managing for quality in the United States. In: J.M. Juran(ed.), *A History of Managing for Quality*. Milwaukee: ASQC Quality Press, pp. 553–602.

Kathawala, Y. (1988) Applications of quantitative techniques in large and small organisations in the United States: an empirical analysis. *Journal of the Operational Research Society*, **39**(11): 981–989.

Klammer, T., Koch, B. and Wilner, N. (1991) Capital budgeting practices – a survey of corporate use. *Journal of Management Accounting Research*, **3**: 113–130.

Klien, J.H. (2001) *Critical Path Analysis*. Basingstoke: Palgrave

Kuempel, E.D., Attfield, M.D., Vallyathan, V. *et al.* (2003) Pulmonary inflammation and crystalline silica in respirable coal mine dust: dose–response. *Journal of Biosciences*, **28**(1): 61–69.

Lane, K. (2003) Making connections at Kings Cross. *Project Manager Today*, May 2003: 8–12.

Lawlor, G. (1999) *Understanding Maths: A Practical Survival Guide for Students in Further and Higher Education*. London: Studymates.

Lewis, C. (2001) *Inventory Control*. Basingstoke: Palgrave.

Mackenzie, D.A. (1981) *Statistics in Britain, 1865–1930*. Edinburgh: Edinburgh University Press.

Mackenzie, R. (1988) More lager, please. In: J. Szymankiewicz, J. McDonald and K. Turner (eds), *Solving Business Problems by Simulation*, 2nd edn. London: McGraw–Hill, pp. 369–375.

Majani, B. (1987) Decomposition methods for medium-term planning and budgeting. In: S. Makridakis and S.C. Wheelwright (eds),

The Handbook of Forecasting: A Manager's Guide. New York: Wiley, pp. 219–237.

McMullen, L. (1970) 'Student' as a man. In: E.S. Pearson and M.G. Kendall (eds), *Studies in the History of Statistics and Probability*. London: Griffin, pp. 355–360.

Meier, P., Sacks, J. and Zabell, S.L. (1986) What happened in Hazelwood: statistics, employment discrimination and the 80% rule. In: M.H. Degroot and S.E. Fienberg (eds), *Statistics and the Law*. New York: Wiley, pp. 1–48.

Mendenhall, W. and Sincich, T. (1989) *A Second Course in Business Statistics: Regression Analysis*, 3rd edn. San Francisco: Dellen.

Middleton, M.R. (2003) *Data Analysis Using Microsoft Excel*. Belmont, CA: Duxbury.

Million, G. (1980) Some problems in forecasting the demand for water in England and Wales. In: O.D. Anderson(ed.), Forecasting Public Utilities: Proceedings of the International Conference held at Nottingham University, March 1980. Amsterdam: North-Holland Publishing, pp. 9–15.

Ming-Yao, L., Devlin, P. and Chi-Tat, T.K. (2000) Development of API RP 2SM for synthetic fiber rope moorings. *Offshore Technology Conference, Houston, Texas, 1–4 May, 2000.*

Montgomery, D.C. (2000) *Introduction to Statistical Quality Control*, 4th edn. Chichester: Wiley.

Morris, P.W.G. (1994) *The Management of Projects*. London: Thomas Telford.

Nonaka, I. (1995) The recent history of managing for quality in Japan. In: J.M. Juran(ed.), *A History of Managing for Quality*. Milwaukee: ASQC Quality Press, pp. 517–552.

North, D.W. (1990) Decision analysis in environmental risk management: applications to acid deposition and air toxins. In: L.A. Cox, Jr and P.F. Ricci(eds), *New Risks: Issues and Management*. New York: Plenum Press, pp. 33–43.

Oakshott, L. (1997) *Business Modelling and Simulation*. London: Pitman.

Oppenheim, A.N. (1992) *Questionnaire Design and Attitude Measurement*. 2nd edn. London: Heinemann.

Pallant, J. (2001) *SPSS Survival Manual*. Buckingham: Open University Press.

Parker, R.H. (1968) Discounted cash flow in historical perspective. *Journal of Accounting Research*, Spring: 58–71.

Pearson, E.S. (1970) 'Student' as a statistician. In: E.S. Pearson and M.G. Kendall(eds), *Studies in the History of Statistics and Probability*. London: Griffin, pp. 360–403.

Phillips, L.D. (1982) Requisite decision modelling: a case study. *Journal of the Operational Research Society*, **33**: 303–311. Also in S. French (ed.), *Readings in Decision Analysis*. London: Chapman and Hall, 1989, pp. 110–122.

Pike, R. (1996) A longitudinal survey on capital budgeting practices. *Journal of Business Finance and Accounting*, **23**(1): 79–92.

Roberts, M.J. and Russo, R. (1999) *A Student's Guide to Analysis of Variance*. London: Routledge.

Ryan, B.F. and Joiner, B.L. (2000) *MINITAB Handbook*, 4th edn. Pacific Grove, CA: Duxbury.

Schimmel, K. and Nicholls, J. (2003) Gender differences and e-commerce behavior and perceptions. *Journal of Internet Banking and Commerce* [online], **8**(1). Available at http://www.arraydev.com/commerce/JOBC/articles.htm [accessed 6 November 2003].

Schonberger, R.J. (1982) *Japanese Manufacturing Techniques*. New York: Macmillan.

Seber, G.A.F. and Wild, C.J. (1989) *Nonlinear Regression*. New York: Wiley.

Simpson, S. (2002) Selection. In: J. Leopold(ed.), *Human Resources in Organisations*. Harlow: Pearson Education, pp. 78–105.

Sparkes, J.R. and McHugh, A.K. (1984) Awareness and use of forecasting techniques in British industry. *Journal of Forecasting*, **3**(1): 37–42.

Sprent, P. (1989) *Applied Nonparametric Statistical Methods*. London: Chapman and Hall.

Sutlieff, H. (1982) Forecasting emergency workload for day ahead. *Journal of the Operational Research Society*, **33**(2): 129–136.

Swart, W.W., Gearing, C., Vas, T. and Cann, G. (1975) Investment planning for the tourism sector of a developing country with the aid of linear programming. In: H.M. Salkin and J. Saha (eds), *Studies in Linear Programming*. Amsterdam: North-Holland, pp. 227–249.

Symonds, G.H. (1955) *Linear Programming: The Solution of Refinery Problems*. New York: Esso Standard Oil Company.

Taha, H.A. (1997) *Operations Research*, 6th edn. New York: Prentice-Hall.

Thorneycroft, T. (1987) *Seasonal Patterns in Business and Everyday Life*. Aldershot: Gower.

Tippett, L.H.C. (1935) Some applications of statistical methods to the study of variation of quality in the production of cotton yarn. *Journal of the Royal Statistical Society*, Supplement 2, 27–55.

Tufte, E.R. (1983) *The Visual Display of Quantitative Information*. Cheshire, CT: Graphics Press.

Tukey, J.W. (1977) *Exploratory Data Analysis*. London: Addison–Wesley.

Velleman, P.F. and Hoaglin, D.C. (1981) *Applications, Basics and Computing of Exploratory Data Analysis.* Boston: Duxbury Press.

Walkenbach, J. (1999) *Microsoft Excel 2000 Bible.* New York: Wiley.

Wardle, P.A. (1965) Forest management and operational research: a linear programming study. *Management Science*, 11(10): B260–B270.

Weaver, J.B. and Reilly, R.J. (1956) Interest rate of return for capital expenditure evaluation. *Chemical Engineering Progress*, 52(10): 405–412.

Wilson, A. (2003) *Marketing Research: An Integrated Approach.* Harlow: Prentice Hall.

Wilson, R.H. (1934) A scientific routine for stock control. *Harvard Business Review*, 13: 116–128.

Wisniewski, M. (2001) *Linear Programming.* Basingstoke: Palgrave.

Zhongjie, X. (1993) *Case Studies in Time Series Analysis.* Singapore: World Scientific.

Index